Leaders and Managers

Pergamon Titles of Related Interest

Related Journals*

Leaders
and Managers
International Perspectives on Managerial Behavior and Leadership

---

Edited by
JAMES G. HUNT,
DIAN-MARIE HOSKING,
CHESTER A. SCHRIESHEIM, AND
ROSEMARY STEWART

This volume covers the contents of a NATO Scientific Affairs Division
Symposium

Pergamon Press
New York   Oxford   Toronto   Sydney   Frankfurt   Paris

Pergamon Press Offices:

U.S.A.	Pergamon Press Inc., Maxwell House, Fairview Park, Elmsford, New York 10523, U.S.A.
U.K.	Pergamon Press Ltd., Headington Hill Hall, Oxford OX3 0BW, England
CANADA	Pergamon Press Canada Ltd., Suite 104, 150 Consumers Road, Willowdale, Ontario M2J 1P9, Canada
AUSTRALIA	Pergamon Press (Aust.) Pty. Ltd., P.O. Box 544, Potts Point, NSW 2011, Australia
FRANCE	Pergamon Press SARL, 24 rue des Ecoles, 75240 Paris, Cedex 05, France
FEDERAL REPUBLIC OF GERMANY	Pergamon Press GmbH, Hammerweg 6, D-6242 Kronberg-Taunus, Federal Republic of Germany

Library of Congress Cataloging in Publication Data

Main entry under title:

Leaders and managers.

    Bibliography: p.
    Includes index.
    1. Leadership – Addresses, essays, lectures.
2. Management – Addresses, essays, lectures.   I. Hunt,
James G., 1932–
HD57.7.L42 1984   658.4′092   83-13342
ISBN 0-08-030943-7

Printed in the United States of America

To Lewis Carroll and Radcliffe-Brown, two Oxford professors
who have contributed more than they intended to leadership theory.

Contents

List of Tables

List of Figures

Preface

This book covers the content of an international symposium on managerial behavior and leadership research held at St. Catherine's College, Oxford University, England, from July 10–16, 1982. As such, it has a double mission. First, it comprises Volume 7 of the Leadership Symposia series that originated in 1971. This series covers the contents of biennial symposia held at the Carbondale campus of Southern Illinois University until the most recent symposium held at Oxford.

Second, its international thrust and its consideration of broader aspects of managerial behavior (in addition to leadership) represent a major commitment to a direction that has received an ever-increasing level of emphasis in each of the last three volumes.

This internationally oriented volume joins the earlier ones in charting the state of the field. The previous volumes are: *Current Developments in the Study of Leadership* (1973); *Contingency Approaches to Leadership* (1974); *Leadership Frontiers* (1975); *Crosscurrents in Leadership* (1979); and *Leadership: Beyond Establishment Views* (1982).

This series was established to provide in-depth consideration of current and future leadership directions and to provide an interdisciplinary perspective for the scholarly study of leadership. Taken as a whole, the books in the series have been designed to build on one another, to show the evolution of the field over time, and to be at the forefront of new developments. The current international focus and broadened managerial behavior emphasis are considered to be at the heart of developments within the very recent past.

The format of the volumes has encouraged the achievement of these objectives in a number of ways. First, a mix of work from well-known scholars, widely recognized for many years, and younger scholars whose work has only recently received attention, has been utilized. Second, expert discussants/critiquers have prepared commentaries for the presentations. Third, interchange has been encouraged at the symposia and issues emerging from this interchange have been woven into the introductory part or chapter materials of the volumes. Fourth, a broad-ranging overview has been prepared to put the book's contents into perspective. That perspective has often ranged far afield from the contents of the chapters themselves. Finally, in more recent volumes, the editors have provided a considerable amount of additional commentary to help balance the content of the volumes in terms of current directions.

To encourage further scholarship in the leadership area and to recognize the contributions of outstanding individuals, the Ralph M. Stogdill Distinguished Scholarship Award was established in 1976. Bestowed on an intermittent basis, the award is given to a leadership scholar "in recognition of his/her outstanding contribution to the advancement of leadership research and for devotion to the development of a new generation of leadership scholars." Thus, the award is intended not only for the scholarly contribution of the chosen individual but, equally important, for the contribution to the development of others in the field. To date, award recipients have been: 1976, Ralph M. Stogdill himself; 1978, Fred E. Fiedler; 1980, Rensis Likert.

The current symposium was sponsored by the NATO Scientific Affairs Division, Special Programme Panel on Human Factors, the Texas Tech University College of Business Administration, and the University of Southern California Graduate School of Business Administration. We are indebted to officials in all of these organizations for their encouragement and support.

Planning and arrangements for this international symposium involved a number of people. First, there was a symposium organizing committee to participate in planning, paper evaluation, and decision making. The committee was composed of the four editors: James G. (Jerry) Hunt (Texas Tech), Dian-Marie Hosking (University of Aston), Chester A. Schriesheim (University of Florida), and Rosemary Stewart (Oxford Centre for Management Studies).

Second, to host the symposium and implement travel and lodging arrangements, Anne Bond at the Oxford Centre for Management Studies provided invaluable help.

Third, graduate assistants Ashok Pawha and Donna Sarchet, along with secretaries Sheila Hatcher and Glenna Merryfield and student workers Beverly Harrell, Cheryl Martin, Lori Rubio, and Rana Wheeler, all at Texas Tech, provided administrative and secretarial help beyond the call of duty (as did Anne Bond at Oxford).

The content of this volume was obtained as follows. First, a call for abstracts was: (1) mailed to a large number of people throughout the world, and (2) advertised in a number of journals with heavy North American and/or international circulation.

Abstracts from the Americas and Asia were sent to Jerry Hunt and Chet Schriesheim. Abstracts from the rest of the world were sent to Rosemary Stewart and Dian Hosking. There was then a panel of reviewers at each location.

Some 200 + abstracts were received from the call. Raters at each location then blind-reviewed these. After consultation between and across the two sets of editors, a group of abstracts was considered to have received ratings indicating that they should be considered further.

The authors of this group of abstracts were invited to prepare complete papers. The completed papers then underwent a review process similar to that of the abstracts. Twelve papers and five "think pieces" (shorter works, in early stages of development and representative of diverse perspectives) were final-

ly selected for presentation along with an invited contribution on participation by Edward E. Lawler III. The contributions included in this volume
represent those presented at the Oxford symposium, with the exception of
works that could not be satisfactorily revised in time to meet publication
constraints.

The review process was aided by a longstanding symposium advisory board,
augmented by a large number of ad hoc reviewers. Advisory board members
are:

CHRIS ARGYRIS
Harvard University

BERNARD BASS
*State University of New York at
  Binghamton*

DAVID BOWERS
University of Michigan

ELMER BURACK
University of Illinois at Chicago

JOHN CAMPBELL
University of Minnesota

MARTIN CHEMERS
University of Utah

JOHN CHILD
*University of Aston in
  Birmingham, U.K.*

LARRY CUMMINGS
Northwestern University

MARTIN EVANS
University of Toronto

GEORGE FARRIS
*Rutgers, The State University of
  New Jersey*

FRED FIEDLER
University of Washington

EDWIN FLEISHMAN
Advanced Research Resources

WILLIAM FOX
University of Florida

GEORGE GRAEN
University of Cincinnati

CHARLES GREENE
Indiana University

EDWIN HOLLANDER
*State University of New York
  at Buffalo*

ROBERT HOUSE
University of Toronto

T. OWEN JACOBS
*Army Research Institute
Alexandria, Virginia*

STEVEN KERR
University of Southern California

ABRAHAM KORMAN
City University of New York

CHARLES LEVINE
University of Kansas

JAMES PRICE
University of Iowa

MARSHALL SASHKIN
University of Maryland

CHESTER SCHRIESHEIM
University of Florida

HENRY SIMS, JR.
The Pennsylvania State University

JOHN SLOCUM, JR.
Southern Methodist University

JOHN STINSON
Ohio University

PETER WEISSENBERG
*Rutgers University, Camden,
New Jersey*

Ad hoc reviewers were:

MICHAEL ARGYLE
Oxford University

IAN MORLEY
University of Warwick, U.K.

ANTHONY BUTTERFIELD
University of Massachusetts

RICHARD MOWDAY
University of Oregon

THOMAS CUMMINGS
University of Southern California

RICHARD OSBORN
*Battelle Human Affairs Research
Centers, Seattle, Washington*

PIETER J. D. DRENTH
Free University of Amsterdam

JANET FULK
University of Southern California

RANDALL SCHULER
New York University

DAN GOWLER
*Oxford Centre for Management
Studies*

CHERYL SEGRIST
Texas Tech University

JOHN SHERIDAN
Texas Christian University

RICKY GRIFFIN
Texas A&M University

RICHARD STEERS
University of Oregon

FRANK HELLER
Tavistock Institute, London, U.K.

PETER STORM
*University of Groningen,
The Netherlands*

EDWARD LAWLER, III
University of Southern California

HENRY TOSI, JR.
University of Florida

BARRY MACY
Texas Tech University

BERNARD WILPERT
Technical University of Berlin

MORGAN McCALL
*Center for Creative Leadership,
Greensboro, North Carolina*

GARY YUKL
*State University of New York
at Albany*

The advisory board and reviewers have been most helpful in providing a critically important perspective to supplement that of the organizing committee.

The present symposium could not have been held without the assistance of all those mentioned above. Neither could it have taken place without financial support. The bulk of such support came from the NATO Scientific

Affairs Division and the United States Army Research Institute for the Behavioral and Social Sciences. This was supplemented by support from the Office of Naval Research and Smithsonian Institution along with the University of Southern California Graduate School of Business Administration. Secretarial and graduate-student assistance was provided by Texas Tech University.

In addition to the above points, a word is in order about the editorship of this volume. If one takes an international emphasis seriously, it is nearsighted to restrict editorship exclusively to those from the United States. Thus, the two American editors have been joined by their colleagues from the United Kingdom. It was agreed that Jerry Hunt, as the founder and principal architect of the symposia series, would be the senior editor and the others would be listed alphabetically.

This ordering is followed for most of the editorial pieces in the book. In one or two cases, however, the ordering is changed to reflect extra preparation effort on the part of the first author. Let there be no doubt about overall contribution, however; this book and the symposium upon which it is based reflect a true team effort on the part of *all* the editors. Had it been possible to prepare a book with no ordering of names, we would have done so.

Last, but not least, Donna Hunt should be recognized for proofreading assistance. We are indebted to her and the others mentioned above for their outstanding efforts.

J. G. Hunt
Dian-Marie Hosking
Chester A. Schriesheim
Rosemary Stewart

Leaders and Managers

1

International Managerial Behavior/Leadership Perspectives: An Introduction

James G. Hunt, Dian-Marie Hosking,
Chester A. Schriesheim, and Rosemary Stewart

In the two most recent volumes in this series *(Leadership: Beyond Establishment Views* and *Crosscurrents in Leadership)*, it was argued that the scholarly study of leadership was in a transitional period. Such a period is one where "the major tasks are to reappraise the existing structure, explore new possibilities . . . and work toward choices that provide a basis for a new structure" (Levinson, 1978, p. 317). It was further argued that we could not yet tell what the new structure would look like but that it would probably be highly pluralistic with "different models for different purposes, in contrast to one or a few grand models" (Hunt, Sekaran & Schriesheim, 1982, p. 6).

This volume not only continues that diverse, pluralistic tradition but adds dramatically to that diversity with its heavy international focus. That focus, which was only a glimmer in *Crosscurrents*, became more marked in *Beyond Establishment Views*, and is now a major driving force in this volume.

As the selections in this book show, the international emphasis clearly adds to the diversity of models and approaches considered. The diversity stems from the different philosophical and empirical assumptions of many researchers outside North America as compared with their North American colleagues.* The diversity is also enhanced by movement away from models concerned strictly with narrow-gauge interpersonal influence and toward consideration of virtually all aspects of managerial behavior.

Finally, the volume is further diversified by the inclusion of a number of "think pieces." These are shorter contributions in an earlier stage of development that are designed to be provocative and to add new insights in ways of thinking about leadership and managerial behavior.

---

*The terms "North American" and (less frequently) "United States" are used generally by us in this book to contrast one set of studies with "European" and (less frequently) "outside North America" work. These terms are meant to be generic and their spirit is to avoid both chauvinism and overgeneralization.

Thus, the volume is the embodiment of the editors' philosophy of "Let a thousand flowers bloom," which we think is clearly called for in the current transitional period of leadership research. The trick is to try to maintain a reasonable level of quality and coherence along with this diversity and, we hope, to retain our former constituency while broadening this constituency perhaps beyond the recognition of traditional North American leadership scholars. This is tied in with how well the book meets a key objective of the symposia series, "to chart the state of the field." Obviously, we believe it does it quite well, in ways that we shall show. Of course, the reader must be the final judge of the volume's success in terms of quality, coherence, and charting of the field.

With this prologue in mind, we will first look at the structure of the book, and then provide a thematic overview of the content.

The book is divided into six parts, each of which begins with a part introduction. These introductions summarize the content of each chapter in the part and point out a number of specific issues relevant to each chapter and how these fit into other areas. These comments are a combination of our own insights and those expressed by the symposium participants and audience.

In the first five parts, the part introduction is followed by three or four content chapters. In addition to these, each of the parts has a concluding commentary chapter. These commentary chapters contain discussants' reactions to one or more of the preceding chapters in the part, and also integrative comments on the part as a whole. It is here that the international flavor of the book is extended beyond that in the content chapters. Commentators were selected from countries other than those represented by the chapter authors. Each part as a whole then tends to contain a diverse set of perspectives from a number of different countries. In general, these commentators go beyond a simple critiquing of the chapters by embedding them within a broader literature base and pointing out some implications for future research.

Part 6 consists of two chapters. The first of these is an epilog providing a brief sampling of work from throughout the world that was not treated or only touched upon in the rest of the book. The second is a conclusions chapter written by the editors. Together these two chapters are designed to extend the content of the book and provide a broad perspective on the state of managerial behavior/leadership research as of 1983.

Let us now take a brief look at the contents of each part.

PART 1. NEW PERSPECTIVES ON LEADERSHIP AND MANAGEMENT

The content chapters in this part provide new ways of conceptualizing leadership/managerial behavior in organizations. Even though all these chapters assume an underlying structural-functional paradigm, they are extremely diverse. In this they are illustrative of the diversity throughout the book. Three of the chapters are entirely theoretical while one is a mix of theory and empirical work.

PART 2. RESEARCH METHODOLOGIES FOR EXPLORING MANAGERIAL BEHAVIOR

Where Part 1 emphasizes conceptual matters, Part 2 emphasizes a number of different methodologies in measuring managerial behavior/leadership. These methodologies range from observational approaches to exploratory experiential methodologies based on epistemological assumptions that differ from work in the other chapters in this part. There is not only a range in the methodologies employed, but also in the breadth and depth with which behaviors are conceptualized and measured.

PART 3. SYMBOLISM, METAPHORS, AND MANIPULATION OF MEANING

Traditional leadership research has tended to focus on a fairly narrow range of behaviors and on outcomes such as satisfaction and performance. In contrast, the chapters in Part 3 are representative of approaches that examine the less direct but quite important symbolic, metaphorical, and thought-shaping aspects of leadership. Organizational culture, metaphorical imagery, and the impact of language in situational interpretations are the key concerns.

PART 4. PARTICIPATION RESEARCH: EUROPEAN AND UNITED STATES PERSPECTIVES

A book purporting to include international managerial behavior/leadership perspectives would not be complete without detailed consideration of participation research. The governmental and organizational systems outside North America often mandate some form of worker-management participation. Of course, such a mandated system has a substantial impact on how one conceptualizes and studies leadership and managerial behavior.

The contributions in this part focus on some of the different forms such participation can take and are representative of major cross-national research streams. Work from two large-scale multi-nation studies is reported and a close look is taken at issues encountered in United States organizations for participative decision making. A number of theoretical issues are dealt with and a "processual" longitudinal design that allows one to track the ongoing decision-making process in this kind of research is discussed in some detail.

PART 5. THINK PIECES ON OVERCOMING THE RULING PARADIGMATIC ORTHODOXY

Though the three think pieces in this part take different points of view, they are tied together by their attempt to move beyond traditional North American leadership approaches. The emphasis is on work ranging from discretion in the role of a manager to a new leadership conceptualization to deal with emerging technologies to leadership in the context of strategic management.

PART 6. EPILOG AND CONCLUSIONS

The first chapter in Part 6 summarizes a very large number of studies from North America and beyond, most of which had not been published as of the beginning of 1983. The second chapter, comprised of the editors' conclusions, focuses on the values and traditions involved in current organizational behavior and leadership research; it examines the implications of these in terms of a paradigm shift in the study of leadership/managerial behavior.

Part 1

New Perspectives on Leadership and Management

Introduction

James G. Hunt, Dian-Marie Hosking,
Chester A. Schriesheim, and Rosemary Stewart

The four chapters in this part share a general lack of concern with distinctions between leadership and management; in many cases the terms are used interchangeably. This seems increasingly to be the fashion, and has been commented on elsewhere (Hosking & Hunt, 1982). The chapters also share an interest in the interpersonal concerns of management *within*, rather than *of* organizations, and in the processes and outcomes experienced by those formally appointed to managerial positions. Three of the four chapters are clearly embedded in the structural-functionalist paradigm, and the fourth (Chapter 2) is an example of structural analysis. These points are returned to in the concluding chapter in this volume.

In Chapter 2, Robert E. Quinn presents a conceptual framework intended to characterize the "perceptual understructure" of social action. Quinn argues that every statement about social phenomena—regardless of whether the level of analysis is traits, behaviors, organization, or whatever—reflects three "core value dimensions." He arranges these in such a way as to describe four "paradigms" or "world views"—perceptual outlooks that are hard to alter, outlooks that reflect certain preferences, for example, for control/objectivity and certainty, or flexibility, subjectivity, and uncertainty.

Quinn argues that structural analysis reveals that we all endorse one of the four "paradigms" much more strongly than the others. In this respect he is consistent with the substantial literature on what some call "world views" or "scripts" (Abelson, 1981; George, 1974; Holsti, 1970). What is perhaps more unique is his argument that the remaining values are subscribed to in such a way that there are two lesser but "more or less complementary" paradigms, with the fourth being evaluated very negatively. Finally, he suggests that the identified values should be held to be no more than "conceptual opposites," that they should be regarded as of equal value.

Quinn's more general purpose may be similar to that of Von Bertalanffy

(1956), who set out to promote the unity of science by identifying the underlying structural dimensions and developing them into a "General System Theory." Equally, a parallel could be drawn between Quinn's efforts and the type of structural analysis long undertaken by social anthropologists (see, e.g., Malinowski, 1944; Radcliffe-Brown, 1952; as well as Moore & Beck, Chapter 13, this volume).

Peter Storm, from The Netherlands, has written the commentary for Quinn's chapter. He was chosen because of his knowledge of the European and U.S. leadership literature and because of his balanced academic/practitioner orientation. He raises a number of very specific concerns about Quinn's chapter and asks for clarification on a number of points. His underlying concern seems to be that Quinn's sophisticated model is simultaneously too simple in some areas and too complex in others. Storm ties the model into a number of other leadership approaches ranging from micro to macro treatments. Finally, Storm shows how this relatively abstract model might be related to some practical concerns of middle managers.

The reader may ask to what extent a person's most strongly endorsed paradigm will remain so over time. It is also instructive to compare Quinn's view with that of others such as Burrell and Morgan (1979) who, unlike Quinn, argue that different paradigms reflect *mutually exclusive world views* such that an individual cannot endorse more than one paradigm.

The thesis of Chapter 3, "A Multiple-Constituency Framework of Managerial Reputational Effectiveness," by Anne S. Tsui is predicated on a distinction similar to that employed by March and Simon (1958): that is, a distinction between questions of fact and questions of value. Given that this is so, different "constituencies" or "stakeholders" will evaluate managerial effectiveness in different ways. More precisely, Tsui uses role theory to argue that "multiple constituencies" of subordinates, peers, and superordinates send expectations to a manager that indicate what they judge to constitute desirable role behaviors. "Reputational effectiveness" is gained when these expectations are met. Higher levels of "reputational effectiveness" are achieved when all of a manager's constituents rate him or her highly. Tsui argues that higher levels of "reputational effectiveness" will result in favorable outcomes for the individual manager and for the organization. Concerning the latter, higher levels of reputational effectiveness will — in the long term — result in a "mutually responsive organization" with high levels of cooperation and functional contributions.

Commenting on Tsui's chapter is Alfred Kieser, from West Germany. Kieser was selected because of his macrosociological orientation and on the basis of his work with organizational variables of the kind dealt with by Tsui. The essence of his commentary is that Tsui's model is too restrictive. He goes on to develop a number of points that he thinks Tsui's model neglects. Among these neglected points are: a heavier emphasis on the dynamic processes of role making; emphasis on attribution; consideration of the myths and ideologies reflected in symbolic actions; and a much more detailed look at constituent expectations.

One issue to be considered by the reader is that of the relationship between "reputational effectiveness" and other outcomes such as organizational effectiveness or commitment. What might be the relationship between "consensual reputational effectiveness" and "hard" performance criteria? Another question is concerned with a key premise of the model that managers act in response to the expectations of multiple "role senders." How might this premise be reconciled with the actions of managers who have such strong beliefs about the role behaviors in which they should engage that they consider those of "constituencies" as largely irrelevant?

In Chapter 4, "Functionalism: Basis for an Alternate Approach to the Study of Leadership," Charles F. Rauch and Orlando Behling attempt to integrate previously unconnected hypotheses and data through the explicit application of a well-known but often unrecognized paradigm — that of "structural-functionalism." They argue that there are two leadership functions: task and maintenance. Given the functionalist perspective, it is argued that these two functions promote the survival of the social system in which they occur. A second premise is that different "structures" — that is, "events, artifacts, and processes" — have *"functional equivalence."* This means that they are deemed to be alike, not in the substantive sense but in the sense that they all contribute the same functions to system survival. The structures that Rauch and Behling argue contribute in this way are: "hierarchical leader behaviors," "self-management," "the task itself" (including "formal organization"), "workgroup influences," and external "environmental influence."

Michael Argyle, from the United Kingdom, was selected to comment on the Rauch and Behling chapter because of his early, classic work in the leadership area and because of his coauthorship of a book relevant to some of the chapter concepts. Argyle first raises some questions about the theoretical aspects of the Rauch and Behling model and then makes suggestions for reanalyzing some of the data in order to focus on a number of questions suggested by the chapter. He proposes some extensions to the current work based on his recently completed book in which a range of different social situations are examined. Finally, he discusses a number of issues related to the substitutes for leadership (Kerr & Jermier, 1978) or nonleader sources of clarity notions (Hunt, 1975) treated in United States leadership literature.

One issue, touched upon by Argyle, concerns whether or not adding in increasing levels of maintenance *structures* will result in concomitant linear increases in the degree to which the maintenance *function* is fulfilled. Osborn, Hunt, and Jauch (1980) call this the "manure hypothesis" and argue that the relationship is *nonlinear*: a little is good, but too much stinks. Hosking and Morley (1980) also deal with related notions.

Another question concerns what problems might be involved in trying to investigate the different kinds of cross-functional task and maintenance relationships suggested by the model. Instrumentation, sampling, and measurement limitations are all important issues. And finally, how realistic is the functional equivalency assumption of the authors? To what extent might it be an oversimplification?

The last content chapter in Part 1, by Janet Fulk and Thomas G. Cummings, is a "modest proposal." The authors' use of the modifier, "modest," is perhaps because their proposal is only intended to deal with "unofficial social-contracting processes." It is argued that these involve negotiation between "leaders" and their subordinates. In other words, they restrict their attention to contracting that occurs "over and above the formal employment contract"—to what they define as leadership à la Katz and Kahn (1978), as opposed to management. As a feature of such negotiations, leaders and subordinates develop certain kinds of "relationships." They also arrive at an "informal work contract" that specifies the subordinates' task content and task boundaries.

The authors identify four "pure types" of social contracting that differ in the amount of influence the subordinate has in relation to others. For example, they include "contractual relations" where mutual influence results in the determination of the subordinates' task content and task boundaries, and "prescribed relations where the leader exercises most influence (of a non-authority-based kind). Using Bateson's theory of logical types (Ruesch & Bateson, 1951), Fulk and Cummings argue that the nature of the relationship between the leader and subordinates will structure the meanings that the latter attach to their task. To put the point slightly differently, the amount of discretion a subordinate has on a particular task will have different meanings (for that individual) depending on the interpersonal processes by which the agreement was reached.

Aspects of the wider system setting are considered in terms of their possible effects on matters such as the leader's ability to influence subordinates (or substitutes for leadership; see Kerr & Jermier, 1978). Various aspects of organization are referred to as possible constraints on the degree to which leaders and subordinates are willing and able to engage in formal social contracting: it is argued that technology and other such "contextual" conditions represent constraints on the kinds of agreements and task characteristics.

The commentator for the Fulk and Cummings chapter is Peter Dachler from Switzerland. A key reason why Dachler was selected was because of his recent concern with developing a new conceptualization of the leadership/management area. He sketches out his reconceptualization in terms of a social-systems approach. Once that is done, he uses it as a base against which to discuss the Fulk and Cummings chapter. His model is of interest in its own right and appears to bear some similarity to the think piece by Osborn, Morris, and Connor in Chapter 21.

One point for consideration is the way in which Chapter 5 distinguishes leadership from management and its focus on informal social contracting over and above the formal employment contract. To what extent might it be possible to apply this in practice where the actual definition of formal requirements and their fulfillment might present difficulties?

One should also consider the circumstances under which social contracting might or might not be appropriate, desirable, or feasible. Personal preferences and economic conditions may make a difference. The employment relationship could serve as a boundary condition: for example, very little social contracting may take place in subcontracted, market-based relations (see Williamson, 1975).

Overall, the chapters in this part raise underlying questions concerning the nature of social structure, the nature of "reality," and the nature of social systems. Dian-Marie Hosking treats these in her integrative commentary. Further elaboration on some of these points is also provided by the editors in the book's concluding chapter.

2

Applying the Competing Values Approach to Leadership: Toward an Integrative Framework

Robert E. Quinn

Seventeen years ago Rinn (1965) expressed frustration with the way knowledge is accumulated in the social sciences. He was particularly chagrined by the fact that "theoretical systems proceed without sufficient attention to structural similarities between diverse universes of content," and that this inattention hinders the discovery of "isomorphic relationships between theories." In hopes of furthering communication and understanding, Rinn offered the following:

> My proposal is that each of us should first identify the domain of phenomena to which he is attending and then describe its structure, that is, identify the major parameters which can be used to rank the domain elements. If we will both do this, my hunch is that we will find some degree of similarity among parameters even when we are concerned with different domains. Hopefully, these common parameters will help us bridge the communication-research gap which now stands in the way of our constructing a broad science of man. (p. 445)

While Rinn's concerns are focused on all of social science, they are particularly appropriate to the study of leadership. Despite an immense investment in the enterprise, researchers have become increasingly disenchanted with the field. The seemingly endless array of unconnected empirical investigations is bewildering as well as frustrating (Greene, 1977; Korman, 1966; Miner, 1975; Salancik, Calder, Rowland, Leblebici, & Conway, 1975; Schriesheim & Kerr, 1977). Not only do we fail to specify the structural similarities between leadership and other fields, but even within the field we fail to specify the parallels between such mainline approaches as the analysis of traits, behaviors, and influence patterns (Yukl, 1981, p. 89). Just as the failure to specify similarities hinders the construction of "a broad science of man," so the problem hinders us from developing a more efficient investigation of leadership. This chapter presents a framework that specifies similarities across traits, behaviors, and influence patterns, organizing these three approaches within the field, and linking them to other areas of organizational analysis.

This is done by making explicit the understructure of leadership theory. While the framework presented here is large in scope, it is clearly a theoretical statement. It goes without question that the dimensions, definitions, and conceptual relationships posited here will be refined or perhaps radically altered by the hard edge of empirical investigation.

TOWARD COGNITIVE UNDERSTRUCTURE

In a program of research on the perception of organizational effectiveness criteria, we developed a scheme called the *Competing Values Framework*. Successive panels of experts in organization theory were asked to make judgments about the similarity and dissimilarity of effectiveness criteria (Quinn & Rohrbaugh, 1981, 1983). In each study, the judgments were analyzed with multidimensional scaling, and in each analysis the resulting cognitive maps were strikingly similar. The results of the research led us to propose that there might be a general perceptual understructure operating when researchers and practitioners make judgments about organizations and their performance (see Figure 2.1. While it is tempting to explain the framework in detail, because

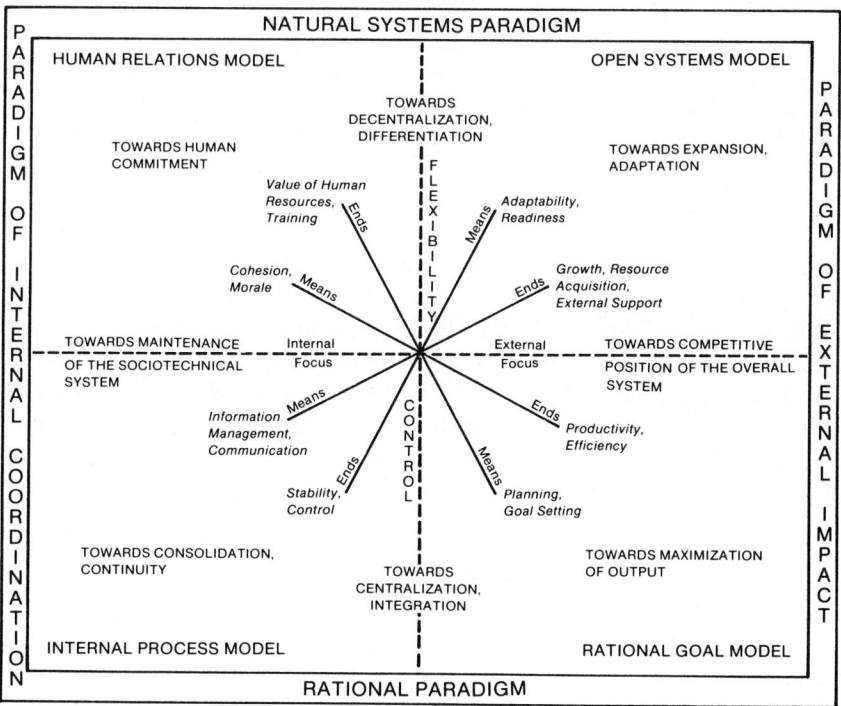

FIGURE 2.1. The competing values framework of effectiveness criteria

of space limitations, we simply present a two-dimensional version of the scheme in this figure and refer the reader to several papers that explain its arrangement and elaborate its implications and applications; Quinn & Rohrbaugh, 1981, 1983; Quinn, 1981; Quinn & Cameron, 1983; Quinn & McGrath, 1982).

In a recent paper we moved our focus from the evaluation of organizational performance to some wider concerns, and argued that the dimensions in Figure 2.1 are representative of value dimensions that are widely employed in the evaluation of social action (Quinn, 1981). These dimensions are control — flexibility, internal focus — external focus, and means or processes — ends or outcomes. Following Jones (1961), we suggested that these values are likely to be manifest in the aesthetic production of a high culture, particularly in such areas as art, poetry, philosophy, and scientific theory. Using organization analysis as an illustration, we showed that strong parallels to the above framework appear at nearly every level of analysis. These include, for example, Jung's (1971) four problem-solving types, the four motive systems of Forgus and Shulman (1979), Driver and Rowe's (1979) four decision styles, Leary's (1957) four personality quadrants, Rinn's (1965) four structural domains, Parson's (1959) four systemic prerequisites, and Burrell and Morgan's (1977) four-quadrant analysis of organization theory. In our paper we explored two possible explanations of why the dimensions emerge. The first is a biological explanation concerning information processing and the structure of the brain and builds on the work of Springer and Deutsch (1981) and Taggart and Robey (1981). The second is from Forgus and Shulman (1979); it is more sociopsychological in orientation, and suggests that the perceptual system is conditioned to differentiate along these axes during the early phases of infant socialization.

In elaborating our arguments about perceptual bias, we proposed the cognitive framework in Figure 2.2. While the framework is clearly a speculative statement, it is highly consistent with theories of individual perception and information processing developed by Jung (1971), Driver and Rowe (1979), Forgus and Shulman (1979), and Taggart and Robey (1981). At the foundation of the diagram are the same vertical and horizontal axes shown in Figure 2.1. The vertical axis has to do with structure and ranges from an emphasis on flexibility to an emphasis on control. Toward the top are subjectivity and uncertainty, while toward the bottom are objectivity and certainty. The horizontal axis has to do with the difference between an internal focus and an external focus. The inner orientation is more receptive and passive; the outer more exploratory and aggressive. At the left are the values of withdrawal, rest, reflection, and serenity. At the right are the values of engagement, tension, impact, and conflict. They suggest two very distinct orientations.

The juxtaposition of the vertical and horizontal axes creates four large quadrants that are labeled according to four motive systems proposed by

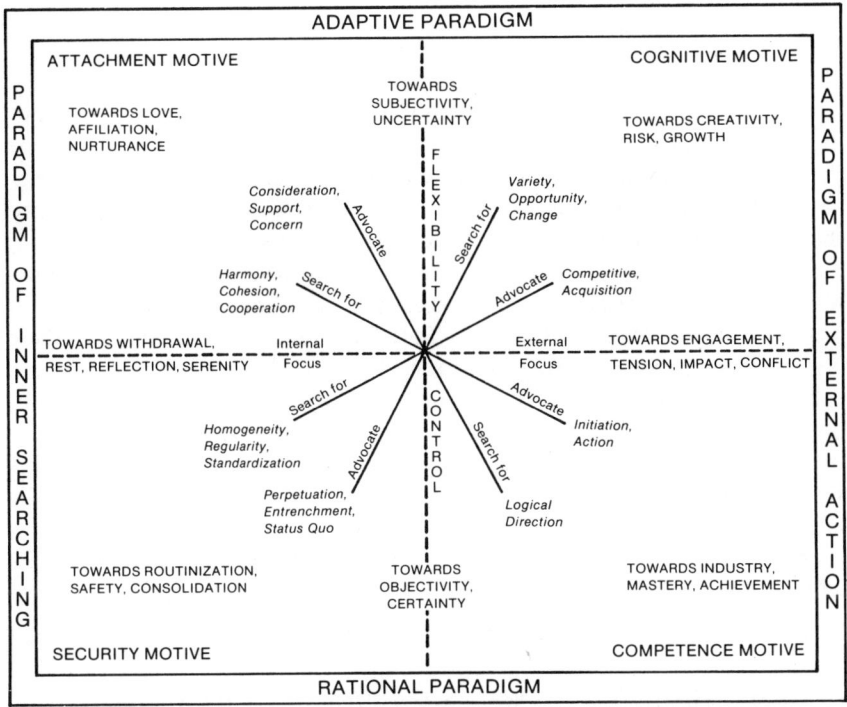

FIGURE 2.2. Toward a framework of cognitive values

Forgus and Shulman (1979). The diagram further suggests that within each motive system there is a dominant bias in terms of searching the environment and advocating a particular set of social values. In the attachment motive (upper left), for example, there is a tendency to search for harmony, cohesion, and cooperation, and to advocate consideration, support, and concern, suggesting a high value on love, affiliation, and the nurturance of human relationships. Each of the other quadrants can be interpreted in the same manner.

In the margins of the diagram are four paradigms. By "paradigm" we mean a widely accepted world view, a basic perceptual outlook that is widely shared and very difficult to alter (Georgiou, 1973). The rational paradigm (bottom) suggests a world view in which there is a strong preference for control, objectivity, and certainty with a tendency to search for logical direction and to advocate perpetuation, entrenchment, and the status quo. In this world view, both the security and mastery motives are important and their related values are espoused. In contrast, the adaptive paradigm (top) suggests a world view in which there is a strong preference for flexibility and a high tolerance for subjectivity and uncertainty. There is a tendency to search for variety, opportunity, and change while advocating consideration, support, and concern. Here, the attachment and cognitive motives are both important and their related values are espoused.

The two paradigms on the sides of the diagram are particularly interesting. The two lines on either side of internal focus are "search" lines, while the two lines on either side of external focus are "advocate" lines. This suggests that the paradigm to the left is highly passive, while the paradigm to the right is highly active. In the paradigm of inner searching (left), there is a tendency to seek harmony, cohesion, and cooperation while also seeking homogeneity, regularity, and standardization. The dominant value is on withdrawal, rest, reflection, and serenity. In the paradigm of external action there is a tendency to advocate the initiation of planned action and to engage in competitive acquisition. The dominant value is on engagement, tension, impact, and conflict. These two world views not only parallel the inner-outer distinctions of a number of scholars, but they are also at the core of the difference in Eastern and Western philosophy (Taggart & Robey, 1981). On the left is the Eastern view which suggests oneness with nature, accepting things as they are, and taking no unnecessary action. On the left is the Western view which suggests the imposition of order onto nature and the manipulating of things in order to bring about desired ends and outcomes.

THE DIMENSIONS IN LEADERSHIP RESEARCH

The orientations in Figures 2.1 and 2.2 are not new to leadership theory. Although usually not clearly articulated, they have been operating for some time. In the *Handbook of Leadership* (Bass, 1981), for example, five chapters are devoted to each of the following dichotomies: democratic versus autocratic; participative versus directive; relations versus task; consideration versus initiation; and laissez-faire versus motivation to manage. Hundreds of studies are reviewed in the 112 densely packed pages. The introduction to this material begins with reference to the 1938 Lewin and Lippitt study, lists 26 labels under which types of relationships have since been dichotomized, defines the five dichotomies to be used in the coming five chapters, and then observes:

> Karmel (1978) drew attention to the ubiquity of initiation and consideration in the study of leadership and efforts to theorize about it. What she primarily offered to add was the importance of the total amount of both kinds of leader activity in contrast to leader inactivity. Thus, she brought us back full-circle to Lewin and Lippitt (1938), who conceptualized leadership as authoritarian (initiating), democratic (considerate), or laissez-faire (inactive rather than active). (Bass, 1981, p. 219)

This statement illustrates two important points. First, the phenomenon of leadership tends to be perceived around the core dimensions in Figure 2.2.

Authoritarian leadership is toward the bottom, rational paradigm, while democratic leadership is toward the top, adaptive paradigm. Active leadership is toward the paradigm of external impact, on the right, while inactive leadership is toward the paradigm of inner searching, on the left. (For a second, very striking discussion of the ubiquity of this phenomenon, see Rinn, 1965, pp. 446–447). Second, as illustrated in the above statement, there is a tendency to conceive of and employ only three of the four values. Here, for example, the action orientation is collapsed onto the authoritarian and democratic orientations. The importance of this second tendency will be elaborated later.

A second, more specific example of the fact that these dimensions are operating comes from MacCoby (1976), who reports a study in which he interviewed 250 managers from 12 major corporations. A psychoanalyst who was not steeped in the culture of corporate life, MacCoby came to the field of management free of many of the prevailing assumptions. Using a variety of psychoanalytic and anthropological techniques, he set out to build a typology of management character. He concluded that there are four types of managers, and his four types closely parallel the four quadrants in Figure 2.2. The *craftsman* is technically oriented, focuses on constraints, is conservative, and has a need for security. This type contrasts sharply with the *gamesman* whose main interest is in challenge, competition, risk, new ideas, and approaches The *company man* is concerned for the human side of the organization, interested in the feelings of people, cooperation, and mutuality. Contrasting with this type is the exploitative, dominant, action-oriented *jungle fighter*. These four tend to fit well into the quadrants in Figure 2.2. The last category, the jungle fighter, is not as well developed as the others and is slightly out of focus, a fact discussed below.

Problems of Bias and the Conceptualization of Opposites

A major proposition of this chapter is that the dimensions in Figure 2.2 enter the world of leadership theory not once but twice. First, the actor in the social situation (the leader) employs them to differentiate and make sense of the social environment and to select an appropriate action. Second, the observer (researcher-theorist) employs these same dimensions in making sense of what is going on in the observed situation. These dimensions influence the research design, the observation process, and the description of the phenomenon. One of the reasons why the four-quadrant framework fails to appear even more often in social science is that our tendencies in information processing hinder us from effectively conceiving of opposites as equally valued (Rothenberg, 1979; Weick, 1977b). Jungian theory suggests, for example, that people are predisposed toward feeling or thinking and toward sensation or intuition. Hence, there is a strong quadrant. Similarly, Driver and Rowe

(1979) point out that people have a dominant decision style with a less strong backup style.

Our own observation is that there is a weak or empty quadrant; that is, that people have a strong quadrant and two more or less complementary quadrants with a fourth that is highly discounted. The values in this quadrant tend to be defined in negative terms. MacCoby's (1976) chapter about the jungle fighter is an excellent example of this phenomenon, standing in sharp contrast to the other three with the least number of pages and a preponderance of negative terms. This may be attributed to the fact that of the 250 people interviewed, only 11 were of this type, or it may be that the researcher's own cognitive bias put him at a disadvantage in so negatively defining this type that it lost its utility for identifying people.

A second and closely related reason why the four-quadrant framework does not emerge more often is the existence of a generalized cultural bias. For example, in Western culture the external values around assertiveness and conflict tend to be much more important than the interval values around passiveness and harmony (Taggart & Robey, 1981). Generally, we have conceived of and confirmed that active, assertive behaviors are more desirable and more effective than passive behaviors. As illustrated in the above statement from Bass, this bias permeates the entire literature on leadership.

Taken together, these two problems—the bias in individual information processing and the existence of a generalized cultural bias—keep us from being more effective in the art of Janusian thinking. Proposed by Rothenberg (1979) and named for the Roman deity whose two faces looked in opposite directions at the same time, Janusian thinking is a complex process in which a simultaneous antithesis is actively formulated. Two ideas or concepts are conceived to be equally operative or equally true. It is a special type of secondary process thinking that has a dreamlike, mirror-image quality. It arises from psychological or intellectual conflict and provides a means for resolution. Janusian thinking often occurs as a creative leap that overcomes apparent contradictions and generates new progress or creation.

In leadership research we could benefit from some Janusian thinking. By this, we mean conceiving of traits, behaviors, and influence patterns as equally valued opposites. Further, we could organize these and derive greater meaning from such definitions if they were located along the dimensions defined in Figures 2.1 and 2.2. In order to accomplish this task, it is necessary to locate desirable elements (traits, for example) and define them in positive terms. An opposite element must also be located and defined positively. Opposites must not be mutually exclusive such as short and tall, but should be conceptual opposites that, at least theoretically, might be simultaneously demonstrated in the experiential world.

In an attempt to accomplish this task, we began to work with Yukl's (1981) lists of effective traits (p. 70), behaviors (p. 121), and influence patterns (p. 11). As we set out to categorize, combine, and organize traits, we were struck

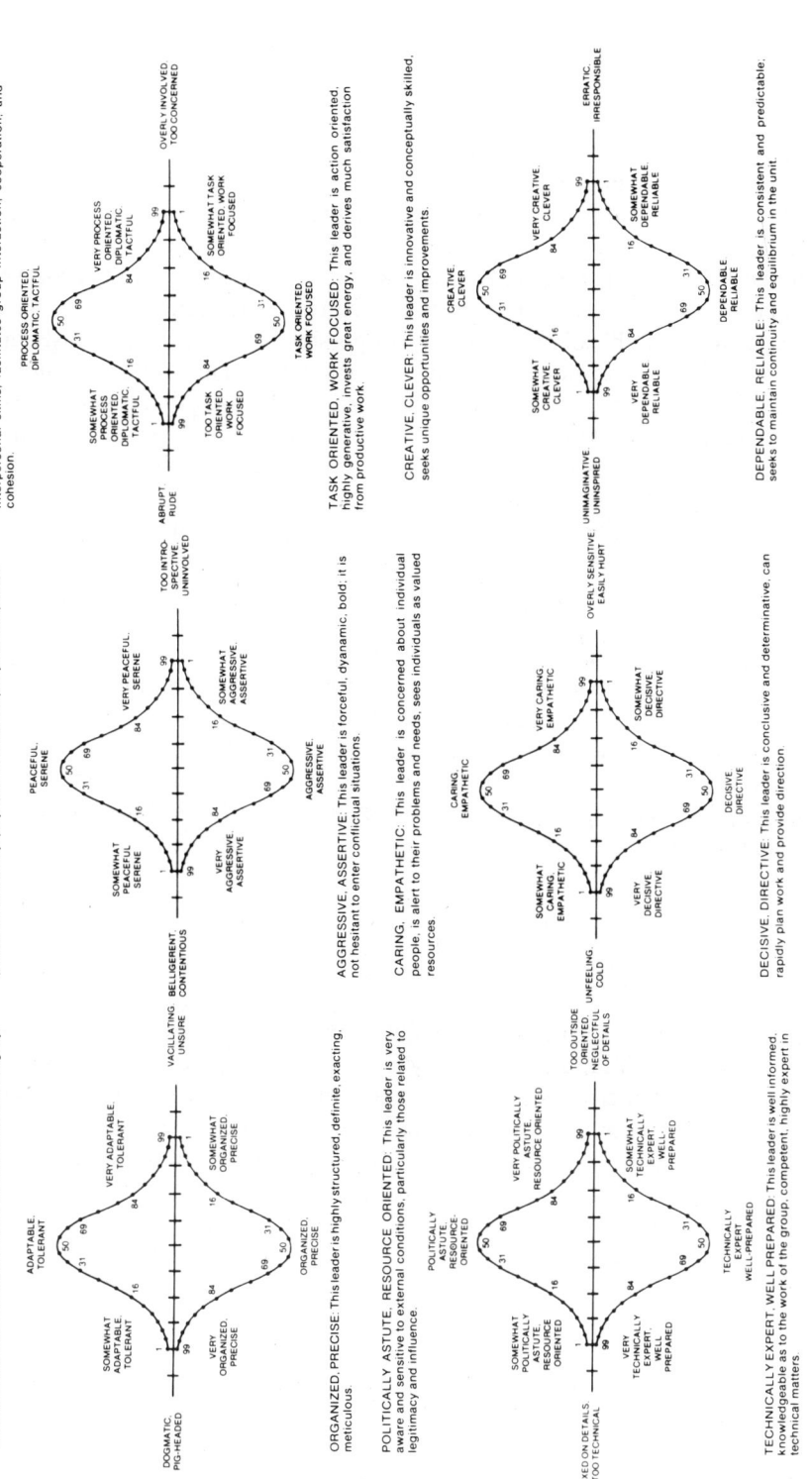

ADAPTABLE, TOLERANT: This leader is flexible, open, adjusts well to turbulent conditions; has a high tolerance for uncertainty and ambiguity.

ORGANIZED, PRECISE: This leader is highly structured, definite, exacting, meticulous.

POLITICALLY ASTUTE, RESOURCE ORIENTED: This leader is very aware and sensitive to external conditions, particularly those related to legitimacy and influence.

TECHNICALLY EXPERT, WELL PREPARED: This leader is well informed, knowledgeable as to the work of the group, competent, highly expert in technical matters.

PEACEFUL, SERENE: This leader tends to be level-headed, unruffled by pressure and adversity, projects a sense of tranquility and composure.

AGGRESSIVE, ASSERTIVE: This leader is forceful, dynamical, bold; it is not hesitant to enter conflictual situations.

CARING, EMPATHETIC: This leader is concerned about individual people, is alert to their problems and needs, sees individuals as valued resources.

DECISIVE, DIRECTIVE: This leader is conclusive and determinative, can rapidly plan work and provide direction.

PROCESS ORIENTED, DIPLOMATIC, TACTFUL: This leader has good interpersonal skills; facilitates group interaction, cooperation, and cohesion.

TASK ORIENTED, WORK FOCUSED: This leader is action oriented, highly generative, invests great energy, and derives much satisfaction from productive work.

CREATIVE, CLEVER: This leader is innovative and conceptually skilled, seeks unique opportunities and improvements.

DEPENDABLE, RELIABLE: This leader is consistent and predictable, seeks to maintain continuity and equilibrium in the unit.

FIGURE 2.3. Six pairs of juxtaposed leadership traits

17

by the fact that each positive trait could be overemphasized and thus redefined in negative terms. A persistent-firm orientation becomes dogmatic and
pig-headed; an orientation toward adaptability-tolerance is seen as a vacillating and unsure position. If the observer, whether an actor in the social situation or a researcher-theorist, is cognitively predisposed in another direction,
then the point at which this shift occurs will come sooner than if the observer is positively predisposed toward the given trait orientation.

Once we made this observation, it was possible to engage consciously in
the generation of overstatements. This, in turn, allowed us to conceive more
precisely of valued opposites with the mirror-image quality that is characteristic of Janusian thinking. In Figure 2.3, for example, we show six pairs of
definitions. In the first we define adaptable-tolerant and persistent-firm. Between the two definitions are two juxtaposed normal curves. The numbers
along the curve at the top suggest movement from a dogmatic-pig-headed
position toward increasing adaptability and tolerance. The inverted curve begins at the vacillating-unsure position and moves toward increasing persistence
and firmness. It then moves to the dogmatic-pig-headed position. There are
12 definitions. Each definition provides an evaluative point for considering
a given leader. In theory it is possible to be high (or low) on two opposite
definitions. That is, a given leader might be seen as both adaptable-tolerant
and persistent-firm, as both peaceful-serene and aggressive-assertive. These
12 definitions are presented at this point, not for measurement purposes, but
as an initial and tentative illustration of a Janusian system for thinking about
leadership.

TOWARD AN INTEGRATIVE FRAMEWORK

In Table 2.1 we expand upon the previous list and present eight definitions
at each of three levels: traits, behaviors, and influence patterns. In the first
row, for example, are process-oriented, diplomatic, tactful traits. In the same
row, under behaviors, are those activities that facilitate interaction. Next,
under influence patterns are involvement and decision identification. The eight
definitions in each of the three columns are constructed to be Janusian concepts defining four dimensions that closely parallel the dimensions in Figures
2.1 and 2.2. Employing the Janusian qualities consciously built into these definitions, we can construct two diagrams that provide an integrated, tension-
based view of leadership.

Traits, Behaviors, and Styles

In Figure 2.4, the appropriate definitions in the first two columns of Table
2.1 are combined and employed to build a framework of traits and behaviors. This scheme is derived theoretically, its construction guided by the framework in Figure 2.2. It must be seen as a hypothetical rather than an empirical

statement about the perceptual understructure of leadership. At the core of the diagram are the same vertical and horizontal dimensions that appear in Figures 2.1 and 2.2. In the upper-right quadrant is the creative-clever leader who envisions, encourages, and facilitates change. At the opposite point on this same dimension is the dependable-reliable leader who maintains structure, does the scheduling, coordinating, and problem solving, and who sees that rules, standards, and deadlines are met. At the next point in the upper-right quadrant is the resource oriented, politically astute leader who acquires resources and maintains the unit's external legitimacy through the development, scanning, and maintenance of a network of external contacts. At the opposite point is the technically expert-well-prepared leader who deeply comprehends the task of the group, constantly collects and selectively distributes critical information, and facilitates the development of shared meanings about the unit's work environment. These leaders tend to provide a sense of continuity and safety.

If we continue in a clockwise direction, at the next point, in the lower right quadrant, we have the task-oriented-work-focused leader who looks to initiate action, to motivate those behaviors that will result in completion of the group's task. At the opposite point is the process-oriented-diplomatic-tactful leader who facilitates interaction, encourages expression, seeks consensus, and negotiates compromise. At the next point is the decisive-directive leader who provides structure. This person engages in goal setting and role clarification, sets objectives, monitors progress, provides feedback, and establishes clear expectations. At the opposite point is the caring-empathetic leader who shows consideration. This person is aware of individual needs, actively listens, is fair, supports legitimate requests, and attempts to facilitate the development of individuals. Given the lists from which these definitions were derived (Yukl, 1981, pp. 70, 121), it is reasonable to believe that all of these traits and behaviors are, at some time and in some situation, desirable characteristics in leaders.

The juxtaposition of these traits and behaviors suggests certain overlapping styles of leadership. The creative and resource-oriented traits suggest an inventive, risk-taking style. This is in contrast to the conservative, cautious style suggested by the technically expert and dependable-reliable traits. Overlapping the inventive, risk-taking style is the dynamic, competitive style which is suggested by the resource-oriented and work-focused traits. These, in turn, are in contrast to the cooperative, team-oriented style at the opposite side of the diagram. Continuing around the diagram in a similar manner, the directive, goal-oriented style is in contrast to the concerned, supportive style and the structured, formal style is in contrast to the responsive, open style. Each is defined by the traits and behaviors closest to the style. Because each style shares a trait with its neighboring style, it overlaps and is similar to its neighbor while it also tends to be in sharp contrast to its opposite.

Each quadrant is labeled according to the skills that are most representa-

Table 2.1. Eight Definitions at Three Levels of Leadership.

TRAITS	BEHAVIORS	INFLUENCE PATTERNS
Process-Oriented, Diplomatic, Tactful: This leader has good interpersonal skills; facilitates group interaction, cooperation, and cohesion.	*Facilitates Interaction:* This leader is interpersonally skilled, facilitates group process, encourages expression, seeks consensus, facilitates compromise.	*Involvement-Decision Identification:* Through participation, the target person is brought to identify with decisions. Through participation and indoctrination, the target person internalizes the values of the group and is committed to them.
Caring, Empathetic: This leader is concerned about individual people, is alert to their problems and needs, sees individuals as valued resources.	*Shows Consideration:* This leader is aware of individual needs; actively listens; is fair, objective; supports legitimate requests; attempts to facilitate individual development.	*Mutual Dependency-Internal Expectations:* Through consideration and fairness, a trusting relationship is developed and valued by agent and target. Because of valued relationship, informal expectations bring desired behavior.
Creative, Clever: This leader is innovative, conceptually skilled, seeks unique opportunities and improvements.	*Envisions Change:* This leader seeks new opportunities, encourages and considers new ideas, is tolerant of ambiguity and risk.	*Anticipation-Generation of Hope:* Influence is drawn from anticipation of the future. Agent develops hopes for a better condition. Agent gains support by showing relative advantage of proposed change.
Politically Astute, Resource Oriented: This leader is very aware and sensitive to external conditions, particularly to those related to legitimacy, influence, and resource acquisition.	*Acquires Resources:* This leader develops interpersonal contacts, monitors the environment, amasses power and influence, maintains the external image of the unit, and secures resources.	*Resource Control-Instrumental Compliance:* Agent controls resources, target complies due to implicit or explicit promise of some desired outcome.

Task Oriented, Work Focused: This leader is action oriented, highly generative, invests great energy, and derives much satisfaction from productive work.	*Initiates Action:* This leader is concerned about the task, stimulates appropriate performance in group members and others necessary to task completion.	*Accomplishment-Rational Persuasion:* Agent builds on the need for goal attainment. Convinces target that suggested behavior is best way to meet target's needs.
Decisive, Directive: This leader is conclusive and determinative, can rapidly plan work and provide direction.	*Provides Structure:* This leader engages in goal setting and role clarification, sets objectives, monitors progress, provides feedback, establishes clear expectations.	*Formal Structure-Legitimate Request:* Agent's position in hierarchy legitimizes his request, target complies because it is the right thing to do.
Dependable, Reliable: This leader is consistent, predictable; seeks to maintain continuity and equilibrium in the unit.	*Maintains Structure:* This leader maintains the stability and flow of the work by scheduling, coordinating, problem solving, and seeing that rules, standards, and deadlines are understood and met.	*Workflow-Situational Engineering:* Agent's responsibility for the workflow allows manipulation of the physical and social environment; altered opportunities and constraints bring compliance. Levers include layout, equipment, job design, schedules, assignments, policies, etc.
Technically Expert, Well Prepared: This leader is well informed, knowledgeable as to the work of the group, competent, highly expert in technical matters.	*Provides Information:* This leader deeply comprehends the task of the group, constantly collects and distributes information, facilitates the development of shared meanings, develops a group sense of continuity and safety.	*Information Flow-Information Control:* Access to information flow allows agent to bring compliance through giving, withholding, or distorting information to the target.

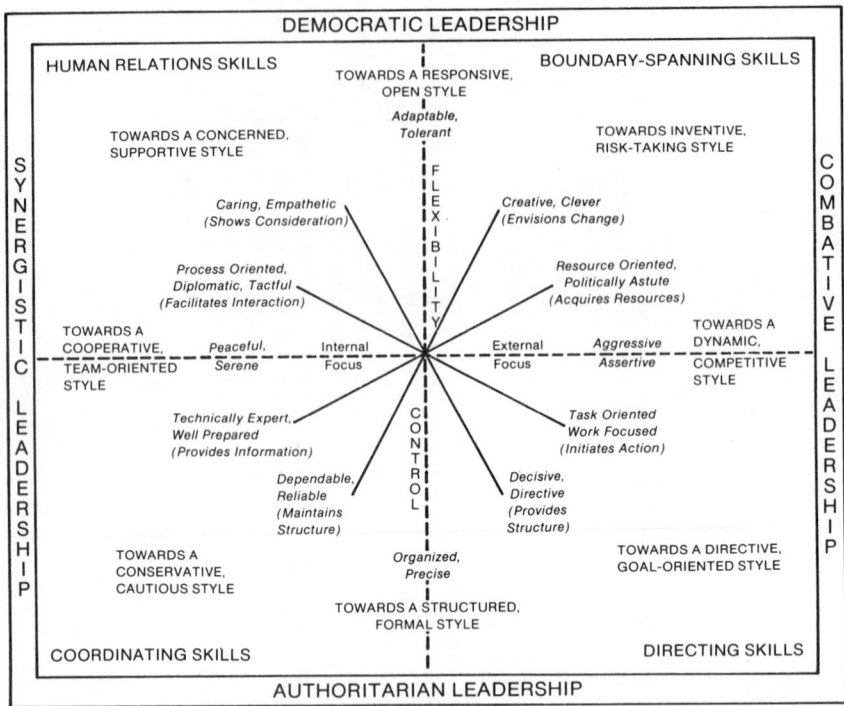

FIGURE 2.4. A competing values framework of leadership traits and behaviors

tive. Boundary-spanning skills in the upper right, directing skills in the lower right, coordinating skills in the lower left, and human-relation skills in the upper left.

As with the schemes in Figures 2.1 and 2.2, the margins contain four paradigms. To the right, for example, is the paradigm of combative leadership. In this world view an effective leader tends to reflect the styles and traits to the right of the diagram with a strong bias toward the dynamic-competitive style and the three most closely associated traits, suggesting that an effective leader is aggressive-assertive, resource oriented, politically astute, and task oriented-work focused. This orientation is very consistent with Western values. Each of the three remaining paradigms can be interpreted in a similar fashion.

The four paradigms may help us to understand some of the confusion in our thinking about leadership. Each paradigm has two overlapping, complementary paradigms and a fourth that is in sharp contrast. It is proposed that many people have difficulty conceiving of their own weak area in positive terms. Hence, for both actors and observers, parts of Figure 2.4 are overemphasized while others are underemphasized and even defined in negative terms.

Influence Patterns and Change Strategies

The concept of influence is deeply embedded in the literature on leadership. Generally, it has to do with the process whereby an agent attempts to alter the perceptions, attitudes, values, or behaviors of a target person. Typologies have been proposed by Dahl (1957), French and Raven (1959), Etzioni (1961), Cartwright (1965), Patchen (1974), Webber (1975), and Lee (1977). Yukl (1981, pp. 11–21) has built a composite of many of the earlier schemes. Most of the definitions in the third column of Table 2.1 and most of the concepts and labels in Figure 2.4 are reflective of the language in these various treatments.

In Figure 2.5 we again begin with the same vertical and horizontal axes and construct a hypothetical arrangement of influence patterns. At each end of the four dimensions are the eight sources and forms of influence from the

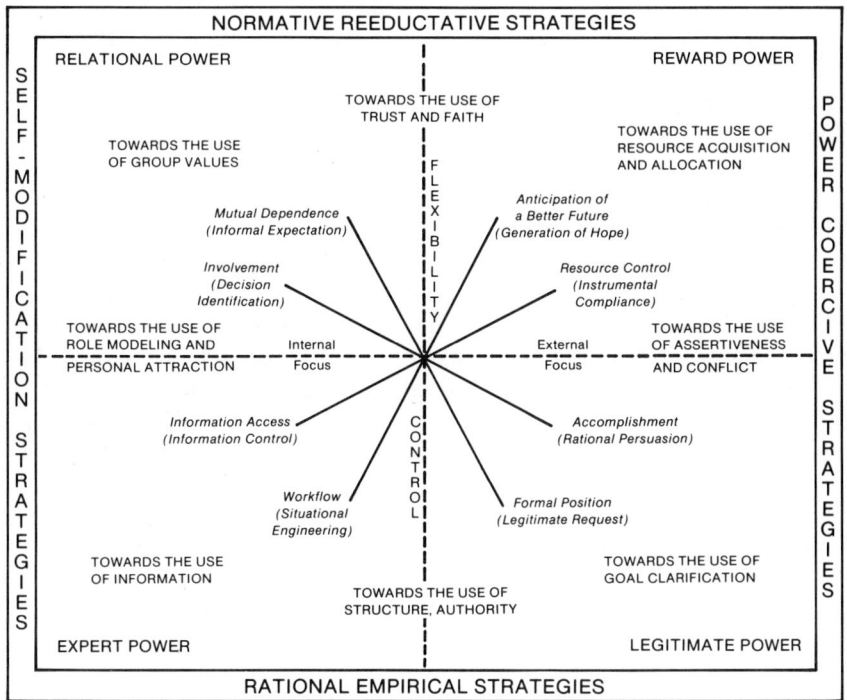

FIGURE 2.5. A competing values framework of influence patterns and change strategies

third column of Table 2.1. Beginning in the upper-right quadrant is the form and source of influence associated with the creative-clever leader who envisions and facilitates change. This person derives influence from the anticipation of a better future. The agent develops the hope of a better condition and gains support by showing the relative advantage of the proposed change to the target person. At the next point in the same quadrant is the source and form associated with the politically astute, resource-oriented leader who is skilled in the acquisition of resources. From the ability to acquire resources comes some degree of control over the distribution of resources. The target person complies because of the implicit or explicit promise of some deserved outcome. In the next quadrant is the pattern associated with the task-oriented, work-focused leader who is action oriented. Here the agent builds on the target's need for goal attainment and uses rational persuasion to convince the target that the suggested behavior is in the target's best interest. The decisive-directive leader who initiates structure through objective setting and role clarification is associated with the pattern at the next point in Figure 2.5. Here the agent makes a legitimate request and the perception of legitimacy flows from the agent's formal position and the appropriateness of the request to the task at hand. In the next quadrant is the source and form associated with the dependable-reliable leader who maintains the structure. Here the source of influence is control over the workflow; change is brought about by situational engineering. The agent manipulates the opportunities and constraints in the physical and social environment in order to bring about the desired end. Some of the levers include layout, equipment, job design, schedules, assignments, and policies. The pattern associated with the technically expert-well-prepared leader has to do with information flow and information control. The agent's access to information allows the person to achieve compliance by giving, withholding, or distorting information.

In the next quadrant is the source and form associated with the group-oriented, diplomatic-tactful leader. Here the agent employs the participative process and achieves influence through decision identification. The target internalizes the values of the groups and carries out decisions in which the target person has invested. The last pattern is the one associated with the caring-empathetic leader. Here the agent derives influence from the individual relationship which is valued by both the agent and the target. Because of this valued mutual dependency, the agent is able to bring compliance through the employment of informal expectation.

The identification of sources and forms of influence allows for a more general specification of influence strategies. At the top of the diagram is reliance on trust and faith. At the opposite point is the employment of structure and authority. In the right quadrant is the use of resource acquisition and allocation, while at the opposite point is the manipulation of information. At the middle, right side is the use of assertiveness and conflict while at the opposite point is role modeling and personal attraction. In the lower-right quadrant is the use of goal clarification, and at the opposite point is the use of group values and pressures. Accordingly, the quadrants are labeled by the type of power that is being employed. These are reward, legitimate, expert, and relational. Referent and coercive power, if shown, would appear at each end of the horizontal axis.

The concept of influence is not only embedded in leadership but also in the literature on change. Indeed, all of the above definitions are written in terms of change. This insight is particularly important as we move to a discussion of the paradigms in the margins of Figure 2.5.

In a classic and wide-ranging article entitled "General Strategies for Effecting Change in Human Systems," Chin and Benne (1969) articulated three general categories of strategies. Rational-empirical strategies assume that people are rational and, once their self-interests are revealed, they will pursue them. This approach assumes that science and research are necessary to overcome ignorance and superstition, and that education (empirical truth) frees people. This approach emphasizes expertise and authority. The expert finds the facts and then tells the target what is rational. The second category, the normative-reeducative approach, is very different. Here, behavior is action supported by norms and commitments that are, in turn, supported by the values and attitudes of the individual. It is not enough to change knowledge, to provide information and rationales. Internalized attitudes, values, habits, skills, and significant relationships must also be changed. The target does not passively await environmental stimuli, but attempts to shape the relationship with the environment. This approach argues that people must "learn to learn from their experiences," emphasizing communality, openness, and trust. Change requires the lowering of status barriers, recognition of mutuality, collaboration, and involvement. Finally, the power-coercive approach has to do with the application of power. In order to bring change, political and economic sanctions must be brought to bear. There is a reliance on the authority of law or administrative policy. People are changed by the manipulation of economic sanctions and/or authority structures.

These three strategies closely fit three of the four paradigms in Figure 2.5. In the rational-empirical approach, at the bottom, there is a heavy emphasis on the value of structure and authority. Both expert and legitimate power come into play. There is a tendency to advocate information control, situational engineering, legitimate request, and rational persuasion. In the normative-reeducative approach the emphasis is on trust and faith. The use of group values (relational power) and resource acquisition and allocation (reward power) are important. Preferred influence strategies are informal expectation, generation of hope, decision identification, and instrumental compliance. In the power-coercive orientation the emphasis is on assertiveness and conflict. Related strategies are rational persuasion, instrumental compliance, generation of hope, and legitimate request. Reward and legitimate power are also complementary to this approach.

One of the most interesting aspects of Figure 2.5 is that it contains a fourth paradigm that was not mentioned at all by Chin and Benne. This world view appears on the left side of the diagram and is far more passive than the others. This absence once again may be an illustration of the Western bias toward impact on and intervention in the environment. It is somewhat paradoxical to think of passivity as a change strategy or of inaction as a source of influence. In this world view the change agent does not focus on forcing change in the target person. Instead, the change agent focuses on altering self. Influence is accomplished through example. In order to increase influence, the change agent must become more attractive in terms of group values, and more expert as to the informational needs of the group. Influence accrues to the change agent because the target person values the character or informational qualities of the leader.

SUMMARY AND CONCLUSION

This chapter began by pointing out the need for the articulation of structural similarities within the various areas of leadership research and between leadership and other research areas. After presenting a framework of cognitive values it was then proposed that leadership research is hindered by bias in individual cognition and in the general culture. By employing Janusian thinking, a tension-based framework of traits, behaviors, and influence patterns was developed.

The diagrams presented here are clearly theoretical statements that are still in need of testing. They are, in essence, complex hypotheses of spatial relationships between concepts. They invite multidimensional analysis. If such analysis were generally to confirm them, then they suggest a number of directions in future inquiry.

These diagrams provide tools to explore for bias in the work of individual researchers. We have already provided an illustration with MacCoby's typology. Another illustration might be Mintzberg's (1973) managerial roles. Although he identifies three interpersonal roles in his typology, when we array all of the roles across the categories in Figure 2.4, they fall into three of the four quadrants, leaving the human-relations quadrant empty. We are left with an interesting question: Is there no "interaction facilitation role" or no "concerned human role" played by top management, or is Mintzberg's predisposition so drawn toward the other quadrants that these are overlooked? In a similar fashion we can begin to locate the values underlying the work of a wide variety of leadership theorists.

At a more macro level we can become more aware of the general biases in the overall literature. Is a less active leadership style always less effective as Bass (1981, p. 608) argues? Is this true for all cultures and situations? Are we even able to conceive of the paradigms at the left of Figures 2.4 and 2.5

as effective? If the answer is yes, then how, when, and why would they be effective? We might learn much from pursuing this issue.

The question of bias also takes on importance at the applied level. In evaluating job candidates, are there inherent biases in the perceptions of individuals on selection committees or judges in assessment centers? The present tools might be useful in clarifying such predispositions and aid the development of a more conscious selection policy. Likewise, the schemes presented here might lead to the design of more balanced management-development programs.

Apart from the issue of bias, the framework allows for some intriguing research about the outcomes of leadership behavior. Quinn and Cameron (1983) have developed a life-cycle model of effectiveness criteria that suggests that patterns of emphasis on effectiveness criteria change over time. How do the patterns of leadership behavior shift during these same periods? Does the shift in leadership patterns bring shifts in effectiveness patterns or vice versa? Because of the parallels in the leadership and the effectiveness schemes, we would expect that some particularly intriguing theory and research might be designed around the issue of outcomes.

At the outset of this chapter we cited Rinn's call for greater attention "to structural similarities between diverse universes of content"; it is hoped that this work will lead us in such a direction and contribute to a more efficient investigation of leadership.

3

A Multiple-Constituency Framework of Managerial Reputational Effectiveness*

Anne S. Tsui

Recent trends in leadership research and theory building are exciting for at least two reasons. First is the reexamination of the leadership concept as evidenced by the efforts to integrate leadership with managerial work (Hunt, Sekaran, & Schriesheim, 1982). Second is the emergence of transactional approaches that focus on both the causes and the effects of leader behavior (T. R. Mitchell, 1979). The broadening of the leadership concept beyond the leader-follower relationship and the increased emphasis on identifying determinants of leader behavior may indeed reflect a paradigmatic shift which has the potential of revitalizing the entire leadership field. This chapter introduces a framework of leader behavior and effectiveness based on models and views consistent with this new, emerging paradigm.

Studies on managerial and leader behavior have progressed along two parallel but noncommunicative paths. Theories on leadership effectiveness, while abundant, have not led to any appreciable understanding of the real phenomenon because of the narrow and highly deterministic way in which they conceive of leader behavior. Theories on managerial effectiveness, on the other hand, are sparse. This had led to a large number of studies with noncumulative and nonintegrative results as well as the selection of managerial effectiveness criteria that are based on convenience or researcher bias rather than on theory. The literature on managerial effectiveness is as much in a state of dismay as the literature on leadership effectiveness. In this chapter, the literature on managerial effectiveness will first be briefly reviewed. Then a theoretical framework of managerial effectiveness will be described in detail,

*This chapter is based upon a portion of a Ph.D. dissertation done at the University of California, Los Angeles, under the direction of Professor Anthony Raia and a thesis committee of W. Fogel, O. Grusky, B. Gutek, and B. McKelvey. Comments on an earlier draft from John C. Anderson, Chester Schriesheim, and several anonymous reviewers are gratefully acknowledged.

This research is supported from grants by the Hewlett-Packard Company, the Control Data Corporation, and the Business Associates Fund of the Fuqua School of Business, Duke University.

along with a series of propositions to guide future research. Those leadership theories that have been useful for the development of the framework will also be discussed.

LITERATURE REVIEW

Existing theories and research on managerial effectiveness have concentrated primarily on the personal characteristics of the managers, such as their abilities (Ghiselli, 1966; Korman, 1968), interests (Nash, 1965), or motivational attributes (Korman, 1968; Miner, 1978; Mitchell, 1974) as predictors or correlates. Organizational and environmental causes of managerial actions have largely been ignored. Campbell, Dunnette, Lawler, and Weick consider this variable to be one on which "everyone suggests the need for research is great, but actual empirical activity is sparse" (1970, p. 385). This set of variables is macro in nature and includes the structural properties of the organization, organizational climate, formal role characteristics, or other environmental factors (Campbell *et al.*, 1970; Cummings & Schwab, 1973). They consist of both structural and social characteristics of the manager's job context. Many leadership theorists have argued for the importance of macro or situational variables (e.g., Kerr & Jermier, 1978; Osborn & Hunt, 1975; Salancik, Calder, Rowland, Leblebici, & Conway, 1975). The lack of attention to these environmental determinants is a major problem that has retarded progress in both leadership and managerial effectiveness research.

Reviews of empirical studies investigating the predictive power of ability, aptitude, interests, and personality factors on managerial effectiveness have yielded disappointing results. The average correlations range from .25 to .30 (Ghiselli, 1966; Guion & Gottier, 1965; Korman, 1968; Nash, 1965). Review of studies using motivational variables in predicting managerial performance also found average correlations of .30 (House, Shapiro & Wahba, 1974; Korman, 1968; Mitchell, 1974). In sum, less than 10 percent of the variance in managerial performance has been accounted for by either abilities or motivational factors.

The slow progress in the understanding, explanation, and prediction of managerial effectiveness has been further delayed by the conceptual confusion and the measurement problem of the construct of effectiveness itself. This "criterion problem" is still with us after 20 years (Dunnette, 1963). A review of 100 empirical studies on managerial effectiveness yielded no commonly accepted conceptual definition or a set of criteria (Tsui, 1982). This seems to be due largely to the lack of a theory to guide in the selection of meaningful criteria. Managerial effectiveness has been indirectly defined as the ability of the manager to meet organizational objectives through supervisory ratings or rankings, to be successful in climbing the corporate ladder or the salary scale. Supervisory rating or ranking is the most frequently used approach. The theoretical validity of this approach is based on the assumption that the hierarchical superior can accurately represent the interests and expectations of the organization or of other organizational members. To the extent that the superior's expectations, perceptions, and judgments are influenced by factors other than organizational interests, the validity of using supervisory judgment to define managerial effectiveness is threatened. At most, it represents effectiveness from the superior's perspective only, which may not correspond to the organization's or other organizational members' judgment of the manager's contribution in meeting the collective goal. Further, it has been suggested that organizational outcomes, supervisory evaluations, and individual outcomes may all be affected by factors other than just managerial behavior or actions (Lombardo & McCall, 1982; Pfeffer & Salancik, 1978). The need for a different conceptualization of managerial effectiveness becomes clear.

A THEORETICAL FRAMEWORK

Effectiveness is a value judgment (Campbell, 1976; Scott, 1977; Steers, 1977), and it can only be meaningfully studied by asking, "Whose judgment defines effectiveness?" (Cameron, 1978; Connolly, Conlon, & Deutsch, 1980). Empirical evidence at both the individual level (Kavanagh, McKinney, & Wolins, 1971; Lawler, 1967) and the organizational level (Friedlander & Pickle, 1968; Molnar & Rogers, 1976) shows little or no convergence among the effectiveness assessment of a focal entity by multiple raters. At the organizational level, a multiple-constituency approach was proposed explicitly to allow evaluations from the perspectives of the multiple stakeholders (Connolly et al., 1980). This approach treats organizations as systems generating differential assessments of effectiveness by different constituencies. Constituents are those who have a stake in the performance of the focal organization. Divergence in expectations and in evaluation criteria is to be expected. In general, the multiple-constituency approach to organizational effectiveness asks: What constituencies exist in a particular setting? What effectiveness assessments does each now reach? What are the consequences of these assessments? These questions seem to be equally meaningful for addressing the issue of managerial effectiveness at the individual level.

Role theory (Katz & Kahn, 1978) and role-set analysis (Merton, 1957) provide the theoretical foundation for a multiple-constituency (MC) view of managerial effectiveness. Managerial behavior is seen to be determined largely by the expectations of the multiple role senders. The role senders comprise the constituencies who communicate specific expectations of desirable behavior by the focal manager, determine the criteria by which the focal manager is evaluated, and deliver rewards or sanctions as feedback on the manager's role behavior. A common set of constituencies for managers with hierarchical responsibility for one or more subordinates consists of superiors, subordinates, and peers or colleagues, all either within or outside their own organizations. Depending on the level, the functional specialization, and the location of the management position in the organizational structure, the size and the composition of the role set may vary. In addition, the focal managers' own expectations and priorities regarding desirable managerial role behavior must also be considered.

According to this MC framework, both the behavior expected of the focal manager and the evaluation of his or her effectiveness are particularistic in nature. Each constituency has interest in and perceptions of different aspects of the focal manager's total role behavior. If perceived behavior is congruent with expected or preferred behavior, the constituent will more likely form a favorable evaluation of the focal manager. This conception of effectiveness is not new. It was inferred in the Expectations-Approach to management control by Machin (1979) and explicitly stated in the social-structure perspective of leadership by Salancik *et al.* (1975). Managerial effectiveness defined from the judgment of the constituencies is termed "reputational effectiveness" in order to distinguish it from the traditional concept and approaches. Reputation is in the eyes of the beholder. Reputational effectiveness ratings among constituencies may not converge. The degree of convergence depends on the nature of the multiple sets of expectations and on the manager's ability to meet these expectations by behaving in a manner that is preferred by his or her critical role senders.

Expectations and reputational effectiveness may be affected by organizational, interpersonal, and personal factors. These factors influence both the clarity and the compatibility of the expectations which, in turn, affect the degree of role stress experienced by the focal manager. They also influence role perceptions and behavior independent of expectations from constituencies. Furthermore, the focal manager engages in behavior that attempts to modify the expectations of the constituencies. Thus, the activities of the focal manager and the expectations of the constituents create a complex social environment in which the dynamic reciprocal influence process develops and continues.

Reputational effectiveness may lead to favorable outcomes both for the focal manager and for the organization. Individual outcomes may include personal success as in higher performance ratings, more promotions, or other rewards. Organizational outcomes may include a more mutually responsive social system resulting in higher productivity, lower turnover, and more satisfied constituencies: superiors, subordinates, peers, and external constituencies such as customers. The central construct of reputational effectiveness, its determinants, and its consequences are represented in Figure 3.1. A detailed description of the central construct and its relationship to its antecedent and outcome variables, as well as the propositions, will follow.

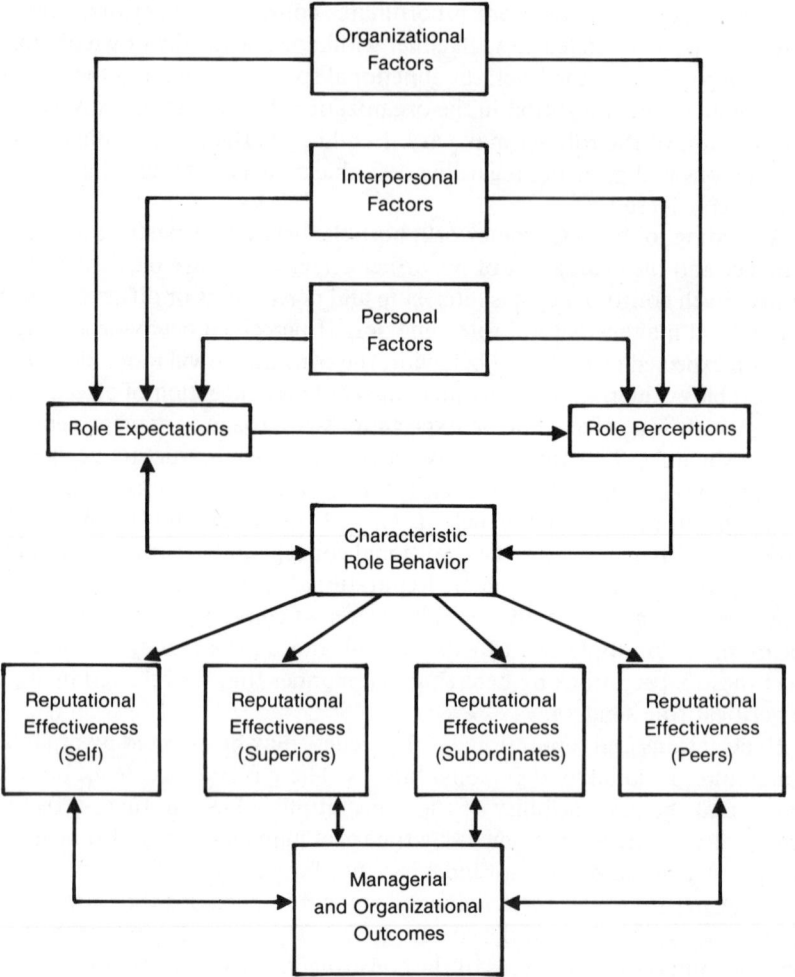

FIGURE 3.1. A multiple-constituency framework of managerial effectiveness

The Construct of Reputational Effectiveness

Reputational effectiveness is defined as the judgment made by the constituent regarding the extent to which his or her expectations are being met by the focal manager's behavior. Other theorists have suggested that being seen as effective may be the most valid and reliable indicator for differentiating good from poor managers (Campbell, 1976; Lombardo & McCall, 1982). Ultimately, managerial effectiveness may be a matter of perceptual consensus, as suggested by Lombardo & McCall (1982) or by Salancik *et al.*, who indicated that "the effective leader is one who is responsive to the demands of all individuals in the social system with whom he must interact and coordinate his behavior" (1975, pp. 99–100).

To the extent that individuals pursue self-interests at work (Argyris, 1964; Barnard, 1938; Williamson, 1975), constituencies would set behavioral expectations based upon the anticipation that such behavior will lead to the satisfaction of their own goals and interests. Conformity to expectations would lead to favorable evaluation by the constituency. According to the idiosyncracy credit theory of leadership (Hollander, 1959), a leader accumulates status (or reputation) by being responsive to the demands and expectations of members. Followers attribute effectiveness to those leaders who are able to meet their expectations. This is also the fundamental thesis of the social-exchange theory of leadership (Hollander & Julian, 1969).

Reputational effectiveness can be established under two basic conditions. First, the focal manager can sacrifice some self-interests in order to meet the expectations of others. This will lead to the accumulation of idiosyncracy credits which become a powerful influence base for future exchange. Fair trade is to be expected in the long run between any two parties, because people have a tendency to reciprocate favors (Gouldner, 1960). The second condition under which reputational effectiveness can be gained is when there is congruence in role expectations. This congruence is present when there is similarity in self-interests or it can be promoted through influence efforts by the focal manager or by the constituency. Influence attempts can be directed upward (Greene, 1975; Mowday, 1978), downwards (Hollander & Julian, 1969; Katz & Kahn, 1978), or laterally (Landsberger, 1961; Lawrence & Lorsch, 1969; Strauss, 1962). Similarity in self-interests between the focal manager and a specific constituency provides the condition for achieving reputational effectiveness with that constituency. Congruence in expectations among multiple constituencies may be unusual but provides the potential for gaining consensual agreement in reputational effectiveness by multiple raters. Reputational effectiveness among multiple constituencies may not converge, owing to the different frames of reference used when evaluating the same set of managerial behavior. Existing research seldom explores the importance of constituencies other than superiors. The manager's effectiveness with subordinates may be constrained by the manager's lateral relations (Osborn & Hunt, 1974) or by incompatible expectations from superiors (Pfeffer & Salancik, 1975). There is a need for more systematic investigation of the impact of subordinate, peer, or self-expectations on managerial behavior. Further, there is a need to link the idiosyncratic judgments of effectiveness to the judgment made by the organization according to organizational criteria. Approaching managerial effectiveness from the reputational framework directly asks the question: Whose judgment defines effectiveness? This approach recognizes that a manager belongs to a larger social network than that of himself and subordinates. It will provide insightful answers to questions such as: Under what conditions will a focal manager be seen as effective by which groups of constituencies? Under what conditions will there be more divergence in expectations? How does divergence in expectation affect managerial behavior? And, what are the consequences of reputational effectiveness, for both the organization and for the focal managers themselves? Reputational effectiveness, a construct comprising three elements — role expectations, perceptions, and actual role behavior — will be discussed in further detail below.

Role Expectations. Superiors, peers, and subordinates depend on certain behavior by the focal manager in order to perform their own tasks or to satisfy their own interests. Expectations are inevitably grounded in the self-interests of the role senders. These self-interests are comprised of the constituency's own role requirements, specific work objectives, or other items in the employment contract as well as personal goals and interests. To the extent that these self-interests differ, the degree of congruence or compatibility in the expectations is also affected. In the managerial role set, the positional requirements form the bases for differential expectations of the focal manager by the multiple role senders. Research by Albrecht, Glaser, and Marks (1964) and Kavanagh *et al.* (1971) suggests that evaluations tend to diverge more when raters are more distant in hierarchical levels. For example, the ratings by two peers tend to have more agreement than ratings between peers and superiors. Based on prior research evidence and the arguments derived from this MC framework, the following proposition is formulated:

PROPOSITION 1: *Divergence in role expectations will be greater across constituencies than among members of the same constituency.*

Unlike the VDL analysis (Dansereau & Dumas, 1977) which suggests the conditions for within-constituency heterogeneity, this hypothesis argues for within-constituency homogeneity but between-constituency heterogeneity in the focal manager's relationship to superiors, subordinates, and peers. Divergent evaluations may be due more to differential demands deriving from positional incompatibility than to individual characteristics. Thus, it is conceived that role behavior expectations between constituencies will diverge greater than expectations between members of the same constituency. The differential expectations across constituencies then serve as the basis for perceptions of role conflict and ambiguity by the focal manager.

Role Perceptions. Role perceptions include an understanding of the requirements for job behavior and performance as communicated by the multiple role senders. The effective manager is supersensitive to the thinking and desires of other organizational members. He or she is other — rather than self — directed. The other-directed manager is responsive to the desires and expectations of the critical constituencies in the role set. He or she may engage in self-sacrificial behavior to assist others and thus accrues idiosyncracy credits.

Role expectations may be perceived to be conflictive and/or ambiguous depending on the compatibility and clarity of the constituencies' expectations. Conflict may occur either between the focal person's own expectations and that of another constituent, or it may arise out of the incompatible expectations among the multiple constituencies. Research on perceived or subjective role conflict is quite conclusive in terms of its negative impact on performance and satisfaction (Kahn *et al.*, 1964; House & Rizzo, 1972; Rizzo, House, & Lirtzman, 1970; Rogers & Molnar, 1976; Whetten, 1978). Studies of the impact of objective role conflict are more sparse (see Katz & Kahn, 1978, chap. 7 for a review). A recent study found that perceived role conflict is affected by objective role conditions, such as role requirements, and the characteristics of the role set (Miles & Perreault, 1976). Overall, there is limited research on the relationship of objective role conflict to role performance and effectiveness by the role receiver. Since a focal manager may attempt to satisfy multiple and perhaps conflicting demands, objective role conflict may not always lead to lower reputational effectiveness. Perceived role conflict, however, is clearly a subjective state that may predispose the focal manager from even attempting to meet the incompatible demands.

Role ambiguity simply means uncertainty about what the role occupant is supposed to do. It may occur because of unclear and insufficient communication between the focal person and the constituency (Rogers & Molnar, 1976). It may also occur because of selective perception. There is substantial evidence that role ambiguity reduces the effectiveness of performance (also see Katz & Kahn, 1978, Chap. 7, for a review). More recently, Miles (1976) observed that perceived role ambiguity is related to negative attitudes toward the role senders and lower self-assessed performance effectiveness. There is less research on the effects of objective role ambiguity. Objective role ambiguity is present when the constituencies fail to communicate role expectations or do not believe that the focal manager understands their expectations. Under this condition, it is unlikely that the focal manager is able to satisfy their desires. The negative effect of perceived role ambiguity will be less if the focal manager takes the initiative to obtain role clarity from the constituencies or to help them define their expectations. The overall impact of role conflict and ambiguity or reputational effectiveness is negative, however, whether it is objective or perceived. The relationship between role perception and reputational effectiveness is thus postulated as:

PROPOSITION 2: *Incompatible and unclear role expectations will be negatively related to reputational effectiveness. Perceived role conflict will be more strongly related to lower reputational effectiveness than objective role conflict, whereas objective role ambiguity will be more strongly associated with lower reputational effectiveness than perceived role ambiguity.*

The nature of managerial role behavior depends on the nature of role expectations, including the range and types of behavior desired, the compatibility of the sets of expected behavioral categories, and the clarity with which these expectations are communicated and received. Relevant behavior categories for managerial positions thus deserve systematic examination in this MC framework.

Managerial Behavior Categories. Research in the past 30 years has produced many lists of managerial behavior categories (e.g., Flanagan, 1951; Hemphill, 1960; Mintzberg, 1973; Stewart, 1967). These lists have many common behavior categories but also many nonoverlapping factors. None of these lists, however, may be considered to be inclusive of the total domain of managerial activities. This is in part due to the methodologies employed. The informants for these managerial activities have ranged from self, superior, and peer to independent observers. The divergence in descriptive behavior categories may result from both selective perception and informational limitations. There is no systematic research that compares description of managerial behavior from different vantage points simultaneously. The MC framework permits such a detailed comparison of the descriptions of observed role behavior, as well as evaluation of effectiveness on the same set of managerial behavior by the multiple observers. Further, the MC framework suggests that there is a need to develop an inclusive list of behavioral categories, including activities that may be performed only by the effective or only by the ineffective managers. Managerial behavior instrumental for gaining reputational effectiveness may differ for different constituencies owing to differential preferences. From this understanding, we derive a third proposition:

> PROPOSITION 3: *Specific managerial behavior instrumental for gaining reputational effectiveness will vary by constituencies. The behavior associated with reputational effectiveness from the superior's perspective may have no or even negative relationships to reputational effectiveness from the peers' or the subordinates' perspectives.*

The differential preferences for managerial role behavior by constituencies suggest the presence of different effectiveness models. The path-goal theory suggests that leadership effectiveness depends on the leader's ability to meet the specific needs of the follower (House & Dessler, 1974). Osborn and Hunt (1974) have offered some tentative evidence that leader attention to lateral relations may be dysfunctional for obtaining effective performance from followers. Research by Salancik *et al.* (1975) indicates that lateral relationships due to interdependence in workflow reduce the supervisor's ability to meet subordinate demands. In summary, the MC analysis suggests that an effective manager adapts his or her behavior and actions to the demands and expectations of the specific role senders. For a further understanding of the conditions under which reputational effectiveness may be gained, a number of organizational, interpersonal, and personal factors have been identified that may be important determinants of both role expectations and role perceptions.

Determinants of Reputational Effectiveness

Organizational Factors. Katz and Kahn (1978) argue that the major determinants of role sending are to be found in the systematic properties of the organization as a whole, the subsystem in which the role senders are located, and the particular position occupied by each. Organizational characteristics may shape both the expectations and the perceptions of role requirements. For example, the authority structure affects the degree to which the focal manager's role requirements may be determined by the expectations of their superiors, subordinates, peers, or themselves. In a highly participative organization, the manager may behave in a manner more congruent with the subordinate's expectations. In a highly coupled, reciprocally interdependent workflow structure such as a matrix, the focal manager's role activities may be determined largely by peer expectations. Organizational strategy affects the focal manager's role behavior through specific expectations transmitted through the hierarchical superior. The structural dimension of formalization was frequently found to be negatively related to perceived role ambiguity (House & Rizzo, 1972; Rogers & Molnar, 1976). The degree of functional specialization may also differentially impact the relative importance of managerial roles (McCall & Segrist, 1978), as well as the behavioral orientation of the management job incumbents (Dearborn & Simon, 1958; Lawrence & Lorsch, 1969).

The more immediate effects of organizational factors on role expectations and perceptions may be found in the immediate task and social environment of the focal manager. Payne and Pugh (1976) reported that role differentiation (differentiation of functional activities at the work-group level) is strongly correlated with the specificity of role definitions and expectations. However, heterogeneity in role specialization may also negatively affect role perception if such heterogeneity is accompanied by divergence in expectations within the role set (MacKinnon & Summers, 1976). Increasing subunit size, if accompanied by heterogeneity in specialization, will reduce consensus of expectations. The location of the focal position in terms of nearness to an organizational boundary may also be related to divergence in role expectations, role behavior, and experienced role stress (Miles, 1976; Miles & Perreault, 1976; Rogers & Molnar, 1976; Whetten, 1978). Living near an intraorganizational boundary, as reflected in those positions that require higher levels of interface with members in other organizational subunits, may reveal many of the same effects but to a lesser extent.

Role expectations, perceptions, and behavior may also be affected by the organization's reward structure. It determines the extent to which managers will engage in individual- or team-oriented behavior. Focal managers rewarded for meeting only bottom-line criteria will engage in activities that maximize short-term results, perhaps at the expense of investment in long-range strategies and development of human resources. On the other hand, focal managers rewarded for group morale, low turnover, and employee development will more likely attend to the expectations of the subordinates.

In summary, the characteristics of the organization such as technology, structure, reward system, and the characteristics of the focal manager's immediate role set determine the nature of expectations held for the focal manager. These characteristics comprise the structural environment of the role set. Their relationship to reputational effectiveness varies, depending on their direct impact on expectations and on role perceptions, leading to different behavioral responses. The following proposition is advanced:

PROPOSITION 4: *Dimensions of organizational and role-set structural characteristics will affect reputational effectiveness by determining the nature of role expectations from multiple constituencies and the nature of role perception by the focal manager.*

Structural dimensions that induce role conflicts and ambiguity will have negative effects. Those that promote congruence in expectations or increase the power base of the focal manager will have positive effects. This proposition relates macrovariables directly to individual-level perception and judgment, an issue considered important by several previous researchers (Osborn & Hunt, 1974; Salancik *et al.*, 1975).

Interpersonal Factors. The multiple-constituency framework, as with several transactional models of leadership, is characterized by active influence activities among organizational members. Role sending and receiving is a dynamic reciprocal influence process and thus highly political in nature. Effectiveness has been referred to as less of a scientific than a political concept (Kanter, 1981). Multiple stakeholders, both inside and outside of the immediate work unit, compete to gain attention of the focal manager in order to advance their own interests or make their jobs easier. Ability to influence the work behavior of others does not lie in the formal authority structure alone. Several other bases of power may be utilized, including personal (French & Raven, 1959; Kipnis, 1976) and structural (Brinkerhoff & Kanter, 1980; Hinings, Hickson, Pennings, Schneck, 1974; Kanter, 1981). The social-exchange theory has indicated that the ability to command scarce and desired resources is fundamental to the ability to influence others (Jacobs, 1971). Kanter (1977) found that effective managers have more credibility and clout than ineffective managers. The constituencies who are perceived to have credibility or clout (or political power), or to possess critical resources (e.g., information, personnel, expertise) will more likely be able to influence the behavior of the focal manager and have their expectations met. Conversely, the focal manager with credibility, political power, or resource power will more likely be able to counterinfluence the expectations of the constituencies, or to cause them to behave in a manner that will lead to the satisfaction of the focal's own goals and desires.

The concept of credibility is similar to the affective bond factor, described by Kahn, Wolfe, Quinn, and Snoek (1964). Individuals with credibility will be liked, admired, and respected. Members of school boards (as focal persons) were found to meet the expectations of the school superintendent (as role sender) more fully when they perceived credibility in the role sender (Gross, Mason, & McEachern, 1958). However, an affective bond may also have negative effects on the role receiver. It can lead to role conflict when the focal person is faced with incompatible demands from two constituencies with whom he or she has established an affective bond, a condition of approach-approach conflict. Political power refers to the manager's position in the informal power system and indicates the manager's capacity to exercise such a power base to influence others. Possession of credibility will especially influence the evaluation by the constituencies. A highly credible focal manager may be evaluated more favorably, even if the constituency's expectations are not entirely met. This may reflect a short-term leniency tendency due to idiosyncracy credit accumulated by the focal manager. In the long run, however, reputational effectiveness will diminish if the focal manager continues to exhibit ineffective or unresponsive role behavior despite the possession of credibility, political power, or resource power.

In summary, the communication of expectations, the behavioral responses by the focal manager, and the effectiveness assessments by the multiple constituencies may be considered a political process that is actively manifested within the formal authority and the informal power structures. It can be postulated that:

> PROPOSITION 5: *Interpersonal factors such as the perception of credibility, political power, or possession of scarce resources will be positively associated with reputational effectiveness. These factors will be negatively or unrelated to reputational effectiveness if the manager consistently exhibits unresponsive behavior.*

Possession of critical resources, credibility, and political power will increase the focal manager's ability to respond to demands. Since there is a danger in being too responsive, focal managers may use these power bases to modify both the content and the level of expectations held by constituencies. The dynamic of these interpersonal influence activities creates a politically charged social environment in which expectations or preferences for the role behavior of the focal manager are formulated, modified, and communicated, and which, in the final analysis, are grounded in the self-interests of each actor.

Personal Factors. Personal factors refer to the attributes of both the focal manager and the constituencies. They may include age, education, experience, or personality traits and may affect the reputational effectiveness of the focal manager. The political nature of sending and receiving expectations suggests at least two personal factors that may be meaningful to a further understanding of the dynamics of the MC framework. They are the concept of power motivation or need to influence (Kipnis, 1976; McClelland, 1961; McClelland & Burnham, 1976) and the expectations or Pygmalion effect (Livingston, 1969; Rosenthal & Jacobson, 1968).

Power motivation is a personality variable that is conceived to enhance the gaining of reputational effectiveness. Power motivation arises when an individual experiences an aroused need state that can only be satisfied by inducing appropriate behavior in others (Kipnis, 1976). The idea of satisfying personal wants is important here, in that the individual is inducing forces in another person in order to achieve some personal goals. An individual with a strong power motivation is expected to be more active in using influence to ensure the fulfillment of expectations by others. Power motivation in the focal person will also be reflected in greater influence attempts at modifying the expectations of the constituencies, to alter the latters' views to be congruent with his or her own. The focal person who is successful in influencing the expectations of others will attribute a higher level of effectiveness to himself or herself, a hypothesis proposed by Kipnis (1976) through his observations in several laboratory and field studies in various settings.

Managers who like power have a desire to have impact and to be strong and influential (McClelland, 1961). They will be particularly effective if the power is exercised on behalf of others (McClelland & Burnham, 1976). These are the managers who are willing to sacrifice some of their own self-interests for the welfare of the organization they serve. Their personal goals are the success of their organizations. They make their subordinates feel strong rather than weak. It can be speculated that these power managers will also tend to be better team players. These institutional managers, by engaging in short-run self-sacrificial acts, accrue long-range obligations. They gain reputational effectiveness in the short run, and accumulate further power to negotiate and bargain in the long run through obligations or idiosyncracy credits.

A longitudinal study by Berlew and Hall (1966) provides insight on a second personal factor that seems meaningful in understanding the effects of expectations on behavior. They found that managers assigned to relatively demanding jobs in the early years of their career performed better than those assigned to less demanding tasks. Research on goal setting also substantiated the relationship between the level of goal difficulty and performance outcomes

(Locke, 1968). Level of expectations seems to be a powerful predictor of effective performance. In a field experiment involving job design and enrichment, King (1974) demonstrated that managers' expectations concerning performance improvement have a stronger impact on the work groups' behavior than job design. Livingston (1969) described this phenomenon as the self-fulfilling prophecy or the Pygmalion effect (Rosenthal & Jacobson, 1968). He concluded from his review of the empirical literature on this effect that a superior with a positive Pygmalion tendency sets high expectations for a target member and has great confidence in being able to develop the talent of this person and in being able to help him or her to be successful. These expectations are inevitably communicated to the target, verbally or nonverbally, through the manner in which the person is being treated.

Research in industry has focused on superior's expectations of individual or group performance. The effects of peer and subordinate expectations are almost unexplored. It seems that focal managers will gain greater reputational effectiveness and be more successful in their careers when they are surrounded by constituencies who are positive Pygmalions, whether they are superiors, subordinates, or peers. This hypothesis rests on the fundamental assumption of role theory: the tendency of people to behave according to the expectations of others. It is thus hypothesized that:

> PROPOSITION 6: *Individual characteristics such as power motivation and positive expectations will favorably affect the reputational effectiveness of the focal manager by the multiple constituencies.*

The focal manager will be most effective when all rather than a subset of the constituencies possess high expectations and have strong power motivation. Power motivation will be instrumental for reputational effectiveness when it is exercised on behalf of the organization or of others. These two personal characteristics add another dimension to the social environment in which role behavior expectations are formulated, modified, communicated, responded to, and in which observed role behavior is evaluated.

Consequences of Reputational Effectiveness

The ultimate significance of reputational effectiveness lies in its relationship to outcomes for both the organization and the focal manager. A focal manager who is responsive to the expectations of others, that is, facilitates the work of others, will contribute more to the collective efforts of the organization. A mutually responsive organization is one in which most members strive to be responsive to the needs of others, resulting in a highly collaborative system with a minimum of dysfunctional, self-interested behavior. A responsive manager will come to be valued by the organization and be appraised favorably according to organizational criteria as defined in the formal performance appraisal system. This reputation and appraisal will lead to rewards such as merit and promotions. Organizational expectations, however, are usually transmitted by the hierarchical superior, who may be biased by his or her own self-interests. The superior may not be able to represent adequately the expectations of the organization, not because of information inadequacy but because of intervening self-interests. Thus, the organization's appraisal of, as well as rewards to, the focal manager will be biased by the superior's idiosyncratic judgment of the focal manager.

Reputational effectiveness may also affect the focal manager's attitude toward others. Reputational effectiveness imputed by the superior will be related to the focal's satisfaction with supervisors. A favorable judgment by peers will be positively associated with satisfaction with co-workers. Reputation with subordinates will increase the focal manager's ability to influence their behavior and priorities. This may lead to satisfaction with these subordinates. High self-perceived effectiveness is expected to be positively related to favorable attitude toward work itself. Discrepancy in reputational effectiveness from multiple constituencies is expected to reduce overall managerial satisfaction, especially if the focal manager's own appraisal is more favorable than those from the constituencies.

In the long run, managers who are able to gain reputational effectiveness from all the constituencies are expected to have contributed most to the effectiveness of the organization. In the short run they may be rewarded for meeting the expectations of a specific constituency only, depending on the overall organizational objectives and strategies, and the practices and philosophies of top management. Since organizational outcomes may be affected by factors other than managerial behavior, an empirical relationship between reputational effectiveness and performance at the subunit or organizational level may be contaminated. Individual consequences for the focal manager deriving from reputational effectiveness will be much stronger. A final proposition states that:

> PROPOSITION 7: *Reputational effectiveness will be positively and strongly associated with favorable outcomes for the focal manager and positively but less strongly with outcomes for the organization.*

Effective managers are most valuable to the organization which may be conceived as a collection of constituencies pursuing both individual and collective goals. It is conceivable, however, that effective organizations or subunits may also contribute to the reputation of the responsible manager. When the situation is ambiguous and cause-effect relationships are unclear, the success of the subunit or of the organization may be attributed to the skills of the leader. This attributional process may be reflected in short-run leniency tendency (i.e., not meeting expectation is positively associated with favorable judgment). In the long run, the MC framework argues that reputation relies on the manager's responsiveness to constituency expectations and demands. Finally, this proposition suggests that individual or organizational outcomes will be the most favorable for the most reputationally effective managers and less favorable for those who have a reputation for being effective with only a subset or none of the constituencies.

SUMMARY

The multiple-constituency framework is a critical departure from traditional models of leadership. The effectiveness of a leader is considered in the context of a social structure comprised of at least three critical constituencies: superiors, subordinates, and peers. The communication of and response to expectations in this social structure result in a complex social environment characterized by influence and counterinfluence activities. Effectiveness of the focal manager is defined from the perspective of the constituency; thus it is idiosyncratic in nature. Meeting the constituency's expectations is the basic condition for gaining reputational effectiveness.

The focal manager may gain reputational effectiveness from one constituency but not from another. Consensual agreement among constituencies is facilitated when there is goal congruence in the role set. Compatibility in role expectations is affected by personal, interpersonal, and organizational factors. These factors comprise a structural and social environment in which expectations about preferred managerial role behavior are formulated, communicated, responded to, and evaluated. The MC framework serves to provide some insight into the conditions under which reputational effectiveness is gained, lost, or preserved. It also suggests how reputational effectiveness is related to managerial success and organizational outcomes.

Reputational effectiveness is similar to the social-test concept in Thompson's framework (1967). When there is lack of agreement on outcome preferences and ambiguity in cause-effect relationships, assessment of performance must rely on the judgement of relevant evaluators. Leader and managers, especially those in the middle level, may face the most uncertain tasks. They are involved in the translation of organizational strategies and the creation of operating procedures to implement objectives delegated by top managers. Ambiguity in evaluation criteria may be a defining characteristic of middle-management jobs. Middle managers cannot be directly evaluated on the basis of productivity at the shop level, nor overall performance at the corporate level. Their effectiveness depends to a large extent on their ability to exercise leadership in all directions and to meet the multiple demands.

The MC approach to managerial effectiveness goes not only beyond the contingency approaches in leadership theories. It also extends the transactional models (Graen & Cashman, 1975; Hollander, 1978; Machin, 1979) by taking into account all the relevant domains of the leader's transactions with others. Stewart (1982) suggests that in some management jobs, leadership influence may be exercised more upward or laterally than downward. The effective leader not only meets the expectations of the most critical constituencies, but also has the ability to identify who the most critical constituencies are, or to enact the "right" constituency set. The effective leader may also attend to competing demands by time-sharing his or her services or resources. When leadership effectiveness accounts for the total management job, it is no longer distinguishable for managerial effectiveness, nor is it meaningful to make this distinction any more.

The framework suggests that the more meaningful determinants of expectations, behavior, and evaluation are the characteristics of the organization and of the constituencies rather than of individuals. Many of the seven propositions have tentative empirical evidence from previous research. Research on this framework will require dynamic as well as temporal research designs. Longitudinal analysis is necessary to investigate the gaining, preserving, and loss of reputational effectiveness in the dynamic and changing social structure. Network analysis, multidimensional scaling, or intensive observations may be some useful methodologies. Machin (1979) used an Expectations-Analysis method to identify and clarify expectations between an interaction pair. His computerized expectations data base can be modified and updated by both role senders and receivers. In brief, methodologies are available to test the dynamic relationship depicted by the MC framework. Empirical research will increase our understanding of the differences in behavioral characteristics between effective and ineffective managers. It will provide insight into the conditions under which a manager may be perceived to be effective by some people but not by others. Further, it will clarify the impact of structural characteristics of the organization and of the role set on the degree of complexity in expectations for the management job. This framework directly considers the impact of macroorganizational variables on behavior and perceptions at the individual level.

Further conceptualization is needed to understand how the manager identifies the critical constituency set, how he or she responds to conflictive and ambiguous demands, and what the consequences of "exceeding" expectations are. This framework, while embryonic, seems promising in providing a new direction of research by extending the focus from the leader-follower dyad to the social structure comprised of both vertical and horizontal networks. The broadening of the leadership concept and the inclusion of both macro and micro variables may be a direction of theory development landmarking the advance of a new paradigm of leadership research.

4

Functionalism: Basis for an Alternate Approach to the Study of Leadership

Charles F. Rauch, Jr. and Orlando Behling

Most organization scholars and practitioners are aware of the significant impact of leadership on the attitudes and performance of people in organizations (Katz & Kahn, 1978, p. 574; Nadler, Hackman, & Lawler, 1979, p. 157). They disagree, however, as to how leadership has its impact, how it should be studied, whether what we have learned is of use to practitioners, and even whether or not we have progressed in our overall knowledge of the field (Argyris, 1979; Bass, 1981, p. 617; Nadler *et al.,* 1979; Schriesheim, Hunt, & Sekaran, 1982). Although Bass remains optimistic that theories are not as conflicting as they seem and that results of theoretical research are being used in practice, Argyris expresses the concern of many with his conclusion that: (a) the number of leadership publications is increasing each year; (b) the additivity of the findings is limited; and (c) their implications for the central, everyday problems of leaders are minimal.

In this chapter we report on our efforts to deal with the problems of additivity and relevance. First, we present a framework for conceptualizing leadership derived from structural functionalism, a widely known but currently rarely utilized sociological paradigm. Second, we report the results of tests of a set of hypotheses derived from the framework. Third, we indicate how the framework provides a relatively simple means for integrating contributions as diverse as Kerr and Jermier's (1978) work on "substitutes for leadership" and Bales' (1953) studies of leadership in groups. Finally, we discuss the implications of the framework for leadership practice.

THE STRUCTURAL-FUNCTIONAL FRAMEWORK

With certain exceptions that will be noted in the discussion section of this chapter, attempts to explain leadership have been based in what Evered (1976) labels the "causal model":

The traditional causal model of explanation is by far the most prominent of all modes of scientific explanation. (p. 264)

With pure causal determinism, S_1 invariably and necessarily follows from the action of the causative agent C, occurring in a situation of the kind S_0, and the transformation $(C + S_0)$ S_1 is described by a law. (p. 263)

The exclusive concern of early leadership theorists with the causative agent C has been replaced in recent years by the greater interest in the moderating role played by the circumstances S_0; and, in discussions of the causative agent C, the emphasis on leader characteristics (commonly labeled "traits") has been supplanted by emphasis on leader behaviors or actions. In the study of leadership, however, the causal model itself has rarely been challenged.

Structural functionalism represents an alternative to the causal model as an explanation of leadership. According to Behling (1980b), structural functionalism "Seek[s] understanding of events, artifacts, or processes (*structures* in the terminology of functional analysis) in terms of their consequences (*eufunctions* and *dysfunctions*) for superordinate systems of which they are parts" (p. 214). Thus, the behaviors and actions of leaders are viewed in conjunction with member self-management and other influences in terms of the effects that all of these influences have on insuring that the work group remains an integral, contributing subset of the larger organization.

Definitions of Key Terms

Certain terms relevant to the work reported here have, unfortunately, several meanings in the social and behavioral sciences. Thus, it is important to explain exactly how we use them here. "Leadership" is defined as the process of influencing the activities of an organized group toward goal achievement (see Stogdill, 1974, pp. 9–10). "Functional" is used as it is used in sociology and anthropology (Merton, 1949, p. 23, and note 4, p. 305) and in the biological sciences, wherein function refers to the vital or organic processes considered in terms of their contributions to the entity in which they occur. (It is *not* used, as employed by Scott, 1977, as a label for the use of the operant paradigm as a basic framework for the study of leadership.) Thus, "leadership functions" refers to the contributions that leadership acts, events, artifacts, and processes make to the achievement of the goals of the organization in which they occur or, minimally, to its survival. "Leadership structures" are those acts, events, artifacts, and processes themselves. (Structure is *not* used in this chapter as it is commonly used in Organizational Behavior/ Theory, to refer to communications channels, authority and responsibility relationships, and the like.)

Major Elements of the Model

Leadership Functions. The literature of leadership contains several cases of paired, roughly parallel ideas about what leaders contribute to organizations. For example, research done at Michigan in the late 1950s and early 1960s (Katz & Kahn, 1978; Likert, 1961) centers on the relative importance of the supervisor's *employee orientation* versus his or her *production orientation* as a determinant of employee performance. Similarly, March and Simon (1958) emphasize the need to influence the employee's *decision to participate* (to join and remain with the organization) and his or her *decision to perform* (to produce). Bales (1953) differentiates between the roles of the *social leader* who helps maintain the unity of the group and that of the *task leader* who helps keep the group engaged in necessary work. Thibaut and Kelley (1959) write of the need for both a (group) *maintenance* function and a *task* function. Cartwright and Zander (1968) suggest that constructive behaviors of leaders serve either to *maintain the group* or are *instrumental to goal attainment.*

Clearly, all these authors imply the existence of two key leadership functions necessary for the survival of the work group. One is a *maintenance function*; if the group is to survive and attain its goals, members must receive adequate incentives to assure that they continue to participate in its activities. The other is a *task function*; if a work group is to survive and attain its goals, it must also import resources, normally from a parent organization. Usually, if these resources are to be forthcoming, the work group must accomplish some task or tasks that contribute to the goals of the superordinate organization. Clearly, task accomplishment and group maintenance are requisite functions of leadership, but they may not be the only ones. Both Stogdill (1974) and Dubin (1979) list additional organizational problems to be solved or functions to be performed. In both cases, however, their lists easily factor into task accomplishment and group maintenance. Accordingly, the functions of leadership examined in this chapter are the task and the maintenance functions.

Leadership Structures. In this section we identify leadership structures that may fulfill the two functions. Miner (1975) lists five sources of control of behavior in organizations: self, hierarchical, professional or ideological, group, and the task itself. Osborn (1974) mentions four sources of influence: environment of the system, internal structure and processes, nature of groups, and characteristics of the individuals. If Miner's professional or ideological influences are considered a subset of environmental influences, and Osborn's internal structure and processes consist of both formal organizational structure as well as hierarchical leader behavior, then six kinds of influence can be drawn from these two sources. However, in the perception of the work-group member, the task itself and formal organizational structure may be difficult to distinguish. Therefore, we postulate that there is a leadership structure that has the potential for filling part or all of each of the two leadership functions under each of the following five sources of influence: hierarchical *leader behaviors, self-management,* the *task itself* and formal organization, work-*group influences,* and *external* environmental *influences.*

In examining hierarchical leader behaviors, limiting the behaviors to those of the immediate supervisor, as has been the practice in much leadership research, is inconsistent with the structural-functional emphasis on examining *all* of the various structures that might fulfill the two leadership functions. Several writers (Stogdill, 1974; Calder, 1977) suggest that we should look beyond the supervisor. Few studies have done so, however, and those that have (Hill & Hunt, 1973; Hunt, Hill, & Reaser, 1973) consider only the level of supervision immediately above the supervisor. In addition to the behavior of higher-level managers, certain peers may also behave in ways that affect work-group outcomes (House & Baetz, 1979; Katz & Kahn, 1978). Thus, the hierarchical leader behavior structure considered here includes behaviors of immediate supervisors, behaviors of other members of the hierarchy, and behaviors of influential peers.

Relations Among Task and Maintenance Structures and Functions. Thus far it has been implied that task functions are accomplished exclusively through task structures and that maintenance functions are accomplished exclusively through maintenance structures. The leadership literature shows, however, that cross-influences are possible. House (1971), House and Dessler (1974), House and Mitchell (1974), Greene (1979a), and others find that in certain situations, usually with low task clarity and/or high subordinate authoritarianism, task-oriented leader behaviors are related to various maintenance outcomes. In the other direction, House and Rizzo (1972), Greene and C. A. Schriesheim (1980), J. F. Schriesheim (1980), and others report situations in which maintenance leadership is correlated with task performance. In addition, Greene (1975) and Miles and Petty (1977) report that maintenance-oriented leader behavior acts to allow sufficient task-related leader behavior for high performance without a loss of group maintenance. Thus, cross-influences are also included in the framework presented here.

Structural-Functional Concept. The proposed structural-functional concept of leadership is as follows: Task-oriented structures of self-management, the task itself, the work group, external influences, and leader behavior of the immediate supervisor, the supervisor's senior, and/or other persons in the hierarchy all influence task-related outcomes such as individual and group performance. Maintenance-oriented structures of self-management, the task itself, the work group, external influences, and hierarchical leader behavior all influence maintenance-related outcomes such as individual job satisfaction, group loyalty, and group commitment to the organization. In addition, task-oriented structures can moderate the impact of maintenance structures on maintenance outcomes and vice versa.

Specific Propositions

The previous section developed the broad framework of a functional analysis. This section explains in more specific terms how the variables of the conceptual framework interact.

Equivalence of Leadership Structures. The idea that the various task and maintenance structures are functionally equivalent and can be combined or substituted for one another can be derived logically from functionalism itself or derived empirically from several lines of investigation. Kerr, Schriesheim, Murphy, and Stogdill (1974) hold that the more the leader is able to provide subordinates with valued, needed, or expected services, the closer the relationship will be between leader behavior measures and subordinate satisfaction and performance. Small-group researchers such as Dubin (1958) contend that the nonformal behavior of an organizational group complements formal communications channels in providing direction. Miner (1975) warns that relying on self-control alone invites organizational anarchy, thus suggesting that structures should be used to reinforce one another. All of these suggest that the leadership structures may combine to fulfill the leadership functions.

Curvilinearity of the Task Function. The results of several lines of inquiry also suggest that while the leadership structures may be combined, the outcome is not linear across the entire range. In the leadership literature, Miner (1975) cautions that the use of two or more types of control at one time results in a high probability of negative outcomes; and Filley, House, and Kerr (1976), in a review of path-goal theory research, report that if leader instrumental behaviors take place where the task itself provides clear structure, insignificant or negative correlations with task-related outcomes may result. In fact, while not writing directly about leadership, Scott (1966) proposes that there is an inverted-U relationship between activation level and total stimulation from all sources, and Keen and Morton (1978) indicate that performance and information relate in an inverted-U fashion. These works suggest that the relationship between performance and the task structures is an inverted U.

Curvilinearity of the Maintenance Function. While the case is not as strong, some organizational behavior research suggests that redundant support mechanisms can be dissatisfying, thus suggesting curvilinearity for the maintenance function also. The Deci (1972) notion that extrinsic rewards decrease intrinsic motivation, for example, suggests that if a person is performing an intrinsically satisfying task, extrinsic rewards have a negative effect on the member's maintenance-related outcomes. Another theory that suggests dissatisfaction with excessive maintenance structures is the overpayment portion of equity theory (Adams, 1965). Neither Deci's nor Adams' theories apply directly to the functional leadership maintenance relationship, but they both support the idea that beyond a certain amount, additional forms of reward and social-emotional support decrease satisfaction. It seems reasonable, therefore, to expect a curvilinear relationship between the total maintenance structures and measures of accomplishment of the maintenance function.

Relations Between Task and Maintenance Functions. In addition to the direct relationship described above, there are four types of objectively verifiable cross-functional influences: (1) overemphasis on the maintenance structures can be shown to counteract task structures so that performance decreases; (2) in the same fashion, extreme emphasis on task structures can have the effect of neutralizing maintenance structures so that maintenance outcomes, such as job satisfaction and organizational commitment, decrease; (3) maintenance structures can moderate the negative effects of extreme task emphasis on performance; and (4) task structures can moderate the otherwise negative effects of extreme maintenance emphasis on maintenance outcomes.

The nature of the interrelationships is illustrated in Figure 4.1, which is produced by reversing the maintenance-function inverted-U curve and superimposing it on the task-function curve. Point C in Figure 4.1 represents the first situation described above, in which a high degree of concern for maintenance is associated with decreases in task performance. This situation is exemplified by the extremes of the "human-relations" movement of the 1950s (Bass, 1981, p. 388; Filley, House, & Kerr, 1976) in which exclusively people-oriented leadership decreases productivity. Furthermore, in view of the curvilinear relationship postulated above for the maintenance function, the excessive amount of support structures would also correspond to a lower level of maintenance outcomes. Consequently, point C indicates that a high value of maintenance structures is associated with a point of less-than-optimum performance and job satisfaction.

The effects of excessive amounts of task structures on maintenance outcomes are represented by point B in Figure 4.1. Here the task processes have been built up to the extent that performance has passed the maximum (point A) and reached point B with a diminished amount of satisfaction and commitment as well as performance. This is probably the most intuitively obvious and is the area that has actually been tested most in path-goal theory research (House & Mitchell, 1974). For example, in situations where the task is very clear and subordinates have considerable self-motivation, attempts by lead-

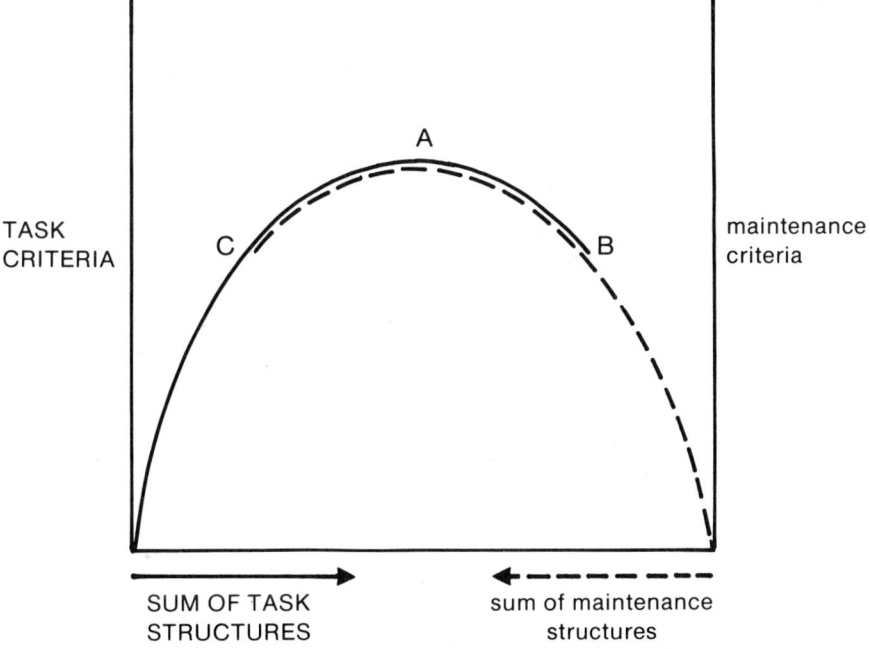

FIGURE 4.1. Interrelationships between task and maintenance curves

ers to clarify paths and goals result in decreased job satisfaction. They are perceived as redundant and as an imposition of unnecessarily close control (Filley, House, & Kerr, 1976).

The path from *B* to *A* represents the moderating effect of the maintenance structures on otherwise excessive task structures. This is consistent with the notion held by Miles and Petty (1975) that supportive activity reduces tension and anxiety resulting from large amounts of task leadership. Thibaut and Kelley (1959) indicate that a social-emotional specialist can compensate for excessive task pressure. And Greene (1975) finds that support moderates the relationship between task structure and performance such that with highly maintenance-oriented leaders, emphasis on task accomplishment causes higher subordinate performance. In other words, supportive leadership would ameliorate the negative effects of highly directive leadership on both task and maintenance outcomes.

Finally, the moderating effects of task structures on otherwise excessive maintenance structures are depicted by the path from *C* to *A*. Support for this cross-functional influence may be found in the stress literature (Benson & Allen, 1980). Task-oriented leadership that increases stress to a healthy point may improve both task and maintenance outcomes. Thus, more task-oriented leadership in this situation would tend to increase both performance and job satisfaction.

TEST OF HYPOTHESES DERIVED FROM THE FRAMEWORK

The structural-functional framework proposed here, then, incorporates the following basic ideas: (1) the task and maintenance functions can be fulfilled partially or entirely by task or maintenance structures, respectively, originating in individual members, hierarchical leader behavior, informal groups, influences external to the organization, or the task performed; (2) these structures can be combined or substituted for one another; (3) the relationship between the number of structures operating and measures of fulfillment of the functions is not linear across the entire range and approximates an inverted U; and (4) maintenance structures can serve to alleviate the effects of otherwise excessive task structures, and vice versa.

The Hypotheses

Two sets of hypotheses can be derived from the structural functional model:

HYPOTHESIS 1A: *With the cases represented by the upper 30 percent of the sums of the maintenance structures removed, the relationships between the sum of the self, leader-behavior, group, external, and task-itself task leadership structures and the task-functional outcomes at both the group and individual levels of analyses are curvilinear.*

HYPOTHESIS 1B: *With the cases represented by the upper 30 percent of the sums of the task structures removed, the relationships between the sum of the self, leader-behavior, group, external, and task-itself maintenance leadership structures and the maintenance-functional outcomes at both the group and individual levels of analyses are curvilinear.*

The removal of cases with high levels of sums of the other functional structures is necessary to remove cross-functional effects in testing the basic curvilinearity proposition. Thus, if these cases are included, and the cross-functional effect is present, we would expect a straightening effect on the inverted-U curve. This effect is investigated by testing the following two cross-functional hypotheses:

HYPOTHESIS 2A: *When all cases are included, the relationship between the sum of the task structures and task-dependent variables will approach linearity.*

HYPOTHESIS 2B: *When all cases are included, the relationship between the sums of the maintenance structures and maintenance-dependent variables will approach linearity.*

Sample

Employees from six major subdivisions of a large Department of Defense activity that supports operating units of all the armed services participated in this study. Of the 493 employees in these six activities, 380, representing 42 work groups, completed the survey questionnaires.

Measurements

Dependent Variables. Dependent variables for the individual level of analysis are all self-reported. The task-oriented criteria are expectancy (EXPECTCY) and individual perceptions of group arousal (GPAROUS). EXPECTCY is the sum of the measures of Expectancy One and Expectancy Two from C. A. Schriesheim's (1978) instruments, and GPAROUS is a five-item scale developed by Stogdill (1965). The maintenance-oriented dependent variable is individual job satisfaction (INDJSAT) measured by the 20-question Minnesota Satisfaction Questionnaire (Weiss, Dawis, England, & Lofquist, 1967).

The task-related dependent variables for the group level of analysis include the group average of the self-reported group arousal (GPAROUS) scores plus a combination of judged and measured group performance (GPPERF). Maintenance variables at the group level consist of a subjective measure of group loyalty (GPLOYAL) and an objective measure of organizational commitment (GPPRSNT). GPLOYAL is measured by the Stogdill (1965) five-item scale, and GPPRSNT is computed by subtracting the nonillness hours of sick leave per person per quarter from 22, the maximum value of absenteeism.

Task Structures. The self-management (INDLOC) task structure is operationalized as individual locus of control as measured by Valecha's (1972) modification of Rotter's (1966) scale. Measurement of hierarchical leader behavior for the task function is accomplished by use of the C. A. Schriesheim (1978) scales for the three facets of leader instrumental behavior — role clarification, specification of procedures, and work assignment — for the supervisor, for the supervisor's superordinate, and for an "other designated leader." A total instrumental leader behavior (TOTILB) score is obtained by summing the scores obtained for the three leaders. The task structure provided by the task itself (TSKCLAR) is measured by a modification of the six role-ambiguity items factored from a role-conflict/role-ambiguity questionnaire by Rizzo, House, and Lirtzman (1970). For the task-function group-influence (GPIINF) structure, and for the external instrumental influence (EXTIINF) measure, selected questions from the C. A. Schriesheim (1978) scales for instrumental leader behavior for role clarification and specification of procedures are modified for use with groups and for the evaluation of the most influential from among the following possible external sources: professional association, labor union, family member, or person of similar cultural background.

Maintenance Structures. A measure of an occupational commitment (IN-DOCCOM) derived from a modification of the Organizational Commitment Questionnaire (OCQ) developed by Mowday, Steers, and Porter (1978) is used to operationalize the self-management maintenance structure. Leader-behavior maintenance structures (TOTSUPLB) are operationalized as the sum of scores on the C. A. Schriesheim (1978) scale for leader supportive behavior completed for his or her supervisor, for his or her supervisor's supervisor, and for that person whom he or she chooses as the other designated leader. To measure the maintenance function by the task itself (TSKINSAT), an intrinsically-satisfying-nature-of-the-task instrument has been constructed from the three items from Kerr and Jermier (1978) plus two additional statements used to tap the role-orientation notion used in the work by Graen and Ginsburgh (1977). The instruments used for the group-influence (GPSUPP) and external-influence (EXTSUPP) structures that may fulfill the maintenance function are measured by appropriate questions taken from the C. A. Schriesheim (1978) leader supportive behavior scales. In the case of both task and maintenance structures, individual scores are averaged to produce group scores.

Analysis. Hypothesis 1A predicts that if the cross-functional impact of high maintenance structures is removed, the relationship between the task-dependent variable (TSKDEPEN) and the sum of the task-functional structures (SUMTSKST) will be curvilinear, where SUMTSKST = TOTILB + INDLOC + GPIINF + TSKCLAR + EXTIINF. First, the cases representing the upper 30 percent of the sum of the maintenance structures (SUMMNTST = TOTSUPLB + INDOCCOM + GPSUPP + TSKINSAT + EXTSUPP) are removed from consideration. Then, a regression analysis of the form, TSKDEPEN = B_0 + B_1SUMTSKST + B_2SUMTSKST^2 is performed, wherein a statistically significant negative coefficient of the squared term is justification for rejecting the null hypothesis. The regression tests are used for both the individual and the group levels. At the group level, where numbers of cases are small, the inverted-U relationship is also tested by dividing the range of SUMTSKST scores into three segments and performing nonparametric tests to determine if the task-dependent variables for the middle segment are higher than those for the two end segments.

The second set of hypotheses predict that high values of the cross-functional structures straighten the curvilinear relationships. Thus, to test Hypothesis 2A, the cases representing the upper 30 percent of the scores for the sum of the maintenance are included, and the entire file is then tested for the regression of TSKDEPEN on SUMTSKST + SUMTSKST^2. In this case, the squared term should not be significant.

In order to test Hypotheses 1B and 2B, the same processes are performed with the roles of the sum of the task structures and the sum of the maintenance structures reversed.

Results

Task Function. For Hypothesis 1A, Table 4.1 shows that going from a simple straight-line regression of EXPECTCY on SUMTSKST to a polynomial regression increases the adjusted R^2, and the F test of the squared term is significant with $p < .05$. Similarly, the results of the individual perception of GPAROUS regressed on SUMTSKPR provide statistically significant support for the curvilinearity hypothesis. The maximum point of both the EXPECTCY and GPAROUS curves occurs near the middle of the x axis.

At the group level of analysis, the regression of GPAROUS on SUMTSKST shows statistical significance. The maximum values of GPAROUS, as determined by the polynomial regression equations also occurs very close to the middle of the range (0 to 100) of possible SUMTSKST scores.

The solid curve of Figure 4.2 is a plot of the regression equation for EXPECTCY with the impact of high levels of SUMMNTST removed. Thus, for self-reported dependent variables, support is provided for an inverted-U relationship between task-functional criteria and the sum of the task structures.

The results of nonparametric tests for the group-level data are shown in Table 4.2. Both the Mann-Whitney U and rank-sum tests show that GPPERF scores in the middle of the curve are higher than at the two ends with a significance of $p < .05$.

The impact of the high levels of the sum of the maintenance structures on the task-function relationship is indicated by the data recorded in Table 4.3. When those higher levels of maintenance structures are taken into consideration, the F test for the squared term for both EXPECTCY and individual perception of GPAROUS drops to statistical insignificance and the maximum point of the resulting regression equations shifts from the midpoint of the x axis to the three-quarters point, thus showing the straightening effect of the opposite structures. The dashed-line curve of Figure 4.3 is a plot of the regression equation obtained for the EXPECTCY variable. Although the moderating effect suggested in Hypothesis 2A is demonstrated at the individual level of analysis for the task function by these comparisons, the group level of analysis provides no conclusive evidence in support of Hypothesis 2A.

Table 4.1. Regressions of Functional Dependent Variables on the Sums of Task and Maintenance Structures Using Those Cases in the Lower 70 Percent of Opposite Structure Sums.[a]

| | | SIMPLE REGRESSION | | POLYNOMIAL REGRESSION | | STRUCTURE SUM |
FUNCTION	DEPENDENT VARIABLE	N	Adj. R^2	Adj. R^2	F TEST FOR SQUARED TERM	AT MAXIMUM[b]
INDIVIDUAL LEVEL OF ANALYSIS						
Task	EXPECTCY	163	.020*	.046**	5.485*	54
	GPAROUS	178	.024*	.064***	8.725**	54
Maintenance	INDJSAT	240	.431***	.449***	9.103**	90
GROUP LEVEL OF ANALYSIS						
Task	GPAROUS	27	.077	.151*	3.36*	52
Maintenance	GPLOYAL	26	.226*	.203*	.28	

[a]For example, for the task function, EXPECTCY and GPAROUS are regressed on SUMTSKST for those cases in which SUMMNTST is less than 64, the lower 70 percent of SUMMNTST scores. For the maintenance function, the lower 70 percent of SUMTSKST scores are used.

[b]The range of possible scores for both SUMTSKST and SUMMNTST is 0 to 100.

*$p < .05$; **$p < .01$; ***$p < .001$

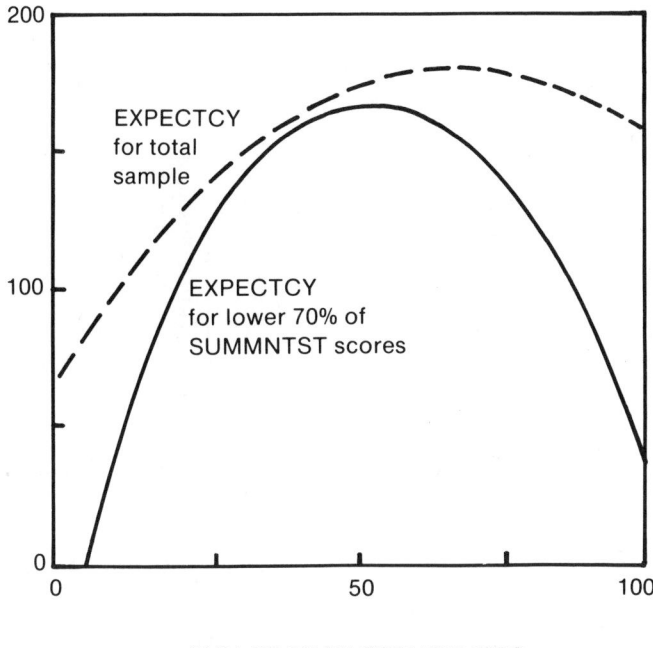

SUM OF TASK STRUCTURES

FIGURE 4.2 Expectancy versus the sum of the task structures for those cases in the lower 70 percent of the sum of the maintenance structure scores (solid lines) along with the same curve for the total sample (broken lines)

Maintenance Function. In the basic test for curvilinearity in the maintenance function, individual job satisfaction regressed on the sum of the maintenance structures provides support for the hypothesis, with the maximum value of job satisfaction occurring at a SUMMNTST of 90. At the group level for the maintenance function, only the rank-sum nonparametric test for the GPBRSNT criterion is significant at $p < .05$. Thus, the support for the basic curvilinearity hypothesis for the maintenance function is limited, though this may be because only a very small portion of the curve has a negative slope in this study. The solid curve of Figure 4.3 is a plot of the regression equation for individual job satisfaction.

The maintenance-function data of Table 4.3 show little impact of the high levels of task-related structure when the test for the basic curvilinearity is compared to the same test with all cases included. However, if just the cases involving the upper 30 percent of SUMTSKST are compared to those involving the lower 70 percent of SUMTSKST, it can be seen that the maintenance

Table 4.2. Nonparametric Tests of Curvilinearity at Group Level Using Lower 70 Percent of Sum of Opposite Structures: Tests that the Middle of the Curves Are Higher than the Two Ends.

FUNCTION	DEPENDENT VARIABLE	MIDDLE SEGMENTS	TEST	SIGNIFICANCE, p
Task	GPPERF	$46 \leq$ SUMTSKST ≤ 54	Mann-Whitney U	.050*
			Rank-sum	.028*
Maintenance	GPPRSNT	$55 \leq$ SUMMNTST ≤ 64	Mann-Whitney U	.070
			Rank-sum	.022*

*$p < .05$

Table 4.3. Impact of Opposite Functional Structure Sums on the Results of Task and Maintenance Polynomial Regression Analysis.

FUNCTION	DEPENDENT VARIABLE	CASES USED IN THE REGRESSION	ADJ. R^2	F TEST FOR SQUARED TERM	STRUCTURE SUM AT MAXIMUM
Task	EXPECTCY	Total sample	.095***	1.85	72
		Lower 70% SUMMNTST	.046**	5.49*	54
	GPAROUS	Total sample	.115***	2.24	73
		Lower 70% SUMMNTST	.064***	8.73**	54
Maintenance	INDJSAT	Total sample	.468***	12.18***	94
		Upper 30% SUMTSKST	.450***	3.11	99
		Lower 70% SUMTSKST	.449***	9.10**	88

*$p < .05$; **$p < .01$; ***$p < .001$

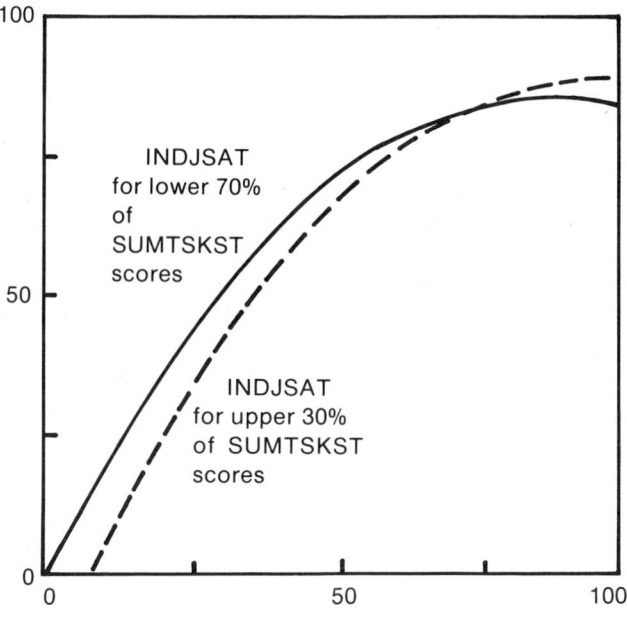

FIGURE 4.3. Individual job satisfaction versus the sum of the maintenance structures for those cases in the lower 70 percent of the sum of the task structure scores (solid lines) along with the same curve for the cases in the upper 30 percent of the sum of the task structures (broken lines)

relationship using only the high level of cross-function influences produces a straighter curve than the relationship without the high level of SUMTSKST cases (see Figure 4.3).

DISCUSSION

The results of the investigation reported here indicate that: (1) the relationship between task criteria and the sum of the task structures is probably an inverted U; (2) the relationship between maintenance criteria and the sum of the maintenance structures is probably curvilinear, but only a small portion of the down side of the curve appears within the operational limits of the data; (3) high levels of maintenance structures probably decrease the slope of the negative portion of the task-function curve; and (4) high levels of task structures probably have a small straightening effect on the far end of the maintenance curve.

Implications for Leadership Theory and Research

The functional analysis described in this chapter builds upon and extends two basic streams of research. The "social-psychological" stream is represented in the works of Bales (1953) and Thibaut and Kelley (1959) through Lord (1977). While this stream is generally well grounded in the concepts of structural functionalism, for the most part it has been oriented toward the laboratory rather than toward field research or application. The "Path Goal-Substitutes" stream, which encompasses the work of Evans (1970); House working alone (1971) and with Mitchell (1974), with Dessler (1974), and with Baetz (1979); and Kerr and Jermier (1978), has served as an important spur to placing the role of leaders within the context of other influences on subordinate performance and has spawned several interesting and important field investigations, but has not tapped the richness that a full functional framework can provide.

The framework presented in this chapter is designed to integrate these two streams of research and to provide a conceptually rich, but at the same time readily testable base for tying together still larger portions of the leadership literature. While space limitations preclude presentation of all the areas in which this is possible, one example may illustrate the potency of the approach in this regard.

Leadership theoreticians and trainers have debated the relative effectiveness of people-centered, task-centered, and people *and* task-centered leadership for years (Blake & Mouton, 1964; Hersey & Blanchard, 1977; Likert, 1961; Reddin, 1970; Stogdill, 1974). This issue is further complicated by the question of whether any person can be high on both dimensions (Filley, House, & Kerr, 1976) as well as by the Larson, Hunt, and Osborn (1976) discussion of "the great hi-hi-behavior myth," in which they report that knowledge of either consideration or of task-oriented leader behavior is sufficient to predict both performance and job satisfaction. Still another related difference in opinion exists over whether or not two levels of hierarchical leaders should have the same or complementary styles (Hill & Hunt, 1973; Storm, 1977). These controversies continue to exist, at least in part, because the real issue is not so much what leaders are doing, as whether or not both leadership functions are being fulfilled. It may well be that much of the confusion on these issues stems from the fact that the researchers usually did not consider the role of structures other than leader behavior in fulfilling task and maintenance functions.

This suggests that in future leadership research, the degree of fulfillment of the two functions by other structures — including leader behaviors of other hierarchical members — should be central. For example, the relationship between group performance and a supervisor's directive leader behavior depends on which portion of the task-function curve is applicable and on the degree of total supportive leadership that exists.

Moreover, the structural functional model itself should be tested further. The maintenance function is of particular interest; there is reason to believe that a significant down side to the curve exists, yet in the sample organization for this study, very little of the decreasing slope was in evidence.

Implications for Leadership Development and Practice

The structural framework also has important implications for the teaching and practice of leadership within organizations, as well as for integration of leadership with other organization behavior concepts. Again, space limitations preclude in-depth discussions of all of them, but it is important to mention two.

First, utilization of the structural-functional model provides a degree of precision and completeness that is lacking in many current situational models of leadership. It provides the trainer and the manager with an indication of not only the functions that must be performed if a work group is to operate effectively but of the major structures—potentially his or her tools—for fullfilling them. Particularly, it permits the leader to relate his or her own hierarchical behavior to the other structures considered capable of fulfilling the important functions.

Second, the structural-functional framework draws attention to a set of leader actions that are rarely considered in traditional concepts of leadership, but which may be more significant than the leader's obvious "leadership" behavior. In order to increase productivity or organizational commitment, a leader may wish to increase or decrease the sum of one or both of the structures, depending on which portion of the inverted U he or she believes that his or her group is operating. If the sum of both of the structures is low, a combination of increased group influence toward the proper goal coupled with leader provision of direction and support would move the unit to higher performance and/or commitment. On the other hand, if the sum of the processes has reached saturation and the leader is not satisfied with the outcomes, he or she may attempt to reduce group influence to move to the lower end of the curve where his or her own influence will have a greater impact. Furthermore, the leader may provide the direction and ensure that an influential assistant provides the support, or vice versa. And still another alternative is to use the cross-functional influences such as moving a group toward optimum performance from a point on the descending portion of the task curve by adding maintenance structures.

In summary, the results of this study lead us to believe that a leader may increase performance or organizational commitment by increasing or decreasing — depending on his or her group's position on an inverted-U curve — the sum of the task or maintenance structures either for a direct impact or a cross-functional influence. To accomplish this, the leader has the following alternatives for increasing or decreasing the task or maintenance structures: (1) changing his or her own instrumental and/or supportive behavior; (2) changing the instrumental and/or supportive leader behavior of another person in the hierarchy who has influence on the group; or (3) changing individual characteristics or group, external, or task-itself influences. The major responsibility of the supervisor is to ensure that the two functions are optimally fulfilled.

5

Refocusing Leadership:
A Modest Proposal*

Janet Fulk and Thomas G. Cummings

Few would disagree that radically new approaches are needed for describing, explaining, predicting, and prescribing that elusive phenomenon labeled "leadership." As a modest step in this direction, this chapter presents an alternative perspective on one facet of managerial leadership: the process by which the subordinate's task boundaries are determined. Our conceptualization focuses on task boundary determination because such activity is generally viewed as a particularly important function within the broader leadership role.

We acknowledge several conceptual debts for portions of the alternative model we propose. The first is to Cummings and Srivastva (1977) from whom we borrow the notions that: (1) work is a social-contracting process; (2) work is comprised of two interrelated components labeled social contract and task; and (3) work agreements can be typified based upon the relative level of influence the role incumbent and related others have in determining how the task will be structured.

The second conceptual basis is a set of interrelated theories of communication in interpersonal relations by Bateson and his colleagues (Bateson, 1972; Bateson, Jackson, Haley, & Weakland, 1956; Ruesch & Bateson, 1951; Watzlawick, Beavin, & Jackson, 1967; Watzlawick, Weakland, & Fisch, 1974) from whom we borrow the application of Bertrand Russell's Theory of Logical Types (Whitehead & Russell, 1910) to interpersonal relationships. Primarily, we employ their notions that: (1) in addition to a content message, interpersonal communications convey a message about the relationship between the two parties; (2) the relationship aspect of a communication is "meta" to content that is, of a higher logical type; (3) the meta level creates a frame within which content messages acquire meaning; and (4) pathological relationships arise from confusions and inconsistencies across these two levels.

A third influence is, of course, the plethora of existing thought on the phe-

*The authors wish to thank Warren Bennis, David Berke, Nancy Hanks, Craig Lundberg, Kurt Motamedi, Stephen Kerr, John Slocum, Will McWhinney, and three anonymous reviewers for helpful comments on earlier drafts of this chapter.

nomena of leadership. While our debts in this area are more diffuse, the most obvious is the absorption of several notions relating to subordinate task discretion and task-role clarity, which have to varying degrees and with varying success been the subject of a vast array of existing leadership models (see, for example, theories by Fiedler, 1967; House, 1971; Graen, 1976; Sayles, 1979; Vroom & Yetton, 1973; and the extensive review of other approaches in House & Baetz, 1979).

We begin by summarizing significant portions of Cummings and Srivastva's conceptualization of work and Bateson's description of the nature of interpersonal communication. We then integrate these thrusts with our borrowings from traditional leadership theory into a conceptual model. We conclude our presentation with a discussion of general theoretical, methodological, and practical implications.

SOCIAL-CONTRACTING DEFINITION OF WORK

Cummings and Srivastva (1977) define "work" as a social process that produces specific agreements between persons performing tasks and others impacting task· definition, execution, and control. Work is seen to be comprised of two interrelated components: a social contract and a task which is the subject of that agreement. The social contract is an agreement between the role incumbent and relevant others as to the relative influence each will have in structuring the role incumbent's task. As such, it serves to establish the structure of the relationship between the task-relevant parties; it also sets up a socially defined boundary specifying the content of the task. Social contracts can be formalized like many employment contracts, or they can involve informal agreements among task-relevant people, such as task performers, co-workers, supervisors, and staff personnel. Social contracts are dynamic and undergo change, often implicitly. This suggests that work is a social-contracting process through which influence agreements and task boundaries are defined and redefined.

Cummings and Srivastva (1977) developed a typology that describes work contracts as comprised of variable weighting of four aspects: contractual, prescribed, discretionary, and emergent. *Contractual* aspects are those parts of a work agreement that are jointly determined by the relevant parties. That is, each party has an important role in determining how the task will be structured. Following Thompson (1967), Cummings and Srivastva (1977) suggested that these aspects reduce uncertainty for each party through the mutual exchange of commitments. *Prescribed* aspects are those parts that are determined by someone other than the role incumbent. They receive legitimacy from others' power over the role incumbent. Such power can derive from a variety of sources, such as expert knowledge, positive identification, control over rewards and punishments, formal authority, and charisma. *Discretionary* aspects of the work agreement are those portions that are determined primarily by the role incumbent. That is, the parties agree that in the discretionary areas, the role incumbent will primarily decide how the task will be structured. *Emergent* aspects of the work agreement are portions that are determined primarily by environmental factors. These parts are not determinable by either party to the work agreement — they arise from the multitude of forces operating within the work context. The four aspects occur simultaneously in a work relationship, although their relative weighting may vary enormously across time or between persons depending upon a variety of circumstances.

THEORY OF LOGICAL TYPES IN INTERPERSONAL COMMUNICATION

Following Bateson (Ruesch & Bateson, 1951), Watzlawick *et al.* (1967) suggest that communication has both a *content* and a *relationship* level. The content level conveys basic information. The relationship level conveys a message regarding the relationship between the communicants. In human communication, the form in which the information is cast provides cues as to how it is to be interpreted (e.g., a command versus a request), and by implication it suggests the relative position of each communicant. Because the relationship level conveys information about the information — that is, meta-information — it is of a higher logical type than the content level. Higher logical types define, limit, and structure the interpretations made of information content. Thus, different metacommunications lead to differences in meanings attributed to the *same* information.

Watzlawick *et al.* (1967) further suggest that disturbed communication can arise because of failure to distinguish between the content itself and the relationship metacommunication. Often, conflicts at the relationship level are difficult to recognize and consequently are misdefined as content-level disagreements. Since the communicants try to resolve differences at a different logical level from the one at which they disagree, they are unable to progress in restoring healthy communication.

A MODEL

In combination, Bateson's distinctions and Cummings and Srivastva's conceptualization are important inputs to modeling leader-subordinate activity surrounding subordinate task boundary definition. In focusing on a subordinate's task, we confine ourselves to those situations in which there is an accepted hierarchical relationship in which a "leader" is responsible for supervising the task activities of the subordinate. In these circumstances leaders participate in social contracting with subordinates about the subordinates' task. The social contracting has both a content and a relationship aspect. The content part concerns the specific subject of the work contract: the task boundaries. The relationship aspect involves the interpersonal process by which leaders and subordinates arrive at those boundaries; that is, it pertains to the relative influence each has in making the decision as to how the boundaries will be constructed. A key point is that the relationship part is of a higher logical type than the content part: it structures the interpretations that are made of specific task content. For example, the amount of discretion a subordinate has on a specific task (content) can have quite different meanings depending upon how the leader and subordinate arrived at that amount of discretion (relationship). For example, a subordinate might perceive a low amount of task discretion as satisfying if he or she had sufficient influence in determining that amount, but unsatisfying if he or she did not. Thus, the leader-subordinate social-contracting relationship is meta to the task content and serves as a central reference point for interpreting it.

The Relationship Aspect of the Social-Contracting Process

Cummings and Srivastva's typology of work agreements is especially suited to describing the relationship aspect of leader-subordinate social contracting. However, whereas Cummings and Srivastva applied their classification scheme to all kinds of work contracts — formal and informal agreements occurring within and outside of organizations — our focus is limited to informal work contracts between subordinates and leaders within organizations. In confining leader-subordinate social contracting to that occurring over and above the formal employment contract, we are following the lead of Graen and Cashman (1975), who viewed leadership (as distinct from supervision) as "the influence of members without resort to authority derived from an employment contract" (p. 153), and Katz and Kahn (1978) who considered "the essence of organizational leadership to be the influential increment over and above mechanical compliance with the routine directives of the organization" (p. 528). Thus, in those cases where leader-subordinate social contracting is negligible, the leader's activity in task boundary definition is merely the enforcement of compliance with the formal employment contract.

Based on Cummings and Srivastva's classification scheme, Figure 5.1 presents four types of leader-subordinate social-contracting relationships, each differing in the amount of determination the respective parties have over defining the subordinate's task boundaries. The relationships are named from the subordinate's perspective, and correspond to the four aspects of work agreements described earlier. Although these four extremes represent only a few of the possible kinds that could be derived from the Cummings and Srivastva model, they provide useful benchmarks for describing social-contracting relationships between leaders and subordinates.

A contractual relationship is characterized by mutual influence in deter-

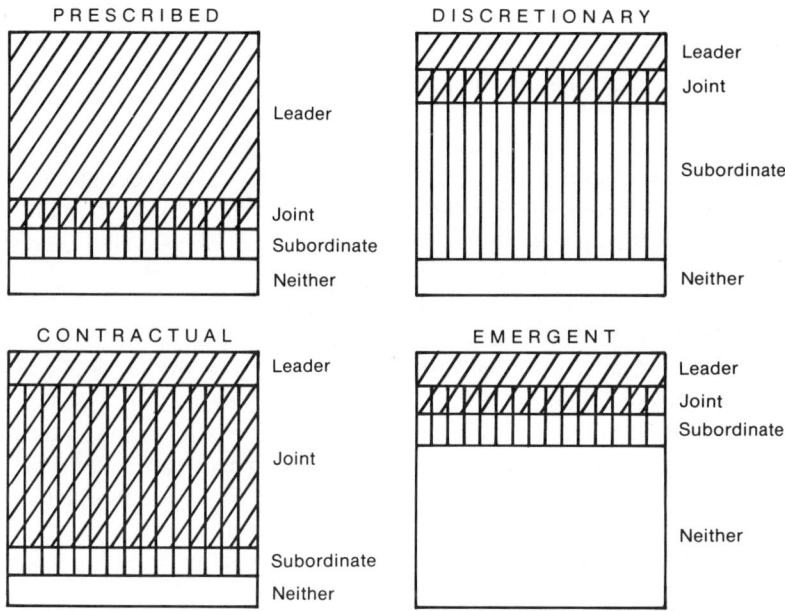

FIGURE 5.1. Relationship social-contracting conditions for determination of subordinate's task boundaries

mining task boundaries. As such, this type of relationship has some commonality with the conception of Graen and his colleagues (Dansereau, Graen, & Haga, 1975; Graen, 1976; Graen & Cashman, 1975) of "in-group exchanges" between leaders and group members. Such exchanges are based on high levels of negotiating latitude between a leader and member; the leader shows a high willingness to give the member individualized assistance in role development, and this leads to negotiated exchanges characterized by high levels of trust, openness to ideas, and reciprocal support.

A prescribed relationship as shown in Figure 5.1 is where the subordinate's task boundaries are determined primarily by the leader. Because we are discussing social contracting over and above the formal employment contract, leader influence must transcend the legitimate authority of the position if subordinates are to engage in this one-sided form of setting task boundaries. Katz and Kahn (1978) proposed that such "influential increment" is likely to come from expert and referent power. They suggested that expert and referent power are relatively free of unintended and undesirable organizational consequences because they are less coercive and externally determined than the formal bases of power. Thus, a particular task content is likely to have quite different meaning to subordinates depending on whether it is based on a prescribed social-contracting relationship or purely on positional, reward and sanction power. In the latter case, there will probably be little social contracting and subordinates will adhere strictly to the formal employment contract.

Figure 5.1 shows that a discretionary relationship is where the subordinate primarily determines her or his own task boundaries. The leader has little or no influence in establishing task boundaries beyond those specified in the formal employment contract. Some discretionary relationships do not represent meaningful forms of social contracting, at least as it is defined in this chapter. These include situations where the leader essentially abdicates her or his role and leaves the subordinate to define whatever task boundaries seem appropriate. Such leadership vacuums can occur either because the leader purposely chooses not to social-contract with the subordinate or, as Kerr and Jermier (1978) have suggested, because powerful neutralizers exist in the leadership situation which destroy or counteract the leader's ability to influence subordinates. They identified several potential neutralizers, such as subordinate need for independence. Kerr and Jermier (1978) raised the possibility, however, that some neutralizers can act as "substitutes for leadership," standing in place of formal leadership to influence the subordinate. The presence of specific substitutes can render a discretionary relationship meaningful if they enable the subordinate to establish appropriate task boundaries that the leader could not effectively establish. For example, a subordinate with professional skills who belongs to a cohesive work group with high performance norms may be able to set informal task boundaries more effectively than a formal leader. Thus, substitutes that provide the subordinate with the necessary expertise, information, and motivation to define informal task boundaries that the leader could not effectively define lead to quite a different discretionary relationship from one produced by leadership vacuums, whatever the cause; the former represents a meaningful social contract between the leader and subordinate, while the latter suggests the absence of such a relationship.

The last diagram in Figure 5.1 is an emergent relationship where neither the leader nor the subordinate determines the latter's task boundaries. This relationship is heavily influenced by forces outside of the leader-subordinate exchange, and because neither party has much task influence beyond that specified in the employment contract, there is essentially little if any social contracting between leader and subordinate. The two parties manage their relationship entirely within the bounds of the employment contract, and the leader's activity with respect to defining the subordinate's task boundaries is simply the enforcement of compliance with the contract. It follows from Kerr and Jermier (1978) that emergent relationships are likely to exist in leadership contexts where extremely powerful neutralizers or substitutes preclude meaningful leader and subordinate informal task definition. For example, organizational structures that are formalized and inflexible can severely constrain both the need and the ability of leaders and subordinates to socially contract regarding task boundaries.

The forms of social-contracting relationship in which a leader participates may vary across task elements, across subordinates, and across time. A leader can have one type of relationship for one part of the subordinate's task and another relationship for another part. For instance, they may engage in a discretionary relationship for defining the performance activities of a particular task and a prescribed relationship for determining the way in which that performance will be evaluated. A leader can also apply the same relationship to all subordinates, or he or she can enter into different kinds of relationships with different subordinates or subgroups of subordinates, as suggested by Graen's (1976) differentiation of members into informal assistants and ordinary members based on in-group and out-group leader/member exchanges. Finally, leaders can engage in different types of relationships with the same subordinates over time. Indeed, the research of Graen (1976) and Katz (1978) suggests that leader-subordinate relationships may progress through a distinct series of phases as employees are assimilated into and adapt to new roles and jobs.

The Content Aspect of the Social-Contracting Process: Task Boundaries

The four extremes of leader-subordinate relationships discussed above occur at the relationship level of social contracting; they are meta to the task boundaries and serve as frames within which task content acquires meaning. The content level of leader-subordinate social contracting is subordinates' task boundaries. Subordinates' tasks have been given considerable attention by leadership theorists. Task structure (i.e., routineness and repetitiveness), in particular, has been hypothesized to be an important moderator of the effectiveness of various leader behaviors (see Fiedler, 1967; Griffin, 1979; House, 1971; Kerr & Jermier, 1978). Although research testing the hypothesized moderating role of task structure has proved at least somewhat successful (see C. A. Schriesheim & Von Glinow, 1977, for a review), it has at least two major limitations. First, in a moderator role, tasks are limited in that they are assumed to be fixed, and also they imply undue restrictions on the kinds of leader behaviors considered acceptable. For example, the task-contingency approach suggests that on highly structured tasks, leaders should minimize the display of directive leader behaviors. Cummings (1982) proposed overcoming the limitations of this task imperative by treating tasks as designable variables, open to leaders' influence and change. Our conceptualization is consistent with Cummings' suggestion in that we consider subordinates' task boundaries as central outcomes of leader-subordinate interactions. The discussion in the paragraphs to follow details the manner in which this is accomplished by leader and subordinate. We recognize, of course, certain limitations to degrees of freedom in task design; organizations generally expect individuals to adapt themselves to job constraints, and technology and other contextual conditions can restrict the kinds of task designs that are possible.

A second major limitation of task moderator research is that it has tended to focus on a relatively narrow band of subordinates' task activity. A number of leadership researchers have called for a broader orientation in studying both task moderators (Schriesheim & DeNisi, 1981; Schriesheim & Schriesheim, 1976, 1980) and the leadership role itself (Fulk & Wendler, 1982; Hunt, Sekeran, & Schriesheim, 1982; Stewart, 1982b). Similarly, we suggest that a task involves a more comprehensive set of activities that should be included under its rubric. All tasks involve a logical sequence of functions commonly identified as planning, executing, and controlling/evaluating. Traditional approaches to leadership have focused primarily on the executing part of this sequence, leaving the remainder to be examined by students of job design and performance appraisal. Clearly, however, subordinates' task accomplishment requires planning, executing, and controlling/evaluating, and we need to reintegrate these elements within subordinates' task boundaries.

Planning involves setting objectives and preparing strategies for attaining those objectives. This typically includes determining resource allocations, developing procedures, and setting time and tolerance targets. *Executing* involves implementing plans and managing new contingencies for which there are no preexisting plans. Obviously, execution is considerably more complex in those instances where there is little ability to preplan task execution because necessary information is not available in advance (see Galbraith, 1973). *Controlling and evaluating* involve setting performance standards, monitoring and measuring performance, providing feedback, and allocating rewards or sanctions.

An important part of the content aspect of the leader-subordinate social contracting is concerned with delineating the *boundaries* of these task elements. This involves two key issues that are fundamental to drawing any boundary: the size of the area which the boundary encloses, and the clarity with which the boundary is marked. With respect to subordinates' task boundaries, the enclosure size can be considered the amount of *discretion* available to subordinates in planning, executing, and controlling their tasks. Discretion refers to the subordinate's latitude of choice and action in task-directed behavior. The clarity of the boundary for a task pertains to *task-role clarity*, which specifies where the subordinate's task begins and ends. This includes the explicitness in formulating and communicating responsibilities and limits, and in specifying mechanisms for evaluating and rewarding task-relevant behaviors and outcomes in the light of those limits.

Overall, then, our conceptualization of task highlights six areas in which important superior-subordinate social contracting can occur — planning discretion, planning task-role clarity, executing discretion, executing task-role clarity, controlling discretion, and controlling task-role clarity. The task boundaries in each area are drawn within the context of the existing frame — that is, according to the influence relationship established by the parties at the meta level. Thus, as they are discussed below they must be considered within the context of *some* frame. For convenience, we describe them all within the context of a contractual relationship.

Planning Discretion. In planning discretion the focus is on how involved the subordinate should be in planning the activities to be carried out, and how much weight should be placed on the subordinate's input in developing the final plan. The types of questions to be addressed include such things as: How much planning can the subordinate do before getting the superior's approval? Should the subordinate simply await assignments from the leader or should he or she initiate? Is the subordinate simply assigned goals, targets, and deadlines or is his or her input to this process an important determinant of goals and deadlines? Is the subordinate expected to develop a set of proposed procedures for task accomplishment?

Planning Task-Role Clarity. This area refers to the clarity with which limitations and expectations regarding planning discretion are formulated and communicated to the subordinate. Does the subordinate know and understand what his or her role should be in planning? Are the subordinate's inputs to plans given careful consideration when they are solicited or are they ignored nevertheless? Role clarification provides both direction and constraint for the subordinate.

Executing Discretion. This pertains to the amount of discretion the subordinate should exercise in executing the task. How much of the task can the subordinate complete without checking with the leader? How much can the subordinate bend rules and procedures, set new procedures as new demands arise, and so on, on his or her own without requesting approval of the immediate supervisor? How much of the execution has been preplanned, and how specific is the plan that is being executed in regard to rules and procedures?

Executing Task-Role Clarity. This area describes task-role clarity with respect to task execution. Basically, this portion pertains to how well the subordinate knows and understands the specific rules and limits that pertain to carrying out the task. It is important to note that high task-role clarity does not imply completely specified rules and procedures that allow for no variation; in other words, high task-role clarity does not mean low discretion. High task-role clarity simply means that the subordinate knows and understands the limits to his or her discretion, however wide or narrow those limits may be.

Controlling Discretion. This area pertains to the amount of discretion the subordinate exercises over control and evaluation. This includes how much input the subordinate has to monitoring his or her own performance, reporting results, setting standards, conducting evaluations of his or her own performance, and specifying appropriate consequences or rewards. It also includes such things as the latitude of the standards, the subordinate's input to specifying the information sources to be consulted in appraising performance, and the flexibility of standards and budgets. Higher discretion would be evident where a subordinate conducted his or her own quality control, largely determined his or her own budget, maintained his or her own performance records based upon criteria which he or she assisted in developing, and so forth.

Controlling Task-Role Clarity. This area pertains to the amount of task-role clarity in regard to control and evaluation. It includes the clarity of the subordinate's knowledge of such concerns as how he or she will be evaluated, when, by whom, according to what criteria, and with what potential consequences or rewards. Also, it includes the subordinate's understanding of the amount of latitude he or she has in participating in the control/evaluation process.

Systematic Aspects of the Contracting Process

Given that the elements of planning, executing, and controlling/evaluating within any task are interdependent, the boundaries of the leader-subordinate social contract regarding these elements are interdependent as well, and this affects the nature of the overall work contract in several ways. First, agreed-upon task boundaries for one area may set limits for agreements in other areas. For example, the discretion inherent in a particular plan may set limits on the latitude of execution, and the ability to preplan may affect the control/evaluation function and vice versa. Second, one party to the contract may compensate the other party for concessions in one area by making concessions in another area. For example, a subordinate who agreed to a smaller role in planning a particular aspect of the job than he or she had expected to assume might be "paid off" by gaining greater latitude in the execution phase. Third, changes from outside of the system that affect one component may indirectly affect other components. The renegotiation of one area as a result of changes introduced from outside the dyad may subsequently require renegotiation in other areas in order to achieve task accomplishment within a work agreement that is acceptable, in total, to both parties.

In addition to interdependencies across the stages of the task, there may also be interdependencies of a different sort across discretion and task-role clarity. For example, the subordinate might find it desirable to have less task-role clarity in those situations where the discretion is not high, perhaps because this affords the subordinate a feeling of greater freedom on the job — not being "boxed in." Or, high task-role clarity might be of great importance to an individual who has agreed to accept a great deal of discretion in a task in order to avoid the debilitating effects of working under a great deal of uncertainty over a large portion of the task. We suggest, however, that the direction of any relationship between the task boundary components will be a function of the expectations and needs of the particular leader and subordinate. While some individuals might thrive under situations of low task-role clarity and high discretion, others might find the high amount of uncertainty implied by such an agreement stressful.

Thus, we have suggested that the six task areas of social contracting form a system in which interdependencies appear both across the task boundaries and within the different portions of the task. Leader-subordinate social contracting is directed at establishing a work agreement that describes the state of the total system at that particular time and within that particular context.

THE ASSOCIATION OF "RELATIONSHIP" AND "CONTENT" LEVELS

We now examine specific associations between the relationship and content levels of leader-subordinate social contracting. Although research must ultimately provide knowledge about such cross-level associations, several logical possibilities are apparent. We discuss these in terms of resolving conflicts occurring at the content and relationship levels, primarily because such conflict resolution can highlight otherwise obscure interactions between the two levels.

Content Conflicts

When leaders and subordinates have disagreements over content or task boundaries, there are at least three major ways to resolve them: (1) adhere to the rules created by the existing relationship; (2) renegotiate the relationship portion of the contract; or (3) resort to an emergent relationship where social contracting is negligible.

In many situations where task disagreements are not highly significant or ego-involving, conflict can be resolved simply by fulfilling the existing relationship part of the social contract, even though this may result in some dissatisfaction. Such responsible behavior is probably the rule rather than the exception in those innumerable cases where task disagreements are relatively minor; living with the resulting dissatisfaction is less costly than breaking the social contract or attempting to renegotiate it.

On the other hand, task disagreements can have major repercussions at the relationship level in those instances where: (1) the issue is highly important to one or both parties; (2) their task boundary expectations diverge strongly; and (3) there is a highly skewed relationship (i.e., prescribed or discretionary frame). Under these conditions, the person with relatively less influence over setting task boundaries may attempt to resolve the disagreement either by seeking to renegotiate the relationship to obtain greater determination, or by reneging on the contract altogether — retreating to an emergent relationship where only the formal employment contract is followed.

Clearly, these two strategies can have drastically different costs and outcomes. Attempting to renegotiate greater amounts of task determination can require considerable time, effort, and the giving of future commitments, but can result in a more permanent and mutually acceptable solution to the contracting problem. Withdrawing to an emergent relationship can quickly resolve the specific disagreement and perhaps protect the relatively low-influence party from the other's possible arbitrary use of influence above that authorized by the employment contract, but can severely damage the relationship and preclude future opportunities to engage in informal social contracting. A key determinant of whether the person with relatively less influence will seek either to renegotiate or to renege on the informal contract is the level of trust he or she has in the other party. If the level of trust is high, the person can be expected to incur the risks of trying to renegotiate because he or she feels that the other will at least treat such overtures fairly, whatever the eventual outcomes. Considerable research suggests that mutual trust is essential for working through problematic and emotionally laden interpersonal problems (see, for example, Rogers, 1961). Conversely, if the trust level is low, the person with less influence is likely to retreat to the relatively safe confines of the formal employment contract because he or she feels that at least within these bounds, there are formally legitimized rules for resolving leader-subordinate task conflicts. Research in labor relations suggests that low levels of union and management trust are associated with low informal cooperation and strict adherence to the formal labor contract (see, for example, Kochan, 1980).

Disagreements at the Relationship Level

Whereas conflicts over task content are relatively identifiable and potentially resolvable within the existing relationship, disagreements over the relationship are particularly difficult to recognize, and moreover, they typically must be resolved by changing the relationship itself. Watzlawick and his colleagues (1967) have argued that "relationships are only rarely defined deliberately or with full awareness" (p. 52), and consequently, relationship conflicts are rarely seen as meta-level issues, but are typically misdefined as content-level problems. An unfortunate outcome of this misdefinition is that people seek content solutions to what are really relationship problems, thus perpetuating the conflict. An example serves to illustrate. A faculty member and a doctoral student spent months in heated argument over the content of the latest revisions made by the faculty member to a joint paper. In the end, the conflict was resolved when a third party assisted them in redefining the issue as a relationship problem: the faculty member had violated an implicit contractual relationship by failing to obtain the approval of the student to diverge substantially from the agreed-on outline and by distributing the revised paper to a variety of colleagues without either showing it to the student coauthor or obtaining her approval for distribution. With the issue redefined, the pair were able to resolve the conflict by explicit agreements pertaining to their coauthoring relationship. Interestingly, the final, mutually acceptable paper had virtually the same content as the initial revision over which they had argued so bitterly.

Given the tacit nature of relationships, the first step in resolving leader-subordinate conflict at this level is to recognize that it is in fact a relationship problem. Two major relationship problems that can be particularly detrimental to task content are relationships that are too unstable, and conversely, relationships that are too rigid. Any ongoing relationship must eventually develop a stable set of rules or agreements that define and guide the interaction. Because the process of establishing such contracts is typically characterized by uncertainty and instability, it consumes energy and resources that could be directed elsewhere. Thus, achieving stable leader-subordinate relationships can have significant resource-saving functions; it can also reduce leader-member uncertainty. If the right to define task boundaries shifts too rapidly, existing agreements may be upset, creating conflict, or consequent changes in discretion and task-role clarity may adversely affect the subordinate's ability to fulfill her or his role, or the parties may become incapacitated at the task-content level. As Watzlawick et al. (1967) noted: "'sick' relationships are characterized by a constant struggle about the nature of the relationship, with the content aspect . . . becoming less and less important" (p. 52).

Because healthy relationships eventually attain stability, the early periods of superior-subordinate interaction are critical determinants of the nature of the long-term relationship, and through it, the nature of the task boundaries. The considerable literature on organizational socialization and role making (see, for example, Graen, 1976; Van Maanen & Schein, 1978; Wanous, 1977) suggests that initial interactions between leaders and subordinates structure and limit future interactions and the interpretations that will be made of those interactions. Leader and member attention to the relationship level of their early exchanges can be expected to increase the chances that the parties will become conscious of their own and each other's expectations about how task boundaries should be defined. This surfacing of expectations can reveal important disagreements, and as such, is a necessary prerequisite to constructive conflict resolution (Walton, 1969).

Whereas leader-subordinate relationship stability has important functions, it can become dysfunctional if it leads to rigidity and resistance to necessary changes in the relationship. Stable agreements about each person's influence in defining task boundaries can become obsolete and ineffective as the work environment or the relevant parties change. Because the costs of renegotiating and reestablishing such relationships are likely to be perceived as high by one or both parties, resistance to change is probably common in stable relationships, especially those achieving high levels of leader-member agreement, as suggested by the extensive literature on group cohesion (see, for example, Cummings, 1982; Hackman, 1976).

One logical way to change the relationship level of social contracting is to replace an existing relationship with a different relationship that fits the content equally well or better, and thus changes the content's entire meaning. Watzlawick et al. (1974) proposed that successful relationship change of this type needs to take into account the views and expectations of the participants. The research of Katz (1978) on time and work provides a possible model to assist this. Katz proposed that employees change their perceptions toward work as they enter and cycle through three transitional stages of job longevity: socialization, innovation, and adaptation. He found that different types of issues preoccupy employees at each of the three stages, leading to different social constructions of work and its context. Albeit speculatively, we may map the leader-subordinate relationships prescribed in Figure 5.1 onto the content issues salient to employees at each transitional stage. During the socialization stage employees are concerned with reality construction, such as deciphering norms, building relationships, and learning about others' expectations. Here a prescribed relationship would reasonably fit the content, since employees would likely expect and welcome assistance from powerful others in defining task boundaries. Over time, as employees move into the innovation stage, their primary concerns shift to influence and achievement. They seek challenging tasks and enlarged scopes of participation. In the early periods of this stage, a contractual relationship seems to fit the content, as employees would expect to engage with leaders in mutually negotiating more challenge and participation. In the latter parts of the innovation stage, employees would likely have gained special skills and higher levels of achievement and influence, and a discretionary relationship appears to frame these contents quite well. Finally, in the adaptation stage, Katz suggested that employees lose interest in the task elements of work, and focus on the contextual aspects including activities outside the work environment; they protect their autonomy and minimize their vulnerability. An emergent relationship where there is little social contracting and the relationship is played entirely within the bounds of the formal employment contract seems a reasonable frame for these content issues.

In summary, content issues may be resolved by reference to the relationship level to enforce an existing contract, to renegotiate that contract, or to resort to an emergent relationship. Relationship issues may be resolved by establishment of a stable contract or by renegotiating the relationship to provide an interpretation of content that is more acceptable to both parties. In the latter case, leader and subordinate attention and energy must be directed toward the relationship itself, since that is the level at which the difficulties occur.

RESEARCH ISSUES FOR REFINEMENT OF THE MODEL

Contextual Influences on Social Contracting

In presenting our conceptualization of leader-subordinate social contracting, we thus far have set aside consideration of the broader context in which such processes take place. Clearly, there are a variety of external influences that may permeate the leader-subordinate system and alter its direction or outcomes. Although space constraints do not permit extensive treatment of contextual considerations here, the following factors quite clearly deserve further discussion and empirical examination:

1. Sources of superior and subordinate expectations about the social-contracting process, including cognitive-structural characteristics such as implicit theories (Lord, Foti, & Phillips, 1982), attributional tendencies (Calder, 1977), egocentrism (Greenwald, 1980; Staw, 1980; Thompson & Kelley, 1981), scripts (Abelson, 1981), schema (Fiske, 1981; Sandelands, 1982), and needs for achievement and independence (Kerr & Jermier, 1978); personal resources such as task expertise, charisma (House, 1977), job security, performance record, and negotiation and communication skills; and norms about leader-subordinate social contracting deriving from specific work groups, organizational culture, and ideologies associated with a particular political and economic system (e.g., capitalism versus socialism).

2. Interdependencies in social contracting across dyads of which the leader is a member, especially those resulting from resource limitations and equity considerations across subordinates.

3. Social-influence inputs/cues from outside the dyad as resources for support and/or role construction (Schriesheim, 1980), as substitutes for formal leadership (Kerr & Jermier, 1978), as sources of direct input for the construction of meaning (Salancik & Pfeffer, 1974), and as bargaining resources though the power of coalition (March & Simon, 1958).

4. Technological characteristics that set limits on task boundaries, such as task interdependencies within or across units (Thompson, 1967), task uncertainty (Galbraith, 1973), and "objective" attributes such as time span of discretion (Jacques, 1965).

5. Structural constraints on leader-subordinate interactions, including organizational formulation and inflexibility (Kerr & Jermier, 1978), vertical and horizontal specialization and coordination (Hunt & Osborn, 1982), unit size,

and embeddedness of the dyad in dual reporting relationships, matrix structures (Galbraith, 1973), or dual or triple hierarchies (Schriesheim, Von Glinow, & Kerr, 1977).

Nontask Outcomes of Social Contracting

We now touch briefly upon outcome variables that have been of interest to leadership researchers: subordinates' satisfaction, anxiety, and performance. Although several suggestions follow logically from the model, research must eventually enlighten us about the multitude of ways in which these variables impact and are impacted by the social-contracting process.

Subordinate satisfaction with task boundaries is likely to vary depending upon how those task boundaries were selected. In general, to the extent that the leader and subordinate: (1) achieve agreement on a social contract, which (2) leads to task boundaries that are not strongly divergent from the subordinate's expectations, and (3) fulfill the conditions of the agreement in their interactions, we may expect the subordinate to manifest a reasonable amount of satisfaction. Subordinate satisfaction is thus seen to be a function of specific expectations, agreements, and interpretations of whether those agreements are fulfilled.

Previous research suggests that subordinate anxiety may be associated with low task-role clarity (Van Sell, Brief, & Schuler, 1981). However, this linkage may vary depending upon the type of leader-subordinate relationship — that is, whether the subordinate is in a prescribed or contractual relationship (in which case he or she is dependent upon the leader for clarification), a discretionary relationship (in which personal choices have been made about the task-role clarity boundary), or an emergent relationship (which completely removes dyadic influence on task-role clarity).

Subordinate performance is likely to be related in fairly complex and particularistic ways to the social-contracting process. The same conditions associated with lower anxiety and/or higher satisfaction may also be related to lower performance. A leader and subordinate may, for example, achieve agreement on task boundaries which the subordinate does not have the skills, abilities, or motivations to occupy effectively. Conversely, they may choose boundaries uniquely suited to the subordinate and the task at hand. Also, because social contracting is a process with systemic characteristics, there are likely to be feedback effects similar to those implied by the work of Lowin and Craig (1968) on the causal nature of subordinate performance on leader behavior, and Greene (1979b) on reciprocal causality in leadership relations with subordinate "outcome" variables.

Although the outcomes of social contracts are highly particularistic to specific dyads, research is likely to suggest the kinds of contracts that are satisfying and productive for certain classes of individuals within certain contexts. When they are applied in these situations, we will probably find high predictability for the class as a whole. For example, we might expect that for highly skilled professional employees working in basic research, a discretionary relationship will be favored and/or effective for many activities, and that the attempted imposition of alternative contracts may lead to conflict for many dyads (see Kerr, Von Glinow, & Schriesheim, 1977). At the same time, of course, we must take care to recognize that there will probably be some dyads in this class for which some other form of relationship will be appropriate.

A Note on Perspective Taking

The social-contracting process we have described involves an oscillating series of interactions between a leader and subordinate over a period of time. The snapshot highlighted here concerns one point in the series and the subordinate's perspective. For example, a discretionary frame describes high subordinate determination and low leader influence, whereas a prescribed frame describes the reverse. This vantage point is arbitrary and could have as readily reflected the leader's perspective. Also, in any ongoing series of interactions, each action is simultaneously an effect of a previous action and a cause of the next action. Thus, cause-effect interpretations vary according to where one intervenes in the sequence (i.e., selects one point which is labeled "cause"). Leaders and subordinates, because of their differing perspectives, are likely to perceive different intervention points and consequently develop different causal interpretations. Awareness of how these different perspectives arise from the same interaction is important to understanding the social-contracting process. The serial nature of interactions reminds us that behaviors do not occur in a historical vacuum, but are intimately tied to prior interactions.

Methodological Considerations

The relationship level of social contracting poses a tremendous methodological challenge for leadership researchers. It is often implicit and sometimes out of conscious awareness of the parties. Furthermore, the healthier the leader-subordinate relationship, the more it will recede from view. This suggests that the more we study effective leaders, the more difficult will be the research task and the deeper we must probe to find relevant information. The kinds of cross-level confusions that are common today—such as confounding a discretionary relationship with discretion as a task boundary—are quite likely the inevitable result of inherent difficulties in studying effective leaders.

One possible path around this difficulty is to study effective leaders at times when relationship social-contracting activity is most likely to be visible, such as during the early stages of social contracting and at periods of instability. Another alternative is to apply research tools that allow us to probe more deeply in order to bring obscure phenomena more readily to view. For example, projective techniques could be applied in the context of clinical studies of leadership. Finally, Fulk and Wendler (1982) suggested that we extend our research horizons to include more study of ineffective leaders. In our terms, the focus would be on troubled leader-subordinate relationships rather than on either or both of the parties per se.

PRACTICAL IMPLICATIONS

In general, our conceptualization suggests that attention to the social-contracting relationship is particularly important for the leadership function pertaining to subordinate task boundary definition. However, relationships are often implicit and this makes relationship social contracting a complex and intricate process. Leaders and subordinates exchange and interpret subtle cues that communicate information about the relative influence of each party in task boundary definition. To assist this metacommunication, leaders and subordinates can explicitly and verbally formulate expectations regarding the roles each individual will play in task boundary definition and thus attempt to reach an overtly expressed agreement. Of course, it is essential that both verbal and nonverbal behaviors of the parties continue to be consistent with the rules of the agreement if this "relationship discussion" approach is to function effectively. Also, both leaders and subordinates will find it useful to be continuously alert to the fact that subtle cues are being interpreted by both participants, and that such interpretations are difficult to make accurately without supplemental verbal feedback aimed at clarifying the implicit message. The importance of feedback in managing the relationship level of social contracting regarding task boundary definition cannot be overstressed.

Social contracting at the relationship level may also be assisted by explicit attention to situational cues that suggest which form of relationship is likely to be most productive. Awareness of specific "substitutes for leadership" may direct efforts away from less tenable social-contracting relationships. For example, where subordinates possess professional skills and belong to a cohesive work group with high performance norms, a leader might be advised to avoid attempts to impose a highly prescribed relationship. Also, leader attention to individual subordinate needs, expectations, and abilities can cue specific areas of potential resistance as well as potentially successful relationship forms. Similarly, Katz's (1978) work suggests that subordinates may require less prescribed relationships over time, and may in more advanced career stages prefer to opt out of social contracting altogether. Awareness of this progression should assist leaders in recognizing the necessary transition points and thus avoiding unnecessary conflict with subordinates as their demands change.

The role of time also suggests that in stable social-contracting relationships leaders may find it useful occasionally to audit the relationship social contract to assess its continuing appropriateness. Such audits may provide early detection of potential problem areas. "Checking in" may also enable leader and subordinate to plan any relationship transitions that may be needed in the future.

Paradoxically, *less* attention to the relationship level is required when the relationship is healthy. In fact, attempts to renegotiate substantially an existing stable relationship that is still functional for either party may meet with considerable resistance. Attention to the relationship is probably most important in periods of instability or conflict. At other times, occasional reaffirmation may be all that is necessary or desirable.

With respect to task content, high leader emphasis on structuring task boundaries is likely to be welcomed in two situations: (1) stable, prescribed relationships; and (2) contractual or discretionary relationships where a low amount of discretion and/or high task-role clarity have been determined to be the contract. High leader emphasis on structuring task boundaries is *not* likely to be acceptable in: (1) an emergent relationship; or (2) a contractual or discretionary relationship where there is agreement for high discretion and/or low task-role clarity; and (3) an unstable or undefined relationship (in which case the leader will have assumed a prerogative that is not yet part of the deal). Moderate amounts of leader emphasis on defining task boundaries are probably acceptable in the remaining situations.

The embeddedness of content and relationship levels means that when conflict arises at the relationship level, it is particularly difficult to detect as a relationship conflict. Instead, it is often misdefined as a content conflict. For example, most of us have experienced a situation in which a disagreement arose as to whether a particular course of action was appropriate, but where the real issue was *who was to decide* which course of action should be taken. A useful solution when faced with a conflict situation is explicitly to define the relationship frame from both leader and subordinate perspectives. In doing so, it may become evident that the major source of disagreement lies in the relationship perspectives rather than in task content. This knowledge should assist the development of appropriate conflict-resolution remedies.

Finally, one practical conclusion that is readily apparent is that a major condition for leadership effectiveness in managing subordinate task boundary definition is good communication skills. An effective leader should: (1) formulate clear, specific, and accurate communications to the subordinate with regard to both task and relationship levels; (2) elicit messages of similar quality from the subordinate; (3) accurately decode transmissions from the subordinate regarding relationship as well as content; (4) recognize and formulate problems at the appropriate logical level and ensure that solutions are directed toward that level; (5) recognize differences in perspective taking that may arise from differences in leader and subordinate interventions in the ongoing series of interactions; (6) recognize when a social contract requires changing; and (7) provide effective feedback.

6

Commentary on Part 1

Chapter 2 Commentary:
A Further Consideration of Competing Values

Peter M. Storm

Robert E. Quinn starts Chapter 2 by reiterating something that has been emphasized for a long time in the scholarly leadership literature: namely, that despite the endless number of both theoretical and empirical investigations during the last three decades or so, the field of leadership is still not bearing the fruit that everybody seems to be expecting from it.

Some people say that this is so because we have been moving in the wrong direction. Many contributions in previous symposium volumes have argued this. In addition, a whole conference has been dedicated to finding a new way of looking at leadership (McCall & Lombardo, 1978).

Now, the message that we should turn in a new direction is *not* the message picked up here from Quinn's contribution. Rather, my interpretation is: let us stop momentarily and see what directions people have been taking. Because, on the surface, different researchers have been following quite different paths. And so, Quinn argues, let us not quarrel about who is right and who is wrong, but let us look beneath the surface and try to find out whether there is something we have in common. This common thing he calls the "understructure of leadership theory."

Quinn's second major point is seen as the reintroduction of "passive leadership." Perhaps these words are not obvious, which is not surprising because they appear only once or twice in Quinn's rather complicated framework. But these are the words that summarize much that Quinn is trying to get across. Specifically, they are seen here as representing the idea of leadership as a highly ambivalent or Janusian concept.

A third and a *major* point, according to Quinn himself, concerns the consequence of accepting the fact that leadership is a matter of contrasting or competing values. As he puts it: patterns of value bias enter the world of leadership not once but twice: first, through the actor being researched; second, through the researcher him or herself. Now, this is indeed a major point in the sense that it has been a point of argument among methodologists for ages. What is relatively new, however, in Quinn's way of presenting this dilemma, is that he urges us not to look for the values that are present and active, but to look for the one set of values that is hidden, forgotten, or pushed away.

This leads to a fourth major point, namely that both those who actually lead and those who observe such leaders are not acting according to one set of coherent values. Rather, they are acting according to competing sets of values. Significantly, this has led Quinn, following Driver and his colleagues (Driver & Mock, 1975; Driver & Rowe, 1979) to the concept of the "backup style." This is, of course, not a completely new concept in the field of leadership. It is used, for example, by Wynne and Hunsaker (1975) in their contribution on a human-information-processing approach to the study of leadership. Even though not new, the concept is an important one. I will show why shortly.

As a fifth and last point, it is important to mention an assumption, not an assertion or a hypothesis, implied by Quinn in his analysis of the understructure of leadership. The assumption is that there is an isomorphic, or one-to-one, relationship among leadership traits, behaviors, and influence patterns. This assumption is open to considerable question and leads to the first of the commentator's roles, that of a critic.

CRITIQUING

First, let us take a closer look at the fundamental concept of "perceptual understructure." Now, there is no quarrel here with Quinn about his assumption that somewhere there must be some similarities in peoples' biases: that is, in the preconceived ways in which individuals tend to talk about leadership and in which they tend to look at leaders in action. The two of us are not alone in this assumption. J. P. Campbell (1977) has pointed out that many tend to value subordinates mostly as passive organisms. Weick (1978) mentioned a common bias in viewing leaders as active and autonomous, rather than as docile and dependent. Pondy (1978) suggested that stability and non-variety in leadership behavior are often preferred. Also, Pondy, as well as Dubin (1979), observed that there is a tendency to look at direct, face-to-face leadership rather than at indirect or symbolic leadership of organizations or, even more abstract, technological processes.

Quinn goes much further than this, however, when he introduces the concept of understructure, for this concept implies a universal *system* of biases — a challenging idea indeed. It reminds me of Geert Hofstede's (1980) seminal work on culture's consequences. By coincidence or not, both frameworks rest on three, albeit very different, dimensions. The question is: What is this perceptual understructure and how deep does it go? The problem is that Quinn does not provide one with a definition of any sort. So, all that can be done is to look at the way he handles it.

Here it appears that there is a lack of consistency in his treatment of the concept. Philosophically, it is supposed to be an unalterable and ordered set of norms that govern the evaluation of social action. But pragmatically, it is an instrument that can be applied in the development of a more conscious and hence, presumably more effective, selection policy.

On a theoretical level, it is treated as something that is governed primarily by instincts, feelings, and emotions (hence the connection with values and traits). On an operational level, however, it derives from an analysis of conscious judgments and it is presented as a set of cognitive maps.

To put it somewhat differently, Quinn appears to suggest that one can manipulate one's own perceptual understructure, while simultaneously being unable to escape from it.

It is perhaps this lack of a clear definition of perceptual understructure that allows Quinn to assume a one-to-one relationship among values, traits, behaviors, and influence patterns. For instance, he equates a diplomatic or tactful leader with someone who is dominantly active as a facilitator of interaction. It is equally logical, however, to equate a tactful person with someone who, for instance, provides information. This raises the following question: What kind of logic did Quinn apply in relating the three levels of leadership to each other in Table 2.1? Are these relationships mainly of a *descriptive* nature? Or are they *predictive* or, rather, *prescriptive*? In the major overviews of empirical leadership research, such as *Stogdill's Handbook of Leadership* (Bass, 1981), very little evidence can be found for descriptive isomorphism among values, traits, behaviors, and influence patterns.

More importantly, there is agreement here with such authors as J. P. Campbell (1977) and Margerison (1980) who have argued that theories and studies of leadership will not provide their full payoff until they are firmly placed in the context of the objectives for which they are intended. In this sense, I think, Quinn should tell us whether he wants us to accept his framework as an empirical taxonomy, as a theoretical typology, or, at the other extreme, as a normative framework that aids him, and perhaps others, in attaining order and control in a specific environment.

To finish the critic's role, it is useful to address a few, more specific issues.

First, according to Quinn, his framework enters the world of leadership twice: once through the subject of study, the leader, and once through the researcher. I agree, but ask, does it not also enter through the one who studies the researcher? Specifically, in this case, Quinn himself? And, more importantly perhaps, does it not also enter through the subordinate? If so, what are the consequences of such a proposition with regard to the dynamics of leader-follower interaction?

Second, it is perhaps because of my own limited information-processing capacities (I have tried to count all the different labels mentioned by Quinn at each of the four levels, but stopped when I reached 120 or so) that I am not able to understand the specific meaning of the *advocate-search* dimension. It appears that the two can be easily exchanged in his framework: for instance, to advocate change and to search for competition, rather than to advocate competition and to search for change.

Finally, it would be helpful if Quinn were a bit more specific regarding the way we should interpret his juxtaposed leadership scales. Would he go so far as to say that, if there are N people on the scale below, among all those who score a particular leader in the middle, about $\frac{1}{2}N$ really means that a person is "adaptable/tolerant," while the other $\frac{1}{2}N$ really means that an individual is "organized/precise"?

The validity of such a proposition is not questioned here. It is very important, however, that we know whether such a proposition follows from the idea of Janusian thinking or not when we try to reanalyze previous studies according to Quinn's framework.

dogmatic _____ vacillating

EXTENSIONS

In taking up the role of integrator and extender, one could follow the direction taken by Quinn himself, and compare his framework with additional fourfold classifications.

However, Quinn has already done an excellent job at that, so there is no need to go further along that path at this time. Rather, let us first back up and see to what extent Quinn's point of view seems to tie in with other, more or less recent, attempts to redirect the mainstream of leadership research. First, and most important, it appears that Quinn's framework — or at least some of its major aspects — can be tied in with that relatively new school of thought that has reintroduced the active subordinate into the picture. For instance, the general proposition — advanced by Graen and his colleagues (Graen & Cashman, 1975); Wynne and Hunsaker (1975); House (1971); Scott (1977) and by Hollander (1978) — that the effects of leadership can only be understood in terms of a specific combination of leader and follower, does not seem at odds with Quinn's approach.

The reader is aware, no doubt, that several different ways of operationalizing followership are being considered here. I am not certain that it would be possible to create a consistent set of relationships among the specific propositions entertained in each of these models, using Quinn's framework. But as it is Quinn's intention to describe the understructure of the leadership field, it seems appropriate that an attempt should be considered, in addition to his own proposals for further study.

Second, it appears that Quinn's framework can be tied in with the work of those who propose a more macro-oriented view on leadership. See, for example, Bass and his colleagues (Bass, 1981; Bass & Valenzie, 1974) and Hunt and Osborn (1982). Specifically, it appears that interesting results could be obtained if some of these macromodels were extended with the concept of what might be called the "hidden culture," that is to say, the quadrant of traits, behaviors, and influence patterns that is valued negatively within a particular organization.

Finally, it appears that Quinn's views tie in, to some extent, with the thoughts of those — such as Kerr (1977), Calder (1977), and Pfeffer (1978) — who believe that leadership is *not* a clearly delineated subset of human behavior. If it is assumed that Quinn's argument regarding an almost perfect correspondance between the multidimensional structures of organizational effectiveness and leadership traits will be supported in future studies, it appears that his framework could well be used in reanalyzing the overlap — if there is any — between leadership and other forms of organizational control.

PRACTICAL APPLICATIONS

At this point, it seems appropriate to change the focus of the commentary and leave the theoretical pros and cons of the competing values approach. It was Henry Mintzberg who introduced the "Bill and Barbara test" in the preceding symposium volume. In essence, he said that, while writing about leadership, one should always try to serve those who actually carry leadership responsibilities in the field.

This is an important point of view, if only because most of the contributors to this volume are not only researchers but also consultants and trainers, and because we should not be telling each other stories about leadership that we could not or would not, tell "them."

Mintzberg's message, however, is not taken here as an indictment against anything that is abstract and descriptive in nature or as an invitation to write only cookbook recipes on leadership — particularly not in the present instance, as I believe that the true qualities of Quinn's framework are in its description rather than in its prescription of leadership. Hence, one can serve those out in the field by restating, rephrasing, or reflecting some of the problems they are experiencing without actually solving those problems (in some cases, perhaps, those problems are unsolvable). In my opinion, Quinn's framework does exactly that. Also, Mintzberg's message does not seem to be to resort to unlimited empiricism or ever-increasing sample sizes. Rather, the opposite seems to be the case. Thus, whenever an individual is contemplating a particular idea, he or she should always be prepared to test this idea openly against his or her own experiences and against the insights gained from those leaders with whom the person is familiar. Hence, in applying the "Bill and Barbara test," I will use my experiences, most of which were gained in training sessions with middle managers.

There are essentially two ideas in Quinn's chapter that relate strongly to those middle managers. The first is the concept of "passive leadership." Whenever the nature of leadership is discussed, these middle managers invariably suggest that, according to their experiences, leadership is essentially impossible.

It is impossible, the middle managers say, because if one really wants to do a job well, things will always have to be done that somehow contradict each other. Sometimes, these contradictory demands are rather specific and concrete, having to do with opposing aims of different groups or persons. In such situations, one can excel in an active way by offering skills in bargaining and negotiation.

Most of the time, however, these contradictory demands are not specific or explicit. They are more like unspoken expectations which, if referred to by a manager, are vehemently denied by those concerned, but which are very real to a manager who is trying to be sensitive to his or her environment. One way out of such a "damned if you do, damned if you don't" situation is to be insensitive, to be active (or even aggressive) in asserting one's own definition of the situation. Another way is to be passive, do nothing, wait and see. And, these managers say, sometimes it is better to be insensitive, but at other times it is better to be passive. All of this is not surprising if one looks up the words "to lead" and "leadership" in the dictionary, where it says that to lead equals: (1) to be ahead of, (2) to serve, to follow. Nor is it surprising if one takes a good look at the old sayings or aphorisms that refer to leadership. At least in Holland, there are about as many sayings that sing the praise of active leadership as there are sayings that warn against the dangers of active leadership.

What is surprising, however, is that there are very few theories or models that allow for a praise of modest or passive leadership, let alone specify when such leadership is needed.

The competing values framework, I believe, has usefulness because it puts this idea back into the center of attention.

The second idea concerns the backup style. Space precludes in-depth treatment of this topic. However, this concept justifies considerable attention in future research. Up to now, we have too easily accepted the view that leadership styles are more or less fixed for the lifetime of a leader. Partly, such an attitude regarding the rigidity of leadership styles is understandable because we have been using such drastically different categories (such as autocratic versus democratic).

But it also appears to have been a matter of convenience: the assumption of style rigidity allows one to rely on cross-sectional data (whether averaged by group or not).

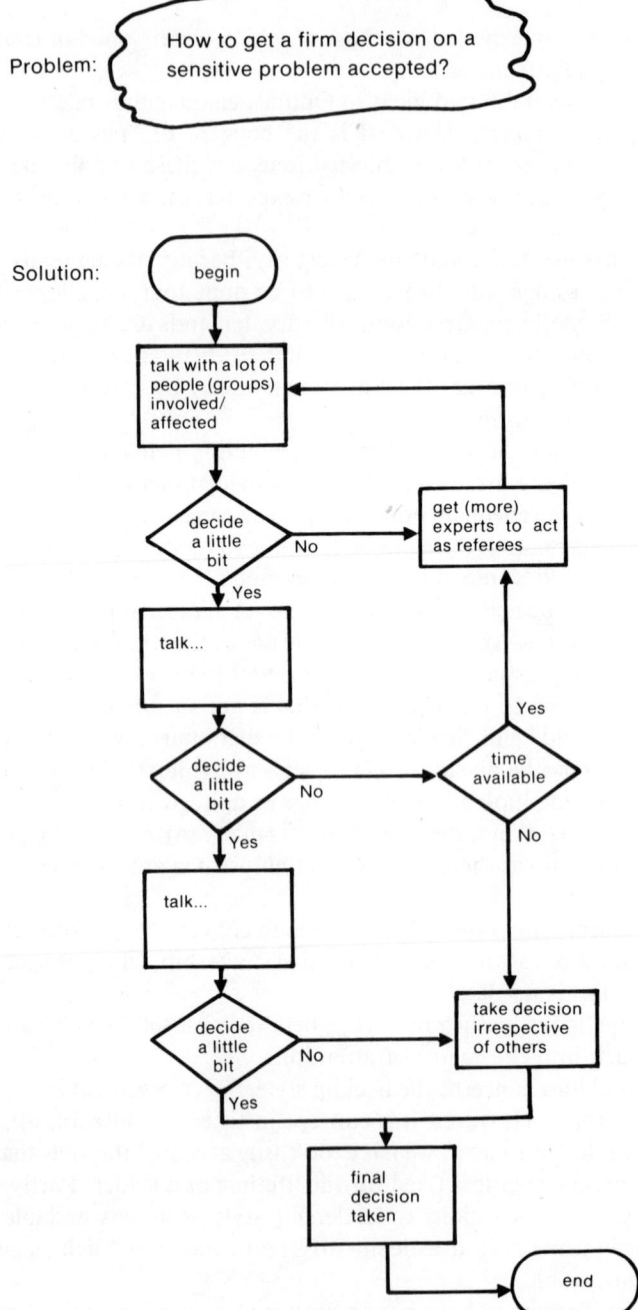

Problem: How to get a firm decision on a sensitive problem accepted?

Solution:

FIGURE 6.1. The backup style

In all our management-training sessions, time is spent discussing "sensitive problems that need firm decisions." Usually, the group is divided into smaller groups. First, each of these groups takes some time (about 1½ hours) to find its own solution, then we get together to compare the different solutions. The surprising thing is that all groups generally come up with the same basic solution.

This basic solution is depicted in Figure 6.1. The solution consists of a primary procedure (which could be called the democratic route or style) and two contingency procedures (which could be called the technocratic route and the autocratic route). What this figure implies is that most of the managers involved prefer a (sort of) democratic style, but that they all want to fulfill the condition of "a firm decision." Whenever they start to get the feeling that the democratic route leads to divergence rather than to convergence on the particular issue at hand (for instance, an RIF), they will resort to one of the other two styles. When time is still plentiful, they will prefer the technocratic route, calling for the involvement of (more) experts who act as referees. When it is not, a firm decision is taken by the manager him or herself.

It surely appears that the order of preference shown in Figure 6.1 is culturally bound. It would be surprising, however, if managers from other cultures came up with one route or style only.

Again, there are very few theories or models that take this sort of phenomenon explicitly into account. In the competing values framework, on the other hand, it plays a pivotal role.

Chapter 3 Commentary:
How Does One
Become an Effective Manager?

Alfred Kieser

How does one become an effective and successful manager? We learn from Anne S. Tsui's chapter that "by performing well" is no longer the correct answer. Why? Because those who are rating the performance of managers in organizations are not able to do this in an objective and consistent way. Formal evaluation systems have proved to be invalid and unreliable. Thus, evaluations of managerial effectiveness remain value judgments in spite of the extended use of formal appraisal procedures (which are widely used, it could be added, because they serve to veil and legitimize the subjective judgments).

But, then, how do judgments on effectiveness come about? Tsui introduces a role concept to answer this question: different role senders or coherent groups of role senders — constituencies — such as superiors, peers, or subordinates hold different expectations toward the focal manager. When constituencies regard the extent to which their expectations are being met by the focal manager's behavior as satisfactory, they judge him or her as efficient. Conflicting or ambiguous expectations create conditions under which it is harder to gain reputational effectiveness. Tsui also points out that interpersonal factors such as credibility, resource power, or liking and admiration, and personal characteristics such as power motivation and positive expectations intervene in the processes of expectation formation, perception of expectations, role behavior, and assessment of effectiveness. Finally, she states that the acquisition of reputational effectiveness has favorable outcomes for the focal manager and for the organization; managers who are able to gain reputational effectiveness from all the constituencies are, in the long run, expected to make great contributions to the effectiveness of the organization. "Evaluate managers positively in order to motivate them to live up to this standard!" Is this the conclusion suggested in Tsui's chapter?

There is little doubt that Tsui is right in pointing out that appraisals of managerial effectiveness are subjective value judgments and that role concepts can be useful for explaining what is going on in this judgment process. A simple test can demonstrate the importance of role expectations in judgments on effectiveness. When we ask somebody to indicate how a person should behave in order to be effective, he or she will probably be lost. The person will probably respond by asking, "In what function or job?" Our respondent will then be in a much better position to answer our question referring to specific roles. That is, he or she could better describe how a cook, a bookkeeper, a professor, a medical doctor, a politician, or even a manager should behave in order to be effective. In doing this, the respondent refers to socially established, accepted standards of behavior associated with these roles. The problem with Tsui's role concept is that it does not take advantage of the analytic power role theory has to offer and which this little test tried to capture. Roles depict behaviors that are characteristic of a set of persons in a specific context (Biddle, 1979, p. 56). Members of a social system — such as a society or a formal organization or a group within a formal organization — *share* expectations with regard to characteristic behavior persons in certain positions (e.g., in management positions) should exhibit.

Applying role analysis to performance evaluations of managers, then, suggests certain questions. Which expectations toward management are shared by all members of an organization? (That bank managers should wear ties during office hours might be an expectation held by all members of a bank.) Which expectations are shared by the groups of subordinates, peers, or superiors? How much consensus in expectations is there within or between groups? Which expectations are central; which are peripheral? Tsui does not ask such questions. For her, the behavior expected of the focal manager and the evaluation of his or her effectiveness are "particularistic in nature." It is a basic feature of role theory, however, that they are not. Thus, referring to the introductory question — how does one become an effective and successful manager? — Tsui's contribution gives a very restricted answer: "By engaging in behavior that is congruent with expected or preferred behavior." The more important question — what kind of behavior is expected from managers — remains unanswered.

It can be argued that since the task-related performance of managers is difficult to measure, symbolic actions are important in gaining reputational effectiveness. As Pfeffer (1981a, p. 5) points out, "It is the task of management to provide explanations, rationalizations, and legitimation for the activities undertaken in the organization." Or, as Pondy (1978, pp. 94-95) has phrased it:

> The effectiveness of a leader lies in his ability to make activity meaningful for those in his role set — not to change behavior but to give others a sense of understanding what they are doing and especially to articulate it so they can communicate about the meaning of their behavior. . . . If in addition the leader *can put it into words*, then the meaning of what the group is doing becomes a *social fact*. . . . This dual capacity . . . to make sense of things *and* to put them into

language meaningful to large numbers of people gives the person who has it enormous leverage.

Managers are expected to exhibit dramaturgical and language skills, though these expectations are seldom expressed overtly. Still, covert expectations can make up roles (Biddle, 1979, p. 119). Those managers are considered effective who, by stylized expressions (Hewitt & Hall, 1973) or by linguistic rituals (Starbuck, 1982), are able to link their actions to organizational ideologies. Nonverbal communication in ceremonials is also essential for demonstrating that a manager is in agreement with the myths, ideologies, and belief systems of the organization (Siehl & Martin, Chap. 12, this volume).

Another aspect of managerial role behavior that is also somewhat underdeveloped in Tsui's chapter is its dynamic character. She points out that political processes are going on between role senders and focal persons and that "personal factors" such as power motivation and positive expectations are influencing the building up of reputational effectiveness. However, she does not properly link these concepts with her role concept.

Expectations of role senders are formed in a dynamic process. The role interpretation of the focal person to some extent forms the expectations of the role senders (Graen, 1976, conceptualizes this process as role making). That manager is effective who is able to build up high expectations with his or her role senders and to fulfill these expectations he or she evoked: it is the manager who is considered for a career — not the one who only responds to mediocre expectations. Thus, a concept of managerial effectiveness should concentrate on the process of role making.

Attribution theory can be quite helpful in explaining the building up of expectations toward organization members (Green & Mitchell, 1979; Mitchell, Green, & Wood, 1981). On the basis of this theory it can be assumed that three critical questions guide the leader's behavior in appraising the subordinate's performance: (1) Is the cause of good or poor performance attributable to the subordinate or to external causes? (2) To what extent does the subordinate have control over the causative agent? (The more control the subordinate is seen to have, the more responsible he or she is seen to be for performance.) (3) Is the causative agent likely to continue to be effective in the future (if it is, the leader will expect future performance to be consistent with present performance). The more a leader attributes a subordinate's success to internal factors such as ability and effort and attributes failures to external factors such as luck, the higher the leader's aspirations should be for that subordinate's future performance. Expectations are self-confirming: when a member's performance is inconsistent with the leader's expectations, the leader is likely to attribute that performance to external causes. Attribution of success or failure is moderated by factors such as empathy, similarity, and liking, and by the focal person's skill in presenting believable, sincere, and adequate accounts of poor performance or in attaching a positive meaning to failures.

The role-making concept and the attribution concept suggest that reputational effectiveness, to a large extent, is a self-fulfilling prophecy. Managers who are evaluated positively will get the chance to prove their worth in more demanding tasks. The reputation of being effective also spreads within an organization. An aura of success is created. But how does the first positive assessment come about? The person's ability to pick up the organization's myths and ideologies and to reflect them in his or her symbolic actions is of crucial importance — at least at higher managerial levels where objective performance criteria are hard to determine.

On the basis of these conceptual modifications, one can come to conclusions that contradict a number of propositions presented by Tsui: role ambiguity and role conflict need not necessarily be negatively linked to reputational effectiveness (Tsui's Proposition 2). Role ambiguity not only characterizes a situation in which managers have difficulties making out what is expected of them, but it is also a chance to define roles in such a way that the managers can be successful on the basis of these self-defined tasks. A specialist who is hired for the newly created post of "marketing research" will probably meet high role ambiguity but the person has the chance to convince his or her marketing manager that the services he or she can provide are valuable ones. The same specialist being assigned to an established role with highly routinized tasks and no role ambiguity would have much more difficulty getting the job revalued and convincing role senders of his or her superior qualities.

The same applies to role conflict. Role conflict is not only a problem, it is also a chance to play Machiavellian politics. The focal person can feed back the role conflict to role senders and, thereby, help the more powerful party in this conflict to gain power. This process will, in turn, increase that person's reputational effectiveness in the opinion of the more powerful constituency. Whether or not the person succeeds in this strategy is certainly dependent on his or her linguistic and bargaining skills. In any case, it is problematic to see only one exit to role ambiguity and conflict, as Tsui does: namely, loss of reputational effectiveness.

The impact of organizational structure on role performance and reputational effectiveness is also conceptualized too narrowly. Structural regulations that reduce role conflicts and ambiguity may also limit degrees of freedom for outstanding managerial activities. On the other hand, routinization of certain activities can enable the manager to concentrate on important unstructured problems and thereby impress his or her role senders. The quantitative aspects of role definitions — the amount of activities defined in written rules — seem less important for the assessment process than qualitative ones: Which activities are programmed and which ones are left to the manager's discretion? How does the manager use this discretion?

To summarize, Tsui is making two important points: (1) performance evaluations of managers are subjective value judgments, and (2) role theory can provide helpful tools for analyzing evaluation processes in organizations. However, Tsui does not exploit the analytic possibilities role theory offers. In particular, she does not deal with the question of *which* expectations are held with regard to managerial positions and to what extent these expectations are shared within an organization or within a constituency. By Tsui's referring to too many concepts and not integrating them, the dynamics of role making and the building up of reputational effectiveness remain vague in this chapter. Attribution theory and the notion of organizations as ideological systems seem promising starting points for efforts to extend the concept of reputational effectiveness.

Chapter 4 Commentary:
A Look at Functionalism as an Alternative Approach to Studying Leadership

Michael Argyle

Rauch and Behling develop the theme that leaders fulfill two main functions — task and group maintenance — that these functions are also met by the task itself and other parts of the working environment, that these sources are additive, and that they produce an inverted-U effect on task performance and on job-satisfaction-type variables.

This commentary first treats various aspects of the theory. As I understand it, a functional theory tells us primarily what to expect will happen to meet the functions postulated; so the main prediction from this theory is not the one that was tested but a quite different one: that is, that leaders will perform a function if that function is not being met from other sources. What is tested instead is the less direct consequence that if a function is not being met at all, there will be trouble of some kind.

The idea that leadership functions may be met in other ways, however, is an important one, especially if the different task functions are separated. Some time ago, my colleagues and I found that different supervisory skills had little effect on output for workers who were machine paced (Argyle, Gardner, & Coiffi, 1958). The same is probably true for those on a wage incentive. When there are high-quality inspectors, or a training department, there is less for the supervisor to do. When these things are lacking, the supervisor ought to fulfill these functions. Other research has shown that the existence, or emergence of, leaders, and of certain group structures, is functional; groups that have them perform more effectively.

The authors are well within that familiar two-dimensional tradition of two kinds of leadership — Initiating Structure and Consideration, but one of the main criticisms made of this tradition in earlier volumes in this series is that these dimensions are too global, and are insufficiently detailed (Hunt & Larson, 1977). A common finding about initiating structure and consideration, however, was that *both* are needed, neither will do the job alone, especially for task performance. This is similar to the findings in Rauch and Behling's chapter about cross-over effects between task and maintenance, which in the end only work for task performance.

The curvilinear hypothesis raises a rather different point. There is some past evidence, and the authors present new evidence, to the effect that too much task direction or control has undesirable effects. However, it does not appear there are grounds for thinking that the same applies to the maintenance function: most people have no objection to being rewarded more!

It now seems appropriate to comment on the research presented. Rauch and Behling's main finding is that there is a curvilinear effect of task function variables on task performance, significant mainly at $p < .05$, with a sample size of 380, and with rather small main effects. There was little evidence for curvilinearity for the *maintenance* variables on job satisfaction, though the main effects were much greater.

The measure of task performance at the individual level was by self-report, which seems unsatisfactory. At the group level, the measure includes "a combination of judged and measured group performance." This too may have problems since presumably the different groups were engaged on different tasks so that output measures could not be easily compared.

The job satisfaction measure at the individual level was directly affected by the job satisfaction function variables; however, one of the latter was satisfaction from the task itself, which is one of the main components of job satisfaction.

Nevertheless, there is an interesting body of data here, and I would like to suggest some other ways of analyzing it. As previously indicated, I believe that the functional hypothesis predicts primarily that if one structure does not fulfill a function, then another structure will. Leadership is of interest here, and it can be predicted that if the other environmental structures fail to meet task or maintenance functions, then the first-line supervisor will adopt a style of leadership that will do so. There should therefore be a negative correlation between supervisors' task or maintenance activities, and those supplied from the remainder of the working environment. This could be easily tested with the existing data.

We could make more detailed predictions of a similar kind about subcomponents of these functions, such as keeping up speed of work, or quality of work, instructing, and training. In the group-maintenance sphere the components could include individual social support and maintaining group cohesiveness.

It probably follows from the functional hypothesis that if a function is being met at a low level from other sources, the effect of the supervisor meeting it will be greater. It has already been found that initiating structure has more effect on productivity in unstructured and ill-defined situations. Further examination of this prediction, however, for both main functions, could be carried out with the present data. Another hypothesis is that a leader must have the expertise required for the job. To know what this is would require a detailed examination of what the leader actually has to do.

EXTENSIONS

In order to teach someone how to be an effective leader, we need to be able to give him or her more detailed information than just general discussion of task and maintenance functions.

How does one carry out task functions without losing out on maintenance functions? The use of democratic-persuasive skills has been suggested as part of the answer — directing the work while keeping some subordinate autonomy. There are different ways of giving orders, and the persuasive suggestion is one of the most effective. What exactly is involved in maintenance skills? *Rewardingness* and use of positive *nonverbal* signals are part of these skills, and as we know from other contexts, these may need special social-skills training (Trower, Bryant, & Argyle, 1978). Providing *social support* is another, and this may involve listening sympathetically, keeping up the social network, bolstering self-esteem, or providing tangible help.

Effective social skills, however, vary with the actual social situation, and situations vary in ways other than the availability of task and group maintenance. The situation that confronts leaders of groups can vary from that of a military commander or the captain of a squash team to that of a research group director. Within more orthodox work settings, there are infinite variations in the actual work done, the technology, physical environment, and the sociotechnical system (Thurley & Wirdenius, 1973), and the decisions taken by the leader vary accordingly. Fiedler (1967) and others have suggested dimensions for classifying situations. My own view, as expounded in a recent book, *Social Situations* (Argyle, Furnham, & Graham, 1981), is different: I believe that situations, including work settings, are distinct social structures and systems, like the atoms of chemistry, and like different games, discrete not continuous. In order to function effectively one needs a good map, showing how the system works.

An important part of the map is the set of relationships between those involved. Let us concentrate on the supervisor-subordinate relationship. Argyle and Furnham (1982) have found that, compared with other relationships, rather low levels of satisfaction are generated — more like neighbors than like friends (Figure 6.2). It is also a relationship with a great deal of conflict (Figure 6.3). The supervisor-subordinate relationship was found by Wish, Deutsch and Kaplan (1976) to be superficial, and somewhat hostile.

In terms of conflict, the supervisor-subordinate relationship is second only to marriage, but without the very strong rewards that marriage may offer. Like other working relationships, it is maintained by other aspects of the system — the organizational constraints, and the incentives. People want to be paid, achieve success, and so on, and working relationships are instrumental to these goals. Supervisors are more a source of instrumental rewards (see Figure 6.1), than of emotional support. The position of a leader is more favor-

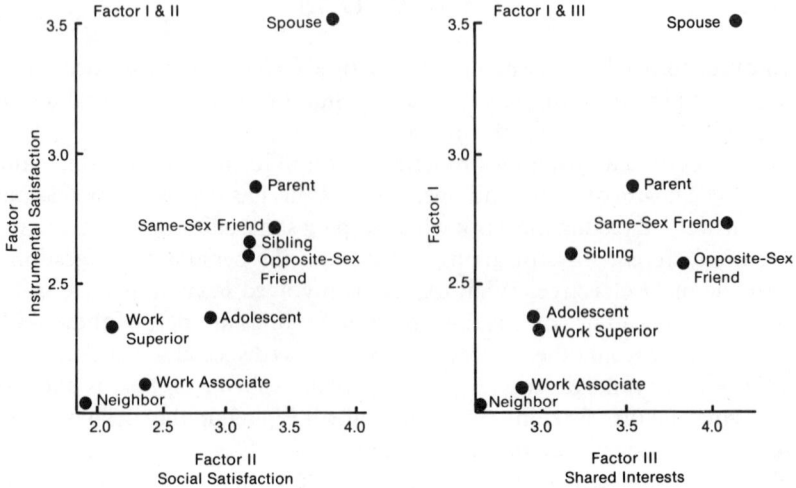

FIGURE 6.2. Relationships plotted on the satisfaction dimensions

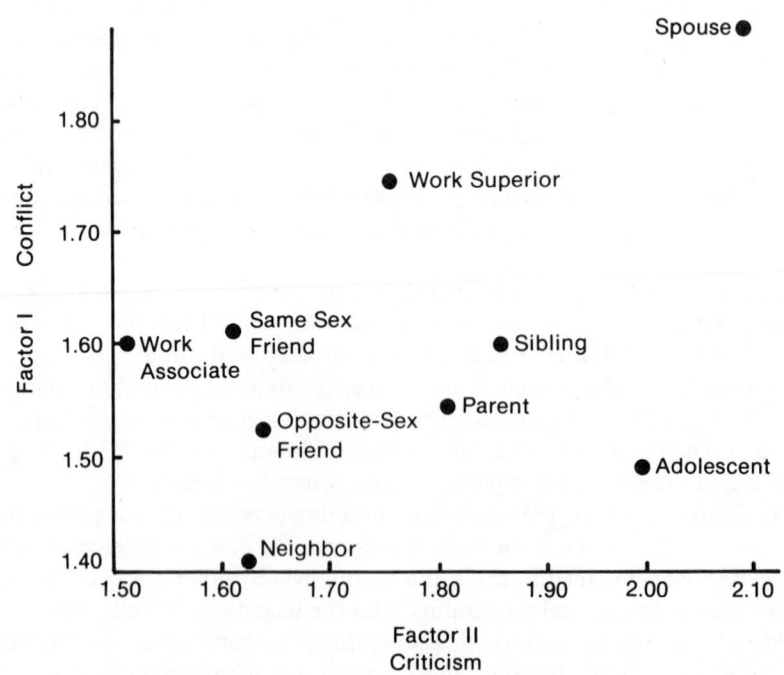

FIGURE 6.3. Relationships plotted on the conflict dimensions

able if the leader is able to provide greater rewards; these can be instrumental rewards, such as providing help or material benefits, or they can be primarily social, as when the leader is high on consideration. In either case, the leader's power over the subordinate is increased, as exchange-theory research has shown.

Work relationships have a somewhat paradoxical characteristic: on the one hand they appear to be superficial and a source of conflict, but on the other they can be a source of job satisfaction and social support. The paradox is partly unravelled if we realize the extent to which these relationships are kept going by processes that are *external* to them.

Part of a leader's skills involves maintaining group cohesiveness, since this affects job satisfaction and related variables, and under most conditions affects task performance. So this is an example of a cross-over effect, where a maintenance function affects task performance. Group cohesion can be promoted by certain leadership skills, of which democratic-persuasive behavior is one. It can also be increased by other organizational arrangements — the use of group incentives and physical proximity, for example.

In designing working systems, should we plan for task and maintenance functions to be met by supervisors or by other aspects of the organization? We would need to study the components separately. Whether or not a wage incentive can be introduced depends on whether production is controlled by the individual or the group, whether it can be measured, and on labor unions, for example. The more jobs the leader has to do, the more difficult the job is, but also the closer the leader's relationship with his or her subordinates. The less a leader has to do, the more we move to a leaderless group situation where any residual leadership functions are performed by informal leaders. The way is open for a new research design: one that compares advantages and disadvantages of the leader in the organization fulfilling these functions. This is suggested as the next step in exploring the functional hypothesis, and we are much indebted to the Rauch and Behling chapter for developing it for us.

Chapter 5 Commentary:
On Refocusing Leadership from a
Social Systems Perspective of Management

H. Peter Dachler

The suggestions made by Fulk and Cummings for refocusing traditional conceptions of leadership are substantial and fundamental in their implications for understanding the phenomenon of management of social systems in general and leadership as a social process in particular. I want to sketch briefly a social-systems perspective of the conceptual problems I see in the leadership literature. This will create a framework within which the fundamental issues raised by Fulk and Cummings can be highlighted, as well as extending and attempting to make more explicit the possible implications of their proposed conceptual alternatives for managerial leadership.

SIGNS FROM THE LAST LEADERSHIP SYMPOSIUM

Among the many interesting contributions in the last symposium volume were two presentations that seemed to highlight, perhaps symbolically, some basic turning points in leadership theory and research approaches to this topic. One was the summary of results Lombardo and McCall (1982) provided from observing some 600 managers slave away in the Looking Glass Inc. simulation. Without really working out in detail their main themes, they found that the issue of leadership and management was intimately embedded in the *nature* of the social system created by the situation. They talked about how problems and not leader behaviors were important; they described how these problems float through the organizational system; they realized that effectiveness was what *made sense* in certain social-political processes; they were surprised by the fact that problem-solving managers could, at times, completely ignore the formal power structure and transcend the position hierarchy, as the *definition* of the problem seemed to require it, and so on. In other words, while Lombardo and McCall set out to study managers or individuals in situations, they actually observed fundamental *properties of social systems*, not behaviors of managers as such and their "effects" on subordinates' productivity and satisfaction.

The other contributions to the previous symposium volume that set off such a heated debate were Mintzberg's (1982) overstated and perhaps somewhat arrogantly presented prescriptions for leadership and management research. He clearly questioned the relevance of traditional leadership conceptions for the nature of the problems faced by management. He correctly implied that traditional leadership questions emerged out of *discipline-embedded* theoretical frameworks which often ignore or are unaware of the crucial properties the pressing problems faced by management entail. This is so because the discipline-related questions start with the basic assumptions inherent in the *discipline paradigms* which carve out theoretically and methodologically relevant parts of a complex phenomenon, thus missing the complexity of the whole phenomenon. Adding together the isolated facts that emerge out of such a reduction process has *never* led to a better understanding of the complex whole phenomenon, as the trait and behavior approach, as well as the contingency approach to leadership have clearly shown. I am freely interpreting and probably extending what Mintzberg expressed in his critique of the relevance of traditional leadership conceptions for understanding the complex phenomena in management. Nevertheless, Mintzberg's prescriptions, overstated as they may be, clearly signal the fact that the *nature* of leadership and management in the real world does not fit well our conceptions of it and the methods we use to research leadership and management.

LEADERSHIP AND MANAGEMENT FROM A SOCIAL-SYSTEMS PERSPECTIVE

How can the signs from the previous leadership volume be extended and made more implicit and specific, so that the present proposal of Fulk and Cummings for refocusing managerial leadership can be more clearly understood within a more general framework of current problems in leadership and management theory?

What follows is a brief sketch of some of what I consider the fundamental problems in current misconceptions of leadership and ways to reconceptualize leadership and management; these are two concepts that need to be clearly separated, despite the tendency in the literature to use "leadership" and "management" interchangeably.

First, nearly without exception, the dominating paradigms of management and of leadership start with the idea that management as well as leadership are basically what is implied by the general formula of "getting things done through people." Fulk and Cummings also take as one of their starting points Katz and Kahn's (1978) often quoted definition that leadership is the "influential increment over and above mechanical compliance with routine directives of the organization." Furthermore, nearly without exception do leadership approaches like those of Graen (1976), Fiedler (1967), Vroom and Yetton

(1973), the Ohio State leadership model, and House and Mitchell (1974) see leadership and presumably management as getting things done by influencing people. Management theorists likewise refer to management functions such as decision making, planning, organizing, and the like which a manager has to fulfill, usually through influencing people. Fulk and Cummings also have incorporated this aspect of managerial leadership into their model. What is missing in these conceptions of leadership and management, however, is the fundamental *nature* of the phenomenon to be led or managed.

It is the central thesis here that the concepts of leadership and management are not crucially tied to given individuals who have been assigned such roles. Furthermore, what is being led or managed are not individuals, nor individual productivity-related behaviors and attitudes; what is being led or managed are, instead, collectivities and social systems — very complex ones at that. Perspectives of leadership or management are intimately tied to the basic assumptions we make about the nature of social systems. Thus, unless we rethink not only our conceptions of leadership but also our assumptions about the nature of social systems in general, our attempts to refocus leadership will by necessity remain obscure and incomplete. We therefore also have to confront current and emerging conceptions of social systems. By doing so, we can derive clear implications for leadership or management that emerge from such a confrontation.

Another fundamental problem is the long-neglected distinction between the concept of management and that of leadership. *Management* from a social-system perspective is fundamentally an issue of *design, change, and development of, and giving directions to total social systems embedded in their environment. Leadership* is defined as the design, change, development of, and giving directions to social *sub*systems embedded in their environment. However, contrary to the prevailing notion of leadership according to which individuals are influenced by individual leaders or managers, social systems are *not* managed by *a* top manager or a powerful coalition of managers. Instead social systems in their environment are designed, changed, developed, and directed by many interconnected managers, some of whom are so designated by their position, others do so in fact. Furthermore, complexly interdependent legal, technical, social, and norm-giving events and circumstances powerfully design, change, develop, and direct social systems. The concept of management therefore refers to *polycentric processes* that evolve out of social, political, evolutionary, self-designing, recursive, and sense-making processes that have their bases in social interaction. Here we are starting to get close to some of the basic issues raised by Fulk and Cummings.

In summary then, whereas *both* management and leadership refer to complex *processes* that design, change, develop, and direct social systems, leadership is tied to a person, but what that person thinks, does, and feels involves a great deal more than simply influencing other people over and above the formal contract obligations. Management, on the other hand, is not tied to any one person or group, but is a social-political-evolutionary-nonlinear and sense-making process. The process operates polycentrically from the heterogeneous actions and intentions of many individuals. In short, management is a fundamental property of social systems, not of individuals.

A QUICK AND DIRTY CONTRAPOSITION BETWEEN TWO PERSPECTIVES OF SOCIAL SYSTEMS

Leadership and management conceptions are embedded in the basic assumptions made of social systems. Thus, a quick and necessarily dirty contraposition between dominant and newly evolving perspectives of social systems may help in explicating some of the crucial problems in traditional leadership theory that Fulk and Cummings have attempted to refocus.

Most of the dominant leadership or management theories are to a greater or lesser degree embedded in a perspective of organizations that might be called the *rational-design perspective*. The basic unit of analysis in the rational-design view is the individual. Individuals are the focus of most organizational phenomena, including leadership and management. Groups are merely the context and provide the structure in which individuals can be located and described. As a consequence, groups are seen as the sum of the properties of individuals.

The crucial data to be collected concern the characteristics of individuals and the characteristics primarily of their immediate environment, from which individual behavior and introspective reports are causally explained. In other words, Lewin's basic and often misunderstood model of behavior is the paradigmatic origin of this view. The *definition of membership*, which also describes the boundary of organizations, is based on individuals' acceptance of preestablished organizational goals and objectives, as well as their participation in the instrumental functions of the organization. The rational-design perspective of organizations sees only certain individual characteristics as relevant to the rational achievement of organizational goals. Other characteristics are considered as either irrelevant or disruptive.

A crucial aspect of the rational-design perspective of organizations is the fact that they are goal oriented; goals, therefore, exist and can be specified a priori. They serve as one of the main directing factors for action. It is assumed that organizations therefore only survive when members have common goals, and when goals are reachable and acceptable. Without preestablished goals, the crucial function of control in organizations cannot be effectively carried out. Therefore, goals serve as the main criteria by which behavior is evaluated.

The rational-design perspective of social systems starts with the fundamental premise that organizations are monocentrically designed. They are the result of intentional-rational design and planning of mostly powerful individuals or coalitions. Functions such as division of labor, coordination of activities, and assignment of authority all serve the rational achievement of preestablished goals. Finally, organizational design for the achievement of specified goals is based on "scientific" (in the positivistic tradition) or assumed cause-and-effect knowledge about the phenomena to be designed.

The scientific paradigm supporting the rational-design perspective is fundamentally out of the positivistic tradition. It is based on the application of disciplinary (in the leadership case, primarily psychology) preconceptions to what managers think are organizational problems. It is assumed that the nature of social systems is knowable in an absolute sense, and controllable. Reality exists objectively out there the way that stones and apples, that fall from trees, exist out there. In summary, the social world can be constructed in rational ways and is controllable on the basis of our cause-and-effect knowledge. Methods of inquiry therefore include primarily analytical, reductionistic, exact, quantitative tools on the basis of which primarily single, one-way causal relationships are sought.

As extreme as this summary may seem (and as many qualifiers as were left out for reasons of space), the fact remains that a good part of our modern textbooks still include many, if not most, of the crucial assumptions about organizations that we have subsumed under the rational-design perspective. Furthermore, I submit, without being able to provide the detailed arguments here, that the established views on leadership, be they from Stogdill (1974), Katz and Kahn (1978), Fiedler (1967), Vroom and Yetton (1973), Graen (1976), or House and Mitchell (1974), basically derive in their *principal* assumptions from the rational-design view of organizations. The question then arises: To what degree do the rational-design perspective of organizations and the conceptions of leadership and management that derive from it accurately reflect the *nature* or the crucial characteristics of the leadership and management problem?

We can only answer this question by looking at an alternative perspective which I would like to summarize under the label of *organismic-evolutionary perspectives* of organizations.

The unit of analysis for the organismic perspective is the issue group, the groups that form around issues or problems, which may or may not be groups defined by an organization chart. The characteristics of individuals are in part a reflection of intra- and intergroup processes (see, for example, Smith, 1977). Attitudes and group climate are a reflection of social and political processes (see Salancik & Pfeffer, 1974). We—they feelings, for instance, and corresponding cognitive schemas or commonsense theories, are increasingly shown to be long-ignored reflections of social and political processes within and between groups (Weick, 1969). These commonsense theories have a bearing on what is perceived and what is ignored and action sequences are embedded in this perceptual, social-processes-reflecting cycle (Neisser, 1976). Therefore, groups have inherent properties that evolve out of mutual influence and social-reality construction processes (Berger & Luckman, 1967; Weick, 1979). Properties of groups are not averages of individual characteristics! The important data within the organismic-evolutionary perspective of organizations are implicit, that is, they are qualitative everyday theories or conceptions of real people, not abstracted individuals in the experimental tradition, as well as behavior patterns, not single behaviors.

Important issues are not personal characteristics of people but rules. That is, they are the implicit and hierarchically ordered schemas or theoretical preconceptions about the world and its relationships and meaning. These rules, which evolve out of collectivities, govern relationships among individuals (in Weick's double-interact sense), and the patterning of interactions is reflected in an order, a form that is enacted by collections of people through in-forming. Thus, a resultant order is a manifestation of rules, and vice versa (see, e.g., Hayek, 1967, pp. 3–132). The boundary question within the organismic perspective is dealt with by recognizing that membership in organizations is not uniquely definable since organizations' boundaries are in constant flux, dependent upon who defines the boundary and on the goals that evolve out of the social-reality construction process. The boundary of the marketplace, for example, is undefinable. It depends upon who does the perceiving, for what commodity, and with respect to what market problem or market-related goal.

Within the organismic perspective, the environment for a person, for a group, or for the organization does not have an independent reality apart from the behavior and cognitive maps and interpretations people or groups give the environment. Environments are socially and cognitively constructed phenomena (Bateson, 1972). To measure them would require a reconstruction of the meaning people attach to environments (including value and ideological issues) and the theories they hold about them.

While in the organismic perspective organizations have goals, these goals are not specifiable in an absolute sense. Instead, they are symbols attached to the inter- and intragroup processes (Pfeffer, 1981a). Goals seem to emerge out of trial-and-error processes. They often function to build constituencies, to define the limits of responsible action, and to impose a certain enactment of reality on the discourse within and outside the organization. They are thus an integral part of the political process in organizations (Brown, 1978). The rational control function of goals is a symptom of social interaction. Rationality is part of the sense-making processes that often functions retrospectively to provide a meaning to what happened or what one did.

What respect to structure and function of social systems, the organismic perspective is best described by an insight from Hayek (1967, pp. 96–105), that social systems are certainly a result of human action but not of human design. The orders of social systems evolve on the basis of the huge variety of interrelated actions and intentions that are involved in the social processes of the collectivity forming organizations. We have looked for constraints on managerial decision making (usually resource related) in order to remove them. But we have not been able to see the fact that managers cannot design organizations unilaterally in the way that engineers can design machines. Here lie the absolute limits on manageability that a certain amount of complexity entails. Alternative scientific paradigms emerging out of diverse approaches like dialectics, evolutionary biocybernetics, phenomenology, hermeneutics must serve as the epistemological bases for knowing the structure and function of organizations. Concepts like contradictions, paradoxes, historical relativism, cultural processes, evolutionary processes, and cyclical interdependence all make one-way cause-and-effect or independent and dependent variable conceptions irrelevant or at least inadequate. However, these concepts may become crucial guides in understanding organizations from an organismic perspective.

THE FULK AND CUMMINGS ANSWERS ON LEADERSHIP

In the context of this very brief and superficial sketch of a framework, it is now appropriate to turn to the Fulk and Cummings' chapter. Their suggested conceptual alternative to leadership within the contraposition of the rational-design and organismic-evolutionary perspective of social systems is discussed. In general this chapter appears to stand with one leg in each of the two social-systems perspectives, but it is eagerly leaning toward the organismic.

Even though Fulk and Cummings initially discuss managerial leadership, in the distinction we have tried to make between management and leadership, they clearly deal with leadership, not management. Their focus is on the *processes* by which subordinates' tasks and their boundaries are determined. Thus, the problem lies with a person who is the designated leader on some organization chart as well as the subordinates who fall into his or her supervisory domain. Fulk and Cummings discuss the definition of work through social contracting as a means for establishing and structuring the relationships between *all* task-relevant parties, not just between leader and subordinates. But in their model, they revert back to only leader-subordinate social contracting. The same is true for the important notion of the two logical types of interpersonal communication. The relationship level of communication is of higher logical type because it represents metainformation which serves as the informational framework out of which the meaning of the content information emerges. The crucial issue, however, regarding the metainformation is that it involves a great deal more than just the relationship between leader and subordinates. Metainformation provides the cognitive schemas, the interpretation or the metarules regarding the total social matrix within which leader-subordinate relations occur. This provides the meaning of the communicated content between leader and follower.

For instance, Graen's (1976) distinction between hired hands, winners, and losers is certainly not just an issue of the reward and punishment outcomes that the supervisor provides, based on his or her evaluation. It is much more an issue of inter- and intragroup processes as described, for example, by the upper, middle, and lower perspectives discussed by people like Kanter, Moss and Stein (1979) or Smith (1977).

But Fulk and Cummings unfortunately restrict their exciting new concept of metainformation to just the leader and the follower, as if that relationship occurs in a social, political, or cultural vacuum. In their illustration (Figure 5.1) of the four types of social-contracting relationships, only leader and subordinates act. And, in the emergent relationship, for instance, Fulk and Cummings argue that it is "heavily influenced by forces outside of the leader-subordinate exchange, and because neither party has much influence beyond that specified in the employment contract, there is essentially little if any social contracting between leader and subordinates." But here Fulk and Cummings miss much of what Watzlawick (1978) as well as other social-systems theorists have tried to show. Much social sense making emerges out of the matrix of social forces even in an emergent relationship. The issue of leader-subordinate relationships is more than simply directional influence and how much leaders and subordinates can grab of the influence pie.

Finally, Fulk and Cummings incorporate into task boundaries basic management functions such as planning and executing. While this is an important addition to traditional conceptions of tasks in the leadership literature, it is not clear from the discussion in their chapter that the managerial task-content dimensions are not an issue of manager and subordinate behaviors per se, but involve system processes. Planning, controlling, and executing are all problems that float through the system. While single people plan, control, and execute, the final forms and processes are always something more or less than the planner, controller, and executor intended or wanted. Systems processes of a more general sort play a crucial part.

A good part of the perspective represented by Fulk and Cummings is therefore tied to the traditional leadership perspective and to the rational-design view of social systems. On the other hand, Fulk and Cummings clearly recognize the basic social nature of leadership. They recognize that meaning and sense making as well as everyday (or implicit) theories are crucial issues in leadership. They also recognize what they call oscillating series of interactions, that imply cycles rather than the traditional action-reaction type of conception of interactions. Although they still believe in the possibility of traditional cause-effect interpretations, they realize that cause-and-effect meanings can vary according to where one steps into the interaction cycle. Thus, the authors provide some crucial and powerful conceptual tools for refocusing leadership toward a perspective that takes into account basic social-systems characteristics.

Further development in this direction, however, will require a careful integration of the more holistic theories of social systems by such, for-the-traditional-leadership-not-yet-relevant, theoreticians, as Gregory Bateson, Jim Bugental, Jim Clark, Friedrich Hayek, Edmund Husserl, Erich Jantsch, Erwin Laszlo, Ian Mitroff, John Rawls, Geoffrey Vickers, Karl Weick, and others. See publications of Bateson, 1972; Hayek, 1967; and Weick, 1979 as representative works. We have to add to our rational-design thinking the organismic-evolutionary conceptions of social systems if we are to overcome the conceptual blinders that we have inherited from basic psychology and the traditional empirical social sciences, and if we are to start understanding some of the complexities that real-world management and leadership entail.

Part 1 Integrative Comments:
On Paradigms and Pigs

Dian-Marie Hosking

In *Alice in Wonderland*, Lewis Carroll observed Alice engaged in conversation with a cat. She inquired "Cheshire puss . . . would you tell me please which way I ought to go from here?" "That depends a good deal on where you want to get to," replied the cat; he might also have said that it depends on where you think "here" is. The authors of the chapters in Part 1 seem to agree on this point — in Wonderland — surrounded "by an endless array of unconnected empirical investigations" (Quinn, Chapter 2).

Perhaps less obvious is their seeming unanimity on the "way we should go from here." In particular, the chapters share three major values regarding the nature of social structures, the nature of "reality," and the nature of social systems. I shall briefly describe first the "dominant" and then the "competing" values (Quinn, this volume) that characterize their perspectives. The nature of the values and their wider implications for research and theory are given detailed attention by the editors in Chapter 25.

SOCIAL STRUCTURES AND THE NATURE OF REALITY

The study of leadership and management has typically been conducted in the context of a tradition that assumes organization structures to have the status of "social facts" (see Durkheim, 1938). These social facts are viewed as the conceptual equivalent of biological structures: both are seen as making functional contributions to the systems in which they occur. This paradigm has developed in such a way that the social structures are usually treated as relatively unchanging, and as constraining activities and interactions in such a way as to serve the common good. This "structural-functionalist" paradigm is present in each of the "new perspectives" in Part 1 — more fully developed and explicit in some chapters than in others, but there nonetheless.

While objectified, constraining social structures constitute the dominant features of the contributions, competing values appear in references to functional processes and subjective realities. For example, Fulk and Cummings refer to functional processes, but this value is largely lost in the wider con-

text of their framework. Only in one contribution does the notion of functional processes receive any prominence — the only chapter in which a functional perspective is explicit (Rauch & Behling, Chap. 4). The authors go
to great lengths to point out that their view of structures differs from the
conventional view just described — that is, that their definition is essentially
processual. In other words, they endorse the minority tradition of structural-
functionalist anthropology which takes the view that social structures can only
be observed in their functioning (see, for example, Radcliffe-Brown, 1952).
Unfortunately, this particular value is rather lost in the empirical translation
of their concepts.

"Unfortunately," those who employ the structural-functionalist perspective typically fail to recognize that the biological analogy can be very misleading where social systems are concerned. In particular, it is important to
appreciate that the perspective incorporates an assumption of "functional
unity": it assumes that cooperation is endemic in the part-whole relationship.

THE NATURE OF SOCIAL SYSTEMS

Given these assumptions, it is assumed that social systems are characterized by a common goal and coordinated by "rational" authority, and that
conflict — if it occurs — arises from the failures of human information processing. The "unitary perspective" (Fox, 1966) characterizes the chapters in this
part. For example, Tsui argues that managers act in response to the expectations of "multiple role senders." While this is a pleasing departure from the
conventional North American literature in the area, it assumes the existence
of shared goals and values. To explain, if the expectations of these various
constituencies conflicted — as they would were functional unity absent — the
poor manager would have the reputation of Shakespeare's Hamlet who
claimed he could "tell a hawk from a handsaw." His friends had no doubt
he was confused, if not mad!

A related issue concerns the extent to which the authors anticipate conflict in their perspectives. The nearest conflict comes to playing any major
role is in the work of Fulk and Cummings. However, their concern is with
conflicting perceptions or "potentially resolvable" disagreements about tasks,
not with conflict at the level of values. Again, there is evidence of competing
values. Some elements of a more "pluralist," political-science perspective are
to be found in all the contributions, particularly in those of Fulk and Cummings and of Tsui. As already observed, the latter makes much of the existence
of multiple stakeholders and multiple criteria for effectiveness. However, as
has already been implied, the full implications of such a perspective are not
developed. If they had been, a very different perspective on leadership and
management would result.

For example, if the assumption of functional unity were rejected, interpretations of action would be in terms of bargaining and compromise between members of an ecological aggregate (see Chapter 25). This being the case, analysis of power relationships would be central to the conceptual framework. While Fulk and Cummings pay *some* attention to power and political processes, such processes are given a fairly minor role. They are only considered in the context of negotiating subordinates' task boundaries, not, for example, in the broader role of organizationwide attempts to "negotiate order" (see, e.g., Day & Day, 1977; Hosking & Morley, in press).

Finally, it is important to draw attention to the fact that the biological analogy that underpins the structural-functionalist paradigm is especially misleading on the question of how social structures develop and change. Biological organisms cannot change their structures without breaking their continuity *but social systems can.* As Radcliffe-Brown observed: "A pig does not become a hippopotamus" (1952, p. 181). To return to the earlier *Alice in Wonderland* analogy: *it is only in Wonderland that babies turn into pigs,* and therefore only there that the biological metaphor is appropriate.

Part 2

Research Methodologies for Exploring Managerial Behavior

Introduction

James G. Hunt, Dian-Marie Hosking,
Chester A. Schriesheim, and Rosemary Stewart

The four content chapters in this part provide an interesting contrast of methodologies. Chapter 7, by Fred Luthans and Diane Lee Lockwood, "Toward an Observation System for Measuring Leader Behavior in Natural Settings," is a cautious step from traditional methods of studying leadership. It is firmly rooted in the quantitative tradition in terms of instrument development work, but differs from traditional methods by the use of short-term observations as well as questionnaires. The focus of the chapter is on the development of observation as a way of improving the reliability and validity of the data collected by questionnaires, and on the development of an observational instrument called the Leader Observation System (LOS).

Chapter 8, by Mark J. Martinko and William L. Gardner, "The Observation of High-Performing Educational Managers: Methodological Issues and Managerial Implications," also focuses on observation. It is similar to the Luthans and Lockwood contribution in that both explore the contribution that can be made by using observation as an additional method. Both also use large numbers of doctoral students, whom they trained beforehand in observational methods, for their observations. At the same time, their chapter differs from that of Luthans and Lockwood in a number of important respects. Martinko and Gardner become increasingly interested in exploring the qualitative data that their observers provide and are more concerned with the methodological issues, problems, and contribution of observation. They are thinking about the nature of their data, and whether the data are the right kind for their study. Luthans and Lockwood are concerned with a much narrower range of questions of validity.

The Martinko and Gardner contribution is especially interesting because the authors are seeking to identify the behaviors, attributions, and competencies of high-performing education managers. They compared 25 high-performing and 25 moderate-performing school principals as part of a series of related studies commissioned by the Florida Council on Educational Management. The emphasis on performance is unusual in a study of this type.

Chapter 9, "An Experiential Approach to Understanding Managerial Action," by John G. Burgoyne and Vivien E. Hodgson is completely different from the first two. It is qualitative and focuses on differences and similarities in descriptions of experiences across different cases. It seeks to develop a new method, whereas the others use methods with a long history. The Burgoyne and Hodgson chapter is therefore more exploratory in its methodology. Its aim is also different in that the authors are seeking to understand the rationale for a manager's behavior rather than to describe its emotional effect. In its focus this chapter appears to possess a number of similarities to the work by Huff reported in Chapter 14.

Beverly Alban Metcalfe's chapter (Chapter 10), "Microskills of Leadership: A Detailed Analysis of the Behaviors of Managers in the Appraisal Interview," is different again in its focus and methodology. The first three chapters are concerned with managerial behavior in general. By contrast, Alban Metcalfe's is a study of a very specific and limited type of behavior, that exhibited in the appraisal interview. Like Martinko and Gardner she is interested in the difference between effective and less effective managers, though she is studying that in a simulated situation of a training course on performance-appraisal interviewing, where managers role play such interviews. She seeks to identify the differences in behavior of those who are rated as conducting "successful," "average," and "unsuccessful" interviews on the basis of the Nemeroff and Wexley (1977) questionnaire completed by the research member who plays the role of the subordinate.

Of particular interest is the specificity and detail with which the manager/leader behaviors are conceptualized and measured. Individuals such as Argyris (1979) have complained about the lack of specificity of consideration and initiating structure behaviors. Chapter 10 shows one way of addressing that concern.

To comment on the individual chapters, commentators from the other side of the Atlantic from the chapter authors were chosen. Commenting on Luthans and Lockwood is Peter Forsblad from Sweden. Forsblad was selected because of his personal experience of observational studies of managerial behavior. He summarizes the long history of studies of managerial behavior and of the need to relate one's research to these earlier studies as Martinko and Gardner have attempted to do for the more recent work from the United States. Forsblad outlines the difficulties and attitudes that explain the limited amount of observational work. He raises some queries about Luthans and Lockwood's approach; particularly whether it is worth employing the observational method without making use of the qualitative possibilities that it offers for obtaining a greater understanding of what one is studying. He also suggests that, from his own experience, some of the categories used in the LOS are not observable.

Philip Strong from the United Kingdom was asked to comment on the Martinko and Gardner chapter because he has extensive experience of observation in a different area: that of how pediatricians handle their interviews with parents and child. His remarks show that someone who is experienced in using the method can make helpful suggestions even if he or she is not a so-called expert in the particular subject being studied. He praises the thorough design of the study and concentrates upon suggestions for developing its qualitative, observational aspects.

Peter Weissenberg, from the United States, was invited to comment upon the Burgoyne and Hodgson chapter because of his long-run perspective concerning how the leadership area has developed over time in North America. He, like Forsblad, points to relevant earlier research, which is not mentioned in the Burgoyne and Hodgson chapter. He suggests that in assessing the value of Burgoyne and Hodgson's methods we ask ourselves whether they help to maximize the natural advantages of field studies. A proper study using their methods — and by proper study he means one that is applied to an appropriate sample size — would take much research time and effort. He concludes that at the present stage of leadership research, we need large-scale types of studies based on larger numbers, rather than the more individualized approach of Burgoyne and Hodgson. However, he suggests that their methods would enable one to understand some individual behaviors that are not well understood. In this he is arguing that their work might contribute to more structured later research involving traditional scientific methods. This is quite a different position from that of Burgoyne and Hodgson, who operate from a different epistemological base. They believe methods such as theirs may be necessary to obtain meaningful information about managers. Throughout, he underlines the need for an integrated theory of leadership.

Bert King from the United States was asked to comment upon the Alban Metcalfe chapter because of his expertise acquired through many years of evaluating organizational behavior projects in terms of funding. He raises a variety of questions about the value of the methods utilized by Alban Metcalfe. He queries whether such intensive microanalysis of 1/100 of a minute, is worthwhile in terms of the results that it can yield and the limitations that it imposes upon the size of the sample. Here his concern is similar to that of Weissenberg. King suggests various reasons why a simulated appraisal interview is likely to differ from an actual one. He points to two aspects that were neglected in the research design: the interaction between the two people and the time dimension required to understand and to assess an actual appraisal interview.

Rosemary Stewart is the integrative commentator for Part 2. Her major focus is on a discussion of the chapters within the context of contributions Europeans and North Americans can make to each other's work.

The four chapters are examples of very different views about what research is worth doing. Luthans and Lockwood appear to be very sure of the value of their approach. To the extent that Luthans and Lockwood are concerned with determining "what managers really do," a question may be raised about the variety of ways in which this can be conceptualized and about the value assumptions implicit in the LOS categorization. The Martinko and Gardner approach is interesting because it starts in the quantitative tradition, but explores what other data their observers can provide. The authors also indicate an awareness of and interest in understanding the complexity of "what managers really do."

This underlying issue of "worthwhileness" of a particular approach also permeates the other contributions in this book. This judgment clearly cannot be made in the absence of the researcher's values. Indeed, this question of values is so important that we return to it again in Chapter 25.

Weissenberg's earlier mentioned treatment of the Burgoyne and Hodgson chapter is a case in point. While he would see it as a precursor to the kind of study he really thinks needs to be done, Burgoyne and Hodgson feel it is valuable in its own right, perhaps potentially more valuable than the positivist studies advocated by Weissenberg.

A question that will no doubt occur to the reader in terms of Alban Metcalfe's chapter is the degree to which a focus on behaviors in the appraisal interview is relevant for other aspects of a manager's role. Is there a separate repertoire of behaviors needed for each of several important aspects of a manager's job or would the behaviors demonstrated in the appraisal interview carry over to other situations? This is not a new question, of course, but it is an important one to consider in Alban Metcalfe's study.

One may argue that it is not so much the behaviors themselves as the methodology used to isolate the behaviors that is important. This then points to a question raised by King concerning what might happen to the results here if an alternative classification scheme such as that of Bales (1950) were used. Also, how might one use a tape-recording system such as Alban Metcalfe's in a real-time manner?

Finally, as one looks at the Luthans and Lockwood chapter, one is struck by the nature of the leadership dimensions revealed. Though the authors set out to "scratch from scratch," as it were, in deriving categories, the final dimensions appear remarkably similar to those in other recent work (e.g., Yukl, 1981). What does one make of this?

7

Toward an Observation System for Measuring Leader Behavior in Natural Settings*

Fred Luthans and Diane Lee Lockwood

In a previous volume in this symposia series a social-learning theory base and observational measurement of leader behavior were proposed (Luthans, 1979). More specifically, a call was made for: (1) getting back to observable behavior in natural settings as the unit of analysis for the study of leadership; (2) a social-learning theoretical framework that recognized leadership as a reciprocal, interactive process involving the leader (including his or her cognitions and traits), the environment (including followers and structural and other organizational and broader environmental variables), and the leader's behavior itself; and (3) alternatives to the commonly used indirect questionnaire measures of leader behavior such as an observational system.

A number of papers and articles have since attempted to refine and expand the first two points either directly (for example, see Davis & Luthans, 1979; Luthans, 1981, pp. 429–432; Luthans & Davis, 1979) or indirectly (e.g., see Davis & Luthans, 1980a, 1980b; Luthans, 1981, pp. 63–71; Luthans & Davis, in press; Luthans, Paul, & Baker, 1981). The interested reader is referred to these sources for a full treatment of the use of observable behavior as the unit of analysis and social learning as the theoretical base for the study, understanding, and research perspective for leadership.

Let it simply be said that the study described here drew from the first proposal of the earlier volume by using observable behavior in situ as the unit of analysis and from the second proposal by using the interactive notion from social learning as the theoretical foundation. The major thrust of this chapter, however, is to explore and report the efforts made on the third proposal of the earlier volume — the need to develop measures of leader behavior other than the questionnaire, such as an observation system.

*Support for this study was provided by the Office of Naval Research, Organizational Effectiveness Group (Code 442), Contract N00014-80-C-0554; NR170-913, Fred Luthans, University of Nebraska, Principal Investigator.

WHY AN OBSERVATION SYSTEM?

An observational measurement approach to leadership behavior seems desirable for two major reasons. First, if leadership is viewed as an interactional process, as in social-learning theory, then as Kerlinger (1973) has pointed out, "Observations must be used when the variables of research studies are interactive and interpersonal in nature" (p. 554). The second reason for the need of an observational system is the apparent inadequacy of existing questionnaire measures. There is a growing awareness and recognition that the questionnaire measures on which leadership research has almost solely depended over the years may be a major reason for the dismal state of the field.

Schriesheim and his colleagues have recently supplied empirical evidence that casts some serious doubts about the reliability and validity of commonly used leadership questionnaires such as the Ohio State LBDQ and Fiedler's LPC instruments (see Schriesheim, Bannister, & Money, 1979; Schriesheim & Kerr, 1974, 1977; Schriesheim, Kinicki, & Schriesheim, 1979). For example, in a comprehensive paper presented in an earlier leadership symposium volume, Schriesheim and Kerr (1977) concluded that, "Leadership is today without any instruments of demonstrated validity and reliability" (p. 33). This finding does not necessarily mean that the instruments reviewed do not possess reliability and validity, but rather that the available evidence simply does not support them. This lack of empirical support has spurred a number of studies to demonstrate the psychometric properties of these instruments (see Bass, 1981 for a review of this literature) and the more careful development of new questionnaires (Yukl & Nemeroff, 1979). However, except for a few preliminary attempts (for example, two chapters that were based on observational research were included in the last symposium volume; see Bussom, Larson, & Vicars, 1982; Lombardo & McCall, 1982; and the present symposium from which this volume is derived contains an observational study of educational managers reported by Martinko & Gardner, Chap. 8), more direct alternative measurement techniques such as observational systems have not been developed or used in leadership research. The purpose of this chapter is to provide at least the beginnings of a possible alternative, a supplement (not a total replacement) to questionnaire measures of leader behavior. This study was undertaken in order to make a preliminary assessment of a newly developing leader observation system (LOS) for the measurement of leader behavior in natural settings.

METHOD

Settings and Subjects

The study utilized five organizational samples that were by design diverse: a fairly large financial institution, a state agency, a medium-sized manufacturing plant, a campus police department, and the Navy and Army ROTC units of a university. All those with supervisory responsibilities (from the president down to first-line supervision) in the financial institution ($N = 52$), campus police ($N = 16$), and professional staff in the ROTC units ($N = 15$) and supervisors/managers (usually within the same department) in selected operational departments of the state agency ($N = 18$) and manufacturing plant ($N = 19$) served as target leaders (total $N = 120$) in the study. Thus, leaders are defined in this study as those in managerial positions (at all levels) with responsibilities for supervising two or more subordinates. These target leaders typically had been with their respective organizations six to ten years and in their present positions one to five years. They were generally distributed throughout the 26 to 55 age range and a great majority had a college education. Their jobs covered the whole range of functions found in their respective organizations. These demographics were compatible with the intent of the study, which was to generalize across levels, functions, and personal characteristics of leaders.

Measures

Leadership behavior measures included in this study were the Leader Behavior Description Questionnaire — Form XII (LBDQ-XII) developed by Stogdill, Goode, and Day (1962), the Managerial Behavior Survey (MBS) developed by Yukl and Nemeroff (1979), and the newly developing Leadership Observation System (LOS).

The LBDQ-XII was used because it represents the most widely used measure in leadership behavior research to date. Many of the leadership theories and research findings to date are based on some variation of the IS (initiating structure) and C (consideration) subscales included in this questionnaire. Yet, as previously pointed out, the LBDQ-XII measure lacks convincing demonstrable support for construct validity. Previously reported reliabilities of the LBDQ-XII have been fairly favorable (Bass, 1981; Schriesheim & Kerr, 1977) and the Cronbach alphas in the present study ($N = 393$) ranged from .74 to .91 for the various subscales. The IS scale was .86 and the C scale was .83.

Although a relatively new and still developing instrument, the MBS was used because, in the words of the authors Yukl and Nemeroff (1979), it was specifically designed to "identify distinct, meaningful, and widely applicable categories of leadership behavior" (p. 169). Thus, it attempts to tap multiple behaviors. In addition, the reported psychometric properties of the MBS reported by its authors are quite favorable. In four separate studies the Cronbach alphas are reported in the .7 and .8 range (Yukl & Nemeroff, 1979) and in the present study ($N = 395$), they ranged from .56 to .90 on the various subscales.

The Leader Observation System (LOS)

The observation system used in this study was developed in two major phases. First, 44 leaders (defined as those in managerial positions with supervisory responsibilities) at all levels in all types of organizations (not the 120 target leaders who were the subjects of the actual study) were observed in a completely unstructured format for a varied hour each day over a two-week period (that is, 440 hours of unstructured observation of leaders in their natural settings). The 44 observers were management students who were given an extensive training workshop. This observer training emphasized the systematic errors commonly found in observing others (it followed the procedures suggested by Thornton & Zorich, 1980). In addition, they practiced writing protocols from several role-playing exercises that were then critiqued by the trainers/researchers. The observers were trained to observe the behavior of the target leader continuously over the hour; to record specific, identifiable behaviors on their logs; and to be reporters concentrating on objective description rather than trying to judge or evaluate the behaviors observed. These observers had not yet studied leadership theory or research; thus the attempt was made to minimize the possible confounding effect that implicit theories may have on observing leader behavior (DeNisi & Schriesheim, 1981).

While true randomization of the observation times was not possible, the observers systematically varied their hours throughout each working day during the two weeks to help assure representativeness. After the two weeks, the observed leaders were shown copies of the protocols of their behaviors and were asked to rate to what extent these were typical of their behavior. On a scale of 1–5, the mean rating was 3.9, which indicated that the behaviors, on the average, were typical "to a considerable extent." These leaders were also asked to suggest any additional behaviors that they considered typical. These additions mainly consisted of activities that might best be described as of a sensitive nature, that is, important policy meetings, disciplining, and managing conflict.

The second major phase involved in deriving the LOS used in this study was the considerable job of constructing comprehensive and workable categories to accommodate (contain) the 440 hours of freely observed behaviors. This task was accomplished by a Delphi process (Delbecq, Van de Ven, & Gustafson, 1975). The Delphi panel consisted of four persons with considerable academic work in management/leadership and three graduate students from outside disciplines who were completely naive with respect to prior leadership research. All panel members were given handouts and required to read and become familiar with the processes of constructing adequate behavioral categories as outlined by Kerlinger (1973) and Crano and Brewer (1973).

In the first Delphi round, the panelists independently reviewed the extensive protocols completed by the observers and suggested general categories with accompanying behavioral descriptors from the protocols. The panelists were instructed to use frequency of behaviors as a guideline in constructing the categories. These categories with accompanying comments were collected (there were about 100 categories resulting from the first round) and fed back to the panelists. Then, through several iterations the panelists further collapsed the categories into smaller but more comprehensive sets that could be readily used by observers to record the frequency of occurrence. Through this Delphi process, the final surviving 12 categories incorporated a multiplicity of opinions and critiques whose purpose was not only to be representative but also to be as exhaustive and mutually exclusive as possible. The resulting 12 final categories and the accompanying behavioral descriptors on the LOS instrument are shown in Table 7.1

The categories in the LOS are conceptually similar to those associated with a managerial activities approach. Both the LOS and a managerial activities approach attempt to determine what managers/leaders actually do in the natural setting and use direct methods of measurement. However, the traditional behavioral approaches to leadership (e.g., the Ohio State or Michigan studies) depend on indirect questionnaire measures and the categories for these measures were not derived from free observation of leaders in natural settings. Instead, the researchers themselves largely determined the response sets of their questionnaires and the resulting behavioral categories are quite different (i.e., usually less concrete) from the LOS categories. Yukl and Nemeroff's MBS instrument, on the other hand, does contain many similar categories. Although drawing from the literature rather than from free observation in natural settings, they did make a conscious effort to select observable, concrete behavioral categories (Yukl & Nemeroff, 1979).

Mintzberg (1973, 1975) is most closely associated with the managerial activities approach, but the "leader" is only one of his ten managerial roles. He states that, "Leadership involves interpersonal relationships between the leader and the led" (1973, p. 60). As such, the manager must engage in activities that provide guidance to subordinates, motivate them, and create favorable conditions for the work. Some of these managerial activities may be classified as primarily concerned with leadership (an example would be staffing, which involves hiring, training, evaluating, remunerating, promoting, and dismissing subordinates). Mintzberg, however, makes it clear that leadership permeates all managerial activities, even those with some other basic purpose. When a manager requests information from a subordinate, for example, he or she may be simultaneously motivating, training, allowing participation in decision making, and/or monitoring the subordinate's performance. Consequently, it appears to be difficult to separate "leadership behavior" per se from the larger domain of managerial activities, and the LOS reflects this difficulty.

Results from Mintzberg-type studies (see, for example, Kurke & Aldrich, 1979) using different organizations and subjects tend to confirm Mintzberg's

Table 7.1. The LOS Categories and Behavioral Descriptors

1. **Planning/Coordinating**
   a. setting goals & objectives
   b. defining tasks needed to accomplish goals
   c. scheduling employees, timetables
   d. assigning tasks and providing routine instructions
   e. coordinating activities of each subordinate to keep work running smoothly
   f. organizing the work

2. **Staffing**
   a. developing job descriptions for position openings
   b. reviewing applications
   c. interviewing applicants
   d. hiring
   e. contacting applicants to inform them of being hired or not
   f. "filling in" where needed

3. **Training/Developing**
   a. orienting employees, arranging for training seminars, etc.
   b. clarifying roles, duties, job descriptions
   c. coaching, mentoring, walking subordinates through task
   d. helping subordinates with personal development plans

4. **Decision Making/Problem Solving**
   a. defining problems
   b. choosing between 2 or more alternatives or strategies
   c. handling day-to-day operational crises as they arise
   d. weighing the trade-offs; cost benefit analyses
   e. actually deciding what to do
   f. developing new procedures to increase efficiency

5. **Processing Paperwork**
   a. processing mail
   b. reading reports, in-box
   c. writing reports, memos, letters, etc.
   d. routine financial reporting and bookkeeping
   e. general desk work

6. **Exchanging Routine Information**
   a. answering routine procedural questions
   b. receiving and disseminating requested information
   c. conveying results of meetings
   d. giving or receiving routine information over the phone
   e. staff meetings of an informational nature (e.g., status updates, new company policies, etc.)

7. **Monitoring/Controlling Performance**
   a. inspecting work
   b. walking around and checking things out, touring
   c. monitoring performance data (e.g., computer printouts, production, financial reports)
   d. preventive maintenance

8. **Motivating/Reinforcing**
   a. allocating formal organizational rewards
   b. asking for input, participation
   c. conveying appreciation, compliments
   d. giving credit where due
   e. listening to suggestions
   f. giving position performance feedback
   g. increasing job challenge
   h. delegating responsibility & authority
   i. letting subordinates determine how to do their own work
   j. sticking up for the group to superiors and others, backing a subordinate

9. **Disciplining/Punishing**
   a. enforcing rules and policies
   b. nonverbal glaring, harassment
   c. demotion, firing, layoff
   d. any formal organizational reprimand or notice
   e. "chewing out" a subordinate, criticizing
   f. giving negative performance feedback

10. **Interacting With Outsiders**
    a. public relations
    b. customers
    c. contacts with suppliers, vendors
    d. external meetings
    e. community-service activities

11. **Managing Conflict**
    a. managing interpersonal conflict between subordinate or others
    b. appealing to higher authority to resolve a dispute
    c. appealing to 3rd-party negotiators
    d. trying to get cooperation or consensus between conflicting parties
    e. attempting to resolve conflicts between subordinate and self

12. **Socializing/Politicking**
    a. nonwork related chit chat (e.g., family or personal matters)
    b. informal "joking around," B.S.
    c. discussing rumors, hearsay, grapevine
    d. complaining, griping, putting others down
    e. politicking, gamesmanship

findings. In general, these studies suggest that subordinates consume about one-half of managers' contact time and the purposes of these contacts usually involve requests, sending or receiving information, and occasionally strategy making. These studies, however, report that some difficulties were encountered in coding "purpose of activities" largely because of the ambiguous or overlapping nature of the categories. In other words, the coding of activity purpose often requires a great deal of inference on the part of the observer to discriminate between, for example, overt and covert purposes, sequential purposes, multipurposes, and changed purposes (Mintzberg, 1973, pp. 274–276). The LOS tries to overcome this coding problem by dealing only with frequencies of observable behavior and not requiring inference on the part of the observer.

The actual format of the LOS instrument used in the present study lists the behavioral categories along the left-hand side and random times along the top. The random times were for 10 minutes every hour over 2 weeks, or a total of 80 observations. There was a separate sheet for each day. A nominal measuring format was used; that is, the observers recorded either the behavior was present ("✓") or absent ("0") for each ten-minute time slot. By judging whether the behavior was present or absent, the problem of inferring covert purposes of the behavior or degrees or magnitude of the behavior was avoided. Only a frequency count of the behavior was recorded by the LOS in this study.

Observers Used in the Study

Partipant observers ($N = 88$) in the study were selected jointly by the researchers and the personnel managers of the respective organizations (or the designated project officers in the case of the campus police and ROTC units) according to the following criterion: Does this person have maximum visual and audible contact with the target leader and a good understanding of the functions, terminology, and nature of the work performed by the target leader? The target leader's informed consent was also needed and secured in all cases.

The selected participant observers in almost all cases turned out to be the target leader's secretary or a key subordinate. Eleven (12%) of the participant observers were responsible for observing two target leaders and seven (8%) of the participant observers had three target leaders. This was discouraged as much as possible and only occurred when it was better in the opinion of the researchers/personnel managers to meet the criterion of selection as a participant observer in the study and observe more than one target leader than to select another observer but not meet the selection criterion nearly as well. This usually was the case where one secretary served more than one target leader. These participant observers had considerable job experience but little formal higher education and had little or no knowledge of the literature on leadership research or theory, thus minimizing the implicit theory problem

(DeNisi & Schriesheim, 1981). Except for the training they received (which will be described next), they had little or no knowledge of the specifics of the study.

The outside observers ($N = 8$) used in the study were graduate students in management. Three were assigned to the financial institution, two to the manufacturing plant, one to the state agency, and one to the campus police and ROTC units. An experienced graduate student (a Ph.D. student with the most knowledge of the study) observed at all the sites and largely coordinated the efforts of the other seven outside observers. These outsider observers had briefly studied leadership theory and research in their course work in management, received training, and had a very general idea of the objectives and procedures of the study.

Observer Training

A training workshop conducted by the researchers was held on the premises of each of the participant observers' respective organizations. Each session followed the same format, used the same trainers (the authors of this chapter plus a graduate assistant), and took approximately 2½ hours to complete.

About the first half of the observer training workshop was devoted to three areas: first, to provide a very general explanation of the purpose of the observations (i.e., to gather data for input into a profile of the leader's behavior); second, to go over in detail the observational instrument, giving special attention and analysis to the 12 behavioral categories and the procedures for filling out the instrument, including what to do if the leader was absent; and third, to give careful instruction on potential observational errors (following Thornton & Zorich, 1980) and how to overcome them. In particular, the potential for errors of description versus evaluation and distortion to please the person being observed was deemed to be particularly relevant to these participant observers and was stressed in the training. For example, the observers were instructed to avoid letting their evaluative biases color their observations: since there are no "good" or "bad" categories on the instrument, the observations would be useful only if they were accurate. By careful explanation and example the trainers showed how the observers could avoid these errors.

The second half of the training was devoted to demonstration and practice. The trainers employed a number of role-playing skits that illustrated the specific leader behavior categories, and the trainees used the instrument to record the behaviors they observed. By following the principles of modeling theory (Bandura, 1977; Latham & Sari, 1979), this aspect of the training was intended to increase observer accuracy through modeling, rehearsal, and repetition. After each role-playing skit, the trainers went over the LOS instrument with the trainees and discussed which behavior category was being illustrated and which specific errors might have been committed during that observation.

In a final role-playing skit, which was rather lengthy and elaborate but realistic, six behavioral categories were represented. The observers' performance on this last exercise served as an evaluation check for the training. A precise evaluation of observer accuracy is possible, of course, only when there is an objective criterion, that is, when the "correct" observations are known. Such an objective criterion was possible in this training exercise because the skit was designed to exhibit the six categories and thus an evaluation of trainee accuracy could be made. Although these data were unavailable in one of the organizations, in the remaining four organizations the participant observer trainees had an overall mean accuracy of 92.5 percent, with no significant differences between organizations. This accuracy was considerably higher than the 69 percent obtained by Thornton and Zorich (1980) in their observer training group, but their exercise was longer.

The outside observers used in the study were given the same training as the inside participant observers. After the training, they were given a tour of the facility, were introduced, and chatted with the participant observers they would be working with over the two-week observation period.

Data-Collection Procedures

Approximately four weeks prior to the collection of the LOS data, all target managers ($N=120$) completed, among other instruments, the MBS and LBDQ-XII. The wording on these instruments was changed to reflect a self-assessment. They were completed on site in the respective organizations under the supervision and instructions of the researchers. The four-week time lag between the questionnaire data collection and the observational data collection was used in order to minimize contamination effects. The target leaders were also asked to fill out a brief questionnaire that asked them to give a self-estimate of the percentage of their work time spent in each of the LOS categories.

Each target leader then distributed the LBDQ-XII and MBS questionnaires to his or her immediate superior ($N=118$), usually two peers ($N=210$), and about three subordinates ($N=362$). The pronouns and instructions were modified in each of these samples to reflect who was filling it out. If a target manager directly supervised a large number of subordinates, the researchers randomly selected out a sample of three to five subordinates to fill out the questionnaires. It was stressed that the anonymity of these raters would be preserved and their names never appeared with the data.

The LOS data were then collected on the target leaders 80 times by the participant observer over a two-week period (a random ten-minute period each working hour over two weeks). This represented a total of 9,600 (120 target managers $\times$ 80 observation periods) possible observation periods when the

LOS instrument was filled out. In addition, all participant observers completed a short follow-up questionnaire at the conclusion of their two-week observational period. The purpose of this questionnaire was to assess the extent to which observed behaviors were representative or "typical" of normal behavior patterns exhibited by the target leaders over the time they had worked with them. That is, the leaders may have attempted to act in exemplary ways not necessarily customary to their typical behavior patterns simply because they knew that they were being observed, or this particular two-week period may not have been representative of their typical workload. Results for this Representativeness Scale indicated that all observed behavior categories on the LOS, on average, were reported to be typical to a considerable or very great extent.

Since it was not feasible to have the outside observers present at all times during the observation data-collection periods, a time-sampling technique was employed to gather their data. The trained outside observer would randomly appear unannounced, and simultaneously with the participant observers, but independently, would record on the LOS sheets the observed behaviors of the target leader. A total of 253 such simultaneous, independent observations took place. Each of the participant observers had two or three times when an outside observer joined him or her unannounced to record simultaneously the behavior of the target leader.

A summary of procedures, in order of sequence, is the following:

1. LBDQ-XII and MBS questionnaire administration to target leaders ($N = 120$) and other rater sources (superior [$N = 118$], peers [$N = 120$], and subordinates [$N = 362$]) and target leader questionnaire on self-estimate of time use.
2. Observer training.
3. Measurement of target leaders' behavior using the LOS instrument filled out by participant observers every ten minutes for two weeks and periodically by outside observers.

RELIABILITY AND VALIDITY

The development of any new measurement system must address the important psychometric issues of reliability and validity. Unless the measurement scheme can be demonstrated to be dependable, consistent, and accurate (i.e., reliable), there is always the possibility that the data gathered by the instrument are loaded with error and the results meaningless. To the extent that measurement error is demonstrated to be slight or minimal, the measure is said to be reliable (Nunnally, 1978). The most common way to assess the reliability of behavioral data gathered by observation has been through interrater agreement (Bijou, Peterson, & Ault, 1968).

Interrater reliability analysis for the LOS is quite encouraging (see Luthans, Lockwood, & Conti, 1981, for a complete discussion and a full data presentation of the interrator reliability assessment). There is 93.5% agreement between the participant observers and the outside observers in this study. When only agreement on observed behaviors (leaving out agreement on behavioral categories that did not occur) is calculated, there is 87.4 interrater reliability. Although reliabilities are not even reported in but a couple of observational studies involving managerial leadership (Bussom, Larson, & Vicars, 1982), in order to rule out the possibility of chance agreement, statistical analysis was also performed on the interrater data gathered by the LOS instrument. Chi-square calculations yielded highly significant values ($p < .001$) ranging from $X^2 = 99.3$ for "staffing" to $X^2 = 119.3$ for "Monitoring/Controlling Performance" and the r_ϕ statistics (Cohen & Cohen, 1975) had highly significant values ($p < .001$) ranging from .89 for "Staffing" to .68 for "Monitoring/Controlling Performance." Perhaps the most revealing statistic, however, is Cohen's (1960) kappa statistic which specifically represents the proportion of joint judgments in which there is agreement, after chance agreement is excluded. The values for this kappa statistic are very similar to those for r_ϕ and the overall was a highly significant ($p < .001$) .81.

The interrater agreement assessment makes a contribution to the reliability of the LOS. More and different analysis, however, is also needed. In addition, more important validity analysis is needed. Reliability, of course, is a necessary but not a sufficient condition for validity. A measurement scheme may consistently and accurately measure something other than the intended construct. Validity basically refers to whether the measurement system is measuring what it is supposed to measure (in this case, does the LOS really measure leader behavior?). This simple definition is not intended to imply that validity can be demonstrated by a single study. Compared to reliability, it is much more difficult to demonstrate validity.

This study uses the multitrait-multimethod (or simply MTMM) approach to extend the relatively simple interrater agreement assessment of reliability and helps *begin* the evaluation of validity. Cascio (1978) points out that the MTMM analysis contributes to both reliability and validity assessment. He states:

> Reliability is estimated by two measures of the same trait using the same method, while validity is defined as the extent of agreement between two measures of the same trait using different methods. Thus, the distinction between reliability and validity is simply a matter of degree—that is, in terms of the similarity of measurement methods. (p. 97).

Besides helping to assess both reliability and validity, the MTMM focused on *construct* rather than predictive validity. The evaluation of construct valid-

ity seems relatively more important at this early stage of development of the
LOS. As Guion points out, "All validity is at its base some form of construct
validity. . . . The most salient of the traditionally identified aspects of validity
—the only one that is salient—is construct validity. It is the basic meaning of validity" (1977, p. 410). Eventually, if subsequent studies can build support for construct validity, then predictive validity will become more important. Once again, however, it must be remembered that this study is only a
beginning. Reliability, and, to a greater extent validity assessment, is both
a logical and an empirical process. The goal over time is to build a type of
nomological network to assess the LOS and leadership in general. In this network, observable leader behaviors would be related to other observables,
observables to theoretical constructs, and one theoretical construct to another
theoretical construct. Only a portion of this long-term goal is realized in this
present study.

RESULTS OF THE MTMM ANALYSIS

The MTMM analysis in this study mainly depended on multiple rater
sources as measurement by more than one method. Some may argue that such
a multirater comparison makes more of a reliability than a validity assessment. As used in this study, it is hoped that this approach contributes to both
reliability and validity assessment. There are important precedents where multiple raters were used in analyzing construct validity. For example, as Lawler
(1967) carefully noted:

> Campbell and Fiske (1959) consider the multitrait-multimethod approach rather
> than the multitrait-multirater approach; however, they point out that use of
> raters that occupy different organizational positions relative to the ratee can
> reasonably be considered to be measurement by more than one method. (p. 372)

In addition, it is important to point out that one of the examples used in the
original Campbell and Fiske (1959, p. 96) paper uses multiraters in the
MTMM matrix. Thus, multiraters are first treated as multimethods in the
MTMM analyses made of the LBDQ, MBS, and LOS. This is then followed
by an MTMM analysis that uses observation and questionnaire methods as
multimethods. The problem with the latter approach, however, is that there
are not directly comparable categories of behavior across the methods.

MTMM Analysis of the LBDQ-XII

A correlation matrix for the LBDQ-XII was constructed. Correlation coefficients between different rater sources were calculated using the Pearson
Product Moment formula. In general, the matrix revealed that different rater

sources (subordinate, superior, peer, and self) did not tend to agree highly enough (on the validity diagonals) to argue that convergent validity existed to any great extent. One possible exception was between superior and self ratings where six of the twelve correlations were slightly significant in the .20s range, but not enough to provide strong support for convergent validity between these two rater sources. In addition, the results did not support discriminant validity among the behavioral categories on the LBDQ-XII.

Kavanaugh, MacKinney, and Wolins (1971) provide a simplified and interpretable technique for quantitatively analyzing and summarizing large MTMM matrices. In addition, this statistical analysis is less subject to judgmental interpretation. In essence, their analysis-of-variance model allows one to assess the relative strength (weight) of variance components attributable to convergent and discriminant validity, method or source bias (halo), and error. Table 7.2 presents the results of variance component and indexed calculations for the LBDQ-XII multirater matrix. In can be seen that a modest amount of the indexed variance (.20) can be attributed to rater source bias (i.e., "halo" in the rating situation). An approximately equal proportion of the variance (.19) can be attributed to convergent validity among multiple rater sources using the LBDQ-XII instrument. Finally, almost none (.01) of the variance is attributable to discriminant validity (that is, the subscales of the LBDQ-XII are highly intercorrelated). In summary, this statistical analysis does not provide strong support for either convergent or discriminant validity (when compared to halo and error terms) among multiple rater sources using the LBDQ-XII instrument.

MTMM Analysis of the MBS

The correlation matrix for the MBS questionnaire showed a pattern of results quite similar to those produced for the LBDQ-XII instrument. The results indicated that different rater sources do not tend to agree highly enough (on the validity diagonals) to argue that convergent validity existed to any

Table 7.2
Components and Indices for the LBDQ-XII MTMM Using Multiraters
(Self, Superior, Subordinate, and Peer).

Source*	Variance Components	Indices**
L (convergent validity)	.168	.19
L × B (discriminant validity)	.009	.01
L × S (halo)	.176	.20
Error	.708	

*L = Target Leader; B = Behavior; S = Source or Rater.
**Variance components standardized error term.

great extent. Also similar to the LBDQ-XII, the results for the MBS did not appear to satisfy the requirements for discriminant validity among the behavioral categories.

The results of the statistical analysis for the MBS shown in Table 7.3 indicate that a moderate amount of the indexed variance (.29) can be attributed to rater source bias (halo). Less of the variance is attributable to convergent validity (.21), and almost none (.01) to discriminant validity. In summary, these results do not provide strong support for either convergent or discriminant validity (when compared to halo and error terms) among multiple rater sources using the MBS instrument.

MTMM Analysis of the LOS

The correlation matrix for the MTMM analysis of the LOS is presented in Table 7.4. Correlation coefficients (calculations used the Spearman Rho because of the nominal data) between participant and outside observers tend to agree substantially enough (see the validity diagonal) to argue that convergent validity exists to a moderate degree, with the possible exception of the infrequently occurring "Managing Conflict" behavioral category. With respect to discriminant validity criteria, the results are also moderately positive. That is, the pattern of correlation coefficients in the validity diagonal is generally greater than the correlation coefficients found in the two adjacent heterobehavior blocks (dotted triangles), with the exception of "Managing Conflict." The pattern of correlation coefficients in the validity diagonal is also greater than the correlation coefficients found in the monomethod-heterobehavior blocks (solid triangles). Finally, the same pattern of behavior intercorrelations is found in all of the heterobehavior triangles of both the monomethod and heteromethod blocks, even though there are some differences in the general level of correlations involved.

Results for the statistical analysis of the LOS matrix are provided in Table 7.5. It can be seen from this table that a substantial proportion of the indexed variance is attributable to discriminant validity (.68), somewhat less to conver-

Table 7.3
Components and Indices for the MBS MTMM Using Multiraters
(Self, Superior, Subordinate, and Peer).

Source	Variance Components	Indices
L (convergent validity)	.167	.21
L × B (discriminant validity)	.009	.01
L × S (halo)	.256	.29
Error	.632	

gent validity (.42), and almost none (.01) to halo bias. In total, the evidence for convergent and discriminant validity appears to be relatively strong for the LOS when multiple rater sources are considered measurement by more than one method. Once again, however, a word of caution is in order. One could question whether the participant and outside observers really represent multiple methods in a validity analysis of the LOS. They are certainly different sources and different sources have traditionally been used as different methods, but there are obviously some problems with making this strictly a validity test. On the other hand, validity assessment is judgmental and this analysis is beginning input into such a judgmental process. In addition, however, this MTMM analysis of the LOS does provide empirical input for an alternative assessment to the interrater evaluation of reliability of the LOS.

The LOS and Questionnaires as Multiple Methods

To get around the potential problems associated with the use of multiple sources as multiple methods, an attempt was made to compare similar categories of the LOS (observation method) and LBDQ-XII and MBS (questionnaire methods). This, of course, represents a classic multiple-methods analysis. Because there are widely different behavioral categories for each instrument, however, a way of collapsing categories for comparison purposes was needed.

The data for the LBDQ-XII and MBS were first submitted to a principal components factor analysis with varimax rotation in order to reduce the individual categories to factors that could be reasonably compared. The factor analysis for the LBDQ-XII resulted in a two-factor solution (consideration and initiation of structure), accounting for 64 percent of the cumulative variance. The factor analysis for the MBS resulted in a three-factor solution (consideration, initiation of structure, and conflict management), accounting for 58 percent of the variance. However, since the third factor (conflict management) contributed only .06 percent to the cumulative proportion of explained variance, the data were subsequently forced into a two-factor solution (consideration and initiation of structure) for comparison purposes. A factor analysis for the LOS was not possible because the observers were instructed to check as many behaviors as occurred within a given ten-minute period. Since more than one behavior was often observed during this time frame, there would be high intercorrelations among LOS categories and thus trying to determine a factor structure would be meaningless. As a result, for comparison purposes the LOS categories were forced on a conceptual basis into consideration and initiation of structure factors comparable to the results from the LBDQ-XII and MBS factor analyses. Table 7.6 shows how the behavioral categories for each instrument were collapsed into consideration and initiation of structure.

The MTMM correlation matrix for this multiple methods analysis is pre-

Table 7.4
LOS Multirater Matrix (Participant and Outside Observers)[a].

Participant Observer

PARTICIPANT OBSERVER		P_1	P_2	P_3	P_4	P_5	P_6	P_7	P_8	P_9	P_{10}	P_{11}	P_{12}
Planning/Coord.	P_1	1.0											
Staffing	P_2	11*	1.0										
Training	P_3	06	08	1.0									
Dec. Making/Prob.-Sol.	P_4	48*	01	06	1.0								
Processing Paperwork	P_5	18*	14*	16*	24*	1.0							
Exchanging Routine Info.	P_6	18*	02	07	21*	06	1.0						
Monitoring/Control. Perf.	P_7	33*	02	02	32*	04	17*	1.0					
Motivating/Reinforcing	P_8	54*	07	03	48*	13*	19*	38*	1.0				
Disciplining/Punish	P_9	10*	02	07	10*	03	06	06	01	1.0			
Interact. W/Outsiders	P_{10}	17*	01	03	06	04	02	24*	15*	05	1.0		
Managing Conflict	P_{11}	07	04	01	10*	02	02	03	11*	02	04	1.0	
Socializing/Politicking	P_{12}	31*	01	10*	26*	15*	25*	30*	44*	10*	09	06	1.0

Outside Observers

OUTSIDE OBSERVERS		O_1	O_2	O_3	O_4	O_5	O_6	O_7	O_8	O_9	O_{10}	O_{11}	O_{12}
Planning/Coord.	O_1	(36*)	16*	09	44*	32*	19*	46*	60*	06	25*	05	30*
Staffing	O_2	11*	(84)*	08	00	09	04	04	08	01	03	03	04
Training	O_3	06	04	(62)*	03	19*	07	07	05	02	04	04	09

Dec. Making/Prob.-Sol. O_4	43*	02	12*	(84)*	10*	19*	38*	52*	06	15*	05	25*
Processing Paperwork O_5	15*	14*	12*	31*	(71)*	06	05	18*	06	02	06	17*
Exchanging Routine Info. O_6	19*	01	07	24*	11	(70)*	25*	24*	03	01·	05	22*
Monitoring/Control. Perf. O_7	36*	03	05	33*	19*	11*	(71)*	47*	04	24*	07	30*
Motivating/Reinforcing O_8	55*	13*	14*	48*	37*	26*	54*	(84)*	03	22*	07	43*
Disciplining/Punish O_9	10*	02	03	10*	08	05	06	08	(38)*	05	01	10*
Interact. W/Outsiders O_{10}	19*	02	03	04	02	05	23*	19	03	(77)*	01	08
Managing Conflict O_{11}	07	04	05	05	11*	04	06	10*	01	09	(49)*	07
Socializing/Politicking O_{12}	26*	02	07	28*	27*	21*	43*	48*	06	06	00	(80)*

1.0	16*	13*	44*	30*	20*	47*	60*	06	28*	05	27*
	1.0	08	02	07	00	09	14*	01	06	03	01
		1.0	15*	12*	04	14*	12*	02	01	03	07
			1.0	49*	22*	40*	56*	06	14*	11*	23*
				1.0	15*	29*	44*	05	04	04	33*
					1.0	23*	26*	03	01	08	21*
						1.0	62*	04	28*	09	42*
							1.0	04	27*	07	48*
								1.0	03	01	06
									1.0	01	03
										1.0	05
											1.0

[a]The figures enclosed in parentheses are the validity diagonals; the figures enclosed within solid triangles are the monomethod-heterobehavior blocks; and the figures enclosed within dotted triangles are the heteromethod-heterobehavior blocks.

This analysis includes the observed behaviors for which the participant and outside observers simultaneously, but independently, filled out the LOS.

*$p < .05$

133

Table 7.5
Components and Indices for the LOS MTMM Using Multiraters
(Participant and Outside Observers).

Source	Variance Components	Indices
L (convergent validity)	.196	.42
L × B (discriminant validity)	.584	.68
L × S (halo)	.003	.01
Error	.268	

sented in Table 7.7. Several different combinations of behavioral categories collapsed into consideration and initiation of structure were also analyzed with results quite similar to those found in Table 7.7. It can be seen that, with the possible exception of the modest degree of convergence between the LOS and MBS consideration factor, there is little evidence of convergence in the validity diagonals between the LOS observational method and either of the LBDQ-XII or MBS questionnaire methods. There is, however, a substantial amount of convergence in the validity diagonal between the LBDQ-XII and MBS—both of which are questionnaire-based methods. None of the criteria for discriminant validity were satisfied to any great extent.

Table 7.6
Collapsing of Behavioral Categories for Each Method into
Consideration and Initiation of Structure

MBS

Initiation of Structure	*Consideration*
Coordinating	Autonomy/Delegation
Planning	Consideration
Problem Solving	Facilitating Subordinate Work
Role Clarification	Criticism/Discipline
Goal Setting	Conflict Management
Training	Facilitating Group Interaction

LBDQ-XII

Initiation of Structure	*Consideration*
Integration	Consideration
Production Emphasis	Tolerance of Freedom
Representation	Tolerance of Uncertainty
Superior Orientation	
Initiation of Structure	

LOS

Initiation of Structure	*Consideration*
Planning/Coordinating	Motivating/Reinforcing
Decision Making/Problem Solving	Disciplining/Punishing
Monitoring/Controlling Performance	Managing Conflict
Staffing	Socializing/Politicking
Exchanging Routine Information	
Training	

Table 7.7
Multimethod Matrix for LBDQ, MBS, and LOS.

	LOS IS	LOS C	LBDQ-XII IS	LBDQ-XII C	MBS IS	MBS C
LOS IS	1.0	.67*	(.08)	.01	(.09)	.14
C		1.0	.10	(.07)	.10	(.19)*
LBDQ-XII IS			1.0	.41*	(.59)*	.40*
C				1.0	.61*	(.57)*
MBS IS					1.0	.82*
C						1.0

*$p < .05$

The results of the statistical analysis of the MTMM matrix are shown in Table 7.8. It can be seen that a substantial proportion of the indexed variance (.54) is attributable to convergent validity (for the most part between the two questionnaire methods). A substantial proportion (.55) of the variance, however, is also attributed to halo bias in the rating situation (i.e., high scale intercorrelations between C and IS for each instrument). Finally, there was only a very modest amount of variance contributed by discriminant validity (.10). In summary, these results provide only minor support for the construct validity of any of the three leadership behavior measures analyzed by the MTMM.

To make a more directly comparable multiple-methods analysis, the LOS and the self-report percentage of a time-usage questionnaire containing the same behavioral categories were used as two different methods. Table 7.9 shows that in the validity diagonal there was significant convergence between

Table 7.8
Components and Indices for the Multiple Methods of LBDQ-XII, MBS, and LOS.

Source	Variance Components	Indices
L (convergent validity)	.381	.54
L × B (discriminant validity)	.038	.10
L × S (halo)	.407	.55
Error	.328	

Table 7.9

Multimethod Matrix: LOS and Self-Estimate of Time-Usage Questionnaire.[a]

Observation Method

OBSERVATION	DM	DP	ER	IO	MC	MCP	MR	PC	PP	SP	ST	TD
Decision Making/Prob. Solv.	1.0											
Disciplining/Punishing	56*	1.0										
Exchanging Routine Info.	73*	55*	1.0									
Interacting W/Outsiders	46*	52*	57*	1.0								
Managing Conflict	53*	65*	50*	40*	1.0							
Monitoring Performance	64*	63*	60*	37*	54*	1.0						
Motivating/Reinforcing	67	69	61	52	58*	67*	1.0					
Planning/Coordinating	73*	57	64*	44*	44*	65*	68*	1.0				
Processing Paperwork	51*	47*	75*	48*	39*	50*	52*	48*	1.0			
Socializing/Politicking	56*	55*	71*	62*	48*	55*	61*	50*	64*	1.0		
Staffing	55*	59*	58*	40*	55*	61*	45*	56*	41*	53*	1.0	
Training/Developing	58	56*	58*	45*	48*	53*	56*	65*	47*	43*	54*	1.0

Questionnaire Self-Estimate Method

SELF-ESTIMATE	DM	DP	ER	IO	MC	MCP	MR	PC	PP	SP	ST	TD
Decision Making/Prob. Solv.	(06)*	13	02	05	03	03	08	13	23*	02	14	05
Disciplining/Punishing	13	(03)	01	05	20*	07	03	10	02	04	21*	18*

136

Exchanging Routine Info.	04	05	(02)	17	04	04	09	01	23*	05	04	10
Interacting W/Outsiders	03	10	06	(49)*	02	07	05	02	14	27*	17	09
Managing Conflict	12	05	01	08	(17)	06	16	11	08	05	13	06
Monitoring Performance	16	01	15	07	22*	(17)	16	16	07	08	20*	15
Motivating/Reinforcing	07	10	06	02	16	12	(19)*	04	05	05	08	02
Planning/Coordinating	02	14	13	06	07	19*	08	(17)	22*	17	18*	11
Processing Paperwork	03	13	11	31*	08	03	23*	15	(30)*	22*	15	23*
Socializing/Politicking	07	10	04	04	11	09	17	03	17	(19)*	04	07
Staffing	07	17	13		21*	13	09	12	07	03	(23)	27*
Training/Developing	04	01	06	04	05	13	08	04	04	15	10	(32)
	1.0											
	15	1.0										
	01	10	1.0									
	02	12	01	1.0								
	28*	38*	04	15	1.0							
	14	34*	21*	02	29*	1.0						
	06	30*	14	00	25*	35*	1.0					
	19*	27*	06	04	21*	20*	16	1.0				
	02	01	16	39*	01	05	01	15	1.0			
	14	24*	28*	19*	18	08	00	01	17	1.0		
	27*	52*	10	14	45*	39*	31*	23*	02	11*	1.0	
	08	44*	11	02	30*	39*	22*	25*	01	03	45*	1.0

[a]The figures enclosed in parentheses are the validity diagonals; the figures enclosed within solid triangles are the momomethod-heterobehavior blocks; and the figures enclosed within dotted triangles are the heteromethod-heterobehavior blocks.

*p<.05

methods (the LOS and the self-report time-usage questionnaire) for six of the twelve categories with three more approaching (.17) significance. There was, however, little evidence of convergence for the categories of "Decision Making/Problem Solving," "Disciplining/Punishing," and "Exchanging Routine Information." It is also interesting to note that there was greater convergence between the *self*-estimate of time usage and participant observers (who in nearly all instances were the *subordinates* of target managers) than in self-subordinate comparisons for either the LBDQ-XII or MBS questionnaire measures. None of the criteria for discriminant validity seemed to be satisfied to any great extent.

The statistical results shown in Table 7.10 indicate that a moderate amount of the indexed variance was attributable to both convergent validity (.31) and halo bias (.33), with the remaining proportion (.15) due to discriminant validity. In summary, these results provide moderate support for convergent validity, but less for the discriminant validity of LOS when the multiple methods are considered to be the observation system (LOS) and a directly comparable self-estimate of time-usage questionnaire.

DISCUSSION

This study provides data to begin an analysis of reliability and validity of a newly developing observation system to measure leader behavior in natural settings. Simple interrater agreement reliability was found to be quite high, but more analysis was provided. In particular, the multitrait-multimethod (MTMM) technique was used. Although there are certain limitations with the MTMM approach (for example, Kalleberg & Kluegel, 1975, have shown that the building-block correlations of the MTMM matrix are all complexly determined, and, therefore, the comparisons involved in the MTMM criteria will also be complexly determined), it was deemed to provide the most apropriate and comprehensive analysis of the LOS possible at this point of its development.

In general, the results of the MTMM analysis indicate that when multiple

Table 7.10
Components and Indices for the LOS MTMM Using Multiple Methods
(Observations and Self-Estimate Questionnaire).

Source	Variance Components	Indices
L (convergent validity)	.239	.31
L × B (discriminant validity)	.097	.15
L × S (halo)	.265	.33
Error	.540	

rater sources (self, superior, peer, and subordinate) were considered as measurement by more than one method (as widely cited MTMM analyses have done in the past, for example, Campbell & Fiske, 1959; and Lawler, 1967), the questionnaire-based LBDQ-XII and MBS measures were not demonstrated to show support for either convergent or discriminant validity. Instead, a rather substantial within-rater source halo bias existed. Raters using these questionnaire methods generally failed to discriminate among presumably independent categories. That is, a given source tended to rate the leader on all behavioral categories in much the same manner (as evidenced by high scale intercorrelations within rater source). In addition, there was little agreement (convergence) in the ratings of the leader among different rater sources. Each rater source apparently perceived the leader's behavior quite differently. This finding has important implications for the evaluation of the validity of these questionnaires and for analyzing the situational determinants of leader behavior.

With respect to the LOS, results of the MTMM analysis indicated at least moderate support for both convergent and discriminant validity when participant observers (generally subordinates) and outside observers were considered measurement by more than one method. In other words, participant and outside observers tended to agree when describing the behavior of a leader and tended to discriminate among behavioral categories.

Compared to the questionnaire methods, the LOS faired better in this analysis using multiple sources as multiple methods. Although the rater sources were somewhat different and more comprehensive for the questionnaire measures, the comparison shows that the LOS indices for both convergent and discriminant validities are greater and the halo problem smaller. This result, of course, is not convincing evidence, nor is there any intent to prove that the observation system is superior to the questionnaire methods. It must be remembered that the LOS data are based on a fixed ten-minute observation period that is common to both rater sources. The LBDQ and MBS, on the other hand, are based on an open-ended and unspecified period of time. Another problem in making direct comparisons is that both rater sources in the LOS are watching the same target leader at the same time while the LBDQ and MBS draw from pooled data representing the average leadership style (ALS) of the target leaders. Despite these and other potential problems with making direct comparisons in this study, the results can serve as a stimulus and point of departure for examining and interpreting some of the problems that questionnaires may have relative to observational methods and can help justify the effort for developing an observational system to supplement questionnaire measures.

For example, one interpretation from these comparative results would be that the leadership questionnaire measures may be susceptible to high degrees of selective recall and halo bias on the part of the raters. On the other hand, an observational system such as the LOS may be less susceptible to selective recall (i.e., the lag between observation and recorded behavior is more immediate than in questionnaires). In addition, halo bias may be minimized when well-trained participant and outside observers are used to gather leader behavior data. For these reasons alone, continued efforts toward the development and use of observational methods for measuring leader behavior seem justified.

The results from this study would also seem to indicate that any one rater source using questionnaire measures would not provide an adequate assessment of leader behavior. The typical practice of correlating subordinate questionnaire measures of leader behavior with performance ratings of leaders based on perceptions by superiors may be like comparing apples and oranges. This study clearly indicates that various rater sources filling out a questionnaire perceive the behavior of a leader quite differently. An "appropriate" rater source would seem to depend more on the criterion measure of interest. For example, if the criterion measure of interest is performance ratings by superiors, then perhaps the appropriate rater source to describe the ratee's behavior is the superior. If subordinate satisfaction is the criterion measure of interest, then perhaps the appropriate rater source is subordinate perceptions of leader behavior, and so on. This approach, however, would also run the risk that any significant results may be due to common source (rater) variance unless there was a considerable time lag between the administration of the measures.

When the MTMM analysis used the LOS (observations) and MBS and LBDQ (questionnaires) as multiple methods, the results were less encouraging for the LOS than when multiple rater sources were used as multiple methods. When consideration and initiation of structure types of factors for the LOS, LBDQ-XII, and MBS instruments were compared, results indicated: (1) a modest degree of convergence between the LOS and MBS consideration factor, but not for initiation of structure; (2) no significant convergence between the LOS and LBDQ-XII for either factor; and (3) a substantial degree of convergence between the MBS and LBDQ-XII for both factors. The latter result could be attributed to a methodological artifact (i.e., both MBS and LBDQ-XII are questionnaire methods). The evidence to support the discriminant validity of any of these instruments was very slight in this portion of the analysis. It must be remembered, however, that especially in the case of the LOS, there were not directly comparable behavioral categories with the other methods. When an analysis was made with two different methods (the LOS and the Self-Estimate of Time-Use Questionnaire) containing the same behavioral categories, then the LOS did fare better. A moderate degree of convergent validity was evidenced, but less support was shown for discriminant validity.

CONCLUSION

It should be emphasized once again that this study only provides a beginning for analyzing a newly developing observation system of measuring leader behavior in natural settings. It is not intended that the results from this study be interpreted as conclusive. Rather, the importance of this study lies in demonstrating the potential reliability and validity of a supplemental method to questionnaires for measuring leader behavior in natural settings. The high interrater agreement percentage contributes to the evaluation of the reliability of the LOS approach, and the MTMM analysis, especially when multiple rater sources are considered to be multiple methods, contributes to its reliability and validity evaluation. The MTMM analysis using observation and questionnaires as multiple methods was not as encouraging. However, without directly comparable behavioral categories across the methods, these results may not be surprising. When the questionnaire method did use directly comparable categories (the Self-Estimate of Time Usage), the results of the validity analysis were more encouraging.

An obvious need for future study would be to make a comparison between questionnaire and observation methods that have directly comparable categories. If there is demonstrated support for the validity of the widely used LBDQ or the new MBS, then the more practical and easy-to-use questionnaire method should be used as an important, but not an *only*, data-gathering technique for leadership research and application techniques. The same is true of the observation system. By using both questionnaires and observational techniques, a network of concordance among multiple methods of measurement can result. Such a multiple-methods approach seems to be the most feasible way of obtaining a reliable and valid measure of extremely complex leader behavior. As Nunnally points out, "Validity usually is a matter of degree rather than an all-or-none property, and validation is an unending process. . . . New evidence may suggest modifications of an existing measure or the development of a new and better approach to measuring the attribute in question" (1978, p. 87). This study represents but one step in this continuing effort to obtain reliable and valid measures of leader behavior.

8

The Observation of High-Performing Educational Managers: Methodological Issues and Managerial Implications*

Mark J. Martinko and William L. Gardner

This chapter describes the theoretical foundation, procedures, and methodological issues associated with a major observational study designed to identify the behaviors, attributions, and competencies of high-performing educational managers. The discussion is particularly relevant to leadership because leadership is a key aspect of educational management and the study incorporates numerous measures of leader behavior.

RELEVANT LITERATURE

Two bodies of literature are relevant to this study: the literature on management and the research on competencies focusing specifically on educational managers.

Management Research

Recent reviews of management and, in particular, leadership, have been critical, noting an almost endless variety of theories predominantly based on surveys and questionnaires with tenuous validity (Campbell, 1977; Davis & Luthans, 1979; Schriesheim & Kerr, 1977). They conclude that we know very little about what effective leaders actually do.

Perhaps the study most responsible for the current state of pessimism is Mintzberg's (1973) study. It had a major impact on the field because Mintzberg questioned the dominant approaches to managerial research, utilized an

*The research reported in this chapter was funded by the Florida Council on Educational Management.

alternative methodology, and obtained findings that directly contradicted existing theory.

Since Mintzberg's precedent-setting study, several management researchers (Davis & Luthans, 1979; Martinko & Gardner, in press; Schriesheim & Kerr, 1977) have advocated greater use of observational methods. Several observational studies have been completed recently and are particularly relevant to the present project. Larson, Bussom, and Vicars (1981) and Bussom, Larson, Vicars, and Ness (1981) investigated the work activities of school superintendents and police executives, respectively. While generally confirming Mintzberg's work, the authors of both studies concluded that the work of public managers often differs markedly from that of business managers.

Another work that is relevant to the present investigation is reported by Morris, Crowson, Hurwitz, and Porter-Gehrie (1981). These researchers used an ethnographic approach to observe and record the behavior of 16 urban school principals. In addition to providing qualitative descriptions of managerial behavior, these authors also used Mintzberg's roles to analyze their subjects' behavior. Their conclusion was that the Mintzberg methodology was inadequate for describing the behavior of educational managers. Like Larson et al. (1981), they suggested that there were considerable differences in the behaviors of educational as opposed to business managers.

As a group, the major limitation of the Larson et al. (1981), Bussom et al. (1981), Mintzberg (1973), and Morris et al. (1981) studies is that they did not differentiate between the levels of performance of the managers they observed. It is therefore difficult to discern from their results which behaviors, if any, are related to effectiveness.

Despite limitations, the above group of studies provides the foundation for developing a methodology that can help identify differences in the behaviors of high versus moderate performing educational managers. Because of the differences found between educational, public, and business managers, however, it does not appear that the results of prior managerial studies generalize well across situational contexts. A study of educational managers is therefore warranted.

The Competency Literature

A comprehensive review of the competency literature considering more than 350 studies was conducted by Lake (1981). The majority of these studies (almost 86 percent) were classified as "competency list" studies (e.g., Mangers, 1979; Payne, Ellett, Perkins, Klein, & Shellenberger, 1975; Sause, 1974). That is, through an iterative process, the researchers develop lists of behaviors potentially related to high performance. The "key" competencies are then identified through a judgment process using a group of "experts" such as school principals, educators, academicians, and superintendents. The judgment processes used often include consensus, nominal, and/or delphi group methods.

As Lake points out, there are substantive weaknesses in these "list" approaches. First, none of these studies adequately differentiates between the competencies of effective versus ineffective performers. The majority of the studies utilize mixed groups including principals with wide ranges of performance and other judges who are not school principals. As a result, there is no assurance or basis for concluding that this process yields competencies related to effectiveness.

A second problem, related to the first, is the perceptual nature of the data generated in the "competency list" studies. Aggregate *opinions* regarding behaviors are not necessarily valid indicators of competencies.

The inability to account for environmental effects, such as urban versus rural settings, is another problem. Moreover, the practice of aggregating opinions and judgments of persons from a variety of environments makes it increasingly unlikely that valid competency data are obtained.

Perhaps the most serious problem is the restrictive notion of competencies that has developed. This problem is manifested in two ways. First, because of the perceptual nature of the data and the nature of the groups from which the data are collected, the competency lists characteristically reflect surface-level perceptions. They do not reflect more complex operations described in the educational and management literature such as attributional processes (e.g., Green & Mitchell, 1979; Weiner *et al.,* 1971). Thus, many relatively powerful predictions from attribution theory are not reflected in the competency literature.

A second and perhaps more critical problem arises from the restrictive connotation of the term "competency." As used in the literature, a competency is a skill, ability, or cognitive schemata used to accomplish a task. There is nothing wrong with this definition except that, in practice, both researchers and practitioners have been using it in isolation from other important variables in the performance environment. More specifically, similar to the old trait approach to leadership, the notion has developed that competencies, in isolation, may be able to differentiate effective and ineffective performers. Thus, most of the competency list studies, like the old trait leadership studies, ask the subjects to identify the characteristics of effective managers without considering the environment. It seems much more realistic to view performance as a complex interaction in which the environment and competencies interact and thereby result in behavior that influences the outcome of teacher and student performance. A development of this nature in the competency literature would parallel the evolution of leadership theory in the management area progressing from unidimensional trait approaches to multivariate contingency models that incorporate the environment (e.g., Fiedler, 1967; House & Mitchell, 1974).

An Integrative Model

In order to guide our research, and in recognition of the weaknesses of prior competency and management research, a social-learning theory model of an educational manager's work motivation is presented in Figure 8.1. While the application of this model to educational managers is original, similar models have recently been developed to explain human motivation in general (Bandura, 1977), and leader behavior (Davis & Luthans, 1980a).

Essentially, the model indicates that the changing external environment and the specific school environment are major determinants of the behaviors that generate effective school performance. The model suggests that the principal processes environmental stimuli, makes decisions regarding the causes of desired performance outcomes (causal attributions), and then behaves in a manner that he or she believes will be effective. The model emphasizes the importance of the environment, cognitive processes, and the interactive nature of behavior.

If it is assumed that social-learning theory is a valid model of managerial behavior, a number of serious issues and implications regarding current approaches to observational studies become apparent.

1. *The Environment.* As the external environment changes, behaviors required for effective management change. Stated another way, there is a contingent relationship between the environment and effective managerial behavior. *Implication*: Observational studies need to take particular care in documenting the environment.

2. *The Specific Environment.* The effective behaviors required in some specific environments will be different from those required in others. For example, there are likely to be differences in the effective behaviors required in large versus small, urban versus rural, and closed versus open school en-

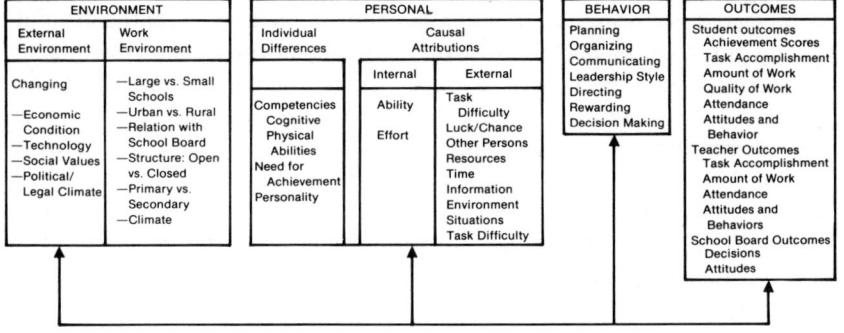

FIGURE 8.1. Social-Learning Theory Model of Managerial Work Motivation

vironments. *Implications*: Observational studies need to control for the specific environment through either randomization or stratification. Valid studies in both situations require large sample sizes.

3. *The Person.* Simply observing and documenting behaviors may not provide data that are adequate to differentiate between effective and ineffective performers. Causal attributions and beliefs about performance mediate the manager's behavior. It is not at all difficult to imagine a scenario of two managers behaving in a similar way for different reasons and having markedly different impacts on performance outcomes. *Implication*: Adequate methods of classifying verbal behavior and obtaining data regarding covert decisional processes in field environments need to be developed and incorporated into observational field studies.

4. *Performance Outcomes.* An important element of the social-learning theory model is the impact of the behavior on performance outcomes. Unless outcomes are observed and related to behavior, inferences regarding appropriate and effective behavior will be exceedingly difficult. *Implication*: Researchers must use performance as either an independent or dependent variable in order to make valid inferences regarding effective managerial behavior.

The following sections describe the methodology and methodological issues relating to an observational study of educational managers based on the social-learning theory model described above.

METHODS

Sample Selection

A complete description of the process of identifying the high and moderate performing principals appears in Lake and Martinko (1982) so only a brief summary is presented here. Five criteria were used. They were: (1) actual versus predicted performance on minimal competency exams; (2) the absolute ranking of the school performance on nationally normed achievement tests; (3) superintendents' ranking of schools; (4) superintendents' ranking of principals; and (5) a requirement of at least two years' tenure.

As discussions of organizational effectiveness indicate (Cummings & Schwab, 1973; Schwab & Cummings, 1973), there are rarely univariate indexes of organizational performance. In most situations, decisions regarding organizational effectiveness are multivariate and satisficing. Similarly, there is no univariate and universally accepted criterion for evaluating the performance of educational managers. The criteria used above represent several different perspectives. Although it may be possible to argue against the use of any single criterion as the standard for identifying the sample, it seems reasonably safe to conclude that the use of all five criteria reliably and validly differentiates between high and moderate performers. In addition to the above, care was taken to ensure that the sample was representative of the total population in terms of geographical location, mixture of primary and secondary schools, and the mixture of urban versus rural schools. The sample includes principals from 28 primary schools, 12 middle schools, and 10 high schools with equal proportions of high and moderate performers. These schools represent 10 of 22 districts and are geographically dispersed throughout the state.

Observers

The observers are 23 doctoral students and 2 professors at 5 major universities in the state of Florida. All attended a two-day workshop on observational methods and are observing two principals, one high and one moderate performer, for nine randomly assigned days during a twelve-month period. In order to avoid bias, the observers have been told that they may have been assigned two high performers, two moderate performers, or a high and a moderate performer.

The Observation Methodology

There were a number of important considerations in designing the observational procedure. First, for the results to be interpreted meaningfully, the methodology needed to be comparable to that of other studies. The observational methodologies of Morris *et al.* (1981), Luthans and Lockwood (in press), and Larson *et al.* (1981) were all incorporated into the present study.

Second, there needed to be a delicate balance between obtrusive and unobtrusive data-collection procedures (Crano & Brewer, 1973; Downey & Ireland, 1979; Miles, 1979; Weick, 1968).

The third major consideration was the balance between qualitative and quantitative research methods. Rather than viewing these approaches as competing, the triangulation strategy recommended by Jick (1979) was employed.

Observation Procedure

The data-collection method is direct, nonparticipant observation. The data-collection instrument, the Field Note Coding Form (FNCF), is illustrated in Figure 8.2. Comprehensive instructions for completing the FNCF are provided in Martinko and Gardner (1981), so only a brief summary is presented here.

The most important column on the FNCF is the "Description/Explanation of Event" column, which is used to develop a detailed narrative description of managerial behavior. As this column is being completed, the observers

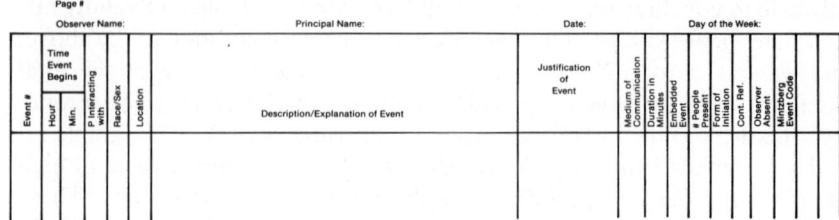

FIGURE 8.2. Field note coding form

are required to record the information in the left-hand columns indicating the beginning and ending of events, time, the person(s) with whom the principal is interacting, the race and sex of people in the event, and the location.

The right-hand columns are completed after the field visit and indicate the medium of communication, duration, whether or not the event took place within the context of another event, the number of persons present, the person initiating the event, whether the observer was present, and the classification of the event according to Mintzberg's (1973) event code. The "Justification of Event" column is completed either in the field or during the process of organizing the field notes. In this column the observers are instructed to record verbal statements indicative of the managers' attributions regarding performance causation.

In addition to the observer coding process, several other coding procedures have been developed and are coded after the observers complete their processes. These procedures include codes for Mintzberg's (1973) purpose of contact, Mintzberg's (1973) roles, the Luthans and Lockwood (in press) Leader Observation System (LOS), and a Principal Competency Index (PCI).

Finally, as suggested by Barker's (1963) notion of the stream of behavior, several other coding processes are developing as the study continues. In order to facilitate their development, periodic site meetings, marginal codes on protocols, and the process of memoing as suggested by Glaser (1978) and Glaser and Strauss (1967, 1970) have been implemented.

Collateral Measurement Processes

In order to achieve triangulation (Jick, 1979), other measurement procedures are being employed such as interviews, a system for monitoring mail, and indexes of managerial behavior, leadership style, and organizational climate. These measures will support the results of the observations and provide a more complete description of the differences between the high and moderate performers.

Observer Training

The observer training process consisted of a two-day program. After the introductory remarks, the participants were immediately immersed in the observation process and asked to record, without guidelines, behaviors observed in a three-minute videotape simulating principal behaviors. They were then asked to describe their observations and frequently included a variety of value judgments. Disagreements regarding appropriate data recording inevitably occurred among the participants. A list of observation errors (Campbell, 1958; Thornton & Zorich, 1980; Weick, 1968) was then provided and discussed. The majority of the remainder of the training (approximately ten hours) consisted of learning the behavior observation process (Martinko & Gardner, 1981) by observing, recording, and receiving feedback regarding videotaped simulations of principal behavior developed for the program.

A reliability check was conducted on the second day. Two videotaped role plays were viewed by the observers. During this segment there were 12 events and 24,661 different coding possibilities. The observers selected the standardized code identified by the investigators 91.9 percent of the time.

Percentage of agreement between the observers and the standardized code was also calculated for each column of the FNCF. Particularly significant is the fact that 96 percent of the events identified by the trainees corresponded to those identified by the investigators. The percentage of agreement for the remaining columns ranged from a low of 81.7 for Mintzberg's event code column to a high of 100 percent for the column indicating the presence or absence of the observer.

As observations continue, observers attend periodic site meetings in order to resolve data-coding problems and discuss behaviors related to high performance.

Reliability Checks

In order to ensure that the field data are reliable, several checks have been incorporated into the design as suggested by Mitchell (1979). Descriptions of each of these reliability checks are summarized in Table 8.1.

RESULTS

The data presented here represent one day of observation for 14 high and seven moderate performing managers. More than 2,200 events are included in this analysis. The final data base will include approximately 25 high and 25 moderate performers, 400 days of observation, and almost 40,000 events.

At this point, conclusions based on the data are tentative. The major pur-

Table 8.1. Reliability Checks.

INTEROBSERVER AGREEMENT	Check #1: Participants of the training program view role plays and films and code their observations using the data coding form. The "correct" coding of the activities determined by the researchers is employed as a standard against which the observers' code is compared. The average agreement percentage is calculated. Check #2: All observers have a second observer spend at least one day with them observing a principal. The interobserver agreement percentage is calculated from the field notes of the two observers.
INTRASCORER RELIABILITY	Each observer codes several field notes more than once and an estimate of intrascorer reliability is obtained. By averaging across observers, the mean intrascorer reliability is calculated.
INTERSCORER RELIABILITY	The researchers randomly select and code 30 sets of field notes. From the researchers' and observers' coding of the same field notes the interscorer reliability is calculated.
SPLIT-HALF RELIABILITY	The events recorded by observers are numbered and divided into even and odd numbered groups. Split-half reliability is calculated.
TEST-RETEST RELIABILITY	Each day of observation is numbered and divided into even and odd numbered groups. Test-retest reliability is then calculated.
G STUDY	The data collected during observation are indexed by observer, subject, type of school, observation category, day, and performance level of the principal. The observation category frequency scores are the dependent variables and are entered into a multi-factor matrix as indexed. Multivariate analysis of variance (MANOVA) is performed on the data to determine the proportion of variance contributed by each factor.

pose of this section is to demonstrate the nature and quality of the data obtained in this and similar studies. These results then serve as a foundation for the discussion of methodological issues which follows.

Comparative Analysis

Although there are a considerable number of studies of managerial behavior (e.g., Carlson, 1951; Kotter, 1982; Stewart, 1967, 1976), the methodologies often differ markedly so that direct comparisons are not warranted. Thus, in this section, only studies that used similar structured observation methodologies are considered as standards for comparison.

Similarities. The results of this study are supportive of other prior research employing structured observation procedures. Mintzberg (1973) found that managerial activities ranged from 86 to 160 events per day and more than half had a duration of less than 9 minutes. The managers in this study have a range of 80 to 200 events per day with a mean of 5.0 minutes. Like Mintzberg's managers who spent 92 percent of their contact time in verbal face-to-face exchanges, these managers also spent a majority of their contact time, 80 percent, in verbal face-to-face interactions. Another similarity is that the managers in this study, as in the others (Bussom *et al.*, 1981; Larson *et al.*, 1981; Mintzberg, 1973), spent about half of their time working with subordinates. There was also comparability in the amount of time spent at desk work by the managers in this study, 17.0 percent, as compared to the range of 15 to 30 percent found in prior studies (Bussom *et al.*, 1981; Kurke & Aldrich, 1979; Larson *et al.*, 1981; Mintzberg, 1973). Finally, the managers in this sample spent about 6 percent of their time on the telephone fitting within the range of 6 to 11 percent indicated by other studies (Bussom *et al.*, 1981; Kurke & Aldrich, 1979; Larson *et al.*, 1981; Mintzberg, 1973).

Differences. While the above findings are generally consistent with those of prior studies, other findings suggest differences. Mintzberg (1973) found that managers spend 59 percent of their time in scheduled meetings and 10 percent in unscheduled meetings. Morris *et al.* (1981), on the other hand, found that principals spend only 3 percent of their contact time in scheduled meetings and 75 percent in unscheduled meetings. The current study indicated that principals spend 18.0 and 26.3 percent of their contact time in scheduled and unscheduled meetings, respectively. In addition, both Morris *et al.* (1981) and this study found that principals spend about 15 percent of their time on tours while Mintzberg's managers spent only 3 percent of their time touring. Thus, the principal's job appears to be less structured and more spontaneous than that of a chief executive.

Performance Contrasts

The purpose of this section is to demonstrate the nature and the power of the methodology in contrasting the behaviors of high and moderate performers. Because of the almost limitless number of possible contrasts, only a small proportion of the data is presented here.

The results from one important variable, the nature of the persons with whom the principal interacts, are summarized in Table 8.2. Although these data reveal few differences in these gross measures of activity, cross-tabulations of these data with other variables yields interesting contrasts. For the purpose of illustration, the results of the cross-tabulations for two interactions, students and teachers, with other variables are described below.

A cross-tabulation of performance level with medium of communication for students and teachers (Table 8.3) indicated that both high and moderate performers prefer verbal face-to-face contacts. It also appears, however, that high performers have a greater diversity of media in communication.

When form of contact initiation is cross-tabulated with performance level for interactions with students and teachers (Table 8.4), few differences are apparent with respect to contacts with students. However, there appear to be differences for interactions with teachers. More specifically, high performers in this sample initiated a greater proportion of contacts with teachers than did moderate performers.

Mintzberg's (1973) event code is broken down by performance level for contacts with teachers in Table 8.5. Again, although differences cannot be tested at this time, it does appear that high performers spend relatively less time in scheduled meetings and more time in unscheduled meetings with teachers than do modeate performers.

Perhaps the most interesting difference in the behavior of high versus moderate performers concerns the cross-tabulation of performance level and leadership style (Table 8.6). The data from this sample suggest that high performers utilize a task-oriented style when interacting with students and teachers more often than the moderate performers.

Finally, it is appropriate to mention again that the sample size is still small and that the differences between the high and moderate performers have not been tested with inferential statistics. Some of the differences described may be a function of chance. Nonetheless, even at this stage the data suggest many interesting differences and the potential power of the methodology. It also should be noted that analyses similar to that displayed above can be performed for each of the positions in Table 8.1. In addition, each of the other variables can be cross-tabulated with one another. For example, managerial roles can be cross-tabulated with Mintzberg's event code to assess the interrelationships between managerial roles and managerial behavior.

Table 8.2. Principal Interacting With Other Parties.

PRINCIPAL INTERACTING WITH	HIGH (N=14)			MODERATE (N=7)			TOTAL (N=21)		
	% of contacts	% of total contact time	Mean duration of contacts (in minutes)	% of contacts	% of total contact time	Mean duration of contacts (in minutes)	% of contact	% of total contact time	Mean duration of contacts (in minutes)
Assist. Principal	6.1	9.2	5.8	2.3	.9	1.8	5.0	6.5	5.3
Secretary and Clerical Staff	20.0	8.3	1.6	17.8	7.6	2.0	19.4	8.1	1.7
Faculty	16.7	13.1	3.0	15.0	14.5	4.6	16.4	13.5	3.4
Students	10.5	7.1	2.5	15.1	8.3	2.6	11.8	7.5	2.6
Parents	2.3	1.9	3.1	3.8	8.9	11.0	2.7	4.1	6.2
Outsiders	4.3	5.7	5.0	2.9	2.1	3.6	4.0	4.6	4.7
Peers	1.1	3.2	11.0	.6	3.8	31.3	1.0	3.4	14.4
Maintenance and Support Staff	3.9	2.5	2.4	2.6	2.0	3.8	3.5	2.3	2.7
Professional Staff	3.1	3.1	3.7	2.9	1.9	3.2	3.0	2.7	3.6
External Admin. Staff	1.2	2.4	7.9	1.9	1.3	4.1	1.4	2.1	6.6
Temporary Inst. Staff	.8	1.1	5.5	.6	.3	2.2	.7	.8	4.8
Mixed Group of People	10.7	26.9	9.6	10.6	28.3	12.8	10.6	27.3	10.5
Observer	9.9	9.7	3.8	14.8	12.2	4.0	11.2	10.6	3.8
Unknown	8.4	4.8	2.2	7.9	6.8	4.1	8.2	5.5	2.7
Other	1.0	1.0	3.6	1.2	1.0	4.1	1.1	1.0	3.8
TOTAL	100.0	100.0	3.8	100.0	100.0	4.8	100.0	100.0	4.1

Table 8.3. Medium of Communication.

	STUDENTS							
	HIGH				MODERATE			
MEDIUM OF COMMUNI-CATION	% of contacts	% of total contact time	Contact duration (min)		% of contacts	% of total contact time	Contact duration (min)	
			Mean	Std Dev			Mean	Std Dev
Verbal Face-to-Face	95.1	95.9	2.6	4.3	100.0	100.0	2.6	3.6
Written	0.0	0.0	0.0	0.0	0.0	0.0	0.0	0.0
Visual	2.8	1.5	1.4	1.3	0.0	0.0	0.0	0.0
Verbal Telephone	.7	.6	2.0	0.0	0.0	0.0	0.0	0.0
Verbal Intercom	.7	1.9	7.0	0.0	0.0	0.0	0.0	0.0
Other	.7	.1	.3	0.0	0.0	0.0	0.0	0.0
TOTAL	100.0	100.0	2.5	4.2	100.0	100.0	2.6	3.6

Table 8.4. Form of Contact Initiation.

	STUDENTS							
	HIGH				MODERATE			
FORM OF CONTACT INITIATION	% of contacts	% of total contact time	Contact duration (min)		% of contacts	% of total contact time	Contact duration (min)	
			Mean	Std Dev			Mean	Std Dev
Principal	63.8	65.9	2.6	4.4	54.5	60.5	2.9	4.4
Mutual	4.2	2.6	1.6	3.1	1.3	2.5	5.0	0.0
Opposite	31.3	27.1	2.2	3.5	41.6	30.1	1.9	2.4
Clock	0.0	0.0	0.0	0.0	2.6	6.9	7.0	1.4
Unknown	.7	4.4	16.0	0.0	0.0	0.0	0.0	0.0
TOTAL	100.0	100.0	2.5	4.2	100.0	100.0	2.6	3.6

Table 8.3. *(continued)*

TEACHERS

	HIGH				MODERATE		
		Contact dura-tion (min)				Contact dura-tion (min)	
% of contacts	% of total contact time	Mean	Std Dev	% of contacts	% of total contact time	Mean	Std Dev
89.8	88.4	3.◌	4.6	93.1	95.3	4.6	7.3
2.9	1.7	1.8	1.4	1.4	3.9	13.0	0.0
1.9	7.6	12.0	11.4	0.0	0.0	0.0	0.0
3.9	2.1	1.6	1.5	1.4	.1	.3	0.0
1.0	.2	.7	.5	4.1	.7	.8	.4
.5	.1	.3	0.0	0.0	0.0	0.0	0.0
100.0	100.0	3.1	4.8	100.0	100.0	4.7	7.2

Table 8.4. *(continued)*

TEACHERS

	HIGH				MODERATE		
		Contact dura-tion (min)				Contact dura-tion (min)	
% of contacts	% of total contact time	Mean	Std Dev	% of contacts	% of total contact time	Mean	Std Dev
46.8	40.8	2.6	3.8	36.8	33.1	4.2	6.2
6.8	4.5	2.0	2.0	2.6	1.7	3.0	2.8
43.9	39.9	2.8	2.8	48.8	27.1	2.6	4.2
1.5	14.0	29.0	14.2	10.5	37.3	16.5	11.6
1.0	.8	5.0	0.0	1.3	.8	3.0	0.0
100.0	100.0	3.1	4.8	100.0	100.0	4.7	7.2

Table 8.5. Mintzberg Event Code.

STUDENTS

MINTZBERG EVENT CODE	HIGH				MODERATE			
			Contact duration (min)				Contact duration (min)	
	% of contacts	% of total contact time	Mean	Std Dev	% of contacts	% of total contact time	Mean	Std Dev
Tours	2.1	3.6	4.3	2.5	0.0	0.0	0.0	0.0
Scheduled Meetings	0.0	0.0	0.0	0.0	3.8	11.6	8.0	2.0
Unscheduled Meetings	93.8	91.8	2.5	4.3	96.2	88.4	2.4	3.5
Telephone Calls	.7	.5	2.0	0.0	0.0	0.0	0.0	0.0
Desk Work	1.4	2.5	4.5	4.9	0.0	0.0	0.0	0.0
Travel	1.4	.8	1.5	.7	0.0	0.0	0.0	0.0
Personnel	0.0	0.0	0.0	0.0	0.0	0.0	0.0	0.0
Other	.7	.8	3.0	0.0	0.0	0.0	0.0	0.0
Unknown	0.0	0.0	0.0	0.0	0.0	0.0	0.0	0.0
TOTAL	100.0	100.0	2.5	4.2	100.0	100.0	2.6	3.6

Table 8.6. Leadership Style.

STUDENTS

LEADERSHIP STYLE	HIGH				MODERATE			
			Contact duration (min)				Contact duration (min)	
	% of contacts	% of total contact time	Mean	Std Dev	% of contacts	% of total contact time	Mean	Std Dev
Task Oriented	65.6	60.1	2.4	4.1	50.7	47.4	2.4	3.4
Human-Relations Oriented	29.9	30.7	3.5	5.0	47.9	51.0	2.8	4.1
Unknown	4.5	1.2	.7	.7	1.4	1.6	3.0	0.0
TOTAL	100.0	100.0	2.5	4.2	100.0	100.0	2.6	3.6

Table 8.5. *(continued)*

TEACHERS

	HIGH				MODERATE		
		Contact duration (min)				Contact duration (min)	
% of contacts	% of total contact time	Mean	Std Dev	% of contacts	% of total contact time	Mean	Std Dev
1.9	6.2	9.8	12.9	1.3	.6	2.0	0.0
4.4	17.8	12.5	14.5	10.5	37.3	16.5	11.6
80.5	66.8	2.6	2.8	80.4	52.1	3.0	4.8
2.9	1.5	1.6	1.1	1.3	.1	.3	0.0
7.3	3.4	1.4	1.3	3.9	9.0	10.7	8.7
0.0	0.0	0.0	0.0	0.0	0.0	.3	0.0
.5	.5	2.0	0.0	1.3	.1	.3	0.0
1.0	1.6	5.0	1.4	0.0	0.0	0.0	0.0
1.5	2.2	7.0	2.8	1.3	.8	3.0	0.0
100.0	100.0	3.1	4.8	100.0	100.0	4.7	7.2

Table 8.6. *(continued)*

TEACHERS

	HIGH				MODERATE		
		Contact duration (min)				Contact duration (min)	
% of contacts	% of total contact time	Mean	Std Dev	% of contacts	% of total contact time	Mean	Std Dev
68.7	68.6	3.2	5.1	44.9	41.9	3.5	4.0
28.6	30.9	3.4	5.0	53.1	49.3	5.0	7.5
2.7	.5	.7	.8	2.0	8.8	7.7	9.1
100.0	100.0	3.1	4.8	100.0	100.0	4.7	7.0

DISCUSSION

It is premature at this point to state definitive conclusions based on the data. It is appropriate, however, to discuss the methodological issues, problems, and contributions of this and similar observational studies.

Inferring Competencies from Behaviors

A critical concern regarding this and prior observational studies is that differences in the behaviors of high and moderate performers may not be detected. There are several reasons for this concern. First, the extensive prior research on trait theories of leadership generally suggests that there are few important traits that reliably distinguish effective managers (e.g., Luthans, 1981). Second, with notable exceptions (e.g., Fiedler, 1967; Likert, 1967), leader effectiveness has only been infrequently used as an independent or dependent variable in *field studies* of leadership. Thus, with the exception of a few early studies (e.g., Guest, 1956; Jasinski, 1956; Likert, 1950; O'Neill & Kubany, 1959; Ponder, 1958), there is little a priori guidance from field work indicating where to look for behavioral differences in effective versus ineffective managers. Third, when performance and/or effectiveness have been used as dependent variables, it has frequently been concluded that the relationship between behavior and performance is contingent upon leadership style and environmental considerations (e.g., Fiedler, 1967; House & Mitchell, 1974). While the environmental characteristics and leader styles from these models can be manipulated in laboratory environments, it is difficult to control or assess their effects in field settings. Thus, in observational field studies, it is entirely possible that environmental differences will "wash out" significant behavioral differences even with large sample sizes.

Finally, a rather substantial body of research on managerial behavior (Stewart, 1976, in press; Stewart, Smith, Blake, & Wingate, 1980) indicates that there is not only great variability between the behaviors of managers in the same position but also that the behavior of individual managers varies greatly over time. If this variation within managerial behaviors is as great as Stewart and her colleagues suggest, it would be extremely difficult to detect consistent differences between samples of high and moderate performers.

Coding Issues

A second issue of concern, closely related to the first, is the inadequacy and/or lack of coding methodologies. These problems fall into two major categories. First is the problem of coding behavior so that it is described accurately and is comparable with prior research. For example, in Mintzberg's event code, interactions with secretaries are coded as Desk Work (DW), but experience suggests that these interactions are extremely important. In this case, our decision has been to maintain the integrity of the Mintzberg system so that the data remain comparable. Another example concerns the Mintzberg (1973), Larson *et al* (1981), and Morris *et al.* (1981) event codes which define all events as mutually exclusive. Thus, if a principal engages in an informal meeting with a teacher during a tour, these systems require that the event be classified as either a tour or an unscheduled meeting, but not both. In this study, the event classification system is revised so that time spent talking is coded as part of a tour but also as an unscheduled meeting within the tour, that is, as an embedded event. If it is desired, embedded events can be pulled out of the data so that the data are comparable with those of the other studies. However, the data indicate that managers are frequently engaged in embedded events and thus, our system provides a more accurate representation of managerial behavior.

Another example of the dilemma and conflict between comparability and accurate reflection of behavior are the Mintzberg (1973) "Purpose of Contact" and "Managerial Role" codes and the LOS code developed by Luthans and Lockwood in Chapter 7 of this volume. Experience at coding indicates that the categories from these schemes are not mutually exclusive; thus, we have changed our coding processes to reflect the "real world" more accurately by recording multiple purposes of contact, roles, and LOS indicators using the SPSS MULT RESPONSE program (Hull & Nie, 1981). It is important to make these changes so that methodological progress continues. However, there must remain a balance between comparability and the need for accurate description.

A second major concern is the current level of sophistication of coding procedures. The differences between highly and moderately effective managers may be more subtle than expected. For example, there may be no difference in the amount of time that highly and moderately effective managers spend in scheduled and unscheduled meetings. Yet, a more sophisticated level of analysis regarding specific behaviors exhibited during meetings may reveal significant differences.

Three methodological processes have been incorporated to address the problem described above. First, sophisticated cross-tabular analyses as illustrated in the results have been developed to examine the full complexity of the interrelationships in the data. Second, particular attention has been given to the protocol via the "Description/Explanation of Event" column of the FNCF. In this way, we can go back through the data and code any behaviors that are later found to be relevant. Third, attention has been given to Barker's (1963) notion of the "stream of behavior." As the study continues, the observers are generating hypotheses regarding key behaviors. This process has been formalized using Glaser's (1978) notion of memoing as hypotheses develop and qualitative descriptions of behavior are evolving into coding procedures. Thus, we are beginning to bridge the qualitative/quantitative gap (Behling, 1980a; Davis & Luthans, 1981) by evolving qualitative observations into quantitative coding procedures. In many respects, this process goes beyond Jick's (1979) notion of triangulation. In addition to validating hypotheses through multiple measures, quantitative methods are evolving from a qualitative foundation.

A third approach adopted is the development of a coding system to classify verbal behaviors according to attributions. The rationale for this approach, based on attribution theory, is that attributions and causal inferences regarding the environment are important determinants of principal behaviors. It is interesting to note that after his observational work, Mintzberg (1976) became very interested in cognitive processes and style but never really developed a method for coding these data. The development of a system for classifying verbal behaviors according to attributions is proving difficult. The majority of the research performed in this area has been conducted in laboratory settings and the classification schemes used in these studies are not readily applicable. For example, it is very difficult to determine whether an attribution is made to internal or external dimensions. A manager who believes that he is controlling the environment is making an internal rather than an external attribution. Yet, environmental attributions are normally considered external attributions in laboratory studies. In summary, the attributional dimensions suggested in the literature (e.g., Green & Mitchell, 1979; Kelley, 1972; Weiner *et al.*, 1971) are extremely difficult to operationalize in field settings.

Qualitative versus Quantitative

The above discussion has already highlighted many of the salient issues regarding the dilemmas of qualitative versus quantitative research. However, some additional emphasis regarding the necessity of the qualitative data collection and analysis process is warranted. As the study is progressing, we are becoming increasingly aware of the need to develop better methods for collecting and processing the qualitative impressions of the observers. As suggested above, both the state of the art regarding observational studies and the present systems of classifying data appear primitive. As the study is progressing we are becoming increasingly aware of the need to develop better methods for processing the qualitative impressions of the observers. Moving from a quantitative to a more qualitative emphasis, of course, has risks. These risks have been minimized by requiring that reflections, value judgments, and hypotheses be separated from the data in parentheses, and by making sure that these reflections are processed after rather than during the data collection. It is also important, however, to note that we are now encouraging rather than discouraging these processes. We have consciously made the decision that the bias that enters into the process through encouraging qualitative analysis and processing of the data is more than offset by the quality of the hypotheses developed.

Reliability and Validity

A few words concerning reliability and validity are also warranted. Up to this point, with one exception (Luthans & Lockwood, Chapter 7, this volume), the major recent observational studies have not included reliability checks (e.g., Larson et al., 1981; Mintzberg, 1973; Morris et al., 1981). As mentioned above, this study incorporates numerous intrarater reliability checks as well as the G study suggested by Mitchell (1979; see Table 8.1). However, even with all of these checks, there are other threats to reliability that have not been discussed in the literature. The data from all of these studies go through several transformations: field notes, final preparation of field notes, coding by research teams, and keypunching. There are possibilities for loss of information in each of these processes.

There is also the problem of measuring reliabilities. On a categorization system such as Mintzberg's (1973) event code, which employs ten different categories, some researchers have calculated reliability extremely liberally by assuming that the observer makes ten independent decisions. Thus, when observers are in agreement regarding the classification, there are ten specific points of agreement: one regarding the classification that is most appropriate and nine regarding those that are inappropriate. Even when they do not agree on the appropriate classification, there are still eight points of agreement regarding the inappropriate classifications. On the other end of the continuum, reliability measures can be extremely conservative. For example, in our study, the observers must have identified the same category as the standard to be scored as having responded correctly.

These discrepancies in reliability-checking procedures have several potential dangers. First is the danger that researchers can artificially inflate reliabilities by using large numbers of classifications with the liberal rating systems described above. The second, and perhaps most serious danger, is that researchers will become sidetracked by arguments concerning reliabilities. Observational systems that artificially inflate reliability might then be used at the expense of systems that reflect behavior more accurately. As a result, the development of more valid observational systems may become retarded. Given the present state of the art, it would seem important to concentrate on systems that accurately reflect behavior rather than becoming overly concerned with the reliability of systems that may have questionable validity. Thus, studies with a decidedly qualitative emphasis are recommended until valid quantitative observational processes evolve.

CONCLUSIONS

This last section has summarized the problems and issues that have been most salient during the development and implementation of the study. There are certainly many more issues and those described could be discussed in considerably more detail.

In summary, our most serious concern, which relates to all of the issues raised, is whether or not observation studies of management, and this study in particular, will be able adequately to identify behaviors related to effective managerial performance. The present study is unique in that performance levels of the managers have been adequately differentiated and the sample size is large enough to identify significant differences if they exist. Despite these features, current observational methodologies may not be sensitive enough to detect differences. We have therefore moved decidedly toward a more qualitative approach to enable us to provide a valid description of the behaviors observed and to develop more valid classification schemes. While reliability is an extremely important consideration in detecting differences between the high and moderate performing managers, validity is our major concern. It is of little consequence if we can reliably observe behaviors that are not related to performance.

9

An Experiential Approach to Understanding Managerial Action

John G. Burgoyne and Vivien E. Hodgson

This chapter is concerned with the appropriateness and potential of a particular approach to research on managerial action, given the current state of theoretical and methodological development of this field. While we have developed and are using the approach to study managerial action, we feel it also has considerable potential for leadership research.

In taking the approach in question we have assumed that human, and therefore managerial, activity is intentional and meaningful and that human beings contribute as well as respond to the social world. The approach therefore attempts to focus upon the managers' world (as experienced by managers) rather than upon managers themselves.

In essence, the approach has its expression, in particular, in the methodologies of "Protocol Analysis" and "Stimulated Recall." Protocol analysis can be loosely described as recording individuals "articulating their stream of consciousness," their thoughts, feelings, and emotions while they actually go about the activity being studied. Stimulated recall, on the other hand, involves playing back the recorded protocol to the individuals and asking them to describe more fully the thoughts, ideas, and emotions that either were going through their mind or of which they were in some way aware at the time or during the particular activity. Thus, stimulated recall allows a person to describe more fully his or her experience at the time of activity and also the reasons and purposes for acting as he or she did.

This chapter is based on a pilot study carried out specifically to explore the potential for this research approach.*

The chapter is structured as follows:

1. The study of managerial action and leadership research: the questions that now need to be addressed and their implications for methodology.

*This was carried out with the support of a grant from the Social Science Research Council, U.K., and is a project entitled: An Investigation of the Generative Process Underlying Managerial Behaviour. Further work is in progress to systematize the methodologies, as a basis for a program of research on substantive questions using the approach.

2. Philosophical considerations: ontological and epistemological positions underlying research approaches, and those that can inhibit and facilitate progress in this field of knowledge.
3. Methodologies available for the study of managerial behavior and leadership processes in comparison with the proposed approach.
4. Research approaches and designs within which the approach can be used.
5. Specific theoretical issues on which the methodology can shed light.
6. Examples of data and how they can be interpreted in relation to the various theoretical issues.
7. Practical, technical, and methodological conclusions for the methodology development study.
8. General conclusions.

MANAGERIAL ACTION AND LEADERSHIP RESEARCH: EMERGING QUESTIONS

The historical development of research on managerial behavior can be roughly described using the following three categories:

1. The *pre-empirical studies,* based on general experience and theoretical speculation, for example, Sloan (1963). This can also be seen as the predominant mode of the early management/organization theorists such as Fayol (1949) and Urwick (e.g., Urwick & Brech, 1957), and the tradition that is continued today by Drucker (1955), who, although viewed somewhat critically by many academic researchers, continues to generate insights and interpretations that practicing managers find meaningful.
2. The *"media" studies,* typified by the earlier work of Stewart (1967), which looked at managerial behavior empirically, and primarily in terms of the medium through which they were working, such as formal and informal meetings, paperwork, telephone conversations, and tours of inspection. Such studies have shown, with a high degree of consistency, a number of important features of managerial work: its fragmented nature, constant change between many short activities, and a high degree of human interaction. Attempts within these kinds of studies to describe what the activities within the medium were about have been more difficult. The problem stems from the need to have some a priori classificatory framework to describe the work, which then limits the conclusions.
3. *Content studies,* a category that is arguably exclusively occupied by the work of Mintzberg (1973) and Stewart (1976). On the basis of detailed observation and data collection from a small number of managers over several weeks, Mintzberg proposed a number of categories of activity that make sense of these data. Although these categories still, in a sense, appear to emerge partly from the eclectic set of management science/organization behavior models in Mintzberg's head, rather than exclusively from the data, his con-

clusions are grounded in direct observations of managerial behavior, and are recognized by some managers as at least a better description of what they actually do.

At this point the study of managerial behavior forks into two streams. One stream focuses on more macro issues such as the similarities and differences between managerial jobs as wholes, in terms of, for example, empirically based categories of managerial roles. The second focuses on more micro issues such as examining the process by which specific episodes of managerial activity come to have their form, and trying, for example, to discover the "programs" that managers follow in choosing their courses of action.

Both of these avenues are useful but the latter has been relatively neglected. As Weick (1974) argues, in his review of Mintzberg's *The Nature of Managerial Work* (1973):

> The difference between programmes and roles is made so clear in this book that subsequent researchers will probably have a healthy pessimism towards further role analysis of managerial work and a healthy optimism towards explicating programmes of managerial work.

It is this problem of studying the process (and/or structure) or programs of managerial work, particularly in the micro sense of understanding specific episodes of managerial work, to which the protocol analysis and stimulated recall methodologies seem particularly appropriate.

Stewart (1982b) has pointed out that leadership research and research into managerial behavior have tended to be pursued independently. While managerial research has always focused largely upon what managers do, leadership research has in the past been more concerned with trying to identify what forms of leadership behavior are associated with different outcomes.

Recently, however, leadership researchers have both recognized the importance of looking at the process of leadership (Hunt & Larson, 1979) and called for more descriptive research "in situ" (Luthans, 1977; Sayles 1979).

As yet, however, most leadership process studies have been conducted through the use of structured questionnaire–type methodologies (Bruning & Cashman, 1978; Schiemann & Graen, 1978).

The use of such research methodologies as protocol analysis and stimulated recall would make it possible to start to look at the leadership process from a different perspective and in a more qualitative, descriptive way.

PHILOSOPHICAL CONSIDERATIONS

Managerial behavior and action, as a field of research, together with leadership research have been influenced by the mainstream of convention about methodology in the social sciences. As has now been well and critically documented (e.g., Harré & Secord, 1972), much social science has attempted to follow the tradition of logical positivism which borrows from the physical sciences (or more accurately from the popular myth of the physical sciences) the assumption that basic reality consists of absolute, stable entities that are accessible to direct, "objective" observations which then provide a bedrock of facts or data on which true theories can be cautiously but solidly built. Such a perspective deals harshly with notions of consciousness, experience, human processes of interpretation, and attaching meaning to events. Such concepts are dealt with either as metaphysical claptrap (not meriting any place at all in proper scientific discourse), or dismissively as possibly there but not accessible to proper scientific observation, and therefore admissible only "in extremis" as explanatory intervening variables, studied only indirectly and inferentially through their effect on properly observable phenomena. The substantial research traditions of leadership style, and correlating personality measures with indices of leadership or managerial "effectiveness," have relied heavily on psychometric methodologies which they seek to treat as if they were objective measuring instruments. What starts off as a process of interpretation of questions and expressions of views, beliefs, and preferences that the researcher assumes to be relevant, often within severe constraints of forced choice response, as a person completes a paper-and-pencil attitude scale/test/personality measure or questionnaire ends up yielding a number that is then treated as an "objective fact," just as objective as one's blood group or height. This sleight of hand of converting base subjective data into supposedly golden objective data is conducted behind a smokescreen of test mystique and statistical manipulation. The dubious assumption is that if such subjective data can be forced, by the conditions of their generation and the suppression of the variety in them by statistical technique, to display some of the properties associated with supposedly objective physical resources (i.e., traditional validity and reliability), then they are objective data. The implicit logic is weak in the extreme.

The epistemological argument has been worked through in many contexts (Reason & Rowan, 1981). The approach under discussion here is clearly related to alternative views that, in order to advance our understanding of human processes, it is necessary to use methods that are in harmony with those processes, and, further, individual experience, consciousness, and human interpretation are all aspects of human process. On the basis of common sense, protocol analysis and stimulated recall are methods that seem to qualify.

There are at least two alternatives to the external objective-reality-only view. One can be described as a dualistic view that assumes both an "absolute" world of external realities and an interacting world of experience, consciousness, meaning, and intention, with both realms influencing each other. In a dualistic methodology, both these realms could be studied by methods that are appropriate to them, and their interaction can be studied. The other view, which can be loosely identified with the phenomenological tradition, is that the realm of experience is the basic unit of analysis and that one should always begin with the concrete behavior and experience of the person in a given situation.

Such issues obviously open up fundamental philosophical questions which, given our main purpose, we cannot go into here. What it is important to note is that the methodological approach under discussion here may be applicable in programs of research that are based on either a dualistic or a phenomenological perspective. It may be important, however, to be clear about which perspective one is working with in any given situation, as this will affect the study's design and interpretation.

THE APPROACH IN COMPARISON WITH OTHER METHODS

The particular characteristics of the approach under discussion can be further explored by comparing it with some of the other methods that have been adopted in attempts to investigate what managers do.

Direct observation and behavior recording are, on the surface, the best possible approach by positivist criteria, if problems of the observer effect can be overcome at the technical level. Observation only, however, gives no insight into the meaning and intention of the observed action. Further, a tight system of observation categories involves making a priori assumptions about the nature of managerial activities, and adopting such a system therefore begs the question that is presumably being asked. On the other hand, a more open-ended approach, possibly as exemplified by Mintzberg (1973), begs the question of what internal and intuitive frameworks the observer uses. It is possible that studies like Mintzberg's owe more to the processes of participant observation as classically exemplified by Whyte (1941) and Lupton (1963) in other fields. In participant observation, conclusions rest much more on the researcher getting in touch with the experiences and ways of thinking of those being studied. This process has difficulty, however, meeting the normal research criterion of having an explicitly describable research process and leads people like Bussom, Larson, and Vicars (1982) to observe:

> There has been little attention to research design and method in the managerial work field. Methodological rigor that has been demanded for some time in other types of organizational and managerial studies (e.g. in leadership) is obviously lacking in most managerial work studies.

However, protocol analysis and stimulated recall offer explicit methodologies and data that give access to managerial action as it is experienced by the manager. That is, they try to understand the managerial process from the perspective of the manager rather than, as generally is the case, that of the researcher.

Critical-incident reporting (Flanagan, 1954) is an interesting methodology in many ways, not least because it was somewhat different from the predominant approach of its era. Having people give accounts of incidents that were critical or exceptional by some criteria (easy, difficult, successful, unsuccessful, satisyfing, unsatisfying) yielded essentially personal and qualitative accounts. In some way the approach has something in common with stimulated recall in asking for accounts of previous episodes. The time gap, however, is typically different, being weeks and months for critical incidents and minutes or hours for stimulated recall. The difference seems critical in practice, and theoretical notions such as short- and long-term memory would predict that this would be so. There is also a difference in the mode of questioning, with critical-incident reporters being pushed more toward self-report of concrete observable happenings, and stimulated recall reports being oriented more toward personal experiences, feelings, and perceptions.

Diary studies (e.g., Horne & Lupton, 1965) tend to have the problem already discussed of needing a categorizing system for reporting activities, which then begs the most interesting questions. This problem also applies to self-report activity checklist studies, which are also subject to some of the criticisms already leveled at psychometric approaches, when they become the raw material for *factor-analytic analysis,* the output of which assumes a false air of objectivity, given the nature of the basic data.

Repertory grid approaches (M. Smith, 1980) are of interest because they can be used at both the macro and micro levels of analysis — by examining the constructs people use to differentiate roles, jobs, and global tasks at the macro level and by doing the same thing for specific activities, people, problems, or any other elements derived from specific job content at the micro level. Repertory grid approaches also belong within the same broad epistemological tradition as protocol analysis and stimulated recall, being centrally concerned with the experience of the people in the situation being studied and the constructs that guide their actions within that situation.

There are, however, a number of problems with repertory grid approaches. In particular, there is the problem of what has become variously labeled as "implicit leadership theories" (Hunt & Larson, 1979) in the context of leadership research and "real" versus "ideal" in the context of educational research where, as early as 1971, Levinthal, Lansky, and Andrews demonstrated that many of the lecturing skills observed by students in their lectures were frequently those they *believed* to be highly desirable. The implication of Levinthal et al.'s results is similar to Hunt and Larson's argument that raters in perception and attribution leadership research are likely to rely heavily on stereotypes and implicit theory of what a "good" leader should be. Basically, it is the problem of espoused versus theory in use (Argyris, 1979).

Thus, it seems highly probable in repertory grid construction, where managers are asked simply to describe and differentiate between people and/or activities, that they may do so according to what they believe are good characteristics and qualities in general. There is no pressure on them to think about the people in a way that is meaningful to their "real" experience of them: they are not asked to describe them within the context of *specific* concrete situations, with all the influences and complexities involved in "real" events and activities. This criticism of repertory grid approaches, of course, applies to any approach that attempts to obtain people's perceptions by methods that in essence isolate perceptions from concrete and specific experience as, for example, in the case of leadership perception and attribution research.

Protocol analysis and stimulated recall on the other hand are very much about trying to obtain people's perceptions within the context of the concrete experience of those perceptions. Thus, they allow inferences to be made not only about the perceptions managers use when describing their actual experience of people or activities, but also about how they use them. Protocol analysis and stimulated recall give better access to, and the meaning of, mental processes. So, for example, whereas approaches such as repertory grid analysis or leadership perception research may shed light on how a manager sees his or her different colleagues, protocol analysis and stimulated recall will shed light on how he or she formulates his or her approach to dealing with them in a meeting or negotiation, and how, through this, different images of them influence his or her actions.

RESEARCH APPROACHES AND DESIGNS

Protocol analysis and stimulated recall represent a methodological approach to the observational part of the research process. As observational methodologies they do not imply any specific research design but are, rather, observational methodologies that could be used in the context of a number of research designs.

Potential research designs can be broadly categorized into the "dualistic" and "phenomenological" in the meanings of these terms already discussed. In "dualistic" designs, data about mental processes could be analyzed against separate observations of related behavior. Newell and Simon (1972) have used protocol analysis in this way in psychological studies of problem solving, where structured problems have been given in a laboratory setting, and outcomes objectively observed. Clarkson (1962) used a loose version of the methodology to derive data from which a model of fund-investment managers' behavior could be developed, and tested the model on the basis of its power to predict or simulate actual behavior.

Within a more strictly phenomenological approach it is the descriptions of cases of the phenomena being studied that constitute the data for analysis.

The aim of the analysis is to detect, delimit, and describe similarities and differences among the cases. This is done by careful and repeated exploration for variation in the set of descriptions of experience. That is, the basis for analysis is the variation within the specific group of cases in a particular study. The aim is not to describe any similarities and differences but to describe the most significant ones, the ones that one might expect to be common to other groups of similar cases. The final outcome aimed at is a number of categories describing similarities (and differences) among the cases.

Thus, taking a more strictly phenomenological approach to descriptions of managerial action obtained using protocol analysis and stimulated recall would mean examining the basic transcripts for similarities and differences in the descriptions of experience and attempting to identify a number of general categories of descriptions that describe the (significant) similarities in the managers' descriptions of their experience. The meaningfulness of such categories can be checked by asking independent judges to assign transcripts to categories of description. It is possible to make a further check on the meaningfulness of categories by checking back with the "researched" to ask whether the categories make sense to their experience. In taking such a step, it is assumed that the "researched" are intelligent and as capable as the "researcher" in interpreting and categorizing experience (e.g., Reason & Rowan, 1981).

To return to the issue of research designs within the broad phenomenological tradition, it is also possible to take a more deductionist approach to data that are essentially descriptive of experience. Transcripts from protocol analysis and stimulated recall can be inspected for evidence of specific processes that certain theories would predict to be there. Such an approach has been used to find out whether students use certain "rational" decision-making processes in evaluating their own learning (Burgoyne, 1975).

THEORETICAL ISSUES EXPLORABLE
WITH THE METHODOLOGY

Any theory of management, leadership, and organizational behavior has the potential to yield predictors and hypotheses about how managers think and interpret their environment and shape their actions. These can all be tested against protocol analysis and stimulated recall data.

Microeconomic and pricing theories would yield predictors about how managers address themselves to decisions concerning resource allocation. Rational decision-making and information-processing models suggest processes that could be looked for in protocols associated with any decision-making situation. Various issues of organizational behavior could be illuminated by protocols for situations where managers are formulating their approach to people.

General models of psychological functioning such as the Test-Operate-Test-Exit model of Miller, Galanier, and Pribram (1960), and more specific ones such as Simon's (1957) concept of "satisficing" in decision making could also be tested.

Protocols can be a useful source of data in relation to theories and models of how managers learn from experience, an area of special interest for the authors. Common sense and our pilot work suggest that longitudinal forms of research design are particularly appropriate here. Protocols of a manager committing himself to a course of action, together with protocols taken days, weeks, or months later when the manager becomes aware of and interprets the repercussions of these actions, suggest themselves as potentially fruitful sources of data about whether and how managers learn from their experience. Such protocols can be inspected for evidence of the learning cycle postulated by Kolb, Rubin, and McIntyre (1971) and the accompanying differences in learning style. The single- and double-loop learning model of Argyris and Schon (1976) could also be tested against this kind of data, as could the various "blocks" models of the learning process and its inhibition (Temperol, 1977).

There are a number of leadership theories that might be illuminated by protocol analysis and stimulated recall data. For example, it would be possible to examine transcripts for evidence of where managers seem to derive satisfaction and whether, as suggested by Fiedler, they seem to be motivated by interpersonal relationships or task-goal accomplishment and the extent to which these two motivations actually influence their effectiveness in more or less favorable situations (Fiedler & Chemers 1974).

Similarly, it would be possible to look at the extent to which managers' actual experience of their subordinates reflects differences in their relationships with them; the Vertical Dyad Linkage theory, of course, suggests that managers establish different kinds of relationships with their subordinates (Graen & Cashman, 1975). The Vertical Dyad Linkage theory could be further illuminated by obtaining protocol analysis and stimulated recall data from a manager's subordinates. Such data could also be used to examine House's path-goal theory (House, 1971).

Finally, this kind of data could be inspected for evidence of the kind of personal contingency thinking implied by Vroom and Yetton's model (1973).

EXAMPLES OF DATA

It is not our intention to present comprehensive data summaries and substantive findings from our pilot study, but we do present one example in order to give an impression of the kind of data yielded by this method. The example we picked might be seen as relevant to leadership issues in an attempt to demonstrate further how this approach could be usefully adopted in leadership studies.

We pick up a discussion in a team meeting of a welfare department:

Protocol at the Time

Senior Officer: Umm . . . I had a final discussion with Janet Smith, who left at the end of the . . . of the week, and in fact she's going to be carrying on a couple of . . . of cases pro tem, umm . . .

Manager: For long? And why?

Senior Officer: No, no, we'll work on that one. Mostly for money I think. No, mostly for love, certainly not for money, umm . . . She's working through to term really.

Manager: It's a bit . . . Ah yes, well it's all very well, but I mean how account-able can she be if she's not a qualified — I don't think . . .

Senior Officer: Well she can . . . she can . . . John Jones is going . . . in fact is taking the cases legally, and Janet's doing some sessional work with them. It's two particular cases that she's . . .

2nd Senior Officer: Is it . . . ?

Senior Officer: Yes.

2nd Senior Officer: Because I think that the concern there is that Janet is still involved with the girl although she's left.

Manager: I'm not sure it's quite as straightforward as that, James.

Senior Officer: Well I don't . . .

Manager: And I share that —

Senior Officer: Well I mean I've talked to David and I've said look, you know, if it's felt that it isn't appropriate because the situation's moved from that when she discussed it with me, that we may have to say look it's not appropriate for her to be involved because of the way the case has moved, and it needs somebody with a . . . with a different view now, yes, so I talked to David yesterday about it. That's all.

Recalling the above episode a little later (after having listened to a playback of the recording), the manager describes his thinking and experience during the episode.

Recall of Protocol

Researcher: He was on to Janet Smith there.

Manager: Yeh, he was. Now I was cross about that.

Researcher: You were.

Manager: Yes, and I shall talk to him about it after. I mean I . . . I realized yesterday I'd said to you a number of times I was cross and irritated, and I perhaps wasn't as strong as that, but I was concerned because I don't think it was appropriate for an individual who isn't employed by the department to be working, ostensibly representing us, however good she is, and however appropriate in one way it is, I think it's inappropriate in terms of accountability, and I think one of my . . . I mean professionally James is very sound, he's first class, very good, but he does sometimes not be aware of the personnel issues of some of the things he does and I was thinking "Oh God, here we go again, Oh God, Janet, really. . . ." (a) that he shouldn't have done it, but (b) if he was thinking of doing it he should have discussed it with her first. Because if something went wrong with that case, I mean the client doesn't know she's not representing us, and yet she's not employed by us, and where do we stand? I mean just supposing, it's a very disturbed woman, suppose she committed suicide?

Researcher: Yeh. Hmm . . . Again, what . . . to what degree did these sort of . . . did you think through?

Manager: Ah well it was all at the back of my mind, about that. I mean it's a question of think . . . when you say "think through," it's sort of like a computer, isn't it?

Researcher: Yes.

Manager: I mean I wasn't just reacting, I knew I was reacting, I was aware of the reasons behind, and at one time I'd . . . I mean the thing that had changed my mind . . . there was a point in the discussion when I was prepared to push it, and then I decided I would deal with it outside the meeting.

Researcher: And would you normally handle it that way?

Manager: Yes, yes. Your being there didn't . . . I just didn't want to get a great hassle with everybody else around, er so um you know I would have dealt with it like that. I didn't think it was appropriate to deal with it in that meeting, but it was . . . That's one of the beauties of having this report back. I don't know if you've noticed, but I mean people exchange information, I find this a marvellous way of cueing into what's going on in the district, and there are a number of threads that I can pick up.

Six months later, the researcher again raised this incident with the manager.

Follow-Up Interview

Researcher: Umm the last one is from the second day, which I've only got the one episode at the moment . . .

Manager: It was Janet Smith, hmm . . .

Researcher: Umm . . . that was James making his report about that.

Manager: Yes, and me feeling that he hadn't understood umm the implications of what . . . and the decision he'd taken, which was about accountability. Well we did discuss it in his follow-up session, er and she didn't continue to keep the cases.

Researcher: Hmm . . . that sounds very straightforward and simple, there must be more . . .

Manager: Well I think the . . . it's interesting you see because when you are in this line of work one of the things you learn is that it's not only what you say to people, it's the work they do on it after you've said it, er so that for example you can talk to somebody about a matrimonial problem and they don't appear to have absorbed it or taken in what you are on about and you go back a week later and they've moved and you're ready to start from the point where they were when you left off and by working on this material you've discussed, they've moved. Now I think the things that were said in that meeting about . . . it was barely only just touched on, umm about accountability, by the time we came to discuss it he'd absorbed that and he'd moved . . .

Researcher: He'd already moved . . .

Manager: . . . and it . . . there wasn't an issue.

Researcher: I see, yes . . . because where were you, you were expecting to have a bit of a thing with him.

Manager: I was . . . I was expecting that we might have to . . . yes I was expecting that I might have to spell it out, and fun . . . I mean the interesting thing is that I had perhaps thought that I might use it as a vehicle to widen out . . . to talk about being more aware of the personnel implications of some of the things that happen. Umm now in fact I didn't, because it wasn't an issue and I . . . some things happened recently of a similar nature, where I'm going to try and take the same opportunity, because I always think it has more impact if you can relate it to something that's actually going on than just out of the blue . . .

Researcher: Because you did mention that was something you had a concern with . . .

Manager: Yes, I mean he's super in so many ways and I think like the rest of us you . . . you take the package, don't you . . .

Researcher: Oh aye yes . . .

Manager: And you don't want to undermine what's good and so you take opportunities as they arise to . . . but it's interesting because there are two senior posts who've recently . . . well are retiring and the jobs are up for um advertisement, and James would be perceived as a contender, um but I don't think he's going to apply, and if he had have done in discussing what I was going to say in his reference, I would have had to talk about perhaps this lack of sensibility to personnel issues, which sometimes can have . . . fairly serious repercussions.

Researcher: I should imagine that's rather important.

Manager: Yes, this is one of the key things, you see.

Researcher: I find it quite interesting that you were aware of this, you were going to take the opportunity, but when it didn't become an issue then you kept it 'til the next time that it did become . . .

Manager: Because it's an ongoing thing between us. Um if I had had a staff development interview with him since, um I would have probably raised it then in a more general context. Er yes, I mean maybe I should have done, you're right, maybe I should have done.

Researcher: No, I'm not necessarily suggesting you should . . .

Manager: No, no, well I'm just reflecting now, maybe I should have done, I . . . I suppose really that you can . . . you don't want to nag, and it's a question of what sort of weighting you give to it, um . . . in that job it's important but it isn't the area of work where there is a major personnel dimension to the job, because it's fairly . . . in terms of bodies within his section it's relatively small compared with I mean Anne's section might have had 300 people in it all together . . . Now James's got about 50 or 60 people, and they are all salaried staff, and you don't get the sort of . . . the sort of personnel issues that you get in a — so I suppose the question of what weight you give to it, um and given the other problems you have to contend with, and the other things he does, it's a question of using the appropriate opportunity rather than saying it's so crucial that we've got to deal with it here and now, because if we don't it's going to be a major factor in limiting his performance in the job. It is something that has an effect but it's . . . in that job it's not important . . . not significant. If he wanted to take a wider role it would have much more serious implications and at some point I've got to tackle it.

Researcher: Yeh. To what extent would you think that that's something that you've unconsciously . . . sort of are aware of and have made a decision on the basis of, or have you actually consciously worked that out as a . . .

Manager: Or have I just ducked it?

Researcher: Or have you ducked it . . .

Manager: I don't know, I don't know, it's interesting, I suppose, I'll have to think about that. I suppose if I'm honest I'd say um that I haven't consciously worked it out that that's the way to deal with it, but nor have I just ducked it, it's an approach but I've thought well in this case . . . this is the way to handle it. I mean I have a similar problem with Anne Brown who's very good at her job, but has . . . but limits her performance because she's not very flexible, and again it's something you are aware of and you deal with it when you can but you can't . . . you don't make an issue of it because the basic performance . . . the overall performance is very good. . . .

In concluding this example it is important to reiterate that it is shown to convey the flavor of the approach and not to draw conclusions from the data. It is useful to keep this flavor in mind in reading the next section.

PRACTICAL, TECHNICAL, AND METHODOLOGICAL CONCLUSIONS FROM THE METHODOLOGY DEVELOPMENT PROJECT

The initial research project, which has been primarily oriented to the development of the methodology itself, has involved data collection on 37 episodes of managerial work, taken from the streams of work of 8 managers. For 5 of these 8 managers, follow-ups have been carried out to study their reflections on the events following on from the incidents studied.

A variety of conclusions of a practical, technical, and methodological nature have been drawn about the approach:

1. A general interview (or "context" interview) is needed as a background to the methodology to give information necessary to interpret data from the protocols. The practical procedure can usefully consist of initial meeting for context interview and setting up a suitable occasion to be with the person at work to collect protocols and carry out stimulated recall discussions. A later follow-up meeting can then look at subsequent events.

2. For obvious reasons, stimulated recall is often the preferred or only feasible methodology because many managerial episodes are themselves interactive and verbal, thus precluding "real-time" protocol analysis.

3. It is useful to use both protocol analysis and stimulated recall on the same episode, since neither yields a complete picture of the experiences concurrent with an episode. Together, they can give a fuller picture.

4. A certain amount of strategy and skill is needed on the part of the researcher to keep protocol analysis and stimulated recall sessions focused on actual episode work. There is a danger that data-gathering encounters can degenerate into ordinary interviews, if the manager steps out of *talking about his work while he is doing it* into *suspending his work and talking in generalizations about how he thinks he approaches his work.*

5. Some evidence of observer effect was collected. It was also found possible, however, to collect information on the nature of the influence from the stimulated recall and follow-up sessions. In particular, managers would point out that they had been conscious of being less severe with subordinates than they would normally be. Thus, while not denying the problem of observer effect, this particular approach has the advantage of being capable of bringing out its nature and extent, which can then be taken into account in interpreting the data.

6. A longitudinal approach with follow-up, or ideally, repeated observation of incidents over time that belong to the same stream of activities would be particularly useful as a basis for understanding some of the more processual aspects of managerial action, including processes of learning from experience.

CONCLUSIONS

We believe that the approach we have described is particularly appropriate for furthering our understanding, through research, of both managerial and leadership processes. We believe the approach to be useful because it fits the kinds of theoretical questions that need to be asked about managerial action and leadership processes, given the state of knowledge in the field. It is also desirable from the point of view of certain philosophical considerations, flexible enough to be used in the context of a variety of research designs, open to both inductive and deductive research approaches, and capable of shedding light on a broad range of theoretical issues. It is also a feasible approach from a practical and technical point of view, and we make no apologies for discussing issues at this level because it is in the crucial area of what happens at the empirical coal face, as it were, that the true validity of a research approach is established or lost.

In terms of the potential for developing theory, the particular strength of the approach is that it makes available a form of data about managerial experience in which a whole variety of processes can be observed going on together.

We hope that it is not overstating the case to suggest that data of this kind may serve as an empirical stepping stone to move from a situation where we have a variety of theories *on* management or leadership to a situation in which we might have one or more integrated theories *of* management or leadership.

10

Microskills of Leadership: A Detailed Analysis of the Behaviors of Managers in the Appraisal Interview

Beverly Alban Metcalfe*

Although, at a theoretical level, there have been conspicuous advances in leadership research over the past years, it is probably true that there has been minimal progress in the development of effective leadership skills training programs. Crucial questions are still posed regarding: (a) what it is that constitutes effective leader behavior; and (b) how it can be identified for the express purpose of skills training.

In planning the research to be presented here, the concept of leadership infers the presence of one who uses interpersonal skills of influence to direct the actions of others toward the achievement of organizational goals. The major objective was to obtain data that might usefully be applied to a social-skills training program for increasing a manager's interpersonal effectiveness with subordinates. A specific situation was selected that was of common occurrence and importance to practicing managers, and the success of which depended largely on the practice of leadership skills. It was important also that the effects of such behaviors could be observed and measured in relation to specific outcomes.

LEADERSHIP AND THE APPRAISAL INTERVIEW

In a previous paper the author (Alban Metcalfe, 1982a) has argued that the appraisal interview represents a situation in which behaviors identified as characteristic of effective leadership, such as those discussed by House and Dessler (1974), Vroom and Yetton (1973), Oldham (1976), and Sims (1977), are prerequisites of its success.

*The research presented in this chapter was conducted while the author was a doctoral student at the University of Bradford Management Centre, under the supervision of Dr. G. A. Randell. The author would like to thank both Linda Marsh of Huthwaite Research Group and Rose Evison for their advice in the use of behavioral analysis, and for co-rating a sample of the data for rater reliability. She would also like to express her thanks to Paul Jackson and Steve McKenna for their statistical advice.

The appraisal interview represents a situation in which many of the leadership strategies advocated by these theorists might be expected to be practiced. The proposed research was intended to reduce the crucial gap that exists between the identification of leadership skills at a macrobehavioral level and the much more specific, operational definitions of the behaviors that constitute those skills.

PAST RESEARCH INTO THE APPRAISAL INTERVIEW

Several studies have attempted to identify those behavioral characteristics of the manager that are associated with a "successful" interview outcome (e.g., Burke, Weitzel, & Weir, 1978; Cederblom, 1982, for reviews). But, with the exception of the seminal study in the GEC Co. by Meyer, Kay, and French (1965), the behaviors of the appraiser are measured by means of the responses of the subordinate to a perceptual questionnaire. The assumption that behaviors of leaders are isomorphic with the highly subjective perceptions of subordinates has been seriously challenged in the literature.

Another source of concern relates to the questionable reliability of impressions set to memory some weeks, or in some cases even *a year or more* after the appraisal has taken place. In view of the finding of Hall and Lawler (1969) that managers and subordinates could not even agree when their last performance appraisal interview was held, one wonders how reliable such specific information is when it is gained so long after the appraisal. In the author's experience of working on interviewing skills workshops with managers, it is not usual for a manager to forget completely (or deny) an event or particular point of discussion that occurred within 20 minutes of the event having taken place; and it is only the fact that the tape recording provides indisputable evidence for that event having occurred that eventually convinces the individual that it has indeed taken place.

Putting aside the arguments relating to the questionable validity of using perceptual measures as accurate measures of leader behavior, the question remains as to the *value* of feedback from a questionnaire to individuals who want to modify their behavior. Since such information is typically imprecise, relying as it does on generalizable *inferences* about behaviors, it is consequently of limited value (see Latham & Wexley, 1977, p. 256). However, this by no means nullifies the importance of these data from questionnaires as measures of the *dependent* variable—usually referred to as interview outcome measures. The very fact that appraiser and appraisee perceive the behavior in the appraisal interview differently is of inherent value to a skills development program, and has been used as such (Nemeroff & Cosentino, 1979).

Another criticism concerns those studies that have attempted to control managers' style by assigning individuals to a particular condition in which they are instructed to be "participative," or "nonparticipative," for example, and then compared conditions with outcome measures. Since it would appear unwise to presume that mere instruction creates the necessary conditions, it might be that such treatments are suspect. What is therefore needed is some measure of the independent variable that is far more accurate and objective than the subordinate's highly subjective and emotive perceptions. These can then be related to outcomes of the interview.

A final point is that data gathered in past appraisal interview research have of necessity involved a variety of totally different performance reviews, since they have been based on real appraisals of individuals with widely differing successes and failures. The present investigation controlled for this variability by employing a standard case study. The analysis concerns the perceptions and behaviors of both managers and subordinates who were role playing the standardized biography. There are a number of methodological issues concerning the design of this study that are discussed.

In summary, the two criteria on which success, and consequently leadership skills, were to be judged were the degree to which the subordinate felt that the appraisal helped improve performance, and equally important, the degree of motivation to do so. These two processes of leadership relate directly to the theoretical literature on leader effectiveness, and to the objectives of developmental appraisal interviews, such as those discussed by Maier (1976).

THE PRESENT RESEARCH STUDY

Background and Method

Data for the research study were collected from senior and middle managers attending two-day appraisal-interviewing-skills workshops. (The format of the two-day workshop is fully described in Randell, Shaw, Packard, & Slater, 1976.) On the first day the managers role played the immediate superior of a middle manager. The subordinates were role played by members of the research group at Bradford who had been briefed to react as naturally as possible, and to respond genuinely to the treatment they received so as to provide the managers with a practical and realistic learning experience.

On the morning of the first day of the workshop the managers were introduced to the objectives of the appraisal interview. Briefly stated, they were twofold: first, to provide a *developmental step*—that is, to adopt a participative problem-solving approach with the subordinate in reviewing past performance and events with a view to identifying what he needs to do next to increase performance; and second, to facilitate *motivational growth* by identifying barriers or frustrations that may be creating obstacles to development, and equally importantly, discussing needs and expectations (Randell *et al.,* 1976). In this way, a certain element of control was introduced in terms of the background information available to the managers, the statement of objectives, and the suggested style to be adopted. It was not presumed, however, as has been the case in some previous studies (cf. French, Kay, & Meyers, 1966), that merely be suggesting that they adopt a particular style, they would *ipso facto* behave in that particular way. Indeed, the differential responses were the prime variables under investigation.

The interviews, which were tape recorded, lasted approximately 25 minutes and were observed by two other managers who were participating on the course, and by one tutor. Immediately following the termination of the interview, both parties to the interaction were given a questionnaire to fill in. This questionnaire, devised by Nemeroff and Wexley (1977), comprises two relatively short scales. The first scale, the Performance Feedback Characteristic Questionnaire (PFCQ), represents a list of descriptive statements that the authors maintain reflected the five major characteristics emerging from the literature. A seven-point Lickert-type scale was used to measure the responses.

The second scale comprises Criterion Measures concerned with Satisfaction with the Interview (SWI), Motivation (MOT), and Satisfaction with the Manager (SWM).

The purpose of this research study was to describe and analyze the behaviors of both managers and subordinates in the interviews who were defined as "successful," "unsuccessful," or "average." Success was determined by the subordinate scoring either 6 or 7 on both criterion variables. These were item 13 ("I think the interview helps me to do a better job") and item 16 ("At the end of the interview I really wanted to improve my behavior").

These particular variables were chosen because they were far more specific than taking a measure of the general "satisfaction with interview" subscale. Furthermore, as has been argued above, these variables reflect two major objectives of developmental appraisal interviews and relate directly to certain tenets of leadership behavior as embodied in some contemporary leadership models (already referred to). "Unsuccessful" interviews were those in which the subordinate scored 1 or 2 on both item 13 (Helpfulness) and item 16 (MOT). Average interviews were those in which subordinates scored 3, 4, or 5 on both variables 13 and 16.

The Procedure for Analyzing the Behavior

Among tape recordings of 78 interviews, 20 were "successful" interviews, 8 "unsuccessful," 29 "average," and 21 interviews did not fit into these categories. In fact, only six interviews were available for transcription in the unsuccessful group. After various types of behavioral analysis were considered, including Flanders (1970), Bales (1950), and a variety of interactional analysis techniques, the Behavior Analysis categories of Rackham and Morgan (1977) were judged most appropriate. The author became trained in their use and the reliability of her (blind) analyses was checked by analysis of a sample of the same data by a Behavior Analysis trainer, using Cohen's Kappa measure of agreement chi-square test. For the two interviews subject to the analysis, Kappa equalled 0.76, $p < .001$, and 0.88, $p < .001$. As recommended by Rackham and Morgan, categories of behavior to be used in this particular situation were modified to reflect the behaviors observed as particularly relating to it. The list of behaviors included in the analysis were those shown in Table 10.1.

The construct of "inviting participation" has consistently shown to be an important factor in the success of an appraisal interview (Greller, 1975, 1978; Meyer, Kay, & French, 1965; Wexley, Singh, & Yukl, 1973), yet it has proved

Table 10.1. Behaviors Included in the Analysis*

PROCEDURAL PROPOSING (PP) — Statements regarding the procedure to be followed.

PROPOSING re JOB (PJ) — Proposals relating to job activities.

GIVING INFORMATION (GI) — Behaviors that offer opinions or feelings.

GIVING INFORMATION (GE) — Behaviors that offer facts or clarifications.

**STATING GUIDELINES (SG) — Principles on which actions are based.

POSITIVE EVALUATION (PE) — Positive reactions to appraisee and his or her performance.

NEGATIVE EVALUATION (NE) — Negative reactions to appraisee and his or her performance.

DISAGREEING (DIS) — Statements of disagreement and objection re issues.

ATTACKING (ATT) — A behavior that attacks another *person* directly.

DEFENDING (DEF) — A behavior that defends an individual's position.

BUILDING (BUILD) — Behavior that extends or develops a proposal.

SUPPORTING (SUP) — Conscious declaration of agreement or support.

SUMMARIZING (SUM) — A behavior that summarizes or otherwise restates.

SEEKING INFORMATION (SI) — Behaviors that seek facts, opinions, or clarification.

SEEKING FEELINGS (SF) — A behavior that seeks the feelings of another person.

SEEKING PROPOSALS (SP) — A behavior that seeks suggestions or proposals.

BRINGING IN (BrIn) — A behavior that invites the other person to contribute.

TESTING UNDERSTANDING (TU) — A behavior in which an individual indicates he or she is seeking to establish whether he or she has correctly understood or not.

CHECKING OUT (ChO) — A behavior inviting agreement or disagreement.

OPEN (Op) — Nondefensive taking of responsibility for mistakes.

INVITING PARTICIPATION (IP) — Behaviors that include an implicit or explicit invitation to respond or contribute to what has just been said.

SHUTTING OUT (ShOut) — Prevents opportunity for others to participate in interaction.

*For further definitions of these categories, see Alban Metcalfe (1982b).
**The author would like to acknowledge Rose Evison for the provision of this category.

to be a difficult construct to describe operationally. It was noticed in trial use of the behavior analysis scale that not only did inviting participation occur when questions were asked, but it was also implicit in some behaviors that one might not expect to be particularly participative, such as proposing a course of action concerning the subordinate's job. A suggestion might be made in such a way as implicitly to invite the subordinate to respond directly to it. Consequently, when the appraiser invited participation, that behavior was recorded in two ways: as inviting participation but also according to the *content* of that behavior.

Each behavior of the manager and subordinate in the interview was timed in 100ths of a minute and recorded as a frequency. Behaviors were recorded in sequence for future analysis. Since interviews lasted varying lengths of time, behavioral measures were standardized by calculating them as percentages.

Behaviors were thus recorded:

1. as a percentage of the total time that the individual behaved in the interview; and
2. as a percentage of the total number of behaviors of that individual in the interview.

Since it was necessary initially to spend about one working week analyzing each interview, the sample was severely limited to the six interviews that constituted the unsuccessful group, and a sample of six chosen at random from each of the other two groups.

Although, as has already been explained, "success" is determined by a combination of two scores to form what shall be referred to as the COMP variable, it was thought that it would be instructive also to look at characteristics of each constituent variable.

Results and Discussion: Perceptual Scale

Regression. Results of the multiple regression analysis of performance feedback characteristics on the criterion measures are shown in Table 10.2. Only two performance feedback characteristics contribute a significant proportion of variance to the criterion measure COMP. The beta weights are given. These two variables were the perceptions by the subordinate of the manager's friendliness, and the manager ending the interview on a positive note. Inspection of the multiple regressions for the single constituent variables contributing to success are also given since the results might be instructive. Interestingly, the same pattern is revealed for variable 13 (Helpfulness) as was for COMP. However, for variable 16 (Motivation), an additional variable, namely, the perception that the subordinate was given an opportunity to state his side of the issues, contributes most variance to the outcome measure. These results support past findings that stress the importance of manager supportiveness and inviting subordinate participation to a successful outcome of an appraisal

Table 10.2. Multiple Regression Analyses of Performance Feedback Characteristics on (a) Variable 13: for Subordinates and Managers; (b) Variable 16 for Subordinates; (c) COMP (Variable 13 + Variable 16), for Subordinates.

(a) *Variable 13 ("I think the interview helps me to do a better job")*

Subordinates

Performance Feedback Characteristic	B	R^2	F	df
Var 2 (M ended interview on positive note)	.39	.20	14.47***	1, 76
Var 1 (M tried to be friendly)	.27	.06	6.91**	2, 75

Managers

Performance Feedback Characteristics	B	R^2	F	df
Var 1 (I tried to be friendly)	.36	.15	12.71***	1, 76
Var 7 (I asked Sub about particular problems concerning the job)	.33	.11	10.93***	2, 75

(b) *Variable 16 ("At the end of the interview I really wanted to improve my behavior")*

Subordinates

Performance Feedback Characteristic	B	R^2	F	df
Var 2 (M ended interview on positive note)	.26	.07	6.47*	1, 76
Var 1 (M tried to be friendly)	.23	.03	3.96*	2, 75
Var 5 (M gave opportunity to state my side of issues)	.22	.17	13.46***	3, 74

(c) *COMP (Variable 13 + Variable 16)*

Subordinates

	B	R^2	F	df
Var 2 (M ended interview on positive note)	.39	.21	15.52***	1, 76
Var 1 (M tried to be friendly)	.34	.10	11.79***	2, 75

$N = 78$ in each sample.
*p < .05
**p < .01
***p < .001

interview (Burke, Weitzel, & Weir, 1978, 1980; Nemeroff & Wexley, 1977; Wexley, Singh, & Yukl, 1973).

Linear Relationships

Analysis of Variance. A one-way analysis of variance was performed on the subordinates' scores on the perceptual questionnaire to test for linearity. With the exception of one case, the relationships between the performance feedback characteristics and dependent variables were linear ($p < .05$). However, the relationship between item 13 (Helpfulness of interview), and item 8 (Amount of time speaking) was significantly nonlinear ($F_{2,75} = 5.94$, $p < .05$). It would seem that the subordinates' perception of having done most of the talking during the appraisal interview was associated both with the interviews judged successful and those judged unsuccessful, with reference to helping the subordinate to do a better job. A perceived lower proportion of time speaking was associated with average interviews. In other words, a high proportion of subordinate talking is not in itself a recipe for a successful (or an unsuccessful) appraisal interview; it would appear that the more important issues are concerned with *what* is said. These findings would seem to support the views expressed by other researchers (e.g., Burke, Weitzel, & Weir, 1978, 1980; Greller, 1975, 1978).

Considering the value of the findings from the analysis of the scores of the perceptual scales to those interested in improving the nature of managerial effectiveness, at least three serious limitations come to mind. First, knowing that being friendly and ending the interview on a positive note are important characteristics of a successful appraisal interview is neither sufficient nor precise enough information on which a skills-training program can be built. Furthermore, these behaviors would appear to contribute only around 30 percent of the variance of a successful appraisal. In addition to these points, it should be borne in mind that these variables refer to subordinates' *perceptions* of the managers' general manner of behaving, and in fact they say very little about which *specific* behaviors create such an impression. Each of these points would seem to suggest the need for an objective and accurate microanalysis of the meaningful units of behavior performed by the managers in each of the groups, in the hope of identifying distinguishing behaviors that may be included in a subsequent interpersonal-skills-training program.

The importance of such an analysis is apparently borne out by the perhaps surprising fact that when an analysis was made between the mean scores of the managers' and subordinates' perceptions of the same interviews, only one performance feedback characteristic yielded a significant difference. Interestingly, this was item 3, which concerned whether a follow-up interview was arranged or not. Since one might reasonably presume that this was perhaps the most clear-cut event of the interview, it is interesting that it yielded the greatest difference in perceptions of both parties. This serves to reinforce the need for an objective analysis of the behaviors.

Results and Discussion: Behavioral Analysis of the "Successful," "Average," and "Unsuccessful" Appraisal Interviews

Since the means and standard deviations of the behavioral measures indicated that the distributions were highly skewed, nonparametric rather than parametric statistical analyses were considered to be both appropriate and more conservative. Consequently, the Kruskal-Wallis one-way analysis of variance was employed. In the cases of behaviors identified by the Kruscal-Wallis, the Mann-Whitney U test was used to establish whether two independent groups had been drawn from the same population.

From a one-way analysis of variance of the behaviors of the managers in the successful, unsuccessful, and average appraisal interviews, several behaviors emerged as significantly differentiating between the groups. Table 10.3 gives a summary of the significant results of a Kruskal-Wallis one-way analysis of variance of behaviors, and states whether the relationships were linear or nonlinear. The average measures of behaviors as percentages of time, and as percentages of frequency, are both given. Because it was considered important to obtain measures of how subordinates behaved in each group, the results of a one-way analysis of variance of subordinates' behavior are also shown.

Figure 10.1 shows the profile for the mean scores of time spent behaving by managers in each group, and indicates the value and direction of the Mann-Whitney U test where significant differences between pairs of groups were obtained. Figure 10.2 shows the analogous profile for subordinates.

The range of behaviors that differentiated between the managers in the successful, unsuccessful, and average appraisal interviews is quite extensive. Perhaps the most outstanding difference exists in the area of behaviors concerned with inviting participation, where the average score for the managers in the successful group considerably exceeds the average score for the managers in the other two groups. This finding is consistent with previous studies measuring perceptions of subordinates as reflecting effective managerial behavior in the appraisal interview (e.g., Greller, 1975, 1978; Maier, 1976; Nemeroff & Wexley, 1977; Wexley, Singh, & Yukl, 1973). The score does not account *precisely* for the way in which time was spent in such interactions, but describes a particular style and suggests a general disposition toward the appraisee. In this study, however, the behavioral *content* was also categorized. How then, apart from adopting a significantly more participative style, did the managers in the successful appraisal behave?

Several differences emerge when comparisons are made between managers in the successful group and those in the other groups. The former spent significantly less time giving facts and clarifying issues and in disagreeing, but spent a significantly greater proportion of their time offering supportive behavior and giving positive evaluation (PE) of aspects of subordinate performance, or about the appraisee in general. The results of the one-way analysis of variance for the three separate measures of seeking information do not reach significance, but a combined score of the various seeking information behaviors S(Info.) does. Interestingly, the relationship is nonlinear, with both successful and unsuccessful groups of managers obtaining higher scores than the average group. Perhaps the scores relate to differences in style

Table 10.3. Summary of the Significant K Values of the Kruskal-Wallis One-way
Analysis of Variance, for Behavioral Analysis Measures of Managers and
Subordinates in the "Successful," "Average," and "Unsuccessful"
Appraisal Interviews, Expressed (a) as a Percentage of Time;
(b) As a Percentage of the Total Number of Behaviors.*

Managers' behaviors		x^2	Linear (L)	Nonlinear (NL)
GI	a) K = 6.61	$p < .05$	L	
	b) K = 7.16	$p < .05$	L	
GE	a) K = 7.82	$p < .02$		NL
	b) K = 7.94	$p < .02$		NL
PE	a) K = 12.57	$p < .01$	L	
	b) K = 9.56	$p < .01$	L	
NE	a) K = 5.65	$p < .06$	L	
	b) K = 5.27	$p > .05 < .10$	L	
DIS	a) K = 7.83	$p < .02$	L	
	b) K = 8.77	$p < .02$	L	
ATT	a) K = 9.57	$p < .01$	L	
	b) K = 9.57	$p < .01$	L	
SUP	a) K = 8.94	$p < .02$	L	
	b) K = 6.49	$p < .05$	L	
SInfo	a) K = 6.04	$p < .05$		NL
	b) K = 3.52	ns		
SUM	a) ns			
	b) K = 8.94	$p < .02$		NL
Ch.OUT	a) K = 8.93	$p < .02$	L	
	b) K = 8.71	$p < .02$	L	
IP	a) K = 11.66	$p < .01$	L	
	b) K = 10.75	$p < .01$	L	
Sh.OUT	a) —			
	b) K = 10.37	$p < .01$	L	
Subordinates' behaviors				
DIS	a) K = 11.88	$p < .01$	L	
	b) K = 8.76	$p < .02$	L	
DEF	a) K = 14.90	$p < .001$	L	
	b) K = 14.90	$p < .001$	L	

*$df = 2$; x^2 approximation recommended for use with three samples when all samples
contain more than five observations (Leach, 1979, p. 154).

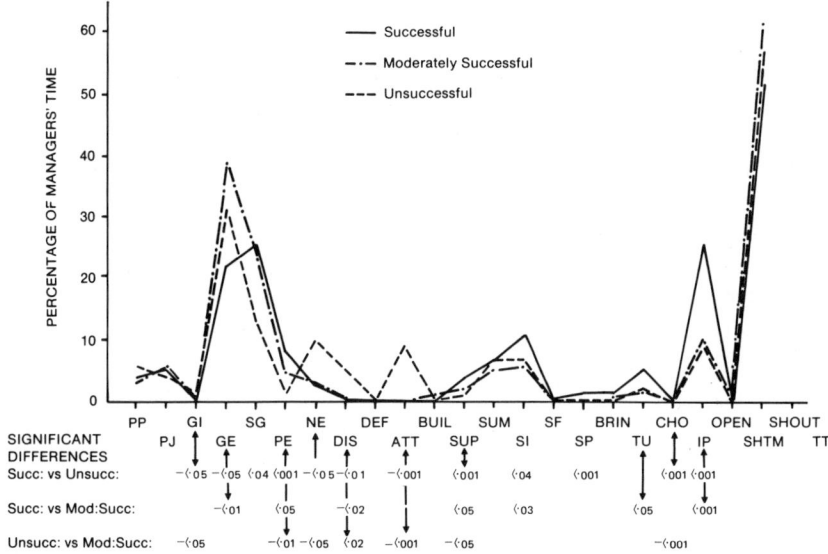

FIGURE 10.1 Graph showing distribution of mean behavioral analysis scores as measured by time for managers in the three groups of appraisal interviews; with a summary of the significant values obtained from the Mann-Whitney U test comparing pairs of groups

adopted by the managers, with the unsuccessful managers sometimes seeking information in an interrogative manner, whereas the style of the successful group was characteristically participative.

These results might help illuminate some of the reasons why a participative style is not always effective. The manager who does not possess the necessary skills might be convinced that by frequently asking questions, he or she is being participative. In fact, a subordinate who is subjected to a barrage of questions might experience this behavior as distinctly threatening. This finding might also have serious implications for research, such as has already been referred to, in which managers are assigned to a condition of being partici-pative and in which it is assumed they will be competent in using the necessary skills. Greller (1978) has referred to the lack of relationship that might exist between "a condition" and the "psychological experience" of participation.

Another characteristic of successful managers, apart from inviting partici-pation and seeking information more often, was that they also appeared to *listen* to the subordinate response since they obtained significantly lower scores for interrupting (ShOut). Furthermore, when they made suggestions or ex-pressed opinions, they tended to check it out with the subordinate since checking-out behavior significantly differentiated between the three groups (K = 8.93, p < .02), with managers in the successful appraisals using more checking-out behavior than managers in the average appraisals ($U = 0$, $p < .001$), and than managers in the unsuccessful appraisals ($U = 0$, $p < .001$). In fact, none of the managers in the unsuccessful appraisals used the behavior. As far as checking out might be considered as a behavior that increases the opportunity for a subordinate to state disagreement or agreement with the point under discussion, it would seem to be related to behaviors that Greller (1978) associated with a sense of ownership of the appraisal, or that Burke et al., (1978) would consider as "treating the appraisee as an equal." Although a relatively brief behavior, it might serve to reinforce or "tie together" other supportive, inviting participation behaviors into a consistent, overall "helpful and constructive style" which is a conspicuous feature of the successful appraisal (Burke et al., 1978).

Not only did successful managers invite participation throughout the interview, but they also differed significantly from the others in their summarizing behavior, that although not longer, was in proportion to other behaviors more frequent than for the less successful managers.

The above behaviors might be critical contributors to Greller's finding that; "'Ownership' was the factor most strongly related to subordinates' reaction to the appraisal; it was also found to be the factor most closely linked to overall management style" (Greller, 1978, p. 646), of which he states: "It may not be far removed from what others have labelled 'psychological participation' (e.g., Wexley et al., 1973), for ownership involves being welcomed and feeling that what needed to be done was done." (Greller, 1978, p. 646)

These behaviors also help to identify more specifically and operationally those behaviors that constitute the somewhat amorphous leadership dimensions of "consideration" and "supportiveness."

As might be expected, a considerable number of behaviors differentiated the managers in the successful appraisal from those in the unsuccessful appraisals. The managers in the successful appraisals spent significantly more time inviting participation, in supportive behavior, and in giving positive evaluations.

In respect to the way in which successful managers gave information, they differed significantly from unsuccessful managers, not only by spending less of their total time giving factual information but perhaps more importantly in expressing themselves by way of *stating principles*. This may take the form of explanations for past action, or give the basis for future action, including statements of aims and criteria applicable to decision making. Perhaps it was the combination of offering information in a way in which it could be applied to future situations and the effective use of summarizing points discussed that the subordinates saw as particularly helpful. This may provide clues as to the more precise nature of the "initiating structure" dimension identified in previous leadership research.

Managers in the unsuccessful group differed significantly from those of the successful group by virtue of their spending significantly more of their time expressing opinions and feelings, in disagreeing, attacking, and in giving negative evaluations of the subordinate and of his performance. They also interrupted more often — a behavior not exhibited by any of the managers in the successful group.

Other behaviors that significantly differentiated the managers in the unsuccessful appraisal from those in the average group involved mainly negatively evaluating the appraisee and his opinions and performance since the average score for the managers in the unsuccessful group was significantly higher than that of the average group for disagreeing, negatively evaluating, and attacking, and significantly lower for positive evaluation. Behaviors in which they scored significantly lower than the other groups were support and positive evaluation. In each case behavioral measures were in terms of time and frequency with the exception of interrupting, which was calculated as a frequency.

The results of the one-way analysis of variance for the subordinates in each of the three appraisal interviews revealed only two behaviors that differentiated between the groups. These were behaviors of defending and disagreeing. In both cases, the subordinates in the unsuccessful groups obtained higher scores.

Managers in the unsuccessful appraisals spent on average a quarter of their time either disagreeing, criticizing, or personally attacking the subordinate whom they were appraising. It hardly seems surprising then that the subordinates in these appraisal interviews spent between a quarter and half of their time disagreeing or defending themselves. Since it is evident that a considerable amount of collective time was spent with manager and subordinate in conflict in the unsuccessful appraisal interviews, the unsatisfactory outcome measures are almost predictable. Previous findings relating perceived criticism and threat to outcome measures of appraisal success have differed markedly. Some cite dysfunctional effects (e.g., Burke *et al.,* 1978; Kay *et al.,* 1965) and others beneficial effects (e.g., Fletcher, 1973; Greller, 1978). Explanations for this apparent ambiguity are given with reference to contextual variables such as the presence of positive evaluation (e.g., Fletcher, 1973), and the opportunity to express one's feelings (e.g., Landy, Barnes, & Murphy, 1978), or by reference to the object of the criticism (e.g., subordinate's performance or person). In the present study, the global term "criticism" was subdivided into three different components of (NE), (DIS), and (Att). The results of the behavior analysis would appear to confirm the value of defining operationally, and as precisely as possible, the different aspects of criticism since the relationship between them and the other behaviors of the managers and subordinates would seem to reflect the pattern of eventual outcomes of the appraisal interviews.

Interestingly, the results show that the subordinates in the successful appraisals used more building and supportive behavior than subordinates in the unsuccessful appraisals (see Fig. 10.2). This would seem to emphasize the need to look more closely at the interactive effects of subordinate and manager behaviors, and at possible causal linkages.

Interviews that achieved successful outcome measures are characterized by subordinates actually communicating far more information than the manager appraising them, who spent more time talking in terms of guidelines or principles of action than in giving facts and clarification.

Overall Results and Conclusions

The frustration experienced by leadership researchers who have relied on perceptual measures to identify characteristics of effective managers was summed up perhaps by Greller (1978) who, like the present writer, was attempting to identify leadership skills in the appraisal interview:

> The most striking feature is that those measures of appraisal behaviour which are most specific and most closely match the actions prescribed for managers have the least effect. Specific behaviours are so loosely linked to each other that they neither produce an independent factor nor load on factors with other descriptions of the appraisal interview. As a consequence it seems unlikely that simplistic changes of manager behaviour in the interview would help. (p. 655)

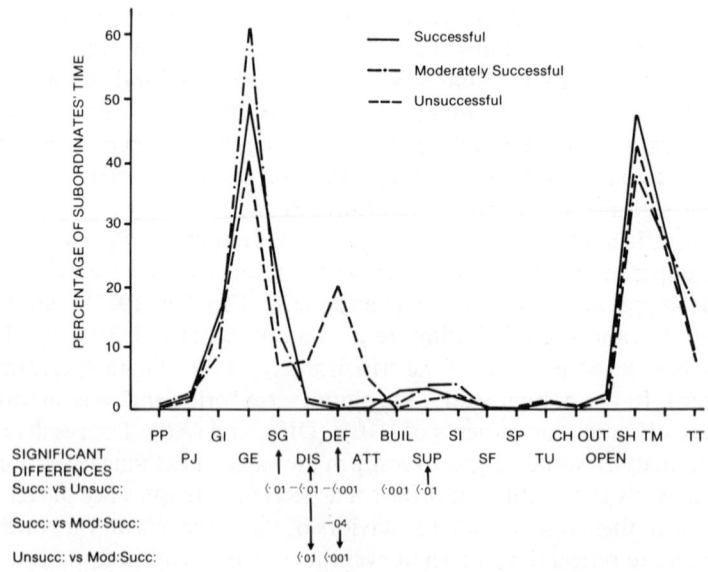

FIGURE 10.2. Graph showing distribution of mean behavioral analysis scores as measured by time for subordinates in the three groups of appraisal interviews; with a summary of the significant values obtained from the Mann-Whitney U test comparing pairs of groups

The present writer challenges this conclusion on the grounds that the above research and perhaps the majority of leadership research has employed perceptual measures as a means of collecting the crucial data. In this chapter it has been argued that not only are perceptions of an event that occurred days or even months in the past a function of distortion, but they cannot be regarded as an accurate or even an appropriate means of measuring actual leader behavior. The example of the significant difference between the certainty of managers and subordinates as to whether a follow-up interview had been arranged perhaps reinforces this suggestion. In addition, the variables that perceptual scales identify as relating to the nature of managerial effectiveness are of limited value to a managerial skills-development program since they are typically imprecise and deal with style rather than specific, trainable behaviors.

In the present study only two perceptual measures consistently provided a significant amount of predictive value to the dependent variables. These were manager friendliness and ending the interview positively. There are at least three additional major problems of applying this information to a training program for increasing managerial effectiveness:

1. How do you help a manager to become more friendly if his or her predominant style could not be described as such? Where does one begin?
2. Ending the interview positively, although perhaps providing the manager with a useful clue as to how to draw final conclusions, says nothing about how the rest of the appraisal should be conducted.
3. How credible would a management educator appear to an experienced manager who was told that these were the most important guidelines?

The results of the behavior analysis, on the other hand, revealed several behaviors that were seen to differentiate the behaviors of managers in the three groups. They are shown in Table 10.4. It must be added, however, that as the sample was relatively small, caution should be adopted in extrapolating from the results. But as far as these results might be accepted as instructive, the behaviors identified as characterizing the successful interviews could easily be incorporated into a leadership-skills-development program.

By providing training in skills in the appraisal interview, it might reasonably be presumed that one is at the same time increasing a manager's skills of leadership in his or her daily contact with subordinates. In a recent study of managers' appraisal-interviewing skills, Burke, Weitzel, and Weir (1980, p. 694) would appear to be supporting the view expressed by the present writer when they conclude that "The specific behaviours examined here were also related to the ways in which managers deal with the day-to-day job performance of their subordinates. Perhaps what is most important is that the behaviours are teachable." A study by Dulewicz, Fletcher, and Walker (1976) investigating whether the introduction of a new appraisal scheme in the Civil

TABLE 10.4. Comparison of the Subordinates' Perceptions that relate to the "Successful" Appraisal Interview, with the Behavioral Analysis of the Managers in the Successful Interviews.

Perceptual Measures	Behavioral Measures	Significant Differences
*Var 1: The manager tried to be friendly during the interview.	+ Checking Out (ChOut)	S vs U
*Var 2: The manager ended the interview on a positive note.	+ Supportive Behavior (SUP)	S vs U
	+ Summarizing (SUM)	S vs M
*Var 4: The manager praised me for what I have done well.	+ Positive Evaluation (PE)	S vs U
		S vs M
		S vs U
*Var 5: The manager gave me the opportunity to state my side of the issue.	+ Inviting Participation (IP)	S vs U
	+ Giving Information: Internal (GI)	S vs U
	+ Giving Information: External (GE)	S vs M
	+ Seeking Information: Cumulative (Seeking Information + Seeking Proposals + Seeking Feelings) (SInfo)	S vs M S vs U
	Stating Guidelines (SG)	S vs U
	+ Shutting Out (ShOut)	S vs U S vs M
	+ Disagreeing (DIS)	S vs U M vs U
	+ Negative Evaluation (NE)	S vs U
	+ Attacking (ATT)	S vs U
	Directive: Cumulative (Proposal regarding job + Stating guidelines) (DIR) PJ + SG	S vs U

S = successful; M = moderately successful; U = unsuccessful managers.

*Indicates analysis of variance revealed significant F values for this item.

+ Indicates analysis of variance revealed significant K values for this item.

Only Var 1 and Var 2 emerge from a multiple regression analysis as significantly predicting a successful outcome to the appraisal interview.

Service had resulted, three years later, in improvements in manager-subordinate communications reported significant improvements in the frequency, quality, and degree of satisfaction of the manager-subordinate communications.

The present writer is not suggesting that by increasing a manager's interpersonal skills in the appraisal interview, one can immediately transform an ineffective manager into one with leadership qualities. Several researchers have stressed the fact that relatively little is achieved in the appraisal interview when existing communications between the manager and subordinate are poor (e.g., Fletcher, 1978; Greller, 1975, 1978). The notion of thresholds is probably pertinent here. Consequently, in order for training in leadership skills to be effective, a certain minimum level of interpersonal competence is probably necessary.

Another major factor is the view that the interpersonal skills between manager and subordinate reflect only one of the possibly many roles required for managers to be all-round effective leaders (e.g., McCall & Segrist, 1980). However, McCall, Morrison, and Hannan (1978) made the following observation:

> The verbal nature of managerial work at all levels is the best documented characteristic of the job. . . . At low to middle levels of management researchers have generally found that well over half the time was spent in verbal communications, with a range of 27 per cent to 82 per cent. . . . Managers at higher levels spent up to 90 per cent of their time in oral communication, with 65 per cent being most typical. . . . Most verbal interactions are face-to-face. (pp. 11–12)

One major variable determining the ultimate success of the appraisal interview is undoubtedly the interpersonal skills of the appraiser. And since, as was argued earlier, these skills are essentially leadership skills, relating both theoretically and empirically to leadership research, it would seem indisputable that training in the skills, in part identified by the research presented in this study, will provide a valid basis for leadership-skills development.

Apart from the caution that must undoubtedly be adopted when extrapolating from these results to a wider population, since the sample here was so small and the interviews were role played, there are also inevitably some questions regarding the methodology employed in this research. Attempts were made in the design of this study to control some important variables. In so doing, three principal factors were taken into consideration:

1. The sample should encompass a wide range of experienced managers from different organizations.
2. Since the appraisal interview may be used by different organizations for a number of different reasons, it was decided highly appropriate to control for the objectives of the appraisals to be studied. As the purpose of the appraisal interview in the present research context was to provide a particular situation in which specific leadership skills may be studied, it was viewed here with respect to its importance as an employee development tool (see Kleinman & Durham, 1981; Randell et al., 1976) where its primary emphasis is in increasing subordinates' motivation to perform and equally importantly, to help subordinates identify what they need to do differently to improve their performance. These were the stated controlled objectives of the course the managers were attending. It may be argued that, by exposing all the managers in the sample to a particular course in appraisal interviewing before performing interviews, the design affected the outcome.

While undoubtedly true, this does not imply that the resultant performances are less valid. Indeed, it would seem to suggest that a further degree
of control has been introduced since each of the managers can be presumed
to have at least some degree of shared theoretical and practical knowledge,
whereas had they performed the interviews before exposure to the course,
their background information of interviewing skills *and* objectives would
undoubtedly be varied. Furthermore, the information imparted in the
course reflected the objectives and styles of appraisal interviewing recommended by the current literature and embodied the aspects of leadership
skills discussed by the models of leadership cited, which again implies some
control.

3. In order to compare the behavior used by the managers appraising, a standard case study and role playing were employed.

Balanced against this is the relative artificiality of imposing role-played
recorded and observed interviews, where the information available is extremely limited. This does, however, in certain important respects correspond to
real-life situations in that it is in the nature of a manager's job to be confronted
with novel situations and limited information with which he or she is expected
to deal effectively.

Second, a *standard* case study was used. Again, this was necessary to
achieve some control over the situation and provides corresponding benefits.
The case study was written by members of a large international organization
and was based on what they perceived as reflecting real-life problems of common occurrence to their managers. The biographical information was given
to the managers at least three days before the interviews. For these two reasons
at least, since the managers were experienced, one might reasonably presume
that the case would become meaningful to them in the light of their previous
experiences.

Third, the criticism that the situation of being observed and recorded is
inherently threatening must undoubtedly be accepted. However, the experimental evidence provided by Weick (1968, p. 369), for example, suggests that
such an influence may be overestimated. Certainly, in this study the managers
appeared to act, after the initial few minutes at least, as if this was unimportant
to them; and perhaps the fact that 10 percent of the interviews obtained extremely low scores on both criterion variables serves as some evidence of the
fact that they seemed somewhat unconscious of their often disastrous behavior.

There is also the obvious and valid criticism that since these were not real-
life appraisals, one could not in fact validate subordinate intentions to improve their subsequent performance. If one bears in mind, however, the experimental evidence from past studies that support the notion that the skills of
using supportive behavior and inviting participation in the appraisal interview
have been found to be significantly related to several outcome measures, including actual improvement in performance (Burke, Weitzel, & Weir, 1980,

p. 690), one can only hope that by attempting to increase these skills, one obtains some degree of improvement in performance.

Finally, perceptions of each appraisal were collected immediately following the termination of the interview. In previous studies, the time gap varied enormously even up to a year or more. The present design makes the perceptions particularly susceptible to recency effects, but these are probably not as distorting as the effects of memory distortion after several months.

Possible Extensions of the "Microlevel" Approach

The fact that attention is drawn to the limitations of the present study, and to other factors that may well be providing an important source of variation between the results collected from different samples, suggests a direction for future research in terms of the use of much wider sampling designs. Another suggestion for future research that might provide valuable data for skills training concerns the application of a variety of different behavioral analyses. The use of content and some process analyses was included in the present study, but other process analyses might include study of underlying dimensions such as those mentioned by Nemeroff and Cosentino (1979); for example, "When my manager and I disagree about my job responsibility, my manager tries to clarify the disagreement" (p. 570), or "The manager helps me establish priorities for the coming period." The author is at present analyzing the data with a view to identifying what appear to be underlying processes that seem to relate individual behaviors to particularly effective, or conversely, detrimental strategies.

At the other extreme, another basis for analysis might include nonverbal behaviors. Yet another is the use of sequential analysis. Implicit in this suggestion of sequential analysis is the possibility of analyzing causal links between manager and subordinate behavior in appraisal interviews. This offers the potential of relating findings regarding skills in appraising with wider conceptual models of leader behavior. It also provides some means of counteracting the criticism that not enough research has been directed at the role of the subordinate in causing leader behavior (e.g., Greene, 1975; Herold, 1977).

As suggested here, the use of follow-up data from subordinate performance and longitudinal studies of perceptions in the manager-subordinate relationship and subordinate-organization relationship could provide rich and increasingly valid data for leadership research. This of course presupposes the use of data from real-life interactions, and could therefore include a range of demographic and personality variables that would facilitate the study of interactional effects. This would also enable research to be conducted on the relationship between leadership skills in the appraisal interview and interpersonal skills of managers in a much wider range of activities.

Finally, it must be noted that the major limitation of using the behavioral analysis technique, as it was used in the present investigation, is the extra-ordinary amount of time required for the process of analyzing the wealth of data available in appraisal interviews. Since the ultimate utility of the technique lies in the value of being able to use it in subsequent real-life situations, it poses a most important question. In answering this question, it should be borne in mind that one of the prime objects of the present research was to investigate the precise nature of leadership skills using a different approach from that adopted by past studies. Consequently, its inherent value lay in iden-tifying as wide a range as possible of objectively observed behaviors that dif-ferentiated successful, unsuccessful, and average managers. Although it was thought important that behaviors be timed carefully, the results indicate (Table 10.3) that in all but one behavior, frequencies yielded the same dif-ferences. Without doubt, some categories of behavior could be collapsed into single, simpler groups: for example, all seeking-information behaviors could form one single group. A final instrument that included the 13 behaviors found to be most crucial would provide no problem to an individual well trained in BA to rate behaviors in frequencies in real time. Indeed, similar instruments are employed without problems by experienced users (Rackham & Morgan, 1977). The importance of training is, of course, as crucial to the instrument's effectiveness as to any other measure, and high reliability of the user is an essential prerequisite.

While clearly advocating a microlevel analysis of leadership skills, the pres-ent author is fully aware of the problems inherent in trying to understand leadership skills by attempting to identify and measure their "constituent" parts. Behavior analysis, for example, would appear to produce far richer and more valuable descriptions of leadership behavior than the scores from perceptual scales (see Table 10.4). Although the present writer advocates the use of such an objective, microlevel analysis, she fears that it may be used to prescribe what *should* be done, and *when*. Since the leadership skills in-vestigated in the present study were concerned with social interaction, the pro-cess requires far richer skills than merely being able to perform a particular verbal behavior at a particular time (Alban Metcalfe, 1981).

A thorough knowledge of the specific behaviors will by no means provide the answers to leadership research. In isolation, they make little or no sense, and can certainly not be extrapolated to the vast, heterogeneous range of leadership activities. They must, undoubtedly, be related to a much broader view of leadership, which encompasses a range of organizational, situational, and individual variables. This would seem to bring the discussion back to the realm of macro theory, and contingency models of leadership. The proposed coexistence of macro- and microlevel research into leadership in no way diminishes the importance of macrolevel theories; indeed, one would appear to enrich the other, since managers, about whom they are essentially con-cerned, require first of all knowledge of, and the facility for, training in the behaviorally based skills of leadership. They also require some form of cognitive framework so that it can be determined in which situation and under what constraints managers need to vary their behavior. As clear as the present results would appear to be, this is only one of a multitude of situations with which a manager is faced in any one day. Furthermore, the present writer would not present a case for the immediate and indiscriminate "conversion" of all managers in every situation to comply with the "successful" managers' profile. However, given the present economic climate which for one reason or another makes the traditional organizational "carrot" of salary increase and promotional opportunities far less common (Morrison & Krantz, 1981), there will indubitably be an urgent need for managers to prove their competence in complex interpersonal skills, such as participation. While the contingency models such as those of Vroom and Yetton, and of House and Dressler can suggest in which circumstances these particular skills will be most efficacious, they do not explain the means by which they can be developed. Therefore, while firmly maintaining an appreciation of the macrolevel models of leadership, the results of the behavior analysis presented in this study would appear to have isolated specific and potentially trainable behaviors that are likely directly to affect the managers' performance in appraisal interviews, and by extrapolation, leadership behavior in general.

11

Commentary on Part 2

Chapter 7 Commentary: Observation for What?

Peter Forsblad

The Luthans and Lockwood chapter is primarily methodological in nature. It focuses on some questions concerning observation as a method for gathering data on leadership, reasons for the development of an observational system, reliability, and validity of the proposed system (LOS), and its relationships to questionnaire methods (LBDQ and MBS). These questions are clearly defined and also treated comprehensively. However, the broader set of issues that relate to the use of observational methods are either merely hinted at or neglected altogether. The most serious omission in this respect is perhaps that there is no discussion of what data a fully developed LOS can be expected to produce or how LOS data can be used to further our understanding of leadership "in natural settings."

One way to start thinking about the proposed observational system, in the context of how it might relate to an increased understanding of leadership, is to look at some earlier studies that have used observation as a method for gathering data on managerial behavior.* An enumeration (in chronological order) of the more important of these would include:

- *Carlson (1951):* the original managerial behavior study in that it was the first to ask how managers actually spend their time, although it was not an observational study in the strict sense since it used a diary method. It was carried out in 1949 and used ten company presidents as subjects.
- *Westerlund (1952):* a carefully designed experimental study using participant observation in a time-sampling mode involving supervisors and their work groups as subjects.
- *Burns (1957):* a time-study of executives (with a frequency count of observed behavior on much the same lines as LOS although with a cruder set of behavioral descriptors).

---

*Since the subjects in the Luthans and Lockwood study are managers and the "leadership" categories and behavioral descriptors used in LOS seem very closely related to those used in studies of managerial behavior, this mode of comparison is less far-fetched than it might appear at first sight.

- *Wirdenius (1958):* supervisors in a variety of natural settings studied by observation under random time sampling.
- *Dalton (1959):* a broad study on how "industrial managers manage." Interviews, diaries, and participant observation are used to gather data. Dalton worked for extended periods in two of the three companies studied.
- *Copeman, Luijk, and Hanika (1963):* a strict time study involving at least some elements of observation.
- *Sayles (1964):* an anthropological parsimonious description and explanation of the behavior of 75 middle and lower managers in an organization in which Sayles "lived" for several years.
- *Dubin and Spray (1964):* one of the first work-activity studies involving managers; particularly concerned with patterns of interaction.
- *Kelly (1964):* a time study of managers extolling the methodological virtues of activity sampling.
- *Brewer and Tomlinson (1964):* a time study of managers.
- *Hodgson, Levinson, and Zaleznik (1965):* an undeservedly forgotten study of managerial roles and work sharing among top executives in a hospital.
- *Horne and Lupton (1965)*: another work-activity study concerned with middle managers.
- *Thomason (1967, 1968):* explores managerial roles and relationships on the basis of observational data.
- *Mintzberg (1968):* provides most of the empirical evidence on which Mintzberg based his 1973 book successfully asking the question, "What do managers actually do?"
- *Stewart (1976):* a broad study on the characteristics of managerial work involving observation as well as questionnaires and interviews.
- *Kotter (1982):* general managers studied through interviews and observation with a particular focus on managerial influence and decision making.

This enumeration covers 30 years of studies of managerial behavior involving at least some use of observation for the collection of data. It can be extended somewhat but not much without searching obscure sources that would only provide endless replication. Therefore, the conclusion that there are not very many of these studies seems warranted.

There are a number of plausible reasons for this sparsity of observational studies. Among the more obvious are the following:

— Observational studies are extremely time-consuming and quickly produce vast quantities of data that are difficult to handle with ordinary statistical data-reduction techniques.
— Access to managers for observational studies usually presents more of a problem than access for a "comparable" study administered by questionnaire.
— Observational studies have generally not been rewarded by the "academic

system," since they, almost without exception, contain elements that are contrary or at least not in full accord with traditional notions of science.

A second conclusion that can be drawn from the above list of studies — substantiated in particular by the second half of the list — is that observational studies have been used mainly to gather data on: (1) what leaders actually do; (2) how much and in what ways that varies in different situations; (3) why leaders behave as they do; and (4) what impact that behavior has. What has been aimed at, in other words, is some form of increased understanding in the broad meaning of the term. This idea seems so ingrained that Stewart (1982a) writes:

> One problem in observation is the insight of the observer. What is wanted is someone who is both capable of observing analytically and detachedly and of thinking creatively about the meaning of what is being observed. An observer who does not have these characteristics can fill up an observer's format but cannot contribute to the understanding of what is being observed. (p. 133)

The Luthans and Lockwood framework has quite a different focus. Here the intent of the study is "to generalize across levels, functions and personal characteristics of leaders." It proposes to accomplish this objective "by dealing only with frequencies of observable behavior [in a way that does not require] inference on the part of the observer." A question that seems to grow naturally out of these statements from the Luthans and Lockwood chapter regarding intent and method of the study is whether it is worth using observation to gather data, a method that is costly and by most considered cumbersome, if one does not want the qualitative information usually so ardently pursued by users of the method. Yes, answer Luthans and Lockwood, it is worth it if it means that more reliable and more valid data are gathered with a greater chance of discriminating between presumably independent categories.

At this point, however, one of the issues which, it was remarked at the beginning of these comments, is curiously missing in the Luthans and Lockwood contribution becomes crucial. This issr , can perhaps most succinctly be expressed in the question: Data for what? Luthans and Lockwood, at least as I understand it, provide something resembling an answer to this question as well.

In their discussion of why questionnaire measures provide inadequate assessment of leader behavior they state that ratings depend heavily on the criterion measure of interest, such as performance ratings or subordinate satisfaction. If this holds true — and I think it does — then it would also seem to hold true for data gathered by observation. That is, for each criterion measure of interest, a different set of observation system categories and behavioral descriptors would be needed. As they now stand, the LOS categories seem mainly to be useful for describing the work of the leader within the conceptualization given or perhaps for time studies.

The data-for-what question can be regarded as the turning point around which the Luthans and Lockwood framework revolves. Unless this question is answered with some precision, even if it only means repeating what is the essence of the Mintzberg (1968) response — data to know what to look for — the entire discussion of reliability and validity in questionnaire versus observation will fall flat.

In closing, I would like to address two additional points:

1. Some of the observational categories used do not seem quite observable. What does the manager do when he or she —

- sets goals and objectives?
- organizes the work?
- defines problems?

2. One of the three stated objectives of Chapter 7 is to recognize leadership as "a reciprocal, interactive process involving the leader, the environment, and the leader's behavior." Meeting this objective would seem to demand more than a frequency count of the leader's behavior along 12 categories.

Chapter 8 Commentary: On Qualitative Methods and Leadership Research

Philip M. Strong

I liked this chapter by Martinko and Gardner. Thus, the major thrust here is not to critique but rather to integrate and extend, to make links and suggest new departures. I shall comment on what the authors' research strategy looks like to someone trained in a very different research genre from that incorporated in the main focus of this project. My own work has been in the qualitative tradition; a tradition that appears to be growing in importance in leadership research and indeed has a valuable place in Martinko and Gardner's chapter.

Let us begin by summarizing what appear to be the strong points in an excellent design: the range of varied and reasonably hard outcome measures; the central emphasis on observation rather than on interview; the large number of educational managers observed; the coding scheme's recognition that two or more activities can occur simultaneously; and the emphasis on the fundamental importance of validity as opposed to reliability that leads to both the inclusion of qualitative as well as quantitative data and, perhaps, to a profoundly modest tone throughout the chapter. Whereas the perspective of a good deal of research combines megalomania with myopia in roughly equal proportions, Martinko and Gardner, it is nice to report, display neither of these traits.

Since I have no serious criticism of this project's design, I shall focus my comments instead on two separate areas. The first and more specific of these concerns various ways in which the project might be complemented by further sorts of research, mostly qualitative in nature. The second contains more general reflections upon the problems of combining the quantitative and qualitative research traditions.

Complementary Research

In the Martinko and Gardner study, the observers were trained and the reliability of their judgment assessed by using videotapes of *simulated* managerial behavior. Confidence in the results would be much increased if a further reliability check could be carried out, based this time on videotapes of *actual* managerial behavior. It is possible, for example, that simulated behavior is easier to code than naturally occurring behavior. All action contains crucial elements of what the conversation analysts call recipient design but one suspects that simulation may heighten this, making it more self-conscious while simultaneously lessening the complexity and multifocused nature of the interaction.

At several points in their discussion, the authors wonder whether their techniques are sufficiently fine-grained to get at the mysteries of effective leadership. Good leadership, they argue, may be a highly subtle thing. This appears to be a crucial point. What it suggests, Martinko and Gardner confess, is that far more detailed observation of managers may be needed to help solve the problem.

Such detailed observation may have a further value. Early in the chapter, the authors point out what is an effective style of leadership in one environment may not be effective in another. As schools vary considerably, so, therefore, may effective managerial behavior. (To this one might also add the possibility that more than one kind of leader behavior might prove effective in any one environment.) But despite this point, in both later discussion in the chapter and the preliminary tables, the only contrast drawn is between the behavior of high and moderate performers. Of course, the data at this stage are possibly too preliminary for analysis of varying behaviors. Nevertheless, for the detailed explanation of individual variation in behavior, further, more intensive study is probably needed. In consequence, given both the possible subtlety and the variability of effective leadership, it is important to outline the different kinds of intensive study that might complement the present research. Before doing so, however, it should be added that even if this research does eventually point up major differences between effective and noneffective educational managers, microscopic inquiry will still be needed if we are to understand what some of these differences mean.

What then are the three major types of inquiry?

One type of inquiry would use *systematic analysis* (using a precoded system) of mechanically recorded managerial interaction — either audio or video. Audio recording alters behavior somewhat less than the pressure of an observer (Samph, 1976) and mechanical recording in general has several distinct advantages: it offers a much greater wealth of data; it places action in a detailed international context; and it is replayable. This should record much finer detail than can be managed by the present system of observation.

A second type would employ *qualitative analysis* of systematically recorded, naturally occurring behavior, whether it is recorded by audio, video, or verbatim note taking. The aim here would be to use, at least initially, a more *inductive* approach to the analysis of the data.

The crucial difficulty in precoded systems is knowing whether or not one has determined the appropriate categories. The qualitative approach treats this as the principal research problem. In doing so, it sacrifices the advantage of ready computation. Ideally, however, this is not a drawback in the long run. Once one is satisfied that valid categories have been produced, one can move forward to more systematic counting.

A simple design for this study would be to take say, two high performers and two moderates, to record what seem to be crucial and readily accessible aspects of their organizational life (for example, their behavior in particular meetings), and to analyze intensively and inductively for any systematic differences. These results become hypotheses to be tested on recorded data from an additional set of managers. The hypotheses would then be modified and broadened in the light of any novelties in this second data set and then retested on a further data set. This process, known as "analytic induction" in the trade (Bloor, 1978; Mitchell, 1979), would be continued until the addition of further data sets produces no further modification in the hypotheses. In practice, of course, we are normally severely limited by constraints of time.

A third mode of inquiry involves using *a detailed ethnographic study.* Clearly, Martinko and Gardner have already taken the first step toward an ethnographic study by getting their observers to take limited field notes during their short period of observation. The study proposed here, however, would take a rather different form. First, it would focus on only a limited number of managers—at most three or four of either type. Second, according to the guidelines of analytic induction, these would be studied in sequence, that is, one set of high and low managers would be observed and hypotheses produced; these hypotheses would then be tested on the next set, and so on. That is, hypothesis generation and testing would be built into the field work in a more systematic way than in the Glaser and Strauss (1967) methodology cited by the authors.

Third, the period of observation would be far longer than the ten randomly assigned days in the present study. Three months would be a minimum for each manager. The key point here is that the present study, for all its virtues, does not intersect, at least on the data produced so far, with what are the crucial problems in running a school. There is considerable emphasis on activities but less on the particular difficulties the managers are trying to solve. The detailed ethnography extending over a reasonable period of time would bring the organization and the problems more into focus, along with its leaders. In this respect, although the authors rightly condemn primitive trait analysis, the present study, perhaps, still tends to focus more on managers than on managers-in-organizations, and in doing so, tends to repeat elements of the old-style trait tradition. At the same time, an extended period of observation would also enable the detailed study of crisis management, which is usually a crucial part of leadership. By watching events over time, one could study how particular leaders calm things down, smooth over problems, decide on confrontation, face unexpected calamities, and so on. Many crises take time to develop and all are complexly embedded in organizational life.

One final point on the subject of ethnography: The best method of doing things (if one were actually to embark on all that has been suggested!) might well be to reverse the order in which these studies have been suggested. Ideally, perhaps, the ethnography should come first. This would suggest both crucial factors and crucial locales for further study. There could then follow systematic recording of behavior in these key locales which could simultaneously be analyzed via both inductive qualitative procedure and systematic precoding, since each would focus on different features. Finally, the inductive analysis should uncover further features that could be turned into a coding schedule for further precoded analysis.

Experimental and Prospective Studies

If it turns out that different school environments demand very different kinds of leadership, then we will still face a considerable research problem. What will need to be discovered now is just how flexible managers can be. Can a manager who has succeeded in one type of environment do equally well in another in which a quite different kind of leadership is required? Which behaviors are closest to other behaviors? And so on.

The research design for this problem would be very different from the ones described so far. The ideal would be an experimental design in which both high and low managers are assigned to different types of schools from those they had previously worked in. In practice, however, one might be obliged to use a prospective or even retrospective study of naturally occurring changes in the past.

Combining Qualitative with Quantitative Research

The problem of combining qualitative and quantitative research methods is an obvious and important topic. First, then, a quick historical sketch. If recent accounts are to be believed, social research some 50 years ago was a kind of Eden in which the two methodologies were seen as complementary rather than antagonistic. The Chicago sociologists of the 1930s seemed to have combined the two and, likewise, Beatrice Webb, the major Fabian researcher of the early part of the century, carried out ethnography as well as the analysis of official statistics.

Then came The Fall. The advent of highly sophisticated quantitative and survey techniques, combined with the relatively weak development of qualitative methods, led to a parting of the ways. Quantitative researchers scorned their qualitative brethren as totally unscientific, and turned to various extreme forms of positivism which tried, unsuccessfully, to model the social on the natural sciences. Qualitative researchers, in defense, elaborated equally implausible and extreme philosophical arguments.

Just recently, however, some signs of mutual accommodation may be discerned, of which Martinko and Gardner's contribution is an excellent example. Both sides have much to learn from each other. (Both also — the qualitative as much as the quantitative — must learn from the nonacademic tradition of qualitative analysis to be found in literature films and documentary. A review of the literature somehow never includes a review of literature; see Strong, 1982.)

As Martinko and Gardner suggest, the key lesson to be learned from the qualitative tradition is the importance of validity, without which reliability is meaningless. As they also argue, the key weakness of the qualitative tradition is the relative absence of systematic method. Both statements, however, need a little qualification.

While naturally approving of the movement toward validity, there is an obvious danger that it may end up in a state of total chaos — interesting chaos perhaps, but still chaos. In this respect, Martinko and Gardner's review of the observational literature on leadership is most instructive, particularly in the great care that successive researchers have taken to ensure comparability between their own and previous studies. Here, then, is a central emphasis on cumulative work. By comparison, the qualitative tradition presents a sad spectacle. For example, Hammersley (1980) in a recent detailed review of qualitative studies of classroom interaction — a major field over the last 15 years or so — comments sadly on the utter fragmentation of the field. If qualitative work is to combine with the quantitative tradition, it must be carried out, by and large, in an equally focused and systematic way. There is still, of course, a place for relatively unstructured and free floating work, as the work of Goffman (1982) in particular should remind us. Nevertheless, it would be utterly wrong if all qualitative work was in this style. We qualitative researchers need a good dose of system, and relaxed interaction with the quantitative tradition can only help us in this.

At the same time, for all our many glaring faults, I do not think, or at any rate do not like to think, that we are quite as primitive as Martinko and Gardner seem to suggest. I have already stressed the importance of analytic induction, and the related method of "deviant case analysis" also deserves a mention (Strong, 1979). Likewise, there is now a considerable body of useful methodological work, of which McCall and Simmons' (1969) reader is perhaps the best collection.

Chapter 9 Commentary: Understanding Managerial Behavior/Leadership: Research Approaches and the Development of New Knowledge

Peter Weissenberg

One of the most long-lasting and difficult problems that all social scientists must solve in order to develop new knowledge from a theoretical perspective is how to examine and how to document what actually happens when theory makes predictions, and action follows theory. This is the problem associated with the measurement and observation of behavior in field or laboratory settings. The Burgoyne and Hodgson chapter continues attempts to solve this problem by applying a particular research approach developed in another area to the examination of leadership behaviors. They point out that, "While we have developed and are using this approach to study managerial action, we feel it also has considerable potential for leadership research." It is apparent from this statement that they do not equate "managerial" behaviors or actions with those flowing from the concept of "leadership."

They discuss two methods in particular: "protocol analysis" and "stimulated recall." Their proposals are examined here in several ways: initially, this approach to studying leadership behavior is placed in context and then its potential usefulness for carrying out this avowed goal is evaluated.

Burgoyne and Hodgson have listed the historical development of managerial behavior research in terms of several periods, or major approaches, the "pre-empirical," "media" studies, and "content studies." A review of their sources and their discussion of these three approaches seem to indicate that they have ignored to some extent what might be called the very solid "empirical" thrust that began with the seminal work done in the 1930s by Moreno (1934) as he developed the sociometric studies that were applied to an examination of leadership. One might also consider here the major studies conducted by the office of strategic services (OSS) in the United States and by other agencies in other parts of the world using observational techniques to study the actual leadership behaviors of a variety of individuals as well as the testing studies carried on during this period by the U.S. Army and other military agencies to examine a variety of so-called "traits" of leadership.

Following this, additional empirical work culminated in the major effort by Stogdill (1948) when he reviewed the trait literature shortly after the close of World War II. Burgoyne and Hodgson make too little of those developments which led to the development of research on leadership behaviors/styles exemplified by Ohio State researchers such as Fleishman (1953). This research was followed by the work of Bass (1960), Fiedler (1964), and ultimately by many other studies. These are given short shrift in the historical development as it is summarized by Burgoyne and Hodgson. And perhaps they are peripheral to the developments in studying managerial behavior that these two authors seek to highlight. On the other hand, in their historical discussion they do a very solid job of distinguishing between what we might call "managerial" research and "leadership" research. And they bring the research efforts up to date by citing some of the more recent symposium volumes.

Before continuing with an examination of some other specific aspects of their suggestions, this commentary takes a step backward into the "context" so that we can have a better understanding of where, indeed, their methods are in the development of leadership research.

Bouchard (1976) provides a thorough review of field research methods. The methods discussed here would fit into that broad classification. In Bouchard's terms, the field "is where the generality, applicability and utility of psychological knowledge are put to the test" (p. 363). Further, he makes certain suggestions for researchers and these suggestions should be kept in mind even as the development of new methods is discussed. Bouchard suggested that researchers "(1) choose the method that is most likely to serve their purpose rather than the easiest method; (2) use more than one method whenever possible; and (3) focus more on the actual behavior of theoretical or practical concern and less on verbal behavior and test responses than they have in the past" (p. 363). Burgoyne and Hodgson's methods fit the latter suggestion about focusing on actual behavior. This, then, in Bouchard's terms, would be one of the strongest recommendations for a modern method. Bouchard correctly stresses the need for this type of approach and if Burgoyne and Hodgson's approaches help us fill this need, then we would have succeeded in acquiring a strong and particularly relevant new technique to help us develop our leadership interests.

Bouchard also points out that there are special characteristics in field settings that are of importance to researchers and will help in the development of valid theory. A field setting can have a greater degree of intensity and will allow for a larger range of phenomena to be observed. In addition, the frequency and duration of behaviors will be greater than it might be expected to be in a laboratory. The natural time constraints of the system, however, operate and natural units are involved. The settings are realistic since they are the settings within which the studied behavior naturally takes place. Generally, there is a greater degree of representativeness of treatments and of subjects in a field setting. If Burgoyne and Hodgson's methods are to be useful additions, they should utilize the natural advantages implied by these areas in field studies.

If, however, this usefulness is to develop, we must face some of the other dilemmas of field studies: that is, the fact that they are costly, take time, and require appropriate funding. As can be seen from the discussion of the methodologies under review, to carry out a proper study using protocol analysis and stimulated recall involving follow-up would take an inordinate amount of research time and effort, and consequently, support. In addition, it would take the support of ancillary personnel to type and prepare the protocols for analysis, to make sure the follow-up takes place, and for other auxiliary tasks. Whether or not the results are worth the cost and effort would depend on the final analysis of the data and their contribution to the development of new insights and theory in the pursuit of knowledge about leadership.

Burgoyne and Hodgson present a convincing argument that their approach qualifies them to do something better than what is being done, and that it accords with a variety of philosophical justifications for carrying out and for defining what is accurate research and theory building. They clearly and explicitly discuss the tensions and conflicts between a variety of theoretical approaches to understanding research methodology and to justifying it, the so-called philosophy-of-science arguments. They indicate that their approaches, using protocol analysis and stimulated recall, would allow them to justify their research through various philosophical bases. So far then, the authors have justified their methodology as necessary and have attempted to provide a sound philosophical basis for its validity and applicability to leadership as a particular field of research.

In the development of leadership, as Bass (1981) has pointed out, the use of research methodologies has often coincided with the development of specific approaches or theoretical directions in leadership. Perhaps the particular stage of research in which we find ourselves (or should find ourselves) today is not what would benefit most fruitfully from the application of the new techniques suggested by Burgoyne and Hodgson. For example, Bass (1981) indicated that in the beginning, since "The study of leadership is an ancient art" (p. 5), there was much discussion and philosophical speculation. During this time, perhaps, those who were involved would have benefited from the ability to do a detailed analysis of the behaviors represented by protocol analysis or the examination of the behavior that results from stimulated recall. The emphasis was on understanding very gross types of behaviors as exemplified by certain major figures, usually in the literature or in significant positions of authority in society. If one could follow some of the characters in Homer's *Iliad*, sit in with them as they carried out their leadership acts, and then examine transcripts of these acts, as well as asking them to think about them in retrospect, one might benefit greatly in understanding what specific leadership behaviors meant, and how they were developed. In our early attempt to emphasize the development of leadership traits we might have benefited from these approaches. Today, however, we seem to be in the later stages of major theory-building efforts. Such stages should require major, large-scale research efforts with large samples, and attempts to use protocol analysis and stimulated recall to observe actual leadership behaviors and to understand them at the micro level, at this stage of our research and theory building, might not be most beneficial.

Perhaps we could, in some cases, benefit from a microlevel analysis of the behaviors and motivations that are implied to exist in various leadership styles. In my own research efforts using Fiedler's (1967) model (Weissenberg & Kupat, 1976, for example), I have often asked whether, indeed, we are dealing with behavior or attitudes and how do we know which? Perhaps, the use of protocol analysis at the appropriate time, and with the appropriate sample, would allow us to put the microscope on certain types of behaviors that are not yet fully understood. This could help to clarify some of the confusion that exists among a variety of our present models and theories of leadership behavior. There is no doubt that we need to reach a common understanding of these behaviors and attitudes if we are ever to pull together the variety of different approaches now existing.

Many seemingly common types of behaviors are described by the different theoretical approaches (C, S; hi/lo LPC: employee and task orientation, for example), but we do not know whether or not they are really the same, or whether there are merely semantic similarities involved in their definitions. The uses suggested by Burgoyne and Hodgson for their protocol analysis and stimulated recall methodologies might allow us to determine whether a considerate leader in the Ohio State sense is indeed the same as a high-LPC leader in the contingency model. The best use of this set of methodologies might be to examine individual behavior within those theories that focus on such behaviors. However, some approaches have considered leadership a group process, for example, and for that type of research it might be difficult to apply these techniques. We can hope, however, that Burgoyne and Hodgson's research methods will help us to reach that stage when we can assist an "Academy of Leadership" (Bass, 1981, p. 15) to establish a standard definition of leadership that will help us clarify our path forward and will assist us in achieving the integration needed at the present stage.

Leadership seems to have a variety of faces even as leaders have a variety of styles, approaches, or behaviors. What is needed is a definitive approach to defining, classifying, and capturing those different "faces" so that we can recognize them when we meet them again, when they may be wearing a different pair of glasses, or have grown a beard. Is this not what we have when we look at the different "theories" to which Bass (1981) and others refer, and which are championed by a host of well-qualified, excellent theoreticians and researchers? Will Burgoyne and Hodgson help us to capture those "faces"? They certainly seem to have added a new dimension by suggesting the use of protocol analysis and stimulated recall. But, just as any new camera has advantages, it also has drawbacks. Some have been mentioned in broad terms above. Perhaps a few others should be mentioned.

A researcher will have to have a good deal of training in both observational and interview skills in order to produce an accurate protocol for future analysis. In addition, it will take careful training to allow the subsequent use of the stimulated recall in a valid, meaningful fashion. Of course, one can say the same for other methods but obviously a questionnaire can be administered by a relatively untrained research assistant and it can be administered to many subjects at one time. To administer any psychological test, particularly a clinical, projective instrument, also takes a good deal of training and many can also only be administered to one subject at a time. So the Burgoyne and Hodgson methods do not possess unique liabilities, but they are liabilities that must be compensated for by advantages in order to make the method worthwhile. It will be necessary to train and prepare researchers a good deal before they can use this approach accurately to describe many of the complex behaviors of leadership. Still, if this method provides some additional accuracy, it may be worth the trouble.

My own research into Fiedler's contingency model continued over many years. It would have been useful if I had been able to gather some very detailed event records such as those that protocol analysis could provide. If it had been possible to stimulate the recall of the subject, additional insights that could have clarified some of the questions about the real nature of the underlying dynamics involved in Fiedler's model might have resulted. Further, if one could apply this approach to a study of Blake and Mouton's (1964) methodology and examine in detail the behaviors of individuals going through the various training stages, perhaps one would gain much clearer insight into the actual dynamics underlying the different styles described in very nonbehavioral terms. Could we learn more about consideration and structure? By applying these techniques, we probably could. Burgoyne and Hodgson are to be applauded for presenting us with a tool that has helped them in understanding managerial behavior. Even if some misgivings continue about its transferability, we should try it because the tool may help and it certainly cannot hurt.

I have tried in this discussion of Burgoyne and Hodgson's method not to be overly critical and negative. I have tried instead to place these authors into perspective within the flow of research and theorizing in the field of leadership research. This review has not been overly concerned with the details of their procedures but has tried to present their place in the spectrum of research methods and has related their approaches to the development of an overall theory of leadership behavior and integration.

Chapter 10 Commentary:
Micro Leadership Skills Reconsidered

Bert King

Alban Metcalfe has a very substantial chapter based on painstaking research that represents very well the empirical, quantitative tradition in the leadership research area. She is to be commended for the behavioral focus she has adopted and for devising a simulated performance appraisal interview which she could record on film and subsequently subject to an exhaustive quantitative analysis. In addition, she deserves praise for her yeoman effort to relate the findings in the different areas of leadership and of performance appraisal.

At the same time, there are some important limitations and additional research directions that are important to consider. One of the objectives of this volume is to consider the advantages and disadvantages of different methodologies and a substantial portion of the book has been devoted to methodological issues. At this point I would like to invite the reader to consider the particular approach used here—that of role playing. Whenever one uses role playing, it is important to consider just how realistic the role-playing situation is and whether, if we had used real-life behavior instead, we would have obtained the same results.

Alban Metcalfe criticizes the excessive use of questionnaires in the fields of performance appraisal and leadership. There is no disagreement here with this criticism and her intention to avoid the biases involved in the use of questionnaire data. There are, however, several ways that one could avoid an exclusive reliance on questionnaire data. One way would be to observe and evaluate, either *in situ* or on film, actual appraisal interviews. Alban Metcalfe decided not to do this and her decision is understandable. It would be quite difficult, of course, to obtain access to real-life appraisal interviews and, in observing them, the presence of the observer could influence the data owing to the subjects' awareness of the observation process and their attempt to look good.

The alternative she selected involved setting up a simulation with subjects who were readily available because they were involved in training programs for managers, either as trainees or as instructors. But this means that the subjects were not naive as to what should go on in an appraisal interview. The staff personnel who played the role of the subordinate who was being appraised could be assumed to have certain beliefs as to which kinds of supervisor behaviors are praiseworthy and which are not, since they were involved as instructors in the management training program in question. To the extent that this is so, we encounter the possibility of certain perceptual biases in spite of the fact that Alban Metcalfe purposely selected the role-playing method in order to avoid perceptual biases. These staff members might, consciously or unconsciously, evaluate certain behaviors in the interview in accordance with the precepts that they communicated as instructors in the training program. Even if this did not occur with respect to the content of their particular training program, it might well occur with respect to their general knowledge of what is recommended in the literature on appraisals. In other words, as professional trainers or managers they cannot be assumed to be representative of the population of supervisors.

Since more than one of these confederates were employed as the simulated subordinate, we must raise the additional question of how much variability might have occurred from one of them to the other. As far as I can tell, this variable was not taken into account. Consequently, one cannot eliminate the possibility that the group results presented were inordinately influenced by certain of the confederates whose behavior in the simulation might have differed from the others. It would have been useful to have some measures of the behavior in the simulation of each of the confederates so that we could assess this possibility.

In light of Alban Metcalfe's criticism of the excessive use of subjective and perceptual data, it is somewhat startling to note that the criterion that she used actually falls in this very category. That is, her criterion consists of the feelings of the subordinates in the simulation about the interview, and she used their "feelings" in order to divide the interviews into successful and unsuccessful ones.

Another point we might make about the use of role playing is that it eliminates the possibility of "historical" analyses relating what goes on in a given appraisal interview to what has happened yesterday, last month, and the like. We expect, of course, that the real-life appraisal interview does not occur in a vacuum but in a context that stems from the personalities of the supervisor and the subordinate and their history of interaction in the past. One supervisor/subordinate pair may have been characterized by a long period of conflict and another by amiable relationships over the period being appraised. We would certainly expect this previous conflict, or lack of it, to have a strong influence on what goes on in the interview.

Furthermore — and this could be even more important — using a simulated interview precludes us from following up to determine what the effects of the interview are on subsequent behavior on the job. In other words, we cannot really get at the job performance bottom line using this approach. This would suggest that role playing might well be more useful in training people how to interview than it would be in discovering what determines the effectiveness of real-life interviews.

Let us turn now to that aspect of the design indicated by the use of the term "microskills." Analyzing behavior of this sort in units of 1/100 of a minute is indeed a Herculean task and Alban Metcalfe notes that it literally took days and days of effort to analyze a single interview. While such a fine-grained analysis is commendable, it also involves certain costs such as the limitation on the number of interviews that one can hope to analyze. Hence, in focusing on the minute aspects of the interview, one has to lose out on the reliability gains that would result from a larger number of interviews.

There is another price one has to pay for a microanalysis of this sort. That is, the microanalysis per se may prevent one from seeing the forest for the trees. Alban Metcalfe's analysis weighted each appearance of a given item equally and did not take into account, for example, trends over time within the interview, rather than just the percentage of interview time in which a given behavior appeared. Of course, this is not a criticism that is necessarily true of microanalysis, since the researcher could plot incidence as a function of time. It is just that with such a laborious procedure, the researcher simply may not have the time or energy to consider this "longitudinal" approach.

Also, in using the microanalysis, one loses sight of the interactional nature of the behavior of the subordinate and the supervisor. Instead of noting that the supervisor engaged in a certain kind of behavior that then led to a particular response by the subordinate, we only know how frequently each exhibited various behaviors.

My own conception of the interview as an interaction seems discrepant with Alban Metcalfe's description of it in terms of an independent variable (the manager's behavior) and a dependent variable (the subordinate's behavior). What this amounts to is that the appealing precision of the microanalysis may blind one to the more macro, interactional aspects of the interview. We need to consider just how micro we need to be. Is dealing with hundredths of a minute necessary? How do the results of such an analysis correspond to what would result from a more macro analysis like that of Bales (1950)? What, if anything, do we get from such an analysis that we would not get by using larger units of analysis?

Extensions

Let us now try to extend the work that was done in terms of generalizations that might be made, of different subject populations that might be used, and of methodological implications and/or lessons learned. In this connection, it is important to indicate, first of all, that explicit theoretical notions or frameworks as to just what one should observe in the appraisal interview would be useful. There is, of course, no explicit theory here that Alban Metcalfe has laid out. Nevertheless, the fact that certain behavioral categories were selected for recording and analysis suggests that there is some implicit theoretical position here as to what is important in the appraisal interview.

Another comment on extending the results involves the use of different groups of subjects including those who are relatively naive as to what we teach supervisors in courses about appraisal. Using larger groups of subjects would be prohibitively expensive, of course, with Alban Metcalfe's methodology since it requires so many days of an analyst's time for each interview. This would constitute additional justification for some theorizing as to just what is important in the appraisal interview and how fine-grained an analysis is necessary. If we could determine that a few variables are critical and design less laborious ways of measuring them, we could then go on to assess the generalizability of the findings for a wide range of different subject groups.

It should be noted that this comment applies to the entire area of research on appraisal interviews in particular and management in general. All too often we settle for samples of convenience that do not represent, statistically, any designated universe and that do not yield adequately reliable results because they are so small. I think we need to consider what we can do to encourage leadership researchers to deal more adequately with these matters of sample size and sample representativeness.

On the matter of extending the results of this study, what is badly needed is more research that compares different methodologies. Such studies, however, are quite rare compared to those—like this one—that rely on a single methodology. In the case of appraisal interviews, one should compare the present microanalysis approach with others (like that of Bales or any of the many content analysis systems that have been devised). If we should find that the laborious microanalysis approach yields data not provided by alternative approaches, then we would feel much better about the high cost of the labor involved.

Perhaps the most important thing of all with respect to extending these results, or any other results based on role playing or simulation, is the matter of external validity: that is, how well do the results predict criteria that are important on the job? To what extent could we, for example, predict the quantity and quality of work produced on the job from what goes on in the appraisal interview? Checking this would require that we use real-life appraisal interview data and relate these measures to the criterion variables. In fact, we would have to use a complex multivariate or systems approach because of the number of interrelated variables involved. That is, there are obviously many things going on in the appraisal interview involving what is said (and what is not said), how it is said, body language, and the like. And what goes on in the appraisal interview is also obviously a function of what happened on the job during the appraisal period. Thus, one can hypothesize that high job performance leads to reinforcement in the appraisal interview which may be followed by high(er) job productivity. But in such a case we need to know just how much of the variance in subsequent job performance is accounted for by what is said (and how it is said) in the interview, and how much to other variables (such as the fact that the subordinate may be at that point in the learning curve at which performance would be expected to continue rising, in which case the appraisal interview might have less impact than in the case of a worker who had reached a plateau in performance).

It should also be noted that Alban Metcalfe's analysis omitted any consideration of salary changes and focused on interpersonal relationships. But we need to know the relative impact of the interpersonal variables and salary changes that enter into the appraisal interview or that come into effect more or less at the same time as the appraisal interview. In real life, salary changes would be expected to be critical in changing performance. Whether or not the supervisor recommends a salary increase—either in the appraisal interview itself or on some other more or less contiguous occasion—might well outweigh the degree of consideration and the amount of time spent talking in the interview. Again, we need a multivariate approach in order to answer such questions.

Another way to extend the results of this study is to determine what mechanisms account for the impact of the supervisor's behavior in the interview. Specifically, we should examine the role of cognitive variables, which would, of course, require that we go beyond Alban Metcalfe's strict behaviorist approach. That is, we need to determine what the subordinate and the supervisor think at each stage of their interaction in the appraisal interview. To do that, we would need to rely on interviews, questionnaires, and protocol analysis in order to get at the emotional reactions, the attitudinal responses, and the perceptions of both members of the dyad. In light of the current social-psychological preoccupation with attributions, we would certainly do well to ascertain how the supervisor and the subordinate explain the other's behavior to themselves.

Also in the cognitive area, we know that goal setting has produced a set of findings over the years that rank among the more substantial achievements in the world of research. What we do not know, however, is how the goal-setting process interacts with the kinds of variables Alban Metcalfe focused on; that is, how large are effects on performance of the supervisor's general demeanor in the interview compared to the effects of his or her goal-setting behavior?

Implicit in a number of the observations made above is the notion that time is a critical variable. We need to know what has preceded the appraisal interview and, of course, what effects show up downstream. In order to deal with such temporal sequences, we should consider using longitudinal designs involving studying personnel over the course of a year or more. In this way we could determine the impact of the appraisal interview on subsequent health/sickness, absenteeism, productivity, and job satisfaction of the worker. Moreover, we could put the appraisal interview in the context of a dynamic interpersonal relationship and determine the extent to which a specific appraisal interview index (e.g., amount of talking) is important compared to the effects of the long-term interaction during the appraisal year.

Alban Metcalfe's work has raised many interesting issues, indeed.

Part 2 Integrative Comments: A Look at Research Methodologies for Exploring Managerial Behavior

Rosemary Stewart

The chapters in Part 2 provide a good opportunity for thinking about what the North Americans and the Europeans can usefully learn from each other. Each has developed somewhat different traditions of research and tends to approach it in different ways. The international flavor of this volume should encourage us to think about how we can benefit from each other's strengths and perhaps learn to modify our own myopias.

The North American strengths are that the researchers pay more attention to reliability, they are more thorough in their research design, and within their ideas of validity they are also more thorough. They are more professional than the Europeans. These strengths were noticeable in the abstracts and papers by North Americans originally submitted for inclusion, compared with those by Europeans. We in Europe can learn from the greater care with which North Americans design their research, write their articles, and criticize others' work.

The volumes in the Leadership Symposia series have tended to emphasize leadership as it is conceptualized in the United States. Hence it is worth trying to spell out what contribution European and perhaps other social scientists outside North America can make to help this research be more fruitful. The distinctive character of the European comments and criticisms of some of the U.S. work highlights three such contributions. The first is the need for Americans to think more carefully about the meaning of the data that are used to form the basis for conclusions—perhaps as a visiting scholar from the United States has said; "One difference between the North Americans and European social scientists is that the latter think more" (Steers, personal communication, 1982). Illustrative of this statement are the questions the Europeans ask about validity. They take a broader view of it than do North Americans and are more concerned with whether what is being done makes sense, with the underlying assumptions, and with what comparisons can meaningfully be made with other studies.

One of the things that strikes me about some North American studies where great care has been taken to get valid measures is that they include things that are not meaningful. Hence, it appears that some North Americans need to ask themselves more often: "Does this particular measure, even though I can say that I have tested its validity, mean what I say it does?" Forsblad, for example, pointed to several reasons for doubting whether some of the data in the Luthans and Lockwood chapter had the meanings that Luthans and Lockwood attributed to them.

Some North Americans also need to examine more carefully the value of the comparisons that they make with previous studies. There are, for example, several meaningless comparisons in the Martinko and Gardner chapter, even though it is otherwise an impressively thorough, as well as most interesting, research report. They draw conclusions about the similarities and differences between their educational managers and other managers. They cite, among others, Mintzberg's (1973) study of five chief executives saying, for example, that he found that "managers spend 59 percent of their time in scheduled meetings"—all five of them during one week! Yet an earlier study (Stewart, 1967) of 160 middle and senior managers who kept a specially designed diary for four weeks found that these managers varied widely in how they spent their time for all the recorded aspects and that individual managers varied from one week to another. This suggests that only large samples of carefully matched managers over several weeks would be likely to provide the basis for any meaningful comparisons.

The second contribution that Europeans can make is their tendency to take a broader view of the subject they are studying. This includes being aware of, and considering, related literature both for the potential relevance of its content and for its use of similar methods. North Americans are more inclined to build a fence around subjects and not to look over the fence. The very professional thoroughness of North American researchers tends to a narrow view. In leadership research the references will be to other leadership researchers and not to other relevant work. This is even true for methodology. Both Luthans and Lockwood in their chapter and Martinko and Gardner in theirs ignore the long history of observational research. The narrower base of American studies makes it easier for them to claim a myopic uniqueness.

The third, and perhaps most important, contribution of the Europeans is that they can help North American leadership scholars to recognize the value assumptions that they are making. Europeans, especially those whose education included training in the philosophy of science, are more alert than North Americans to the value assumptions made in research. The utility of leadership studies, and the categories included in leadership questionnaires, have tended to be taken for granted by North Americans working in the area. A number of the European commentaries in this book help sensitize one to the problematic character and cultural bias of such work.

An international volume such as this can interest the reader because of specific chapters and because it offers the reader the opportunity to learn of work going on in other countries. However, since leadership studies have traditionally mainly concerned North Americans, the latter is of less interest, although the inclusion of managerial behavior opens up more possibilities for cross-fertilization between North American and other researchers. Potentially of most value for readers from both sides of the Atlantic is the opportunity to understand and learn from a different approach to research.

Part 3

Symbolism, Metaphors, and Manipulation of Meaning

Introduction

James G. Hunt, Dian-Marie Hosking,
Chester A. Schriesheim, and Rosemary Stewart

The chapters in this part are representative of approaches that tend to look at leadership/managerial behavior in a rather different way from the typical approach of North American scholars. Indeed, as James G. Hunt points out in his integrating commentary, these approaches are different enough from those used in traditional North American leadership research to be labeled "radical" by Larry Cummings, a leading United States organizational behavior scholar.

These studies are different and interesting because of their emphasis on the infrequently considered symbolic and interpretative aspects of a manager's role. As such, they are representative of other recent work focusing on symbolic aspects of management (see, e.g., Pondy, Frost, Morgan, & Dandridge, 1982).

The flavor of this statement as applied to the chapters in this part can be better understood by looking at a brief summary of each.

Chapter 12, "The Role of Symbolic Management: How Can Managers Effectively Transmit Organizational Culture?" by Caren Siehl and Joanne Martin, begins with a description of what the authors mean by organizational culture. It is seen as embodying the content (core values), form (language, rituals, stories, etc.), and strategies necessary for transmitting the culture in the organization. The authors then discuss how a manager can create, maintain, and transmit a shared culture to obtain commitment and control. Results from a study done in a large, high-technology firm are summarized. The study combines a first-phase qualitative methodology to determine relevant cultural concerns followed up by quantitative methodology designed to ascertain results of a training program. The training program was designed to transmit to new employees core cultural values ascertained from the earlier qualitative methodology.

Chapter 13, "Leadership among Bank Managers: A Structural Comparison of Behavioral Responses and Metaphorical Imagery," is a think piece in which Larry F. Moore and Brenda E. F. Beck see a key aspect of the manager's/ leader's job as the manipulation of meaning for subordinates. Like Siehl and Martin, these authors also see leaders as the key persons in the process of constructing or at least shaping culture. Leaders must help provide imagery for subordinates by identifying key sets of meanings that a particular culture provides for given types of social institutions.

Moore and Beck use metaphorical questions as a part of structural analysis to elicit basic frames used by a sample of Canadian bank managers. They argue that these metaphors provide an indication of underlying principles that will be related to a leader's behavior choices. In turn, this knowledge is believed to be potentially useful in managing conflict, meeting client needs, and performance of other roles.

The third in the trio of symbolic and interpretative chapters is by Anne S. Huff. In Chapter 14, "Situation Interpretation, Leader Behavior and Effectiveness," Huff focuses on the importance of the changing use of language in getting a top-level decision made and accepted. She argues that an organizational manager ("leader," in her terms) is concerned with framing a decision situation and transmitting that frame to others. Framing involves setting forth a series of arguments concerning a key decision situation and then finding an argument strong enough to warrant action. Huff's framing process is clearly related to the "manipulation of meaning" which is such an important part of Moore and Beck's contribution.

Huff follows through a school superintendent's decision-making sequence and shows how a simple model she has developed can help explain the sequence of action. Her work shows the importance of interpretation, language, and other highly subjective aspects of a manager's work. In this respect, her study is in the same mold as the chapters by Siehl and Martin and Moore and Beck.

In his commentary on Chapter 12, Nigel Nicholson, from the United Kingdom, adds considerable richness to Siehl and Martin's work. Nicholson was selected to comment on this chapter because of his grasp of related literature, his strong interest in the topic, and his familiarity with the managerial behavior/leadership scenes in both the United Kingdom and the United States.

For Nicholson, a key question underlying the Siehl and Martin chapter is their definition of organizational culture and how that might resemble or differ from organizational ideology. In addressing this concern he leads the reader through an array of provocative literature from both sides of the Atlantic. He also raises a number of research issues such as: the significance of the difference between organizational cultures, the extent to which management is what he calls the "agent" or the victim of culture, and how one induces change in organization cultures.

Commenting on both Moore and Beck's Chapter 13 and Huff's Chapter

14 is Ian Morley from the United Kingdom. Morley was selected for almost precisely the same reasons as Nicholson. He orients his commentary on the two think pieces around three themes. First is the nature of leadership and leadership roles. Here he focuses on the role of the leader in structuring subordinates' thoughts, motives, feelings, and behaviors. In addressing this area, he brings to bear a broad range of literature from social psychology and political science.

Second is the conceptualization of decision making and stages within the decision-making process. This focus moves him into a discussion of the cycling and recycling involved in decision making and he embeds the Huff piece within this discussion. Again, a rich social-psychological and political science literature is presented.

Finally, leaders' general orientation to their role is presented. Here Morley brings in related work on entrepreneurs, policy orientations of leaders, and the like to add additional perspective to the work of Moore and Beck.

Hunt's integrative comments place the studies within the context of work that deviates both epistemologically and methodologically from mainstream or establishment North American leadership studies. Much of his commentary is based on recent treatment of the related organizational behavior area by Larry Cummings. The underlying issues are considered important enough to be picked up again by the editors in Chapter 25.

One issue of importance to the reader in considering organizational culture is the precise nature of its definition and its relation to such concepts as ideology, organizational climate, external culture, managerial philosophy, and socialization. The Siehl and Martin chapter perhaps raises more questions than it answers in this regard. The commentators shed some light here, as do a number of the cited references.

While the nature of organizational culture is one question that comes to mind, what follows are a number of others suggested by the Siehl and Martin chapter.

To what extent might the training program described by Siehl and Martin as a cultural transmission device serve as a manipulative "keep 'em happy" device? To what extent might such a program promote group think (Janis, 1972)? What might be the relative impact of organizational culture versus that of the external culture within which it is embedded? To what degree does the cognitive knowledge gained in a cultural transmission training program lead to assimilation of organizational values?

In terms of the Moore and Beck think piece, there are a number of conceptual and methodological issues that are prevalent throughout. While these should not divert the reader from the overall contribution and message of that chapter, nevertheless, he or she will probably want to recognize some of these. Morley deals with a number of them in his critique.

The reader may also want to be alerted to the importance of time in the Huff chapter. Morley again adds insight by emphasizing this within the decision-making cycling and recycling. In this the piece bears a relation to those treated by Clark in Part 5, where time is a key variable. Finally, there appears to be an underlying kinship with the Burgoyne and Hodgson contribution from the United Kingdom (Chapter 5).

12

The Role of Symbolic Management: How Can Managers Effectively Transmit Organizational Culture?

Caren Siehl and Joanne Martin

The success of an organizational leader is contingent upon the development of shared meaning through a coherent system of beliefs and guiding values (Peters, 1981). Selznick (1957) clearly argued that:

> The formation of an institution is marked by the making of value commitments, that is, choices which fix the assumptions of policy makers as to the nature of the enterprise, its distinctive aims, methods and roles. The institutional leader is primarily an expert in the promotion and protection of values. Leadership fails when it concentrates on sheer survival. Institutional survival, properly understood, is a matter of maintaining values and distinctive identity. (pp. 152 & 153)

While chairman of the board of IBM, Thomas J. Watson, Jr. (1963) posited a similar argument when he said that, "The basic philosophy, spirit, and drive of an organization have far more to do with its relative achievements than do technological or economic resources, organizational structure, innovation, and timing. All these things weigh heavily on success, but they are transcended by how the people in the organization believe in its basic precepts and how faithfully they carry them out." (p. 13)

Previous research and theory, as the preceding paragraph indicates, suggest that one of the critical tasks of management involves the construction and maintenance of a system of shared values. Such values are one component of the phenomenon known as organizational culture.

Although definitions of culture are available, their primary shared attribute is vagueness. An amalgamation of some of the more interesting definitions would result in the following: organizational culture can be thought of as the glue that holds an organization together through a sharing of patterns of meaning. The culture focuses on the values, beliefs, and expectations that members come to share (i.e., Baker, 1980; Gamst & Norbeck, 1976; Pfeffer, 1981a; Van Maanen & Schein, 1979).

It is important to reduce the vagueness of such definitions if culture is to be developed and managed by organizational leaders. A more concrete and complete definition of organizational culture would suggest that a culture consists of three components: content, forms, and strategies.

The first component, the content of an organizational culture, can be viewed as the core values of the organization. These values define the basic philosophy or mission of the company. Sometimes the core values concern technical issues such as one which Ken Olson, the founder and president of Digital Equipment Corporation expresses as: "Our job is to make a good product. Growth is not our primary goal. After making good products, growth is the natural occurrence" (*Fortune,* Apr. 23, 1979). Or they can be financial in nature, as is reflected in an underlying value of Data General: "We're in this business to make money. It just so happens that the computer business is the best way to do that. But if we could make more money selling rye bread, we should consider doing that" (Herb Richman in *Fortune,* Apr. 23, 1979). Oftentimes the core values are humanistic and emphasize the importance of the people and customers of the organization. Values of this type include Dana Corporation's "Productivity through people" and IBM's "IBM means service" and "Respect for the individual." DuPont's "Better things for better living through chemistry," and GE's "Progress is our most important product" are other examples of underlying beliefs that shape the way people interact and process information about the organization.

It is suggested that the content of the culture can be communicated through the second component of culture, cultural forms. Such forms are oftentimes indirect, implicit, and subtle means of value transmission. Organizational researchers have studied a number of potential cultural forms including: special language or jargon (e.g., Edelman, 1977; Hirsch, 1980; Pondy, 1978); organizational stories and scripts (e.g., Clark, 1970; Martin, 1982; Wilkins, 1978); rituals and ceremonies (e.g., Gephart, 1978; Moch & Huff, 1980; Smircich, In press, 1983); and physical arrangements, such as dress and decor (e.g., Edelman, 1971; Pfeffer, 1981a).

The third component of culture, not dealt with in previous culture research, consists of strategies that managers can use as a means of reinforcing the content or underlying values of the culture. Strategies teach, support, and demonstrate behavior and attitudes that are appropriate for a particular cultural context. Potential strategies include recruitment policies, training programs, compensation, promotion practices, and other management systems. For example, if a culture values a people-oriented management style, successful users of this style should receive more promotions than other managers.

The development of strong organizational culture is important because cultures serve four, perhaps five, useful functions. First, cultures offer a shared interpretation of organizational events, so that members know how they are expected to behave (e.g., Bougon, Weick, & Binkhorst, 1977; Lodahl & Gordon, 1972; Martin, Harrod, & Siehl, 1980; Martin, 1982). Second, in addition to these cognitive functions, strong cultures have emotional impact, lend-ing an aura of excitement, if not inspiration, to employees' work lives. For example, cultures can generate commitment to a set of corporate values or management philosophy, so that employees feel they are working for something they can believe in (e.g., Clark, 1970; Edelman, 1977; Martin & Powers, in press; Ouchi, 1980; Selznick, 1957; Sproull, 1979; Wilkins, 1978). Organizational cultures also generate commitment by giving members a sense of community. Values shared among employees provide for the integration of individuals into the work setting, a kind of individual-to-organization linking (Louis, 1980a). Such a sharing of values can bind members to the organization (Ouchi, 1981; Wilkins, 1978). Third, culture creates and maintains boundaries. In- versus out-groups arise that help to define who is and who is not behaving appropriately within the organizational context. Fourth, cultures also serve as organizational control mechanisms, formally labeling some patterns of behavior as prohibited (e.g., Ouchi & Price, 1978; Salancik, 1977; Wilkins, in press). Finally, the presence of a strong humanistic culture has been tied by implication, if not firm empirical evidence, to increased productivity or profitability (Ouchi, 1981; Pascale & Athos, 1981).

Although earlier research provides support for the important functions served by culture, questions remain as to how a manager can create, maintain, and transmit a shared culture in order to reap the benefits of increased commitment, cognitive sense making, and control. The study that is the subject of this chapter addresses two issues that are central to furthering the understanding of the process by which managers can transmit and reinforce the content of culture, or the underlying value system.

First, how can managers transmit the content of culture, the core values, in a believable, credible manner? One way that managers could communicate the values would be to use explicit forms of communication. Examples of explicit forms include quantitative figures, broad policy statements, and rules and procedures. Managers might prefer to use explicit, unambiguous means of communication so that misunderstandings and differences in interpretation will not occur.

It is predicted, however, that managers will do just the opposite and use implicit forms of communication to transmit values. Previous research, as described earlier, suggests that the values may be transmitted through one or more of the following implicit forms: jargon, organizational stories, and rituals. Other forms that have been relatively unexplored in previous research include humor and the role modeling of appropriate behavior.

Managers may use implicit forms because the core values, especially those of a humanistic nature, tend to be abstract and hypothetical. Research has shown that people have a difficult time remembering or believing information when it is communicated directly in an abstract manner (Martin, Harrod, & Siehl, 1980; Martin, Patterson, & Price, 1979). If managers use explicit language and quantitative figures to express values, their remarks may be forgotten or considered less than credible, particularly if those values have a humanistic tone and are hard to justify in purely financial terms. Without the use of implicit, cultural forms, it is likely that values would be dismissed by employees as propaganda or superficial platitudes. Cultural forms are concrete, yet they communicate values indirectly. For example, the value-relevant message of an organizational story is usually implicit while the events, characters, and action line of the story are specific, detailed, and concrete.

Second, can managers use a strategy, such as a formal training program, to reinforce the core values? Earlier research findings suggest that structured training programs, because they remove new employees from the work setting, do not increase cultural understanding (Louis, 1980b).

Contrary to previous research, however, it is predicted that the use of a formal training program by management can be more effective in reinforcing the core values than continued on-the-job interaction. A training program is predicted to be a powerful management strategy because new employees are isolated from the daily demands of learning a new job. The training manager can indirectly and subtly focus attention on core values. Values can be consistently and redundantly reinforced in the controlled environment of a training program.

In summary, the present study addresses several basic issues left unresolved by previous research on the development and management of a shared value system. First, how can managers transmit the cultural content or value system? It is predicted that managers will communicate the values implicitly using such forms as: rituals or ceremonies, humor, and role modeling. Second, can the strategy of a structured training program be used by management to reinforce the value system? It is predicted that a formal training program is more effective than continued on-the-job interaction.

METHOD

This study was conducted in a field setting at a large, high-technology corporation, referred to below as XYZ. This organization was selected because it has consciously attempted to create and maintain a distinctive organizational culture in the face of changes caused by sustained organizational growth.

Design: Stage One

The study had a two-stage design. The first stage utilized qualitative methods to determine the content and form of this particular organizational culture. The first author conducted open-ended, in-depth interviews with managers at various levels of the corporate hierarchy. In addition, she attended as an observer a one-week recognition event for top-level and rising middle-level managers. Activities included observation of formal group sessions on such topics as the company's unique culture and philosophy of management, informal socializing, and participation in organizational rituals, such as award ceremonies. By the end of this stage of the research process, the researchers were familiar with and understood the shared interpretation of many elements of XYZ's organizational culture. A brief description of the results of the qualitative stage of the study is included in a later section of this chapter.

Design: Stage Two

The second stage of the study had a two-group quasi-experimental design. The subjects were newly hired sales trainees. Within two days of beginning work, all subjects were asked to complete a questionnaire. A cover letter with the questionnaire requested the voluntary assistance of the trainees. The trainees were assured that the confidentiality of their responses would be maintained and that no one at XYZ would have access to their individual responses. The response rate was 87 percent.

During the first six weeks of an eight-week period, all subjects studied written orientation material, which included cultural information, and participated in a one-day orientation session. During the last two weeks of this eight-week period, half of the subjects (group 1) participated in a ten-day structured training program, while the training of the other half of the subjects (group 2) was deferred for scheduling reasons until after the study was completed. Although the subjects could not be randomly assigned by the researchers to the two groups, the subjects whose training was deferred did not differ in any apparent way from the trained subjects. Subsequent analyses, as described below, confirmed this. The training program was led by a first-line manager and guest speakers included the regional manager, district manager, and other first-line managers. Those subjects (group 2) who did not attend the formal training class continued to study product and market information at their home offices. Their activities during the last two-week period did not differ from those of the preceding six weeks. The first author attended the orientation session and eight of the ten days of the training class, including several after-hours social events.

At the end of the eight-week period, all subjects completed a second version of the questionnaire. At this time only half of the subjects had participated in the training program and consequently had been exposed to the management strategy. Figure 12.1 summarizes the two-group design and the timing of this second stage of the study.

Questionnaire Design

Qualitative data collected during the first stage of the study were used to design questionnaires for use in the second stage of the study. All versions of the questionnaire (items were counterbalanced across two time periods) had four sections: special language/jargon; organizational stories; questions about

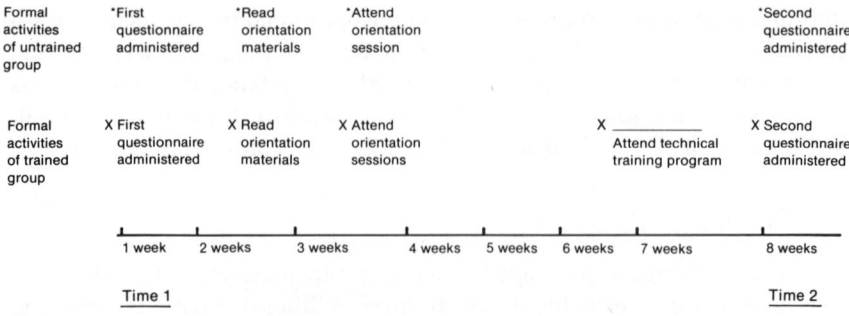

FIGURE 12.1. Design of second stage of study: Timing of the management strategy. (Note: the exact timing of some activities may vary slightly)

company goals; and an indirect measure of ideological commitment. The content of the items in each of these sections was tailored to reflect the culture of XYZ. Although these items were closed-ended quantitative measures, they represent an attempt to provide subtle and sensitive measures of cultural knowledge and commitment. For this reason, the items are described in some detail below.

Special Language/Jargon. This section of the questionnaire consisted of a vocabulary test of 20 words or phrases of particular relevance to XYZ employees. The jargon was obtained during interviews with managers of XYZ. Subjects were asked to define each word or phrase. Twelve of the words or phrases had technical meanings, such as MOF (Master Order Form), while eight were used by managers to transmit underlying values of the culture, for example, "working the issue" (confronting disagreement and continuing the discussion until genuine consensus is reached). Definitions were coded as totally correct, partially correct (a synonym or more abstract form of the word), or incorrect. Intercoder reliability was perfect, with coders reaching 100 percent agreement after a brief training session.

Organizational Stories. Four stories, frequently told during the in-depth interviews, were summarized. Subjects were first asked how much of the story they had heard. (Subjects responded to these and other items on 11-point scales, with higher scores indicating greater cultural knowledge and more commitment.) Three morals to the story were then offered and subjects were asked to decide the extent to which each represented the appropriate interpretation of the story. Although all three morals for each story were logically plausible, data from the first stage of the study indicated that one moral was generally considered to be the "correct" interpretation by management, one moral was obviously "incorrect," and one was ambiguous. The "correct" moral reflected a shared value of XYZ. To the extent that a subject's judgment followed management's pattern, the subject would be demonstrating knowledge of a shared interpretation of meaning particular to this organizational setting. For example, one study concerned a lower-level employee:

Susan Sanders, a secretary of a sales unit in Northern California, had been working for XYZ for about two years. She was well respected by everyone — her manager, the sales people, and other secretaries. She was extremely skillful and her performance had been rated as excellent. Owing to her efforts, Susan's manager did not need to direct his attention to proofreading or correction tasks. Susan also had a pleasant personality. In fact, she was one of those people who was generally cheerful, even on bad days. During her second year with XYZ, Susan's husband, who worked for another company, was promoted to a new job in Arizona. Although he would be losing a valued employee, Susan's manager approved her request for a transfer to an XYZ office in Arizona. This office was not hiring at the time but gladly accepted her transfer, knowing that her skills would be helpful in some capacity in the future.

The three morals offered for this story were:

"We believe that people are clearly our most important asset and we take pride in treating our employees well." ("Correct.")

"Employees are one part of the financial structure of XYZ and are as important as their contribution to the bottom-line." ("Incorrect.")

"Because good employees are hard to find, we feel it is to XYZ's advantage to try to meet the needs of such people." ("Ambiguous." Logically plausible, pragmatic rather than humanistic, an interpretation or moral not offered by XYZ management.)

Company Goal Identification. In stage one of this study, the top managers had identified a number of XYZ's corporate goals that embody the underlying values of the company, for example, meeting social and environmental commitments to communities surrounding corporate facilities. Subjects were asked to rate the importance of each of five such goals to XYZ and to themselves personally. This provided a measure of the accuracy with which subjects perceived the company's values and a measure of the subjects' personal ideological commitment to those values.

Indirect Measure of Ideological Commitment. Direct measures of subjects' commitment to the corporate ideology are subject to social desirability effects, even given anonymity, and thus, have unavoidable demand characteristics. To overcome this problem, commitment was also assessed using an indirect measure of error-choice. These measures consisted of statements taken from published material about XYZ company. A key numerical fact in each statement was left blank. Subjects were instructed to fill in the blank with one of two predesignated choices. Subjects were not aware that both alternatives were actually incorrect. One of the choices was biased in a direction designed to make the company look better than in fact it was; the other choice was biased in a negative, anti-company direction. For example, one item estimated sales-force turnover at either 12 or 16 percent, when the actual turnover rate was 14 percent. Ideological commitment to the company should be reflected in a disproportionate preference for the positive bias, pro-company alternatives. The plus or minus difference is not meaningful in itself. It is the change in the cumulative bias from Time 1 to Time 2, irrespective of the bias at Time 1, that will indicate an increase or decrease in commitment.

RESULTS AND DISCUSSION

The qualitative data are presented first, so that the richness and the texture of XYZ's organizational culture are familiar. These data are used primarily to address the first question raised in the introduction to this chapter. The quantitative data are then presented and discussed in the context of both questions.

Qualitative Results

During the course of the in-depth interviews, the observation of the managerial recognition event, and the training class, four core values were emphasized by management: (1) The family of an employee is an integral concern of the company; (2) XYZ doesn't undercut the future by considering only the short-term consequences of decisions; (3) XYZ believes that people are clearly the most important asset of the company; and (4) XYZ is different: we build a unique product and our people are unique also.

The qualitative data answer the question of how managers can transmit values in a believable, credible manner. The four shared values were transmitted in several different forms. One form was the organizational story. For example, the following story, or a slight variation of it, was told repeatedly: A prospective employee was qualified for a sales position with XYZ but had specific family constraints on his ability to relocate. XYZ offered the salesman a job in his desired location even though his experience made him better suited to sell to a different market. This story clearly articulates the first shared value, as stated above, of commitment to be supportive and understanding of employees' families.

The observation of the orientation day suggested that managers can also transmit the underlying values or content of the culture in the form of organizational rituals. Rituals are repeated behavior patterns that are stylized or formalized (Smircich, in press). XYZ's orientation session was designed by management to be highly ritualistic. The setting, the sequence of events, and the controlling characters did not vary from one session to the next. The ritual had the specific purpose of introducing aspects of XYZ culture and, in general, of demonstrating the third central value of XYZ: the company cares about people. As the orientation manager told us, "Most new employees go through buyer's remorse. They aren't totally confident that they made the right job decision. All we want to do today is let them know that XYZ really is happy to have them on board. We want them to share our ideal of giving 100 percent to each other and to XYZ."

In addition, within the ritual of the orientation session, other aspects of XYZ's culture were communicated by the leader of the organization (the company president and founder) through the use of a special videotape. The videotape portrayed the president giving a tour of the historic company headquarters. He related the pivotal values of the philosophy of management and the culture in the form of organizational stories, drawing on incidents from the company's history to make his points. For example, one story concerned the leader's commitment to the second central value: avoid the folly of considering only the short-term consequences of decisions.

Organizational values were also transmitted in the form of special language. By definition, this language should be unique to XYZ and best understood by XYZ employees. Interestingly, the content of the language also emphasized the fourth of the central values as discussed, the value that stressed the uniqueness of the company, its people, and its products. Managers used the jargon to express the underlying values and to help emphasize organizational boundaries.

Humor was also used by management to convey the content of XYZ culture. For example, in the beginning of the training program, laughter was scarce. Most jokes were understandable to an outsider. They contained little jargon and the causes of laughter were fairly universal objects such as foolish mistakes, sexual innuendo, and general tension. By the end of the training program, laughter was more frequent. This could be due to increased cohesion and openness among the participants. Understanding of these jokes, however, required more knowledge of the unique culture as well, as the jokes contained considerable XYZ jargon. In addition, the targets of the jokes were usually out-groups, such as competitive companies. Thus, humor tended to define the in-group, out-group boundary, with the new employees gradually, through their laughter, coming to act like in-group members. In accord with the fourth core value of XYZ, the new employees were coming to define the in-group, their company, as unique and distinct from other groups.

The observation of the training class also provided support for the hypothesis that cultural information may be transmitted by managers through the role modeling of appropriate behavior. The training managers modeled behavior as a means of teaching the new employees what would be expected in this particular corporate environment. The employees observed a specific instance of behavior and developed a minitheory concerning situations in which this behavior pattern would be appropriate. For example, one role-modeling incident concerned the third of the central values of XYZ, that the company's employees are its most important asset. A minitheory illustrating the application of this value was built around the belief that the company should not give up on low-performing employees.

A powerful enactment of this minitheory was observed during the second day of the training program. The trainees had been made aware of the need to be prepared for a test to be given during the afternoon of the second day. Just before breaking for lunch, the manager held an "impromptu" review session. She asked several sample exam questions of each individual, beginning with the last person in the last row and moving sequentially through the class. One trainee appeared to be completely unprepared and failed to answer a single question correctly. Rather than reprimanding this employee publicly or privately, the manager was encouraging and offered additional study help during lunch. Later that afternoon, the manager summarized the relevant minitheory, saying, "We believe that if an employee is failing to perform, we owe that person assistance."

Discussion of Qualitative Results

The purpose of gathering the qualitative data was twofold. The first objective was to address, to the extent possible, the two issues raised in the introduction to this chapter. The first issue concerned the transmission of values by managers. The qualitative data provided evidence that managers can transmit underlying values using at least five forms: organizational stories, special language, rituals, humor, and the role modeling of appropriate behavior. The first three of these forms have been suggested by previous culture research. The latter two forms represent an understudied means by which managers can transmit cultural information and values, particularly new information that has not yet been institutionalized in the company's history, language, or ritualized ceremonies.

The qualitative data cannot provide a test of the second issue to be addressed: whether a structured training program can be an effective management strategy for reinforcing underlying values. The qualitative data do provide a basis for the subsequent quantitative investigation of this issue. Observation of the training program indicated that subjects were learning the company jargon and organizational stories. Whether they were gaining an equivalent or better understanding of the values than those subjects not involved in the training class can be tested using quantitative methods. Comparisons of the two groups would yield information about the efficacy with which one cultural strategy, a structured training program, transmitted values.

The second objective of collecting the qualitative data was to gain a sense of the content of the culture of this particular organization. The highlights of the qualitative data, summarized above, indicate that the content of XYZ's culture primarily concerned four values central to the company's philosophy of management. Some aspects of this information about the content of XYZ's culture were used to develop the quantitative measures discussed in the next section of this chapter.

To summarize, the qualitative data answered the question of how a manager can transmit values. In addition, the data provided a picture of the richness and complexity of the content and forms of the corporate culture. The quantitative data, discussed below, build on this qualitative information to address the question of whether managers can use the strategy of a training program to reinforce values.

Quantitative Results

To ensure that any difference at Time 2 between the trained and untrained groups was due to the presence or absence of the structured training class, the Time 1 results for the two groups (prior to any training) were compared. As expected, at Time 1 both groups' responses to the questionnaire items were generally not significantly different more often than would be expected by chance. There was, therefore, no reason to suspect that the two groups differed initially in any substantive way.

Changes in knowledge of the value system and commitment to the values that occurred between Time 1 and Time 2 were then examined. First, the results for the trained group (those employees exposed to the management strategy) will be described. (More detailed presentation of these data and analyses are available in Siehl & Martin, 1982.) By Time 2, after the formal training program, the trained group of new employees had come to interpret the values transmitted by the organizational stories in a fashion similar to that of the managers interviewed in stage one of the study. Averaging across the stories, at Time 2 the "correct" morals to the stories were rated as highly appropriate interpretations of the stories, the "neutral" morals were rated near the midpoint of the scale, as they had been at Time 1, and the "incorrect" morals to the stories received lower ratings. For the "correct" and "incorrect" morals, these differences between Time 1 and Time 2 were strongly significant for each of the stories. These results clearly support the conclusion that by Time 2 the subjects exposed to the training program had come to adopt the shared interpretation of the meaning of the values transmitted by these organizational stories.

At Time 2, the trained group showed high levels of ideological commitment to the values and goals underlying the XYZ corporate culture. Averaging across the five corporate goals articulated by top management, at Time 2 the trained subjects felt that these goals were highly important to the company and to themselves personally. Although these ratings of the importance of the goals to the company at Time 2 represented an increase over the Time 1 ratings for the trained group, two of these differences were not significant, two were marginally significant, and one was significant. A similar pattern of effects was found in the analysis of the ratings of the personal importance of these corporate goals. Although at Time 2 ratings were higher, or for one goal equal, the differences between Time 1 and Time 2 for the personal importance ratings were significant for only two of the five goals. For each of these measures of ideological commitment, the patterns of results are similar and the same explanation for that pattern can be offered: ideological commitment was at a high enough level at Time 1 that a ceiling effect prevented some of the Time 2 differences from being significantly higher. Nevertheless, as expected, commitment increased over time for these trained subjects.

The second type of ideological commitment measure minimized demand characteristics. The indirect error-choice test showed that the trained subjects had a strong tendency to make errors that were favorable to the company. For the trained subject, this bias, indicating ideological commitment, was significantly stronger at Time 2 than at Time 1. To summarize the commitment results for the trained group, the high levels of ideological commitment found at Time 1 increased following participation in the management strategy of a structured training program, and, for measures where ceiling effects were not present, these increases in commitment were significant.

Turning now to the untrained group (employees not exposed to the management strategy), a quite different pattern of results was found. By Time 2, there was no significant improvement in the untrained subjects' abilities to identify the "correct" or "incorrect" morals to the stories. Unlike the trained group, the untrained subjects showed no significant change in their willingness to endorse the shared values expressed by the organizational stories. The various measures of ideological commitment also showed relatively little change for the untrained group. The untrained subjects showed only slight increases in commitment, smaller increases than were shown by the trained group. None was significant.

An additional set of analyses were done comparing the trained and untrained groups at Time 2. The results confirm those reported above, with the trained group showing greater overall understanding of the value system and higher levels of commitment to the values of the company than the untrained group.

Discussion of Quantitative Results

The quantitative data addressed both questions raised in the introduction. The first of these questions concerned the cultural forms used to transmit knowledge about the corporation's values. The quantitative measures used two such forms: jargon and stories. Over time the subjects came to understand the meaning of words and phrases unique to this organizational setting, became more familiar with the organization's stories, and came to endorse the same interpretation of those stories as management. Both of these forms, then, were successfully used by management to communicate the content of the organization's culture, that is, the underlying value system.

The second question concerned the use by managers of a cultural strategy, a formal training program, to reinforce the underlying value system of the company. Over time the trained subjects showed a significant increase in their familiarity with the shared values transmitted by the organizational stories. A similar change in ideological commitment levels was also found for the trained subjects. In contrast to the trained subjects, the untrained subjects showed no significant increases in cultural knowledge or commitment. These results suggest that a formal training program is a powerful strategy that managers can use to reinforce underlying values.

CONCLUSION

As was proposed earlier, one of the critical tasks of the manager and leader is the creation and maintenance of a system of shared values. The present study makes the contribution of addressing several issues that are basic to furthering the understanding of how a manager can create such a value system. First, managers can use implicit, cultural forms, such as organizational stories, rituals, and role modeling, effectively to express and communicate core values. Second, the use by management of a strategy, such as a formal training program, can be a powerful means of reinforcing the value system and generating employee commitment.

The present study also suggests several questions that are worthy of future research. It was learned that managers can communicate values through a variety of cultural forms. This gives rise to such questions as the following: Under what circumstances are the different forms used by managers? When are they more or less effective?

In addition, it is acknowledged that culture is a powerful phenomenon that plays important functions in organizational life. Do managers want to allow such a phenomenon with far-reaching effects to develop and change in an uncontrolled manner? One would think not. What other specific strategies can be employed to promote the development of a widely shared value system? How can new strategies be designed?

It would be useful if managers could know how to recognize culture, how to control culture, and ultimately, how to change culture. Continued research efforts that attempt to extend present theory would be of value to both practicing managers and social scientists.

13

Leadership Among Bank Managers: A Structural Comparison of Behavioral Responses and Metaphorical Imagery*

Larry F. Moore and Brenda E. F. Beck

The present chapter reports the use of structural analysis (Levi-Strauss, 1963) to elucidate the organizational behavior and social imagery of a particular leader figure (the branch bank manager) relative to important subunits that constitute his or her leadership setting. We will illustrate how structural analysis, a technique widely used in anthropology, can help identify key social dimensions that underlie the attitudes a leader holds, the assumptions the leader makes, and the behaviors that characterize the leader's style in a given setting. Structural analysis provides an analytical approach that can be used to define and understand the various dimensions that frame a leader's subculture and offers illumination on why particular behaviors have been chosen and why they are more, or less, effective. Because leaders are responsive to the social systems in which they function, this approach can offer important insights into the cultural influence process that helps shape leadership style — a process that is not well understood (House & Baetz, 1979).

The authors, one an organizational behaviorist and the other a cultural anthropologist, have recently undertaken a study of 77 experienced Canadian branch bank managers using, via interview, seven critical incidents written especially for the situational demands of branch bank management. A number of possible behavioral responses were proposed to interviewees in connection with each incident. A specific metaphor set followed every behavioral decision and each manager was then asked to use these images to discuss the conceptual framework in which he or she had cast the associated behavioral response. Additional metaphor sets were subsequently used to explore abstract concepts such as bank power and business climate. Finally, a mail-in ques-

*This research was supported by grants from the Social Sciences and Humanities Research Council of Canada, the Canada Department of Industry, Trade and Commerce, and the Canada Secretary of State, Multiculturalism Branch.

tionnaire provided measures of personal values, managerial attitudes, person-thing preferences, and other related issues. This research has been conceived as a case study concerned to identify and to conceptualize analytically a specific Canadian management style. The present chapter is based on data from three of the critical incidents used and their associated metaphors.

According to structural theorists, social situations are always framed by general principles or dimensions of meaning. Usually the key themes relate to a limited set of dichotomous value-laden oppositions, for example, pure versus impure. Charismatic leaders are persons who are especially skilled in the manipulation of such meanings, doing so through their symbolic use of speech and other key behaviors (House, 1977). Leaders thus become recognized through making such general principles especially salient and clear to others. This implies that leaders are key persons for the process of constructing culture and should be key subjects for researchers interested in unpacking that construct. Thus, the quality or character of the imagery a leader uses in relating various contextual influences and tensions constitutes the essence of personal style. The specific combinations of attitudes, assumptions, and behaviors a leader uses to define such sets of meanings are termed "leadership style" in this chapter.

To do research on style one must first identify key sets of meanings a given culture provides for social situations of a particular type. Next, one must look at participants assumed to have leadership roles in that kind of setting and test for references to these meanings. When a person translates those general principles into specific attitudes and behaviors, he or she has defined a personal style (Hodder, 1982). It must be made clear, however, that no person's style can be seen as a simple behavioral blueprint that exactly replicates some wider frame of meanings. Just as a picture can blend with, complement, or fight against its frame, so leaders view their actions in relation to a set of general principles that a culture supplies. Specific leader actions may blend, assert independence, or even conflict with these larger themes. A manager may try to make his or her style "democratic," for example, in a conscious effort to stand apart from the authoritarian setting of the corporation for which he or she works. Hence, such relationships are often subtle, dialectical, and creative. Rarely are they blatant, stencil-like, or mechanical. In understanding this dynamic, a structuralist perspective can contribute to current leadership research.

The interviews in the present study show that modern bank managers see themselves caught between senior bank officials, the staff of their branch, and members of the public at large. To understand the differences among these constituencies and differences in leader requirements relative to each, it is useful to understand leadership styles by reference to the wider corporation milieu. Although anthropologists have worked extensively on systems of meaning used by non-Western peoples, they have not yet applied their tools (except in passing) to mainstream North American life. Nevertheless, a few cultural analyses have been completed in our own milieu and those insights can sometimes be cross-linked with a business context. In order to make a preliminary identification of basic meanings present in the Canadian banking milieu, the research reported here used an extant study of one popular film type: the Western. These Wild West adventure stories capture many of the key values important to North American culture and help to articulate a "frame for action" familiar to both Canadian and U.S. residents. In particular, Will Wright (1975) isolated four "periods" in the Western film industry, and showed that a gradual evolution has taken place. He argues, with much evidence, for a shift from the "classical plot" of the 1930s to a "professional plot" during and since the 1960s. These changes in character and world view in top-grossing films paralleled key changes in the economic and social base of North American society at large.

The authors of this chapter took the four principles Wright outlined as important to the "professional plot" in Western films and attempted to translate them into terms appropriate to the Canadian business setting. This articulation of parallels rests, in particular, on a 1966 film called *The Professionals*. In that story, a set of professional gunslingers (a weapons expert, a horseman, a tactician) are hired by a wealthy client to bring home his kidnapped wife. The bandits who take her, however, soon turn out to be good guys and old friends of the lead gunslinger (a tactician). The audience quickly comes to realize, furthermore, that the captured wife is also an old girlfriend of the key bandit. It was her father who had unfeelingly broken up her romance and "sold" her as a bride to the gunslinger's wealthy client. In the end, therefore, the hero-lead-gunslinger refuses any salary offered him by his employer and bravely refuses an order to recapture and return the now-happy wife.

Consider, next, the translation of this film plot into business terms. A banker, like the new Western hero, is required to act as part of a team of skilled fighters. In each bank, employee roles are highly specialized. Furthermore, in *The Professionals* the hero's men remain loyal to assigned teammates, even at some personal cost. They wish to earn their pay as professionals, and not just to acquire money per se. Much like bankers, these Western heroes feel themselves to be rather separate from the wider society. The villains they face, what is more, are not classically immoral adversaries. Indeed, the skilled activities required of gunslingers are often valued more highly (by recent story writers) than are the outcomes of their specific struggles. The modern Western film does not, therefore, resolve a simple contest between good and bad so much as it juxtaposes several different structural viewpoints: those of a hero, a client, an adversary, and the professional team.

One may also note that a hero's association with the wilderness was highly valued in early Western films. But in the modern Western a hero's association with the wilderness is used to show off his knowledge about how to deal with uncharted settings. Heroes today do not ride into town out of a natu-ralist's paradise. Instead they must meet various threats or challenges that exist inside settled society. In this way such key figures (leaders) keep themselves firmly rooted in a primarily professional identity (Wright, 1975).

The above description provides a structurally useful frame for understand-ing a branch bank manager's job. A banker is a professional, both by self-definition and by corporate labeling. Such a person works with other man-agers and professionals, but also identifies strongly with one particular bank. A banker wishes to earn wages through a legitimate knowledge of the bank-ing milieu. The branch bank manager, furthermore, must work with a team that has specialized skills related to one specific part of that milieu. Bankers who survive the threats of our society's economic "wilderness" and manage to turn high profits are rewarded as "heroes" by senior management. A villain, meanwhile, can surface anywhere in a banker's life. Such an adversary can be a customer, a member of the local branch staff, or perhaps even a senior official. A villain is simply someone who disturbs the smooth functioning of the banker's job (a person's professionalism). As a hero, he or she must keep operations moving and effective in the face of all such challenges.

An analysis of the professional plot, in Wright's book *Sixguns and Society* (1975), develops the significance of four key oppositions in North American culture. These are defined in terms of a classical plot, and several of them are shown to weaken by the time the professional plot takes centerstage (Table 13.1). Taking these four basic oppositions as a starting point, therefore, plus Wright's discussion of historical developments, the present researchers, using inductive analysis (Patton, 1980) of their interview responses, have modified these to produce six thematic pairs thought to apply to the current banking milieu in Western Canada. As a cross-check on the inductive analysis that generated the six dimensions, an independent card-sort of the relevant raw responses was conducted, revealing very little ambiguity in interpretation. The dimensions are not necessarily mutually exclusive (independent), nor do they necessarily exhaust all possibilities for dimensionality in the branch bank

Table 13.1

Original Oppositions (Wright, 1975)	Modified and Modernized Oppositions (Beck and Moore)
1. Inside/Outside	1. Inside/Outside
2. Hero/Villain	2. (Center/Periphery) (Professional/Lay)
3. Strong/Weak	3. (Strong/Soft) (Background/Foreground)
4. Wilderness/Civilization	4. Universal/Personalistic

management subculture. However, these six are deemed to hold major importance for the analysis of leadership. A detailed description of these six key oppositions in relation to the bank management milieu is presented in Table 13.2.

The authors also mapped the specific situation depicted by *The Professionals* onto the position of the branch bank manager, as shown in Figure 13.1. This procedure provided a set of general principles believed likely to frame actions and attitudes in a Western Canadian branch bank. Through a detailed set of interviews with local bank managers, and various attitudinal measures managers administered to them, those key oppositions were then studied empirically. In particular, contrasts between the metaphoric image discussions (the frame materials) and responses to specific behavioral incidents were discovered. As said above, this was to be expected. Persons in positions of management need to define their actions as distinct from frame concepts if they are to create a "personal leadership style."

To obtain more insight on how such an analytic approach provides an effective explanation of contrasts found between behavioral and metaphoric response patterns in the empirical data, let us now turn our attention to the critical incidents used in interviews.

Each of the seven critical incidents represented a managerial problem or dilemma quite commonly encountered by branch bankers. Together, the incidents covered a wide range of managerial roles. In most of the incidents multiple roles were involved. After considering each incident, the respondent was instructed to choose, from a set of possible behaviors, the one that the typical branch manager would be most likely to follow. Next, the respondent was asked to explain his choice, thus revealing details about the typical manager's action or behavior alignment. Finally, the respondent was presented with a set of metaphors and asked to select the one that best represented the typical branch manager facing the problem just considered. An example metaphor set might contain these body parts: hand, brain, eye, ear, teeth, tongue, breast, leg. Once the most representative metaphor was selected, the respondent was again asked for an explanation, this time to reveal his background thinking regarding the relevant variables impinging on the problem setting and how he perceived them to be interrelated. The resulting cognitive structuring provided an image or frame alignment that could be compared and contrasted with the behavioral alignment previously derived.

The behavioral and metaphor responses in these interviews were coded according to a relationships model developed by Kluckhohn and Strodtbeck (1961). They posit three value orientations or value frames: lineal (L), collateral (C), and individualistic (I). A lineal orientation is hierarchical and associated with the father-son model of authority relations. A collateral orientation is characterized by horizontal support concerns, such as those commonly found in groups of peers. An individualistic orientation tends to be person-specific, so that individuals are encouraged to act on their own. The responses bank managers provided were generally found to orient in contrasting directions, suggesting that managers often do present themselves in contrast to a wider frame (see Table 13.3).

Incidents 2, 4, and 5 in the interview used were particularly germane to leadership. Each incident depicted a leader in relation to one or more of three important social subsets: customers, superiors in head office, or subordinate staff. Hence, these reflect the three corners of the triangular situation most managers face (diagrammed in Figure 13.1).

Let us now consider Incident 2, concerned with subordinates and with customers. This scenario takes place in the branch bank's inner office. The manager is required to placate an irate customer whose accounts have been mishandled. Simultaneously the manager is pressured to protect the reputation of the loan officer, a subordinate employee. Here an inside/outside opposition provides one important frame concept. The loan officer is clearly a company employee, while the customer is not. The bank manager himself is also an employee yet his professional performance is strongly linked with pleasing customers, even at the expense of his own team members. It is therefore no surprise that the typical behavioral response provided by managers (action alignment) is collateral (treating the customer as an equal and placating him). At the same time, the manager's use of metaphor material (the image or frame) is lineal in that now hierarchical relations within the bank staff are highlighted. In the metaphor discussion most managers placed themselves above both the customer and the employee involved. Indeed, this research on imagery shows that a manager's metaphor responses contain very suggestive, holistic material about the general background or frame surrounding the social situation being worked in. What follows are the details from Incident 2 that illustrate these principles in operation.

Incident 2

Sample Behavioral Response: The manager calls both the loans clerk and the customer into his office. He then accepts the blame on behalf of his staff, and assures the customer that this will not happen again.

Sample Metaphor Response: The brain. This is the coordinating part of the body. The customer has asked to go to the top, the control part of the body in order to get satisfaction.

Incident 4, focused on the interaction of a manager and superior bank official, provides a second example of frame and behavior contrasts. Here, inadequate physical facilities and overcrowded conditions have resulted in staff turnover and employee dissatisfaction. Managers' behavioral responses to this situation show a predominantly lineal action alignment. A branch official

Table 13.2. Definition of Six Oppositions Important in the Branch Bank Setting.*

1. INSIDE
The manager's primary concern is for the staff. He/she sides with the employees in a dispute or conflict situation with a customer. The manager emphasizes the internal operations of the bank.

2. PROFESSIONAL
The manager's approach tends to increase, emphasize, or maximize the vertical distance between him/herself and the public or staff. The manager would like people to look up to him/her. The manager is concerned with reputation and image; he/she always wants to look "professional," "competent," "in control," etc.

3. CENTER
The manager focuses or concentrates on the "center" of the organization. This could be head office, regional headquarters, or him/herself as manager, or some other central power figure. He/she sees action originating from the center. Problems or change may originate from, have the most impact on, or be dealt with from the center. The manager conceptualizes the bank as being in two parts, and identifies him/herself with the central part.

OUTSIDE
The manager's primary orientation is toward the customer. He/she is mostly concerned with placating the customer in a dispute or conflict situation. The manager emphasizes public or client relations.

LAY
The manager tries to minimize the distance between him/herself and the public or staff. He/she refuses to put on airs, or to make him/herself appear infallible or larger than life. He/she is one of the gang, or a part of a team. The manager does not associate competency or being a professional with authoritarian style, titles, or stereotypes.

PERIPHERY
The manager focuses or concentrates on the periphery of the organization. This could be the branch, the staff, etc. He/she sees action originating from the periphery. Problems or change may originate from the periphery, or be dealt with most effectively from the periphery. The manager places him/herself on the periphery.

4. UNIVERSALISTIC

The manager's strategy or approach to a situation is based on a common standard that is applicable to everyone. Also, a single goal or orientation exists for the whole branch. There is a usual way of doing things or of dealing with people. The manager has an attitude of "this is the way things are" or "this is the way it is supposed to be."

5. BACKGROUND

The manager's approach is to stay out of the public eye (that of either the customer or the staff). He/she is concerned with being discreet, tactful and considerate of other people's privacy. He/she handles the problem with the individual concerned, without involving others or seeking a group solution.

6. STRONG

The manager has a strong approach. He/she is action/achievement oriented. There may be a sense of urgency about the need to "do something." The manager makes his/her own decisions and carries them through or makes sure they are carried out.

PERSONALISTIC

The manager's understanding is that neither all situations nor all people can be approached in the same way. Each individual is considered to be unique. Each action chosen is seen to depend on the particular situation or individual.

FOREGROUND

The manager is very open about a problem and/or solution. He/she is not overly concerned with how it looks, or with protecting a subordinate's privacy. The manager may use public notices or memos to communicate with staff. The manager may involve other people in a problem or decision (supervisors, employees, etc.), or make the issue a group concern, involving the whole branch/staff.

SOFT

The manager may have a slower or more passive style, adopting a "we'll see" approach. Action without urgency. He/she allows others to influence, give input, make suggestions or otherwise modify his/her decisions and/or actions. He/she may feel impotent in the face of larger powers.

*Generally managers do not choose, but rather recognize the importance of both principles, depending on the specifics of the situation.

247

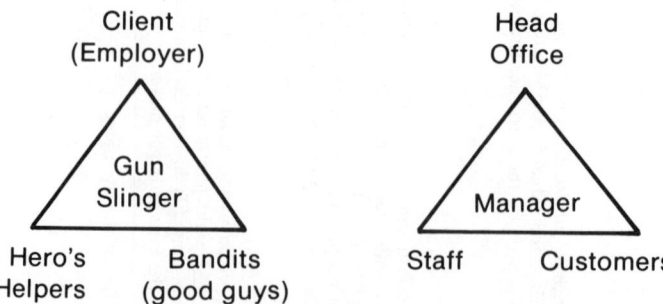

FIGURE 13.1. Movie and bank manager analogy

typically decides to make strong, direct appeal to the head office on behalf
of the local team of employees. Here a strong/soft dimension is added to the
general structural frame. A soft approach to superiors is reserved for situations where subordinates' needs are less easily defined in team terms. Here,
there is collateral metaphor usage (image alignment) because the cognitive
background frame is one of sharing a problem with employees that is not
of their making. A manager must have enough knowledge of the organization to suggest possible solutions that the head office can afford. Hence the
key opposition is center (leader's contacts or network) versus periphery (de-
pendents' suffering). In this case, then, the manager's behavioral choice is
lineal while the frame imagery used is collateral. Again, therefore, a leader's
actions are distinguished from the frame issues involved. Here are the details
from Incident 4 that illustrate these principles in operation:

Incident 4

Sample Behavioral Response: In a letter to the district office, outline the facts
and request a meeting with the district manager, plus a site visit.

Table 13.3 Bank Manager Behavioral and Metaphor
Interview Responses.

	Incident Number and Predominant Alignment Found						
	1	2	3	4	5	6	7
Behavior responses (action alignment)	I	C	I	L	I/C	C	I
Metaphor responses (imagery alignment)	C	L	C	C	C	L/C	C

I = Individualistic, C = Collateral, L = Lineal

Sample Metaphor Response: Oil. There is a need for something that will flow easily. One needs to keep the staff and the customers happy.

The first example discussed above (number two in the interview sequence), required a decision about where the blame lay, and the second (Incident 4 in the interview) concerned information access. The third example provided is from incident five, where interpersonal relations with a subordinate are at stake. In this case, a sensitive personal matter (body odor) can be seen to contain racial and perhaps feminist overtones. This issue places the manager in a very delicate bind vis-à-vis a female subordinate. The predominant behavior choice (action alignment) on the part of the manager here was to encourage the person with body odor to help herself. Hence, the behavior or action alignment is now largely individualistic. Yet, the frame or metaphor material suggests a siblinglike approach to such persons, clearly a collateral principle. Here are the relevant details:

Incident 5

Sample Behavioral Response: Privately and tactfully discuss the complaint with the immigrant person.

Sample Metaphor Response: A brother. One will hopefully come across as a brother. If one is female, then a sister. This is not a matter of a senior figure talking to a junior figure. It is a peer talking to a peer.

The structural concern in incident five is now background/foreground. By taking the role of sympathetic peer and treating the problem discretely (placing it out of direct view), a subordinate's self-esteem and dignity are maintained vis-à-vis the rest of the team.

Here, too, the cognitive alignment of the manager shifts with the use of metaphor. The choice of a sibling image directs attention firmly toward a collateral perspective. Yet in commenting on the behavior required, several people mentioned multicultural and human-rights issues. For example, one manager said, "This is probably the most difficult of all staff problems one can have. . . . Had this here, thought we handled it well, but then we got a call from the Human Rights Commission. If an immigrant person is involved they will immediately read discrimination into the incident. It is a real problem." In this case the frame principles involve a behavioral treatment of the subordinate that is universalistic and a conceptual one that is more personalistic.

Returning to the concept of the branch bank manager as hero/leader, the foregoing discussion highlighted six key oppositions:

A. Incident 2
   1. inside versus outside

   2. professional versus layman
B. Incident 4
   3. strong versus weak
   4. center versus periphery
C. Incident 5
   5. background versus foreground
   6. universalistic versus personalistic.

   An examination of parallel cultural institutions, such as the use of themes in Western films, can provide useful insights, therefore, into the actions of business managers. Both types of leaders face multifaceted environments in which mental maps play a primary role in framing (though not necessarily determining) social action. Where there are many cross-cutting possibilities for organizing and conceptualizing a given milieu, the use of structural analysis seems particularly promising.

   Robert E. Quinn (Chapter 2, this volume), based on an examination of the perceptual understructure or value orientations in the leadership literature, has developed a "conceptual tension system or Janusian framework of desired, but competing values." Quinn's analysis of leadership posits a general framework of cognitive value orientations represented by four opposing quadrants. He illustrates, using Janusian thinking, how a leader may be simultaneously influenced by opposing alignments. The six cultural oppositions identified in the present study through an adaptation of key principles found at work in Western films appear to fit nicely into Quinn's general leadership scheme. This suggests that his larger model reflects similar cultural principles and that both of us (independently) may have uncovered related frame concepts. A tentative fit between Quinn's work and this discussion can be seen in Figure 13.2. Inside, center, and foreground orientations would seem to suggest a concern for coordinating skills, whereas outside, periphery, and background orientations more closely suggest a concern for boundary-spanning skills. Similarly, lay, soft, and personalistic orientations suggest a concern for human-relations skills while professional, strong, and universalistic orientations appear to relate to directing skills.

   The focus on personality characteristics in leadership research has now been replaced with the realization that both leaders and their groups generally belong to broader, highly complex organizational systems. Thus, an "appropriate" leadership style will necessarily be a function of interactions involving the leader, the group, the task, and also the environment (Coltrin & Glueck, 1977). Salancik and Pfeffer (1977) have shown that the impact of the leader is significantly constrained by cultural and historical factors related to a particular situational setting. Moreover, Salancik et al. (1975) found that leadership power and political influence stem from positions in an organization's social structure. Further, they found that major dimensions of social

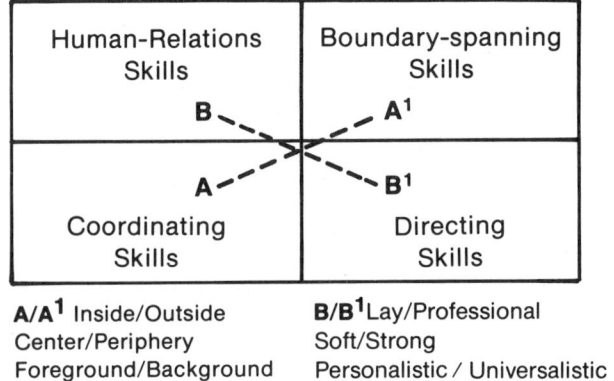

Human-Relations Skills **B**	Boundary-spanning Skills **A¹**
A Coordinating Skills	**B¹** Directing Skills

A/A¹ Inside/Outside   **B/B¹** Lay/Professional
Center/Periphery   Soft/Strong
Foreground/Background   Personalistic / Universalistic

FIGURE 13.2. Fit between Quinn's work and present study

structure vary across organizations and that the effective leader will be responsive to the social system in which he or she functions. House and Baetz (1979) cite the need to develop better ways to conceptualize the leader's environment and to determine its dimensions and dynamics vis-à-vis leader behavior. Recently, a number of scholars have recognized the promise of investigating complex relationships between the leader and specific social constituencies through the analysis of stories, myths, symbols, symbolic language, and metaphor (see Huff, 1978; Mintzberg, 1973, 1979; Pfeffer, 1981a; Pondy, 1978; Weick, 1977a; Wilkins, 1978). Specifically, these narrative forms may be examined to determine how people make sense of what is going on in their organizations and what behaviors are appropriate in particular kinds of situations.

The above chapter falls partway between a strictly empirical study and a more theoretical attempt to talk about meaning. In a sense it represents an attempt to operationalize both the assertion that frames of meaning exist and that such frames need not coincide directly with specific behavioral choices a manager or leader makes. If these findings are representative, then it would seem that such leaders must be sensitive to larger social themes, as well as skilled in relating their own actions to them. The metaphor questions used here were designed to elicit such basic "frames." This "cultural projection technique" aids in identifying the particular principles that direct an individual's thought. It is not that such metaphors directly guide managers in their work. Rather, these images colorfully outline a set of abstract principles that can be related (usually by contrast) to a leader's specific behavior choices. Culturally grounded constructs obtained through structural analysis may ultimately provide leaders with a means of being more articulate about their values and more confident in their behavioral choices. Such classification can ultimately improve the management of staff conflict, the meeting of customer needs, and the performance of other leadership roles. The authors plan to use these constructs to compare the imagery of high- and low-performing bank managers as identified by a performance index. Image and behavior comparisons of male and female bank managers are also in progress.

14

Situation Interpretation, Leader Behavior, and Effectiveness*

Anne S. Huff

More often than they would like, leaders find that an issue they thought was "solved" reasserts itself and becomes a problem again. In fact, 70 percent of the situations managers described for Lyles' (1981) study of problem formulation began with vague feelings of unease about the solution to a situation that had been acted upon previously. In a 2½-year study that Louis Pondy and I have made of over a dozen issues facing three school districts, one situation in particular had this character.

Several years before we began studying "Allison Park" (pseudonyms are used throughout this chapter), the school board had decided to close Tope School in response to a number of factors, including declining enrollments. When we began interviewing, in November 1979, the Tope issue appeared to be moving toward a final phase of razing the building and selling the land for residential lots. In the next year and a half, however, the focus of decision making shifted a number of times and finally involved a widely debated option of closing one or more neighborhood schools and reopening Tope as one of several centrally located buildings.

Dick Ingram, the superintendent of Allison Park, found it initially difficult to resolve in his own mind how these options should be compared. The Tope issue was politically volatile and had both financial and educational ramifications. Only after six months of conversation, intensive public hearings, committee consideration, outside consultation, and other problem-formulating activities was Ingram confident of the choice to be recommended to the board. This chapter discusses the way in which Ingram reformulated the Tope School issue in his own mind and then speculates about the potential tension between the task of problem formulation itself, and the task of influencing others to accept a given formulation.

*Louis R. Pondy was co-investigator for the project cited in this chapter. Support by the National Institute of Education, Grant No. G-80-0152 is gratefully acknowledged.

DATA AND CODING

The data for this investigation are drawn from the verbatim transcripts of 14 interviews with Ingram conducted between November 1979 and July 1981 by Lou Pondy and myself. (Three other telephone interviews could not be transcribed verbatim.) The interviews were transcribed into the computer and coded for easier access. A complete record of school board minutes was also coded by subject, as were articles published in the local newspaper. Our understanding of the Tope issue was further enhanced by attending seven board meetings, interviewing two board members and one principal twice each, attending a faculty planning committee, and other less formal contacts with the school district and its personnel. Tope School was not the only focus of our investigations at this site, but during the spring of 1981 it dominated most of the district's attention, and therefore most of our attention.

To understand Ingram's attempt to make sense of the Tope issue the study focuses on the language he used, and the arguments he made, in our interviews. The interviews have the advantage of being collected during the process of deliberation, in contrast to most studies of decision making that rely on retrospective or laboratory evidence.

The scheme of content analysis applied to the interviews comes from a philosopher, Steven Toulmin (1958, 1979). Toulmin suggested that in most natural situations individuals make assertions without being sure that those assertions are true. This perspective fits the policy maker very well. The issues about which policy decisions must be made almost always involve considerable uncertainty. Policy makers try to find evidence that is *strong enough* to justify making a decision, even though that evidence is rarely conclusive. Because the links between evidence and conclusions often are not immediately apparent, policy makers can be thought of as having "arguments" with themselves and others. The purpose of these arguments is to find a logical structure of sufficient strength to warrant action.

Toulmin offers five categories for analyzing arguments. The main line of the argument consists of a "claim" and the "data" offered in support of that claim. Since uncertainty is involved, additional support, or "warrants," are often added which suggest why the jump from evidence to claim should be taken. In fact, the speaker sometimes provides "backing" to support the warrant further. Finally, the claim may be "qualified" by the speaker to indicate the conditions under which it might not be true.

For this analysis, the 14 interviews (20,006 lines, or about 670 double-spaced pages of text) were coded by topic. Toulmin's categories of argument were then applied to the 9,423 lines of interview material that involved the Tope issue. As an example of the material that resulted, Figure 14.1 diagrams this statement:

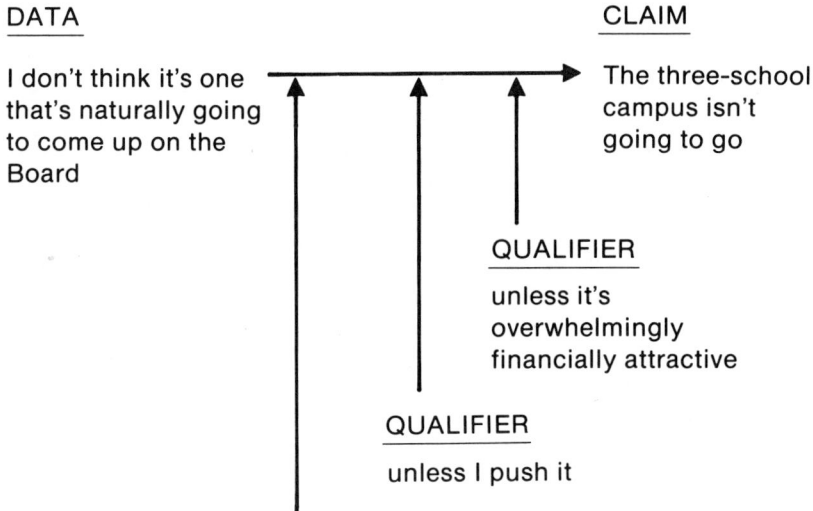

FIGURE 14.1. Argument diagrammed using Toulmin's categories

The three school campus isn't going to go unless I push it, I think. I don't think it's one that's naturally going to come up on the Board. It will be presented as an alternative and unless it's overwhelmingly financially attractive I think the inclination would be to stay in the neighborhood pattern, go for a referendum, sell Tope, escrow the money, invest it, and take security in the fact that there'll be money in the bank if we need to add some more space at some time.

To further structure the vast amount of material available in the interviews, the 350 claims that were identified using Toulmin were further coded for the main subject of each claim. A summary of some of the results of this coding procedure is included in Table 14.1.

Table 14.1. Summary of Coding Data.

Interview	Date	Approx. Length (ms pages)	% Tope	# claims¹	# action claims²	# predicting claims	# claims specifying alternatives	# claims applying specific criteria	# references to "future"
1.	11/2/79	51	27%	10	—	—	1	—	—
2.	2/21/80	58	33%	17	2	2	5	—	5
3.	9/5/80	75	26%	25	6	4	2	—	—
4.	9/16/80	43	20%	14	1	6	—	—	—
5.	10/02/80	40	8%	5	4	1	—	—	—
6.	10/29/80	43	34%	17	5	5	—	1	5
7.	11/06/80	34	14%	7	1	1	—	—	1
8.	12/05/80	71	29%	37	—	2	4	11	5
9.	1/22/81	59	60%	38	—	6	—	1	2
10.	2/11/81	21	67%	17	—	2	4	7	2
11.	4/26/81	24	99%	21	5	5	1	2	5
12.	5/21/81	52	98%	56	8	10	3	4	11
13.	6/9/81	19	100%	14	2	2	2	1	—
14.	6/16/81	76	87%	72	10	5	—	3	42

¹The number of claims includes direct response to interviewer questions, unless answers are factual.
²Claims that involve what the superintendent, board, or other actors are doing, or have just done.

ANALYSIS

The coding summarized in Table 14.1 indicates a significant break around December 1980, first in the kind of claims Ingram was making, and then in his attentiveness to the Tope issue. Before the December interview, many claims, and indeed much of the data offered to support them, involve present or anticipated actions.

Then, in response to events that will be described below, Ingram began to have doubts about the district's overall approach to the Tope issue. A clear signal of this shift back to problem formulation is that the claims being made directly involve the criteria for decision making. The end of this reformulation period is not well defined, but by the end of April Ingram had again begun to focus on action. In June, the month of the board decision on the Tope issue, his action-oriented assessments often involve how individual board members were likely to vote, and how he thought they should vote.

Our data on the Tope issue provide a unique opportunity to look at executive problem formulation, or in this case reformulation, in an organizational context. Very little research has been done in this area (Lyles, 1981, p. 61), especially in nonlaboratory settings. Lyles' work (1981), based on recollective interviews with 33 middle and upper managers, led to a heuristic model with three general phases: (1) a period of individual awareness and incubation, which is activated by some triggering event, into (2) an organizational phase of information gathering, problem rationalization, and debate, until (3) some resolution is reached. Lyles documents, however, that most problem-formulating episodes cycle through the steps of problem formulation more than once. Quinn (1980), who studied strategic change in a number of major corporations, supports the notion that redirection of organizational efforts is an iterative and time-consuming process, with both analytical and political components.

The Tope issue follows this broad outline of the problem-formulation process. Our data collected during the period of decision making allow, however, for a more detailed look at the *content* rather than the process of decision making. This examination of the Tope issue focused on three questions:

1. What causes departures from an established line of decision making?
2. What feeds the recycling involved in the period of reformulation?
3. How is a new direction established?

The results of this analysis can be summarized in the following way:

1. *The appearance of new alternatives did not, per se, dislocate the established flow of decision making.* Ingram identified four alternatives for Tope in our first, November 1979, interview. They were to rent, lease for a nominal fee, turn the building over to the town for senior housing, or tear the build-

ing down and sell the land. By February 1980 Ingram claimed that "we are leading to the logical conclusion of razing the building." He also noted, however, that a fifth "central campus" alternative had received some attention. Interest in this alternative stemmed from the financial advantages of operating out of fewer buildings, and the ease with which the district could offer a school lunch program.

The constellation of alternative resolutions of the Tope issue had changed, to our surprise, when we began interviewing again in the fall of 1980. The town planning commission had revitalized the senior housing option Ingram had previously dismissed. Then, a local church interested in expanding their facilities contacted the district. In October Ingram expected that Tope would go to one of these two buyers. These changes in the Tope issue, which demanded adaptation in Ingram's activities and his predictions, did not, however, cause him to rethink the general direction established several years earlier.

2. *Indistinguishable alternatives, on the basis of criteria already established, did not, per se, disrupt the established flow of decision making.* The criteria for deciding what to do with the Tope building were rarely mentioned directly in this period. Ingram was concerned with being financially responsible. He also wanted to maintain the district's independence in the decision, while being responsive to town and neighborhood welfare in choosing a user of the building. Neither the church nor the town appeared to have a clear edge over the other on these dimensions, but Ingram suggested several times that the more general criteria of expediency or "a bird in the hand kind of thing," might be the deciding factor.

3. *Reconceptualization of the Tope issue was triggered by an argument presented as part of an unrelated, short-term problem facing the district. This argument challenged not the set of alternatives (though it revitalized a previously dismissed alternative) but the key criteria by which the original decision to close Tope had been made.* In December 1980, an apparently unrelated event changed the focus of attention on the Tope School issue. Third-grade parents from one building in the district, dissatisfied by a class size larger than third grades in other buildings, and unable to persuade the principal or superintendent to add another teacher, organized and brought their complaint to the school board. During several public meetings the administration argued that the size of the class was within the bounds of normal practice in the district over time. One parent, however, using some of the same data presented by the administration, suggested that *inequities among* classes had increased and that even greater variation in class size should be expected as enrollment continued to decline.

This argument highlighted for Ingram an educational disadvantage of the neighborhood schools that had previously been universally characterized as an expensive, but educationally preferable, way to organize the district. Centralizing students in fewer buildings could now be seen as providing more options for matching individual students with appropriate class configurations, a particularly important aspect of Allison Park's educational philosophy. However, if students would benefit from larger numbers in one building, it was important to make that decision before disposing of one of the largest, and most centrally located, buildings in the district. Ingram therefore decided to push the board to consider a central campus alternative. In his words, the central campus concept "was real to me before . . . but [the analysis of class-size inequities] gave a different dimension to it than it had before."

4. *Expanding the criteria considerably expanded the scope of the decision and necessitated new kinds of analysis, which lengthened the reformulation process.* Once educational criteria were introduced, additional actors (notably teachers, principals, parents, and the public) became involved. A series of public meetings were held. A teacher committee was appointed by the board to consider "qualitative" aspects of the issue in its expanded form. District administrators prepared figures on class size, classroom space, and projected costs under various assumptions. At the same time an external demographics consultant was asked to look again at his projections, an architect was asked for renovation estimates under various assumptions, and a financial consultant helped project district finances. Commissioning and hearing these reports took almost four months, even though many extra meetings were held.

5. *Reformulation was shaped by the last decision about Tope and by the concern with class size that triggered reformulation.* In our first interview, when Ingram recapitulated the board's initial decision to close Tope, he indicated that some members of the community felt "sandbagged" by the fact that identifying Tope as the building to be closed was a last-minute compromise decision. A parent group explicitly referred to this incident in one of the first meetings held in 1981 and demanded the right to fully discuss any alternatives the board considered. During the spring, parent representatives often called daily to ask if special meetings had been arranged. Typically one or more members of the public exercised their right to attend such meetings. In retrospect Ingram felt that the board, unused to this level of public attention, delayed conversation which would have indicated to each other the position each was beginning to take on the Tope issue.

Throughout deliberations, a continued concern with class size could be seen. Alternatives discussed by teachers, administrators, and the board included comparisons of class-size implications.

6. *Reformulation continued through the period of analysis.* An interesting aspect of the public debate about "the" central campus alternative was the lack of specificity about which buildings would be closed or the grade configuration that would be assigned to remaining buildings. Various options continued to be explored through May, when the board considered relocating junior high students to Tope and maintaining all of the neighborhood grade schools.

7. *The development of a new framework, involving "future flexibility," finally allowed one alternative to be viewed as having a significant edge over other alternatives.* Ingram tried various ways of reframing the Tope issue. In January, for example, he said, "I think I would have more comfort with a three school central campus decision because I know it's got some room for error, it's reversible." In February, he felt that, "from a space point of view the current pattern is a pretty inefficient use of space, we're going to have the equivalent of a whole building of unused space." In April he said the majority of the teaching staff would accept the central campus concept because of "a need to grow and change" and he felt that this concept was also responsive to changes in the community. In May he said that in a central campus mode, "people are going to be much more highly motivated, with much greater sense of responsibility."

Despite these and other potential framing concepts, however, Ingram was not able to support the central campus concept confidently. In May, for example, he said: "I'm scared about it. I'm not sure we're right for this key decision. It's not such a black and white clear-cut kind of decision." The frame that finally allowed him to support the central campus alternative and urge the board to support it as well was expressed in terms of "future flexibility." Concern with the future needs of the district can be found throughout our interviews, but are not frequent. The word "future" is used from 0 to 5 times an interview until May, when it is used 11 times. On June 16, however, Ingram uses the concept of the future 42 times; talking, for example, about "how the future of the district can best be spent," "the kind of participation that's required to take bold action in the future," and "the discomfort of thinking about the future of the district in [the neighborhood] configuration."

This brief overview of the Tope School issue suggests some initial answers to the three questions asked about the content of problem reformulation. First, Ingram's initial formulation of the Tope issue was able to withstand considerable variation in potential resolutions of the issue. It was only when another event raised explicit questions about the criteria around which the original decision was made that he began to reconsider his way of framing the issue. (It might also be noted, in support of Lyles, 1981, and Quinn, 1980, that Ingram had already begun to have doubts about a firm offer for Tope actually materializing, thus making reconsideration more likely.)

Second, the introduction of new criteria considerably expanded the scope of the Tope issue. New analysis was required. Teachers became important actors as educational criteria were reintroduced. Parents and the community wanted to be involved. Throughout this period various alternatives were experimented with, which necessitated more complicated analysis and required additional interaction.

Finally, Ingram had considerable difficulty finding a satisfactory way of framing the Tope issue in its expanded state. It took several months before the flow of events and the "trial arguments" he generated led to a formulation strong enough to warrant his commitment. The successful distinction among alternatives was arrived at after many possible ways to frame the decision were considered.

A LEADERSHIP DILEMMA

Finding a frame is only part of the leadership task. The second part of the task is using the frame to influence others. As Bower and Doz (1979) suggest, a central task of the chief executive officer is to "shape the premises of other executives' thoughts" (p. 157).

Ingram was very unaware of his obligation as superintendent to "take a position" on the Tope issue. The behavior necessary to find an appropriate frame for the Tope issue, however, may well have stood in the way of the behavior needed to influence others. To find a suitable frame one might expect the attributes of creative problem solvers, including "a questioning attitude" and "fluency and flexibility of thinking" to be important (Adams, 1974; pp. 76, 79). The Tope issue illustrates why these characteristics are necessary: new actors need to be informed and heard; new information will (or might) appear as soon as various analyses are completed; the exact nature of alternatives cannot be specified until this information has been gathered; and so on. As Quinn (1980) suggests:

> Strategy deals with the unknowable, not the uncertain. It involves forces of such great number, strength and combinatory powers that one cannot predict events in a probabilistic sense. Hence it is logical that one proceed flexibly and experimentally from broad concepts toward specific commitments, making the latter concrete as late as possible in order to narrow the bands of uncertainty and to benefit from the best available information. (p. 56)

Flexibility, experimentation, and delayed commitment, however, can also defer the second leadership task of influencing the framework others apply to the issue. Quinn points out the necessity of building other's knowledge of the situation and increasing their commitment to the general direction emerging from the reformulation period. Yet he is vague about the way in which executives can do this. In fact a difficult double requirement seems to be placed on leaders. On the one hand they are asked to delay their own commitment until reformulation activities are well underway. On the other hand they must have enough vision and commitment to channel the thoughts of others during this process.

Ingram largely achieved this difficult task within the schools. The rhetoric of future flexibility was partially discovered and advanced in the teachers' committee of which he was part. He also increased his interaction with and reliance upon the principals. By May all of the principals and many of the more vocal and respected teachers were supportive of a central campus alternative. The board, however, was not brought along by the same developments. Although two board members sat on the teacher committee, they left communication of the results to a formal report from the teachers at the end of their deliberations. (As noted above, the public nature of the decision may have been an important factor in suppressing interaction among board members while they were still in a data-gathering posture.)

Ultimately Ingram did try to persuade the board that the future needs of the district strongly favored the central campus alternative, but the final vote supported selling Tope as originally planned and maintaining the neighborhood schools. Many factors appear to have had a hand in this divergence of opinion. Ingram felt that there were strong positive aspects to the traditional pattern. He was reluctant to be seen as a partisan debating with pro-neighborhood forces in the community. He felt that a sophisticated board should be presented with a sophisticated analysis of alternatives.

While these and other factors are unique to the Tope issue, I believe that the quandary Ingram found himself in typifies a generic problem of leadership. Leaders hope that situations will unfold in an orderly enough way that their worst doubts will be past before the situation requires a public voice. Even to have the first broad outline of an assessment will then help channel the discussion. But that is not always possible. The leader, in fact, begins at a disadvantage, because of the broader perspective the position requires and the time that the process of reformulation often requires. It is likely that special interest groups – in this case, parents protecting neighborhood schools – will be able to articulate more quickly and easily a position and begin to influence others since their interests are more focused and narrowly defined.

15

Commentary on Part 3

Chapter 12 Commentary: Organizational Culture, Ideology, and Management

Nigel Nicholson

Caren Siehl and Joanne Martin have made a highly original contribution to the management literature by reporting research that is methodologically innovative and conceptually divergent from the dominant paradigms in the field. The importance of culture and cultural variables is increasingly recognized in organizational studies, but this is probably the first documented attempt by behavioral scientists to use quasi-experimental, longitudinal field research (as opposed to more commonly used case methods) to assess directly the content of cultural transmission and its consequences. This careful piece of work deserves to be built upon by others and should encourage researchers to view the issues as less intractable than is commonly believed.

The issues raised, however, are frighteningly large — for example, what is the societal function of complex organizations and the practice of management? — and bewilderingly complex — how are the multiple layers of meaning in organizational behavior created, sustained, and changed? I shall not attempt to resolve such weighty questions here, but only try to bring to the surface and explore some of the important issues evoked by the Siehl and Martin chapter.

First, let us reaffirm the authors' conviction of the utmost relevance of cultural variables to understanding organizational behavior. The point is well made by Salaman (1979) when he says that, "organizational culture or subculture is no optional extra . . . (but) an essential component in the structure of organizational control of middle level and expert members" (p. 177). This statement also implies that cultural control of behavior becomes more crucial the higher one ascends in the organizational structure, and that participation in the manipulation of cultural forms is a management and a leadership skill. This is the issue that Siehl and Martin address, though they leave room for us to explore further here what is meant by culture and its contents.

The issue is not merely that there might be some need for semantic refinement of what Raymond Williams (1976) has called "one of the 2 or 3 most complex words in the English language" (p. 76), but for us to question which

dimensions of culture are affected by management practice. The broad definitions of culture offered by the authors and other writers on organizations
(notably Pettigrew, 1979) are, of necessity, imprecise, encompassing the way
of life and shared meanings of a collective. The breadth of such definitions
leads us to an important logical point — that the practice of management is
itself a component of culture and therefore logically subordinate to it. Management cannot control culture for attempts to control cultural variables
themselves constitute part of the culture. The values that inform management
behavior are derived from cultural forms that permit or encourage such attempts. This point is better appreciated if one considers how organizational
cultures are embedded in the wider culture of the social system. According
to this view, management practice reflects, transmits, and contributes to culture but does not create or control it. What Siehl and Martin's chapter shows
is that *some* of the contents of culture may be accessible to management control, principally what may be termed "ideology" (see Hartley, in press). By
separating these two ideas — culture and ideology — we can explore further
what their chapter tells us about the range of managerial control over cultural
variables.

At the broadest level of analysis, to understand organizational culture requires a willingness to reinterpret the culture in terms that are applied externally, rather than the interior language and definitions of the actors. The analysis
of power relations and the sources of legitimacy is a case in point, for the
structure of the rights and obligations of organizational members is the
skeleton upon which hangs the rich fabric of culture — stories, folkways,
mores, and the like. Salaman (1979) identifies the two major strands in the
organizational culture of most capitalist enterprises: "structuralism," the conviction that organizational structure is a given and not the outcome of choice
or the exercise of will; and "psychologism," the shared belief that individuals'
efforts bear a major responsibility for organizational performance. More empirically grounded is Bate's (1982) recent study of organizational culture in
three enterprises. Across the three, Bate identifies some common themes in
their cultures: impersonality, depersonalization, subordination, conservatism,
autonomy, and pluralism. The implication of this kind of analysis is that
organizational actors are usually unaware of the cultural assumptions that
guide their own behavior, and hence, contrary to the rhetoric of leadership,
usually have less power to change and control culture than they have the skills
to be its handmaidens. So it was that Sofer (1970) found in his case studies
that a "culture of ambition" was dominating management's judgments about
performance. A shared optimistic mythology about promotion prospects and
work values obscured the reality of routinized work and restricted opportunities.

In Siehl and Martin's organization there might be similar scope for some
reinterpretation of signs. For example, could it be said in this case that control via commitment is induced by the strategies of "organizational seduction"

that Lewicki (1981) has identified, via the medium of inculcating a "human-relations" ideology? Could the training program they describe also be portrayed as a ceremonial to convey organizational myths (Trice, Balasco, & Alutto, 1969) whose ideological content socializes new entrants to accept the legitimacy of existing practices and arrangements? There are points and episodes in their account where there is scope for distinguishing the manifest values of managerial ideology and what might be the latent values of organizational culture.

A possible case in point is the treatment of the trainee who failed to answer correctly any of several "sample exam questions." The manager's "minitheory" that: "We believe that if an employee is failing to perform, we owe that person assistance," could, in many organizations be euphemistic code for: "Performance is a matter of individual achievement, and if you don't do better after we've given you all the help we can, you *really* will have failed!" This example is used only to illustrate how contrary meanings and values may deceptively enclose one another, not to rewrite the research material. Secondary sources are usually inadequate for this kind of reinterpretation, and only the authors, from their close familiarity with the living reality of this organizational culture, could take such speculations further.

As it stands, Siehl and Martin's is an extremely effective demonstration of the transmission of some ideological elements of an organizational culture. The literature on ideologies accords them the status of "morally sustaining ideas" (Selznick, 1966), which are much less often created within organizations than they are imported and transformed (Beyer, 1981) and which serve as instruments of control rather than as ends in themselves (Pettigrew, 1973). Starbuck (1982) and Starbuck, Greve, and Hedburg (1978) draw attention to the ubiquity of organizational ideology, and to the need for ideologies to adapt or be transformed for major shifts in organizational functioning in order to be feasible. The management of ideology is, therefore, as Siehl and Martin assert, absolutely central to organizational effectiveness, though it is less easy to agree with their implication that the maintenance of ideological cohesion is a recipe for managerial "success." As Meyer (1982) points out, although potent ideologies may "engender devotion, create élan, lend drama, and accord dignity to everyday activities [they can also] cause organizations to become excessively deviant, rigid and stagnant" (p. 80). Lewicki (1981) sounds a similar warning that too much managerial emphasis upon building loyalty and commitment readily leads to the "pathology" of "confining corporate mentality." In other words, the effective transmission of a dominant ideology can result in organizational "nest fouling," to use the graphic phrase of Pondy and Mitroff (1979). Rather, organizational effectiveness may depend upon management's ability to help the organizational culture to incorporate conflicting ideologies (Beyer, 1981) or unlearn the values and beliefs that have brought success in the past (Hedburg, 1981).

This brings us back to the question of how much management has it in its power to control organizational culture. The logically self-defeating nature of attempts to change organizational culture could be said to be the dominant theme of Argyris and Schon's analyses of individual and organizational learning (1974, 1978). This suggests that the "double-loop learning" necessary for adaptive change requires recourse to external agencies who can help to "reframe" how problems and solutions are perceived (Watzlawick, Weakland, & Fisch, 1974). Acceptance of this analysis, however, need not lead us to pessimism about management efficacy or to a determinist view of the relationship between the culture and managerial behavior.

If one accepts Schon's (1971) assertion that only the top three to seven persons' ideologies are of practical importance in many organizations, then the levers of change could certainly be said to be clearly visible, even if they are hard to handle. The relationship of influential individuals to the surrounding culture(s) is dialectical. Ideology both transforms and is transformed by consciousness. Cultures generate leaders who generate cultures. James Macgregor Burns' (1978) brilliant analysis of political leadership is studded with notable examples: Hitler's enculturation within outcast cliques of embittered ultra-nationalists providing the seedbed for his own virulent strain of ideological fervor; Ghandi's cross-fertilization of ancient Hindu values with a political pragmatism learned in British prisons; Lenin's capture of revolutionary subculture by infusing it with his bitter personal learning at the hands of centralized authority. In each case it is not possible to say whether the circumstances produced the man or the man engineered the circumstances for his own success.

The relevance of such cases to organizational management is less remote than might appear if one accepts the premise of the centrality of cultural variables to organizational practice (Pfeffer, 1981a). House's theory of charismatic leadership (1977) is one of the few recent attempts in the literature to grapple with the issue. He is primarily concerned with questions about the means management can employ to evoke the collective will of subordinates. His reading of the literature suggests that one indispensable element of this is the articulation of an ideological goal, though he does not discuss the content of organizational ideologies. If, however, the organizational literature does not shed much light on the relationship between leadership influence and the ideological content of workplace interaction, there is growing literature that does, by focusing on more overtly political organizations: trade unions. Research at the Warwick University SSRC Industrial Relations Unit (Batstone, Boraston, & Frenkel, 1977, 1978) and at the Sheffield University MRC/SSRC Social and Applied Psychology Unit (Hartley, Kelly, & Nicholson, 1983; Nicholson, Ursell, & Blyton, 1981) has documented how the power of leaders varies as a function of their ability to mobilize and exploit shifting ideological themes. From these data and ideas one can conclude that the "language game" of leadership (Pondy, 1978) depends upon the characteristics of the surrounding cultural and subcultural milieux, the personality characteristics of the actors, and the quality of leader-follower interactions. From this or similar interactive perspectives in the leadership literature (e.g., Hollander, 1978) one is drawn to the crucial insight that individual managers differ in the kinds of ideologies they need to promote to maximize their effectiveness, as well as the more usual observation that certain types of organizational cultures require particular styles of management.

One interesting corollary of this is that the role transitions of leaders, that is management succession, is one of the major means by which organizational cultures have the opportunity to change and evolve (Nicholson, 1982). The fact that the succession process is not a traumatic event or revolutionary stimulus wherever it occurs is a tribute to the compulsive force of most organizational enculturation and socialization (Van Maanen, 1976, 1980), the comprehensive nature of organizational mechanisms for making change a stable process (March, 1981), and the widespread tendency for succession to be used as a scapegoating *response* to organizational crises rather than an instrument of change (Brown, 1982).

These qualifications notwithstanding, there has been no systematic research looking at how executive succession can be a stimulus for changes in organizational *cultures* (as distinct from changes in organizational performance) though unscientific evidence to the effect that it does abounds in the popular media of the business and political arenas.

The purpose of this digression has been to underline the need for balance in how one evaluates the impact on organizational behavior of collective values and individual agency. Siehl and Martin are surely right when they advocate raising managerial consciousness about cultural variables as a strategy for change and control, though this "enlightment effect" can never be transcendental to the culture that permits or produces it (Gergen, 1973). As an afterthought one can reflect that this paradox is one that applies equally to we who research and write about such questions. The knowledge about organizational behavior that our efforts produce is potentially freedom and power enhancing to organizational actors, but we should also be aware of the extent to which we can be the prisoners of cultural definitions, linguistic conventions, and institutional practices. So it is that research on leadership and other topics does produce genuine change insofar as it helps the meanings and values of scientific subcultures to evolve, but at the same time we are often like scriptwriters or mythmakers for a vast ceremonial whose dimensions we are unable to grasp fully, and that we are consequently powerless to change radically.

Let me conclude by briefly considering what issues this discussion suggests should provide the focus for the future investigation of symbolic management. Four major questions are implied:

1. What is the significance of differences between organizational cultures? Comparative organizational research has in the past tended to be overly structural, and future cross-cultural or interorganizational studies should focus more upon differences in the meaning and value of organizational behavior in contrasted settings. These contrasts should be analyzed as exemplifying the different ways organizations manifest, amplify, modify, and use the cultural themes and values of their occupational and societal contexts.

2. What is the relationship between organizational ideology and organizational culture? Previous research on the problematic relationship between subjective and objective dimensions of climate has suffered from an overly static and quantitative bias. Future research requires a fresh approach to the seeming paradoxes of conflicting meanings and definitions through longitudinal qualitative strategies that construe them historically and dialectically.

3. Are managers the agents or the victims of organizational culture? The decomposition of management to measurable dimensions, traits, and behaviors has obscured the fundamental duality of managerial roles. A holistic qualitative appreciation of managerial individuality is needed to understand better how important are individual differences in the balance between the functions of management roles: as purveyors and maintainers of cultural themes, and as agents and innovators of subcultural variation.

4. How can change be induced in organizational cultures? There is scope for new approaches to the study of the planned and unplanned events that precipitate alterations in cultural configuration and ideological value. The role of change agents, consultants, and external information sources can be reassessed in terms of the opportunities they provide for the reframing of dominant themes, with attention focused on the political processes that mediate the reinforcement or change of collective definitions.

These are challenging questions and offer little scope for the methods and schema that have predominated in the past, but by the same token, they offer a way forward to methodological innovation, interdisciplinary insights, and a richer set of ideas for understanding the subtle complexities of management and organizational behavior.

Chapters 13 and 14 Commentary: On Imagery and the Cycling of Decision Making

Ian E. Morley

This commentary locates the Moore and Beck and Huff thinkpieces within three related traditions of research in social psychology and political science. The first is concerned with the nature of leadership and leadership roles. The second is concerned with attempts to conceptualize decision making and stages within the decision-making process. The third is concerned with leaders' general orientation to their roles.

The Nature of Leadership and Leadership Roles

It has been estimated that there are well over 100 different definitions of the term "leadership" (e.g., Burns, 1978; Stogdill, 1974). However, there seems to be general agreement that: (1) leaders lead groups; (2) leadership structures the cognitions, conations, affects, and behaviors of the led; (3) leaders are differentiated from other group members; and (4) leaders form part of the organization of a large social system.

It is element 2 that is important here: that leadership functions to structure the thoughts, motives, feelings, and behaviors of the led. First, there is the leader's "executive" role: the "exercise of power, vested in the leader by the norms, including norms which give others authority to appoint him to leadership" (Kelvin, 1970, p. 226). Second, there is what might be called the leader's symbolic role: the exercise of influence "derived from the leader's personal status irrespective of whether he has or does not have power to enforce his wishes" (Kelvin, 1970, p. 226). Kelvin's thesis is that: "Inasmuch as the leader has power he may exercise leadership by determining the behaviour of his followers: inasmuch as he (also) has status and is valued, he will influence the beliefs and feelings of his followers" (p. 226).

The symbolic role of the leader reflects the fact that he or she brings special kinds of resources to the group. Leaders help to define reality for others: they interpret actions, give meaning and perspective to events. Karl Weick (1978) has pointed out, leaders "provide pictures": they acquire power to the extent that people rely on them because they get "more accurate and more diverse or more suggestive pictures than do any of the followers" (p. 47). They get more accurate pictures if they are experts because they gain information from their position in the organization, and because they form networks of informal relationships (Bacharach & Lawler, 1980; Batstone, Boraston & Frenkel, 1977). They get more suggestive pictures because, to borrow from Pettigrew (1979), they create "symbols, languages, beliefs, visions, ideologies and myths" (p. 572). That is to say, leaders obtain normative power to the extent that they act as "sponsors," providing images for those they lead. It is this sponsorship that is so important when we consider the generation of purpose, commitment, and order in organizational groups (Pettigrew, 1979). It should be noted, however, following Huff, that the influence process is by no means one-way. Leaders set the policy for the group but monitor opinions and negotiate agreements that ensure the commitment of (at least) the key members of the groups they lead.

In some cases the pictures leaders provide derive from "philosophical" beliefs defining threats and opportunities in the (political) environment of work (George, 1969, 1974; Holsti, 1970; Morley, 1981b). In political science, writers like George (1969, 1974) and Holsti (1970) treat such beliefs as part of an "operational code" defining for each actor a "fundamental orientation to the problem of leadership and action" (George, 1974, p. 188). To establish the philosophical content of the code they ask questions such as:

- What are the prospects for eventual realization of one's political values and aspirations?
- Is the political future predictable?
- How much control and mastery can one have over historical development?
- What is the role of chance and accident in historical development?

Answers to such questions can be revealing, as Holsti's (1970) studies of John Foster Dulles have shown.

I agree with Moore and Beck's concern that neither the effects of leader imagery on subordinates nor the relationship of a leader's own imagery to the leader's behavior in different settings is well understood. The inclination here is to treat metaphorical images as a small subset of the more general class of beliefs about the purpose, character, and identity of an organization. As Sproull (1981) has said, beliefs of this kind "can strongly influence organizational actions" (p. 214). They serve the same purpose as constructs such as operational codes (George, 1974; Holsti, 1970), images (in Jervis', 1976, sense), attitudes (Abelson, 1972; Winkler, 1974), ideologies (Marengo, 1979), sagas (Clark, 1972), and frames (Huff, this volume). That is, they function as *scripts* that define *in ordinary language* the threats and opportunities implied by given kinds of input. They provide guidance for action because they function as plans, directing the search for information, and because they exemplify "the reasoning of the *practical* syllogism, the choice of action that is appropriate in the light of informational precises" (Eiser, 1980, p. 43). They provide justification for behavior and a "mechanism for creating a community of interest" (Sproull, 1981, p. 214). Constructs of this kind have been utilized in studies of political leadership (George, 1974; Hermann, 1980; Holsti, 1970) and organizational design (Beyer, 1981; Sproull, 1980). I think they are important for studies of leadership, generally, because they are important components of a theory of action (Abelson, 1972). To the extent that these think pieces suggest further analysis of this kind we should be grateful.

Decision Making and Stages within the Decision-Making Process

Writers such as Bales (1950), Bales and Strodtbeck (1951) and Morley and Stephenson (1977) have used category systems to describe stages in group decision making. Bales' categories were designed to chart the ebb and flow of task and socioemotional problems implied by his analysis of the "equilibrium problem" in small task-oriented groups (see Parsons, Bales & Shils, 1953). The categories used by Morley and Stephenson were designed to chart the movement between person and party climates in negotiation, implied by Douglas' (1957, 1962) studies of industrial peacemaking. In one sense the piece by Huff lies squarely within this tradition, although the system of categories is much less clearly tied to a theory of the psychological processes supposed to underlie decision making in (or by) groups. (Incidentally, I have found the categories extremely difficult to apply to data from experimental and real-life negotiation groups.) Huff, however, pays more attention than others to the idea that stages in decision making are "notional": that a group in one stage of decision making may interrupt the process and go back over old ground. This is an important emphasis, and one that has been brought "centerstage" in the work of Janis and Mann (1977) and Burnstein and Berbaum (1981).

According to Burnstein and Berbaum (1981), decision making may be described as cycling and recycling through stages of *identification* (of problems), *development* (of solutions), and *selection* (of policy). The "interrupts" that initiate recycling may be determined by events *endogenous* or *exogenous* to the decision-making group (Burnstein & Berbaum, 1981, pp. 39–40).

With respect to endogenous cycles, considerable attention has been devoted to ways in which skilled performers structure interaction so that: (1) the capacities of group members are efficiently linked to the demands of the task; (2) disagreement is organized to prevent premature selection of a policy, and to root out ideas that are plausible, but false or incomplete. Consider the work conducted by Snyder and Diesing (1977), Lockhart (1979), and Morley (1981a, 1981b; Morley & Stephenson, 1981) which attempts to analyze the skills involved in negotiations between representatives of groups. If pressed I will argue that people like Ingram act as negotiators and that systematic attempts to integrate literature on leadership and literature on negotiation are long overdue. Further, it should be noted that Huff's distinction between finding a frame and using the frame to influence others is somewhat similar to Walton and McKersie's (1965) distinction between integrative and distributive bargaining.

Attention has also been paid to ways in which negotiators exploit continuity in their relationship with members of the other side. This work is particularly relevant to Huff's argument that leaders participate in discussions to test the strength of a particular script or frame. In their *Shop Stewards in Action,* Batstone, Boraston, and Frenkel (1977) have noted that, *given a broad balance of power between the participants,* "leader" shop stewards sometimes develop relationships with managers that are affectively positive, particularistic, and high in terms of information exchange. Confidential information is exchanged off the record (privately), much of it preventing the other from "getting into difficulty" or "being conned" (Batstone, Boraston, & Frenkel, 1977, p. 173). Furthermore, participants help each other to work out how goals can be achieved and made to look legitimate in terms of previous agreements or rules of custom and practice. Here the construction of dual arguments merges into problem solving that contains an irreducibly political component.

Burnstein and Berbaum (1981) argue that interrupts to the decision process owing to disagreement, "should be most frequent during selection, but may also be observed at earlier stages" (p. 33). For example, disagreement may occur during diagnosis if A sees that B's definition of the problem will lead to a solution unacceptable to A.

Other common endogenous cycles are "associated with turnover in membership, exacerbation of the equilibrium problem, and refusal of authorization" (Burnstein & Berbaum, 1981, p. 40).

Exogenous cycles occur when outside events prevent continuation of the decision-making sequence. Psychological research has concentrated upon reasons why "obvious" warning signs were ignored in cases such as the Bay of Pigs fiasco (Janis, 1972), the bombing of Pearl Harbor (Janis & Mann, 1977), and the decision to cancel projects such as Skybolt (Burnstein & Berbaum, 1981). Both Janis and Mann (1977) and Burnstein and Berbaum (1981) consider cases in which decision makers foresee high costs whatever they do (however the issue is defined). In such cases, apparently, they are motivated defensively to avoid (wrongly) signs that things are going wrong.

To summarize: there is quite a large body of research in social psychology and political science that has considered the kinds of questions posed by Huff. Her piece provides a valuable addition to this literature.

From Huff's perspective, the leader is seen as needing to find an argument that is strong enough to warrant action. This perspective is reminiscent of Steinbruner's (1974) analysis of uncommitted thinking. If he is correct, this appears: (1) at high levels of an organizational hierarchy; (2) when actors are under pressure to treat problems in a fairly abstract way; (3) when the decision process extends over a considerable period of time; and (4) when officials experience an intense workload with competing demands on their time. Under such circumstances the official him or herself looks for sponsors who can structure the decision problem for the official. Further, at different times the official may adopt different (and competing) patterns of belief (relating outcomes to alternatives via causal theories) (Steinbruner, 1974, p. 129). It is tempting to say that the decision maker is trying out new arguments in an attempt to select an appropriate frame of reference. However, he has "difficulty in establishing his beliefs and protecting them against the pressures of inconsistent information" (Steinbruner, 1974, p. 129). Typically, oscillation occurs between two or three patterns of belief, each pushed by a sponsor. According to Steinbruner, the "syndrome of the uncommitted thinker" is readily observed in the behavior of U.S. presidents (e.g., F. D. Roosevelt) ("he was of the mind of the last person he talked to") and in the behavior of high officials in public-sector organizations (many of whom come to their jobs through political channels).

Leaders' General Orientation to Their Roles

The study of metaphorical imagery is not new in research on leadership. It is associated, particularly, with the study of entrepreneurs (defined as persons "who take primary responsibility for mobilizing people and other resources to initiate, give purpose to, build, and manage a new organization"; Pettigrew, 1979, p. 573). According to Pettigrew (1979), entrepreneurs are typically portrayed as heroes who are successful because they exemplify qualities of "courage, persistence and ability" which make them resourceful (see, e.g., Boswell, 1972). Other literature has attempted to compare and contrast (in different contexts) the psychological profiles of those who are entrepeneurs and those who are not (Pettigrew, 1979).

I have three main comments to make about the piece by Moore and Beck. First, it is not clear that the *data* show that bank managers' actions are guided by metaphorical imagery of any kind, although the idea has a good deal of plausibility. Rather, the data show that when asked to think metaphorically, people can do so. For the most part, Moore and Beck used a forced-choice format, although some kind of free-form response was also involved. Second, the six key oppositions identified by Moore and Beck may be agreed upon without reference to the concept of the bank manager as hero/leader. They relate to dilemmas built into the nature of the managerial task. Third, it is hoped that this research will encourage others to pursue the concepts and methods suggested by cultural anthropology. Furthermore, it is the contention here that Moore and Beck are wise to combine studies of leaders as heroes (or whatever) with those traditional kinds of research (measures of personal attitudes and the like). At least part of the emphasis Moore and Beck might wish to preserve could be contained in studies of leaders' policy orientations, reflecting "general operating goals or reasons for being actors in the political arena" (Hermann, 1980, p. 4). Hermann (1980) has, for example, combined research on leaders' operational codes with research on personal character- istics, identifying six orientations "setting the tone for the foreign policy behaviour that political leaders urge on their governments," each "characterized by a particular type of strategy and style" (Hermann, 1980, p. 9). (The six orientations are the expansionist, active independent, influential, mediator/ integrator, opportunist, and developmental orientations.) It may be, as Her- mann says, that it will "take information about the impact of such things as leaders' . . . policy orientation before we can develop adequate criteria for deciding what is effective, rational or high quality decision-making" (Hermann, 1980, p. 28). If so, let us hope that such research is forthcoming.

Part 3 Integrative Comments: Managerial Behavior from a "Radical" Perspective

James G. Hunt

A few years ago a section such as this would not have appeared in a book of this kind in the United States. Even had the individual contributions been written, they would not have been accepted. They would have been considered too "soft" for a book purporting to report leadership findings. The chapters do not dwell heavily on their data and little is said about traditional reliability and validity, the use of sophisticated multivariate statistics, and the like — all hallmarks of the traditional scientific method as currently applied.

Furthermore, the areas they investigate are unusual for traditional North American leadership research. Symbolism, the place of metaphors in the role of the leader, and tracing through the thought shaping, manipulation of meaning, or framing process involved in a single decision do not fit obviously with research that examines the relationship of a given aspect of leader behavior to satisfaction and performance as a function of given task variables, and the like.

Indeed, the former kinds of studies have traditionally been so unusual in the positivist, North American leadership literature as to be termed "radical" by Cummings (1981). In reviewing organizational behavior trends for the 1980s, Cummings argues that there will be two camps — the radical and the "conservative." Though applied by Cummings to the broader organizational behavior area, it is the position here that the camps are applicable to leadership and managerial behavior research, which are a subpart of organizational behavior.

The epistemological base differs dramatically between the radical and conservative approaches. The conservative camp essentially argues for doing what is already being done more rigorously or extending and refining current models. Those in the radical camp argue that study of the same phenomena, no matter how rigorous, is a deadend. Proponents of this approach call for what they term a "paradigm shift" or new way of conceptualizing the leadership field. Indeed, this notion of a paradigm shift is so important that the editors devote much of the final chapter in the book to it and Clark uses it as the theme for his integrating commentary for Part 5.

Let us now look at the major directions that Cummings sees each of these camps taking in the 1980s. In terms of the conservative approach, these directions are:

1. **Improved construct validity.** An example in this volume is the work of Luthans and Lockwood (Chapter 7) to develop improved leader behavior measures.
2. **More careful selection and measurement of dependent variables, including a change in those deemed important.** Traditionally used variables such as satisfaction, performance, absenteeism, and turnover will be treated with increasing sophistication. They will also be joined by other variables such as those involved in group processes. While new variables may join increasingly sophisticated older ones, all will fit within variations of current paradigms.
3. **New applications of experimental and longitudinal research designs.** These are designed to root out causality and are reflected in some of the studies in the epilog chapter.
4. **Increased and more appropriate use of multivariate statistical designs.** Such designs are important, for example, where there are multiple predictors along with multiple contingency and/or criterion variables.

While some might term this as an elegant maintenance of the status quo, that certainly cannot be said for the radical directions summarized below:

1. **Rather than treating organizations as objective reality, study them as social constructions of reality.** Applied to leadership, this means treating it as a perceptual or attributional phenomenon.
2. **Study the symbolic nature of management as a process.** This is illustrated by an emphasis on stories and myths and the significance of these for various aspects of organizational and individual functioning.
3. **Treat processes linking different levels of analysis.** Cummings uses an example of combining frameworks from organizational psychology and organizational sociology in examining the organizational effects of the external environment.

If Cummings is right, work from both camps will be represented in new research developments. Thus, studies similar to those in this part will not be just fads. This view is reinforced by other recent literature (e.g., McCall & Lombardo, 1978) that argues that current positivist approaches to leadership do not capture the essence of the phenomenon and that drastically different approaches are needed.

To what extent might there be a merging of the two camps? The assumptions about how knowledge is generated are so different for purists from each camp that, though clearly desirable, conceptual reconciliation will be difficult. Nevertheless, conservative models are beginning to incorporate some concepts from the radical camp (e.g., attribution, processual variables) and studies such as Siehl and Martin's are concerned with some of the conservative tenets. This is so even though the underlying knowledge base is different. This integration issue is treated in more detail in the concluding chapter.

At this point it is tempting to touch briefly on European versus North American approaches. Interestingly, both camps are represented in both European and North American work in this volume. For example, the Burgoyne and Hodgson chapter from the United Kingdom clearly falls into the radical camp. Yet the Drenth and Koopman chapter from Holland is just as emphatically in the conservative camp.

In an epilog on European leadership research in the previous symposium book (Hosking & Hunt, 1982), it was concluded that Europeans were more diverse in their treatment of the field than were North Americans. For example, the Europeans were less likely to concentrate on leadership (typically defined as some variations of interpersonal influence) as a unique phenomenon than were the North Americans. The Europeans were far more likely to embed an interest in leadership within an investigation involving other aspects of management. They were also likely to use "softer," less positivist approaches than their North American colleagues. In other words, they were more likely to embrace studies such as those in this part than their more "conservative" North American colleagues.

While these conclusions may be an oversimplification and the reader should examine the original source (Hosking & Hunt, 1982), it is tempting to speculate here that European and North American approaches to leadership may now be growing closer together. This is particularly true if one considers both managerial behavior and leadership research together. It may well be that the differences between conservatives and radicals are greater than the differences between Europeans and North Americans.

At first glance, this speculation appears to be at variance with some of Stewart's commentary in Chapter 11. The difference may be more apparent than real, however, if one recognizes that Stewart is primarily referring to more traditional North American work and not that represented in Part 3.

Part 4

Participation Research: European and United States Perspectives

Introduction

James G. Hunt, Dian-Marie Hosking, Chester A. Schriesheim and Rosemary Stewart

Participation has been a topic of extreme interest in the United States and other parts of the world for many years. However, the meaning of the concept differs substantially both within and between various countries. The commentary and three content chapters in this part illustrate the range of ways in which the term participation may be used. They also illustrate quite clearly the different contexts in which participation typically takes place within different nations.

The part starts with two chapters that are representative of directions in current European participation research. The first of these (Chapter 16) by Frank Heller, is entitled, "The Role of Longitudinal Method in Management Decision-Making Studies." Chapter 17, "A Contingency Approach to Participative Leadership: How Good?" is by Pieter Drenth and Paul Koopman. Chapter 18, by Edward Lawler III, "Leadership in Participative Organizations," then describes a number of issues involved in current U.S. participation research and contrasts these with some of the European concerns.

The comments by John W. Slocum further highlight some issues involved in participation research and concentrate on the European-oriented chapters by Heller, Drenth and Koopman. Bass then has an integrative commentary for Part 4 that emphasizes participation from a decision-making perspective.

It is important at this point to provide additional background so that the reader can have a better understanding of the context for the participation studies included here.

In Europe, and some countries such as Israel, growing recent demands for greater employee participation, either directly or via representatives, have led to legislation on industrial democracy and other participation frameworks within Western Europe and Yugoslavia (Industrial Democracy in Europe International Research Group [IDE] 1981). This legislation has, in turn, led to a considerable amount of interest from organizational scholars.

Two important multination research projects examine some of the organizational implications of these different European participation contexts and one includes Israel as well. These projects are important not only in their own right in terms of what they reveal about participation, but because they are illustrative of the strengths and weaknesses of large-scale studies conducted by scholars from many nations.

The first of these projects is being conducted by the Industrial Democracy in Europe International Research Group (IDE). The IDE research is an international collaborative effort among more than 20 organizational researchers from 12 countries (Belgium, Denmark, Finland, France, Germany, Great Britain, Italy, Israel, The Netherlands, Norway, Sweden, and Yugoslavia). The project began in 1973 and is still continuing. Major findings to date are summarized in two volumes published by the Oxford University Press (*Industrial Democracy in Europe,* 1981a; *Industrial Relations in Europe,* 1981b). The focus of the project is on assessing the impact of different legally prescribed participation systems upon involvement, influence, and power in organizations and to assess employee reactions to the different participation patterns (Industrial Democracy in Europe International Research Group, 1981).

The underlying model guiding the research is a contingency one consisting of *de jure* participation patterns, *de facto* participation patterns, outcomes, and a wide range of contingency variables hypothesized to influence various relationships in the model.

The second project is the Decisions in Organizations (DIO) one started in 1974. Whereas the IDE project is a cross-sectional, large-sample research effort that makes generalizations across countries, the DIO project is a longitudinal in-depth study of a large number of decisions in a small number of organizations (Decisions in Organizations, in press). The DIO project was derived from the IDE and involves teams from Great Britain, Yugoslavia, and The Netherlands.

The two initial chapters in this part focus on aspects of the DIO project related to leadership and decision making. The Heller chapter takes a methodological perspective and describes the "processual longitudinal method" involved in the work. In it, a four-phase decision cycle is studied processually, i.e., the nature of the decision-making process is examined within each of the decision-making phases. Whereas one can use the analogy of a series of snapshots to characterize typical U.S. longitudinal leadership research work, the analogy of a motion picture best depicts the perspective discussed by Heller. Not too long ago, Melcher (1977) lamented the lack of such designs in leadership work and made a strong argument for their importance. Thus, it is refreshing to see the approach treated here.

Heller then moves beyond the DIO study to show how the approach is being used in an ongoing study of a major London airport.

The debt that the DIO project owes to the IDE project is clearly shown in the Drenth and Koopman chapter, in which a more narrowly focused version of the IDE contingency model is used to examine type of decision as a contingency in the participation-outcome relationship. And following Heller, it considers the four-phase decision cycle as part of the analysis.

With these chapters (together with any desired additional reading from the IDE and DIO references here and in the Heller and Drenth and Koopman chapters), the reader is then prepared to put into perspective the Lawler chapter which treats participation leadership implications in U.S. organizations where participation is not mandated by law.

The commentaries add still more perspective. A key reason for selecting the two commentators, John Slocum and Bernard Bass, was because of their broad grasp of diverse but related literatures.

Slocum argues for a finer-grained, more conceptual look at participation than is currently available in the participation literature, including the Heller and Drenth and Koopman chapters. He then derives a participation model based on the conceptual refinements that he develops.

Slocum's look at the underlying conceptual aspects of participation is complemented by Bass' treatment of participation within a decision-making mode. Bass' integrative commentary considers some methodological concerns and focuses on conceptual issues by drawing on different aspects of the decision-making literature from those treated by others in this part. He also elaborates on an important point in Lawler's work — the difference between participative leadership and the way an organization is arranged to share power in the decision process. This difference is also a key one in contrasting participation systems in Europe and Israel with those in the United States.

Now let us look at some issues to which the reader should be sensitized as he or she pursues the chapters in Part 4.

First is a concern related to the broader managerial behavior/leadership question that is both explicit and implicit throughout this volume. To what extent is participation related to leadership? It is not always clear — just as it is not always clear in discussing managerial behavior/leadership — where a given concept stops and another begins. For some readers this may present a problem; for others, not.

Second is the significance of the problems for which subordinate participation is allowed or encouraged. Many, if not most, would agree that subordinates are likely to resent being allowed to participate only where trivial problems are involved. Indeed, one may be worse off with such participation than with none at all. A key question, however, is who defines triviality? Management's definition of significant and trivial decisions may differ from that of subordinate workers.

Triviality may be further subdivided into two dimensions: one is the impact a decision may have on work unit or organizational functioning; the other is the package of satisfactions an individual subordinate obtains as a consequence of the decision. Some decisions will be trivial on both counts, some trivial on one, some trivial on the other.

Apropos of Part 3, this whole question can also have symbolic overtones. Apparently trivial decisions such as the color of restroom walls may be a symbolic issue. People may want to participate on a seemingly trivial issue such as this not because they care about the color of the walls but because they care about the relationship. The question of triviality is also likely to vary as a function of the traditions of the country involved.

Also, of course, as pointed out earlier, we should not forget the context within which participation takes place. In Europe and Israel many of the issues will be influenced by legislation. In the United States this is not the case.

A third issue has been mentioned earlier; that is, the difference between a participative system or organization and that of participative leadership behavior. The two are quite distinct.

16

The Role of Longitudinal Method in Management Decision-Making Studies

Frank A. Heller

This chapter has three aims. First, it seeks to present a logical and theoretical argument for a longitudinal approach to decision-making studies in which some aspect of leadership plays a part. Second, as a vehicle for the longitudinal approach, we will describe the outline of a study on decision making in the complex environment of an airport. Third, this chapter serves as an introduction to the Decision in Organization (DIO) project in relation to which the Dutch team (Drenth & Koopman, Chapter 17, this volume) presents an approach and supportive data.

The three aims are closely related. The airport study is a follow-up and development of the DIO research and both are longitudinal.

With the objectives stated in positive terms, it will further clarify our position if we explain limitations and exclusions. This chapter, the airport study, and the DIO do not aim at a theory of decision making or leadership. The objective is to use what can be called a transitional model, based on specific assumptions and capable of giving rise to testable hypotheses. In my view, scientific explanations require a theoretical framework: that is to say, a postulated pattern of variable interaction described by a model. They do not require a theory. This term should be reserved for a highly articulated and extensively tested system of predictive relationships that have received a substantial measure of acceptance by scientists working in the relevant disciplines. Mitchell (1968, p. 211) is correct when he says that "the term 'theory' is one of the most misused and misleading terms in the vocabulary of the social scientist." The advantage of the less ambitious transitional model concept (see also Bass, 1974) is its ability to adapt to the process of growth, refinement, and the inclusion of relevant complexities. The open-systems model used in the airport study has moved substantially from earlier formulations (Heller, 1971, 1976a) without losing its essential contingency or basic variable framework.

While the airport study will be used to explain the reasons for a certain longitudinal design, it will give no data. Preliminary evidence in support of such an approach is given by Drenth and Koopman in Chapter 17, and in

Rus, Odar, Heller, Brown, Drenth, Koopman, Wierdsma, Bus, and Kruyswyk (1977) and Drenth, Koopman, Rus, Odar, Heller, and Brown (1979). When figures are given for the airport study, they are meant to illustrate the method, not to elicit evidence. For this reason I also avoid, for the time being, the need to enter into arguments about the most appropriate statistical designs for assessing our longitudinal data, although I am aware of the complexity of such an undertaking (Kimberly, 1976). Instead, the chapter briefly explains the field research methodology that we judge appropriate for our purpose. The quality of longitudinal data depends substantially on our choice of data-gathering techniques.

BACKGROUND TO THE STUDY

The Decision in Organization project started in June 1974 and completed field work in January 1979. It derives in part from a 12-country cross-sectional study of Industrial Democracy in Europe (IDE, 1976) that has recently resulted in two detailed publications (IDE, 1981a, 1981b). The longitudinal study shares with IDE the outline theoretical contingency model and some variables. In the 12-country team's planning it was felt that certain hypotheses required a follow-up, in-depth approach of some kind. Resources were not available to do this in all countries, but teams from The Netherlands, Yugoslavia, and Great Britain planned the four-year study that we now call DIO (Heller, Drenth, Rus, & Koopman, 1977). This research took more than four years to complete and has not yet been extensively reported (but see Drenth *et al.,* 1979; Koopman *et al.,* 1981; Rus *et al.,* 1977). A very substantial data base was accumulated in the three countries and some data processing is continuing. It was felt that because the study makes certain claims of originality and development from previous cross-sectional research, it should be discussed in the present volume although it was not possible to produce all relevant findings.

It is not claimed that longitudinal research is appropriate for all research questions or that it will always produce superior results. In fact, a good case can be made for moving from cross-sectional to longitudinal designs as part of a deliberate program, which may even include a further cross-sectional stage later on. This is what happened in our case.

A number of leadership decision-making studies preceded DIO and used the concept of transitional models. These are evolving sets of relationships and hypotheses that adapt gradually to incorporate findings from previous research, using cross-sectional designs (Heller, 1971, 1976b; Heller & Wilpert, 1981; Heller & Yukl, 1969). Several findings from this work are now confirmed, questioned, or elaborated by the longitudinal approach of DIO. An important positive support relates to the role of skill utilization, which emerged from cross-sectional results in an eight-country comparative study (Heller & Wilpert, 1981, pp. 116–123) but has shown up much more clearly in a more elaborate instrument used in DIO (for preliminary results, see Drenth *et al.,* 1979, p. 299; Drenth & Koopman, this volume, Table 6; DIO, in press, Tables 6 and 7).

In many research programs a time will come when the logic of the situation suggests the need for a longitudinal design. This stage, it seems, has now been reached with studies of leadership and decision making.

Characteristics of the Longitudinal Design

Two main characteristics are shared by the airport study and DIO. Both use *decisions as the unit of analysis* and a *processual method of measuring events over time.* Because our samples are of decisions and decision categories, not people, the leadership aspect of our study is necessarily restricted and different from the mainstream of leadership research. Such research is not issue-oriented as is the case with the present research. The emphasis on decisions is a development of previous findings that the nature of tasks is a major contingency in understanding the behavior of decision making (Fiedler, 1964; Heller, 1971; Heller & Yukl, 1969; Vroom & Yetton, 1973). It is also felt that the use of decision or task as a unit of analysis is suitable for a longitudinal study of organizations, where the duration of some decision cycles may be longer than the time a particular manager occupies the leadership position relating to that decision. In fact, this happened during the DIO and the airport research.

Longitudinal research can take many different forms. A "before and after" design or at least two time-separated assessments are the most frequently used. One part of the DIO study administered questionnaires to comparable samples of workers with an interval of 18 months. Even if these studies extend the number of time-separated assessments, they are quite distinct from what are called processual studies. The characteristic of processual studies is the emphasis on continuity. Segmental longitudinal studies assume that the chosen interval represents a meaningful dimension or is in some sense representative of the total process.[1] Continuous assessment of organization life is difficult to organize, and costly (Busson *et al.,* 1982). Case studies sometimes attempt to do this but without quantitative methods.

The longitudinal study of airport decision making as well as DIO do not use fixed or random time intervals. Two strategies are used. One is based on a simple a priori structure of the decision process consisting of four phases:

---

[1]It could be claimed that in logic, all processual studies are time separated, but this is as unrealistic in practice as claiming that there is no essential difference between a series of photographs taken by a still camera and a series taken by a film camera.

For problems with the segmental design, see Sheridan et al. (1975), and for critical appraisals of this study, see Hunt & Larson (1975), pp. 121–129.

Start-up, Development, Finalization, and Implementation. These phases were developed by the three-country team in September 1975 and extended Mintzberg's phase approach by adding "Implementation" of the decision process. For operational purposes, the four phases were carefully described so that each team would measure similar divisions. For the categories of decisions used, see Chapter 17, this volume, by Drenth and Koopman. The identification of the phases depends on whether we are using *retrospective tracing* or *process analysis*. The distinction is illustrated in Figure 16.1.

Since decision cycles often take weeks, months, or even years, the researcher first enters the observation of the process at an unpredictable point. In Figure 16.1 we assume this is halfway through the development phase. The researcher will then trace events back to the beginning, by an analysis of written documentation (where it exists) followed up by interviews. From the point of entry to the end of the decision cycle, the researcher has a wider repertory of methods, which in our case includes observation of all major group meetings and all committee meetings, again followed up by interviews. Since the airport research, as well as DIO, concentrates on tactical and strategic decisions (see Drenth & Koopman, Chapter 17, this volume, Scheme 2), there is always a reasonable amount of fairly reliable information to help with the identification of phases through retrospective tracing. The identification is easier through observation of meetings and, in both cases, clarification can be obtained through interviews.

The duration of the phases varies from decision to decision. The development phase is usually the longest and includes Simon's process of the imperfect search for alternatives through satisficing (Simon, 1957). The implementation phase can also be very long. Although we used a careful description for the starting point of each phase, there were difficulties from time to time in agreeing on the endpoints of the start-up and finalization phases. In the airport

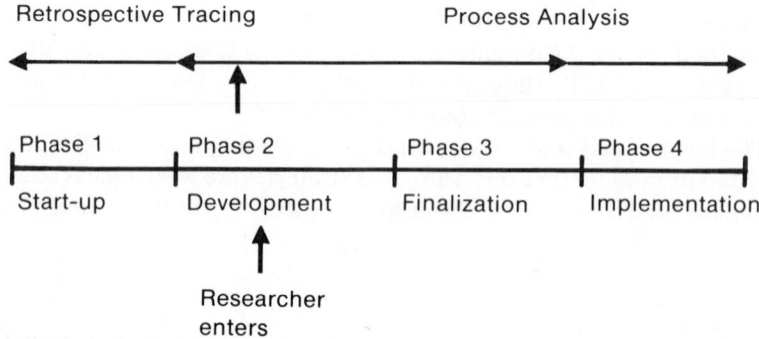

FIGURE 16.1. The four-phase decision cycle and data gathering through retrospective tracing and process analysis

project we have eliminated this problem by making the arbitrary assumption that the start-up and finalization phases last one day. We have found this a workable assumption.

The four phases constitute a logical continuum but it is recognized that in real life complex decision processes do not always follow this pattern (Mintzberg, Raisinghani, & Theoret, 1976). The development phase is sometimes unsuccessful and it becomes necessary to make a fresh start and other loops can occur. For the airport study, which we will describe later, we hypothesize that the most frequent variations from the sequential four-phase cycle will be those shown in Figure 16.2.

Although our unit of analysis is "issues" and "decisions," it is recognized that these events operate through people, that is to say, through management and other employees. It is therefore possible to follow the tradition that describes the resolution of issues through a leadership process. Our assessment of this process is through the style of decision methods used in relation to each issue. The measurement unit is the Influence-Power Continuum (IPC), variations of which have been used in a number of previous research projects (Drenth *et al.,* 1979; Heller, 1971; Heller & Wilpert 1981; IDE, 1981). We now use six defined alternative positions on the IPC as shown in Figure 16.3 (see also Drenth & Koopman, Chapter 17 this volume, Scheme 3).

In previous studies from Likert (1961) to IDE (1981), the measurement of a leader's decision style was cross-sectional. While there are exceptions, this type of measurement makes a number of important assumptions about the representativeness of the "snapshot" which freezes a potentially extended series of events at an arbitrary moment (Fleishman, 1973; Melcher, 1977). Do we assume that the leadership behavior is the same over time or that the respondent is able to smooth out any variations by giving the researcher a mentally calculated average? If so, what are the deviations around that average?

It is a critical aspect of the processual longitudinal approach to decision analysis to answer some of these questions. The IPC is therefore measured for each of the four phases and similar phase-specific measurements are made for several other dimensions, like conflict, that are usually measured only once. We hypothesized that various dimensions of the longitudinal decision process would vary significantly for some or all of the four phases and that this would apply to leadership style or, more broadly, to the distribution of influence and power in organizations. Specific assumptions about the impact of such differences were made (Rus *et al.,* 1977). If a person or group, for instance top management, has extensive influence over phase 1 (Start-up) and phase 3 (Finalization), this is qualitatively different from having little influence in phases 1 and 3 but instead extensive influence over events in phase 2 (Development) and phase 4 (Implementation). We hypothesize that different hierarchical levels in modern organizations will show varying profiles of IPC and this could apply to other variables.

(i) 1 ——→ 2 (No finalization; the decision is not made.)

(ii) 1 ——→ 2 (The development phase is unsuccessful and a fresh start has to
     be made.)

(iii) 1 ——→ 2 ——→ 3 (No implementation.)

(iv) 1 ——→ 2 ⇄ 3 ——→ 4 (The implementation encounters difficulties and
     further work has to be done on developing the issue.)

FIGURE 16.2. Variations from sequential four-phase cycle

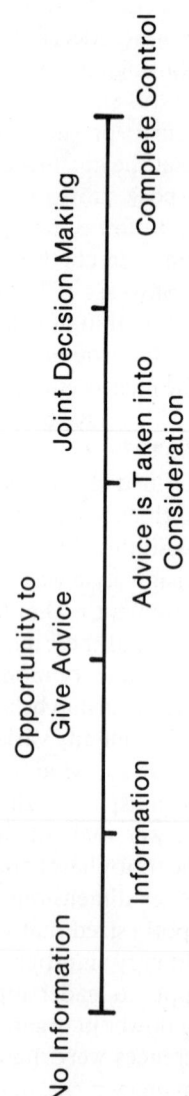

FIGURE 16.3. The extended influence-power continuum

288

Processual longitudinal analysis should aim at the identification of different patterns of variable interactions *within* phases, for instance IPC with satisfaction. The difficulty of using satisfaction as a dependent variable in organization research has frequently been identified (for instance, Campbell, 1976; Katz & Van Maanen, 1976; Strauss, 1974; Vroom, 1964; Wall & Lischeron, 1977). The problems seem to be particularly great with measures of "general satisfaction" rather than with specific aspects of this variable (IDE, chap. 8). It would seem reasonable to examine the possibility that satisfaction with work or with leadership is phase-specific.

Finally, processual studies of the kind we have described should give us a more realistic answer to many causal assumptions in the organizational behavior and leadership literature than is possible with cross-sectional measurements. We would hypothesize, for instance, that highly centralized decision styles in the Development and Implementation phases would create more conflict than centralized styles in phases 1 and 3. This hypothesis is based on the observation that subordinates, at least in England, do not expect to exert very much influence in phases 1 and 3 but believe that they can make useful contributions to phases 2 and 4 (Heller, 1976b).

We have presented some logical and theoretical arguments in support of a processual longitudinal approach to decision-making research, and have described aspects of the method. At the same time we have given preliminary details of the Decisions in Organizations project, which has set out to test some of these assumptions. Preliminary evidence in support of our model and hypotheses is being presented by Drenth and Koopman (Chapter 17) from Dutch data.

THE AIRPORT STUDY

The rest of this chapter will attempt to reinforce and extend the case for processual studies by reference to a current three-year research on airport decision making. This project is supported for three years by the Behavioral and Social Science Liaison Office of the United States Army in Europe. Processual studies are not suitable or necessary for the analysis of all organizational problems. Moreover, we believe that where they are appropriate, the theoretical framework will usually evolve through cross-sectional research until it reaches a certain stage of maturity. This can be illustrated by the variable *skill utilization*. It was used in a simple overall measure of leadership decision making in an eight-country comparative study and produced interesting and consistent patterns and correlations in each country and overall (Heller & Wilpert, 1981). A much more detailed assessment of skill utilization was used in the two-stage questionnaire study of the Decision in Organization project where it yielded significant correlations with the Influence-Power Continuum in six out of seven companies (Drenth *et al.*, 1979, p. 299). The results were particularly clear-cut in the two British companies (Heller, 1976a). The same measure was a dependent variable in the processual part of the DIO study (Drenth & Koopman, Chapter 17, Scheme 3), but was only assessed once, while other variables, like IPC and conflict, were measured in each phase and satisfaction was measured twice.

The theoretical importance of skill utilization as a contingency (see Farris, 1974), and in particular its underutilization as a predictive variable in organizational studies (for instance, Lawler, 1976a), added to our own previous experience, and led to the extension of the processual model in the Airport Study and the inclusion of skill utilization as a phase-specific variable (see Table 16.1 below).

Table 16.1. Unfinalized Raw Data Before Feedback

VARIABLES		TYPE OF DECISION		
		A	B	C
Turbulence-Uncertainty:				
Internal		3	1	1
External		4	1	1
	A	1	5	2
	B	1	2	2
Status Power	C	1	4	3
Levels	D	1	5	6
	E	6	2	2
	F	1	2	2
Effective		1	3	3
Achievement		3	3	3

		TIME STAGES											
		Start	Dev.	Fin	Impl.	Start	Dev.	Fin	Impl.	Start	Dev.	Fin	Impl.
Delay			3		1		2		2		1		1
Meta-P. Intens		3	1	2	1	1	1	1	1	3	1	1	3
Meta-P ±		+	+	+	+					+	+	+	+
Conflict Intensity		4	3	3	2	1	1	1	1	1	1	1	1
Conflict Resolution		1	2	1	3	3	3	3	3	3	3	3	3
Skill Requirem		1	2	2	3	1	1	1	1	1	1	1	1
Skill Use Man		1	2	3	3	3	3	3	3	1	1	1	1
Skill Use Work		1	1	2	3	3	3	3	3	3	3	3	3
	Level A	1	1	1	5	5	2	5	2	2	2	2	2
The Influence –	Level B	1	2	2	2	5	2	5	2	1	2	2	2
Power	Level C	2	2	3	3	5	2	5	2	1	4	4	4
Continuum	Level D	4	6	6	5	5	6	5	6	1	6	6	6
	Level E	6	2	2	2	2	2	2	2	6	2	2	2
	Level F	2	4	4	5	2	2	2	2	3	4	4	2
	*Average	26	28	30	37	40	27	40	27	22	32	33	30
PE = D-A		3	5	5	0	0	4	0	4	0	4	4	4

*Divide by 10

Stansted Near London: A Medium-Size Airport

A certain amount of background will be helpful.

The research is taking place in Stansted near London. The airport is currently the subject of an intensive government-sponsored enquiry to determine whether Stansted should be expanded to become the long-delayed third airport, serving London and the catchment area immediately to the north of it. While the research concentrates on the internal decision process, it is intended to use the turbulence of the environment created by this difficult public choice process as one of the dimensions to be considered. Several external factors have to be taken into account. The relationship between the external

Table 16.1. Unfinalized Raw Data Before Feedback *(continued)*

TYPE OF DECISION

D	E	F	G
4	1	1	4
4	1	1	2
1	5	1	1
2	5	1	1
2	5	1	3
5	5	6	6
5	1	1	5
2	2	1	2
1	3	1	2
1	3	1	3

TIME STAGES

Start	Dev.	Fin	Impl.	Start	Dev.	Fin	Impl.	Start	Dev.	Fin	Impl.	Start	Dev.	Fin	Impl.
	3		1	2		1		1		1		2			2
3	3	3	3	1	1	1	1	3	3	3	1	3	1	1	1
+	+	+	+	−	−	−	−	+	−	+	+	+	−	−	−
4	4	2	2	1	1	1	1	3	1	4	1	1	2	4	2
2	2	2	2	3	3	3	3	3	2	2	2	3	2	2	1
3	3	3	3	2	2	2	2	3	3	3	3	2	3	3	3
2	2	2	2	3	3	3	3	2	3	2	1	2	3	3	3
2	2	2	2	3	3	3	3	1	1	1	3	3	3	3	3
1	2	3	2	5	2	2	5	1	2	2	2	1	2	2	2
1	2	3	2	2	2	2	5	2	2	2	2	2	2	3	3
1	2	3	2	2	6	6	5	2	3	3	2	2	2	3	3
1	4	4	4	5	2	2	5	3	3	5	6	3	3	6	6
6	6	6	6	1	1	1	1	6	6	5	2	4	4	2	2
2	2	2	2	2	2	2	2	2	3	4	3	4	4	2	2
20	30	35	30	28	25	25	38	28	32	35	25	27	28	30	30
0	2	1	2	0	0	0	0	2	1	3	4	2	1	4	4

and internal structures relating to the decision process is illustrated in Figure 16.4.

The macroexternal environment is drawn as a large triangle because it includes, in addition to the elected government, the opposition political parties (who might have to execute the decision of the current government if they come to power in a future election). The third corner accommodates various national pressure groups, including Birtish Airways and other airlines that might be expected to use Stansted instead of or in addition to the two existing London airports.

Inside the macro-environment operate the very powerful local pressure groups, most of them vehemently opposed to the designation of Stansted as the third airport. Within this circle of opposition there are four structural entities operating at a middle level: the British Airports Authority (designated *A*) which operates Stansted and six other national airports; Gatwick Airport

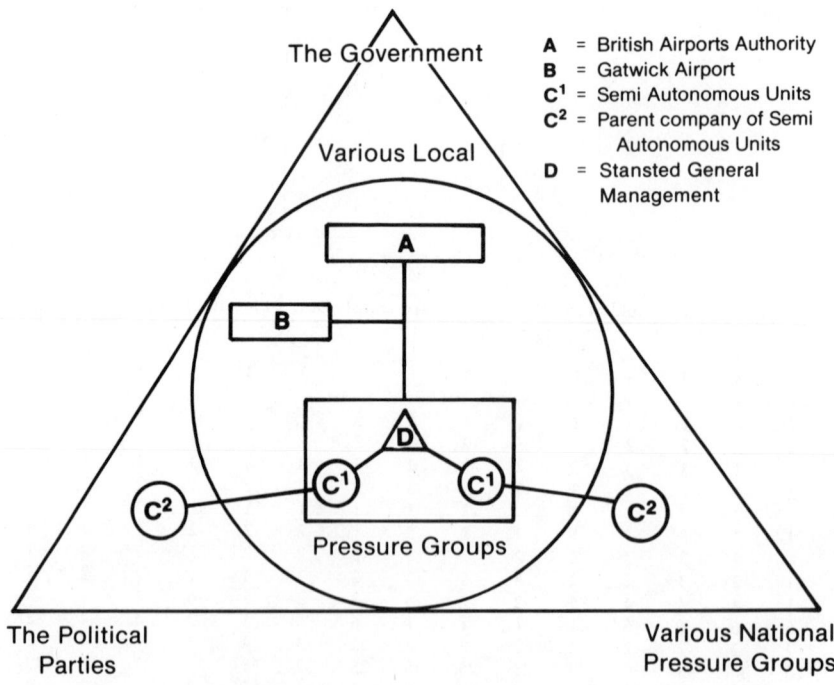

FIGURE 16.4. The airport and its environment

(designated *B*) which has a special executive responsibility for Stansted through its director, who is also the director of Stansted; thirdly, there are a number of subcontractors (designated *C*) often operating on a regional or national level, who service specified activities inside Stansted Airport; and finally, there is the focal airport itself (designated *D*) with its management structure and subcontracting units.

The complex decision process operating the structures within Figure 16.4 has an extended space-time dimension. This is not the primary objective of our research but will be mentioned because it has important repercussions on the decision process within the focal unit of our analysis (the airport). The Stansted issue goes back nearly 30 years to a Government White Paper of 1953 which mentioned Stansted as a "reserve airport." Then followed three Committee Enquiries in 1955, 1961, and 1964, a Public Enquiry in 1965, a Government White Paper in 1967, another major Public Enquiry in 1968, the setting up of a Development Authority in 1973, two government consultative documents in 1975–1976, and a further Government White Paper in 1978. In that year two major advisory bodies were set up that reported in 1979 when the present government was elected. In 1981 a new Public Enquiry was set up by a government that clearly favors Stansted as the third airport. As of this writing the report has not been published, and indeed it is possible that if the report does not come out soon, subsequent government election results might lead to a government not prone to follow the enquiry's recommendations. Such a lengthy decision process would be not unlike those examined by Janis (1982) and Janis and Mann (1977) using a longitudinal decision tree model (Janis & Mann, p. 70).

This extended process, which will eventually lead to a decision, is itself worthy of analysis and is fairly obviously an example of a phenomenon that cannot be scientifically investigated without a longitudinal model. Even within the three-year current project concerned with the internal decision processes of Stansted Airport, there are variations in the uncertainty experienced by the management and unions, as well as the subcontractors operating the airport. The period before the establishment of the latest Public Enquiry led the Airports Authority leadership to very optimistic forecasts about Stansted's likely rate of growth. This was assumed to move from its current underutilization of a 2 million passenger per year capacity to a 15 million capacity by 1992. Such a rapid rate of expansion would require immediate action on some decisions, like the purchase of land and houses. In fact this purchase activity has taken place and has been accompanied by a reorganization of the management structure and a large number of other changes resulting from the anticipation of growth. The expectations were modified to some extent when the Enquiry was set up in September 1981 and have undergone several changes during the last four months as new "evidence" was put forward and interested parties presented their case to the media as well as to the inspector heading up the Enquiry.

Characteristics of Airports

While airline operations have been researched, the management of airports has not. It seems, however, that airports have certain sharply delineated characteristics, that are less prominent in other organizations. This sharpening up of organizational dimensions may enable one to study these phenomena more easily in airports than elsewhere. In addition, it will be recognized that airports are worthy of study in their own right, since they are part of the rapidly expanding transport and leisure industry.

One of the well-established myths in the management literature is the belief that management is or should be in de facto control of situations for which it is given formal responsibility. Studies of the informal organization have thrown doubt on this notion ever since the detailed Bank Wiring Room study at Hawthorne, but the idea lives on. The management of airports does not seem to require such a theoretical position. A large part of airport activity is carried out by highly decentralized semi-autonomous units that report to senior managers who belong to other organizations than the airport. The semi-autonomous groups are called concessionaires and subcontractors, and while there are important technical differences between these two groups, they are all removed from the day-by-day leadership of the airport management. The degree of influence exerted on them by the general manager and his team varies. Both concessionaires and subcontractors have legal time-limited formal arrangements with the airport and several work through main contractors or concessionaires that have formal contracts with other airports as well. These outside semi-autonomous units have their own national organization so that the semi-autonomous unit within the airport has its own leader who operates under the management policy of his own organization, which is quite independent of the British Airports Authority (C_2 in Figure 16.4). We have identified the following semi-autonomous units at Stansted:

Baggage Handling	Duty Free Facilities
Aircraft Servicing	Banks
Passenger Servicing	Post Office
Cleaning of Airports	Airport Expansion Work
Maintenance of Buildings	Civil Aviation Authority Work
Security	

Even though other organizations, such as retail businesses, have decentralized, semi-autonomous units, the above units give airports an element of uniqueness because of their formally contracted diversity. From the theoretical point of view and relevant to the analysis of the leadership role under these conditions is the literature on semi-autonomy most usually related to job design or matrix decision making (for instance, Davis & Taylor, 1972; Emery & Trist, 1973; Katzell & Yankelovich, 1975; Trist, Higgin, Murray, & Pollock, 1963).

Each semi-autonomous group has made contractual arrangements with the airport management. The contracts run for a period of two to five years and therefore start and end at different times. Aircraft servicing may end in 1982, cleaning of airports in 1983, and maintenance of buildings in 1984. But many of the central activities to which the semiautonomous units address themselves are identical, for instance, safety, speed of operation, and throughput of passengers and aircraft. There are regular committee meetings and less regular other meetings between the airport management and semi-autonomous units; workmen and trade unions overlap in various degrees.

The main activities of an airport like Stansted vary considerably at different times of the day, month, and year, while such management processes as accounting and preventive maintenance carry on at an even pace. The Public Enquiry adds uncertainty to some decisions but not to others; every now and again there is an emergency landing alert when other airports are fogged in and recently Stansted experienced the turbulence of a hijack operation. We believe that variations of this kind lend themselves to, and may even require, a processual longitudinal analysis.

Some Aspects of Method

We want to address ourselves to two main considerations: cost and accuracy. Longitudinal research and in particular the processual methods developed in the DIO research are costly of time and manpower. This is probably one of the reasons why cross-sectional studies are usually preferred. The airport research attempts to halve the time taken to collect longitudinal data. This is done by relying extensively on retrospective tracing and much less on process analysis (see Figure 16.1). For this purpose, it is necessary to use decision issues that are heavily documented and work in organizations that use committee procedures. At Stansted we have obtained access to six internal airport committee minutes and two that link the airport with its external environment. Several decision issues are common to a number of committees and allow for cross-referencing and checking. The research team attends three of the main committees on a regular basis, the others occasionally.

The theoretical framework for the analysis of the airport decision process is shown in Figure 16.5. It is an extension of the DIO model and uses a subset of DIO variables with the addition of turbulence. Turbulence is derived from the theoretical considerations of Emery and Trist (1965) and a previous operationalization (Heller, 1976a; Heller & Wilpert, 1981). A brief description of these variables with scoring categories is given in Appendix A. The subset

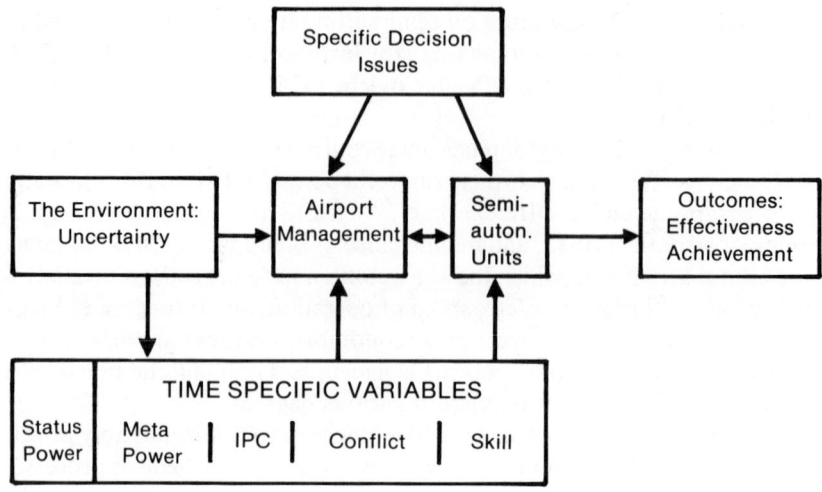

FIGURE 16.5. The model used for the Analysis of the Complex Airport decision process

was chosen on the basis of DIO results related to the airport requirement. The shorter list of variables reduces the cost of the field work.

The data are collected through the analysis of committee minutes and interviews, using an Interview Schedule with the variables listed in Table 16.1. The results in Table 16.1 are illustrative only; *A* to *G* are seven distinct decision issues; issues *A, B,* and *C* come from the management team; issues *D* and *E* from one semi-autonomous group and issues *F* and *G* from a second semi-autonomous group. We hypothesize variations of the phase profiles between these groups of issues and particularly between issues that are handled by the management team and one or more semi-autonomous units. Meta power and status power would be more important in influencing airport management; skill utilization is expected to be much higher in semi-autonomous units. In general, phases 1 and 3 would show higher IPC concentration in airport management decisions since there is likely to be a greater accountability upward to the British Airports Authority and Gatwick Airport than with parent companies of semi-autonomous units (see Figure 16.4).

Quality Considerations

As the cost of processual analysis is reduced, the quality of data may decrease. To some extent this is inevitable and one is aware that cost-benefit problems apply to many choices relating to alternative research methods.

The possible distortions and errors of analysis from retrospective tracing are not due to interrater differences among researchers, but to the inevitable fading of memory traces and the imperfections of minute taking. Such "imperfections" of minutes is a major and somewhat neglected field for research. Deliberate distortion is probably greater than accidental error or omission. Power and value differentials play a large part. We try to reduce the scope for error by having regular meetings with small groups of people involved in each committee. The method is an elaboration of Group Feedback Analysis (GFA), which has been used in a variety of cross-sectional and cross-national studies (Graves, 1973; Heller, 1969). At each feedback meeting we present in very simple format parts of our descriptive data analysis. While the layout will differ, the data will be similar to that shown in Table 16.1. Previous to the meeting we ask each committee member to look at minutes between certain dates. They bring this documentation with them to the GFA meeting when they are presented with our data. The first question is nondirective: "What do you make of this information?" Gradually, more specific questions are asked and we test out our interpretations.

Some individuals have better memories than others; values, objectives, and impressions vary between committee members but they often challenge each other openly and "think aloud" about past events. This semireconstruction of what happened in previous meetings gives us valuable additional insight into the dynamics of the decision process. When a committee consists of managers and trade union members, we have one GFA meeting with each group separately and occasionally a joint meeting. We press groups to reach an agreement on scores and usually obtain it. (If not, we make our own assessment or, if we are doubtful, leave the scores out.) Substantial errors in interview questionnaire scoring are occasionally detected. This can happen even in process analysis or the more conventional questionnaire method. Group feedback methods have been able to deal with some of these problems (see Brown & Heller, 1981).

DISCUSSION

This chapter presents arguments for the appropriateness of a longitudinal approach in studying certain kinds of organizational events, including decision-making styles. While psychology has in the past tended to treat leadership from the point of view of a single individual, a dyad, or a small group, our research has taken the decision as the unit of analysis and included some environmental variables. The wider the frame of reference, the greater the number of conceptual and methodological problems (Bass, 1974; Kimberley, 1976, 1980). One way to handle the requirements of extra complexity is to relax some criteria of rigor, for instance, the traditional preferences for parametric measurements. This is a persuasive argument and should be explored (Argyris, 1976). Some of this exploration — for instance of processual longitudinal methodology — involves difficulties and costs that present almost impossible conditions (Combey, 1980); other explorations lead into purely descriptive case studies that serve well as a beginning rather than an acceptable end to a scientific study. As so often happens in complex fields of research, including the biological sciences, a large no man's land opens up between the requirements of rigor and relevance. Penetration into the no man's land can be attempted from either end of the methodological spectrum, from the pole of precise measurement or from the pole of descriptive analysis and philosophical speculation. More important than the starting point is the degree of penetration achieved and the extent to which it enables other researchers to challenge findings, to reexamine the data, or to repeat experiments if this is thought desirable.

The DIO research and the airport study attempt such an excursion into a relatively unexplored area. Judgments will have to be made about whether the exploration has produced evidence to justify the additional complication of moving from cross-sectional to processual longitudinal studies. Will this approach generate new insights or a deeper understanding of existing models? Will the methods achieve the essential objectives of challenge, reexamination, and repetition we have set out to fulfill? There is an unfortunate, though long-established tendency in social science to oscillate between extremes. The academic purist, faced with the challenge of unsatisfactory results — as is the case with leadership studies at the present time — tends to search for more refined definitions, more precise measurement scales, and above all, for more sophisticated statistical data manipulation (for instance, Bales & Isenberg, 1982; Greene, 1975, pp. 121–126; Salancik, Calder, Rowland, Leblebici, & Conway, 1975). At the other end of the pendulum are the advocates of relevance prepared to retreat into vague case descriptions, anecdotal evidence, and proof by analogy. (Mintzberg, 1982, pp. 250–259). There are a number of important but not very popular methodological positions in between these extremes (for instance, Argyris, 1968, 1976; Bass, 1974; Bussom et al., 1982; Heller, 1969, 1976b). The DIO-type research attempts to introduce a greater measure of relevance than obtains in many studies and to put considerable emphasis on the quality of data gathering. For the time being we are content with using fairly traditional, relatively simple data-analysis methods.

The airport study increases the emphasis on longitudinality, for instance by measuring skill utilization by phases and by covering greater distances more economically through retrospective tracing. We are also increasing the emphasis on qualitative data by relying more heavily on the content analysis of discussion triggered by the feedback of data.

The findings up to now are encouraging (DIO, in press; Drenth et al., 1979). The main conclusion is that the styles of leadership and the methods of influence-power sharing vary significantly between the four phases of the decision cycle and these variations apply also to different levels of the hierarchy. Secondly, the variations between variables like meta power, status power, IPC, conflict, and satisfaction vary significantly within the different phases. Thirdly, it seems that contingency or situational variables in the specified model also show variations by phase of decision process. In some phases, contingencies are unimportant moderators of relationships, while in others they are essential explanatory categories.[2]

This chapter concentrates on the exposition of the theoretical framework and the explanation of a field methodology designed to produce acceptable repeatable results with reasonable attention to economy and parsimony in a highly complex setting. The complexity of the setting derives from the multiplicity of leadership-based decision processes in an organization that has to achieve its objectives through interaction with a variety of semi-autonomous groups with intra- and interorganizational lines of communication and consequently a dispersed pattern of power relations.

The practical implications of phase-specific findings for an understanding of organizational processes are fairly obvious though they are not spelled out here. If the results were substantiated, one could expect them to be particularly relevant for training and organizational design.

CONCLUSIONS

In the first leadership symposium volume in 1973, Fleishman identified the urgent need for longitudinal studies and for a time dimension in research designs (Fleishman & Hunt, 1973, pp. 183–184). There has been very little follow-up from this suggestion. In part this could be due to difficulties with designing appropriate methods and with the problem of persuading funding bodies to support long-term studies.

There has also been a reluctance to move away from traditional assessments of leadership centered on personality or individual difference measures. This was pointed out by Korman in the second leadership symposium (Hunt & Larson, 1974, p. 191) and again by Miner in the third symposium (Hunt & Larson, 1975, pp. 197–206). Miner argued that, "the concept of leadership itself has outlived its usefulness" (Miner, 1975, p. 200), and he suggests "control" as an alternative focus for research. Under hierarchical control he mentions the work of Heller (1971) and Vroom and Yetton (1973) but it seems that very few studies have considered hierarchical power an important aspect of the leadership process. This is surprising and may explain many of the difficulties with leadership research. Our recent projects suggest that while hierarchical control (we call it IPC) is an essential dimension of leadership, the

---

[2]Substantiation of these preliminary findings are not yet available.

unit of analysis could shift from individuals or dyads to issues without weakening the theoretical framework. The assessment of issues and their resolution into decisions may turn out to be more capable of objective assessment than the relatively volatile descriptive leadership measures. Such an approach is also congruent with the widely accepted finding that task — i.e., decision issue — is a major contingency in leadership behavior.

Furthermore, when issues are the focus of analysis, it brings with it the requirement to cover a deeper dimension of organizational space. Issues are often handled at three or four hierarchical levels and the link-up between levels may turn out to be very important. Such a deeper analysis would also follow from using "control" as a central concept (see, for instance, Tannenbaum, 1968). Top management leadership studies have tended to hover at one or two senior levels of a multilevel organization while the effectiveness of top leadership behavior may be very important at the lowest level, where the largest number of employees usually carry out their task.

The review of the European research tradition by Hosking and Hunt (1982) shows that there is a tendency in Europe for a broader and more diversified approach to the study of managerial and organizational behavior and a much greater willingness to see leadership as a political process. The DIO and airport research underline the possibility and maybe even the need to pay more attention to the relatively neglected arguments of Fleishman, Korman, Miner, and Hosking and Hunt.

APPENDIX: THE STANSTED INTERVIEW SCHEDULE

Scoring Definitions

1. *Turbulence — Uncertainty:*
     1 = None
     2 = Little
     3 = High
     4 = Very High

2. *Outcomes*

   Effectiveness:
     1 = Very poor use of time, money, etc.
     2 = Reasonable use of time, money, etc.
     3 = Very good use of time, money, etc.

   Achievement:
     1 = Very poor results in terms of implementation
     2 = Reasonable results in terms of implementation
     3 = Very good results in terms of implementation

Time and Stages Categories

1. *Delay* (over and above what the decision process appears to require):
    1 = No delay
    2 = Moderate delay
    3 = Extensive delay

2. *Meta Power* (External influence. External is from outside Stansted, i.e., BAA or other source. In comments column, state which source):
    1 = None
    2 = Some
    3 = Extensive

3. *Conflict*

    INTENSITY: 1 = Agreement; 2 = Agreement after difference (consensus); 3 = Mild disagreement; 4 = Conflict; 5 = Irreconcilable difference.

    Resolution of Conflict:
    1 = Forcing (one party unilaterally overrides objections.)
    2 = Smoothing (finding a cosmetic or temporary solution.)
    3 = Open Facing (realistic tackling of the problem; can include compromise.)

4. *Skill*

    Requirement (How much experience and skill does the work on this decision require from the participants?):
    1 = None or very little
    2 = Fair amount
    3 = High amount

    Use (How much skill and experience is actually used by the decision makers? Separate management = M and workers = W):
    1 = No use or almost no use is made of available experience and skill
    2 = Some use is made
    3 = Extensive use is made

Influence-Power Continuum

    1 = No or minimal influence
    2 = Information only
    3 = Opportunity to give advice
    4 = Advice taken into consideration

5 = Joint decision making
6 = Complete control

Status Power

As in the case of the IPC, it is a range of Influence-Power.

It is a measure of the *formal* influence each group (or committee) has with regard to each decision. Formal influence can be due to a legal backing or to a company's accepted policy, or to the written rules governing the procedure of a committee. The word "formal" does not, however, require written documentation in all cases. Long-established and accepted custom is sufficient.

The scale is:

1 = None
2 = Unspecified information must be given
3 = Specified information must be given
4 = Consultation is obligatory (or invariably given)
5 = Joint decision making (with the objective of consensus)
6 = One party or group has complete control (veto power is the negative aspect of this).

17

A Contingency Approach to Participative Leadership: How Good?

Pieter J. D. Drenth and Paul L. Koopman

One of the leading questions in research and theory on leadership is how and how much those who will have to implement the decisions should participate in the decision-making process. A number of studies have shown recently that the extent to which this participation will be successful seems to depend on a number of conditional factors. The present study shows that this statement, again, is not generally correct but that its validity depends on the kind of decisions involved.

The present chapter is based on research data collected in three Dutch organizations.[1] The study was part of a larger longitudinal study of participative decision making in organizations (DIO) that was started in late 1974. Research teams in three countries (United Kingdom, Tavistock Institute of Human Relations, Dr. Heller; Yugoslavia, University of Ljubljana, Dr. Rus; Netherlands, Free University of Amsterdam, Dr. Drenth and Dr. Koopman) were involved in the project. Some results of the international fieldwork have been published in Heller, Drenth, Rus, and Koopman (1977) and Drenth, Koopman, Rus, Odar, Heller, and Brown (1979). Some of the Dutch findings have been published in Koopman, Drenth, Bus, Kruyswijk, and Wierdsma (1981). For a more complete account of the Dutch part of the research, see Koopman (1980).

THE EFFECT OF PARTICIPATION

It is still not long ago that researchers in social science proclaimed that a participative style of leadership had more chance of being successful than an authoritarian style. Success in this context refers to both effectiveness and satisfaction (Argyris, 1964; Likert, 1967). In general, research results seemed to confirm this premise (Blumberg, 1968; Filley, House, & Kerr, 1976).

[1]The Dutch study was supported by the Netherlands Organization for the Advancement of Pure Science (ZWO).

Decision making seems more successful if those who have to implement the decisions are given a chance to be involved and to have influence on the decisions in question. Some recent review studies, however, question the correctness of this conclusion (Andriessen & Drenth, 1982; Locke & Schweiger, 1979; Wall & Lischeron, 1977). Their conclusions can be summarized as follows:

— Participative decision making does lead to satisfaction with the decision-making process. It is not always clear which factors are responsible for these relationships. It is not unlikely that participation both satisfies the need for involvement and participation as such, and offers the possibility to achieve secondary goals, such as better relationships, more information, better decision making.
— Participative decision making generally does not lead to a higher motivation, better performance, and higher production. The relationship between participation and performance is very complex and depends strongly upon situational variables. There are situations in which relations are to be found, but other conditions have a negative effect in this respect.
— A set of conditions that has to be fulfilled in order to expect a positive relation between participation and performance has to do with (a) need for participation as well as ability and capacity to contribute to the decision-making process on the part of the participant, and (b) the type of task that offers sufficient room for improvement as a consequence of input and participation by the individual who performs that task (for example, routine tasks as opposed to complex tasks that require cooperation among group members; House & Baetz, 1979).

These findings inspired leadership theorists to propose various forms of the so-called "contingency model" (see Heller, 1976a; Kerr, Schriesheim, Murphy, & Stogdill, 1974; Schriesheim & Kerr, 1977). The essential characteristic of the contingency approach is that no general laws about the relationship between participation and performance can be formulated, but that these relationships are contingent upon a number of (moderator or contingency) variables. The main question is, then, under what *conditions* participation is the most successful. Suggestions in this respect include organizational factors (Porter & Lawler, 1965), task or group characteristics (Fiedler, 1967), nature of decisions (Vroom & Yetton, 1973), or situational variables (Schriesheim & Murphy, 1979).

THE DIO RESEARCH MODEL

This contingency model has also been the basic model of our own study (see Figure 17.1).

One of the most important contingency variables seems to be the nature and complexity of the decision itself (House & Baetz, 1979; Vroom & Yet-

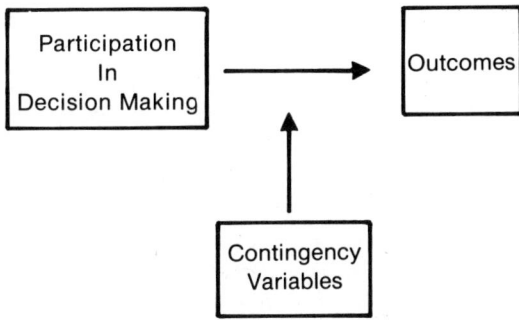

FIGURE 17.1. The basic model DIO

ton, 1973). A distinction has therefore been made between *operational* decisions on the one hand, and *complex* decisions on the other. Operational decisions can be characterized by a relatively short time span, a high frequency, and a concern with operations that can be found "low" in the organization. Scheme 1 lists the operational decisions.

Complex decisions occur less frequently, have a medium- or long-time perspective, and concern issues that find themselves higher in the organization (middle or top). The complex decisions can be further divided into *strategic* decisions (having direct relevance for the continuity of the organization) (see Bacharach & Aiken, 1976; Mintzberg, Raisinghani, & Theoret, 1976) and *tac-*

Scheme 1. List of Operational Decisions.

1. Arranging the layout of your workplace (position of machinery, desks, and the like).
2. How to arrange and plan the work *within your group.*
3. How to carry out your group's work.
4. Changing the amount to be produced by your work group.
5. Purchasing of equipment (costs within the limits of the departmental budget).
6. Transferring someone to another job within the work group.
7. Improving the physical work conditions (noise, temperature, ventilation, draught, etc.).
8. Who works on which shift.
9. Who can go on a training course.
10. Activities within your production unit designed to save costs.
11. Safety procedures.
12. Who gets overtime work and how much.

tical decisions (more related to the control systems with respect to personnel, or to adequate execution of the work; see Child, 1972).

In Scheme 2, the list of strategic and tactical decisions used in the study is reproduced. These two categories of decisions turned out to require a different design and different ways of operationalizing.

With respect to the *operational* decisions, the unit of analysis was the working group in which the decisions were taken. A study was made of a large number of work groups in which some form of joint decision making or consultation took place on a regular basis (the so-called "werkoverleg"; hereafter to be indicated by "work consultation"). In three Dutch organizations (a municipal transport organization, a regional division of the Dutch railways, a plant of a steel works) 22 groups ($N = 191$), 12 groups ($N = 156$) and 9 groups ($N = 160$), respectively, have been included in the study.

For the collection of data, use has been made of questionnaires and scales that were administered groupwise. The *independent* variable, "participative leadership," has been measured by a participation list (IPC, Influence-Power Continuum) with the six levels of participation and involvement as indicated in Scheme 3. The respondents filled in the perceived level of participation with respect to the operational decisions listed in Scheme 1.

With respect to the *complex* decisions, a quite different approach and design seemed appropriate. In the first place, the unit of analysis was not a group in which the decision took place (by its very nature, it is often difficult to determine a particular group in which the decision making takes place, since it is a longitudinal process that takes its path through various levels and groups in the organization). The unit of analysis was the decision process itself. In the three organizations, a total of 56 such decisions were analyzed.

Scheme 2. Strategic and Tactical Decisions.

STRATEGIC
1. Setting up a consultative procedure.
2. Initiating a new product or service.
3. Deciding on medium-size capital investment.
4. Budget forecasting.

TACTICAL
5. Changes in methods of operation.
6. Job-grading procedures.
7. Training methods.
8. General work conditions.
9. Disclosure of information.
10. Safety procedures.
11. Cost-saving methods.
12. Appointment of department head.

Scheme 3. Influence-Power Continuum.

1. No information is given.
2. Fairly detailed information about the decision is made available.
3. Opportunity to give advice.
4. Advice is taken into consideration.
5. Joint decision making.
6. Complete control.

For the operational decisions, the dependent variables* were:
- Effectiveness (Eff; .85),
- Utilization of skills (SU; .85)
- Satisfaction in general (SATG; .74)
- Satisfaction with participation (SATP; .70)

These outcome variables were measured by means of questionnaires as well.

The following contingency variables** were included in the research:
- Reasons for underutilization of skills (.76)
- Expectations from work consultation (.90)
- Group climate (.77)
- Group size
- Organizational climate with respect to participation (.64)
- Seniority in the present function
- Seniority in the company
- Age
- Educational level
- Frequency of the work consultation meetings
- Union membership
- Relevance for productivity of the topics to be discussed in work consultation.

*The numbers in parentheses indicate the average reliabilities.
**Measured by questionnaires and scales.

As far as the data collection goes, questionnaires could hardly be used. The decisions concerned often center on politically sensitive issues, and questionnaires would certainly not reveal the subtle and complex social mechanisms. Two methods of data collection have been utilized:

- *Tracing:* after the decision making was finished, an attempt was made to reconstruct or to "trace" a number of aspects of the process through inter-

viewing with "key persons" and by studying further relevant material, such as documents, agenda minutes, and memoranda.
- *Process registration:* in this form of data collection, the analysis did not take place after but during the decision-making process. Direct observation provided additional information alongside information obtained by means of interviews.

After aggregation of the data and scoring in a simple three-point scale, these scores and descriptions were fed back to the respondents for comments. Amendments and additions were incorporated and the final version of the description and scores were given a final check in two meetings: one with management and one with the Works' Council. In all cases the informants agreed with the final scores.

It turned out to be essential, in accordance with Mintzberg *et al.* (1976) to distinguish four different phases in the decision-making process: (1) Start-up; (2) Development; (3) Finalization; and (4) Implementation. A more elaborate description of the four phases and a justification of the distinction is given in DIO Research Team (1982). An analysis was made for each of these four phases of the extent to which groups and hierarchical levels in the organization had been involved in the decision making, and of which level of participation had been realized in each particular case.

These groups and hierarchical levels have been defined as follows: (A) workers; (B) first-line supervisors; (C) middle management; (D) top management; (P) staff; and (Q) members of the Works' Council. Top management (D) includes the director and the first level below him. Middle management consists of the levels between D and the first-line supervisor (B).

The independent variable was similar to the one with the operational decisions. The same Influence-Power Continuum list (Scheme 3) has been used for the evaluation of the level of participation.

The dependent variables were: satisfaction with the decision-making process; satisfaction with the outcome of the decision; success in terms of the extent to which the goals have been achieved; satisfaction after implementation; efficiency as an estimated relation between input and output; utilization of knowledge and capacities; and time (i.e., the total time of the decision-making process).

The following contingency variables have been included in the analysis:

- Level and nature of the group involved in the decision making (A, B, C, D, P, Q; see above).
- The four phases: start-up, development, finalization, and implementation.
- Nature of the decision; here, the distinction between strategic and tactical decisions was used.
- Status power of the group involved in the decision making; on a six-point scale, quite similar to the IPC scale (ranging again from "no information

given" to "complete control"), the formal power of each group has been registered through written documents, acts, regulations, but sometimes also through unwritten but enforceable laws (the scale was derived from IDE, 1981).
- Metapower, defined as a set of external interventions or influences on the decision making that become visible during the decision-making process but originate outside the work unit (firm or part of firm) under study (Buckley & Burns, 1974; Rus *et al.*, 1977).
- Level of conflicts that may occur during the decision making.
- Clarity of goals of the decision-making process; a distinction has been made between: (1) very clear goal (one dominant goal); (2) several equally ranked goals; and (3) opposite or very unclear goals.
- The amount of trust and openness between the participants during the decision-making process as a whole.

RESULTS

We will first present the results for the operational and the complex decisions separately, and then conclude with an overall observation.

Operational Decisions

In Table 17.1 the relations between the IPC scores and the dependent variables per organization are presented. Organization A is a municipal transport organization with approximately 4,000 employees. Organization B is one of the regional divisions of the Dutch railways, with some 750 employees. Organization C is a plant of a steelworks, employing some 450 employees in the operating factory and supportive departments. The short descriptions indicate the variety of organization types included in the study, but, of course,

Table 17.1. Pearson Correlations ($\times 100$) between the Influence-Power Continuum and Dependent Variables.

Dependent Variables	A (Municipal Transport)	B (Dutch Railways)	C (Steel Works)
Skill utilization	38**	08	24**
Effectiveness	42**	38**	10
Satisfaction, general	14*	19*	31**
Satisfaction, particular	44**	57**	35**
N	175	154	153

$^*p < .05$
$^{**}p < .01$

no claim can be made with respect to the representativeness of the sample.

One can see a reasonably consistent pattern of relationships with the exception of the dependent variable, "general satisfaction." This lack of correlation has been found frequently in the literature, owing to the complex nature of the concept of general satisfaction and because it is usually determined by a large number of variables (Koopman, 1980, p. 140).

The possible moderating effect of the contingency variables has been analyzed in two ways: first, through a subgroup analysis. The total group was divided into two subgroups on the basis of the contingency variable in study (the dichotomy was made as close as possible to the median). A possible difference in correlation between the two groups was taken as an indication of the contingency effect of the variable in question.

In the second method of analysis, a multiple regression analysis was carried out, in which the interaction term "IPC times moderator" has been introduced. If this interaction term should contribute significantly to the predicted variance, that would, again, be taken as support for the moderating influence of the contingency variable.

About the results of these two analyses, we can be brief. Even with rather lenient criteria (a significant difference in at least two of the three organizations, two-sided test, $p < .10$ and the 5 percent significance level for the multiple regression), none of the listed contingency variables showed any significant effect. Only one of the variables showed a consistent trend, although the differences are not significant (see Table 17.2), and the interaction term with IPC gives a significant contribution only in two out of the twelve cases (three organizations, four dependent variables). This variable is "frequency of work consultation." This trend may be interpreted as a tendency for the consulting groups that met more frequently to show a greater connection between participation and positive results and attitudes.

Table 17.2 Pearson Correlations ($\times 100$) between the
Influence-Power Continuum and Dependent Variables in
Subgroups on the Basis of "Frequency of Work Consultation."

DEPENDENT VARIABLES	A HIGH	LOW	B HIGH	LOW	C HIGH	LOW
Skill utilization	44	33	02	−04	30	16
Effectiveness	41	41	34	40	33	08
Satisfaction, general	27	10	21	04	36	29
Satisfaction, particular	48	35	57	39	37	30
$N>$	67	94	45	57	68	49

Complex Decisions

The analysis of the complex decisions shows quite a different picture. Here there are hardly "main effects," but considerable contributions of the contingency variables could be identified.

In the first place, this is true for the contingency-variable *phase* of the decision making. Hardly any significant correlations were found between IPC scores and the dependent variables if the data are summarized over the four phases. But specification per phase generates a number of interesting (and interpretable) correlations. The data are presented in Table 17.3.

Some conclusions may be drawn from Table 17.3. Participation of the workers in more complex decision making in organizations generates satisfaction,[2] especially in the development phase. For the influence of top management, the reverse is true: too much influence in this phase leads to stronger dissatisfaction among workers.

Moreover, too much interference and influence by middle management and staff members in the finalization phase does not seem very efficient. The influence of the Works' Council in the implementation phase can be associated with a more negative evaluation of the success of decision making.

A second important contingent variable turns out to be the nature of the (complex) decisions. Because of the multitude of Influence-Power Continuum–indices (four phases and six groups), this analysis has been restricted to the two more interesting indices:

1. the average IPC score for level A (IPC-A), and
2. a score for power equalization, operationalized as the difference in average IPC score for middle management (C), top management (D), and staff (P) on the one hand, and workers (A), supervisors (B), and Works' Council (Q) on the other. This score is indicated with PE.

Without further specifications rather few and very low correlations between IPC-A scores and PE scores with the dependent variables were found, as shown in Table 17.4.

A further distinction in tactical and strategic decisions, however, produces a different and subtler picture (see Table 17.5). Note that the (positive) correlations are concentrated in the area of tactical decisions, which are closer to the daily experience of the worker than the strategic decisions. The correlation between participation of the workers and success of the decision making for strategic decisions is significantly negative.

The variables, "Status power" and "Metapower" did not show a significant moderating effect in our analysis. They were, however, directly related

---

[2]The fact that the independent variable is measured at an earlier stage than the dependent variable may justify this causal interpretation.

Table 17.3 Kendall Tau Correlations* ($\times 100$) between the Influence-Power Continuum and Dependent Variables ($N = 56$).

DEPENDENT VARIABLES LEVEL	IPC SCORES FOR ALL GROUPS AND LEVELS PER D.M. PHASE																	
	A			B			C			D			P			Q		
PHASE**	2	3	4	2	3	4	2	3	4	2	3	4	2	3	4	2	3	4
Success										−26		−41		−25				−37
Efficiency								−30						−27				
Satisfaction, process	25				−35					−32				−22				
Satisfaction, outcome	25									−31	−21	−34						−39
Satisfaction after implementation	26			28						−27		−41						−31
Use capacities								−21						−34				
Time					−20													−33

*The nature of the data did not permit the use of Pearson correlations as with operational decisions.
**Phase 1 not shown since not significant.

Table 17.4. Kendall Tau Correlations ($\times$ 100) between
Influence-Power Continuum-scores (averaged over 4 phases)
and Dependent Variables ($N = 56$).

DEPENDENT VARIABLES	IPC-A	PE
Success	-02	02
Efficiency	-08	10
Satisfaction, process	12	19*
Satisfaction, outcome	14	07
Satisfaction, after implementation	21*	28*
Use capacities	28	21*
Time	09	00

*$p < .05$

to the IPC score. This is not difficult to understand. The formal power is one of the determinants of the actual power (IDE, 1981), and restrictive influences from outside are not unrelated to the influence and power of the parties cooperating in the decision making.

For the other contingency variables, again, significant effects could be established. In Table 17.6 the correlations are shown for decisions with a high versus low degree of clarity of goal, and in Table 17.7, the correlations for

Table 17.5. Kendall Tau Correlations ($\times$ 100) between Influence-Power Continuum and Dependent Variables for Tactical and Strategic Decisions ($N = 56$).[1]

DEPENDENT VARIABLES	TACTICAL DECISIONS		STRATEGIC DECISIONS	
	IPC-A	PE	IPC-A	PE
Success	31*	22	$-35*$	-18
Efficiency	07	27	-18	-01
Satisfaction, process	09	19	17	19
Satisfaction, outcome	31*	26	04	-11
Satisfaction after implementation	34*	40**	08	13
Use capacities	20	46*	01	02
Time	06	08	26	-02

*$p < .05$
**$p < .01$
[1]Differences between Kendall tau correlations cannot be tested, so additional Pearson correlations have been calculated, allowing for difference testing after Fisher-Z transformation. For "success" and "satisfaction with outcome," the differences T-S were significant for both indices. The other variables generally show a trend in the same direction.

Table 17.6 Kendall Tau Correlations ($\times 100$) between Influence-Power Continuum and Dependent Variables for the Conditions High and Low Clarity of Goal ($N = 56$).

DEPENDENT VARIABLES	LOW CLARITY OF GOAL		HIGH CLARITY OF GOAL	
	IPC-A	PE	IPC-A	PE
Success	− 03	03	04	05
Efficiency	23	35*	− 20	05
Satisfaction, process	36*	20	04	19
Satisfaction, outcome	30	11	13	11
Satisfaction after implementation	22	21	25*	36*
Use capacities	37*	40*	− 15	00
Time	08	19	07	− 16

*$p < .05$

the decisions with a high versus low degree of conflict (the variable "trust" has more or less similar effects).

It appears that participation of employees at lower levels in the organization is most successful under conditions of a lower clarity of goals. Under those conditions participation seems to guarantee better use of the capacities and skills, and seems to be more effective and to lead to more satisfaction than under conditions of a high clarity of goals.

Conflict seems to be an important condition as well. Only if little trust and a high level of conflict are found, a positive correlation between participation and a better use of capacities and skills and more satisfaction with the

Table 17.7 Kendall Tau Correlations ($\times 100$) between Influence-Power Continuum and Dependent Variables for the Conditions High and Low Level of Conflict ($N = 56$).

DEPENDENT VARIABLES	HIGH LEVEL OF CONFLICT		LOW LEVEL OF CONFLICT	
	IPC-A	PE	IPC-A	PE
Success	− 05	00	− 03	14
Efficiency	03	06	− 34	21
Satisfaction, process	27*	14	− 38	31
Satisfaction, outcome	21	03	− 13	08
Satisfaction after implementation	27*	27*	00	32
Use capacities	24*	18	− 31	31
Time	11	07	16	− 42

*$p < .05$

decision making emerges. With a low level of conflict there even seems to be a tendency to a negative relationship between participation on the one hand, and efficiency and satisfaction on the other.

CONCLUSION

This research has produced a number of results that may bring a further differentiation in the theory of participative leadership. Particularly with respect to the contingency model which has become quite popular in the recent publications and empirical studies on participative leadership, it has generated some interesting findings. The distinction between short-term operational decisions on the one hand and tactical or strategical decisions of a longer term on the other turned out to be an important one. With respect to the former type of decisions, none of the selected potential contingent factors had any moderating influence on the relationship between participation and the criteria. With respect to the latter type of decisions, a number of contingent variables did indeed show an effect.

On the basis of the results, it can be formulated that even the statement, "the effect of participative leadership is contingent upon a number of other variables," itself depends at least on whether it concerns routine or more complex decisions. This study gives empirical support to an ironical consequence of the contingency theory: the contingency theory cannot have general validity!

The findings may also lead to some practical consequences. As far as operational decisions are concerned, it may be concluded that as a general rule, positive effects in terms of both effectiveness and satisfaction are a function of the degree of participation. It does not seem necessary to meet a great number of procedural or sociopsychological conditions before a participative system can be expected to be effective. The effects that participation produces seem to be rather straightforward and unconditional.

This is not the case with respect to more long-term and complex decisions. If participation is introduced in decision making at this level in order to make the process more effective and satisfactory to the participants, it may be wise to analyze a number of conditions under which the decision making takes place. Our research results suggest that positive effects are to be expected with tactical rather than strategic decisions. Furthermore, these positive effects can be expected particularly under conditions of disagreement, tension, distrust, and conflict. In those circumstances especially, a more centralized, autocratic way of decision making runs the risk of encountering negative repercussions and delay in the implementation phase.

18

Leadership in Participative Organizations

Edward E. Lawler III

Research on participative leadership has a long and indeed often quite successful history. Students of management are taught the results of the classic study by Lewin, Lippitt, and White (1939) and the results of the Michigan and Ohio State leadership studies (see Bass, 1981, for a review). These studies help to clarify some of the advantages and disadvantages of democratic and autocratic leadership styles. Leadership research concerned with participative behavior on the part of the supervisor, however, is quite different from leadership research concerned with the behavior of leaders in participative organizations. At first glance, this distinction may seem to be trivial, but it is not. The key issue here is that of organization. The premise of this chapter is that participative leadership behavior has quite different impacts, depending upon the type of organization setting, context, and history in which it is practiced. In addition, it is argued that the leadership functions that need to be performed are quite different in participative organizations than they are in more traditional ones.

Few studies have focused on studying leadership in participative work organizations. This lack of research is hardly surprising since the opportunity to study leadership in participative work organizations rarely existed until recently. At least, participatively managed organizations did not exist in the United States in significant numbers until the last few years. Thus, researchers were limited to studying participation either in laboratory settings or in traditional work settings. The situation was somewhat different in other countries and this probably accounts for the fact that much of the research on leadership in participative organizations, in the literature and in this volume, comes from Europe.

My interest in trying to understand the role of leadership in participative organizations has grown significantly over the last ten years as a result of my research on participative organizations. During the last ten years I have had the chance to evaluate a number of participative management projects that were designed to improve organizational effectiveness through moving power, knowledge, and information to lower levels in organizations (see, for example, Seashore, Lawler, Mirvis, & Cammann, 1983). These projects typically have fallen into one of three categories: (1) new plant start-ups where a green field situation exists and from the beginning management has set out to design high-involvement, high-performance work systems (elsewhere, I and other people have reported on the design elements of these projects; Lawler, 1978; Walton, 1980); (2) union-management quality of work life projects in which a participative, cooperative problem-solving structure is set up to change the nature of traditional union-management relationships (results of these projects have also been reported on elsewhere and they have been intensely studied; Goodman, 1979; Lawler & Ledford, 1982); (3) gain-sharing projects in which a plantwide bonus system is used as a lead factor in installing a more participative work climate (there are numerous reports of successful experience in setting these up; Moore & Ross, 1978).

There is no question in my mind that a key element in the success of all the participative projects that I have studied in the last ten years is the effectiveness of the leaders. Indeed, in working on these projects, I found myself regularly being queried by managers about how they should behave in their leadership roles, trying to explain the behavior of executives and managers in these situations, and trying to explain the effectiveness of these plants in terms of leadership effectiveness. Interestingly, the traditional literature on leadership was frequently of little use. Many of the questions that were asked simply are not addressed by the traditional research on leadership and many of the differences observed between effective and ineffective leaders simply are not covered in the traditional literature on leadership. At once, this is both disturbing and not terribly surprising. In essence, the study of leadership in a participative setting is a relatively new topic. Thus, the fact that the literature has relatively little to say about it is not very surprising. Indeed, studying it presents the opportunity to learn a great deal about leadership since it broadens the context in which the topic has been studied and forces theories of leadership to be more robust if they are going to include concepts that are applicable to leader behavior in all settings.

In this chapter I focus on what I think are the key leadership issues in managing participative work organizations. In the discussion the focus is initially on the kind of strategic decisions and design issues that face a manager in a participative organization. The next focus is on the leadership function and what needs to be done in order to make a participative organization effective. Here the concern is with leadership that is distinct from traditional supervision. Thus, the focus is on the process of establishing an organization climate or culture, influencing behavior, and setting direction for an organization that is over and above the traditional managerial role—topics that, as will be noted, are considered by some of the other chapters in this volume but noticeably absent in many others.

STRATEGIC AND DESIGN ISSUES IN PARTICIPATIVE WORK SYSTEMS

There are a number of important strategic and design issues that regularly occur in participative work systems. Research suggests that how they are decided is crucial in determining the effectiveness of participative leadership behavior. In reviewing them, the emphasis will be on noting what the existing literature and the chapters in this volume have to say about them and on sharing my observations which are derived from the study of various participative organizations.

Leadership Islands

A key design issue in the management of work systems is the effects of having multiple decision-making styles within the same work setting. In traditional work organizations this usually involves the question of whether a group or several groups can operate in a participative manner with respect to decision making while the rest of the organization operates in a more traditional manner. In highly participative organizations such as new plants the issue usually revolves around whether most of the organization can operate in a participative manner while certain groups operate in a more traditional, authoritative manner.

The existing literature on leadership is rather silent on this issue, as are the other chapters in this volume. The focus of much of the literature is either dyadic or small group, and tends not to look at the social context in order to predict the effectiveness of a particular leadership style. There is, of course, the literature on social comparison which suggests that different decision-making styles may have trouble existing in the same setting. And there is the classic study by Morse and Reimer (1956) which tends to show that participative islands can be very disruptive in traditional organizations even though they may have effective operating results. Recent research on organizational changes tends very strongly to confirm this early finding (see, for example, Goodman, 1979).

Less evidence is available with respect to what happens to traditional islands in participatory organizations, but in my experience they can be equally as disruptive and have as much difficulty surviving as do participative islands in traditional structures. The overall conclusion, then, seems to be that it is not advisable to design organizations in such a way that multiple leadership styles and decision-making processes exist in the same work setting. In essence, the suggestion is that the dominant style tends to drive out the other style or styles such that the setting becomes relatively homogeneous in its decision-making approach. The exception to this is settings where clear-cut boundaries or walls can be set around small groups or work areas.

The reason for the failure of islands probably rests in the social comparison phenomena that exist in contiguous work settings and the general desire for more participative decision making. In the case of the traditional organization with a participative island, pressure builds up for the rest of the organization to change, and this typically results in the island being eliminated because it produces pressures to which the rest of the organization is unwilling to respond. In the case of the participative organization with the autocratic style, the resolution generally seems to be to move toward the dominant style because it is desired by those people in the autocratic part of the organization and ultimately the pressure becomes irresistible. Indeed, this is one of the most important reasons why traditional supervisors tend not to survive in highly participative work organizations. Reports of high-participation work organizations suggest that as many as 50 percent of traditional supervisors do not succeed in these settings (see, e.g., Walton & Schlesinger, 1979).

Situational Determinants

The current literature on leadership is full of contingency models that try to help the manager decide what type of leadership style to use. Several of the contributions in this volume also look at this issue. These models argue that such things as the type of decision to be made, knowledge of the people, and the importance of decision acceptance be used in deciding what type of leadership style to use. (See, for example, Fiedler, 1964; Hersey & Blanchard, 1969; Vroom & Yetton, 1973). Strangely missing in most of these discussions is any attention to what emerges in many participative organizations as a key factor: the social contract that the leader develops around the decision-making style that will be used. As Fulk and Cummings point out in Chapter 5, leadership can best be thought of as a social-contracting process; and this element warrants considerable attention in deciding what type of decision-making style to use.

In the case of participative organizations, from the beginning the emphasis is upon involvement in decisions and, thus, making decisions in other than a participative management style can be seen as a violation of a social contract. The key issue in these settings is under what conditions it is appropriate to move from a participative style to a more top-down one. It is also clear that if decisions are made in a more top-down manner very often, the entire social contract upon which the organization is managed will be broken and the effectiveness of the organization endangered.

This is not to suggest that in certain cases traditional decision-making approaches cannot be used in highly participative organizations — they certainly can be — but it is to suggest that the kind of decision-by-decision style change that is suggested by many of the contingency models is simply out of the question. For example, the kinds of changes suggested by the Vroom and Yetton model seem unrealistic and counterproductive. The data presented by Drenth and Koopman in this volume suggest a more realistic model in which certain types of decisions might as a matter of course not be subject to a fully participative decision process. What seems to be effective is a style in which an occasional decision that stands out for certain, often prespecified, reasons can be made in a different manner. For example, in many participative organizations, issues concerned with whether or not new products will be added to the plant, certain kinds of financing arrangements, and certain quality-control issues are excluded from the participative process in the organization because of corporate mandate, government regulations, or other issues. When this is done as part of the initial contracting process, then there seem to be no serious problems if these decisions and only these decisions are removed from the participative decision process in the organization.

The key to the perceived legitimacy of removing these decisions is the fact that there are many other "tough" decisions left to the participative process. If this does not occur, that is, if enough tough decisions are not left for the participative process and if the guidelines about what decisions will be made participatively are not adhered to, then ultimately the participative process in the organization is destroyed and the organization ceases to operate as an effective participative organization.

Although the research on participative organizations suggests that it is possible to change leadership styles for certain kinds of decisions, the discussion so far argues for having a core decision-making style. This core decision style, where there is any doubt, should override all else and be the decision-making approach. One advantage of having a core style that leans toward participative decision making is that it allows the attraction of people who are comfortable with this decision style and, of course, it also allows effective participative decision-making skills to develop. These conditions are often noted as necessary if participation is to be effective and can best be achieved in a participative organization. The suggestion then is that there is a cumulative effect from having decisions made in a participative style that is greater than simply the sum of the number of participative style decisions made. It seems that once a critical mass of decisions in the organization is made in a participative style, the whole nature of the organization, the people's commitment to it, the skills of the participants, and the climate of the organization change. The organization becomes a different type of organization from one that does not have a core style of participative decision making and as a result, decisions about what type of leadership style to use must involve different issues.

Group versus Individual Participation

Participative decisions can be made in many different arenas. For example, they can be made in a dyadic discussion between two people, in small groups, based on an organizationwide vote, or by a representative sample of people from the organization. The traditional literature on leadership and managerial behavior provides very few guidelines as to how to decide among these options for decision making. All too often, decision making is simply placed on a continuum from autocratic to democratic (see, e.g., Vroom & Yetton, 1973), and no consideration is given to how to make the decision in a participative manner. In Chapter 17, Drenth and Koopman provide some clues here, suggesting that the nature and complexity of the decision may be critical. Among other things, they point out some of the complexities involved in deciding how different participative decision processes should be used.

In my experience, managers in participative organizations spend a considerable amount of their time analyzing which is the best way to get decisions made. The issue is not whether or not to participate, but what kind of participative process to invoke in order to get specific decisions made. I think it is possible to develop a decision tree not unlike the one developed by Vroom and Yetton which would lead to a prescription about whether to make the decision on a dyadic, small-group, organizationwide, or representative basis. The key variables here would be such things as the decision complexity, importance of decision acceptability by a wide range versus a small number of people in the organization, and the kind of information that people in different parts of the organization have.

Interestingly, in many participative organizations decisions concerned with hours of work, movements in the pay structure, and reduction of work hours due to business slowdown tend to be assigned to small groups that are representative of the organization as a whole. Most shop-floor day-to-day workplace decisions get allocated to the small-group or work-team setting. Very few decisions get made in dyadic interactions between superior and subordinates. Even decisions that are traditionally considered private between the individual and the supervisor typically get made in a group setting. For example, pay increase and performance appraisal actions are typically decided in a small-group discussion. The rationale for this emphasizes the importance of decision acceptability and the fact that everyone in a work team has information relevant to the performance of each other. Indeed, in many cases it would be seen as a violation of the participative contract in the organization if these decisions were made on anything other than a small-group basis.

In my work I have typically used plantwide representative groups to design gain-sharing plans and skill-based pay plans (Lawler, 1981b). The rationale for this is that these plans have a plantwide impact and that people throughout the organization have knowledge and information that are relevant to the design process. In addition, the success of these plans depends on wide acceptability and commitment to making them work. One way to get this is through a plantwide representative group. The development of these plans requires considerable technical expertise since they are complicated issues and, as Drenth and Koopman point out, it is difficult to bring everyone in an organization along to the point where full participation is possible. The disadvantage to this approach is that it is relatively slow compared to a top-down expert design approach and can lead to members of the organizations feeling left out of the process. A possible way to deal with the latter problem is to work with the representatives so that they function as effective links back to their own work areas or units. Still, it is a form of indirect participation and as such is likely to lead to a limited sense of involvement on the part of many people in the organization.

Overall, the suggestion is that a considerable amount of research needs to be done on the advantages and disadvantages of different decision processes where there is employee involvement in decisions. Ultimately, a framework needs to be developed that can guide practitioners to the most effective way to get certain decisions made. Again, it is important to emphasize here that this issue is not one of whether a particular decision should be made in an autocratic or participative manner, it is a question of which type of participative process is most effective in dealing with the issue.

Maturation of Participative Process

Several existing leadership theories recognize that the decision-making processes in organizations need to change over time (see, e.g., Hersey & Blanchard, 1969). This particular phenomenon is very evident in the creation of new highly participative work organizations. Walton and Schlesinger (1979) comment on this extensively in their piece on leadership in high-involvement work settings. With respect to work teams and probably with respect to the overall decision-making processes in organizations, as time goes on more and more decisions can be made in a participative manner because with proper training, experience, and so on, a maturation process occurs in which knowledge and decision-making skills become broadly present in an organization. This means that decisions that early on need to be made in a top-down manner can later be located lower down in the organization.

From a strategic point of view, the existence of a maturation process raises two key issues. First, what needs to be done in order to be sure that the maturation process proceeds as rapidly and effectively as possible, and second, what kinds of decisions can reasonably be made in a participative manner at different stages in the maturation process.

Looking first at the issue of moving the maturation process forward, clearly there are some skills that need to be learned in both the process and the content areas. The recent work on quality circles makes this point quite clearly. For groups to function effectively, individuals need to have both group-process and problem-solving analysis skills. In some new high-involvement organizations the assumption has been made that these can develop without the investment of a great deal of supervisory time and effort. In most cases, this assumption has turned out to be false. It seems that, particularly in the early history of work teams, considerable supervisory/trainer presence is necessary in order for groups to develop correct norms and skills. In the absence of supervisory input early in their history, groups tend to have problems confronting process issues and poor performance by individuals, and they tend to make decisions that are in their narrow self-interest.

Interestingly, the ultimate maturation of a group may depend upon the allocation to it of difficult decisions. If strictly contingency leadership theory were followed, most decisions concerning pay, for example, would always be made in a top-down manner. Obviously, there is a great deal of self-interest motivation in the case of pay decisions, and good decisions require peer evaluation and feedback in participative organizations. Thus, the general recommendation would be to have them made in a dyadic, superior/subordinate mode. On the other hand, it may be that making these kinds of decisions in a participative manner is critical in the evolution and development of effective participative decision-making groups.

Dealing effectively with an issue that is as visible and difficult as pay can potentially give the group a sense of heightened self-esteem and effectiveness to the point where it moves to another level of maturity. The same can be said for decisions about other personnel issues, such as hiring and firing. Most contingency theory prescriptions would say that these should never be left to a group decision, but they are often made by groups in high-participation organizations; and in my observations the act of handling these decisions effectively is an important step in the development and evolution of work teams. If these decisions are removed from the group, as they are in some participative organizations, the case can be made that the ultimate evolution and development of the group will be restricted.

Groups develop skills and a sense of competence by dealing with difficult problems, not easy problems. On the other hand, if they are to be successful, they probably need to move incrementally in the kinds of decisions they make. Thus, pay decisions and personnel decisions may need to come up later rather than sooner in the evolutionary history of groups. Interestingly, contingency theories can help here by identifying those decisions that are likely to be most difficult for groups to make in a participative manner. Walton and Schlesinger (1979) also address this issue in their piece on supervision in high-involvement work settings.

In general, the topic of when different kinds of decisions should be turned over to groups and how rapidly they should be turned over to the participative process is one that could profit from considerable research that follows the longitudinal mode suggested by Heller in Chapter 16. It seems quite likely that an "ideal" chronology of group development could be developed with some research so that it would be possible to talk about the sequence in which management-type decisions are turned over to groups and to a participative process in an organization that is moving toward an overall participative management structure. This chronology would need to include such things as complexity of the technology and the skill levels of the employees.

Whom to Select for Managerial Positions

Walton and Schlesinger (1979), as well as most others who study high-participation work settings, note that it is often difficult to know who will be an effective manager in these settings. Indeed, there is often little agreement on what skills should be looked for in managers. Surprisingly, none of the chapters in the present volume deals with the issue of selecting successful leaders for either participative or traditional work settings.

One key strategic issue in selecting managers concerns the degree to which the emphasis will be on technical skills versus leadership and managerial skills. The early writings on participative organizations emphasized the importance of managerial and process skills. Recently this has changed somewhat because several failures have been reported that were at least partially due to lack of technical skills on the part of managers. The thinking in this area now argues for the importance of technical skills at least in new organization start-ups (see, e.g., Perkins, Nieva, & Lawler, 1983).

But perhaps the real question is just how learnable are the process and leadership skills that are needed to operate effectively in a high-participation work setting. Again, the traditional literature on leadership gives little evidence on this point. There are indeed some classic Ohio State studies that suggest that unless the participative behavior is rewarded and supported in the work environment, it will not persevere subsequent to a training program. But this is not usually the issue in participative organizations. Rather, the issue, given the training and the support of the environment, is what percentage of the managerial work force will be able to demonstrate the new behaviors.

As Walton and Schlesinger point out, there is reason to believe that many supervisors who are quite successful in traditional organizations cannot make the transition to more participative ones. Indeed, sometimes the suggestion is made that people without supervisory experience should be selected for participative organizations because they have less to unlearn. In any case, we do not know the answers to a whole series of important questions about what kind of experience people should have to prepare them for management in a participative work setting and to what degree people can be changed through training and experience to manage effectively in participative work settings.

My experience is that only a few managers who have grown up with the traditional approaches to management can change to be effective in participative systems. There simply seems to be too much to unlearn and too many roadblocks to new learning. Of course, there is the exception who has been a "closet" participative manager all along. This person already has values favoring participation but has been coerced by traditional settings to manage in a more traditional way. I have also encountered convert types who went from being rigidly traditional in their management style to being rigidly participative in their management style. In short, they profess to have discovered a new truth and, in their own dogmatic way, pursue it with the same vigor and effectiveness with which they had pursued their old leadership style. This type of change is rare and in some ways leads to managers of limited effectiveness because they tend to be intolerant of others who are in the process of trying to change and because they are so rigid in their use of participative management.

The most dramatic conversions I have seen have occurred when traditional managers whose only experience has been in relatively top-down organizations have been placed in already exisiting participative work climates. After several months of confusion, they have come to "see the light" and have dramatically changed their views of leadership and managerial behavior. It would be nice if this kind of process could be counted on to work for everyone, but unfortunately it cannot. There are a number of interesting research issues that suggest themselves around this phenomenon. Most of them have to do with what kinds of experiences lead to these changes and whether it is possible to predict with any degree of accuracy who will change in this manner when confronted with taking on a role in a more participative organization and who will resist.

Design of Support Systems

Work organizations are made up of a number of subsystems. The behavior of the managers is just one of these subsystems. Others include the information system, the reward system, the organization structure, the way jobs are designed, and the personnel policies and practices, to mention some of the more important and visible ones. The literature in organizational behavior has increasingly emphasized the interdependence of the subsystems, but little of this seems to have been taken into account in the research on leadership. Because of connectedness of various organizations subsystems, it is impossible to pull out any one system such as leadership and look at it as a stand-alone item.

Leadership effectiveness and appropriateness can only be evaluated in the context of the surrounding systems that support or negate it. This kind of thinking leads to a call for congruence in the subsystems that make up an organization. Indeed, carried to an extreme, this view suggests that the degree of congruence may be more important than the type of overall organizational system that is ultimately put in place. Thus, an internally congruent, authoritarian system may, for example, be much more effective than a generally participative system which is handicapped by inconsistencies and incongruities, and vice versa. In any case, this argument suggests that for a participative style to be effective in an organization, the other systems in the organization must be congruent with it. Much of the research on leadership does not address this issue, nor do the other chapters in this volume. They take the other systems in the organizations as givens (e.g., the reward system, the information and control system) and then ask the question, "How should the manager behave?"

My studies of successful participative organizations suggest that the correct way to view the problem is as a part of an overall design issue. Managerial behavior is just like the reward system, the job design, and the other features of an organization in that it must be designed to interface in a congruent manner with the other systems. These studies suggest that any managerial behavior or leadership style will only be as effective as the degree to which it is congruent with the other subsystems in an organization. Interestingly, the most effective participative organizations seem to be those new organizations where all the systems in the organization were designed from the ground up to be supportive of employee involvement in decision making. This finding supports the view that a key strategic design issue in the establishment of participative work settings is the congruent design of all systems in the setting.

Elsewhere, I have elaborated in more depth on what kind of information and control systems, job design systems, reward systems, and so on, are congruent with a participative approach to decision making (Lawler, 1981a). To mention just a few examples, such things as skill-based pay, job security guarantees, decentralized information and control systems, and group-process skill training seem to be very supportive of participative decision making. It still remains an open question as to what kind of support systems need to be designed in order to have participative decision making and how important each subsystem is in making participative decisions successful. It is hoped that future research will be able to analyze these relationships so that greater specification can be made of the types of overall organization designs and policies that are supportive of participative decision-making processes.

LEADERSHIP IN PARTICIPATIVE ORGANIZATIONS

A number of definitions of leadership emphasize that it is the influence on organizational behavior that is over and above the resort to authority and the mechanical compliance with routine directives of the organization (see, e.g., Zaleznik, 1977). In other words, it is that something extra that an individual does to influence behavior in organizations that is over and above job descriptions and traditional authority relationships. This definition calls for a focus in participative organizations on what it is that a leader needs to do and on how much time should be spent doing it. These two issues will be considered in the sections that follow.

The Role of Leaders

It is one thing to say that leaders are responsible for bringing those things to a work setting that influence behavior over and above the traditional controls, prescriptions, and rewards. It is quite another to say how this is accomplished. The traditional research on leadership provides few clues here, although several of the chapters in this volume provide some interesting thoughts. Siehl and Martin (Chapter 12) identify corporate culture transmission as an important leadership function. Prahalad and Doz (Chapter 22) point out that top management has as an important part of its role influencing "mind sets," "motivations," "power bases," and "building consensus." My observations of successful leaders in participative systems suggest that leadership is done through a combination of factors that can be captured by words like vision, communication, symbols, and charisma. Although most of the literature on leadership is notably silent on issues like vision, symbolism, and charisma, there are a few exceptions that can help us understand what is involved from a behavior point of view in providing direction in a participative organization.

The recent work by Bennis (1982) on chief executive officers gets at some of the issues involved in providing leadership. Bennis talks about successful leaders spending their time not on the "how to do it, nuts and bolts," but on the purpose of the organization and on paradigms of action. In short, they are not concerned with doing things right—the overriding concern of many managers—but with doing the right things. In many cases, they communicate this by talking about a compelling vision of a desired state of affairs. Sometimes they translate this vision into concrete terms through the use of a metaphor or through the description of goals and end states that they wish to achieve. Interestingly, they rarely specify in great detail how these goals are going to be achieved. In a sense, they tend to use what can be called a minimal specification design for mobilizing energy in the organization. This allows individuals to develop their own approaches to reaching the goals and, in the process, to become psychologically committed to the goals of the leader.

Closely related to the issue of vision and the ability to communicate is the skillful use of the symbols and symbolic events. As Bennis points out, effective leaders use a set of symbolic forms, ceremonies, and insignia to show that they are in fact leading and to point the direction in which they are leading. In my observations, effective leaders of participative organizations are often particularly skillful in this area. The use of symbols often includes the creation of very egalitarian perquisites and physical spaces in the organization. For example, in plants everyone enters through the same door, parks in the same lot, uses the same dining room, and so forth, while in large, high-technology companies like the one described by Siehl and Martin, no special benefits are given to executives in parking spaces, airplane travel, and many other areas.

The symbolism here is a strong way of saying that decisions are not to be made on the basis of power, but are to be made on the basis of expertise. Symbols that reinforce traditional power structures work strongly against making decisions on the basis of expertise. Few subordinates, for example, can overcome the symbolism of the typical chief executive officer's palatial office in order to deal with him or her as just another member of the organization. Admittedly, symbolism is only one step in changing the nature of decision making in organizations, but it can be an important one.

Symbolic rewards and events can also be used to influence the culture of participative organizations. Letting the work force off early or personally buying pizza for everyone when a new production goal is reached are examples of climate setters of symbolic value that help to define what the organization is all about. Similarly, in participative systems, having production employees host visitors — including the president of the company — can be another way of symbolizing and communicating the desired culture.

In most effective participative systems that I have studied the cumulative effect of a strong vision on the part of the leaders and communication of that vision is to create a work setting that is supportive of people performing at a high level. "Supportive" in a sense that leaders help provide the tools, skills, and coordination that are necessary for the organization to perform effectively and thus allow people to adapt the vision to their own definition of the situation. In a sense, the leader's job gets defined as creating an environment in which others are encouraged to perform well and in which they have the necessary skills and resources to perform well.

An interesting description of this way of thinking about management is provided by a manager in a large food chain: "We challenge ourselves to seek ways in which we can lead by helping, by teaching, by listening, and by managing in the true democratic sense, that is, with the consent of the managed. Thus the satisfaction of leadership comes from helping others to get things done and changed and not from getting credit for doing and changing things ourselves."

When this kind of setting is created, there is a powerful motivation for effective organizational performance. As Bennis (1982, p. 55) notes, "people knock themselves out in this kind of setting. In the cases of really successful leaders, they create and express an overall set of intentions which is attractive enough to both involve people and empower them. The space generated by such visions makes transformative leadership genuinely participative and noncoercive."

In short, Bennis is arguing that visions, when properly articulated and communicated, empower people because they provide a sense of direction and goals for people to strive toward and, when they are supplemented with providing the resources necessary to reach the goals, can be quite intrinsically motivating. In essence, as I have argued elsewhere, it is possible to create a work climate in which individuals are motivated toward seeing the organization be effective because they identify with its goals, objectives, and vision, and because they feel responsible for goal accomplishment (Lawler, 1980). This is quite consistent with the research on intrinsic motivation and suggests an interesting definition of successful leadership in a participative system. Leadership becomes the creation and communication of goals and visions that people accept as their own. It also includes the empowerment of people through providing resources and the capability to shape methods, procedures, and approaches to achieving the goals to fit their own skills, capabilities, and sense of social reality. When empowerment is combined with a vision, then greater self-management becomes possible and individuals become motivated to achieve the general goals of the organization.

In participative organizations, the most important part of the leadership culture may be the vision of how people will relate to the organization. Often this vision is clearly articulated in a set of operating principles or in a philosophy of management. In my experience, it is this component of participative management vision that sets the participative management organization off from other organizations. Many organizations have leaders who are able to articulate and to a degree symbolize the vision of how the organization should function. Often a poorly articulated part of this vision or a part that is articulated in a very traditional way is how people will relate to the organization. For example, traditional bureaucratic organizations such as the automobile companies and the public utilities have a fairly clearly articulated vision of how people will function in the organization. The problem with this vision is that it is not a very empowering one for individuals, nor does it deal very effectively with their needs for development, growth, and self-esteem.

Quite different is the empowering vision that exists in effective participative organizations. In these, the vision of human resource management is one that talks of personal growth and development, trust, moving knowledge and decisions to lower levels in the organization, and allowing people to define their own work environment. In my experience, it is this feature of the leadership vision that makes for effective participative organizations. The other part of an effective vision, of course, is the sense of what the organization needs to do in the business arena to be effective. As Bennis and others have pointed out, this vision needs to be not only technically correct, but compelling to others in the organization.

Time Spent on Leadership Activities

Because an important part of an effective leader's vision is how decisions are made, leaders often spend considerable time managing the decision-making process. This is certainly true in participative organizations. My studies of participative organizations suggest that top managers focus a great deal of attention on the decision-making process. They attend to such things as building a creditable decision process and deciding how various types of decisions will be made. This means doing such things as creating and working with task forces and committees. It means deciding where in an organization different decisions should be made. These issues are at the very core of participative approaches to management and, thus, if they are not handled well, the vision can become a farce that is quickly dismissed.

Most of the studies of how managers spend their time have been done in traditional work organizations. Similarly, the studies in the present volume were done in the laboratory or in traditional organizations. These studies suggest that many managers spend very little time engaging in what would be called leadership behavior (see, e.g., Mintzberg, 1973). Indeed, the results of these studies have led some to suggest that leadership is not a very important part of the manager's role in organizations. This may be quite true in traditional work organizations. After all, there are so many givens in traditional work organizations that not much time has to be spent doing things like defining directions, deciding on decision-making styles, influencing the climate, providing a sense of direction for the organization, and so forth. Indeed, it hardly seems surprising that in traditional work structures managers seem to focus primarily on the technical aspects of the work and that they often end up being involved in many routine day-to-day decisions about how the work is to be done.

My observations with respect to participative work organizations suggest a quite different picture. Particularly in the case of higher-level managers, a great deal of time is spent on leadership functions. Some comments during a recent interview captured this very nicely. The interview was with a manager of a new high-participation plant, and the question was, "How do you spend your time?" He commented that about 95 percent of his time was spent managing the culture and climate of his plant. He said the remaining 5 percent was spent on traditional production and technical management issues. Interviews with his subordinates suggested that the 95 percent estimate may be a bit high, but that he did spend most of his time worrying about the climate, decision-making styles and processes, and performing what may be called leadership functions.

As was mentioned earlier, quite a few managers have trouble adapting to situations where they need to spend their time performing leadership activities, and as a result end up being ineffective in participative management systems. In essence, the argument is that the job of a manager in a participative system is dramatically different from the job of a manager in a more traditionally managed system. It can be argued that this may change in future years. That is, as people begin to understand and begin to come into a participative system with a clear expectation about how they will operate and with the skills necessary to function in it, then the managers may not have to spend as much time managing and training people for the participative side of the venture. In the case of traditionally managed organizations, clearly, this happens now. People have, as a result of their education and other experiences in life, a well-developed sense of how a top-down system works. Thus, when they enter into traditionally managed organizations, they are already well socialized into the system and know "how to behave appropriately." Typically, when they enter into participative systems they do not have this preparatory socialization; indeed, they have things to unlearn. Hence, it is particularly critical that managers spend their time providing support for the participative structure of the organization.

Although there is some basis for the view that when participative organizations are more common in the society, managers will have less training to do, they may not be able to decrease the proportion of their time spent on leadership behaviors. Leadership behaviors in participative systems are the glue that holds it together and provides the sense of direction that is so necessary for it. Without these, even if people understand the participative process, it is unlikely that the organization could operate effectively without a strong input of appropriate leader behaviors.

Overall, leadership appears to be a particularly important influence on the success of participative organizations. Perhaps more so than in traditional organizations, managers need to be effective leaders. The effectiveness of these organizations depends on employees becoming committed to organization goals and on their accepting a vision of what the organization should be. In the absence of a leader who can communicate the vision and spend a major portion of his or her time in implementing it, participative organizations are unlikely to be effective.

CONCLUSIONS

This review of the key issues in managing participative organizations has suggested some interesting conclusions about some key strategic decisions in managing participative organizations, what constitutes effective leadership behavior, and some potential future directions for leadership research. It suggests quite strongly that all choices about which decision-making approach to use need to be made with an integrated organizational model in mind. When this is done, highly situational approaches become inappropriate, as does dividing organizations into islands with different leadership styles.

In the case of effective leadership behavior, it suggests that, at least in participative organizations, and perhaps in others, effective leaders spend their time in very different ways from ineffective ones. Concepts like vision, use of symbols, communicating goals and ideals, using metaphors to capture climate, managing climate, and managing participative decision-making processes seem to capture what effective leadership is all about. This is quite different from the picture of managerial behavior that emerges from some studies of how managers in organizations spend their time.

With respect to future research directions, a number of issues have been identified. To mention just a few: research is needed on how to choose among alternative participative decision processes, on the maturation of participative decision processes in groups, and on selection, training, and identification of managers for more participatively managed organizations. This research agenda has some important implications for the approaches to research which are appropriate. As Burgoyne and Hodgson mention in Chapter 9, data-collection methods need to be in harmony with the human processes that are being studied. The study of participative organizations would therefore seem to call for the use of participative research methods in which the "subjects" are partners in the research (see Seashore *et al.*, 1983). The issues also seem to call for the use of longitudinal designs that combine observation with other methods. Observation would seem to be particularly important if we are to understand better such things as how visions are communicated and climates defined.

One note of caution is in order here. Most of the existing observation-coding systems seem to be poorly suited to studying such issues as culture setting, empowering, and vision. The approach proposed by Luthans and Lockwood (Chapter 7) gets at some of the relevant issues (e.g., motivation), but does not seem to deal with others (e.g., goal setting, vision). It is hard to see how lab research has much to contribute to this research agenda. Recall approaches such as those advocated by Burgoyne and Hodgson may be useful, but they suffer from enough biases that they need to be cross-validated with other methods, such as longitudinal case studies, that contain a large amount of direct observation and objective data.

Perhaps the best way of summarizing the research situation is to reemphasize the point made at the beginning of the chapter. Perhaps without knowing it, we have developed findings and theories that are applicable to traditionally structured, designed, and managed organizations. Because of the lack of opportunity to study leadership and managerial behavior in participative organizations, we know very little about it. This strongly suggests that our knowledge of managerial behavior and leadership can be greatly increased by studying these phenomena in the kinds of settings that are typical of participative organizations. Not only does this hold the promise of enriching our approaches to studying and thinking about leadership; it holds the promise of creating more effective participative organizations.

19

Commentary on Part 4

Chapters 16 and 17 Commentary: Problems with Contingency Models of Leader Participation

John W. Slocum, Jr.

The concept of participation is an extremely useful tool for studying the process of leadership. Comprehensive reviews of the salient literature (see Kerr & Slocum, 1981; Locke & Schweiger, 1979; Strauss, 1977, 1982; Yukl, 1981) aver that forms of participation are functional when the following conditions are present: (1) the leader has the authority to make a decision; (2) the decision can be made without stringent time limitations; (3) subordinates have the relevant knowledge to discuss and implement the decision; (4) subordinates' characteristics (needs, values, personality traits) are congruent with the decision to participate; and (5) the leader is skilled in the use of participative techniques.

One underlying theme of participative leadership is self-control. Lawler comments that self-control is likely to exist when control systems have participatively set standards (1976b, p. 1282). Thus, when people are given the opportunity to participate in decisions, they are more likely to exercise self-control than when this opportunity is not available. Strauss concludes that "participation — in terms of employee influence — seems to work best in small firms, with simple labor-intensive technologies, where the work force is relatively homogeneous, where the work layout permits communications, and where the external environment is stable and predictable" (1982, p. 235). Others, such as Hackman (1976) and Zander (1982), explicate other conditions. Unfortunately, the literature is replete with studies supporting and disconfirming the success of various forms of participative leadership.

One of the reasons why the literature is a quagmire of results is a lack of a proper theoretical framework. The chapters by Drenth and Koopman and Heller are representative of this problem. The authors have not provided any paradigm that integrates various "contingencies" assumed to affect participation and a host of outcome variables. This problem is further exacerbated by the myriad of ways various authors have used to define "participation."

Participation is a metaconstruct (Schwab, 1980). A construct is any variable of a conceptual nature. Therefore, a construct is nothing more than a mental definition of a variable. If we treat participation as a construct, then the literature is full of contradictions. If we treat participation as a category, then many of the contradictions can be resolved. Most authors (e.g., Strauss, 1977, 1982) treat participation as a construct. According to Cronbach and Meehl (1955), metaconstructs are rarely linked to other variables with any precision at all because it is rare for two studies to measure the same construct in similar ways, under controlled settings. Drenth and Koopman, and Heller, in their chapters, attempt to link a construct (participation) with a categorical variable (nature of the decision and four phases of decision making). Unfortunately, one cannot hypothesize that there will be linkages between categories and constructs very well.

The Influence-Power Continuum, or IPC, is a metaconstruct. It is a series of categories that represent a behavioral decision process. That is, employees are asked to respond to how various operational decisions were made, for example, by the boss, by subordinates, jointly, and so on. Most behavioral decision-making research (Ungson & Braunstein, 1982) involves intensive case studies that involve observation of the bodies in action, interviews, collection of data from meetings, and unobtrusive measures. The methodology used by Drenth and Koopman and by Heller used these data bases. It is refreshing to see that these methods were employed instead of the usual paper-and-pencil measures that have been more typically used.

The problems with the participation/leadership literature range from a simple lack of clarity surrounding the construct of participation into theoretically testable hypotheses to explicit statements about empirical relationships expected when a contingency variable is believed to be operating. These problems are paramount in the work by Drenth and Koopman and Heller. In an insightful review of the contingency literature, Schoonhoven (1981) states that while the contingency approach is widely accepted (Hellriegel & Slocum, 1982), there are five problems with contingency theory. First, it is not a theory because it does not contain a well-structured set of propositions. Rather, she proposes that it is a metatheory or one that enables researchers to conceptualize how various constructs relate. The lack of an adequate theoretical framework has led to ambiguously worded statements, such as "fit," and "appropriate for," among others.

Second, most researchers fail to explicate what interaction is being predicted. When theorists assert that there is a relationship between participation in decision making and a contingency variable that predicts a third variable, effectiveness or satisfaction, they are stating that there is an interaction between the first two variables. Unfortunately, Drenth and Koopman do not give clear recognition to the fact that contingency arguments produce interactive propositions.

Third, most contingency researchers fail to specify the form of the interaction intended. That is, the mathematical function between IPC and each contingency variable was not made explicit. One consequence of this is that a mathematical function can take on several properties. The mathematical function that is used to express the interaction should be grounded in theory.

Fourth, because most contingency researchers assume a linear model and use correlational procedures, the relationships studied within a contingency framework are assumed to be linear. In Woodward's (1965) seminal work, she alerted researchers at least to check for nonlinear effects. While Drenth and Koopman use Kendall's tau in the analysis of complex decisions, the use of Pearson correlations for operational decisions assumes that contingency relationships are symmetrical.

Fifth, most contingency theorists implicitly assume symmetrical effects. For example, Fry and Slocum (1982) hypothesize that more formalized police units facing fewer exceptions and using analyzable search procedures would be more effective than those units using less formalized structures, facing fewer exceptions, and using analyzable search procedures. The implication of their argument is that if low values of formalization are combined with a routine technology or vice versa, then effectiveness will be lowered because no congruence exists between structure and technology. This argument suggests a nonmonotonic effect of structure on the range of uncertainty, rather than the usual assumption that an effect is constant over all values of the independent variable.

A Taxonomy

A taxonomy is proposed that incorporates many of the variables proposed in the Drenth and Koopman and Heller chapters. It provides a conceptual framework for describing and understanding the diversity of conditions under which participation may lead to desired outcomes. Unfortunately, the numerous dimensions on which organizations may vary makes the identification of a single taxonomic scheme extremely difficult. Instead, I have chosen to identify major sources of organizational and personal variation prevalent in the participation literature. For the purposes of this analysis, participation is bounded by the organization's technology, amount of information required to be processed by the individual, modes of control and coordination exercised by the organization, and the opportunity for the individual to engage in self-regulation.

Task Characteristics. The task characteristics identified by Perrow (1967) represent elements of uncertainty that have been the basis for several studies of organizational structure and process (see Daft & Macintosh, 1981). The basic dimensions are task variety and analyzability.

Task variety is the frequency of unexpected and novel events that occur in the transformation process. Variety represents the stimulus of uncertainty (Perrow, 1967). Low variety means that employees experience considerable certainty about the occurrence of future activities, when these activities will arrive for processing, and the form (Slocum & Sims, 1980). High variety means that participants typically cannot predict problems in the future, when they might be called upon to perform activities, and what form these problems will take.

Task analyzability concerns how individuals respond to problems that arise during the transformation process. When the transformation process is analyzable, employees typically follow an objective standard operating procedure to resolve the problem. A correct response can usually be identified by both the employee and the manager. Most managerial work is unanalyzable (Mintzberg, 1973). Few computational procedures will tell the manager exactly how to respond. The employees will have to spend time thinking about what to do, and they may actively search for solutions beyond normal procedures (see, for example, Heller's discussion of Stansted Airport).

Information-Processing Requirements of the Task. The proposition that task characteristics affect the information-processing requirements of the individual has been addressed by Daft and Macintosh (1981, pp. 209–211). These researchers outline two dimensions of information processing: amount and equivocality. The amount of information processing is defined as the volume or quantity of data about organizational activities that is gathered and interpreted by employees to complete the task successfully. In a work setting where an individual's understanding of the task is adequate and additional information is not sought, the amount of information processing required by the individual will be low. Conversely, in settings where the individual's knowledge of the task is limited, additional information will be sought.

Information equivocality is defined as the multiplicity of meanings conveyed by information about organizational activities. Originally proposed by Weick (1969), when information is clear and specific, it generally leads to a single uniform interpretation by individuals. This type of information is unequivocal. Information that lends itself to different and perhaps conflicting interpretations about the task is considered equivocal. In Drenth and Koopman's framework, operational decisions rely on unequivocal information processing; complex decisions rely on equivocal information processing.

Modes of Managerial Control and Coordination. According to Ouchi and Maguire (1975), Van de Ven and Delbecq (1974), and Van de Ven, Delbecq, and Koenig (1976), participation is linked to the organization's control and coordination systems. Van de Ven and his colleagues found that units with higher task difficulty and variability relied less on impersonal coordination mechanisms (i.e., rules, procedures, regulations) and more on personal modes.

They also found that group rather than impersonal modes of control in situations of higher task difficulty and variability were more effective. Increasing job interdependence among personnel had an additive effect in greater use of all modes of control. In following this line of research, it is proposed that modes of organizational control will typically vary according to uncertainties encountered by the employee and the amount of job interdependence. To explicate these differences, the three modes of control proposed by Van de Ven and his colleagues have been utilized.

A *systematized* mode entails: (1) a detailed set of procedures to be followed by the employee; (2) the standards to be attained at each step in the transformation; and (3) built-in monitoring devices that allow the manager to detect deviations from standards so that corrections can be made. Since the procedures are impersonally codified, their use requires little problem-solving communication between management and the employee. The systematized mode is designed by managers to create a program for efficiently organizing and managing tasks that occur repetitiously, and are generally understood by the employee. The employee is expected to give the same response each time the task is performed.

A *discretionary* mode generally consists of: (1) a repertoire of alternative plans for handling various problems; (2) a set of guidelines for exercising discretion in these situations; and (3) the specification of an expected quantity and quality of outputs to be achieved by the employee. The discretionary mode is created for handling problems that recur periodically, but exhibit moderate variation so that different methods or procedures are required of employees. Generally, however, the repertoire of responses is programmed in advance.

A *developmental* mode of managerial control consists of: (1) general goals to be achieved within a specified time; and (2) a set of norms and expectations regarding the general nature of behaviors and interactions among employees. The development mode is created by management for handling tasks that have not been encountered before and/or are sufficiently complex that they require search, evaluation, and judgment.

Self-Control. The discussion by Van de Ven and his colleagues has concentrated on modes of organizational control in relative absence of self-regulation. Cummings (1978) and Manz and Sims (1980) have suggested that in a self-regulated job, many functions traditionally reserved for management (i.e., determining the methods of work, control of variances, assigning members to tasks, allocating social rewards, and interfacing with the client) are taken over by the employee or a group of employees. This does not mean that some mode of managerial control is unnecessary, but that a possible shift in the mode of managerial control is required to achieve self-regulation. This notion of self-regulation can be tied to Van de Ven *et al.*'s three modes of managerial control. The systematized mode allows for the last amount of self-regulation. In this mode, the short-term behaviors of the employee are closely monitored. Conversely, the developmental mode allows the greatest amount of self-regulation. Overall managerial control is still present, but this control is focused on the outputs as opposed to the activities of the employee, and tends to be concentrated at the boundaries of the employee's task. The employee has considerable discretion as to how, when, where, in what order, and so on, the task is carried out. The intermediate discretionary mode allows for a moderate amount of self-regulation.

Table 19.1 illustrates how these variables can be systematically linked to participation. When the task is analyzable, low in variety, and the information-processing requirements of the task are small and unequivocal, participation in decision making (either operational or strategic) is not likely to affect the outcomes posited in the Drenth and Koopman or Heller research. According to Strauss (1982, p. 185), participation under these conditions is likely to deal with "tea and toilet" issues, rather than major issues. Under these conditions, the knowledge gap between employees and managers is large and participation accentuates rather than reduces the differences. Management does

Table 19.1. Participation taxonomy.

Task Characteristics		Type of Technology	Information-Processing Requirements of Task		Managerial Modes of Control and Coordination
Analyzable	Variety		Amount	Equivocality	
Analyzable	Low	Routine	Small	Low	Systematized
Analyzable	High	Engineering	Large	Low	Discretionary
Unanalyzable	Low	Craft	Small	High	Discretionary
Unanalyzable	High	Nonroutine Technology	Large	High	Developmental

not provide the employees with information they need to make a meaningful contribution to either operational and/or complex problems. Therefore, it is not surprising that few of the contingency variables proposed by Drenth and Koopman moderated the relationships for employees making operational decisions. To the extent that participation improves communication between management and the employees, one might expect to find that "frequency of work consultation" might be linked to affective responses. The following hypothesis is advanced from this logic:

> HYPOTHESIS 1: *Task characteristics, information-processing require- ments, management modes of control, and the nature of the decision positively interact to affect the extent of participation and its impact on outcomes.*

The argument assumes a positive monotonic effect of four contingency variables on outcomes. The monotonic assumption is incompatible with the symmetrical property of contingency arguments identified by previous re- searchers. As a consequence, we should expect a nonmonotonic effect of these contingency variables over the range of outcome variables. Therefore, this hypothesis should be partitioned to reflect this problem. The following propo-

Table 19.1. Participation taxonomy. *(continued)*

Self-Control	Nature of Decision[1] Operational	Complex	Outcomes of Participation[2]	Examples
Low	Small	None	Low satisfaction with participation Low general satisfaction Low utilization of skills	Assembly line Clerical Machine operator
Medium	High	Small	Moderate utilization of skills Moderate satisfaction with parti- cipation Moderate general satisfaction	Engineering Computer program- ming Accounting
Medium	High	Medium	Moderate to high utilization of skills Moderate to high satisfaction with participation Moderate to high general satisfaction	Master chefs, Stockbrokers Faculty members Elective surgery members
High	High	High	High utilization of skills High satisfaction with participation High general satisfaction	R&D Strategic planners Disaster workers Social scientists

[1]The adjectives indicated assume that participation is desired by managers and reflect probable employee reactions.
[2]Assumption: Workers have the requisite needs, abilities, and values for participation.

sitions are examples of contingency propositions using effectiveness as a dependent variable:

> PROPOSITION 1: *When the task is analyzable and low in variety, increases in participation involving operational decisions have a negative influence on effectiveness.*

> PROPOSITION 2: *When the information-processing requirements of the task are low in amount and unequivocal, increases in participation involving operational decisions will have a negative influence on effectiveness.*

> PROPOSITION 3: *When the mode of managerial control is systematized, increases in participation involving operational decisions will have a negative influence on effectiveness.*

What is needed is an elaborate set of contingency propositions arguing that task characteristics, information-processing requirements of the task, modes of managerial control, and the nature of the decision interacting with participation will increase or decrease effectiveness. One should be looking at the explanatory power of an interaction after controlling for the main effects of variables comprising the interaction term. This model will permit one to explore fully the range of the contingency variables' influence on effectiveness.

Conclusion

Participation is a sharing of information, power, and influence between employees and managers. Participative leader behavior features the treatment of subordinates as equals and allows for employees to influence leaders' actions and decisions. It is necessary to specify under what conditions participation is likely to improve effectiveness. With a focus on the contingency variables posited in Table 19.1, certain circumstances must be present for participation to promote effectiveness. First, the level of participation must be appropriate to the task itself. If participative leadership is employed when the task is analyzable, has little variety, requires a small amount of processing of unequivocal data, and is imbedded in a systematized management control system, participation may actually direct subordinates' motivations away from work-related issues. Second, the employees must have values, needs, and abilities that support this kind of leadership. Third, the extent of participation will vary according to the phases of the decision-making process. Fourth, the type of decision (operational versus complex) will influence the extent to which participation is likely to influence effectiveness.

Part 4 Integrative Comments: Leadership, Participation, and Nontrivial Decision Making

Bernard M. Bass

In an earlier publication (Bass & Rosenstein, 1977), we suggested that the practice of participative management and industrial democracy should be contingent upon the issues to be decided. Neither seemed appropriate generally for dealing with ways of floating long-term bond issues. Participation by worker representatives on management councils seemed more suited for examining employee benefit plans while informal participative leadership, face-to-face joint consultation of superior and subordinate, seemed best for dealing with the problems in work design. The chapters in this part lend support to such a contingent rationale that participation is more likely with tactical rather than strategic decisions. Moreover, they do so by showing such contingent effects over time. In addition, they provide evidence that differences in participation by workers and management at various levels depend upon which phase of the decision process is examined.

Before an attempt at integration and extension of the chapters, some problems are mentioned.

First, it is necessary to elaborate on what Slocum has said about possible nonlinear effects. Several times in the Drenth and Koopman study, there may be much potential for fan-shaped distributions of the covarying data to appear. On the one hand, where a leader or a system permits participation, it is possible to obtain considerable variation in subordinate participation, in whether people are satisfied with the status quo, and with contingent effects. For example, a leader may continually call for worker inputs into deliberations. Competent workers may respond a great deal; incompetent workers may be content to remain silent. On the other hand, where the leader or the system does not tolerate worker participation, then little variation in worker influence is possible from one situation to the next. Neither competent nor incompetent workers will be able to have much influence. So, when correlating such results, one ought to scatter-plot the data, or to examine the data for heterogeneity of variance, to see whether or not fan-shaped distributions of influence emerge.

The Drenth and Koopman chapter, based on Heller's earlier methodological contribution, raises an interesting question. An important part of their work involves breaking up the decision process into four sequential phases: start-up, development, finalization, and implementation. Manager and worker influence are seen as greater and better for the decision, depending on which phase of the decision is examined. One problem is that most such decisions do not move ahead in an orderly, sequential fashion. More often, they are likely to proceed by fits and starts, by cycling backward almost as much as forward. One may think the decisions are in the development stage when in fact higher authority has already made up its mind and is seeking justification and political support for its position. Huff (this volume) and Bass (1983) elaborate on this point. Awareness of a problem may have been seen three years before the right executives meet fortuitously and discover mutual interest in starting work on the problem (March & Romelaer, 1976). Again, how to plot data along the abscissa of time is a challenging question. If one breaks the total profile of decision activity from its inception to its final implementation into equal time intervals, documentary analyses disclose that after a flurry of start-up activity, the decision lies almost dormant as it gestates until 40 to 50 percent of all participation and activity occurs in the last few periods of time. That is, most of the work on a decision that takes four years to resolve occurs in the fourth year. Most of the work on a decision that takes four days to resolve occurs on the fourth day (Witte, 1972).

What is most gratifying about the work of Heller and Drenth and Koopman is that they have moved leadership research into the empirically under-researched area of organizational decision making. For applying his methodology, Heller returned to the Stansted Airport deliberations, an earlier phase of which Alexander (1979) had examined a decade earlier to focus attention on the impact of premature closure on the decision. This marks the coming together of longitudinal leadership study and what has before been done by people primarily not in the same subset of investigators in the field of organizational decision making. Huff's think piece in this volume (Chapter 14) might also be considered in a similar manner.

As an aside, it is clear that such studies will require long-term support, particularly if one pursues the innovative Heller design. Here decisions are studied both retrospectively, then prospectively, before the results are integrated. Retrospective study is by interviews with informants and analyses of available documents. Prospective study is by observation of meetings and interviews.

In the statement of the analysis of the expected flows in Heller's chapter, the analysis of conflict becomes rather important. There is a decided paucity of studies on the subject. Narayanan and Fahey (1982) emphasize that the organizational decision-making process is a political one. It does not follow the rational, task-oriented, flow that one would expect from problem to search for solution, and then on to evaluation and choice of solution. Rather, it starts with an activation process that begins with a fuzzy idea in one person's head. This leads the person to mobilize other people to agree with him or her. This, in turn, moves on to the formation of a coalition in which a consensus is developed about the nature of the problem and what needs to be done about it. Next come encounters with the opposition – other coalitions. These are other groups that advocate the status quo or working against the proposals of the initiating coalition. Finally, a decision emerges that develops out of a process of conflict resolution between the opposing coalitions. This framing of the decision process in a political context will add much to our understanding of the performance of many more successful organizational leaders.

There is much needed research in this field of organizational decision making. It intermingles with other issues of leadership and decision making that have been discussed above.

There is actually a surplus of theory but a shortage of empirical research on processual studies of leadership and organizational decision making. Optimists tend to feel that there is great opportunity here. Heller points out that these decisions are particularly available to study because they are made in committee. One can observe what is happening. Nevertheless, pessimists note that what is heard and what is really happening are two different things.

Even if it were possible to hear all the discussions and arguments that went on before an organizational decision, it would often be impossible to separate out the business justifications from the personal rationalizations – the hidden agenda, the blind agenda, and personal motivations. This is what makes it particularly difficult to tease out what happened and why. Nevertheless, I feel that there is great opportunity here for sophisticated research.

Until recently, in the West at least, decision making was conceived as an orderly, forward-moving, causal, means-to-ends phenomenon. Orientals, on the other hand, have tended to pursue a more cyclical kind of thinking about it. In the last quarter-century, thanks to March and Simon (1958) in particular, in considering this issue of how organizational decisions are made, we have moved toward description and away from prescription. The fixed, ideal goal of the classical decision maker has been replaced by a readjusted, displaced objective. The logic-driven complete search has become limited. The infinite perfection of information has been rejected as impossible. Rationalization has become as important as rationality. Disorderliness, incrementalism, serendipity, and contiguity of persons and problems have been elevated to key aspects in the organizational decision process.

Consider the Cohen, March, and Olsen (1972) garbage-can model of organizational decision making. If we really want to understand how organizational decision making gets done, how decision processes develop, it is just a matter of looking into the garbage can and seeing who happens to meet with whom, about what issues, at what time. For contingent analyses, this model is the most contingent of all. It emphasizes that executives carry around a portfolio of problems in their back pockets. When they happen to meet, sometimes in a hallway or an elevator, they pull out these different kinds of problems. In fact, it is suggested that effective managers, depending on whom they fortuitously encounter as they move around the hallways or enter elevators, carry on decision processes with the relevant others they happen to meet.

While this garbage-can model seems an appropriate fit for anarchic organizations and universities, I believe it fails to encompass many other possible decision flows. There are numerous other causal linkages between the idealized phases of organizational decision making from scanning to problem discovering and diagnosis, to search and innovation, to evaluation and choice, and to authorization and implementation (Bass, 1983).

It seems reasonable to suggest that all these cause-effect linkages are likely to be seen, but in differing amounts and in varying significance. It becomes an empirical question of how much each causal linkage is present. It is likely that effective organizational decision processes will tend to display more of some linkages than others. For example, organizations that focus mainly on search for justification where managers must primarily be naive advocates rather than naive scientists are likely to be in a state of decay. But organizations that demand only naive scientists, and exclude naive lawyers, also do so at the peril of losing the support of higher and outside authority.

In the garbage-can model, preferences are ill defined, inconsistent, unclear, uncertain, problematic. This means that the organization uses are unclear and misunderstood by their own members. Learning and precedence are matters of accident and trial and error. Such organizational anarchy is characterized by weakened linkages in the model discussed above.

Some degree of contiguity in time or place of problems and persons is mandatory for an easy flow of process. (Try to get together a selected set of faculty members on a college campus and it is easy to see what I mean about the problems of trying to maintain contiguity.) We can't take advantage of contiguity by making it easier for certain executives to be closer together in time and space. We put the offices of some people who would most normally work together as close as possible. But total dependence on contiguity to drive the system will make for organizational disaster.

It appears that organizational decisions are likely to be most effective if characterized by strong forward linkages but with bursts of accompanying backward linkages. Such linkage analysis may be an important guide to effective decision making. This is consistent with Maier's (1963) staging and Kepner and Tregoe's (1965) training for effective decision making.

Cross-cultural effects are likely. Cartesian-trained Frenchmen should more likely emphasize formal, orderly, forward linking in contrast to the Japanese who are more likely to pursue non-Western logic.

Whether or not this model is the basis for empirical research is of less consequence than the fact that the Heller and Drenth and Koopman chapters illustrate the fruitfulness of the merging of longitudinal leadership studies and what in the past has been seen separately as the study of organizational decision making.

In Bass and Rosenstein (1977), attention was focused on the distinction between participative management (a style of management emphasizing power sharing in the decision process) and industrial democracy (legislated power sharing through elected representatives). Lawler, in Chapter 18, adds another important distinction. Participative management may take the form of participative leadership in supervisory-subordinate relations or it may be seen in the way the organization is arranged to share power in the decision process. Lawler mentions three such organizational circumstances as examples. Management designs plans and policies to involve employees at all levels in the decision process. In a second instance, unions and management set up cooperative, problem-solving projects. A third approach builds around plantwide bonus systems, and by its nature encourages participation at all levels to be successful. The research literature has focused on participative leadership rather than participative organizations. Lawler offers a number of propositions about the latter. For example, he suggests that islands of participative management in a sea of traditional authority are likely to be disruptive; contingent approaches to leadership style become illegitimate. A core style is needed with variations associated with different kinds of participation — dyadic, group, representative. What needs to be learned by both supervisors and subordinates seems close to what was preached at Bethel in the 1950s — how to be a good group member. But Lawler offers some interesting specific advice. Groups need supervisory structuring early in their history to avoid narrow, self-interested decisions and inability to confront issues. Groups should be permitted to deal with their own pay, and difficult personnel decisions are seen by conventional wisdom as better left to higher authority. As with Bass and Rosenstein, Lawler feels that research is needed on which kinds of substantive decisions can best be handled by participation. Particularly important is the group's maturity level and the phase in which the decision happens to be. Heller's and Drenth and Koopman's work, of course, support the latter point.

Lawler notes the difficulty of changing traditional autocrats into participative democrats. One reason seems to be that autocrats tend to be happy with their own ways of behaving (Farrow & Bass, 1977). Also, the change is often superficial. The new democrats spout the right words, but their behavior fails to change with their verbalizations.

With reference to the need for designing support systems to accompany participation, it should be noted that the reverse is happening in the command-and-control structures of the modern management information systems. Computers make participation in the input phase of decision making easy at all levels; nevertheless, centralization of decision making is increased as information from throughout the system can be processed and integrated (not necessarily too well) at the most central or highest level.

Lawler points to what a few of us have been saying about leadership in recent years. It is not only a transactional process; it can also be transformational (see Bass, 1981, pp. 609–611). Transformational leaders promote participation because they provide visions and metaphors that rarely specify the needed details that remain to be filled in through participation by all concerned. The transforming leader creates the vision and the environment in which subordinates can grow. Much of his or her time continues to be spent in leadership rather than nonleadership managerial functions. Lawler sees leadership as more important to participative than to traditional organizations. (This is true for process, but certainly not for substance. The autocrat or directive leader in the traditional organization can place a heavy hand on everything and anything. Yet, more leadership, in the aggregate, is seen in the participative organization.)

Lawler has made an important contribution here in focusing on the peculiarities of the participative organization and the failure of most leadership research to deal adequately with the challenges it presents to our understanding of effective leadership when, as a matter of policy and planning, organizations are committed to a participative approach.

Part 5

Think Pieces on Overcoming the Ruling Paradigmatic Orthodoxy

Introduction

James G. Hunt, Dian-Marie Hosking,
Chester A. Schriesheim, and Rosemary Stewart

There are three think pieces in this part: Chapter 20, "Leader Discretion as a Key Component of a Manager's Role," by Ilene F. Gast; Chapter 21, "Emerging Technologies: The Challenge to Leadership Theory," by Richard N. Osborn, Frederic A. Morris, and Patrick E. Conner; and Chapter 22, "Managing Managers: The Work of Top Management," by C. K. Prahalad and Yves L. Doz.

In this introduction, we first summarize their individual content in some detail. We then look at them in terms of Peter Clark's integrating commentary theme — as questioning the paradigmatic orthodoxy in the leadership literature. A key reason why Clark was chosen to write an integrative commentary was because of his background in both micro and macro aspects of organizations. The diversity of the contributions makes such a background particularly important.

We suggest that the reader treat these think pieces in the way we treat them here; that is, each can first be read for its own contribution. This will reveal a range of innovative ideas offering much future research potential. The reader can also keep Clark's key points in mind as he or she reads them as an integrated set.

Let us now look at the individual content of each chapter. Gast addresses a concept that is receiving increasing emphasis in the leadership and organizational literature — discretion. Discretion is conceptualized and measured in different ways by different researchers and, indeed, comparison and contrast among these researchers is a major aspect of her chapter. In general, however, Gast sees the concept as concerned with a manager's freedom to make decisions and choices and the power to make judgments and act. Gast emphasizes the importance of the concept in expanding our knowledge of managerial behavior and leadership. She also points out a number of managerial and research implications that stem from the various models using discretion which she reviews.

In the Osborn, Morris, and Conner piece it is argued that there is a tendency for the emergence of new kinds of technologies to deal with the increasingly sophisticated problems of society. These new technologies are considered to possess at least two important attributes. First, they are controversial — politically sensitive, emotionally charged, publicly visible. Second, they must typically accommodate the goals and requirements of several political actors.

The authors contend that leadership models, as currently conceptualized, cannot deal effectively with these kinds of technologies. What is needed, they say, is a new perspective on leadership which involves the patterning of attention, activity, and reinforcement. Osborn and his associates then define and elaborate on this patterning concept. One key question throughout is concerned with who establishes the patterns, and how. Whereas typical leadership models would focus on one individual ("the leader"), in the Osborn, Morris, and Conner approach the unit of analysis for patterning may be sets of individuals, units, and even whole organizations. In this, the chapter appears to bear a close relation to Dachler's commentary (in Chapter 6). The piece ends with a series of loosely stated but insightful propositions for readers to ponder on the road to operationalizing the concepts in the chapter.

The Prahalad and Doz chapter focuses on the activities involved in managing or leading top-level managers. Interestingly, it is one of only a handful of works concerned with a *systematic* study of the activities of top-level managers (see Kotter, 1982).

The chapter summarizes an ongoing study of top-level managers in complex corporate organizations who are confronted with significant changes in the business' strategic and managerial requirements. The study was designed to help bridge the gap between concrete descriptions of activities (e.g., Mintzberg, 1973; Martinko & Gardner, Chapter 8, this volume) and abstract analysis of tasks. Using extended interviews, the authors develop a model that describes the key elements involved in managing upper-level managers where there is a major strategic redirection.

In terms of a common thread, Clark argues in his commentary that there are three sets of problems which the chapters raise. First is the question of the degree to which the "ruling paradigmatic orthodoxy" is imposing restrictions on future work. In other words, is a paradigm shift needed or can current leadership models such as those by Fiedler, House, Vroom and Yetton, and the like be modified to meet theoretical and practical research needs?

Second, what kinds of theoretical inquiry are necessary to meet the goals set by each of the three diverse chapters? Accompanying this is the question of the methods of research necessary to accomplish these goals. Clark argues that all of the pieces call for a theoretical reformulation away from simple control models and toward various kinds of process models.

Third is the question of how the temporal, processual, and historical dimensions involved in the second question should be addressed.

Clark uses the above points as an integrative theme. He goes beyond this, however, by using elaborations of open-systems theory to build on a number of areas treated in the chapters.

Finally, his commentary brings out some of the differences in perspective often found between European and North American or at least *traditional* North American scholars.

As already mentioned, Clark emphasizes the importance of time in these pieces. The reader may want to relate that to other chapters in the book where time appears to be particularly important. Heller's chapter (16) and Huff's think piece (Chapter 14) are perhaps two of the most obvious of these. These, plus the think pieces in this part all involve processual analysis in one way or another. This kind of analysis is a useful melding point for both radical and conservative approaches (a radical conceptualization that could utilize conservative methodology).

An issue that emerges from the Osborn, Morris, and Conner chapter concerns operationalizing the concepts — especially activity patterning. How might one do this? What modifications are needed in the concept to make it operational? If the concept is viable operationally, to what extent might it be applicable in traditional technologies as well as the "innovative" ones discussed by the authors? What seem to be the similarities and differences between this approach and the social-systems approach discussed by Dachler in Chapter 6?

Finally, as one reads Gast's think piece on managerial/leader discretion, a key concern is how one might extend her work into an operational model that would overcome some of the shortcomings in the current literature.

20

Leader Discretion as a Key Component of a Manager's Role*

Ilene F. Gast

In recent years, researchers have begun to focus on the influence that an organization's context and its environment have on managerial effectiveness. With the shift has come an increasing interest in the processes that enable managers to interact successfully with their environment. One such process is the use of discretion, or the manager's freedom or authority to make decisions and choices, and power to make judgments or to act.

A manager's ability to use discretion effectively is important because so many of the manager's duties are not spelled out by formal job descriptions. Although the position description may generally address the organization's mission and describe some key tasks and the methods used to accomplish them, the burden remains on the manager, who must fit the pieces together and get the job done. In exercising discretion, the manager must also prioritize duties and responsibilities, juggle conflicting demands, and balance his or her goals with those of the organization.

Discretionary actions enable managers to mobilize their authority and personal power in an attempt to influence individuals and features of the organization. How well managers can exercise discretion depends on their ability to assess constraints imposed by the organization's environment, structure, technology, policy, and procedures. Success also depends on how accurately managers assess social and political relationships within the organization and limitations placed on their discretion by other individuals in the organization.

At this time, only a limited body of theoretical and empirical work on managerial discretion exists. This chapter attempts to present, critique, and integrate the existing literature. Implications of this material for managers, practitioners, and directions for future research are discussed.

---

*The author wishes to thank Dr. Lynn Offermann of George Washington University and Robert Anderson of the U.S. Office of Personnel Management for their valuable advice and comments on earlier drafts of this chapter.

A REVIEW OF THEORY AND EMPIRICAL FINDINGS ON MANAGERIAL DISCRETION

The Multiple-Influence Model of Leadership

Hunt and Osborn (1980) have developed a detailed leadership theory that incorporates the concept of leader discretion. Their Multiple-Influence Model of Leadership views the leader as a link between the formal organization and the members of the work group. The effectiveness of a leader's performance is determined by a wide range of factors including variables at the environmental, organizational, group, task, and individual levels of analysis.

The Multiple-Influence Model differentiates between behavior that is under the leader's control—discretionary leadership—and behavior that is not—required leadership. *Required leadership* consists of "those minimal interactions with subordinates dictated by the position occupied by the leader in the organizational hierarchy" (Martin, Hunt, & Osborn, 1981, p. 234). Requirements are set by the leader's position in the organizational hierarchy, the leader's span of control, the technology employed, the work group's mission, and the organization's structure and environment. All leaders at a given organizational level will share similar requirements if these factors are held constant. Conversely, *discretionary leadership* consists of "those leader behaviors or influence attempts under the control of the leader which are over and above that typically vested in the role" (Martin, Hunt, & Osborn, 1981, p. 234).

Discretionary leadership can improve organizational effectiveness. The formal role requirements as dictated by organizational structures, rules, and procedures are often too generalized to deal with specific conditions in work units, especially in complex and unstable organizations. Through the use of discretion, the effective leader supplements the formal properties of the organization and fills in the "gaps" that arise between role requirements and organizational processes.

Discretionary leadership can also positively affect the attitudes and perceptions of subordinates and improve the leader's ability to exert influence. Martin and Hunt (1981) draw on reinforcement theory and exchange theory to explain how discretionary leadership affects employee performance and satisfaction. When the reinforcement contingencies are adequate and operate well, required leadership will be sufficient. Employees can easily determine what they have to do in order to obtain favorable outcomes. Gaps, however, disrupt these contingencies. Through the use of discretion, the effective leader clarifies the desired performance and its relationship to favorable outcomes. By filling in these gaps the leader acquires influence.

Exchange theory explains why a leader acquires influence by filling in the gaps. By exercising discretionary leadership, leaders contribute to the group effort. Over time, bonds or positive exchange relations develop between leaders and subordinates. An individual acquires influence within the group when he or she has the opportunity to make a contribution that helps a group attain shared objectives and makes the contribution. Eventually, control shifts from the formal properties of the organization to the leader and legitimizes the action of the leader. Higher levels of organizational complexity and uncertainty offer leaders greater opportunity to help group members reach shared goals; leaders can, thus, acquire and exercise influence over the group.

Attribution theory provides an alternative explanation. When subordinates attribute behavior to the leader personally rather than to the role requirements inherent in the position, a leader's behavior carries more weight with subordinates. Thus, they will react more favorably to the leader and work harder to help him or her achieve unit goals.

Martin and Hunt used Schriesheim's (1978) modification of the Leader Behavior Description Questionnaire (LBDQ) to assess discretion in four leadership activities: role clarification; work assignments; rules and procedures; and support. Martin and Hunt modified the LBDQ response categories to reflect both theoretical frameworks. For the reinforcement/exchange-theory framework, subordinates rated the 16 LBDQ items as follows: can and does; could but doesn't; can't and doesn't; and can't but tries anyway. For the attribution-theory framework, subordinates indicated whether they believed the leader or the environment was in control of each of the four leadership activities above by dividing 100 points between the leader and the organization.

Because the Multiple-Influence Model is the best articulated of the models to be discussed in this chapter, it is also the easiest to critique. The model is a detailed and reasonable representation of what leaders face in organizations. Nevertheless, the theory is in need of some refinement. First, some of its underlying concepts, particularly discretionary leadership and required leadership, need to be clarified. The proposed dichotomy between discretionary and required leadership does not hold up under examination. Leaders often make decisions and choices (i.e., exercise discretion) in carrying out their formal role requirements. They can choose how to organize their time, what methods and procedures to use, and whom to assign to various tasks. In other situations, leaders may appear to be exercising discretion when they really have no choice in the matter; peers and superiors may be forcing them to take certain actions. Finally, there are situations in which a leader appropriately chooses to do nothing. Thus, discretionary leadership and the exercise of discretion may not be the same thing, and this can be confusing. What happens if the subordinates who are being influenced by discretionary leadership become similarly confused? Will the exchange relations develop as proposed?

Second, the theory could benefit from improved means of operationalizing discretionary leadership. The LBDQ behavior categories are limited to interactions between supervisors and their subordinates. Leaders often exercise discretion beyond the confines of the work group and in areas that remain hidden from subordinates. Further, subordinates are often not in a position to observe all the things their supervisors do. For this reason, a wider range of leader behaviors should be included in this model, and ratings also might be obtained from a leader's peers and superiors.

A final concern stems from the implicit assumption that discretionary leadership is always desirable. Leaders may use acquired influence to build empires or to protect their turf without regard to overall organizational effectiveness. Although the work unit and its members may continue to prosper and support their leader, the organization as a whole may suffer.

Leadership as Incremental Influence

Katz and Kahn (1978) consider the essence of leadership to be incremental influence or "the influence over and above mechanical compliance with routine directives" (p. 528). Incremental influence is similar to Hunt and Osborn's (1980) discretionary leadership since both concepts address the influence a leader acquires by giving more to the job than would be specified by the position's expressed minimal requirements. The two concepts, however, have different roots. Katz and Kahn draw on French and Raven's (1959) power typology to explain incremental influence. Katz and Kahn differentiate between *formal* power bases which derive from the organization and include legitimate power (or power vested in the position), coercive power, and reward power; and *informal* bases of power which derive from the leader and include expert power and referent power (power based on identification with or liking for another person). Incremental influence results from the successful use of both informal power bases.

The effective leader is able to use all five power bases. All leaders have access to the formal power bases, but optimum use of these power bases depends on the individual's ability. Informal power bases cannot be conferred by the organization. Leaders who can utilize expert and referent power have an edge. They have access to power bases beyond those that stem from the organization. Thus, incremental influence increases the control that leaders can exert over employee performance. In addition, subordinates respond more willingly to these informal bases of power than they do to the coercion and manipulation inherent in the formal power bases.

Katz and Kahn's discussion raises important questions about the role played by power in the exercise of discretion. One involves the relationship between discretionary leadership and incremental influence. Since both are proposed to increase a leader's influence over employees, they might be causally related. Each of the power bases utilized by the leader might also be examined for its role in determining specific decisions and choices that an individual leader can make. Finally, it seems likely that powerful leaders may be able to exercise more discretion than those who lack power.

Executive Discretion and Organizational Decision Making

Pfeffer and Salancik (1978) examine the role individuals play in shaping the structure and activities of organizations. They believe that the environment constrains the organization's structure and activities, but reject the idea of environmental determinism. There is much empirical evidence demonstrating how organizational administrators not only affect organizational decisions, but also benefit from the results at the expense of long-range organizational goals. Pfeffer and Salancik therefore, propose that a more realistic view of organizational action "would recognize that organizational actors mold organizational activities but do so within constraints which limit their discretion to take action" (p. 245).

Pfeffer and Salancik emphasize the social and political constraints faced by managers. They claim that one of the most important things about discretion is that it is rarely unilateral; more often it is shared. In order to exercise discretion, managers must depend both on their superiors who provide support and their subordinates who control resources or performance.

Pfeffer and Salancik cite three of their own studies demonstrating the social constraints on leader discretion. A first study illustrates how supervisors' activities were in part determined by those in their "role set." When supervisors' characteristics and work activities resembled those of subordinates, supervisors tended to behave according to their subordinates' demands. Supervisors were more likely, however, to conform to their superiors' demands if supervisors resembled their bosses and faced performance pressure. A second study found that when supervisors were required to engage in a high degree of interdepartmental coordination, they were less likely to attend to their subordinates' demands. A third study examined the amount of discretion mayors had in determining items for their cities' budgets. Mayors who had to confront potent organized interest groups (managers, professionals, and unions) had less discretion over the budget than those whose cities had a higher proportion of nonwhites, government employees, and construction workers and a lower median income — people who intended not to rally for or against issues.

Pfeffer and Salancik have not developed a theory involving discretionary behavior by managers but they do recognize that one is needed. Such a theory would assess how much constraint an administrator faces in formulating action and would specify how much effect an administrator can or should have and under what conditions. Pfeffer and Salancik also emphasize the social implications of shared discretion. Because discretion is shared, a leader must consider and obtain the support and collaboration of other people before he or she can exercise discretion. Further, they emphasize the need to evaluate the effectiveness of a leader's use of discretion since managers often act in their own self-interest.

Competing Sources of Control in Organizations

Kerr and his associates (Kerr, 1977; Kerr & Jermier, 1978; Kerr & Slocum, 1981) also address constraints that leaders face when they attempt to exercise discretion, particularly in controlling employee performance. Kerr and Slocum (1981) point out that within an organization, there are a number of potential sources of control over employee performance. The formal leader is only one such source. Others include formal job descriptions, training programs, task specifications, work groups, and professional norms and values. Each of these sources is capable of providing workers with: (1) *information* about the task at hand, how to do it, and upon task completion, how well it has been done; and (2) *incentives* that motivate employees to perform tasks and pursue organizational objectives. Generally, the formal leader is responsible for providing information and incentives. However, the other sources of control may act as "substitutes" for the formal leader (Kerr, 1977; Kerr & Slocum, 1981).

Depending on the leader's characteristics and the role he or she plays, substitutes may enhance or hinder supervisory effectiveness. Substitutes can offer plausible alternatives to supervisory control. First, the leader often has other critical duties that conflict with monitoring employee performance. Second, the supervisor's skills may be inadequate to qualify him or her as the primary agent of control. Third, the supervisor may be too busy or too far away to provide employees with timely feedback. Finally, if a supervisor has a tendency to overcontrol employees, intentionally or not, a climate may be created that impedes the growth and development of employees. Conversely, substitutes can interfere with supervisory effectiveness. This can occur when substitutes are strong enough to entirely negate the supervisor's ability to influence subordinate performance.

The work of Kerr and his associates details a number of sources with whom the leader must share his or her discretion. It also suggests a number of consequences that may result if the leader exerts influence when none is necessary. Thus, choosing not to act may be the most effective alternative in certain circumstances; not taking action can represent discretionary behavior. This theory, however, lacks a systems perspective. It narrowly focuses on the relationship between the leader and each individual substitute without considering the organizational context. The organization more probably mediates the effect substitutes have on each other and on the leader.

Demands, Constraints, and Choices in Managerial Positions

Rosemary Stewart's perspective differs from those presented so far. Her primary interest is in the position rather than the manager holding it. Stewart (1982a) has developed a model for describing the differences between managerial jobs. She sees all managerial jobs as consisting of three components: an inner core of demands; an outer boundary of constraints; and an in-between area of choices. *Demands* are the activities the manager must do, lest he or she invoke organizational sanctions. Some factors determining demands include output specifications, requirements for personal involvement with work, bureaucratic procedures that cannot be delegated, and required contacts and relationships. *Constraints* are factors inside and outside the organization that limit what the manager can do. They include resource restrictions; laws, policies, and regulations; technology; people's attitudes toward the manager; the extent to which the manager's area of responsibility is defined; and the probability of outcome acceptance. Given the demands and constraints within any managerial position, some *choices* remain. Generally, the manager has some choice about which aspects of the job he or she cares to emphasize, how much time to devote to various responsibilities, which responsibilities to delegate, and how much time to spend with people.

Stewart developed and refined her model over the course of several years. She validated it using a variety of research methods including lengthy open-ended interviews with managers and their bosses, group discussions, on-site observation of managers, specially designed diaries kept by managers, and records of incoming mail. She tested it in managerial training programs by having middle- and senior-level managers use it to analyze their jobs.

Stewart's focus on the manager's job is important. With her model, a managerial position might be evaluated according to its potential for the amount and kind of discretion a manager could conceivably exercise. Such a measure could serve as a baseline against which a manager's use of discretion could be assessed. This model also suggests a means of clarifying the concept of discretionary leadership described in the Multiple-Influence Model. Stewart's demands are "musts," rather than the "shoulds" that required leadership behaviors are. Because required leadership includes an element of choice, the distinction between discretionary leadership and required leadership is muddied and leader requirements become subject to individual interpretation.

The Organizational Assessment Inventory

Like Stewart, Van de Ven and Ferry (1980) focus on the position rather than its incumbent. As part of their attempt to assess all aspects of organizational functioning, Van de Ven and Ferry constructed an instrument that measures the discretion of employees and supervisors and the discretion available in jobs. They define discretion as "the decisions and judgments that role occupants are to make during task execution" (p. 165). Supervisors and employees are asked to judge the amount of authority they have in making decisions in four areas of their jobs: (1) determining what tasks the employee will do; (2) setting quotas; (3) establishing rules and procedures; and (4) determining how work exceptions are to be handled.

Van de Ven and Ferry operationalize discretion in terms of the authority that people have in making job-related decisions. The decisions addressed, however, are internal to the work group and therefore do not involve upward or lateral influence by supervisors. If the instrument were expanded to include a wider range of typical supervisory and managerial decisions, it could provide an alternative to Hunt *et al.*'s LBDQ-based questionnaire. Further, since Van de Ven and Ferry's measure compares supervisory authority with subordinate authority, it has the potential for tapping some aspects of shared discretion.

INTEGRATION AND IMPLICATIONS

Discretionary leadership is one of the most fascinating recent developments in leadership research. It has the potential for providing us with a new focus on the role the individual manager plays in the functioning of organizations. At the present time, however, no one of the existing theories can adequately predict or describe the range of conditions under which a manager will choose to exercse discretion. Nevertheless, the existing work offers a number of insights that can facilitate future research and development.

First, the organization imposes constraints that limit the amount of discretion that can be feasibly exercised. Managers must attend to the organization's policies and practices, and its structural limitations. The manager is also restricted by resource constraints and other restrictions imposed by the external environment. Organizational and environmental conditions determine how critical the individual's ability to exercise discretion will be to organizational effectiveness. As Hunt and his associates point out, it is possible that the same organization that has a critical need for managerial discretion can simultaneously pose restrictions that hamper the manager's ability to use discretion.

Second, social and political factors interfere with the exercise of discretion. Sometimes, as Pfeffer and Salancik's "role-set analysis" suggests, social and political influences can be so subtle that a manager may not be aware of their effect on his or her behavior. At other times, managers are painfully aware of their effects. Managers compete with other individuals who are trying to make similar decisions and choices involving overlapping responsibilities and the same pool of resources. Managers also contend with other individuals who are attempting to exert influence over the same superiors, peers, and sub-ordinates.

Not only do managers share discretion, but they also encounter situations in which it is best to choose not to act. In their work on substitutes for leadership, Kerr and his associates suggest that it is important for formal leaders to recognize that they are not always the best source of influence over employee performance. By yielding to others, managers may improve both their own effectiveness and that of the organization. Conversely, the work of Hunt and his associates and that of Katz and Kahn suggest that when managers yield influence to other sources, managerial influence and impact within the work group could be reduced. Thus, a manager may be forced to choose between personal influence and group effectiveness.

Finally, despite the many constraints on managerial discretion, most managerial jobs offer individuals some choice of which activities to emphasize and how to go about accomplishing them. Choice appears to be a prerequisite for full discretion, for it is within such undefined areas that managers can exercise the most discretion. Individual managers, however, vary in their ability to make optimum use of available discretion. They differ in their ability to perceive opportunities for discretion and to make sound decisions. They also differ in their propensity to use discretion to further their own goals rather than those of the work group or organization. These differences may be based on skill, personality traits, and psychological processes such as attribution of causality and motivation. More research is needed at the individual level of analysis.

Another area requiring further investigation is the relationship between influence, power, and discretion; the nature of this relationship is not clear. Both incremental influence and discretionary leadership are seen as reaching the same end—increasing a leader's influence over subordinates. The means by which they achieve this end differs. Incremental influence requires that subordinates like the leader and respect his or her expertise. The influence that derives from discretionary leadership depends on the degree to which the organizational setting provides the leader with an opportunity to clarify reward contingencies and contribute to group goals. It also depends upon the leader's ability to use that discretion when it is called for. Further research is needed to determine if these two processes complement each other, and if so, in what way.

The success of further research on managerial discretion depends, to some extent, on the ability of researchers to develop improved measures of leader discretion. As yet unresolved are questions involving the best indicators of leader discretion and the most appropriate raters of discretionary activities. The success of further research also depends on how well researchers can evaluate and integrate the contributions that other available theories might make to our knowledge of leader discretion. Some examples include psychological theories of person perception, information processing, personality and motivation, and models from political science.

The study of discretion sensitizes us to the limits of organizational control and planning and processes by which individuals are able to affect organizational functioning. It provides a focal point for examining organizational concerns such as decision making, power, planning and coordination, and identifying potential leaders. Continued work in this area is important because of the implications it has for managers and organizational consultants. Managers could benefit from knowledge of the conditions under which discretion can and cannot be exercised. Managerial effectiveness might also be improved if managers increased their awareness of opportunities for exercising discretion, other individuals with whom they share their discretion, and their own style in exercising discretion. Organizational consultants might help managers by designing training programs and leadership assessment instruments and by working with organizational design to optimize effective managerial use of discretion.

21

Emerging Technologies: The Challenge to Leadership Theory

Richard N. Osborn, Frederic A. Morris, and Patrick E. Connor

Within the next several decades, a number of emerging technologies promise to introduce a revolutionary array of new goods and services: repeated launchings of the United States space shuttle presage the construction and use of large structures in space, including manufacturing facilities, astronomical observatories, communications equipment, and solar-energy systems (see Colombo, 1981); development of deep-mined geologic repositories for the disposal of high-level radioactive waste may finally close the back end of the nuclear fuel cycle (U.S. Department of Energy, 1980). Such technologies share several traits, including: (a) their engineering feasibility is fairly well established; (b) potential markets are promising, but products/services have not yet been produced or sold; and (c) many are controversial.

To say that a technology is controversial is to say that it is politically sensitive, emotionally charged, and publicly visible. Moreover, resolving the various technical, social, political, and psychological difficulties that such technologies typically involve requires accommodating the goals and requirements of several political and social actors; in short, it requires leadership. The problem for us, however, is that this leadership will not likely benefit much from what we already know about the subject. In fact, we suggest that the emergence of these technologies requires a new perspective on leadership. The purpose of this chapter is to describe such a perspective.

LEADERSHIP AS PATTERNING

At the last leadership symposium, Osborn (1982) argued that the European view of leadership is that it is neither a single act nor even a set of behaviors. Rather, it is a "patterning" over time. This concept of leadership emphasized a *recognized consistency of the influence attempts made by those in leadership positions.* We can extend this notion by defining leadership as the patterning of attention, activity, and reinforcement over time.

The Patterning of Attention

The patterning of *attention* deals with the central question of what is important. From a historical perspective, patterning of attention may be seen as the articulation of an organizational culture. The values, attitudes, beliefs, and organizational affiliations of the sets of decision makers needed for problem resolution may be divergent (see Smith & Morris, in press). Transformation of these distinct "cultures" may begin by redefining history to focus on common areas (see Bass's, 1981, transformational leadership). Thus, articulating areas of congruence and prior success may be an unrecognized aspect of leadership.[1]

From a futuristic perspective, the question of what is important may frequently be seen in the guise of goals, goal priorities, and strategic choices (see Child, 1972a; Connor, 1980; Osborn, Hunt, & Jauch, 1980). As House (1977) has noted in his analysis of charismatic leadership, those whom we deem charismatic redefine and reinterpret goals. In normal times, leadership involves providing new visions of demands, coinstraints, and choices (Stewart, 1982a). In extremes, leadership may involve articulating a new set of ideologically based choices that circumvent popular views of existing constraints.

To return to our concern with emerging technologies, in such instances there may be little sense of history or concept of future that is shared among the various political and social actors. There is an ever-constant babble of conflicting choices, demands, constraints, and opportunities. Since goals as guidelines for the future are not articulated in forms that elicit recognition and commitment by the diverse decision makers needed to help develop the technology, the patterning of attention becomes a critical leadership task.

The Patterning of Activity

For the patterning of *activity,* the central questions are: what decisions are made; which actions are taken; and who is involved. In regard to the decisions and actions, there are issues of priorities, sequencing, training, scheduling, and the development of appropriate processes. In most organizations, these questions are partially resolved by the organization's technology, structure, procedures, and control systems (see Connor, 1980; Osborn, Hunt, & Jauch, 1980). In complex emerging technological systems the natural flow of needed actions from the technology is missing. *What* is to be done, and how, thus predominate over issues of the best methods.

Task assignments within a unit, initiating structure, and negotiations across

---

[1]Identification of symbiotic relationships (where participants benefit from a number of secondary spillover effects via association in or with a particular area (e.g., legitimacy, prestige, demand for their services) is expected to be more important than congruence viewed in terms of compromise or benefit/cost maximization.

units are aspects of leadership mentioned in numerous studies (see Bass, 1981). But for emerging technologies, the questions are broader. Which technical specialties are used? What organizations are employed? Which constituencies are coopted? These are not one-time choices; thus, leadership must focus on recognized consistency. Activity patterning may therefore only emerge as an aspect of leadership across events, individuals, specific circumstances, and time.

The Patterning of Reinforcement

Perhaps one of the most fundamental changes in the new series of contingency theories is the emphasis on the pattern of *reinforcements* the leader provides to subordinates (see Bass, 1981). The degree to which the leader makes rewards contingent on an identified series of behaviors and outcomes is continually identified by those who stress behavioral modification (e.g., Sims, 1977). Those identified with the attribution view of leadership (e.g., Mitchell, Larsen, & Green, 1977) have also focused attention on reinforcement, although from a different perspective. Here, the effects of perceived group performance—particularly the attributions of causes of poor performance—are linked to leadership effectiveness.

What are the central leadership aspects of reinforcement patterning? We propose that many center on: (1) articulating attributional linkages that unite diverse actors; (2) providing recognized and acceptable rewards based on action; and (3) developing rewards tailored to the decision arenas of key decision makers.

For emerging technologies, the definition of acceptable outcomes should be added to the issues of contingent rewards and attributions. The reinforcement view reminds us that repeated contingent reinforcement is a key. The attribution perspective alerts us to a related issue of equity: each type of actor is likely to see his or her contribution as critical and the major impetus for progress. Conversely, any lack of progress is likely to be attributed to the inaction and recalcitrance of other key decision makers.

WHO ESTABLISHES THE PATTERNING, AND HOW?

An unmentioned central theme in most leadership analyses can now be challenged. Leadership research normally examines individual action, behavior, personality, or attitudes as they affect an individual or collection of individuals. When leadership is defined as the patterning of attention, activity, and reinforcement, the basic unit of analysis need not be the individual leader. Organizations, units, and sets of individuals may be leaders.

This view of leadership is not as radical as it sounds if we consider who (or what) establishes the pattern, and how that is done. Where the patterning is primarily established by a manager or supervisor via direct, face-to-face contact with subordinates, we find leadership defined in a very traditional manner. A focus on individual interactions yields the dyadic approach embodied in Graen's analysis (e.g., Graen & Schiemann, 1978). By focusing on the interplay of the unit head and the group, the focus of leadership becomes group process (see Stogdill, 1950). Here questions of influence, persuasion, exchange, and relative power may be incorporated.

A comparatively simple change in who and what establishes patterning and how patterns are maintained helps link the macro and micro views of leadership. Presuming that the patterning is historically established, as it is within a bureaucratic setting, yields analyses of leadership roles. When it is also presumed that the pattern is maintained and augmented by the leader, one finds a distinction between required and discretionary leadership. Here the more traditional dimensions of leadership may be used if the focus remains on the leader as a key party in maintaining and augmenting the role (see Hunt, Osborn, & Martin, 1979).

Other views of leadership have mixed the questions of who or what establishes patterning, and how it is achieved and maintained. With analysis of emergent leadership, particularly in laboratory settings, we find such a mix. The experimenter often provides some patterning of attention and activity but allows reinforcement to emerge. For example, an artificial group may be given a task, told the ostensible measures of performance, and then allowed to solve the problem as the members see fit. Thousands of fine-grained variations can be developed depending upon the degree of patterning within and across attention, activity, and reinforcement. Still, the experimental setting typically allows face-to-face (or at least simulated individual-to-individual) contact.

An emerging complex technological system, such as that exemplified by radioactive waste disposal, provides another set of parameters. Patterning across the interest institutions and actors is absent. Direct face-to-face contact is less frequent. However, our view of leadership as patterning of attention, activity, and reinforcement may still apply if we consider that noninteracting sets of individuals may develop and maintain the requisite patterning through their institutions.

DISCUSSION

Development and deployment of what we have called emerging technologies involve four principal dimensions. First, they can be readily construed as a critical *managerial* challenge. In outer-space commerce, for instance, means of financing expensive, high-risk ventures must be identified. Satisfactory relationships among NASA, operators, and entrepreneurs must be established, and so forth. Second, *technological* aspects are also important. Fundamental scientific uncertainties must be reduced, and then translated from scientific insight to lab-scale technology to full-scale hardware. Third, virtually all emerging technologies are subject to environmental, health, safety, antitrust, and other yet to be formed *regulatory* requirements. And finally, emerging technologies almost always involve *political* choices that are inevitably molded by citizens and elected officials. As a consequence, decisions and actions are often parcelled into distinct decision-making arenas: managerial, technical, regulatory, and political. Thus, it is necessary to maneuver an emerging technology through a managerial, technological, regulatory, and political maze.

In short, it is our view that the setting for emerging technologies appears to have little correspondence to the setting factors so prominent in traditional leadership research. Group characteristics, task and job perceptions, and subordinate characteristics may represent different contingencies of comparative salience toward the bottom of large bureaucracies (e.g., Bass, 1981). However, they do not appear to be particularly useful in describing the leadership setting in emerging complex technological systems.

Moreover, in much leadership research the actions of the unit head form the basis for analysis. And the question of who is to be led is comparatively simple—the leader's subordinates. In emerging technologies, however, it is not easy to spot one or even a handful of individuals with formal positions of authority. Without a specific enumeration of who the leaders and followers might be, it is natural to turn to the literature on emergent leadership (see Bass, 1981). But even here the normal leadership approach appears constrained by the necessity to identify individuals who have the most influence over the others. Questions of roughly equal influence that is unequally distributed across different domains are rarely analyzed. Instead, there is more emphasis on the control of interaction, there are small numbers of individuals, and/or there are retrospective looks at why a particular individual emerged as the leader.

More macro extensions, notably by Bass (1981) and the Southern Illinois group (e.g., Hunt, Osborn, & Martin, 1979), provide only a partial starting point. These analyses suggest that an organization's environment, context (size and technology), and structure substantially affect the work and style of leaders as well as the effectiveness of leader attempts to influence both subordinates and peers. But the conceptual base for these descriptions of the setting still presumes that leaders operate predominately within an organizational setting. For emerging technologies, the setting is a broad array of often highly politicized organizations, interest groups, and legislatures. As such, it requires an array like patterning of attention, activity, and reinforcement if it is to be managed.

SUMMARY

We can summarize the analysis with four major propositions. First, we propose that there is a large, significant category of nontrivial, socially important problems in the emergence of complex technological systems. Second, we propose that the situational factors associated with these systems, their evolution, and the definition of leadership are not consistent with those posited by existing leadership theory, and that therefore such theory, as currently formulated, can do little to help analyze these systems. Third, we propose that formulating leadership as a patterning of attention, activity, and reinforcement provides the beginning of a useful perspective. Fourth, we propose that such a view of leadership may help reconcile conflicting research findings by asking by whom (what) and how patterning is established and maintained.

These propositions are both bold and modest. They are bold in the sense that they pose a significant challenge to a well-developed body of literature, not on the grounds of weakness but on the grounds of irrelevance to a set of new and major technological and social developments. They are modest in the sense that they are only vague propositions without full development or empirical support. They are extremely tentative. We would be the first to admit that we have gone a short way down a path that could turn out to be a blind alley.

22

Managing Managers: The Work of Top Management

C. K. Prahalad and Yves L. Doz

This chapter is an inquiry into the work of top managers in large complex industrial organizations. The setting is that of complex corporate organizations confronted with significant changes in the strategic and managerial requirements of their businesses.

Conceptually, our research attempts to shed light on an underresearched area: the work of top managers in complex organizations. Relatively few studies have focused attention on the activities of top management and these studies still leave gaps in our understanding. Most notable are studies that concentrated on how top managers use their time and developed classifications of activities and tasks to organize their findings (Carlson, 1951; Kotter, 1982; Mintzberg, 1973; Stengrevics, 1982; Stewart, 1967). Some went further to provide frameworks to interpret and understand the job of managers in addition to classifying activities (Stewart, 1982a).

Most studies of management have been content with a very abstract definition of top managers' tasks. Even though he had extremely rich data on some companies, such as DuPont, Chandler (1962) boils down the role of top management to planning, appraising, and coordinating and does not conceptualize the extremely rich top-management process data he gathered (Chandler & Salsbury, 1971). The process school of policy research has usually defined the role of top management in the large complex firm as the shaping of structural context (Bower, 1970). While researchers were conscious of the actual complexity of the task and depicted it in specific cases (e.g., Dennison Manufacturing), their conceptualization lagged behind their data.

Our research attempts to bridge a gap between these two largely separate lines of inquiry—the concrete description of activities and the abstract analysis of tasks—by relating the specific actions of top managers to a broader strategic and organizational intent in the context of one particular type of strategic transition. We have considered in detail the process through which top managers carried out a shift from a strategy based on subsidiary autonomy to one of worldwide integration and specialization in a multinational business. After a pilot study in 1974–1975 (the results of which are reported in detail in Prahalad, 1976), a small number of major international companies were selected for intensive study. Some company studies were carried out by doctoral students and the sample now includes more than 20 companies. The evolution of the strategy of a business in each company was documented through internal company documents and interviews that involved executives at headquarters and at subsidiaries. Interviews numbered between 20 and 60 per company. In some companies, events were followed as they unfolded, since the researchers got involved before the strategic transition was completed. Other company studies were retrospective.

Detailed descriptions of the various strategic shifts were then written and checked with managers in the particular company for accuracy and completeness. These detailed descriptions were then further abstracted into patterns of change processes and their underlying chronological structure was analyzed. From these studies of top managers in action as they changed and redirected strategies of large multinational businesses with a complex organizational structure — some with success and others without — an understanding of their work evolved.

THE ORGANIZATIONAL CONTEXT OF TOP-MANAGEMENT ACTION

In response to conflicting demands imposed upon them by competitors and host governments, major companies often adopted complex structures to manage their international operations (Doz, 1979; Doz, Bartlett, & Prahalad, 1980). These structures usually involve overlays of product (or business) managers, geographic (regional and country) managers, and functional managers in some network of matrix relationships (e.g., Goggin, 1975). The three groups — product, geographic, and functional managers — share information, responsibility, and power in complex patterns. Within the product and geographic groups at least, these structures often embody multiple levels of general managers. In these structures, we defined top managers as having more than one general manager reporting to them: our research is concerned with the actions of general managers who have the responsibility to direct the action of other general managers.

Simple models of top-management behavior cannot account for the complexity observed in a multidimensional, multilayered organizational context. We chose such a complex research territory because it would reveal more fully and more visibly the difficulty of top-management work than a simpler informal context such as that of the small entrepreneurial firm. Research on organizational adaptation — and managerial behavior in guiding such adaptation — has usually foundered by adopting too simple a view of adaptation or by focusing on one phenomenon only. Power relationships within the organization, or between organizations alone (Crozier, 1964; Pfeffer & Salancik, 1978), or leadership traits alone, for instance, cannot explain management, behavior. Nor can simplistic structural models, even when they grope for complex contingencies, even out management action from organizational adaptation convincingly (for a critique, see Miller & Friesen, 1980a; Salaman, 1979).

We report in this chapter our exploratory findings as a step toward the development of a middle-ground theory of top-management action in guiding the adaptation of complex firms to shifting competitive and political imperatives.

TOWARD A FRAMEWORK

As we mentioned in our introduction, Bower suggested that beyond the formal structure of reporting relationships, top managers could use management systems to provide direction: information, measurements, and incentives would focus the energies of self-interested managers in the desired strategic direction. The task of top management, in Bower's view, is therefore carefully to manage the context of decisions by using a variety of systems. Several questions remain unanswered. First, what are the underlying dynamics of strategic change? Second, how do structural and systems changes provide the "signals" or the "cues" for change? And finally, is there a logic that helps top managers pick a set of tools — be it structure or systems — to help redirect strategy; is there a logic to sequencing and timing of these administrative changes?

Strategic redirection involves three closely interrelated changes:

1. *Changes in the "cognitive maps" (or the concept of "relevant domain") of key managers.* Each manager, based on his or her own experience, background, network of relationships and the information available to him or her, develops a map of the competitive world over a period of time. This map usually comprises only a few dimensions that become constantly monitored (Ashby, 1952; Lindblom & Cohen, 1979; Neisser, 1967). For example, in a business traditionally with local subsidiary autonomy, managers accept the local market as the only relevant domain. A shift in strategy toward a centralized worldwide operation requires that the "cognitive maps" be changed, from one emphasizing competition in a given country or area to worldwide competition.

2. *The emergence of a new consensus on how to compete among key managers affected by the change.* In order to face conflicting forces, the various groups of managers — product, geographic, and functional — have developed different cognitive maps and may perceive the need for a change differently. Uniform cognitive maps could make the organization too rigid (Meyer, 1982) and prevent it from handling contradictory tensions in its environment (Doz, Bartlett, & Prahalad, 1981; Pondy & Mitroff, 1979). Top managers must, therefore, ensure enough convergence of cognitive maps to

allow for the emergence of a consensus among key managers on how to compete yet make sure not to suppress dissenting views.

3. *A realignment of the power balance among managers* in the organization such that resource-allocation decisions are consistent with the new cognitive map and emerging consensus on a new strategy (Prahalad, 1976).

In other words, strategic change involves the management of the cognitive maps, the consensus process, and the balance of power, among a group of key managers whose commitment is critical to successful implementation.

A consistent strategy for a business results from the alignment of: (1) the cognitive maps of key managers; (2) what consensus they reach on how to compete; and (3) a distribution of power among them that makes resource-allocation choices consistent with that consensus.

The structural view of multinational management has subsumed the three dimensions above under the formal structure and, therefore, considered structural change as the way to change strategic direction (Brooke & Remmers, 1970; Stopford & Wells, 1970). For instance, changing from a geographic to a product organization will — automatically? — shift the strategy from one of national responsiveness to one of multinational integration. There are several practical difficulties with such a simple view: major reorganizations are not without costs: they do not always succeed and usually cause great trauma among affected executives. Even more fundamentally, given the inherent tensions between responsiveness and integration forces in most multinational businesses, a capability to trade off responsiveness as opposed to integration flexibly from decision to decision, country to country, function to function, and product line to product line is increasingly called for. Structural change provides a capability for responsiveness *or* integration, but not for both.

In sum, complex strategies require complex networks of relationships among managers; in these networks, formal structures do not provide a basis for managing the cognitive, strategic, and power orientations of key managers. The appropriate unit of analysis in managing strategic redirection in a complex organization is the individual manager, not abstract subunits.

MANAGING MANAGERS: THE KEY TO STRATEGIC DIRECTION

In order to achieve strategic redirection, top managers in complex organizations actively influence the cognitive, strategic, and power orientation of their key subordinates. The cognitive orientation can be influenced by bringing new data, by proposing new apprehension schemes (Berger & Gluckman, 1966) and alternate interpretations, and by reframing existing data into a different overall context (Davis, 1982). Ideological metaphors may provide consistent new schemes that do not have—immediately—to be close to current reality (Starbuck, 1982).

In the companies we studied, conventional data-management mechanisms and tension-management mechanisms were used to bring about shifts in the cognitive orientation of key managers. (Table 22.1 lists the mechanisms used by the companies we studied.) Different accounting systems were used to gather and organize business-performance data to support new ways of conceptualizing and assessing the value of interdependencies and cross-shipments between subsidiaries (Prahalad & Doz, 1982). Data-management changes could also regulate the flow of information and modify the access of individual managers to relevant information (Prahalad & Doz, 1982; Doz & Prahalad, 1981). Patterns of management socialization could also affect cognitive maps. Further, in the early stages of strategic redirection, top managers worked actively with key executives to develop and advocate multiple perspectives on key business priorities. Multiple coordination committees, planning teams, and task forces were usually created and managed.

Shifting cognitive maps was usually the longest task in the change processes we observed. Following the appointment of a new top manager who brought a different cognitive map and was perceived as a signal of change, it usually took 18 months to 3 years of active work—on data-management mechanisms and tension management mechanisms—before the legitimacy of the current position was sufficiently weakened (analytically and emotionally) to attempt to create explicitly new strategic consensus.[2]

Only once alternative strategies were independently "discovered" (sometimes following on a broad vision the new executive had brought with him),

Table 22.1 Top Managers' Repertoire of Administrative Mechanisms.

DATA MANAGEMENT	MANAGER MANAGEMENT	TENSION MANAGEMENT
• Accounting	• Choice of key managers	• Business teams
• Budgeting system	• Career paths	• Committees
• Planning process	• Executive evaluation & compensation	• Task forces
• Measurement systems	• Management development	• Integrators
• Information systems	• Patterns of socializaton	• Decision responsibility assignments
• Agenda for meetings		• Issue resolution processes

---

[2]Only in the aftermath of critical profit crises was that stage of the change process significantly reduced in length.

and analyzed, and once they elicited potential commitment from a substantial subgroup of key executives, could the process of building consensus toward one particular choice start. In some cases the process was accelerated by an obvious strategic model (e.g., General Motors' managers in Europe were aware through the 1970s that Ford was enjoying high pay-offs from the European manufacturing integration strategy it had implemented in 1967). Changes in the structure of selected data-management mechanisms — such as the planning process or the technological coordination procedures — were the main vehicles used to bring about a convergence of strategic options toward a new consensus.

Creating such a consensus, however, was not followed by action unless the managers' motivations and power bases were also modified (Doz & Prahalad, 1981). Obvious managers' management mechanisms such as changes in compensation schemes, career progression patterns, or key executives were being used at that stage. More critical than how they directly affected one individual or another was how their use was interpreted by other managers.

In sum, top managers we observed successfully managing a major strategic redirection started by introducing and developing new cognitive maps among a small group of key managers. Then, once the issues and alternatives had been explored with the help of the new cognitive maps, they helped the development of a new strategic consensus. Finally, once enough legitimacy for the need to change and some sense of desired direction of change had been created within a core group of managers, it became possible for top managers to identify the power structure within the firm (or the business) to ensure that organizational resource-allocation outcomes would, by and large, contribute to the accomplishment of the desired change.

Each of these three successive changes was accomplished by drawing on a repertoire of administrative mechanisms available to top management. Although the sequencing and timing in the use of the various mechanisms obviously varied from company to company, successful strategic changes exhibited a broadly similar structure over time and unsuccessful changes departed significantly from that structure (Doz & Prahalad, 1981). Successful strategic changes followed the sequence summarized below:

Simplified Chronological Structure of Observed Successful Strategic Redirections

1. A well-regarded top manager — experienced in the business and the company — is appointed to take charge of the business. He or she brings an alternative strategic design or (at least) creates the possibility for alternate perspectives to become legitimate.

2. This new manager uses a range of data-management mechanisms to develop an understanding of the business based on multiple sets of premises.

He or she brings to key subordinates new cognitive maps or helps them develop them. A series of tension-management mechanisms is used to design and manage interactions with subordinates. The need to coordinate or integrate activities (e.g., technology transfers, export sales) selectively emerges from these interactions. Data-management mechanisms (e.g., cost accounting) are refined and redesigned to allow these coordination actions and provide clearer legitimacy for their need.

3. The internal debate moves from specific coordination tasks to changes in the overall strategic direction of the business. Further data-management mechanisms are changed (e.g., planning and budgeting processes). A new strategic consensus emerges from the interactions triggered by these changes; in some cases it closely resembles an early design that the top manager brought with him or her; in others a genuinely new strategy emerges from the organization.

4. Formal reallocation of power by key executives takes place at the end of the process when it has become extremely difficult for managers to disagree with the new strategic direction. Signals of relative power changes among key managers are provided by managers' management mechanisms, visible career path changes for instance, and these in turn make operating managers who have to contribute to implementation fall in line.

SUMMARY PROPOSITIONS

Based on the analysis of a number of strategic redirection processes, we can propose the following generalizations:

1. The administrative acts of top managers, while apparently unconnected and fragmented, can have an underlying coherence. It is the collection of a variety of actions, taken at different times, apparently unconnected, that as a whole provides the direction for change.
2. Major strategic shifts can be accomplished in a multidimensional organization without structural change through the use of administrative mechanisms.
3. The choice of mechanisms has to be made by using criteria such as:
     i. What orientation (cognitive/strategic/power) does it affect?
    ii. How selective is this in its impact?
   iii. What is the strength and symbolic value among managers affected?
    iv. How easy is it to reverse its impact?
     v. What is the time horizon for effect?
    vi. What is the nature of top-management support needed?
4. Strategic redirection will not take root if changes in the structure of the power subprocess are not successfully affected.
5. Legitimacy to power shifts is provided by changes in the cognitive and stra-

tegic orientations. In a crisis, however, change is seen as legitimate and power shifts can take place more swiftly.

6. Since the time frame for implementing strategic redirection is between two and seven years, constancy of purpose is crucial. Further, permanency of key executives involved in the change may be critical.

7. Explicit attention to the characteristics of the tools used to change the three subprocesses, and to the interaction over time among those tools, helps top management to implement strategic redirection without organizational upheavals.

8. The historical evolution of a firm as a social system may inhibit the use of certain tools. As such, the choice, timing, and sequencing of tools may be partly situational.

MAPPING TOP-MANAGEMENT ACTION

The change chronologies that we studied provided the raw material for understanding the meaning of work for the top manager. However, they were primarily retrospective studies, and a reinterpretation of the causes of success and failure. In no firm in our sample did the top-management group conceive of a series of changes ahead of time. Both sequencing and timing of changes were very much matters of judgment. In most cases, top managers could not coherently explain the basis for a series of steps they had taken. The framework presented in this chapter provides a basis for (a) mapping a sequence of steps before large-scale change is initiated, and (b) using administrative actions initiated at different times to accomplish strategic purposes.

In order to enhance the usefulness of this framework for managers, we ought to develop mechanisms that help managers evaluate, on an ongoing basis, the direction and pace of intended change. Further, we need a methodology for assessing the difference between compliance and commitment. For commitment to a new strategy to develop, managers not only should accept the need for change intellectually, but also must cope with deep-seated emotional commitments. Further, the shifts in the balance of power must be seen as necessary and not arbitrary. We believe that the future direction of research is best focused on the issues above.

CONCLUSION

We suggest in this chapter that top managers in multinational corporations face a complex task of shifting strategies to cope with changing competitive conditions. In such complex organizations, structural change is not an appropriate mechanism for effecting the change. Top managers must conceive of their task as one of changing the cognitive, strategic, and power orientation of key managers using a wide repertoire of administrative actions taken over a long period of time. This view requires that we conceive of the task of top management as one dealing with specifics (individual managers) rather than aggregates; not just grand design but a series of administrative acts that mold the behavior of managers. In other words, while the importance of analytical and conceptual rigor in developing a strategic vision is not to be underestimated, the work of top managers remains one of managing other managers to move toward that vision.

23

Commentary on Part 5

Part 5 Integrative Comments: Leadership Theory: The Search for a Reformulation

Peter A. Clark

The three think pieces that comprise Part 5 claim that there is an identifiable "ruling paradigmatic orthodoxy" in leadership studies that is inadequate for future leadership research and for the study of managerial behavior. The authors all argue that existing leadership theories do not provide the analytical basis for understanding and researching commonly occurring contemporary situations in organizations. Further, it is claimed that the established theories are of little value to the training of potential leaders. Hence the several authors propose that the theories of leadership should be reformulated.

There are three sets of problems that the chapters raise. First, to what extent is the "ruling paradigmatic orthodoxy" imposing restrictions on further developments and to what extent do previous points of departure require dramatic revision rather than modification? Second, what kinds of theoretical inquiry can achieve the goals set by these pieces and what are the implications for methods of research? Third, given that the chapters all focus on the temporal embeddedness of the exercise of top-level discretion, how should the temporal, processual, and historical dimensions be addressed? In discussing these three questions it will be suggested that elaborations to open-systems theorizing (e.g., Katz & Kahn, 1978) do provide a fruitful basis for reformulating leadership theory to describe and explain managerial behavior, but that this reformulation must take greater account of social-stratification dimensions of organizations in capitalist societies.

The Ruling Orthodoxy

It is important to start the discussion by scrutinizing the claim about the "ruling paradigmatic orthodoxy." From these pieces and others in this volume it may be observed that leadership research and theorizing is being characterized by reference to a handful of exemplars, namely: Fiedler's contingency theory (1967); House's path goal (1971); Vroom and Yetton's "normative model" (1973); Hunt and Osborn's "multiple-influence" framework (1980); and Katz and Kahn's open-systems concept (1978). Probably the most common theme in these exemplars is that they all adopt a regulative, one-dimensional viewpoint rather than a "radical" view of leadership, and they are all implicitly and most obviously angled toward the preservation of the status quo in organizations. However, there are considerable differences in their modeling of the leadership process and in their objectives. This can be most clearly seen by comparing and contrasting the approach of Fiedler with that of Katz and Kahn's open-systems perspective.

From a European viewpoint, Fiedler's theory may be regarded as very typical of one of the major varieties of North American microorganization behavior. There is an explicit focus on a cogent, prescriptive theory containing a small number of identifiable, measurable variables that are, at least implicitly, argued to account for a high proportion of the variance in leadership effectiveness. The theory is codified and supported by empirical studies conducted under replicable conditions. In addition, there are certain variables that are both potent and open to manipulation. Hence, the theory suggests specific forms of action, or, as Gast rightly notes in Chapter 20, the theory seems to specify clear lines of action. In common with a great deal of micro-organizational behavior, there is very little attention to the cognitive, discretionary, and politically problematic aspects of leadership. There is a neglect of problems of managers in formulating operable theories to guide their actions. By comparison, the perspective of Katz and Kahn (1978) on the open-systems approach to leadership is much more analytical and holistic. In their chapter on leadership (Katz & Kahn, 1978, Chap. 16), the treatment is somewhat conventional although it does explore the extent to which leaders are constrained within existing structural features. In their introduction, however, they propose to define structure by reference to the patterns of events — not activities — which managers cognitize and decode as a basis for action. Their theorizing on events is incomplete, awkward, and certainly not reconciled with the chapter on leadership or with the existence of multiple centers of control in occupational groupings and trade unions. Yet, their concept of structure as streams of events is a promising point of departure.

When the differences between Fiedler and Katz and Kahn are considered, it becomes rather difficult to agree that the ruling orthodoxy is homogeneous or that it is closed off from further development. It is arguable that the open-systems approach can be taken as a fruitful basis for reformulating a theory of management and of leadership. However, this may mean giving much greater attention to the notion of control in organizations, especially to notions of coregulation and to the ways in which capitalism is seeking to adapt organizations to the contradictions that arise from previous concepts of control derived from Taylorism.

Toward Processes

Apart from the approach of Katz and Kahn, much of leadership theory and research contains a mechanistic view of the kinds of knowledge that are useful to the learner. Hence, much leadership theory neglects the problems of its operability, particularly of the extent to which potential leaders can be active agents in the learning process. Here we note the "action theory of learning" proposed by Argyris and Schon (1976) because this theory starts from the processes and cognitions by which managers' intentions are given a guiding role in shaping organizational life. In the action theory, the manager as a learner is concerned with a very wide range of variables or facets, including many events that not only cannot be controlled, but are very awkward to detect, describe, and accommodate.

Each of the three pieces implicitly strives toward the nonmechanistic form of theorizing sketched by Argyris and Schon. Hence, Gast searches for the degree to which as a trainer she can use theories that neglect the exercise of discretion. Similarly, the other two chapters compare the "thin" theorizing of Fiedler or Hunt and Osborn with the "thick" and rich analysis required when treating managerial actions and leadership as a complex cognitive and political enterprise. It is therefore important to recognize that these pieces require a reformulation of the type of theorizing about leadership, away from the simple control models and toward a reflective understanding of the events and processes by which managers' intentions and plans are anticipating and adapting to the complex arrays of events within and between organizations. Osborn, Morris, and Conner rightly stress in Chapter 21 that there is a strong political, competitive, and conflictual dimension. Indeed, they imply that many situations may not be regulated by implicit rules of the game, or, that the rules of the game may contain recipes for future disaster.

Processes over time are central to the proposed reformulation. Osborn, Morris, and Conner suggest that leadership must take account of certain structural phenomena—multiple decision arenas, complex and interdependent "technologies," widely disparate and ecologically dispersed sets of actors, extensive political and coalitional activity. They propose to conceptualize leadership as a patterning over time and specifically recommend that the unit of analysis could be that managerial role set, but they go further than Merton's (1957) seminal formulation by introducing a historical perspective including special attention to how organization leaders write organizational histories as part of the "articulation of the organization culture." Hence, their cognitive theorizing suggests that leadership does involve the "articulation of a new set of ideologically based choices which circumvent popular uses of existing constraints." That is, the double-loop learning proposed by Argyris and Schon is suggested. Finally, their point of departure holds out the possibility of a new theoretical reformulation with the "pattern of attention, activity and re-inforcement" at its core which might provide a basis for reconciling previous research findings.

Processes and their patterning over time are also central to the reformulation proposed in Chapter 22 by Prahalad and Doz, who share the same conception of open-systems theorizing, albeit with a stronger emphasis on the production of "lessons." Their approach is essentially that of the case-oriented, business-policy perspective, somewhat in the Harvard tradition. Great attention is given to the cognitions of managers about organizing themselves and others. They contend that top managers possess a repertory of administrative tools for transforming existing "organization maps" and "dominant logics" as a prerequisite for the establishment of new power balances containing the new "dominant logics." Their case illustrations support the claim that adaptations take years, possibly decades, and that change includes cascading transformations in the "dominant logics" through a plurality of distinct yet interdependent decision arenas. The case study also shows that leaders experience considerable difficulties in scanning in the environment, modeling the intentions of competitors, and interpreting puzzling events.

From a European perspective, the pieces tend to adopt a too restricted theory of control and one that completely neglects the wider social stratification and the institutionalized roles of trade unions. Clearly there are differences in the zones of maneuver occupied by unions in the United States, in Canada, and between European countries. However, given the geographical diversity of many significant organizations, it is simply foolish to neglect the possible existence of coregulation and of the issues this raises concerning managers' legitimacy.

The reformulation of leadership as a historically shaped process located within specific chronological codes — in plural — implies certain methodological shifts that the authors do not discuss, or, debate. Previous leadership research has followed the rigorous model rather than comparative cases studies, but the comparative case-study approach adopted in Chapters 21 and 22 occupies an uneasy position in microorganizational behavior. So far the application of open-systems theorizing through case studies has not been very satisfactory. For example, Katz and Golomb's (1974) case study of the adaptive potential in the kibbutz movement is interesting rather than convincing (Clark, 1978; Miner, 1982, p. 185). The Osborn, Morris, and Conner case illustration relies quite heavily on the ideal-type form of analysis, but this is not made clear. Further consideration should be given to these methodological choices.

The Time Dimension

Clearly, the case analysis and the construction of theorizing involves the time dimension. For example, nuclear waste disposal is undertaken on a bewildering array of time frames, namely, viz: yesterday's politician, the accountant who agrees to accept a 30-year bond, the scientist who treats decay rates in terms of centuries. Prahalad and Doz attempt to reconstruct some of the varied and quite heterogeneous chronological codes operating within organizations. Interestingly, these cases provide instances of managerial work being episodic and their groping toward a processual form of analysis tends to suggest continuity rather than fragmentation (see Mintzberg, 1973).

The three chapters all raise the problem of dealing with the time dimension of managerial behavior and leadership. Gast's approach requires revision to incorporate the concept of the time span of discretion (see Jacques, 1957; Lawrence & Lorsch, 1967) in order to break out of the "time-free" theorizing of microorganizational behavior and to converge with the open-systems theorizing of the other two pieces. Explicating the time dimensions is complex (Clark, 1982), but several points of departure can be suggested.

First, open-systems process theories should make an analytical distinction between recurrence and transformation (P. A. Clark, 1976). According to P. A. Clark (1982), recurrence in organizations is typical, pervasive, taken for granted, yet always contingent. There are a variety of contingent periodicities that require detection and management. Detecting and planning for contingent, recurrent periodicities is central to managerial work at all levels (see Mintzberg, 1973). Recurrences and their momentum (Miller & Friesen, 1980b) are often difficult to disrupt.

For example, Prahalad and Doz illustrate the problem of disrupting recurrence, once established, in order to create transformational change. New concepts are required for the analysis of recurrence. Theories of multiple structures, of collateral structures, and of structural repertoires should be developed further (P. A. Clark, 1975; Duncan, 1972; Zand, 1974). The concept of structural poses as the unit of analysis that relates events and event patterns provides a useful framework for relating organizational features and leadership actions within an approach that incorporates the time dimension adequately (P. A. Clark, 1982).

Second, the treatment of the time dimension in the case-based chapters raises the issue of the degree to which the episodic nature of managerial tasks can be characterized as "fragmentation" (Mintzberg, 1973) because they reveal a high degree of continuity in managerial work. Further, they show that leadership includes constructing images of the future that are perceived as legitimate by colleagues and subordinates while also permitting the transformation of the existing "dominant logics" into future action plans.

Following Katz and Kahn's claim that managers at different levels undertake different kinds of work, then it becomes possible to consider the situations under which episodes may be part of continuity rather than fragmentation. For example, in Figure 23.1 it is assumed that chief executives face both periodic and new problems and that they locate these on the organiza-

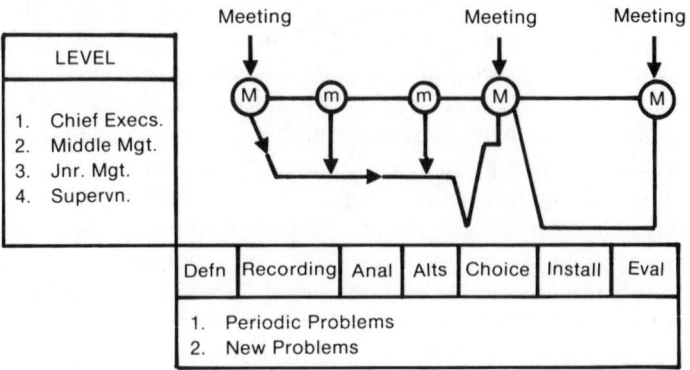

FIGURE 23.1. managerial level and problem-solving time frame

tion's agenda at long meetings. The assumption is that successive stages
and their iterations are dealt with by subordinates, but that the chief executive keeps in touch with developments by small, brief meetings and the occas-
sional major meeting.

Evidence in support of this formulation of continuity in managerial behavior and hence in leadership is contained in Friedman's (1982) analysis of managerial control strategies in the British automobile industry. He suggests that
over a period of six decades there are regular switches of leadership behavior
that covary with the state of product demand for automobiles. Friedman's
analysis goes beyond the time frame of Figure 23.1 and supports these authors'
contentions about continuity.

These pieces raise an important question about the *times* of top leaders.
We know that these executives establish the temporal horizons of their organization and we have good reason to believe that in the United States these
horizons have been progressively attenuated (Abernathy, Clark & Kantrow,
1981) to the point where overall productivity is reduced. Further, we know
that these executives play a central role in strategic time management of deciding the meaning to be attributed to ongoing, past, and anticipated events.

The current corporate struggle over the future civilian aircraft market between American and European executives clearly illustrates the degree to
which there are "unknowns" and the magnitude of the time spans of discretion. We need to know much more about strategic time reckoning, especially if transformational change is to be understood and managed more successfully as a consequence of our researches and theorizing.

Further, these chapters suggest that we need to examine the internal
temporal logistics of organizations, their management, and how leaders seek
to introduce complex interdependencies. Logistics refers to flows of people,
materials, money, and information and the decision as to their tightness.

British managements have typically gone for loose coupling while – contrary to the impression conveyed by the loose-coupling school (Weick, 1974) – U.S. managements have often favored tight coupling, at least within the U.S. The tightness of the coupling directly affects functional autonomy and therefore leadership discretion. Increases in tightness of the type described by Prahalad and Doz indicate that the balance between differentiation and integration is a delicate one. Managing complex interdependencies through time probably requires an extensive organizational repertoire of leadership competences and managerial behaviors.

Conclusion

Within the so-called ruling paradigmatic orthodoxy of leadership studies there is more diversity and potential than these authors have claimed, especially with respect to open-systems theorizing. This commentary has argued that open-systems theorizing provides the most fruitful basis for reformulating leadership studies, but that this shift will require alterations in the type of theorizing in research strategies and in the theory of times and of time reckoning within organizations.

Part 6

Epilog and Conclusions

Introduction

James G. Hunt, Dian-Marie Hosking, Chester A. Schriesheim, and Rosemary Stewart

The two chapters in this final part have been written by the editors in order both to provide broad integration and to extend the scope of the material previously covered. The first of these chapters, "Managerial Behavior/Leadership Perspectives: An International Epilog," attends to the latter. It reviews briefly a large number of studies categorized into major themes that represent the managerial behavior/leadership areas.

Chapter 24 continues a tradition started in the 1977 volume which a number of readers indicate that they have found to be useful. Its coverage is far more extensive than the earlier epilogs, however, in that it: (1) is international; (2) considers both managerial behavior and leadership areas; and (3) covers a much larger number of studies. The material here is at the cutting edge of new developments for it is composed almost entirely of work in various prepublication stages.

Chapter 25, "Conclusions: On Paradigm Shifts in Studying Leadership," is written both to integrate and to take a detailed look at the kinds of paradigms used in leadership/managerial behavior research and the social sciences in general. As pointed out in Part 3 and elsewhere, many authors have argued that the systematic study of leadership is in the throes of a paradigm shift away from a structural-functional perspective.

The concluding chapter examines this contention within the context of European as well as North American research values and traditions. By looking at contributions from this volume as well as other work, conclusions are drawn concerning the degree to which there has been such a paradigm shift in the leadership literature. These conclusions are compared and contrasted with those in the concluding chapter by Schriesheim, Hunt, and Sekaran in the previous symposium book (see Hunt, Sekaran, & Schriesheim, 1982). The conclusions also have a bearing on the way in which one interprets and deals with the diversity so reflective of the field today.

In closing, we remind the reader once again that the two chapters in this concluding part are designed to provide an accurate reflection of the state of the leadership/managerial behavior field, circa 1983.

24

Managerial Behavior/Leadership Perspectives: An International Epilog

Chester A. Schriesheim, James G. Hunt,
Dian-Marie Hosking, and Rosemary Stewart

The epilogs in previous volumes in this series summarized new and emerging research in the field, and the editors feel that this coverage should be continued in the present volume as well. Here, as in previous volumes, we attempt to provide a more complete picture of the state of the field and its probable future directions by summarizing a diversity of current work.

Like previous epilogs, reported below is a summary of studies currently in various stages of development, from theory to empirical research, in the early "idea" phase through fully completed papers. Unlike previous epilogs, however, the number of studies covered here is nearly 200 (previous epilogs summarized only 60 or so works), and this has forced us to treat this material in a somewhat different manner from the format used in past volumes.

As previously indicated, the chapters comprising the bulk of this volume were obtained through a competitive selection process in which authors submitted abstracts of proposed or completed papers, these abstracts were reviewed by a panel of referees for suitability, selected abstracts were then invited for further development as full-length papers, these papers were then reviewed again and revised as necessary (sometimes several times), and the final revisions are included in this book. This process left the editors with about 200 abstracts charting current work in the field, and it was decided to rely heavily on these to form the bulk of this epilog.

Since we are attempting to cover a large volume of work, our summary of each individual piece is necessarily very short. The only place where we depart from presenting very concise summaries is in the material in the first two sections. These works deal with cross-cultural research and research on the nature of managerial work. Since these are a key aspect of the theme of this volume, they are given more detailed coverage. Of course, our briefer treatment of works in other areas is in no way meant to imply lesser importance or quality. It simply reflects the large number of works summarized, and our emphasis on the areas that were the focus of this book.

Perhaps we should also note that whereas previous epilogs included some currently published papers to help "round out" the picture, the amount of material contained herein simply precludes this same treatment. Previous epilogs also generally included a sizeable number of papers obtained from proceedings or presented at professional meetings, but owing to space constraints, the current epilog does not. Provided here, however, as in previous epilogs, are summaries in response to a blanket request by the editors to researchers working in the leadership and managerial behavior fields, as well as solicited and unsolicited unpublished papers from scholars working in these fields.

We attempt to present a reasonable summary of these studies below and, as appropriate, link these to the 1982 epilog (Hunt, Sekaran, & Schriesheim, 1982) and suggest possible future trends in research. As in previous epilogs, we group these works by major themes, recognizing that many have several themes and therefore could be grouped differently. We also discuss some of these works in greater detail than others, depending upon the amount of information we have and upon the stage of development of each work. We do not attempt to integrate these materials tightly or to provide a comprehensive or critical review of the field; as noted above, the purpose of this epilog is simply to paint a more complete picture of the field and to chart its current and probable future directions.

The studies that we summarize below are grouped into the following categories: (1) Cross-cultural research; (2) The nature of managerial work; (3) Leadership behavior and style; (4) Leadership and management characteristics; (5) Power, influence, participation, and conflict; (6) Behavioral reinforcement, modeling, and feedback; (7) Leading and managing professional employees; (8) Communication, information processing, and decision making; (9) Top management and strategic leadership; (10) Leader-follower relations; (11) Management-organizational structure interactions; (12) Leadership, management, and organization development issues; (13) Organizational effectiveness; and (14) General issues of theory development, hypothesis generation, and hypothesis testing.

Before beginning, we should add two brief notes. First, unpublished papers discussed below appear in the "References" section of this book, along with the published and unpublished sources cited earlier in this volume. The abstracts and reports of work in progress are numbered from 001 to 197, and these appear in the "Abstracts and Works in Progress" section that follows the "References" section. Here, it might be noted, an attempt has been made to give readers a short but usable address at which the author(s) of cited works may be contacted for further information. Also, most of the untitled works were submitted in response to the editors' call for summaries of current work in progress. Finally, the editors wish to apologize in advance for any errors of omission or commission that may follow. We have tried to capture accurately the essence of each work described. With so many works being summarized it seems unlikely that we have not made at least a few errors, and we hope that anyone so affected will understand and forgive us.

CROSS-CULTURAL RESEARCH

Perhaps because of the international nature of the symposium upon which this book is based, and also perhaps due to the editors' attempts to obtain works from outside the United States and the United Kingdom, a fairly large number of such works were submitted and are summarized in the sections that follow. The research considered below is explicitly cross-cultural and the author(s) devote considerable effort to cross-cultural comparisons or discussions. Many additional non–U.S. and non–U.K. works are included in the sections that follow this one; these works are not included here because they are either not explicitly cross-cultural or because the author(s) do not devote substantial effort to cross-cultural comparisons or discussions. In many ways this cross-cultural work departs substantially from the content of previous symposium volumes. In these earlier volumes only a few such works may be found. While we certainly do not believe that this difference signals an increase in the amount of cross-cultural research currently being conducted, we do believe that it suggests a healthy broadening of perspective for those interested in studying leadership and managerial behavior.

General Theoretical Treatments

Roberts (138) presents a theoretical and review paper with the central thesis that one of the major shortcomings of cross-national research is a failure to define key constructs adequately. Further, Roberts suggests that conceptualization of the nation-state is a particularly problematic concern, and that most researchers do not deal with the issue of why the nation-state should be significant in studying behavior in organizations. Roberts then reviews how organizational theorists have conceptualized the nation-state, how other disciplines conceptualize the nation-state, and based upon this analysis, which variables appear theoretically meaningful for organizational studies. The final section discusses other alternatives to the nation-state for grouping organizations, as well as other, possibly more appropriate, approaches.

In a related work, Roberts (137) presents the results of a survey of 50 cross-national researchers with respect to their opinions about currently important theoretical and empirical issues in cross-national organizational research. A review of 129 journals (84 of which were scholarly) and 41 popular managerially oriented publications was also conducted to determine what editors appear to think managerial audiences feel is relevant to cross-national management. The results of the survey and the review are compared, and conclusions drawn about what is and what should be investigated in cross-national research.

Along a somewhat different path, Chemers (025) presents a model that integrates current empirical knowledge on managerial effectiveness with a model of cultural differences. The integration focuses on status-bestowal processes, the evolution of leadership styles, and current directions in cross-cultural managerial effectiveness research. A tentative systems-theory framework is offered for the cross-cultural study of leadership effectiveness, as well as some guidelines for assessing the cross-cultural transferability of management techniques. Keilson (077) offers a somewhat similar perspective, arguing that theory in this area will not advance until the psychology of cultural differences is explored, but no theory or model is proposed.

Schoenfeldt (151) presents a cross-cultural model that relates leadership to the managerial role and is based upon empirical research with eight high-technology companies. The model concentrates on what managers do (functions and roles), how they act (styles), and with whom they interact (targets). The relationship between managerial competencies (functions and roles) and leadership (style) is discussed, and initial evidence presented showing that managerial functions, roles, and targets transcend the cultural context but that effective leadership (style or the delivery of managerial competencies) is culturally specific.

Mitchell (116) presents a cross-cultural framework dealing with forces that impact on social-service managers, as well as some preliminary information concerning the effectiveness of various approaches in the United States, Europe, and Japan. Guidelines for effective management action are also presented.

Conceptual Work on Japan

In addition to the more general theoretical cross-cultural work summarized above, Seror (161), Futamura (047), and Calista (020) offer more specific treatments, dealing specifically with Japan.

Seror (161) presents a cultural contingency framework for the comparative analysis of Japanese and American organizations. She also defines culture as a construct, summarizes and critiques research on cultural contingencies, and offers suggestions for future comparative U.S.-Japanese research.

Futamura (047), on the other hand, takes a more narrow perspective, and treats the concept of organizationism as a key concept in Japanese management. He defines organizationism in terms of individual preferences for dealing with the environment as an organizational member (rather than as an independent agent), and relates this to Japanese management effectiveness.

Calista (020) suggests that Japanese managers are more concerned than American managers about fulfilling the intimacy and esteem needs of subordinates through work-group involvement, and that Japanese managers employ a dual process of group involvement and allowing the establishment of individualistic leadership relations. Calista argues that Japanese workers actively seek work-group participation because of this dual approach, and that it is one of the major distinguishing characteristics of successful Japanese management.

Empirical Research

Bass (013) presents a broad-based view of cross-national aspects of leadership, drawing on both his own extensive empirical research and that of others. He places special emphasis on managerial values that are embedded in different cultures and how they affect organizational leadership goals and strategies. Also discussed is a whole broad spectrum of issues, including factors affecting leadership emergence, patterns of displayed leadership behaviors, and leadership effectiveness.

Schou and Storm (153) present a series of longitudinal studies that are organized around a conceptual model portraying leader-subordinate interactions as a regenerative model in which current behaviors and performances amplify (or decrease) subsequent behaviors and effectiveness. Some of the topics covered include societal differences, national perceptions about superior-subordinate relationships, comparative leadership profiles (using established measures), and comparative power, persuasion, and influence profiles.

Erez (040) outlines two uncompleted laboratory studies that examine differences between participative and nonparticipative goal-setting strategies, and their effects on performance and satisfaction within different social value and cultural contexts. Briefly, it is hypothesized that participatory goal setting will be more effective when an individual's prior intentions to accept imposed goals are low and when cultural and social values are congruent with participative goal setting.

Jenner (072) explores differences and similarities in business management ideology as measured by a standardized survey involving a stratified sample of U.S., Australian, Japanese, Korean, and Philippino executives. Emphasis is placed on internal and external issues, such as personnel policies, privacy, government regulation, labor unions, and corporate social responsibility.

In a follow-up to his previous research, Dickinson (034) reports a policy-capturing study using social-judgment theory to assess host national and expatriate policies for selecting American managers for overseas duty. Seven dimensions were used with 54 candidate profiles and a sample of 26 international bank firm employees, either host nationals or American expatriates, from Belgium, the United Kindom, or Japan. As expected, the cue dimensions were weighted differently by the host nationals and the expatriates, and an interaction was found between cue dimension and country of assignment. Implications for future practice and research are discussed.

Senger (160) compared authoritarian attitudes of U.S. and international military officers among enrollees at the Naval Postgraduate School, and found the U.S. officers to be significantly less authoritarian. Cultural differences that might explain the obtained results, as well as implications for cooperation among officers from different countries, are discussed.

Kustin (088) presents the results from a survey of 33 chief operating officers of American corporations and U.S.-based Japanese subsidiaries. It is concluded that the essential difference in leadership style is philosophical, based on doctrines concerning family, society, and government and military leadership that have existed for 2,000 years.

In a similar vein, Obi (124) presents evidence from ongoing research in several Nigerian industries that Western-based leadership and managerial effectiveness models have not been successful in Nigeria because of key differences in traditions and cultural beliefs. He argues that managerial styles and effectiveness are culture-bound, and that cultural differences must be considered for each specific and unique culture considered.

Finally, Miller and Crespy (114) provide a rather specialized discussion of factors lying within the realm of managerial decisions that influence the degree of foreign exchange gains and losses that American international corporations experience as a result of recently implemented government regulations. Emphasis is placed on how these managerial decisions affect the performance of international American corporations in terms of foreign exchange gains and losses.

THE NATURE OF MANAGERIAL WORK

The epilog to the previous volume (Hunt, Sekaran, & Schriesheim, 1982) began with a summary of studies on the nature of managerial work, and it was noted that this work involved many investigators, and a whole range of data-collection and analysis methods. It was also mentioned that the editors saw this diversity of approach, as well as the volume of work in this area, as highly encouraging and as leading to an advancement in our knowledge about managerial roles and effectiveness. The studies summarized below suggest a continuation of this research trend and, again, the editors believe it to be a very positive sign of progress in this field.

Pavett and Lau (126) conducted a study to identify the types of managerial roles and skills that were predictive of managerial and departmental performance. They began by improving scales they had previously developed to measure the importance of Mintzberg's (1973) managerial roles, as well as refining a measure of the importance of managerial skills. These instruments were then administered to a sample of managers at different hierarchical levels, and organizationally generated measures of managerial and departmental performance were obtained. The final part of this research involved examining the relationships between time spent in each managerial role, role importance, skill importance, and the two performance criteria. A number of implications for future research in managerial behavior and effectiveness emerged from these analyses. As a follow-up, Pavett and Lau also compared the perceptions of MBA students with managers in terms of correspondence between the two groups on these same kinds of variables.

In a theoretical analysis, M. G. Evans (041) uses Mintzberg's (1973) ten managerial roles as a framework, and literature relevant to understanding the effective functioning of each role is reviewed. An inventory of required managerial skills and practices is also developed from this review, as are the main interrelationships between the ten roles. Evans also develops a brief framework to show how effective or ineffective performance of one role affects performance of other roles.

Kelly (080) describes a completed small-scale study and a larger planned study dealing with the work of chief executive officers of different organizations. The first study involved the observation of two construction company presidents and a military general for two to three weeks. Analysis of the observational data produced interesting results that are at variance with those of Mintzberg (1973) and others. The executives studied worked short hours, spent much time on personal matters, and set aside considerable blocks of time to deal with specific and important managerial activities. Further analysis of the data suggested two possible explanations for these findings: executive behavior might be a function of technology, or it might be a function of the time period selected for observation. A follow-up study is being planned to explore these and related issues, along with a review of research on chief executive officers.

Globerson (054) conducted a managerial behavior study as a first step in designing a training program to improve managerial behavior through knowledge of key activities performed. The initial research involved analyzing the activities of 199 managers from three hierarchical levels, and 13 army and police officers in 84 different organizations. Of about 2,000 tasks included by the sample as part of their activities, 11 clusters were identified. Based upon these clusters, management workshops were conducted and training effectiveness assessed. It was concluded that the impact of the combined activity analysis and workshop procedure results in significant improvement in managerial and organizational performance when the focus of this approach is on a single organization.

Similar to Globerson (054), Bresnick (017) used both diaries and direct observation to investigate the behavior of middle-level managers and first-line supervisors in a municipal social-services agency. With the results of the data, collected over a one-week interval, training sessions were then conducted to improve the participants' work patterns. Finally, the participants were asked to assess the usefulness of the training in improving their performance.

A paper by Aldrich (006) reports a study of four chief executive officers over a one-week interval by direct observation and unobtrusive means. The results indicate that four dimensions of organizational and environmental constraints influence managerial allocations of time: organization size, the degree of organizational autonomy, the need for legitimacy, and the degree of competition faced by the organization. Also discussed are several implications of these findings for current organizational decision-making theories, as well as implications for future studies of managerial behavior.

Kriger and Barnes (086) report an intensive study of several paired companies in which they explored how difficult and critical organizational decisions are made by senior executives. They focus on decision time phases, influence networks, information flows, human involvements, leadership patterns, and executive roles, as well as on how senior executives move back and forth across different roles in the process of solving complicated issues and problems. The informal processes behind the formal ones are also given some consideration.

Levin (092) conducted a study using loosely structured interviews of six bank and school-system managers. From the interviews, a description was written of each manager's view of his or her work, and these were then given to each manager for further discussion and validation. The analysis of the descriptions and the interviews indicated the importance of the individual's definition of the specific job and situation, and the results provide a picture of managers as lay theorists whose own ideas about what they are doing are fundamental to understanding their work and behavior.

Turning to more quantitative investigations, Rusmore (144) reports the results of a study of 208 managers, using Hemphill's (1960) Executive Position Description Questionnaire. For each manager, two descriptions were obtained, one from the manager and one from the immediate superior. The resultant 208 position scores along 10 different position dimensions were then subjected to a cluster analysis, producing 10 different position clusters. These are described in some detail, although two different clustering methods failed to yield equivalent clusters. Rusmore also discusses the results of correlating a battery of intelligence tests with performance ratings for these same managers, as well as factor-analytic groupings of the intelligence tests themselves.

Segrist (158) reports a study dealing with the outside membership activities of managers and how these activities relate to managerial effectiveness. About 300 bank managers were surveyed concerning their outside-the-organization membership activities, the importance of various managerial work activities to their jobs, and their self-assessed effectiveness in three domains. Promotion-rate data were also obtained. The results of this study indicate that the relationship between outside membership activities and managerial effectiveness depends upon the kinds of activities that are most important to the job and on the effectiveness criterion involved. Implications of the findings for organizational policies on outside activities are discussed, along with possible links between membership involvements and managerial career paths.

South (171) conducted a study of 114 nurses and nursing students using a questionnaire containing vignettes, with graphic rating scale and free response blanks for each vignette. Qualitative and quantitative analyses were conducted to determine the types of behaviors most associated with perceptions of leadership, job competency, and the possession of managerial skills. The results indicated a lack of clear perceptual agreement about what constitutes leadership, competency, and managerial skills, and South discusses some of the more serious implications of this finding for theory, research, and practice.

LEADERSHIP BEHAVIOR AND STYLE

As in previous epilogs, a fairly large volume of current research may be summarized as pertaining to leadership behavior and style. Included here are studies dealing with various aspects of style, studies examining leader behavior or style flexibility, tests or extensions of current leader behavior theories, and studies linking leader behavior to issues in the careers domain. Whereas previous epilogs included studies on participation in the summaries on leader behavior studies, these are treated separately here. Participation, power, influence, and conflict are key themes in European research, and, as a result, they are treated in a separate section below. Also, some of the other sections that follow contain materials that might be considered part of this section; they are treated separately simply because of the volume of research in each of these areas.

General Studies of Leadership Style

Wright (193) studied the effects of "accounting" and "nonaccounting" leadership style on budget- and nonbudget-related performance criteria, satisfaction with supervision, and role conflict. The two styles were found to have different underlying behavioral dimensions, as well as to relate differentially to the criteria. Hendrix and Ovalle (067) examined the effects of different managerial behavior and situational variables on four organizational effectiveness criteria among 4,786 U.S. Air Force and civilian personnel. The obtained results indicated that behaviors contributing toward effectiveness varied depending upon the criterion and situational moderators. Similarly, Eckerman (039) examined relationships among leader behaviors and drug abuse in U.S. Army personnel. Here, however, no significant relationships were obtained.

Ayman and Chemers (011) examined relationships between leader behavior and personality characteristics, situational moderators, and several outcome measures among 160 middle managers in 8 Mexican industries. Factor analyses of the leadership descriptions were also undertaken but the results of this study have not yet been finalized. S. R. Chatterjee (024) is examining relationships between leader behaviors and several outcome measures for a sample of managers in Western Australia. The data have not yet been analyzed, but the results that are obtained will be compared with those existing in the literature.

Faltot (043) examined managerial orientation toward outcome variables (results) and process variables (how results are obtained) and how these relate to various organizational criteria. The obtained results are compared with those in the literature, and the author integrates his conceptualization of leadership style with more established viewpoints. Similarly, Gillespie (053) conducted a study relating leadership styles on the autocratic-participative continuum to various demographic (e.g., age) and organizational structure (e.g., hierarchical level) dimensions. Although relationships were found, no one approach was best, and the executives tended to operate on the consultative part of the continuum.

Shiflett (166) examined the factor structure of one version of the Ohio State leadership scales, and found a five-factor solution. Supplemental analyses of variance indicated that each of these dimensions was related to situational cues, and that it may be possible to integrate older, two-dimensional, approaches to leadership behavior with some of the more complex ones now used in the field.

Studies Examining Leadership Flexibility

Roskin (141) conducted a study of 36 British managers exploring the relationship between their being situational (cognitively and perceptually complex) and their effectiveness. Preliminary analyses disclosed a number of interesting findings, and further analyses are being undertaken. McGuire (110) examined how leaders either adapt their styles to fit the organization or how they attempt to change the organization itself, in two case studies involving U.S. school superintendents. The data indicated that superintendent effectiveness was related to adaptive ability, with the more effective being able to pursue their own goals and preferences within constraints imposed by the organization and the situation.

Connolly (028) offers a theoretical treatment of how leaders become flexible and adaptive, perhaps complementing the McGuire study (110) summarized above. His model treats the leadership process as an ongoing, interactive one that is designed to reduce the cognitive demands placed on leaders sharply and thereby make possible the emergence of finely tuned adaptive behavior. Another possible complement to the McGuire study is the research of Neel, Tzeng, Tekarslan, and Baysal (120), who studied the effect of a department head's leadership style on the styles of subordinate foremen in three small Turkish industries. They found such effects to be strong, and the obtained results are compared and contrasted with earlier research conducted in America.

Speroff (172) presents a theory of leadership style development, arguing

that as leaders mature, they tend to become more team oriented and participative. Speroff also discusses the impact of participative leadership within
his evolutionary model. In a complementary study, Maillet (098) is in the middle of a five-year study of leadership style change among officer-cadets en-
rolled in a Canadian military academy. No results are currently available but
when obtained they might be useful for exploring some of Speroff's ideas.

Finally, Suojanen (176) presents an integrative theory of managerial and
leadership behavior based upon brain neurophysiology. He also links his approach to current theories of motivation and interpersonal relations.

Tests or Extensions of Current Approaches

Harpaz and Vardi (060) examined the effects of task- and relationship-
oriented leader behaviors among Israeli firefighters and found the "high-high"
style to be most effective. Since they had used Hersey and Blanchard's (1977)
measure of leadership style, they also examined the data for support of the
Hersey and Blanchard model. Partial support was obtained, and the authors
discuss implications for improving leadership effectiveness.

Wofford (191) reports a study testing his earlier leader-environment-follower interaction theory of leadership (Wofford, 1981). Support was found
for his theory, showing that ability, environmental constraints, role perceptions, task-goal specificity, and task-goal commitment are important factors
affecting the performance of subordinates.

House's (1971; House & Dessler, 1974) path-goal theory of leadership has
been tested in studies by Schuler, Todor, and Podsakoff (155) and Oppenheimer (125). Schuler *et al.* present strong theoretical reasons why role ambiguity and not task structure should be a central moderator variable in the
path-goal theory, and they report results that are very supportive of their arguments. These authors also report a similar, related study in which leader
credibility was found to be a moderator of relationships between leader behaviors and subordinate role ambiguity and role conflict. They also suggest
that consideration of leader credibility may allow a reconciliation or explanation of why role ambiguity and task structure sometimes do not moderate
leader behavior-subordinate outcome relationships. Oppenheimer (125), on
the other hand, reports the results of a study exploring three-way interactions
among leader behaviors, task structure, and subordinate personal characteristics (authoritarianism, locus of control, task ability, need for clarity, tolerance of ambiguity, and need for direction) and subordinate satisfaction, motivation, and performance. The relationships examined were those proposed
by the path-goal theory or derivable from it, and the cross-validated results
were not strongly supportive of the theory. Possible reasons for the findings
are discussed.

The substitutes-for-leadership approach of Kerr and Jermier (1978), which
may be viewed as a path-goal theory extension (Schriesheim & DeNisi, 1981),

has recently been further clarified and tested by Sheridan (165) and Howell (070). Sheridan broadened this approach by considering some of Mintzberg's (1973) roles instead of the usual leader behaviors, and tested this approach via structural modeling (path and regression analysis). Howell, on the other hand, offers a typology that builds upon the Kerr and Jermier (1978) work by further differentiating among the variables that inhibit the impact of leader behaviors, increase their effects, supplement and replace them. He also considers how the proposed typology helps explain replication problems in moderator variable research and illustrates his discussion with examples from the literature.

Leader Behavior-Career Linkage Research

The final three works to be considered in this section attempt to link the study of leader behavior to research in the careers area or attempt to discuss style and career issues simultaneously. Mark (105) reports the results of a study on career orientations in higher educational administration in the United States. Her results are then linked to leadership performance by considering leadership as an aspect of career development. La Van and Welsch (089) report a study expanding Fiedler's (1967) theory of leadership effectiveness and linking it to career stage models. Linkages are also offered to other leadership theories, such as path-goal theory. Finally, Krieger (085) discusses the results of a survey he conducted on a large number of suggested "guides" for managerial behavior and effectiveness. He compares the results of his survey with those obtained in 1955 and discusses their implications with respect to managerial career development.

LEADERSHIP AND
MANAGEMENT CHARACTERISTICS

Previous epilogs have not contained separate sections summarizing research on leadership and management characteristics, and few studies of this type have usually been reported in previous symposium volumes. The studies summarized below, then, represent a marked departure from previous epilogs, and it is difficult to determine whether the number of studies in this vein has increased or decreased in comparison with the past. These studies are included here, however, because of recently renewed theoretical interest in the study of leader and manager characteristics (e.g., House & Baetz, 1979). Perhaps these studies signal a reemergence of scholarly interest in this domain.

General Theoretical Treatments

Tivendell (182) presents a theoretical treatment that argues that current developments in personality theory and personality testing may allow substantial advances in the study of leader characteristics as compared with earlier approaches. Holliday (068) likewise presents a conceptual work that attacks the older "trait" approach to the study of leadership and, as an alternative, offers a taxonomy of manager types that he believes is supported by the literature. He also summarizes some evidence suggesting that specific characteristics distinguish managers in each of his taxonomic classes. Poppleton (133) outlines a yet-to-be completed project summarizing and integrating existing research on leader and manager characteristics and how these may be developed into a situational-process model.

Studies of Intelligence

Rusmore reports two related studies examining relationships among indicators of executive intelligence (143) and relationships between intelligence and creativity and executive job-performance ratings (145). This later study examined hierarchical level as a moderator, and found intelligence to be less important at higher organizational levels and creativity to be more important. Lear (091) is conducting an unstructured and structured longitudinal observational study of managers, and intends to develop a model of how intelligence, emotion, motivation, and insight interact to affect managerial performance.

Personality Characteristics Studies

Campbell (021) reports results from data obtained by the Center for Creative Leadership on several thousand leadership training course participants. The preliminary results show that people in leadership roles tend to be more intelligent, more dominant, more analytical, and more varied along other dimensions than nonleaders. Discussion is also presented about the situational nature of these findings, and which characteristics seem to be less situation-specific.

Wong (192) offers a new conceptualization of the locus-of-control variable, and argues that managers who are high on internal and external orientations simultaneously are most likely to be adaptive and effective. A. Chatterjee (023) presents an analysis and some limited data supporting a systems-perspective view of leadership effectiveness, and that leaders need two essential skills—environmental sensitivity and environmental compatibility.

Noty (123), on the other hand, is conducting a study relating a large number of personality, value, interest, and ability tests to several criteria of management effectiveness. He expects the obtained results to show that at least several characteristics are needed for effectiveness in his sample.

Start (173) presents a theoretical discussion of relationships between personality dimensions and managerial stress. Also discussed are hierarchical differences in perceived managerial job pressures. Neel (119) explored the relationship between rated leadership ability and democratic, authoritarian, and insecure personalities, and obtained several interesting findings.

Hendrick (066) argues that the reason for the failure of past research on leader characteristics is a general focus on lower-order personality factors instead of more basic predispositional dimensions. Based upon a review of the literature, a model of leader cognitive complexity and situational moderators is developed, along with a proposed program of research. Baril (012) also argues for the importance of complexity, but complexity in self-image. He reports the results of a study of supervisors in seven organizations in which self-esteem and self-image complexity significantly predicted rated supervisory performance. He also discusses research under way to explore his findings further.

Harrell and Harrell (061), Lifson (093), and Terris and Jones (180) have reported studies relating various predictor variables to career success and advancement (Harrell & Harrell), ratings of managerial performance among retail store managers (Lifson), and measures of managerial integrity (Terris & Jones). The results of these studies are relatively complex, and they highlight diversity in both research approach and findings.

The final two studies of managerial characteristics deal with sex. Shapiro and Dessler (164) present a study of men and women managers in terms of differences in types of leader behaviors displayed and the relationships between these behaviors and measures of leadership effectiveness. Several moderator variables are also considered. Niehoff (122) presents a conceptual analysis concerning the integration of women into the U.S. work force. This presentation also devotes considerable attention to normative issues and to how on-the-job relationships between men and women can be productively fostered.

POWER, INFLUENCE, PARTICIPATION, AND CONFLICT

Previous epilogs have usually included summaries on participation in one form or another, usually dealing with participative leader behavior. Research on participative leader behavior was presented above, in the section concerned with leader behavior and style. Below, we summarize research on participation in a broader context, as well as research on influence, power, and conflict. As the reader might infer, the research summarized below represents a considerable change in focus from previous work reported in epilogs. This seems to reflect both a new focus on the part of U.S. researchers as well as a substantial European influence (these areas are usually dealt with by European scholars).

Power and Influence Research

Beginning with what might be labeled "more traditional approaches," Martin (106) presents a model that focuses on leader-subordinate relations and the ability of leaders to secure compliance through the use of normative, informational, and organizational influence. The model is discussed in terms of more established leadership models, and its utility is demonstrated by showing how it can be used to integrate key concepts from these more established approaches.

Dessler (032) presents an integrative review of the leadership area and uses this to develop a new theory of leadership, based upon personal and positional power. This approach is tested by Dessler and Shapiro (033) in a U.S. hospital, and is partially supported.

Trentini (186) provides a theoretical treatment of power, authority, and freedom. These three concepts are first analyzed semantically and are then used to describe several types of interpersonal relations. These relationship types are illustrated by Italian historical examples. Mangham (101) is currently working on analyzing results from a qualitative, nonobtrusive study of managerial behavior and the stimulation of creativity. Preliminary findings conflict with some of the established ideas in this domain, and they seem to suggest that status and status-related power are key aspects of managerial concern in work organizations.

Kuipers (087) is completing two experiments testing two alternate process explanations of subordinate striving to reduce a leader's power: Mulder's (1977) model, and expectancy theory. Early results suggest a slight explanatory advantage for the Mulder model. Chitayat (026) reports a study predicting leadership styles along the participative-directive continuum by individual and organizational characteristics. This study also examines sources of power in business and nonbusiness organizations, as well as how leadership style varies by hierarchical level.

Greene and Podsakoff (056) conducted a large-scale longitudinal study of how subordinates and superiors influence each other and their peers. This study examined the use of different sources of influence, and considered several possible moderators of influence utilization. The obtained results are considered in some detail, along with important research implications and suggestions for future research.

Finally, Michael (113) presents a model of control as an aspect of managerial influence. The model provides for feedforward and feedback aspects of control; it is currently being examined in field settings.

Participation Research

Agersnap and Dreisler (003) present a report on the Danish part of the "Industrial Democracy in Europe" project, exploring issues related to worker influence in 16 decision areas in 10 companies. The relationship between worker participation and leadership styles is examined, and the data suggest that delegation in many areas may be a precondition for worker participation and influence.

Along somewhat similar lines, Drenth and Koopman (038) are currently testing whether the Japanese theory and practice of "quality circles" is similar to a form of work consultation in The Netherlands, called "werkoverleg." Based on the similarity between "werkoverleg" and "quality circles," Netherlands experience may be useful to predict the conditions needed for an effective system of "quality circles," and their current research is concerned with testing this possibility.

In the United States, Macy and Peterson (097) are completing a six-year longitudinal study on the effects of a quality-of-work-life intervention program on participative leadership processes. The effect of direct versus indirect involvement in the QWL program is also being examined, along with a comparison of the effects of objective (i.e., structural) versus psychological participation.

Research on Conflict

Grunwald (059) presents a conceptual analysis of differences among conflict, competition, and cooperation, along with an exploratory study of the connotative and denotative meanings of cooperation and competition. The consequences of cooperation and competition are also explored, as well as their antecedents and situational contexts.

Tjosvold, Andrews, and Jones (183) performed a field study on correlates of different supervisory conflict orientations. It was found that leaders can improve their relations with subordinates by emphasizing shared goals, by assisting subordinates in goal accomplishment, and by rewarding subordinates for goals that are attained. Galicia (049) also explored the impact of different supervisory conflict styles, in a laboratory study using U.S. graduate business students. The obtained results supported the idea that supervisors who employ an integrative (as opposed to distributive or avoiding) orientation toward conflict will be more effective, as measured by several criteria.

Along similar lines, Kremer (084) presents the results of a study designed to explore preemptive behavior in mixed-motive laboratory games, as well as to demonstrate the feasibility of such an experimental approach for differentiating among different styles of leader behavior. His results indicated that whether "preemptors" are nominated for leadership positions by their groups depends upon the nature of the group task, and that such an approach might be profitably used in research situations where there are established status hierarchies.

Finally, Krau (083) reports the results of a transactional analysis of two medium-sized business organizations in terms of violation of worker expectations as a cause of industrial unrest. In both organizations, unrest occurred when management departed from its usual pattern of dealing with employees, and normal relations were reestablished only when management reverted back to its previous pattern of interaction.

BEHAVIORAL REINFORCEMENT, MODELING, AND FEEDBACK

Previous epilogs have contained some material dealing with behavior modification, reinforcement, modeling, and supervisory feedback, but generally within an organizational development-training context. The studies summarized below, then, depart radically from this trend; they are oriented more toward basic theory and research than toward application.

Reinforcement Research

Manz (102) presents a theoretical analysis of the self-management process. Included in his work are the various elements of the process, along with an in-depth consideration of why self-management may be a core determinant of both self and organizational effectiveness. Mawhinney (107) provides a similar but broader theoretical analysis of the functional approach to behavioral analysis. He also argues the need for integrating laboratory and field methods of studying leadership, and presents a laboratory analog that may be used in bridging the gap between lab and field settings.

Komaki (082) presents a proposed series of empirical observational studies that focus on managers' provision of performance consequences for subordinates, as well as on contrasting the actions of effective and ineffective managers in providing performance consequences. She argues that such an approach will lead to more useful findings than the usual observational studies, because of the focus on managers as reinforcement providers. A somewhat similar train of logic is used by Dragon (037), who presents a theoretical paper with the central thesis that a leader's major role is to reinforce subordinates' values about being high performers. She notes that if productivity is not reinforced, it ceases to be valued by employees, with consequent falloff in organizational performance and productivity.

Jones (073) reports a study exploring the use and interpretation of leader reward and punishment behaviors. In the first part, subjects identified leader behaviors that they viewed as rewarding, punishing, neutral, or variable (depending upon the individual or the task). The second part of the study had a new sample describe supervisory responses to different employee behaviors, and these supervisory responses were then related to individual and work-group performance.

Along a somewhat similar line, Arvey, Davis, and McGowen (010) developed a model of supervisory discipline and tested parts of it in a field setting. Their work delineates various aspects of punishment and discipline and assesses its effect on employees, as well as providing further understanding of the effects of punishment and aversive control systems in work organizations.

Finally, in a series of four laboratory studies conducted in India, Singh (169) explored the allocation of rewards by managers for subordinates' performance. Three studies were conducted examining recency effects in reward allocation, while the fourth examined the bases upon which managers allocate rewards.

Modeling and Feedback Research

Adler (002) presents a laboratory study examining the effects of subordinate self-esteem and supervisory behavior on the modeling behavior displayed by subordinates. The basic thrust of this paper is to link leadership theory with social-learning theory, and to demonstrate the effect that supervisors have as models for their subordinates. In some respects, then, this paper is a companion to the reinforcement studies summarized above, since supervisors undoubtedly reinforce subordinates for the appropriate modeling behaviors that they display.

Graeff (055) presents a performance-based normative model linking expectancy theory with social-learning theory and reinforcement theory. Although in its early stages, Graeff believes that his model will prove highly useful in integrating research findings from these three different approaches.

Larson (090), on the other hand, is currently working on a model of the supervisory performance feedback process. He is dealing with antecedents and consequences of the feedback process, and has completed several experiments testing basic aspects of his model. Quaglieri (134) is also performing research in this domain. He is developing a model of the antecedents and consequences of accepting job-performance feedback, and is placing feedback acceptance in a central position in his model. He is also conducting several tests of the preliminary model, which will be used to modify it as necessary.

LEADING AND MANAGING
PROFESSIONAL EMPLOYEES

Previous epilogs contained studies that used professional employees as samples or subjects but their focus was generally not on specific issues related to managing professional employees. The studies summarized below have an explicit focus on professionalism, and as such depart radically from material contained in previous epilogs. This may reflect an increased concern on the part of organizations today in attracting, retaining, and motivating higher-level professionals, or it may merely reflect the broader focus of the symposium itself. In any event, we view these works as important, since the management of professionals in organizations is likely to become ever-increasingly important in the coming years.

Allen and Katz (008) report a study examining relationships between project performance and the relative influence of project and functional managers in a matrix-type organizational structure. The analyses showed performance to be highest when internal influence is balanced and when external influence is centered in the project manager. In another study on project-team effectiveness, Katz (075) explored managerial behaviors that are related to keeping project teams effective when their membership is stable over relatively long time periods. Briefly, it was found that certain types of managerial behavior proved more useful in maintaining project-group effectiveness, and implications for future theory and research are suggested. Katz and Tushman (076) also conducted another study on the turnover and promotion patterns of engineering subordinates in project teams, and how these were affected by the behavior of project managers. It was found that key boundary-spanning supervisors significantly increased both the retention and promotion rates of younger engineers by engaging in behaviors that were aimed at providing a supportive professional work environment. Again, implications and future directions are discussed by Katz and Tushman.

Toren (184) presents an empirical study dealing with the inherent conflict between professional employees' desire for autonomy and organizational pressures for coordination and control. Using a sample of Western and Soviet scientists, she found that scientists do not value autonomy equally in all role areas, and that the importance of autonomy in different roles may be related to differences in experience and in professional socialization.

Schoorman (152) has developed a theory focusing on the leadership of professional subordinates, based upon two activity dimensions (internal-external activity focus, and proactive-reactive activity initiation) and a review of the literatures in leadership and professionalism. He has also conducted an empirical test of the theory, which obtained results at least partially supporting it. Saxberg (148) presents a model of management applicable to engineering and research subordinates, based upon a literature review and an extensive interviewing program in engineering organizations, research centers, and interdisciplinary project teams. Some linkages are also provided to matrix management and project-team management issues considered by Katz and his associates in the studies summarized above. Coelho (027) also presents a model of project-team management, focusing particularly on managing international research projects. Data from a case study and a pilot survey are also presented, as are implications for future theory and practice.

COMMUNICATION, INFORMATION PROCESSING, AND DECISION MAKING

Research on perception, attribution, and implicit leadership theories was discussed in previous epilogs, and the most recent epilog contained an entire section devoted to research in this domain. Summarized below is also work in this area, but there appears to be less of it currently being conducted than in the recent past. Also summarized below is research dealing with communication, information processing, and decision making. This research is a radical departure from that contained in previous epilogs, as it attempts either to integrate traditional leadership approaches with these other approaches or to expand conceptualizations or treatments of leadership and management effectiveness by considering informational and decision-making aspects of leadership and managerial roles.

Attribution and Implicit Theory Research

Niebuhr, Manz, and Davis (121) report on a study of individual differences in attributions about leader behaviors. Using videotapes of leader behavior episodes and measures of individual differences, they expect to find that key individual differences substantially impact upon leader behavior perception and attribution processes.

Zalesny (196) is currently conducting a study of the factor structures of open-ended descriptions provided by students of imaginary leaders. She notes that support for implicit theories would be strengthened if the open-ended descriptions obtain similar factor structures to those of commonly used questionnaire measures of perceived leader behavior.

McElroy and Downey are (109) currently completing a laboratory study that shows that the performance-attribution effect in leadership attribution studies (where performance causes leadership descriptions) is a byproduct of the vantage point of the subjects, and that performance data are more salient cues for observers of groups than for active group participants. Butterfield (019) is also completing a quasi-experimental study exploring the interactive effects of leader sex, behavior, and performance attributions. His preliminary data suggest different performance attributions for "high-high" and "low-low" leadership styles, as well as differences depending upon the sex of the leader. The preliminary results, however, show that the "high-high" style generally leads to higher attributions of performance for leaders, regardless of the leader's sex.

Gioia (051) and Gioia and Manz (052) are currently working on models of automatic versus controlled information processing by leaders and on a specific automatic process, "script processing" (Abelson, 1981). The first model (Gioia) concerns the use of automatic or controlled processes in leader evaluations of subordinate employee performance, and it is oriented toward elaborating the cues and situations that lead to the use of one processing mode over the other. The second model (Gioia & Manz) deals with the use of stereotyped event sequences (script processes) that are activated when a person perceives cues that lead to the expectation that certain actions will occur in a set sequence. This second model is also used by Gioia and Manz to explain poor subordinate and supervisor performance, and several ways of improving performance based on the model are considered.

Research on Decision Making

Wedley and Field (188) are currently developing a theoretical model that integrates and extends the Vroom and Yetton (1973) and Stumpf, Freedman, and Zand (1979) leadership and decision-making models. They are also planning several normative and descriptive tests of their model, as well as potential applications for managerial training.

Rowe (142) has developed a cognitive contingency model that integrates several different approaches to leadership, information processing, and decision making. He has also tested his model in a large number of organizations, and has developed an approach to matching job requirements with leadership and decision-making styles.

Frohman (046) is developing a theoretical paper integrating the strategic decision-making processes used by managers with individual differences and managerial effectiveness. Also being considered are the various pressures that managers face, and the decision-related mechanisms they use to cope with such pressures.

Schappe (149), on the other hand, is developing a model integrating key concepts in the areas of decision making, leadership style, and organizational climate. His model is also designed to incorporate research results on situational approaches to leadership style and decision making, and to provide managers with a diagnostic and prescriptive framework for their use.

Finally, Pendergrass (130) examines the theoretical underpinnings of the "groupthink" phenomenon (Janis, 1972) and develops prescriptions for training to prevent groupthink in the military. He focuses, in particular, on combatting groupthink by changing perceptions of invulnerability and invincibility, and on the effects of poor performance on future groupthink episodes.

Research on Information Processing

Braunstein (016) presents the results of a large-sample field study of the effects of centralized information-processing facilities on leadership and supervisory functions. Briefly, he found that the use of such facilities led to an increased power to initiate and monitor workflow by operative employees, and to a corresponding increase in confusion among first-line and middle-level managers about their supervisory responsibilities. The importance of lateral relationships increased for technical and managerial personnel as well, and lateral coordination was found to be strongly related to managerial performance at the three research sites.

Algera and Koopman (007) are examining a related issue, the consequences of different decision-making strategies in automation projects upon various dependent variables. They are also planning to examine the effects of different possible moderators on their outcome measures. Hatcher (062) is also working on a related theoretical paper, summarizing decision support system characteristics and how they relate to managerial decision making and managerial effectiveness. Haynsworth and McDonald (063) are taking this line of research even further by theoretically exploring information-processing factors that may result in the unscrupulous creation of misinformation and distorted communications, as well as how managers can guard against this.

Sadek (146) presents a theoretical treatment of relationships among communication and information from computer-based information systems and various aspects of managerial effectiveness. Rosenberg (140) presents what might be considered a companion piece in which it is argued that much managerial and leadership success depends upon communication skills, and that terminology plays a central role in managerial success.

TOP MANAGEMENT AND STRATEGIC LEADERSHIP

The material summarized below represents a radical departure from previous epilogs, for in previous volumes very few works are reported in the area of top management and strategic leadership. As we noted with respect to several other areas above, it is difficult to determine whether this represents the more narrow perspective of previous symposia and volumes or whether it is indicative of previously narrower research interests by scholars in the field. In any event, the works reported below represent a very worthwhile widening of our perspective on leadership and managerial behavior and effectiveness, and this is in no small part due to the diversity of material involved. To present this material as coherently as possible, work in this area is presented in three subsections: top-level leadership and managerial behavior and effectiveness, top-level manager-environmental interactions, and specialized problem issues in top-level management and leadership positions.

Top-Level Behavior and Effectiveness

Kimmel (081) presents a broad-based review of knowledge in the areas of senior leader job characteristics (functions, roles, and behavior patterns), competencies (skills, knowledge, and personal qualities), and training, with an emphasis on highlighting areas needing future research. Buchan (018) reports a study of the boards of directors of several large commercial banks in Canada, California, and Australia, focusing on the composition and role of these boards. Personal interviews were used, along with a detailed analysis of the financial performance of each bank, and the changes in board membership over a ten-year period.

In a somewhat similar work, Abelson (001) developed a conceptual model relating chief executive officer attributes, environmental characteristics, organizational structure dimensions, and organizational performance. He is also engaged in a study exploring his model, using data from 488 companies in 11 different industries over a 10-year time period. The emphasis in his empirical research is on exploring causal relationships, while the conceptual model focuses on how environmental turbulence, and changes in organizational size and structure, are managed according to attributes of top management.

Sekaran (159) is also exploring the effects of top-manager attributes on system performance. She is conducting a qualitative study of the effects of Indian prime ministers' values, attitudes, and behaviors on indicators of national economic, cultural, social, and quality-of-life variables for the period 1947 to 1981.

Shrivastava (168) reports the results of an empirical study of strategic decision-making processes in 32 business organizations. Top-management decision makers were found to follow one of four approaches to strategic decision making, and Shrivastava argues that it is the strategic decision process that determines the roles and functions of organizational leaders. Jacobs (071) provides a conceptual integration of the strategy, strategic planning, and strategic management literature with current theory and research on leadership. The outcome of this integration is a model of strategic leader behavior that might prove a useful adjunct to the research of Shrivastava.

Along a different line of research, Kelley and Young (079) argue that the primary management function is the effective management of organizational task processes. In this respect, they agree somewhat with Tichy (181), who also sees top-management effectiveness as requiring attention to technological-task processes. Tichy, however, also views effectiveness as requiring attention to political allocation and cultural/ideological issues, as well as to maintaining a balance among key elements in an organization's technical, political, and cultural subsystems.

A different perspective is taken by MacCrimmon (094), who argues that an essential part of top-level leadership is the willingness to take risks. MacCrimmon presents the results of a study of the risk-averting behaviors of over 500 business leaders in the United States and Canada, and integrates his findings into a contingency theory of risk, which he also relates to current theories of leadership. Schwenk (156) also deals with managers' attempts to structure decisions and reduce environmental uncertainty. He reviews research on biases in ill-structured decisions, managerial uncertainty reduction mechanisms, and various techniques that may be used to improve strategic decision making.

Management-Environment Interactions

Tracy (185) uses J. G. Miller's theory of living systems to treat leadership as consisting of two subprocesses: making decisions in accordance with the needs of the environment, and influencing others to implement the decisions.

He discusses problems and approaches arising from this conceptualization, and provides linkages to current theories of leadership. A similar approach is used by Taylor (179), who examines the role of top managers in receiving environmental stimuli, implementing strategic changes in accord with those stimuli, and overcoming constraints in developing and implementing strategic organizational changes. Besides providing a theoretical perspective, Taylor also reports the results of a study exploring his concepts, using an intensive analysis of four organizations over a 30-year period involving major periods of strategic change.

Fisher (045) also focuses on manager-environment interfaces, but from the perspective of resource-exchange networks. He reports the results of a study identifying managers who are effective resource-exchange networkers, and identifies factors that impact on their efforts to link needs and resources effectively at the community level. He also suggests useful avenues for future research and practice.

Heller (065) presents a theoretical analysis of what she calls the "leadership crisis" in contemporary societies. She discusses leadership ineffectiveness as a developmental and maturational issue, and focuses on changes in society that have produced the crisis. McPhail (112) takes a more macro-oriented, but narrower, view, and examines the potential impact of what he calls the "New World Information Order" (NWIO) on the management of transnational communications organizations. He discusses alternative models for the management of international environmental information, and the impact of these models on corporate strategy in the coming years.

The final management-environment work considered here comes from Dess (031), who focuses on the objective measurement of organizational task environments, using measures similar to those of the Aston researchers. Dess reports results showing that three factors (munificence, complexity, and dynamism) are common to organizational task environments, and he discusses implications for organizational strategy formulation and further research on linkages between management strategic decision making and organizational environments.

Specialized Top-Management Problems

The works summarized below deal with top or strategic management issues in special or unusual circumstances. Although each is different, the general emphasis on special or unique problems is a binding thread that unites this material.

In what might be considered the only "optimistic" work of this group, Kassover (074) examines the interrelated problems that arise in managing communities with high growth rates. A conceptual model is presented, dealing with key areas requiring integration and coordination for successful growth management, and she suggests that community managers need to pay particular attention to process issues and involvement of all groups affected by growth.

Mirvis (115) presents theoretical and conceptual arguments about current perspectives on crisis management, and he suggests that the conventional view is basically a prescription for failure. He argues that instead, a model of crisis management is needed that emphasizes that top managers must adopt a learning-from-errors perspective, and he illustrates his model with examples drawn from his research on organization development failures. He also highlights societal, organizational, and personal consequences of poor crisis management and provides directions for future research and practice.

Along a somewhat similar vein, Zammuto and Cameron (197) present theory and data on managing organizations faced with environmental decline. A typology of environmental decline is presented, along with managerial strategies required to cope effectively with each type of decline. Zammuto and Cameron also discuss several related issues and implications for strategic adaptation and organizational theory. Murray and Jick (118) also deal with "decline," but from the vantage point of managing public-sector organizations in times of severe financial constraints. They present a review of the literature on managing organizations in difficult times, and the results of a six-case comparative study of the effects of financial cutbacks on Canadian hospitals. They also discuss the relative effectiveness of different actions in dealing with the financial cutbacks, as well as employee responses to the cutbacks and the accompanying management actions.

Also using a public sector perspective, Young (194) discusses the diversity of motives for working in public-sector organizations, and how these motives might be more effectively related to incentive systems for improving organizational performance. This work reviews both theory and research in this area, and proposes a new model of public goods for application to the area of employee incentives. Obviously, with more public-sector organizations in more countries being faced with financial cutbacks, this work might be a provocative companion for the Murray and Jick (118) paper.

The final "special problem" paper considered here is that of Gawthrop (050), who deals with public-sector management ethics. Briefly, Gawthrop argues that ethics must be dealt with in holistic terms, and that managers must ensure that ethics are treated as individual, not collective, responsibilities.

LEADER-FOLLOWER RELATIONS

The studies summarized below deal with research on leader-follower relations and, as such, studies in this general domain have typically been included in all of the previous epilogs. The one difference here is that in previous epilogs there usually were not a large enough number of studies to form a separate section, so they were treated under different topic areas (e.g., in the previous volume, they were contained under sections dealing with perception, participation, process studies, and extensions to currently emphasized approaches). Also, several of the studies summarized below deal with charismatic leadership, a topic that we noted in previous epilogs could use additional research. All in all, then, it seems that research in this general area has increased over the past few years, and this is probably a positive development for the field.

Research on Charisma and Related Topics

Shiflett (167) builds on House's (1977) formulation of charismatic leadership by suggesting that it might be conceptually similar to a concept called "personal leadership." This theme is then elaborated by discussing characteristics of personal leadership that have been discussed in the literature, and emphasis is placed on how the leader communicates his or her values to followers. The implications of this approach to charismatic leadership are then discussed, and the possibility of training people to behave in a charismatic manner is considered.

Pearce (128) appears to be working on a conceptual model that shares some similarities with the work of Shiflett. Her model deals with the antecedents and consequences of subordinate loyalty to immediate supervisors, and she uses the model to speculate on situations under which subordinate loyalty is important. A similar approach appears in the work of McKnight (111), who argues that for leadership to exist, followers must be willing to follow, and thus that leadership involves the values of individuals toward such issues as loyalty and commitment. Savoie (147) is also beginning work along what appears to be a similar vein, with his attempt to measure components of charismatic processes among leaders, followers, and situations empirically.

Kelley (078), Dowling (036), Tucker (187), M. K. Evans (042), and Griffin (058) appear to be doing work that might be highly complementary. Kelley (078) completed a field study indicating that just spending time working for a supervisor is not adequate to allow subordinates to estimate their supervisor's values accurately. This suggests that supervisors need to be concerned with issues such as openness to subordinates, accessibility, trust building, and fair use of power. These are some of the key variables being considered by Tucker (187) in her development of a theory of leader-subordinate interactions.

Dowling (036) is also engaged in research that appears to be complementary. He is examining legitimation, ritual, and the creation of meaning in large organizations. Griffin (058) has developed a theory that might be useful in this area as well. He focuses on the leader's role in subordinates' social constructions of reality and, obviously, issues such as those considered by Dowling play a large part. Finally, research by M. K. Evans (042) helps round out some of our knowledge about components of charismatic leadership. She conducted a qualitative study and found that leaders who were strong advocates for their subordinates had higher levels of subordinate performance and lower levels of turnover. This supports some of House's (1977) notions about the charismatic leader being a spokesperson and advocate for followers.

New Approaches and Extensions of Current Work

Manz and Sims (103) present a process-oriented view of the leadership of self-managing groups, using data collected by a variation of the nominal group technique. These data are related both to substantive issues dealing with self-managed groups and to methodological issues in conducting qualitative research.

Conover (029) presents a rather novel piece of work, arguing for the need to conduct research on managerial secrecy, reviewing the limited literature on secrecy, and presenting a preliminary framework for future secrecy research.

Argyle (009) reports a number of new studies that build on his previous work in analyzing leadership relations and situations (Argyle, Furnham, & Graham, 1981). This work considers goals and goal structures, behavior repertoires, activities engaged in, and rules employed; it also examines cross-cultural findings on rules for leaders in five different cultures.

Seers (157) reports on concurrent, longitudinal, and mixed studies designed to explore his newly developed dual-attachment model. This model is based upon integrating major concepts from the job design and leader-follower exchange literatures, and his preliminary tests seem to support the model over models from either of the other two domains.

Sweney and Sweney (177) report an empirical dyadic study of role congruence between supervisor and subordinate roles. This research is an elaboration and examination of Sweney's (1979) earlier work, and it provides moderate support for his response-to-power model.

Shani and Pasmore (163) conducted a field study exploring the Pygmalion effect. They found such an effect to exist, and that leaders who expected subordinates to be higher performers generally displayed higher levels of support, goal emphasis, interaction facilitation, and work facilitation. They also discuss implications for practice in the leadership of subordinates.

MANAGEMENT-ORGANIZATIONAL STRUCTURE INTERACTIONS

Previous epilogs contained few studies relating leadership or management behavior or effectiveness to organizational structure, and the same is generally true here. We do, however, have several studies in this domain, and we view that as encouraging, since more macro approaches are clearly needed to supplement the more traditional micro approaches that have generally been used. Perhaps we should also note that about half of these studies have been conducted outside the United States and the United Kingdom. This might be suggestive of cultural differences in what researchers typically consider, but of course, our sample data are just too small and unsystematic to allow us to draw any firm conclusions.

Carroll and Gillen (022) explored the correlates of rated managerial skill (in six skill areas) with managerial effectiveness in mechanistic and organic organizations. A number of different skill-effectiveness correlations were found among the two types of organizations, although only a few were significantly different. Implications are discussed with respect to structural factors affecting managerial effectiveness and needed skills.

Wlodarczyk (190) conducted a study of the effects of centralization and the use of uniform organizational structures on various aspects of managerial functioning and on relationships between superiors and subordinates in Polish health-care organizations. Many of his structural concepts appear highly related to those used by Blau and by the Aston group in their studies of organizational structure, and Wlodarczyk presents some interesting theory on the effects of centralization and uniformity that complements his empirical findings.

Aldemir (005) examined the relationship between managerial style and organizational structure in ten Turkish industrial firms. Differences in several organizational structure dimensions were found between managers with "professional" and "traditional" styles, and the data generally supported a strong relationship between managerial style and organizational structure. Aldemir also discusses implications for future research.

Shani and Eden (162) present a descriptive study of parallel organizational structures in a military organization. Parallel structures involve conventional line structures with an added structure that focuses on providing participatory problem-solving assistance. Shani and Eden's paper describes the functions, development, and use of such a structure, and it discusses possible applications in other organizations.

Pennings and van Wijk (131) report on a large-scale study of the organizational climates in boundary-spanning units. Their approach is largely methodological, aimed at improving understanding of the correlates by climate by the use of multiple measurement methods and different samples of respondents. Although not explicitly tied to leadership and management issues, this work would seem useful for researchers wishing to explore climate within a leadership or management perspective.

Calista (020) is conducting an exploration of whether generalist managers can be effective in running public agencies that have been formed by folding previously independent bureaus into one organization. His preliminary findings suggest that generalists do not function well in these types of organizations, as they do not articulate effectively with specialized bureau functions. A similar research topic is currently being explored by Ahn and Taylor (004), who are investigating whether decentralized organizational structures lead to improved leadership and impact on rural U.S. communities. Ahn and Taylor also plan to present implications of their findings for rural development in other nations.

LEADERSHIP, MANAGEMENT, AND ORGANIZATION DEVELOPMENT ISSUES

Leadership and management training, and organization development research has typically been summarized in previous epilogs, and from the number of works summarized below, it appears that this area has continued to maintain its interest level for both practitioners and scholars. Since many of these works are highly specialized and applied, they are summarized more briefly than were the works discussed above. This is not meant to suggest that they are unimportant, but that they are of more limited interest than the previous works.

Margerison (104) presents survey results from 250 British executives on their perceptions of important factors in the development of their careers. These factors are then grouped into five summary categories, and implications for management development are discussed. Field (044) reviews the existing literature on leadership theories and discusses how each might be applied by managers under different situations.

Dolan and Tziner (035) present a detailed study of a military leadership assessment center, including information on criterion development and predictive validity results. Schuler (154) also describes the development of an assessment center, and a training program, for leadership potential. Also discussed is an implicit comparison of trait versus behavioral approaches to leadership. Swezey and Mietus (178) discuss a complex management simulation and assessment system that is designed to provide information to participants on the fit between their method of processing information and the information loads and complexity that they face.

Straessle (174) discusses the importance of context learning, and presents examples of its importance and how managers might be trained in it. A similar approach seems to be suggested by Pekerti (129), in his three-tier transorganizational model of management development. This model is particularly designed to foster joint work by consultants, trainers, and researchers, and so it may be useful for combined practical-scholarly work.

Horney (069) describes a personalized development program for managers that is tailored to their individual needs. This approach could possibly be integrated with the Straessle and Pekerti approaches, to yield individualized learning programs aimed at helping managers deal with organizational contexts and environments.

In two highly specialized works, Boyce and Otalora (015) describe an evaluation study of an MBA program in Mexico, while Healy-Sesno and Newman (064) describe how an evaluation process model was used to change the leadership and managerial behaviors of a group of U.S. school superintendents.

In more macro works, Macy and Mirvis (096) describe some approaches to estimating the costs and benefits of change programs, in terms of both monetary impacts and social utility. They also provide examples of the application of these approaches. Moskal (117) presents an empirical study of a team-building intervention in a U.S. hospital. Experimental and control groups were examined, and process and outcome variables were measured. A similar study appears to have been conducted by Boss (014), who studied problems in team-building interventions over a three-year time period in 21 organizations. McCann (108) reports a framework to guide managerial interventions in dealing with complex social problems such as crime. The intervention involves recognizing the dominant developmental process, operating at both a task and conceptual level, working with "stakeholders" at more than one level of analysis, and linking the multiple interventions through an independent coordinative mechanism. Finally, Mangelsdorff (100) presents a survey of U.S. Army interventions in health-care settings. The purpose of this study was to determine the types of interventions currently in use, and to obtain estimates of the effectiveness of each intervention type.

ORGANIZATIONAL EFFECTIVENESS

Previous epilogs did not summarize material pertaining to organizational effectiveness, unless the works were somehow linked to leadership and/or managerial behavior. Because the thrust of the symposium upon which this volume is based was considerably wider than that of previous symposia, several works on organizational effectiveness were submitted for consideration, and these are summarized below, along with two works by Ramsey (135, 136) that link an aspect of organizational effectiveness (employee retention) to managerial behavior.

Macy and Mirvis (095) present a standardized approach for identifying and measuring indicators of organizational effectiveness, and for expressing these indicators in financial terms. They also present data from a five-phase (56-month) longitudinal assessment of a cooperative labor-management change program using their approach.

Withane (189) presents a theoretical analysis of current approaches to the conceptualization of organizational effectiveness, critiques them, and offers a new approach that is based upon structures, values, and environmental elements. Gaerthner and Ramnarayan (048) also review current approaches to organizational effectiveness, critique them, and offer a new approach. Their model classifies organizations according to how they account for their performance: whether the account is constructed for internal or external audiences, and whether the activities accounted for deal with creating frameworks or performing within an established framework. Their classification leads to four types of organizational effectiveness processes, and the authors discuss all four, including measurements issues for each.

In a more specialized vein, Schneider and Bowen (150) develop a theoretical and methodological approach to the measurement of effectiveness for service organizations. Their approach uses client evaluations of effectiveness to avoid response-response biases typically troublesome in organizational effectiveness research and to provide diagnostic data useful for research and management interventions. Another specialized work is reported by Mangelsdorff (099), who discusses the development of a managerial effectiveness indicator system for U.S. Army dentists. He also reports data collected on his indicators for various aspects of organizational functioning.

Finally, Ramsey (135, 136) presents a completed study of the effects of managerial behavior on U.S. military officer and enlisted personnel retention, and an in-process study of general reasons for job switching and possible communication problems between supervisors and subordinates as antecedents of turnover. In this respect, perhaps it should be noted that Stybel (175) is developing a conceptual model dealing with methods of helping managers and employees cope with job dismissal. Since some job switching and turnover is undoubtedly related to the threat of dismissal (or is a direct result of dismissal itself), Stybel's work may be pertinent for scholars and practitioners in this area, such as Ramsey.

THEORY DEVELOPMENT, HYPOTHESIS GENERATION, AND HYPOTHESIS TESTING

Previous epilogs usually contained material with a methodological orientation, particularly with respect to statistical analysis and instrument construction. Here, again, the current epilog does as well. It should be noted, however, that the few works summarized briefly below do not encompass all of the new methodological work of which we are currently aware. Many of the qualitative and observational studies summarized in the earlier sections of this epilog devote considerable explicit and implicit attention to methodological concerns, and we would be remiss if we did not mention this here. We will also briefly discuss methodological concerns in the conclusion to this epilog, which immediately follows the material presented below.

Dansereau (030), in conjunction with several groups of his colleagues, is continuing his earlier work on the unit of analysis issue in leadership research. He has several papers in progress concerning differences between the average leadership style and vertical dyad-linkage approaches to leadership, as well as a book that focuses on multiple levels of analysis from both theoretical and empirical perspectives.

Yukl and Clemence (195) are completing a paper that follows up on Yukl's (Yukl & Nemeroff, 1979) previous work on the development and validation of new measures of leader behaviors. Their current work refines and extends Yukl's earlier work, includes multimethod validations using observations, critical incidents, interviews, and diaries, and compares their new behavioral taxonomy with Mintzberg's managerial roles. Multiple factor analyses are reported, as well as data linking different leader behaviors to different dimensions of organizational effectiveness.

On a more theoretical note, Sooklah (170) suggests that researchers have tended to emphasize research designs for hypothesis testing and have ignored the process of hypothesis generation. He is currently finishing up a project that develops methodology for hypothesis-generating research, and is completing a paper outlining his approach and illustrating it by presenting results from an investigation of the acquisition and use of power in the Canadian public bureaucracy. Perczel (132) is also working in a similar domain, exploring how theory and empirical research relate to each other and how each complements the other. He is completing a paper using experimental field data illustrating his approach, and showing how it might be applied to other research settings.

CONCLUSION

If the reader feels a bit overwhelmed by the amount and diversity of theory and research summarized above, perhaps we, the editors, should note that we feel somewhat overwhelmed ourselves. We have tried to present this material as concisely and coherently as possible but, with such a large volume of work to be summarized, we cannot imagine that we have fully accomplished our task. We therefore commend the diligent reader who has struggled through to this conclusion, and we apologize for any unnecessary hardships we have imposed in our presentation of the above material.

If the reader reflects back on the contents of this epilog, he or she cannot help but be struck by the diversity of research topics, approaches, methodologies, and so on. Although one might be distressed by this seemingly diverse polyglot collection of research in the field, the editors feel that it is a sign of vigor and health. It was argued in the previous symposium volume (Schriesheim, Hunt, & Sekaran, 1982) that such diversity is needed if the field is to advance, and the contents of this epilog, then, seem to provide documentary evidence supporting great diversity.

The previous symposium volume also called attention to differences between U.S. and European research on leadership and management effectiveness (Hosking & Hunt, 1982), and we believe that the contents of this epilog, as well as of this entire volume, further highlight some of these differences. Much of the cross-national research, research on the nature of managerial work, and research on power, influence, participation, and conflict, come from non–U.S. scholars. In addition, the contributions from outside the United States have substantially broadened the treatments of the other areas that are summarized above. We think that the inclusion of this work in this volume has therefore been highly useful for advancing the field, and we intend to continue to seek such works for future volumes.

The work summarized above can be seen to continue some encouraging trends that were noted in the epilog to the previous volume (Sekaran, Hunt, & Schriesheim, 1982). There is clearly a trend toward more exploration of broader conceptualizations of leadership and management behavior and effectiveness, and this seems to be coupled with less reliance on strictly questionnaire-based methods of inquiry. Many of the studies summarized above employ nonquestionnaire methods of data collection, and many have used multiple methods as well. Since what we know is intimately tied to how we conduct our research, we feel that the continuation of this general trend is encouraging and should be further encouraged. This general trend is clearly due in part to our inclusion of much non–U.S. work, since, as was noted in the previous volume (Hosking & Hunt, 1982), Europeans seem to prefer broader conceptualizations of leadership and management, as well as more diverse data-collection methods. It should be noted, however, that many of the U.S. studies summarized above are also less "traditional" in both respects, and we view this as encouraging as well.

In conclusion, then, we believe that the contents of this epilog, and this volume as a whole, are highly encouraging, and they are indicative of a fundamentally diverse and healthy field. Some of the major positive trends that were noted in the previous volume appear to have continued, and we are hopeful that the future will bring even more positive developments for those interested in studying leadership and managerial behavior and effectiveness. The field seems to have finally broken free of its past reliance on narrow theories and approaches, a single methodology (the questionnaire), and a limited focus of inquiry. Although we are not all marching the same march to the same drummer, we seem to be collectively moving ahead. While we could debate whether we should all march along together, the current diversity seems to be highly encouraging and suggestive of good future development.

25

Conclusions: On Paradigm Shifts in Studying Leadership

Dian-Marie Hosking, James G. Hunt,
Chester A. Schriesheim, and Rosemary Stewart

In this concluding chapter, we present an analysis of what we consider the most important general issues revealed by the arguments in this volume. We attempt to do so by locating them in the context of what seems to be conventional in the European and North American traditions. The vehicle we use for this purpose consists of trends observed by a variety of reviewers of the social sciences. We conclude by noting that the diversity of values that underpin research and theory in the areas of leadership and management is now so great that they extend beyond the "structural-functionalist" paradigm. This being the case, we feel it necessary to qualify the conclusion of the previous volume in this series, that is, to promote diversity in order to serve different markets (Schriesheim, Hunt, & Sekaran, 1982). While diversity within a paradigm can only be healthy, it is important to recognize that paradigms may be mutually exclusive and therefore individual preferences for particular paradigms must be recognized and debated.

CURRENT TRENDS

A number of major reviews of relevant literatures have appeared in the last few years (see e.g., Cummings, 1981, 1982; Mitchell, 1979; Tyler, 1981). One author identified the following developments: First, that there is an increasing emphasis on the role of *choice* as compared with constraints and determinants in attempts to explain human conduct. Second, conceptualizations of human action are changing in ways that emphasize *processual* characteristics. Thus, *time* is being given a more central role and simple notions of causation are increasingly being questioned. Third, *idiographic* approaches are once again becoming respectable and attention is being turned to the possibility that variance might be *qualitative* as well as quantitative. These developments are seen as located in the context of a changing "world view" or paradigm where the metaphors derive from evolutionary as opposed to functional biology.

Interestingly, these developments are identified as characterizing research and publications in the discipline of psychology (see Tyler, 1981). Such trends have also been observed in critical summaries of the literature of organizational behavior—literature in which North American discussions of leadership and management typically occur. A central feature of these reviews is that the theoretical richness of the field is seen to be considerably greater than has hitherto been the case (see Cummings, 1982, p. 544). Of particular importance for our present purposes is the general argument that conventional values regarding methodological, epistemological, and related issues are being subjected to major challenges, challenges that are generally held to be promoting or having already resulted in a "paradigm shift."

Given the larger purpose of this series of symposium volumes to chart the state of the field, we feel it is important to examine these kinds of trends in the literatures of leadership and managerial behavior. To do this we first briefly summarize the main features of the traditions in these areas. The traditions, at least in terms of the size of the literature, are best defined by reference to the publications in organization theory and organizational behavior and by analysis of the values that dominate.

First, it seems fair to say that these literatures have long been dominated by a so-called "positivist" tradition. This favors the standpoint of the observer and the accumulation of data that may be expected to reveal regularities and causal relationships. The tradition reflects a view of "reality" as a matter of social fact (see Durkheim, 1938), as something that exists outside the individual, as a set of objects that have an independent existence and constrain or determine the experiences and behaviors of all human beings. An associated value, also drawn from a natural-world model, is a view of social systems as comparable to *biological* systems. This means they can be conceptualized in terms of their "parts" (structures), which make functional contributions to the whole (i.e., the system in which they function—the group, organization, society, or whatever).

Those interested in leadership and management have made important contributions to this "structural-functionalist" paradigm and, in particular, to the analysis of social structures or what might be called "social morphology." Unfortunately, less attention has been devoted to questions such as how structures come into existence or to the conditions that have to be met before the paradigm has any validity when applied to social (rather than biological) systems. Consequently, when this approach is applied to organizations we typically find that the existence of structures is taken for granted, and their status treated as a matter of "fact." In other words, they are treated as static elements of external "reality"—as objects that can be examined independent of process. Hence, such structures are assumed to be amenable to "objective measurement" such that any and all observers could describe them similarly. Little attempt is made to deal with their conceptual status, and their functions are assumed to be the same for one and all, that is, to constrain and coordinate activity for the common good.

As Hosking noted in Chapter 6, these values dominate the "new" perspectives presented in Part 1 of this volume. At the same time, there are indications of a more processual perspective, both in Part 1 and in other contributions (see e.g., Heller, Chapter 16; Huff, Chapter 14). It seems important to note, as Hosking did earlier, that those who endorse a processual definition of social structures will typically argue that any other position results in the kinds of insanities described in Alice in Wonderland—a land where babies turn into pigs! In pursuing a structural-functionalist perspective it is important to explore the differences between social and biological systems and to examine the assumptions on which the analogy is based. As Radcliffe-Brown points out, biological systems are based on the *fact* of functional unity while social systems are based on the *hypothesis* of the same. In other words, it is essential to question the existence of shared values, goals, and interests in the system being studied. Furthermore, it is essential to do so at the level of participants' subjective realities—the level of analysis would have to shift from "macro" to "micro" and focus on the perceptions of individuals.

These observations suggest the importance of two related issues: the level of analysis and conceptualization of the particular organizational setting in which leadership and management occur. These issues are of considerable importance since: "the particular level of biological organization that is chosen as the basis for a model—determines whether we see [organization] as preeminently cooperative or basically conflictual" (Buckley, 1967, p. 12). Research and theory into leadership, management, and organization have typically assumed that the unit studied—total organization, division, or department—is the conceptual equivalent of a single biological organism and therefore has functional unity at this level. Thus, the unit must be basically cooperative. In other words, the inevitable result of the above perspective is what Fox (1966) called a "unitary perspective" of organization.

The values that characterize a unitary perspective are as follows. First, all parts of the system strive toward common or "congruent" goals; activity judged to be inconsistent with "the common goal" is defined as "irrational" and dysfunctional. Second, conflict is not expected; if it is considered at all, then it is usually in terms of divergent perceptions and cognitions rather than values or interests. Third, power and influence processes receive relatively little attention compared with "formal authority" and "formal organization."

As with conceptualizations of social structures, it seems appropriate to note that much of the contemporary theorizing in the areas with which we are immediately concerned continues to reflect these traditional values with only minor modifications (we should also note that this is less true of the European contributions, a point to which we shall return). Thus, a "unitary" perspective predominates and functional unity is assumed to exist at the level of the total organization. An alternative perspective would be to treat the latter as the conceptual equivalent of an "ecological aggregate" in which competition and conflict are to be expected. Such a perspective would have profound implications for theories of leadership and managerial behavior — implications that have yet to receive widespread attention in the relevant North American literature.

Examples of such implications may be briefly outlined in the context of interests in the leadership of organization. If organization is conceptualized as an ecological aggregate, leaders would have the job of structuring relationships between groups, that is, subsystems characterized by functional unity. These would be likely to differ in their values, interests, frames of reference, bargaining strength, and the like. If this were the case, the question of what functional processes might look like would have to be answered in terms of the defined local values and interests of identified functional unities. Such questions could only be addressed by examining beliefs and perceptions as experienced by the "actors" involved, that is, their "subjective realities."

One further implication of the biological analogy demands attention since it again indicates deficiencies in traditional conceptualizations of leadership and managerial behavior. This concerns the etiology of social structures — how they are created, changed, and eradicated. Such issues have received relatively little attention in the organizational behavior or organization theory literature. As Hosking noted earlier when discussing the chapters in Part 1, it is in this area that the biological metaphor has been most misleading since biological organisms are not constantly changing their structures while social systems, even when they are not effecting such changes, are always capable of doing so.

To summarize, it appears that mainstream research and theory in the literatures of leadership and managerial behavior continue to be dominated by metaphors from functional biology. Even so, there are signs of the trends to which both Tyler and Cummings referred: the increasing popularity of anthropological approaches (see e.g., Huff, Moore & Beck, Siehl & Martin, this volume); attention to the importance of the way in which processes are played out over time (Heller, Clark, Prahalad & Doz, this volume); and interest in how individuals construct their social worlds (Burgoyne & Hodgson, Chapter 9). To put the point another way, there is evidence of increasing differentiation, even though there is still clearly a dominant paradigm.

THE IMPORTANCE OF VALUES

Many seem to be of the opinion that increasing differentiation is healthy (e.g., Hunt, in press). One reason for this opinion seems to be a "requisite variety" argument. For example, in his review of organization behavior, Mitchell averred that "no one theory or approach is best for all people in all settings" (Mitchell, 1979, p. 270). A slightly different argument is that different approaches depend on different values and these are in some sense "equal" (see, e.g., Quinn, Chapter 2). If this is so, the way to proceed is certainly as indicated in the last volume of this series: that is, to make value differences explicit and rather than debate the relative merits of different approaches, take a pluralist position and thereby "serve different markets" (Schriesheim, Hunt, & Sekaran, 1982).

Whether or not a particular researcher sees such differentiation as healthy will depend on his or her perceptions of the nature and degree of differences; this will in turn depend on each person's own world view. Given that dimensions of difference can be characterized in a great many ways, researchers will also differ in their judgments regarding the desirability and probability of integration. Recall, for example, Hunt's discussion in Chapter 15 of the "conservative" and "radical" approaches seen by Cummings (1981, 1982) as characterizing organizational behavior research in the 1980s. Cummings characterizes the former by the assumption that "no major shift in paradigm or philosophical approach is necessary" (1981, p. 366). Dominant concerns are essentially validity and reliability, research design, and multivariate analysis.

The radical approach, on the other hand, argues for "new foci, new paradigms and newly applied methodologies": radicals either advocate or practice an approach that focuses on *actors'* perceptions and meanings rather than on those of the observer. As pointed out in Chapter 15, the radical's more subjective, interpretive emphasis reflects interest in symbolic processes and those that link different levels of analysis.

Cummings (1981) sees these approaches as supplementary rather than contradictory (p. 366). In his view, integration should involve recognition of their respective strengths and weaknesses, and, therefore, of their differing potential. In advocating his desire for synthesis, albeit of a particular kind, Cummings voices a popular call for integration. As we have implied, integration can mean many things: for Mitchell (1979) it means conducting competitive tests of theories and retaining only those favored by the "data." Others judge integration to be facilitated by structural analysis which goes beyond particular milieux (see, e.g., Quinn, this volume).

Given that the desire for integration is widely shared, less consensus is evident regarding the likelihood of its being achieved. For example, in his reply to Cummings, Rose (1981, p. 380–383) argues that "synthesis has received little or no attention" and this is unlikely to change. Integration is felt to be unlikely because market forces on both the supply and demand sides operate to discourage it. Rose argues that new ideas have been accommodated by forgetting old ones; little diffusion occurs between disciplines or between specializations within disciplines; and the infrastructure of the profession does not promote synthesis, theory building, or long-term research programs. This point has also been made in previous volumes in this series (see especially Hunt & Larson, 1977, 1979).

The material contained in the present volume clearly indicates that many researchers are concerned about the possible implications of value differences. The relative merits of differing values or "world views" seems an important issue. It is our view that the nature and extent of the differences is often misperceived with the result that certain kinds of integration are felt to be possible when they are not. A particularly vivid example concerns the use of experiential methodologies and the uses to which the resulting data may be put. Beliefs about the latter are often erroneous: we shall describe why this is the case in order to illustrate some of the problems that follow from diverse values in epistemological, methodological, and related areas.

Experiential approaches are designed to examine the "social construction of reality" (Berger & Luckman, 1967). They are based on the belief that an understanding of the social world requires knowledge of individuals' own experiences, meanings, and interpretations. A potential source of confusion arises in that such methods can be employed in the service of widely differing, antagonistic values regarding the validity of differing epistemologies and the nature of "reality" (what Burrell & Morgan, 1979, refer to as the "ontological debate"). The more subjective, phenomenological tradition rejects the natural-science model and reflects a value for individuals' own appreciations of the social world—the latter can only be understood through knowledge of the actor's frame of reference. Knowledge of this kind is held to be of value in its "own right"—not as a contribution to some accumulating stock such that general "laws" might finally be identified.

As indicated, experiential techniques may also be employed in the service of a more conventional, natural-science paradigm that is rooted in what some refer to as a "positivist" epistemology. In this case, such methods are used to explore the relationship between "objective" reality (which the interpretative theorist rejects) and an individual's subjective experience of the same. This "realist" position is associated with a set of epistemological values that support the search for consistencies and causal relationships, and therefore in turn reflect the assumption that knowledge is cumulative.

These approaches are examples of what Burrell and Morgan have respectively labeled "interpretive" and "functionalist" paradigms. To these they added a further two: "radical structuralist" and "radical humanist." Having differentiated approaches in this way, Burrell and Morgan demonstrate that the various paradigms are mutually exclusive—"they offer alternative views of social reality" (Burrell & Morgan, 1979, p. 25). This poses particular problems when it is recognized that a characteristic of world views is that they hinder recognition of alternative perspectives, and are typically held with considerable tenacity. Many social scientists are ignorant of paradigms other than their own; consequently, they interpret the methodologies, data, and the like in the context of their own values and their own criteria. There are misinterpretations of this sort in the discussions summarized earlier in this volume. One in particular appears frequently, that is, that qualitative data are largely of use as "thick" description (see Clark, this volume). In other words, it is often assumed that such data provide a valuable precursor to more rigorous, quantitative investigation and that this is the reason for collecting them. As we have already indicated, many who employ such techniques do so because they reject the structural-functionalist values and the assumption that "knowledge" consists of cumulative social facts.

Confusions of this kind appear in the literature as well as in this volume. Whether or not paradigms are mutually exclusive has a profound bearing on, for example, whether integration can be achieved across paradigms or only within them. If the degree of differentiation in the leadership and managerial-behavior literatures now spans more than one paradigm, and if the paradigms are mutually exclusive, integration of the literature as a whole will be impossible. Furthermore, it becomes inappropriate to take the position that the values are "equal" and therefore to argue for a "pluralist approach" to "serve different markets" (see Schriesheim, Hunt, & Sekaran, 1982, p. 292). While "interpretive," "radical humanist," and "radical structuralist" paradigms have been almost entirely absent from the North American literature with which we are concerned, this is changing. The trends in the literature, small though they may be at present, suggest that other paradigms may come to be more popular. Furthermore, the increasing incorporation of thought from outside the North American tradition now necessitates a refinement to the "pluralist" marketing approach advocated in the last volume of this series. This is simply because the functionalist paradigm is less characteristic of the European tradition (see, e.g., Berger & Luckman, 1967).

These observations show that it is important to recognize cross-national differences not only in what we study but also in the way in which we "understand the world." These differences have important implications for whether or not exchanges will be fruitful. The point is well made by the distinction between "radical" and "conservative" approaches identified by Cummings in his earlier-mentioned review of organization behavior. While such a characterization is appropriate for the North American literature, contributions such as those in this volume, along with knowledge of the European traditions, show it to be inaccurate outside that context. Particularly paradoxical is Cummings' use of the term "radical" for approaches that have long been conventional in many branches of European social science. A radical perspective, when judged in the context of European thought, would include greater attention to theorists such as Alfred Schutz, Marx, Weber, Althusser, Poulantzas, and others.

When put in this wider perspective, a new light is cast on what critics have claimed represents evidence of a "paradigmatic shift." Thus, for example, while Mitchell diagnoses that this has happened because some are now arguing leadership is a "perceptual phenomenon in the mind of the observer" (Mitchell, 1979, p. 269), such arguments are perfectly consistent with a functionalist perspective. Based on this wider perspective, it may be argued that there is relatively little evidence of a paradigm shift in the North American literature on leadership and management. There is, however, greater recognition of alternatives within the functionalist paradigm, especially in the greater attention being paid to subjective assessments of social situations, in idiographic approaches, and in the social contexts of action and interaction.

To summarize, we endorse the conclusions of the previous symposium volume in the sense that greater diversity within a paradigm puts the conventional in a new light and may also provide new resources to a restricted pool. In the light of more recent developments and the European contributions, however, it seems apparent that it is impossible to value all perspectives, methodologies, and the like, as being of equal value—you can't "dance with different partners" when the rules say that the acceptance of one necessitates the rejection of others.

References

Abelson, R. (1972). Psychological status of the script concept. *American Psychologist, 36,* 715-729.

Abernathy, W.J., Clark, K.B., & Kantrow, A.M. (1981, September/October). The new industrial competition. *Harvard Business Review,* 68-81.

Adams, J.L. (1974). *Conceptual blockbustering.* Stanford, CA: Stanford Alumni Association.

Adams, J.S. (1965). Inequity in social exchange. In L. Berkowitz (Ed.), *Advances in experimental psychology,* New York: Academic Press.

Adams, J.L. (1974). *Conceptual blockbusting.* Stanford, CA: Stanford Alumni Association.

Agersnap, & Pederson, P.H. (1981). Explaining workers' responses by technology or by life experience. In J. Forslin, A. Sarapata, & A. Whitehill (Eds.), *Automation and industrial workers, a fifteen nation study* (Vol. 1, pt. 2). New York: Pergamon Press.

Alban Metcalfe, B.M. (1981). Model of psychological processes in social interaction. *Perceptual and Motor Skills, 52*(3), 2.

Alban Metcalfe, B.M. (1982a). Leadership: Extrapolating from theory and research to practical skills training. *Journal of Management Studies, 19*(3), 295-305.

Alban Metcalfe, B.M. (1982b), *Microskills of leadership.* Unpublished doctoral dissertation. University of Bradford, U.K.

Albrecht, P.A., Glaser, E.M., & Marks, J. (1964). Validation of a multiple assessment procedure for managerial personnel. *Journal of Applied Psychology, 48*(6), 351-360.

Alexander, E.R. (1979). The design of alternatives in organizational contexts: A pilot study. *Administrative Science Quarterly, 24,* 382-404.

Andriessen, J.H. T.H., & Drenth, P.J.D. (1982). Leiderschap: theorieen en modellen. In P.J.D. Drenth, H. K. Thierry, P.J. Willems, & Ch.J.de. Welff. *Handboek arebeids* — En organisatiepsychologie. Amsterdam: Deventer Kluwer.

Anstey, E., Fletcher, C., & Walker, J. (1976). *Staff appraisal and development.* London: Allen & Unwin.

Argyris, C. (1964). *Integrating the individual and the organization.* New York: Wiley.

Argyris, C. (1968). Some unintended consequences of rigorous research. *Psychological Bulletin, 70,* 185-197.

Argyris, C. (1976). Problems and new directions for industrial psychology. In M. D. Dunnette (Ed.), *Handbook of industrial and organizational psychology* (pp. 151-184). Chicago: Rand McNally.

Argyris, C. (1979). How normal science methodology makes leadership less additive and less applicable. In J.G. Hunt & L.L. Larson (Eds.), *Crosscurrents in leadership.* Carbondale, IL: Southern Illinois University Press.

Argyris, C., & Schon, D.A. (1974). *Theory in practice.* San Francisco: Jossey-Bass.

Argyris, C., & Schon, D.A. (1976). *Organisation learning: A theory of action perspective.* Reading, MA: Addison-Wesley.

Argyle, M., & Furnham, A. (1982). *Sources of satisfaction and conflict in long-term relationships*. Unpublished manuscript. Wolfson College, Oxford, Univ., U.K.

Argyle, M., Furnham, A., & Graham, J.A. (1981). *Social situations*. Cambridge, U.K.: Cambridge University Press.

Argyle, M., Gardner, G., & Coiffi, F. (1958). Supervisory methods related to productivity, absenteeism and labour turnover. *Human Relations, 2,* 23–45.

Ashby, (1952). *Design for a brain*. London: Chapman & Hall.

Bacharach, S.B., & Aikan, M. (1976). Structural and process constraints on influence in organizations: A level-specific analysis. *Administrative Science Quarterly, 21,* 623–642.

Bacharach, S.B., & Lawler, E. E. (1980). *Power and politics in organizations*. New York: Jossey-Bass.

Baker, E. (1980, Autumn). Managing organizational culture. *The McKinsey Quarterly*, 51–61.

Bales, R.F. (1950). *Interaction process analysis*. Cambridge, MA: Addison-Wesley.

Bales, R.F. (1953). The equilibrium problem in small groups. In T. Parsons, R.F. Bales, & E.A. Shils (Eds.), *Working papers in the theory of action*. New York: Free Press.

Bales, R.F., & Isenberg, D.J. (1982). SYMLOG and leadership theory. In J.G. Hunt, U. Sekaran & C.A. Schriesheim (Eds.), *Leadership: Beyond establishment views*. Carbondale, IL: Southern Illinois University Press.

Bales, R.F., & Slater, P.W. (1955). Role differentiation in small decision-making groups. In T. Parsons & R.F. Bales (Eds.), *Family socialization and interaction process*. Glencoe, IL: Free Press.

Bales, R.F., & Strodtbeck, F.L. (1951). Phases in group problem-solving. *Journal of Abnormal and Social Psychology, 46,* 485–495.

Bandura, A. (1977). *Social learning theory*. Englewood Cliffs, N.J.: Prentice-Hall.

Barker, R.G. (1963). *The stream of behavior: Explorations of its structure and content*. New York: Appleton-Century-Crofts.

Barnard, C. (1938). *The functions of the executive*. Cambridge, MA: Harvard University Press.

Bass, B.M. (1960). *Leadership, psychology and organizational behavior*. New York: Harper & Row.

Bass, B.M. (1974). The substance and the shadow. *American Psychologist, 29,* 870–886.

Bass, B.M. (1981). *Stogdill's handbook of leadership: A survey of theory and research*. New York: Free Press.

Bass, B.M. (1983). *Organizational decision making*. Homewood, IL: Irwin.

Bass, B.M., & Rosenstein, E. (1977). Integration of industrial democracy and participative management: U.S. and European perspectives. In B.T. King, S.S. Streufort, & F.E. Fiedler (Eds.), *Managerial control and organizational democracy*. Washington, D.C.: Victor Winston.

Bass, B.M. & Stogdill, R. (1978). *Revised handbook of leadership*. New York: Free Press.

Bass, B.M. & Valenzie, E. (1974). Contingent aspects of effective management styles. In J.G. Hunt & L. Larson (Eds.), *Contingency approaches to leadership*. Carbondale, IL: Southern Illinois University Press.

Bate, P. (1982). *The impact of organizational culture on approaches to organizational problem-solving*. Paper presented to Conference on Qualitative Approaches to Organizations, University of Bath, U.K.

Bateson, G. (1972). *Steps to an ecology of mind*. New York: Chandler.

Bateson, G., Jackson, D., Haley, J., & Weakland, J. (1956). Toward a theory of schizophrenia. *Behavioral Science, 1*, 251-264.

Batstone, E., Boraston, I., & Frenkel, S. (1977). *Shop stewards in action*. Oxford, U.K.: Blackwell.

Batstone, E., Boraston, I., & Frenkel, S. (1978). *The social organization of strikes*. Oxford, U.K.: Blackwell.

Behling, O.C. (1980a). The case for the natural science model for research in organizational behavior and organizational theory. *Academy of Management Review, 5*, 483-490.

Behling, O.C. (1980b). Functionalism as a base for midrange theory in organizational behavior/theory. In C.C. Pinder & L.F. Moore (Eds.), *Middle range theory and the study of organizations*. Boston: M. Nijhoff.

Bennis, W. (1982, May 31). Leadership. *Industry Week*, 54-56.

Benson, H., & Allen, R. L. (1980). How much stress is too much? *Harvard Business Review, 58*(5), 86-92.

Berger, P.L., & Gluckman, T. (1966). *The social construction of reality*. Garden City, NY: Doubleday, Anchor.

Berlew, S.E., & Hall, D.T. (1966). The socialization of managers: Effects of expectations on performance. *Administrative Science Quarterly, 11*, 207-224.

Beyer, J.M. (1981). Ideologies, values, and decision-making in organizations. In P.C. Nystrom & W.H. Starbuck (Eds.), *Handbook of organizational design* (Vol. 2). New York: Oxford University Press.

Biddle, B.J. (1979). *Role theory. Expectations, identities, and behavior*. New York: Academic Press.

Bijou, S.W., Peterson, R.F., & Ault, M.H. (1968). A method to integrate descriptive and experimental field studies at the level of data and empirical concepts. *Journal of Applied Behavior Analysis, 1*, 175-191.

Blake, R.R., & Mouton, J.S. (1964). *The managerial grid*. Houston: Gulf.

Bloor, M. (1978). On the analysis of observational data: Discussion of and uses of inductive techniques and respondent validation. *Sociology, 12*, 545-552.

Blumberg, P. (1968). *Industrial democracy*. London: Constable.

Boswell, J. (1972). *The rise and decline of small firms*. London: Allen & Unwin.

Bouchard, T.J. Jr. (1976). Field research methods: Interviewing questionnaires, observation, systematic observation, unobstrusive measures. In M.D. Dunnette (Ed.), *Handbook of industrial and organizational psychology* (Ch. 9). Chicago: Rand McNally.

Bougon, M., Weick, K., & Binkhorst, D. (1977). Cognition in organizations: An analysis of the Utrecht Jazz Orchestra. *Administrative Science Quarterly, 22*, 606-639.

Bower, J.L. (1970). *Managing the resource allocation process*. Boston: Harvard Business School Division of Research.

Bower, J.L., & Doz, Y. (1979). Strategy formulation: A social and political process. In D.E. Schendel & C.W. Hofer (Eds.), *Strategic Management*. Boston: Little, Brown.

Brewer, E., & Tomlinson, J.W.C. (1964). The manager's working day. *Journal of Industrial Economics, 12*, 191-197.

Brinkerhoff, D.W., & Kanter, R.M. (1980). Appraising the performance of performance appraisal. *Sloan Management Review, 21*(3), 3-16.

Brooke & Remmers, (1970). *The strategy of multinational enterprise*. New York: Elsevier.

Brown, A., & Heller, F.A. (1981). The application of group feed-back analysis to questionnaire data in a longitudinal study. *Human Relations, 34*(2), 141-156.

Brown, M.C. (1982). Administrative succession and organizational performance: The succession effect. *Administrative Science Quarterly, 27*, 1–16.

Brown, R.H. (1978). Bureaucracy as praxis: Toward a political phenomenology of formal organizations. *Administrative Science Quarterly, 23*, 365–382.

Bruning, N.S., & Cashman, J. (1978, August). *Leadership: Studying the developmental process.* Paper presented at the 38th Annual Academy of Management Meeting, San Francisco.

Buckley, W. (1967). *Sociology and modern systems theory.* Englewood Cliffs, NJ: Prentice-Hall.

Buckley, W., & Burns, T.R. (1974, August). Power and meta power. Relational control and the development of hierarchical control systems. *Eighth World Congress of Sociology,* Toronto.

Burack, E.H. (1979). Leadership findings and applications: The viewpoints of four from the real world. In J.G. Hunt & L.L. Larson (Eds.), *Crosscurrents in leadership.* Carbondale, IL: Southern Illinois University Press.

Burgoyne, J.G. (1975). The judgment process in management students' evaluation of their learning experiences. *Human Relations, 28*(6), 543–569.

Burke, R.J., Weitzel, W., & Weir, T. (1978). Characteristics of effective employee performance reviews and development interviews: Replication and extension. *Personnel Psychology, 31*(4), 903–919.

Burke, R.J., Weitzel, W.F., & Weir, T. (1980). Characteristics of effective interviews of employees' performance review and development. *Psychological Reports, 47*, 683–689.

Burns, J.M. (1978). *Leadership.* New York: Harper & Row.

Burns, T. (1957). Management in action. *Operational Research Quarterly, 8*(2), 45–60.

Burnstein, E., & Berbaum, M. (1981, June 24–27). *Stages in group decision-making: The decomposition of historical narratives.* Paper presented at Fourth Annual Scientific Meeting, International Society of Political Psychology, University of Mannheim, Federal Republic of Germany.

Burrell, G. & Morgan, G. (1979). *Sociological paradigms and organizational analysis: Elements of the sociology of corporate life.* London: Heinemann Educational Books.

Bussom, R.S., Larson, L.L., & Vicars, W.M. (1981). Unstructured, nonparticipant observation and the study of leaders' interpersonal contacts. In J.G. Hunt, U. Sekaran, & C. Schriesheim (Eds.), *Leadership: Beyond establishment views.* Carbondale, IL: Southern Illinois University Press.

Bussom, R.S., Larson, L.L., Vicars, W.M., & Ness, J.J. (1982): *The nature of police executives' work: Final report.* Carbondale, IL: Southern Illinois University Press.

Calder, B.J. (1977). An attribution theory of leadership. In B. Staw & G. Salancik (Eds.), *New directions in organizational behavior.* Chicago: St. Clair Press.

Cameron, K. (1978). Measuring organizational effectiveness in institutions of higher education. *Administrative Science Quarterly, 23*, 604–632.

Campbell, A. (1976). Subjective measures of well being. *American Psychologist, 31*, 117–124.

Campbell, D.T. (1958). Systematic error on the part of human links in communication systems. *Information and Control, 1*, 334–369.

Campbell, D.T., & Fiske, D.W. (1959). Convergent and discriminant validation by the multitrait-multimethod matrix. *Psychological Bulletin, 56*, 81–105.

Campbell, J. (1976). Contributions research can make in understanding organization effectiveness. *Organization and Administrative Science, 7*(1 & 2), 29–48.

Campbell, J., Dunnette, M., Lawler, E., & Weick, K. (1970). *Managerial behavior, performance and effectiveness.* New York: McGraw-Hill.

Campbell, J. (1977). The cutting edge of leadership: An overview. In J.G. Hunt & L.L. Larson (Eds.), *Leadership: The cutting edge.* Carbondale, IL: Southern Illinois University Press.

Carlson, S. (1951). *Executive behavior: A study of the work load and the working methods of managing directors.* Stockholm: Stromberg.

Cartwright, D. (1965). Influence, leadership, and control. In J.G. March (Ed.), *Handbook of organizations.* Chicago: Rand McNally.

Cartwright, D., & Zander, A. (1968). *Group dynamics: Research and method* (3rd ed.) New York: Harper & Row.

Cascio, W.F. (1978). *Applied psychology in personnel management.* Reston, VA: Reston.

Cederblom, D. (1982). The performance appraisal interview: A review, implications, and suggestions. *Academy of Management Review, 7,* 219-227.

Chandler, (1962). *Strategy and structure.* Cambridge, MA: MIT Press.

Chandler & Salsbury, (1971). *Pierre S. DuPont and the making of the modern corporation.* New York: Harper & Row.

Child, J. (1972a). Organization structure, environment and performance: The role of strategic choice. *Journal of British Sociology, 6,* 1-22.

Child, J. (1972b). Organization structure and strategies of control: A replication of the Aston study. *Administrative Science Quarterly, 17,* 163-177.

Chin, R. & Benne, K.D. (1969). General strategies for effecting change in human systems. In W.G. Bennis, K.D. Benne, & R. Chin (Eds.), *The planning of change.* New York: Holt, Rinehart & Winston.

Clark, B. (1970). *The distinctive college: Antioch, Reed and Swarthmore.* Chicago: Aldine.

Clark, B. (1972). The organizational saga in higher education. *Administrative Science Quarterly, 17,* 178-184.

Clark, P.A. (1982). A review of the theories of time and structure for organizational sociology. In S. Bacharach, (Ed.), *Perspectives in organizational sociology: Theory and research,* (Vol. 2). Greenwich, CT: JAI Press.

Clark, P. A. (1975). *Time reckoning systems in modern Western organizations.* (Mimeo). Paper presented at the 34th International Conference Society for Applied Anthropology.

Clark P. A. (1976). Some analytic requirements of an applied organization science. In R.H. Kilmann, L.R. Pondy, & D.P. Slevin (Eds.), *The management of organization design: Strategies and implementation.* North Holland.

Clark, P.A. (1979). Temporal innovations and time structuring in large organizations. *The Study of Time, 3,* 391-416.

Clarkson, G. (1962). *Portfolio selection: A simulation of trust investment.* Englewood Cliffs, NJ: Prentice-Hall.

Cohen, J. (1960). A coefficient of agreement for nominal scales. *Educational and Psychological Measurement, 20,* 37-46.

Cohen, J., & Cohen, P. (1975). *Applied multiple regression/correlation analysis for the behavioral sciences.* Hillsdale, NJ: Lawrence Erlbaum Associates.

Cohen, M.D., March, J.D., & Olsen, J.P. (1972). A garbage can model of organizational choice. *Administrative Science Quarterly, 17,* 1-25.

Colombo, G. (1981, October). Space technology: Where will fiction meet reality? *Technology Review,* 68-72.

Coltrin, S., & Glueck, W.F. (1977). The effect of leadership roles in the satisfaction and productivity of university professors. *Academy of Management Journal, 20*, 101-116.

Combey, P. (1980). A tracer approach to the study of organization. *Journal of Management Studies, 17*, 96-126.

Connolly, T., Conlon, E., & Deutsch, S. (1980). Organizational effectiveness: A multiple-constituency approach. *Academy of Management Review, 5*, 211-218.

Connor, P.E. (1980). *Organizations: Theory and design.* Chicago: Science Research Associates.

Connor, P.E., & Becker, B.W. (1981, March). *Value systems of engineers and engineering.* Paper presented at the University of Delaware's Center for the Study of Values.

Copeman, G.H., Luijk, H., & Hanika, F. (1963). *How the executive spends his time.* London: Business Publications.

Crano, W.D., & Brewer, M.B. (1973). *Principles of research in social psychology.* New York: McGraw-Hill.

Cronbach, L., & Meehl, P. (1955). Construct validity in psychological testing. *Psychological Bulletin, 52*, 281-302.

Crozier, M. (1964). *The bureaucratic phenomenon.* London: Tavistock Publications.

Cummings, L.L. (1982). *Annual Review of Psychology, 33*, 541-579.

Cummings, L.L., & Schwab, D. (1973). *Performance in organizations: Determinants and appraisal.* Glenview, IL: Scott, Foresman.

Cummings, T.G. (1978). Self-regulating work groups: A sociotechnical synthesis. *Academy of Management Review, 3*, 625-634.

Cummings, T.G. (1981). Designing effective work groups. In P. Nystrom & W. Starbuck (Eds.), *Handbook of organizational design* (Vol. 2) *Remodeling organizations and their environments.* Oxford, U.K.: Oxford University Press.

Cummings, T.G., & Srivastva, S. (1977). *Management of work.* Kent, OH: Comparative Administration Research Institute, Kent State University.

Daft, R. & MacIntosh, N. (1981). A tentative exploration into the amount and equivocality of information processing in organizational work units. *Administrative Science Quarterly, 26*, 207, 224.

Dahl, R.A. (1957). The concept of power. *Behavioral Science, 2*, 201-218.

Dalton, G.W. (1959). *Men who manage.* New York: Wiley.

Dansereau, F., & Dumas, M.S. (1977). Pratfalls and pitfalls in drawing inferences about leader behavior in organizations. In J.G. Hunt & L.L. Larson (Eds.), *Leadership: The cutting edge.* Carbondale, IL: Southern Illinois University Press.

Dansereau, F., Graen, G., & Haga, W. (1975). A vertical dyad linkage approach to leadership within formal organizations: A longitudinal investigation of the role-making process. *Organizational Behavior and Human Performances, 13*, 46-78.

Davis, L.E., & Taylor, J.C. (Eds.). (1972). *Design of jobs.* Penguin.

Davis, S.M. (1982, Winter). Transforming organizations: The key to strategy is context. *Organizational Dynamics*, 64-82.

Davis, T.R.V., & Luthans, F. (1979) Leadership reexamined: A behavioral approach. Academy of Management Review, 4, 237-248.

Davis, T.R.V., & Luthans, F. (1980a, Summer). Managers in action: A new look at their behavior and operating modes. *Organizational Dynamics,* 64-80.

Davis, T.R.V., & Luthans, F. (1980b). A social learning approach to organizational behavior. *Academy of Management Review, 5*, 281-290.

Davis, T.R.V. & Luthans, F. (1981). *Integrating qualitative and quantitative research in organizations.* Interim Report for the Organizational Effectiveness Research Programs, Office of Naval Research.

Day, R., & Day, J. (1977). A review of the current state of negotiated order theory: An appreciation and a critique. *Sociological Quarterly, 18*, 126–142.

Dearborn, D.C., & Simon, H.A. (1958). Selective perception: A note on the departmental identifications of executives. *Sociometry, 21*, 140–144.

Deci, E. L. (1972). The effects of contingent and non-contingent rewards and controls on intrinsic motivation. *Organizational Behavior and Human Performance, 8*, 217–229.

Decision in Organizations International Research Team. (in press). A contingency model of participative decision making. *Journal of Occupational Psychology, 54*.

Decision in Organizations. (in press). A book on the three-country research is being prepared.

Delbecq, A.L., Von de Von, A.M., & Gustafson, D.H. (1975). *Group techniques for program planning*. Glenview, IL: Scott, Foresman.

DeNisi, A.S., & Schriesheim, C.A. (1981). Implicit theories of leader behavior. In G. Reeves & J. Sweigart (Eds.), *Proceedings of the American Institute of Decision Sciences*. Boston: AIDS.

Douglas, A. (1957). The peaceful settlement of industrial and intergroup disputes. *Journal of Conflict Resolution, 1*, 69–81.

Douglas, A. (1962). *Industrial peacemaking*. New York: Columbia University Press.

Downey, H.K., & Ireland, R.D. (1979). Quantitative versus qualitative: Environmental assessment in organizational studies. *Administrative Science Quarterly, 24*, 630–637.

Doz, Y.L. (1979). *Government control and multinational strategic management*. New York: Praeger.

Doz, Y.L., Bartlett, & Prahalad, C.K. (1981, Spring). Global competitive pressures vs. host country demands: Managing tensions in multinational corporations. *California Management Review*, 63–74.

Doz, Y.L., & Prahalad, C.K. (1981, Summer). An approach to strategic control in multinational companies. *Sloan Management Review*.

Drenth, P.J.D., Koopman, P.L., Rus, V., Odar, M., Heller, F.A., & Brown, A. (1979). Participative decision making in organizations: A three country comparative study. *Industrial Relations, 18*, 295–309.

Driver, M.J., & Mock, T. (1975). Human information processing, decision style theory and accounting information systems. *Accounting Review 50*, 490–508.

Driver, M.J., & Rowe, A.J. (1979). Decision-making styles: A new approach to management decision making. In C. Cooper (Ed.), *Behavioral problems in organizations*. Englewood Cliffs, NJ: Prentice-Hall.

Drucker, P.F. (1955). The practice of management. London: Heinemann.

Dubin, R. (1958). *The world of work*. Englewood Cliffs, NJ: Prentice-Hall.

Dubin, R., & Spray, S.L. (1964). Executive behavior and interaction. *Industrial Relations, 3*, 99–108.

Dubin, R. (1979). Metaphors of leadership: An overview. In J.G. Hunt & L.L. Larson (Eds.), *Crosscurrents in leadership*. Carbondale, IL: Southern Illinois University Press.

Dulewicz, S.V., Fletcher, C.A., & Walker, J. (1976). Job appraisal reviews three years on. *Management Services in Government, 31*, 134–143.

Duncan, R.B. (1972). Characteristics of organizational environments and perceived environmental uncertainty. *Administrative Science Quarterly, 17*, 313–327.

Duncan, S., Jr., & Fiske, D.W. (1977). *Face to face interaction*. Hillsdale, NJ: Lawrence Erlbaum Associates.

Dunnette, M.D. (1963). A note on the criterion. *Journal of Applied Psychology, 47*(4), 251–254.

Durkheim, E. (1938). *The rules of sociological method*. Glencoe, IL: Free Press.

Edelman, M. (1971). *Politics as symbolic action*. Chicago: Markham.

Edelman, M. (1977). *Political language*. New York: Academic Press.

Eiser, J.R. (1980). *Cognitive social psychology: A guide to theory and research*. London: McGraw-Hill.

Emery, F.E., & Trist, E.L. (1965). The causal texture of organizational environments. *Human Relations, 18,* 21–31.

Emery, F.E., & Trist, E.L. (1973). *Towards a social ecology*. New York: Plenum Press.

Etzioni, A. (1961). *A comparative analysis of complex organizations*. New York: Free Press.

Evans, M.G. (1970). The effects of supervisory behavior on the path-goal relationship. *Organizational Behavior and Human Performance, 5,* 277–298.

Evered, R.D., (1976). A typology of explicative models. *Technological Forecasting and Social Change, 9,* 259–277.

Farris, G. (1974). Leadership and supervision in the informal organization. In J.G. Hunt & L. Larson, (Eds.), *Contingency approaches to leadership*. Carbondale, IL: Southern Illinois University Press.

Farrow, D.L., & Bass, B.M. (1977). *A phoenix emerges: The importance of manager and subordinate personality in contingency leadership analyses* (Army Research Institute Technical Report T7-1). Rochester, NY: University of Rochester.

Fayol, H. (1949). *General and industrial management*. London: Pitman.

Fiedler, F.E. (1964). A contingency model of leadership effectiveness. In L. Berkowitz (Ed.), *Advances in experimental social psychology*. New York: Academic Press.

Fiedler, F.E. (1967). *A theory of leadership effectiveness*. New York: McGraw-Hill.

Fiedler, F.E., & Chemers, M.M. (1974). *Leadership and effective management*. Glenview, IL: Scott, Foresman.

Filley, A.C., House, R.J., & Kerr, S. (1976) *Managerial process and organizational behavior* (2nd ed.). Glenview, IL: Scott, Foresman.

Fiske, S. (1981). What does the schema concept buy us? *Personality and Social Psychology Bulletin, 6,* 105–118.

Flanagan, J.C. (1951). Defining the requirements of the executive's job. *Personnel, 28,* 28–35.

Flanagan, J.C. (1954). The critical incident technique. *Psychological Bulletin, 51,* 327–358.

Flanders, N. (1970). *Analyzing teaching behavior*. London: Addison-Wesley.

Fleishman, E.A. (1953). The measurement of leadership attitudes in industry. *Journal of Applied Psychology, 37,* 153–158.

Fleishman, E. A., & Hunt, J.G. (1973). *Current developments in the study of leadership*. Carbondale, IL: Southern Illinois University Press.

Fletcher, C. (1973). An evaluation study of job appraisal reviews. *Management Services in Government, 28*(4), 188–195.

Ford, R. G., (1977) Functional leadership behavior: measurement and relation to social power and leadership perceptions. *Administrative Science Quarterly, 22,* 114–133.

Forgus, R. & Shulman, B.H. (1979). *Personality: A cognitive view*. Englewood Cliffs, NJ: Prentice-Hall.

Fox, A. (1966). *Industrial sociology and industrial relations*. (Research Paper 3). London: Royal Commission on Trade Unions and Employers Associations, HMSO.

French, J.R.P., Kay, E., & Meyer, H.H. (1966). Participation and the appraisal system. *Human Relations, 19,* 3–19.

French, J.R.P., & Raven, B. (1959). The bases of social power. In D. Cartwright (Ed.), *Studies in social power.* Ann Arbor, MI: Institute for Social Research.

Friedlander, F., & Pickle, H. (1968). Components of effectiveness in small organizations. *Administrative Science Quarterly, 13,* 289–304.

Friedman, A.L. (1982). *Management strategies, market conditions and the labor process.* Working paper for SSRC/WORC Conference, University of Bristol, U.K.

Fry, L., & Slocum, J. (1982). *Technology, structure, and workgroup effectiveness.* Unpublished manuscript, Cox School of Business, Southern Methodist University, Dallas, TX.

Fulk, J., & Wendler, E. (in press). Dimensionality of leader-subordinate interactions: A path-goal investigation. *Organizational Behavior and Human Performance.*

Galbraith, J. (1973). *Designing complex organizations.* Menlo Park, CA: Addison-Wesley.

Gamst, F.C., & Norbeck, E. (Eds.). (1976). *Ideas of culture: Sources and uses.* New York: Holt, Rinehart & Winston.

George, A.L. (1969). The "operational code": A neglected approach to the study of political leaders and decision-making. *International Studies Quarterly, 13,* 190–222.

George, A.L. (1974). Adaptation to stress in political decision making: The industrial, small group and organizational context. In G. Coelho, D. Hamburg, & J. Adams (Eds.), *Coping and adaptation.* New York: Basic Books.

Georgiou, P. (1973). The goal paradigm and notes towards a counter paradigm. *Administrative Science Quarterly, 18,* 291–310.

Gephart, R.P. (1978). Status degradation and organizational succession: An ethnomethodological approach. *Administrative Science Quarterly, 23,* 553–581.

Gergen, K.H. (1973). Social psychology as history. *Journal of Personality and Social Psychology, 26,* 309–320.

Ghiselli, E.E. (1966). *The validity of occupational aptitude tests.* New York: Wiley.

Glaser, B.G. (1978). *Theoretical sensitivity.* Mill Valley, CA: Sociology Press.

Glaser, B.G., & Strauss, A.L. (1967). *The discovery of grounded theory: Strategies for qualitative research.* Chicago: Aldine.

Glaser, B.G., & Strauss, A.L. (1970). Discovery of substantive theory: A basic strategy underlying qualitative research. In W.J. Filstead (Ed.), *Qualitative methods: First-hand involvement with the social world.* Chicago: Markham.

Goffman, E. (1982). *Interaction ritual.* Harmondsworth, Middlesex, U.K.: Penguin.

Goggin, (1975). A decade of progress: Multidimensional organization structure. *University of Michigan Business Review.*

Goldberg, S. (1980). Controlling basic science: The case of nuclear fusion. *Georgetown Law Journal, 68,* 683–723.

Goodman, P. (1979). *Assessing organizational change: The Rushton quality of work experiment.* New York: Wiley Interscience.

Gottman, J.M., & Bakeman, R. (1979). The sequential analysis of observational data. In M.E. Lamb, S.J. Suomi, & G.R. Stephenson (Eds.), *Social interaction analysis.* London: University of Wisconsin Press.

Gouldner, A.W. (1960). The norm of reciprocity: A preliminary statement. *American Sociological Review, 25,* 161–179.

Graen, G. (1976). Role-making processes within complex organizations. In M.D. Dunnette (Ed.), *Handbook of industrial and organizational psychology.* Chicago: Rand McNally.

Graen, G., & Cashman, J.F. (1975). A role-making model of leadership in formal organizations: A developmental approach. In J.G. Hunt & L.L. Larson (Eds.), *Leadership frontiers.* Kent, OH: Comparative Administrative Research Institute, Kent State University.

Graen, G., & Ginsburgh, S. (1977). Job resignation as a function of role orientation and leader acceptance: A longitudinal investigation of organizational assimilation. *Organizational Behavior and Human Performance, 19,* 1–17.

Graen, G., & Schiemann, W. (1978). Leader-member agreement: A vertical dyad linkage approach. *Journal of Applied Psychology, 63,* 206–212.

Graves, D. (Ed.). (1973). *Management research: A cross-cultural perspective.* London: Elsevier Scientific.

Green, S.G., & Mitchell, T.R. (1979). Attributional processes of leaders in leader-member interactions. *Organizational Behavior and Human Performance, 23,* 429–458.

Greene, C. (1975). Empirical frontiers: A critical appraisal. In J.G. Hunt and L.L. Larson (Eds.), *Leadership frontiers.* Kent, OH: Comparative Administration Research Inst., Kent State Univ.

Greene, C.N. (1975). The reciprocal nature of influence between leader and subordinate. *Journal of Applied Psychology, 60*(2), 187–193.

Greene, C.N. (1979a). A longitudinal investigation of modifications to a situational model of leadership effectiveness. *Proceedings of the Academy of Management Meeting,* Atlanta, GA.

Greene, C.N. (1979b). Questions of causation in the path-goal theory of leadership. *Academy of Management Journal, 22,* 22–41.

Greene, C.N., & Schriesheim, C.A. (1980). Leader-group interactions: A longitudinal field investigation. *Journal of Applied Psychology, 65*(1), 50–59.

Greene, C.N. (1977). Disenchantment with leadership research: Some causes, recommendations, and alternative directions. In J.G. Hunt & L.L. Larson (Eds.), *Leadership: The cutting edge.* Carbondale, IL: Southern Illinois University Press.

Greenwald, A. (1980). The totalitarian ego: Fabrication and revision of personal history. *American Psychologist, 35,* 603–618.

Greller, M. (1975). Subordinate participation and reactions to the appraisal interview. *Journal of Applied Psychology, 60*(5), 544–549.

Greller, M. (1978). The nature of subordinate participation in the appraisal interview. *Academy of Management Journal, 21*(4), 646–654.

Griffin, R. (1979). Task design determinants of effective leader behavior. *Academy of Management Review, 4,* 215–224.

Gross, N., Mason, W.S., & McEachern, A.W. (1958). *Explorations in role analysis.* New York: Wiley.

Guest, R.H. (1956). Of time and the foreman. *Personnel, 32,* 478–486.

Guion, R.M. (1977, November–December). Content validity: Three years of talk — what's the action? *Public Personnel Management, 6,* 407–414.

Guion, R.M., & Gottier, R.F. (1965). Validity of personality measures in personnel selection. *Personnel Psychology, 18,* 137–164.

Hackman, R. (1976). Group influences on individuals. In M. Dunnette (Ed.), *Handbook of Industrial and Organizational Psychology.* Chicago: Rand McNally.

Hall, D.T., & Lawler, E.E. (1969). Unused potential in research and development organizations. *Research Management, 12,* 339–354.

Hammersley, M. (1980). Classroom ethnography. *Educational Analysis* 2, 2, 47.74.

Hammersley M., & Atkinson, P. (1982). *The logic of participant observation.* Unpublished manuscript, Open University.

Harré, R., & Secord, P.F. (1972). *The explanation of social behavior.* Oxford, U.K.: Blackwell.

Hartley, J.F. (in press). Ideology and organizational behavior. *International Studies in Management and Organization.*

Hartley, J.F., Kelly, J.E., & Nicholson, N. (1983). *Steel strike.* London: Batsford.

Hayek, F.A. (1967). *Studies in philosophy, politics and economics.* Chicago: University of Chicago Press.

Hedburg, B.L.T. (1981). How organizations learn and unlearn. In P.C. Nytsrom & W.H. Starbuck (Eds.), *Handbook of organizational design* (Vol. 1). New York: Oxford University Press.

Heller, F.A. (1969). Group feed-back analysis: A method of field research. *Psychological Bulletin, 72*(2), 108–117.

Heller, F.A. (1971). *Managerial decision making: A study of leadership styles and power sharing among senior managers.* London: Tavistock Publications.

Heller, F.A. (1976a). The decision process: An analysis of power sharing at senior organizational levels. In R. Dubin (Ed.), *Handbook of work, organization and society.* Chicago: Rand McNally.

Heller, F.A. (1976b). Towards a practical psychology of work. *Journal of Occupational Psychology, 49,* 45–54.

Heller, F.A., Drenth, P.J.D., Rus, V., & Koopman, P. (1977). A longitudinal study in participative decision making. *Human Relations, 30,* 567–587.

Heller, F.A., & Wilpert, B. (1981). *Competence and power in managerial decision making: A study of senior levels of organization in eight countries.* Chichester, U.K.: Wiley.

Heller, F.A., & Yukl, G. (1969). Participation, managerial decision-making and situational variables. *Organizational Behavior and Human Performance, 4,* 227–241.

Hellriegel, D., & Slocum, J. (1982). *Management* (3rd ed.). Reading, MA: Addison-Wesley.

Hempel, C.G. (1959). The logic of functional analysis. In L. Gross (Ed.), *Symposium on sociological thought.* Evanston, IL: Row, Peterson.

Hemphill, J.K. (1960). *Dimensions of executive positions.* (Ohio Studies in Personnel, Research Monographs, Vol. 98). Ohio State University, Bureau of Business Research. Columbus, OH.

Hermann, M.G. (1980, March 19–20). *The implications of leaders' foreign policy orientations for the quality of foreign policy decisions.* Paper presented at the International Studies Association meeting, Los Angeles.

Herold, D.M. (1977). Two-way influence processes in leader-follower dyads. *Academy of Management Journal, 20,* 224–237.

Hersey, P., & Blanchard, K.H. (1969). Life cycle theory of leadership. *Training and Development Journal, 23,* 26–34.

Hersey, P., & Blanchard K.H. (1977). *Management of organizational behavior: Utilizing human resources.* Englewood Cliffs, NJ: Prentice-Hall.

Hewitt, J.P., & Hall, P.M. (1973). Social problems: Problematic situation in quasi-theories. *American Sociological Review, 38,* 367–374.

Hill, J.W., & Hunt, J.G. (1973). Managerial level, leadership and employee need satisfaction. In E.A. Fleishman & J.G. Hunt (Eds.), *Current developments in the study of leadership.* Carbondale, IL: Southern Illinois University Press.

Hinings, C.R., Hickson, D.J., Pennings, J.M., & Schneck, R.C. (1974). Structural conditions and intra-organizational power. *Administrative Science Quarterly, 19,* 22–44.

Hirsch, P. (1980, August). *Ambushes, shootouts, and knights of the roundtable: The language of corporate takeovers.* Paper presented at the meeting of the Academy of Management, Detroit.

Hodder, I. (1982). *Symbols in action.* Cambridge, U.K.: Cambridge University Press.

Hodgson, R.C., Levinson, O.J., & Zaleznik, A. (1965). *The executive role constellation: An analysis of personality and role relations in management.* Boston: Harvard Business School, Division of Research.

Hofstede, G. (1980). *Culture's consequences.* New York: Sage.

Hollander, E.P. (1959). *Emergent leadership and social influence.* St. Louis, MO: Washington University.

Hollander, E.P. (1978). *Leadership dynamics.* New York: Free Press.

Hollander, E.P., & Julian, J.W. (1969). Contemporary trends in the analysis of leadership process. *Psychological Bulletin, 17,* 381-397.

Holsti, O. (1970). "The operational code" approach to the study of political leaders. John Foster Dulles: Psychological and instrumental beliefs. *Canadian Journal of Political Science, 3,* 123-157.

Horne, J.H., & Lupton, T. (1965). The work activities of "middle" managers: An exploratory study. *Journal of Management Studies, 2*(1), 14-33.

Hosking, D.M., & Hunt, J.G. (1982). Leadership research and the European connection: An epilogue. In J.G. Hunt, U. Sekaran, & C.A. Schriesheim (Eds.), *Leadership: Beyond establishment views.* Carbondale, IL: Southern Illinois University Press.

Hosking, D.M., & Morley, I.E. (1980). *Interrelationships between consideration and initiating structure: A further experimental investigation of some leadership traits* (University of Warwick Working Paper Series). Warwick, U.K.

Hosking, D.M., & Morley, I.E. (in press). Communications and decision-making in organization. In T. Wall & M. Gruenfeld (Eds.), *Social psychology and organizational behavior.* New York: Wiley.

House, R.J. (1971). A path-goal theory of leader effectiveness. *Administrative Science Quarterly, 16*(3), 321-338.

House, R.J. (1977). A 1976 theory of charismatic leadership. In J.G. Hunt & L.L. Larson (Eds.), *Leadership: The cutting edge.* Carbondale, IL: Southern Illinois University Press.

House, R.J., & Baetz, M.L. (1979). Leadership: Some empirical generalizations and new research directions. In B.W. Staw (Ed.), *Research in organizational behavior* (Vol. 1). Greenwich, CT: JAI Press.

House, R.J., & Dessler, G. (1974). The path-goal theory of leadership: Some post hoc and a priori tests. In J.G. Hunt & L.L. Larson (Eds.), *Contingency approaches to leadership.* Carbondale, IL: Southern Illinois University Press.

House, R.J., & Mitchell, T.R. (1974, Autumn). Path-goal theory of leadership. *Journal of Contemporary Business,* 81-97.

House, R.J., & Rizzo, J.R. (1972). Role conflict and ambiguity as critical variables in a model of organizational behavior. *Organizational Behavior and Human Performance, 7,* 467-505.

House, R.J. Shapiro, H.J., & Wahba, M.A. (1974). Expectancy theory as a predictor of work behavior and attitudes: A re-evaluation of empirical evidence. *Decision Sciences, 5,* 481-506.

Huff, A.S. (1978, August). Multilectic methods of inquiry. Paper presented at the 38th Annual Meeting of the Academy of Management, San Francisco.

Hull, C.H., & Nie, N.H. (1981). *SPSS update: New procedures and facilities for releases 7-9.* New York: McGraw-Hill.

Hunt, J.G. (1975). Different nonleader sources of clarity as alternatives to leadership. In B.J. Kolasa (Ed.), *Proceedings of the 12th annual Eastern Academy of Management Meeting.* Pittsburgh: College of Business Administration, Duquesne University.

Hunt, J.G., & Blair, J. (1982). *Leadership requirements for the future battlefield.* A research document for the Army Research Institute, Alexandria, VA.

Hunt, J.G., Hill, J.W., & Reaser, J.M. (1973). Correlates of leadership behavior at two managerial levels in a mental institution. *Journal of Applied Social Psychology, 3*(2), 174–185.

Hunt, J.G., & Larson, L.L. (1974) (Eds.). *Contingency approaches to leadership.* Carbondale, IL: Southern Illinois University Press.

Hunt, J.G., & Larson, L.L. (Eds.). (1975). *Leadership frontiers.* Kent, OH: Comparative Administration Research Inst., Kent State Univ.

Hunt, J.G., & Larson, L.L. (1977). *Leadership: The cutting edge.* Carbondale, IL: Southern Illinois University.

Hunt, J.G., & Larson, L.L. (1979). Towards transition to a new stage of development: An epilog. In J.G. Hunt & L.L. Larson (Eds.), *Crosscurrents in leadership.* Carbondale IL: Southern Illinois University Press.

Hunt, J.G., & Osborn, R.N. (1980). A multiple influence approach to leadership for managers. In J. Stinson & P. Hersey (Eds.), *Perspectives in leader effectiveness.* Athens, OH: Center for Leadership Studies.

Hunt, J.G., & Osborn, R.N. (1982). Toward a macro-oriented model of leadership. In J.G. Hunt, U. Sekaran, & C. Schreisheim (Eds.), *Leadership: Beyond establishment views.* Carbondale, IL: Southern Illinois University Press.

Hunt, J.G., Osborn, R.N., & Martin, H.J. (1979). *A multiple influence model of leadership* . Alexandria, VA: Army Research Inst.

Hunt, J.G., Sekaran, U., & Schriesheim, C. (Eds.). (1982). *Leadership: Beyond establishment views.* Carbondale, IL: Southern Illinois University Press.

Industrial Democracy in Europe International Research Group. (1976). *Social science information, 15,* 177–203.

Industrial Democracy in Europe International Research Group. (1981a). *European industrial relations.* Oxford University Press.

Industrial Democracy in Europe International Research Group. (1981b). *Industrial democracy in Europe.* Oxford University Press.

Jacobs, T. (1971). *Leadership and exchange in formal organizations.* Alexandria, VA: Human Resources Research Organization.

Jacques, E. (1957). *The measurement of responsibility.* London: Tavistock.

Jacques, E. (1965). National income policy. In W. Brown & E. Jacques (Eds.), *Glacier project papers.* London: Heinemann.

Janis, I. (1972). *Victims of groupthink.* Boston: Houghton Mifflin.

Janis, I. (1982). *Groupthink.* Boston: Harcourt Brace.

Janis, I., & Mann, L. (1977). *Decision making: A psychological analysis of conflict, choice and commitment.* New York: Free Press.

Jasinski, F.J. (1956). Foremen relationships outside the work group. *Personnel, 33,* 130–136.

Jervis, R. (1976). *Perception and misperception in international politics.* Princeton, NJ: Princeton University Press.

Jick, T.D. (1979). Mixing qualitative and quantitative methods: Triangulation in action. *Administrative Science Quarterly, 24,* 602–611.

Jones, W.T. (1961). *The romantic syndrome: Toward a new method in cultural anthropology and the history of ideas.* The Hague: Martinus Nijhaff.

Jung, C.G., (1971). *Psychological types* (R.F.C. Hall, trans.). Princeton, NJ: Princeton University Press.

Kahn, R.L. (1960). Psychologists in administration. Productivity and job satisfaction. *Personnel Psychology, 13*(1), 275–287.

Kahn, R.L., Wolfe, D.M., Quinn, R.P., & Snoek, J.D. (1964). *Organizational stress:*

Studies in role conflict and ambiguity. New York: Wiley.

Kalleberg, A.L., & Kluegel, J.R. (1975). Analysis of the multitrait-multimethod matrix: Some limitations and an alternative. *Journal of Applied Psychology, 60*, 1–9.

Kanter-Moss, R., & Stein, B.A. (Eds.). (1979). *Life in organizations.* New York: Basic Books.

Kanter, R.M. (1977). *Men and women of the corporation.* New York: Basic Books.

Kanter, R.M. (1981). The definition and measurement of system and individual effectiveness, productivity and performance in organizations: Critical issues, dilemma and new directions. *Annual Review of Sociology, 7.*

Karmel, B. (1978). Leadership: A challenge to traditional research methods and assumptions. *Academy of Management Review, 3*, 475–482.

Katz, D., & Golomb, N. (1974). *The kibbutzim as open social systems.* Ruppin Press.

Katz, D., & Kahn, R.L. (1978). *The social psychology of organizations* (2nd ed.). New York: Wiley.

Katz, R. (1955). Skills of an effective administrator. *Harvard Business Review, 33*(1) 33–41.

Katz, R. (1978). Job longevity as a situational factor in job satisfaction. *Administrative Science Quarterly, 4*, 204–223.

Katz, R., & Van Maanen, J. (1976). The Loci of work satisfaction. In P. Warr (Ed.), *Personnel goals and work design.* New York: Wiley.

Katzell, R., & Yankelovich, D. (1975). *Work productivity and job satisfaction, An evaluation of policy-related research.* New York: The Psychological Corporation, Harcourt Brace Jovanovich.

Kavanagh, M.J., McKinney, A.C., & Wolins, L. (1971). Issues in managerial performance: Multitrait-multimethod analysis of ratings. *Psychological Bulletin, 75*(1), 34–49.

Kay, E., Meyer, H.H., & French, J.R.P. (1965). Effects of threat in the performance appraisal interview. *Journal of Applied Psychology, 49*(5), 311–317.

Keen, P.G.W., & Scott Morton, M.S. (1978). *Decision support systems: An organizational perspective.* Reading, MA: Addison-Wesley.

Kelley, H.H. (1972). Causal schemata and the attribution process. In E. Jones, D. Kanouse, H. Kelley, R. Nisbett, S. Valins, & B. Weiner (Eds.), *Attribution: Perceiving the causes of behavior.* Morristown, NJ: General Learning Press.

Kelly, J. (1964). The study of executive behavior by activity sampling. *Human Relations, 17.*

Kelvin, P. (1970). *The bases of social behaviour.* London: Holt, Rinehart, & Winston.

Kepner, C.H., & Tregoe, B.B. (1965). *The rational manager.* New York: McGraw-Hill.

Kerlinger, F.N. (1973). *Foundations of behavioral research.* New York: Holt, Rinehart, & Winston.

Kerr, S. (1977). Substitutes for leadership: Some implications for organizational design. *Organization and Administrative Sciences, 8*, 135–146.

Kerr, S., & Jermier, J. (1978). Substitutes for leadership: Their meanings and measurement. *Organizational Behavior and Human Performance, 22*, 375–403.

Kerr, S., Schriesheim, C.A., Murphy, C.J., & Stogdill, R.M. (1974). Toward a contingency theory of leadership based upon the consideration and initiating structure literature. *Organizational Behavior and Human Performance, 12*, 62–82.

Kerr, S., & Slocum, J. (1981). Controlling the performances of people in organizations. In P. Nystrom & W. Starbuck (Eds.), *Handbook of organizational design.* New York: Oxford University Press.

Kerr, S., Von Glinow, M.A., & Schriesheim, J. (1977). Issues in the study of professionals in organizations: The case of scientists and engineers. *Organizational Behavior and Human Performance, 18*, 329–345.

Kimberly, J.R. (1976). Some issues in longitudinal organizational research. *Sociological Methods and Research, 4*(3), 321–346.

Kimberly, J.R. (1980). Problems in data aggregation: The temporal dimension. *Organization Studies, 1, 4.*

King, A.S. (1974). Expectation effects in organizational change. *Administrative Science Quarterly, 19,* 221–230.

Kingdon, D.R. (1973). *Matrix organization: Managing information technologies.* London: Tavistock.

Kipnis, D. (1976). *The powerholders.* Chicago: University of Chicago Press.

Kleinman, L.S., & Durham, R.L. (1981). Performance appraisal, promotion and the courts: A critical review. *Personnel Psychology, 34*(1), 103–121.

Kluckhohn, F., & Strodtbeck, F. (1961). *Variations in value orientation.* Evanston, IL: Row, Peterson.

Kochan, T.A. (1980). *Collective bargaining and industrial relations.* Homewood, IL: Richard D. Irwin.

Kolb, D.A., Rubin, I.M., & McIntyre, J.M. (1971). Organizational psychology: An experiential approach. Englewood Cliffs, NJ: Prentice-Hall.

Koopman, P.L. (1980). *Besluitvorming in organisaties: een onderzock naar de effecten van participatie in operationele en komplexe beslissingen.* Assen, Van Gorcum, Vrije Universiteit.

Koopman, P.L., Drenth, P.J.D., Bus, F.B.M., Kruyswijk, A.J., & Wierdsma, A.F.M. (1981). Content, process, and effects of participative decision making on the shop floor: Three cases in the Netherlands. *Human Relations, 8,* 657–676.

Korman, A.K. (1966). Consideration, initiating structure, and organizational criteria—A review. *Personnel Psychology, 19,* 349–362.

Korman, A.K. (1968). The prediction of managerial performance: A review. *Personnel Psychology, 21,* 295–332.

Kotter, (1982). *The general managers.* New York: Free Press.

Kurke, L.B., & Aldrich, H.E. (1979). *Mintzberg was right: A replication and extension of the nature of managerial work.* Paper presented at the 39th Annual Meeting of the Academy of Management, Atlanta, GA.

Lake, D.G. (1981). High performing principals: A synthesis. In *Review of literature and resources on high-performing principals.* Report presented to the Florida Council on Educational Management.

Lake, D.G., & Martinko, M. (1982). *The identification of high performing principals* (Working paper). Tallahassee: Florida State University.

Landsberger, H.A. (1961). The horizontal dimension in bureaucracy. *Administrative Science Quarterly, 6,* 298–333.

Landy, F.J., Barnes, J.L., & Murphy, K.R. (1978). Correlations of perceived fairness and accuracy of performance evaluation. *Journal of Applied Psychology, 63*(6), 751–754.

Larson, L.L., Bussom, R.S., & Vicars, W.M. (1981). *The nature of a school superintendent's work: Final technical report.* Carbondale, IL: Southern Illinois University Press.

Larson, L.L., Hunt, J.G., & Osborn, R.N. (1976). The great hi-hi leader behavior myth: A lesson from Occam's Razor. *Academy of Management Journal, 19,* 623–641.

Latham, G.P., & Sari, L.M. (1979). Applications of social-learning theory to training supervisors through behavioral modeling. *Journal of Applied Psychology, 64,* 239–246.

Latham, G.P., & Wexley, K.N. (1977). Behavioral observation scales for performance appraisal purposes. *Personnel Psychology, 30*(2), 255–268.

Lawler, E.E. (1967). The multitrait-multirater approach to measuring managerial job performance. *Journal of Applied Psychology, 51,* 369–381.

Lawler, E.E. (1976a). Conference review: Issues of understanding. In P. Warr (Ed.), *Personal goals and work design.* New York: Wiley.

Lawler, E.E. (1976b). Control systems in organizations. In M. Dunnette (Ed.), *Handbook of industrial and organizational psychology.* Chicago: Rand McNally.

Lawler, E.E. (1978). The new plant revolution. *Organizational Dynamics, 6*(3), 2–12.

Lawler, E.E. (1980). Motivation: Closing the gap between theory and practice. In K.D. Duncan, M.M. Gruneberg, & D. Wallis (Eds.), *Changes in working life.* London: Wiley.

Lawler, E.E. (1981a). *High involvement work organizations: Design and change theory.* Paper presented at Organization Change Seminar, Carnegie-Mellon University, Pittsburgh, PA.

Lawler, E.E. (1981b). *Pay and organization development.* Reading, MA: Addison-Wesley.

Lawler, E.E., & Ledford, G.E. (1982). Productivity and the quality of work life. *National Productivity Review, 1,* 23–36.

Lawrence, P.R., & Lorsch, J. W. (1967). *Organization and environment: Managing differentiation and integration.* Cambridge, MA: Harvard Business School.

Lawrence, P.R., & Lorsch, J.W. (1969). *Organization and environment.* Homewood, IL: Irwin.

Leach, C. (1979). *Introduction to statistics: A non-parametric approach to the social sciences.* London: Wiley.

Leary, T. (1957). Interpersonal diagram of personality: A functional theory and methodology for personality evaluation. New York: Ronald Press.

Lee, J.A., (1977). Leader power for managing change. *Academy of Management Review, 2,* 73–80.

Levi-Strauss, C. (1963). *Structural anthropology.* New York: Basic Books.

Levinthal, L.F., Lansky, L.M., & Andrews, E.D. (1971). Student evaluation of teacher behaviors as estimates of real-ideal discrepancies. *Journal of Educational Psychology, 62,* 104–107.

Lewicki, R.L. (1981, Autumn). Organizational seduction: Building commitment to organization. *Organizational Dynamics,* 5–21.

Lewin, K., Lippitt, R. (1938). An experimental approach to the study of autocracy and democracy: A preliminary note. *Sociometry, 1,* 292–380.

Lewin, K., Lippitt, R., & White, R.K. (1939). Patterns of aggressive behavior in experimentally created social climates. *Journal of Social Psychology, 10,* 271–301.

Likert, R. (1950). Foreword. In D. Katz, N. Maccoby, & N. Morse (Eds.), *Productivity supervision and morale in the office situation.* Ann Arbor: University of Michigan, Survey Research Center.

Likert, R. (1961). *The human organization.* New York: McGraw-Hill.

Lindblom & Cohen, (1979). *Usable knowledge.* New Haven, CT: Yale University Press.

Livingston, J.S. (1969). Pygmalion in management. *Harvard Business Review, 47*(4), 81–89.

Locke, E.E. (1968). Toward a theory of task motivation and incentives. *Organizational Behavior and Human Performance, 3,* 157–189.

Locke, E.E., & Schweiger, D. (1979). Participation in decision-making: One more look. In B. Staw & L. Cummings (Eds.), *Research in Organizational Behavior* (Vol. 1). Greenwich, CT: JAI Press.

Lockhart, C. (1979). *Bargaining in international conflicts.* New York: Columbia University Press.

Lodahl, J., & Gordon, G. (1972). The structure of scientific fields and the functioning of university graduate departments. *American Sociological Review, 34*, 57-72.

Lombardo, M.M., & McCall, M.W., Jr. (1982). Leaders on line: Observations from a simulation of managerial work. In J.G. Hunt, U. Sekaran, & C.A. Schriesheim (Eds.), *Leadership: Beyond establishment views.* Carbondale, IL: Southern Illinois University Press.

Lord, R.G., Foti, R.J., & Phillips, J.S. (1982). A theory of leadership categorization. In J.G. Hunt, U. Sekaran, & C.A. Schriesheim (Eds.), *Leadership: Beyond establishment views.* Carbondale, IL: Southern Illinois University Press.

Lott, A., & Lott, B. (1965). Group cohesiveness as interpersonal attractions: A review of relationships with antecedent and consequent variables. *Psychological Bulletin, 64*, 259-302.

Louis, M.R. (1980a, August). *"Learning the ropes": What helps new employees become acculturated.* Paper presented at the meeting of the Academy of Management, Detroit.

Louis, M.R. (1980b). Surprise and sense making: What newcomers experience in entering unfamiliar organizational settings. *Administrative Science Quarterly, 25*, 226-251.

Lowin, A., & Craig, J.R. (1968). The influence of level of performance on managerial styles: An experimental object-lesson in the ambiguity of correlational data. *Organizational Behavior and Human Performance, 3*, 440-458.

Lupton, T. (1963). *On the shop floor.* London: Pergamon.

Luthans, F. (1977). *Organizational behavior.* New York: McGraw-Hill.

Luthans, F. (1979). Leadership: A proposal for a social learning theory base and observational and functional analysis techniques to measure leader behavior. In J.G. Hunt & L.L. Larson (Eds.), *Crosscurrents in Leadership.* Carbondale, IL: Southern Illinois University Press.

Luthans, F. (1981). *Organizational behavior.* New York: McGraw-Hill.

Luthans, F., & Davis, T.R.V. (1979). Operationalizing a behavioral approach to leadership. In E.L. Miller (Ed.), *Proceedings of the Midwest Academy of Management.* Ann Arbor, MI: University of Michigan, Graduate School of Business.

Luthans, F., & Davis, T.R.V. (in press). An idiographic approach to organizational behavior research: The use of single case experimental designs and direct measures. *Academy of Management Review.*

Luthans, F., Lockwood, D.L., & Conti, M. (1981). *A reliability assessment of participant observational measures of leader behavior in natural settings* (Office of Naval Research Technical Report No. 3, Contract No. N00014-80-C-0554; NR170-913, Fred Luthans Principal Investigator). University of Nebraska, Lincoln.

Luthans, F., Paul, R., & Baker, D. (1981). An experimental analysis of the impact of contingent reinforcement on salespersons' performance behavior. *Journal of Applied Psychology, 66*, 314-323.

Lyles, M. (1981). The formulation of the nature of strategic problems. *Strategic Management Journal, 2*, 61-75.

MacCoby, M. (1976). *The gamesman.* New York: Simon & Schuster.

Machin, J.L.J. (1979). A contingency methodology for management control. *Journal of Management Studies, 16*, 1-29.

MacKinnon, M.J., & Summers, G.F. (1976). Homogeneity and role consensus: A multivariate exploration in role analysis. *Canadian Journal of Sociology, 1*(4), 439-462.

Maier, N.R.F. (1963). *Problem-solving discussions and conferences: Leadership methods and skills.* New York: McGraw-Hill.

Maier, N.R.F. (1976). *The appraisal interview: Three basic approaches.* LaJolla, CA: University Associates.

Malinowski, B. (1944). *A scientific theory of culture.* N. Carolina.

Mangers, D. (1979). Need for administrator training voiced by legislative task force. *Thrust for Educational Leadership, 8,* 4-7.

Manz, C., & Sims, H. (1980). Self-management as a substitute for leadership: A social learning theory perspective. *Academy of Management Review, 5,* 361-367.

March, J.G. (1981). Footnotes to organizational change. *Administrative Science Quarterly, 26,* 563-577.

March, J.G., & Romelaer, P. (1976). Position and presence in the drift of decisions. In J.G. March & J.P. Olsen (Eds.), *Ambiguity and choice in organizations.* Bergen, Norway: Universitesforlaget.

March, J.G., & Shapira, Z. (1982). Behavioral decision theory and organizational decision theory. In G. Ungson & D. Braunstein (Eds.), *New directions in decision making: An interdisciplinary approach to the study of organizations.* Boston: Kent.

March, J.G., & Simon, H.A. (1958). *Organizations.* New York: Wiley.

Marengo, F.D. (1979). *The code of British trade union behaviour.* London: Saxon House.

Margerison, C. (1980). *Practical research in management and organization.* Cranfield, Cranfield School of Management.

Martin, H.J., & Hunt, J.G. *Dictionary Leadership: Theory and Measurement.* Paper presented at the 24th Annual Meeting of the Midwest Academy of Management, April 1981.

Martin, H.J., Hunt, J.G., & Osborn, R.N. (1981). A macro-organizational approach to leadership. *Proceedings of the 41st Annual Meeting of the Academy of Management,* pp. 234-243.

Martin, J. (1982). Stories and scripts in organizational settings. In A. Hastorf & A. Isen (Eds.), *Cognitive social psychology.* New York: Elsevier.

Martin, J., Harrod, W., & Siehl, C. (1980, September). *The development of knowledge structures.* Paper presented at the meetings of the American Psychological Association, Montreal.

Martin, J., Patterson, K., & Price, R. (1979, June). *The effects of level of abstraction of a script on accuracy of recall, predictions and beliefs* (Research paper No. 520). Stanford, CA: Stanford University, Graduate School of Business.

Martin, J., & Powers, M. (in press). Truth or corporate propaganda: The value of a good war story. In L. Pondy, P. Frost, G. Morgan & T. Dandridge (Eds.), *Organizational symbolism.* Greenwich, CT: JAI Press.

Martinko, M., & Gardner, W.L. (1981). Identification of key competencies of high performing principals: Data coding manual (Working paper, Florida State University, Tallahassee, FL.)

Martinko, M., & Gardner, W.L. (in press). Mintzberg-type studies: Methodological problems and alternatives. In D.F. Ray (Ed.), *Contributions of theory and research to the practice of management.* Starkville, MS: Mississippi State Univ., Southern Management Association.

McCall, G.J., & Simmons, J.L. (1969). *Issues in participant observation.* Reading, MA: Addison-Wesley.

McCall, M., & Lombardo, M. (Eds.). (1978). *Leadership: Where else can we go?* Durham, NC: Duke University Press.

McCall, M.W. Jr., Morrison, A.M., & Hannan, R.L. (1978, March). *Studies of managerial work: Results and methods?* (Technical Report No. 9). Greensboro, NC: Center for Creative Leadership.

McCall, M.W., Jr., & Segrist, C.A. (1980). *In pursuit of the manager's job: Building on Mintzberg.* (Technical Report No. 14). Greensboro, NC: Center for Creative Leadership.

McClelland, D.C. (1961). *The achieving society.* Princeton, NJ: Van Nostrand.

McClelland, D.C., & Burnham, D.H.J. (1976). Power is the great motivator. *Harvard Business Review,* 100-110.

McGregor, D. (1957). An uneasy look at performance appraisal. *Harvard Business Review, 34*(3), 89-94.

Melcher, A.J. (1977). Leadership models and research approaches. In J.G. Hunt & L.L. Larson (Eds.), *Leadership: The cutting edge.* Carbondale, IL: Southern Illinois University Press.

Merton, R. (1949). *Social theory and social structure.* Glencoe, IL: Free Press.

Merton, R. (1957). *Social theory and social structure* (2nd ed.). Glencoe, IL: Free Press.

Meyer, H.H. (1982). How ideologies supplant formal structures and shape responses to the environments. *Journal of Management Studies* (19), 45-62.

Meyer, H.H., Kay, E., & French, J.R.P. (1965). Split roles in performance appraisal. *Harvard Business Review, 43*(1), 123-129.

Miles, M.B. (1979). Qualitative data as an attractive nuisance: The problem of analysis. *Administrative Science Quarterly, 24,* 590-601.

Miles, R.H. (1976). Role requirements as sources of organizational stress. *Journal of Applied Psychology, 61,* 172-179.

Miles, R.H., & Perreault, W.D., Jr. (1976). Organizational role conflict: Its antecedents and consequences. *Organizational Behavior and Human Performance, 17,* 19-44.

Miles, R.H., & Petty, M.M. (1977). Leader effectiveness in small bureaucracies. *Academy of Management Journal, 20,* 238-250.

Miller, D., & Friesen, P.H. (1980a). Archetypes of organizational transition. *Administrative Science Quarterly,* (25), 268-292.

Miller, D., & Friesen, P.H. (1980b). Momentum and revolution in organizational adaption. *Academy of Management Journal, 23*(4),591-614.

Miller, G.A., Galanier, E., & Pribram, K.H. (1960). *Plans and the structure of behavior.* Holt, Rinehart, & Winston.

Miner, J.B. (in press). Further thoughts on the uncertain future of the leadership concept. *Journal of Applied Behavioral Science.*

Miner, J.B. (1975). The uncertain future of the leadership concept: An overview. In J.G. Hunt & L.L. Larson (Eds.), *Leadership frontiers.* Kent, OH: Comparative Administration Research Inst., Kent State Univ.

Miner, J.B. (1978). Twenty years of research on role-motivation theory of managerial effectiveness. *Personnel Psychology, 31,* 739-760.

Miner, J.B. (1982). *Theories of organizational structure and process.* Dryden Press.

Mintzberg, H. (1968). *The manager at work—Determining his activities, roles and programs by structured observation.* Doctoral dissertation, Massachusetts Institute of Technology.

Mintzberg, H. (1973). *The nature of managerial work.* New York: Harper & Row.

Mintzberg, H. (1975, July-August). The manager's job: Folklore and fact. *Harvard Business Review, 53,* 49-61.

Mintzberg, H. (1976, July-August). Planning on the left side and managing on the right. *Harvard Business Review,* 79-90.

Mintzberg, H. (1979). *The structuring of organizations.* Englewood Cliffs, NJ: Prentice-Hall.

Mintzberg, H. (1982). If you're not serving Bill and Barbara, then you're not serving leadership. In J.G. Hunt, U. Sekaran, & C.A. Schriesheim (Eds.), *Leadership: Beyond establishment views.* Carbondale, IL: Southern Illinois University Press.

Mintzberg, H., Raisinghani, D., & Theoret, A. (1976). The structure of "unstructured" decision making processes. *Administrative Science Quarterly, 21,* 246–275.

Mitchell, C. (1981). *On inductive analysis,* unpublished manuscript, Nuffield College, Oxford Univ., U.K.

Mitchell, D. (Ed.). (1968). *A dictionary of sociology.* London: Routledge & Kegan Paul.

Mitchell, S.K. (1979). Interobserver agreement, reliability and generalizability of data collected in observational studies. *Psychological Bulletin, 86,* 376–390.

Mitchell, T.R. (1974). Expectancy models of job satisfaction, occupational preference and effort: Theoretical, methodological, and empirical appraisal. *Psychological Bulletin, 81*(12), 1053–1077.

Mitchell, T.R. (1979). Organizational behavior. *Annual Review of Psychology, 30,* 243–281.

Mitchell, T.R., Green, S.G., & Wood, R. (1981). An attributional model of leadership and the poor performing subordinate. In L.L. Cummings & B.M. Staw (Eds.), *Research in organizational behavior* (Vol. 3). Greenwich, CT: JAI Press.

Mitchell, T.R., Larson, J.R., & Green, S.G. (1977). Leader behavior, situational moderators and group performance: An attributional analysis. *Organizational Behavior and Human Performance, 18,* 254–268.

Moch, M., & Huff, A.S. (1980, August). *Chewing out ass: The enactment of power relationships through language and ritual.* Paper presented to the meetings of the Academy of Management, Detroit.

Molnar, J.J., & Rogers, D.C. (1976). Organizational effectiveness: An empirical comparison of the goal and system resource approach. *Sociological Quarterly, 17,* 401–413.

Moore, B.E., & Ross, T.L. (1978). *The Scanlon way to improved productivity.* New York: Wiley.

Moreno, J.L. (1934, 1953). *Who shall survive?* Beacon, NY: Beacon House.

Morgan, G., & Smircich, L. (1980). The case for qualitative research. *Academy of Management Review, 5,* 491–500.

Morley, I.E. (1981a). Bargaining and negotiation. In C.L. Cooper (Ed.), *Psychology and management: A text for managers and trade unionists.* London: Macmillan/ British Psychological Society.

Morley, I.E. (1981b). *Negotiation and bargaining.* In M. Argyle (Ed.), *Social skills and work.* London: Methuen.

Morley, I.E. (1981c, June 24–27). *Negotiation as a social skill.* Paper presented at Fourth Annual Scientific Meeting, International Society of Political Psychology, University of Mannheim, Federal Republic of Germany.

Morley, I.E., & Stephenson, G.M. (1977). *The social psychology of bargaining.* London: Allen & Unwin.

Morris, V.C., Crowson, R.L., Hurwitz, E., & Porter-Gehrie, C. (1981). The urban principal: Discretionary decision-making in a large educational organization. Unpublished manuscript, University of Illinois, Chicago.

Morrison, A.M., & Krantz, M.E. (1981, July–August). The shape of performance appraisal in the coming decade. *Personnel,* 12–22.

Morse, N.C., & Reimer, E. (1956). The experimental change of a major organizational variable. *Journal of Abnormal Social Psychology, 52,* 120–129.

Moses, J.L. (1979). Lack of application of leadership findings to real world problems. In J.G. Hunt & L.L. Larson (Eds.), *Crosscurrents in leadership.* Carbondale, IL: Southern Illinois University Press.

Mowday, R.T. (1978). The exercise of upward influence in organizations. *Administrative Science Quarterly, 23*, 137–156.

Mowday, R.T., Steers, R.M., & Porter, L. (1978). *The measurement of organizational commitment: A progress report* (Technical Report No. 15). Eugene, OR: University of Oregon, Graduate School of Management.

Mulder, M. (1977). *The daily power game.* Brussels: Martinus Nijhoff.

Nadler, D.A., Hackman, J.R., & Lawler, E.E., III. (1979). *Managing organizational behavior.* Boston: Little, Brown.

Narayanan, V.K., & Fahey, L. (1982). The micro-politics of strategy formulation. *Academy of Management Review, 7*, 25–34.

Nash, A.N. (1965). Vocational interests of effective managers: A review of the literature. *Personnel Psychology, 18*, 21–37.

Neisser, U. (1967). *Cognitive psychology.* New York: Appleton-Century-Crofts.

Neisser, U. (1976). *Cognition and reality.* San Francisco: Freeman.

Nemeroff, W.F., & Cosentino, J. (1979). Utilizing feedback and goalsetting to increase performance appraisal interviewer skills of managers. *Academy of Management Journal, 22*(3), 566–576.

Nemeroff, W.F., & Wexley, K.N. (1977). Relationships between performance feedback interview characteristics and interview outcomes as perceived by managers and subordinates. *Proceedings of the Academy of Management, 30*–34.

Newell, A., & Simon, H.A. (1972). *Human problem solving.* Englewood Cliffs, NJ: Prentice-Hall.

Nicholson, N. (1982). *A theory of role transitions* (MRC/SSRC Social and Applied Psychology Unit, Memorandum No. 487). University of Sheffield, U.K.

Nicholson, N., Ursell, G., & Blyton, P. (1981). *The dynamics of white collar unionism.* London: Academic Press.

Nunnally, J.C. (1978). *Psychometric theory.* New York: McGraw-Hill.

Oldham, G. (1976). The motivational strategies used by managers: Relationships to effectiveness indicators. *Organizational Behavior and Human Performance, 15*, 66–86.

O'Neill, H.E., & Kubany, A.J. (1959). Observation methodology and supervisory behavior. *Personnel Psychology, 12*, 85–95.

Osborn, R.N. (1974). Discussant comments. In J.G. Hunt & L.L. Larson (Eds.), *Contingency approaches to leadership.* Carbondale, IL: Southern Illinois University Press.

Osborn, R.N. (1980). *Overview: European workshop or leadership and managerial behavior.* Unpublished manuscript, Dept. of Administrative Sciences, Southern Ilinois Univ. at Carbondale.

Osborn, R.N., & Hunt, J.G. (1975). An adaptive-reactive theory of leadership: The role of macro variables in leadership research. In J.G. Hunt, & L.L. Larson (Eds.), *Leadership frontiers.* Kent, OH: Kent University Press.

Osborn, R.N., Hunt, J.G., & Jauch, L.R. (1980). *Organizational theory: An integrated approach.* New York: Wiley.

Osgood, C., Succi, G., & Tannenbaum, P. (1957). *The measurement of meaning.* Urbana, IL: Univ. of Illinois Press.

Ouchi, W.G. (1980). Markets, clans, and hierarchies. *Administrative Science Quarterly, 25*, 129–141.

Ouchi, W.G. (1981). *How American business can meet the Japanese challenge.* Reading, MA: Addison-Wesley.

Ouchi, W.G., & Maguire, M. (1975). Organizational control: Two functions. *Administrative Science Quarterly, 20*, 559–569.

Ouchi, W.G., & Price, R. (1978). Hierarchies, clans and Theory Z: A new perspec-

tive on organizational development. *Organizational Dynamics, 7*, 25–44.
Parsons, T. (1959). General theory in sociology. In R. Merton, L. Browns, & L.S. Cotrell, Jr. (Eds.), *Sociology today: Problems and perspectives.* New York: Basic Books.
Parsons, T., Bales, R.F., & Shils, E. (1953). *Working papers in the theory of action.* New York: Free Press.
Pascale, R.T., & Athos, A.G. (1981). *The art of Japanese management.* New York: Simon & Schuster.
Patchen, M. (1974). The locus and basis of influence on organizational decision. *Organizational Behavior and Human Performance, 11*, 195–221.
Payne, D.A., Ellett, C.D., Perkins, M.L., Klein, A.E., & Shellenberger, S. (1975). *The verification of principal competencies and performance indicators: Assessment design-procedures-instrumentation-field test results* (Project Report). Georgia State Department of Education, College of Education, University of Georgia.
Payne, R., & Pugh, D.S. (1976). Organizational structure and climate. In M.D. Dunnette (Ed.), *Handbook of industrial and organizational psychology.* Chicago: Rand McNally.
Pelz, D.C. (1952). Influence: A key to effective leadership in the first-line supervisor. *Personnel, 29*, 20–217.
Perkins, D., Nieva, R., & Lawler, E. (1983). *Managing creation: The challenge of building a new organization.* New York: Wiley.
Perrow, C. (1967). A framework for the comparative analysis of organizations. *American Sociological Review, 32*, 194–208.
Perrow, C. (1972). *Complex organizations: A critical essay.* Glenview, IL: Scott, Foresman.
Peters, T.J. (1981). *Putting excellence into management.* Unpublished manuscript, Stanford University, Stanford, CA.
Pettigrew, A. (1973). *The politics of organizational decision making.* London: Tavistock.
Pettigrew, A. (1979). On studying organizational cultures. *Administrative Science Quarterly, 24*, 570–581.
Pfeffer, J. (1978). The ambiguity of leadership. In M. McCall & M. Lombardo (Eds.), *Leadership: Where else can we go?* Durham, NC: Duke University Press.
Pfeffer, J. (1981a). Management as symbolic action: The creation and maintenance of organizational paradigms. In L.L. Cummings & B.M. Staw (Eds.), *Research in organizational behavior* (Vol. 3). Greenwich, CT: JAI Press.
Pfeffer, J. (1981b). *Power in organizations.* Marshfield, MA: Pitman.
Pfeffer, J., & Salancik, G.R. (1975). Determinants of supervisory behavior: A role set analysis. *Human Relations, 28*(2), 139–154.
Pfeffer, J., & Salancik, G.R. (1978). *The external control of organizations: A resource dependence perspective.* New York: Harper & Row.
Ponder, Q.D. (1958). *Supervisory practices of effective and ineffective foremen.* Unpublished doctoral dissertation, Columbia University.
Pondy, L.R. (1978). Leadership is a language game. In M. McCall & M. Lombardo (Eds.), *Leadership: Where else can we go?* Durham, NC: Duke University Press.
Pondy, L.R., Frost, P.J., Morgan, G., & Dandridge, T.C. (Eds.). (1983). *Organizational symbolism.* Greenwich, CT: JAI Press.
Pondy, L.R., & Mitroff. (1979). Beyond open system models of organization. In B.M. Staw (Ed.), *Research in organization behavior* (Vol. 1). Greenwich, CT: JAI Press.
Porter, L.W., & Lawler, E.E. (1965). Properties of organization structure in relation to job attitudes and job behavior. *Psychological Bulletin, 64*, 23–51.
Poul, D. (1982). Indflydelsesfordelingen i danske virksomheder. Handelshojskolen i Arhus, Denmark.

Prahalad, C.K. (1976, July–August). Strategic choices in diversified MNCs. *Harvard Business Review,* 67–78.

Prahalad, C.K., & Doz, Y.L. (1981, Fall). Headquarters influence and strategic contingencies in multinational companies. *Sloan Management Review.*

Prahalad, C.K., & Doz, Y.L. (1982). *The work of top management in multinational companies.* Unpublished manuscript, Univ. of Michigan.

Quinn, J.B. (1980). *Strategies for change.* Homewood, IL: Irwin.

Quinn, R.E. (1981, November 11). *The understructure of organization theory.* Distinguished Research Lecture presented at the State University of New York at Albany.

Quinn, R. E., & Cameron, K. (1983). Organizational life cycles and the criteria of effectiveness. *Management Science, 29(1),* 33–51.

Quinn, R.E., & McGrath, M.R. (1982). On killing grids and raising amoebas: A new direction in organization development. *Journal of Applied Behavior Science, 18(4),* 463–472.

Quinn, R.E., & Rohrbaugh, J. (1981). A competing values approach to organizational effectiveness. *Public Productivity Review, 5,* 122–140.

Quinn, R.E., & Rohrbaugh, J. (1983). A spatial model of effectiveness criteria: Towards a competing values approach to organizational analysis. *Management Science, 29(3),* 363–377.

Rackham, N., & Morgan, T. (1977). *Behavior analysis in training.* London: McGraw-Hill.

Radcliffe-Brown, A. (1952). *Structure and function in primitive society.* London: Cohen & West.

Randell, G., Shaw, R., Packard, P., & Slater J. (1976). *Staff appraisal.* London: IPM.

Reason, P., & Rowan, J. (1981). *Human inquiry: A source book of new paradigm research.* Wiley.

Reddin, W.J. (1970). *Managerial effectiveness.* New York: McGraw-Hill.

Rinn, J.L. (1965). Structure of phenomenal domains. *Psychological Review, 72,* 445–466.

Rizzo, J.R., House, R.J., & Lirtzman, S.I. (1970). Role conflict and ambiguity in complex organizations. *Administrative Science Quarterly, 15,* 150–163.

Rogers, C.R. (1961). *On becoming a person.* Boston: Houghton Mifflin.

Rogers, D.L., & Molnar, J. (1976). Organizational antecedents of role conflict and ambiguity in top level administrators. *Administrative Science Quarterly, 17,* 598–610.

Rose, G.L. (1981). Organizational behavior and decision making in the 1980's: A critique. *Decision Sciences, 12* (3), 380–383.

Rosenthal, R., & Jacobson, L. (1968). *Pygmalion in the classroom.* New York: Holt, Rinehart, & Winston.

Rothenberg, A. (1979). *The emerging goddess: The creative process in art, science and other fields.* Chicago: University of Chicago Press.

Rotter, J.B. (1966). Generalized expectancies for internal versus external control of reinforcement. *Psychological Monographs, 80* (1, Whole No. 609).

Ruesch, J., & Bateson, G. (1951). *Communication: The social matrix of psychiatry.* New York: Norton.

Rus, V., Odar, M., Heller, F.A., Brown, A., Drenth, P.J.D., Koopman, P., Wierdsma, A., Bus, F. & Kruyswyk, A. (1977, September). *Participative decision making under conditions of uncertainty.* Paper for the Second International Conference on Participation, Workers' Control and Self-Management, Paris.

Salaman, G. (1979). *Work organization: Resistance and control.* London: Longman.

Salancik, G.R. (1977). Commitment and the control of organizational behavior and belief. In B. Staw & G.R. Salancik (Eds.), *New directions in organizational behavior.* Chicago: St. Clair Press.

Salancik, G., Calder, B., Rowland, K., Leblebici, H., & Conway, M. (1975). Leadership as an outcome of social structure and process: A multi-dimensional analysis. In J. Hunt & L. Larson, (Eds.), *Leadership frontiers.* Kent, OH: Comparative Administration Research Inst., Kent State Univ.

Salancik, G.R., & Pfeffer, J. (1974). A social information processing approach to job attitudes and task design. *Administrative Science Quarterly, 4,* 224-253.

Salancik, G.R., & Pfeffer, J. (1977). Constraints on administrator decisions. *Urban Affairs Quarterly, 11,* 474-498.

Samph, T. (1976). Observer effects on teacher verbal classroom behavior. *Journal of Educational Psychology, 68,* 736-741.

Sandelands, L.E. (1982). *Self-schema and task perceptions.* Unpublished manuscript, Northwestern University.

Sause, E.F. (1974, September). A check list: Demonstrating competency as a principal. *NASSP Bulletin,* 19-28.

Sayles, L.R. (1964). *Managerial behavior: Administration in complex organizations.* New York: McGraw-Hill.

Sayles, L.R. (1979). Leadership: What effective managers really do and how they do it. New York: McGraw-Hill.

Schermerhorn, J., Hunt, J., & Osborn, R. (1982). *Managing organizational behavior.* New York: Wiley.

Schiemann, W.A., & Graen, G. (1978). *The predictability of communication in organizations: An empirical investigation and integration.* Unpublished manuscript, Georgia Institute of Technology, College of Industrial Management.

Schon, D.A. (1971). *Beyond the stable state.* London: Smith.

Schoonhoven, C. (1981). Problems with contingency theory: Testing assumptions hidden within the language of contingency theory. *Administrative Science Quarterly, 26,* 349-377.

Schriesheim, C.A. (1978). *Development, validation, and application of new leadership behavior and expectancy research instruments.* Doctoral dissertation, Ohio State University (University Microfilms No. 7908210). Ann Arbor: University Microfilms International.

Schriesheim, C.A., Bannister, B.D., & Money, W.H. (1979). Psychometric properties of the LPC scale: An extension of Rice's review. *Academy of Management Review, 4,* 287-290.

Schriesheim, C.A., & DeNisi, A. (1981). Task dimensions as moderators of the effects of instrumental leadership: A two-sample replicated test of path-goal leadership theory. *Journal of Applied Psychology, 66,* 589-597.

Schriesheim, C.A., Hunt J.G., & Sekaran, U. (1982). Conclusion: The leadership-management controversy revisited. In J.G. Hunt, U. Sekaran & C.A. Schriesheim (Eds.), *Leadership: Beyond establishment views.* Carbondale, IL: Southern Illinois University Press.

Schriesheim, C.A., & Kerr, S. (1974). Psychometric properties of the Ohio State leadership scales. *Psychological Bulletin, 81,* 756-765.

Schriesheim, C.A., & Kerr, S. (1977). Theories and measures of leadership: A critical appraisal of current and future directions. In J.G. Hunt & L.L. Larson (Eds.), *Leadership: The cutting edge.* Carbondale, IL: Southern Illinois University Press.

Schriesheim, C.A., Kinicki, A.J., & Schriesheim, J.F. (1979). The effect of leniency on leader behavior descriptions. *Organizational Behavior and Human Performance, 23,* 1-29

Schriesheim, C.A., & Murphy, C.J. (1979). Relationships between leader behavior and subordinate satisfaction and performance: A test of some situational moderators. *Journal of Applied Psychology, 61,* 634–641.

Schriesheim, C.A., & Von Glinow, M.A. (1977). Tests of the path-goal theory of leadership. A theoretical and empirical analysis. *Academy of Management Journal, 20,* 398–405.

Shriesheim, J.F. (1980). The social context of leader-subordinate relations: An investigation of the effects of group cohesiveness. *Journal of Applied Psychology, 65*(2), 183–194.

Schriesheim, J.F., & Schriesheim, C.A. (1976). A test of the path-goal theory of leadership across multiple occupational levels in a large public utility. In L.K. Bragaw & E.K. Winslow (Eds.), *Proceedings of the Eastern Academy of Management* (Thirteenth Annual Meeting). Washington, D.C.: Eastern Division, Academy of Management.

Schriesheim, J.F., & Schriesheim, C.A. (1980). A test of the path-goal theory of leadership and some suggested directions for future research. *Personnel Psychology, 30,* 349–370.

Schriesheim, J.F., Von Glinow, M.A., & Kerr, S. (1977). Professionals in bureaucracies: A structural alternative. In W. Starbuck & W. Nystrom (Eds.), *Prescriptive models of organizations,* Amsterdam: North Holland, 55–69.

Schwab, D. (1980). Construct validity in organizational behavior. In B. Staw & L. Cummings (Eds.), *Research in Organizational Behavior* (Vol. 2). Greenwich, CT: JAI Press.

Schwab, D.P., & Cummings, L.L. (1973). Theories of performance and satisfaction. In W.E. Scott & L.L. Cummings (Eds.), *Readings in organizational behavior and human performance* (Rev. ed.). Homewood, IL: Irwin.

Scott, W.R. (1977). Effectiveness of organizational effectiveness studies. In P.S. Goodman & J. Pennings (Eds.), *New perspectives on organizational effectiveness.* San Francisco: Jossey-Bass.

Scott, W.W. (1966). Activation theory and task design. *Organizational behavior and human performance, 1,* 3–30.

Scott, W.W. (1977). Leadership: A functional analysis. In J.G. Hunt & L.L. Larson (Eds.), *Leadership: The cutting edge.* Carbondale, IL: Southern Illinois University Press.

Seashore, S., Lawler, E., Mirvis, P., & Cammann, C. (1983). *Observing and measuring organizational change: A guide to field practice.* New York: Wiley.

Sekaran, U., Hunt, J.G., & Schriesheim, C.A. (1982). Beyond establishment leadership views: An epilog. In J.G. Hunt, U. Sekaran, & C.A. Schriesheim (Eds.), *Leadership: Beyond establishment views.* Carbondale, IL: Southern Illinois University Press.

Selznick, P. (1957). *Leadership and administration.* Evanston, IL: Row, Peterson.

Selznick, P. (1966). *TVA and the grass roots: A study in the sociology of formal organizations.* New York: Harper & Row.

Sheridan, J.E., Downey, K.H., & Slocum, J.W., Jr. (1975). Testing causal relationships of House's path-goal theory of leadership effectiveness. In J.G. Hunt & L.L. Larson (Eds.), *Leadership frontiers.* Kent, OH: Comparative Administration Research Inst., Kent State Univ.

Sheridan, J., Vredenburgh, D., & Abelson, M. (1981). *Contextual model of leadership influence in hospital units.* Unpublished manuscript, Texas Christian University, School of Business.

Siegal, S. (1956). *Nonparametric statistics.* London: McGraw-Hill.

Siehl, C., & Martin, J. (1982). *Learning organizational culture.* Unpublished manuscript, Stanford University.

Simon, H.A. (1945). *Administrative behavior*. New York: Macmillan.

Simon, H.A. (1957) A behavioral model of rational choice. In H.A. Simon (Ed.), *Models of man*. New York: Wiley.

Sims, H.P. (1977) The leader as a manager of reinforcement contingencies: An empirical example and a model. In J.G. Hunt & L.L. Larson (Eds.), *Leadership: The cutting edge*. Carbondale, IL: Southern Illinois University Press.

Sloan, A.P. (1963). *My Years with General Motors*. New York: Doubleday.

Slocum, J., & Sims, H. (1980). A typology for integrating technology, organization, and job design. *Human Relations, 33,* 193–212.

Smircich, L. (in press). Organizations as shared meaning. In L. Pondy, P. Frost, G. Morgan, & T. Dandridge (Eds.), *Organizational symbolism*. Greenwich, CT: JAI Press.

Smith, K.K. (1977). An intergroup perspective on individual behavior. In J.R. Hackman, E.E. Lawler, & L.W. Porter (Eds.), *Perspectives on behavior in organizations*. New York: McGraw-Hill.

Smith, M. (1980). An analysis of three managerial jobs using repertory grid. *Journal of Management Studies, 17*(2), 203–213.

Smith, R.F., & Morris, F.A. (in press). The political and regulatory framework for high level radioactive waste management. *Underground Space.*

Snyder, G.H., & Diesing, P. (1977). *Conflict among nations: Bargaining, decision making and system structure*. Princeton, NJ: Princeton University Press.

Sofer, C. (1970). *Men in mid-career*. London: Cambridge University Press.

Springer, S.P., & Deutsch, G. (1981). *Left Brain, Right Brain*. San Francisco: Freeman.

Sproull, L.S. (1981). Beliefs in organizations. In P.C. Nystrom & W.H. Starbuck Eds.), *Handbook of organizational design*. London: Oxford University Press.

Starbuck, W.H. (1982). Congealing oil: Inventing ideologies to justify acting out ideologies. *Journal of Management Studies, 19,* 3–28.

Starbuck, W.H., Greve, A., & Hedburg, B.L.T. (1978). Responding to crises. *Journal of Business Administration, 9,* 111–137.

Staw, B.M. (1980). Rationality and justification in organizational life. In B. Staw & L. Cummings (Eds.), *Research in organizational behavior* (Vol. 2). Greenwich, CT: JAI Press.

Steers, R.M. (1977). *Organizational effectiveness: A behavioral view*. Santa Monica, CA: Goodyear.

Steinbruner, J.D. (1974). *The cybernetic theory of decision*. Princeton, NJ: Princeton University Press.

Stengrevics, (n.d.). *The role of group executives in large diversified firms* (tentative title). Doctoral dissertation in progress at the Harvard Business school.

Stewart. R. (1967). *Managers and their jobs*. London: Macmillan.

Stewart, R. (1976). *Contrasts in management: A study of the different types of managers' jobs, their demands and choices*. London: McGraw-Hill.

Stewart, R. (1979). The managers contacts: Demand or choice? *Journal of European Industrial Training, 3,* 2–5.

Stewart, R. (1982a). A model for understanding managerial jobs and behavior. *Academy of Management Review, 7,* 7–13.

Stewart, R. (1982b). The relevance of some studies of managerial work and behavior to leadership studies. In J.G. Hunt, U. Sekaran, & C.A. Schriesheim (Eds.), *Leadership: Beyond establishment views*. Carbondale, IL: Southern Illinois University Press.

Stewart, R. (in press). *Choices for the manager: A guide to understanding managerial work and behavior*. Englewood Cliffs, NJ: Prentice-Hall.

Stewart, R., Smith, P., Blake, J., & Wingate, P. (1980). *The district administrator in the national health service.* London: King Edward's Hospital Fund for London, distributed by Pitman Medical.

Stogdill, R.M. (1974). Personal factors associated with leadership: A survey of the literature. *Journal of Psychology, 25,* 35-71.

Stogdill, R.M. (1950). Leadership, membership and organization. *Psychological Bulletin, 47,* 1-14.

Stogdill, R.M. (1965). *Work group descriptions: Manual of directions.* Columbus, OH: Bureau of Business Research, The Ohio State University.

Stogdill, R.M. (1974). *Handbook of leadership: A survey of theory and research.* New York: Free Press.

Stogdill, R.M., Goode, O.S., & Day, D.R. (1962). New leader behavior description subscales. *Journal of Psychology, 54,* 259-269.

Stopford & Wells, (1970). *Managing the multinational enterprise.* New York: Basic Books.

Storm, P.H. (1977). Lateral and hierarchical leadership style congruence. In J.G. Hunt & L.L. Larson (Eds.), *Leadership: The cutting edge.* Carbondale, IL: Southern Illinois University Press.

Strauss, G. (1962). Tactics of lateral relationships: The purchasing agent. *Administrative Science Quarterly, 7,* 161-168.

Strauss, G. (1974). Job satisfaction: Review of the literature. *Organization Behavior Research,* Industrial Relations Association.

Strauss, G. (1977). Managerial practices. In J.R. Hackman & L. Shuttle (Eds.), *Improving life at work.* Santa Monica, CA: Goodyear.

Strauss, G. (1982). Workers' participation in management. In B. Staw & L. Cummings (Eds.), *Research in organizational behavior* (Vol. 4). Greenwich, CT: JAI Press.

Strauss, G., Schatzman, L., Erlich, D., Bucher, R., & Sabshin, R. (1963). The hospital and its negotiated order. In E. Friedson (Ed.), *The hospital in modern society.* New York: Macmillan.

Strong, P. *The ceremonial order of the clinic.* London: Routledge & Kegan Paul.

Strong, P. (1982). The rivals: An essay on the sociological trades. In R. Dingwall & P. Lewis (Eds.), *The sociology of the professions: Law medicine and others.* London: Macmillan.

Strong, P., & McPherson, K. (1982). Natural science and medicine; Social science and medicine: Some methodological controversies. *Social Science and Medicine, 16,* 643-657.

Stumpf, S.A., Freedman, R.D., & Zand, D.E. (1979). Designing groups for judgmental decisions. *Academy of Management Review, 4,* 589-600.

Sweney, A.B. (1979). *Leadership: The management of power and obligation* (Prepublication edition). Wichita; KS: Test Systems, Inc.

Taggart, W., & Robey, D. (1981). Minds and managers: On the dual nature of human information processing and management. *Academy of Management Review, 6* (2), 187-195.

Tannebaum, R., & Schmidt, W.H. (1958). How to choose a leadership pattern. *Harvard Business Review 36,* 95-101.

Tannenbaum, A.S. (Ed.). (1968). *Control in organizations.* New York: McGraw-Hill.

Tannenbaum, R. & Cooke, R. (1979). Organizational control: A review of studies employing the control graph method. In C. Lammers & D. Hickson (Eds.), *Organizations alike and unlike.* London: Routledge, Kegan & Paul.

Temperol, P.M.E., & Boydell, T.H. (1977). Barriers to Learning. *B.A.C.I.E. Journal, 31* (9), 154-155.

Thibaut, J.W., & Kelley, H.H. (1959). *The social psychology of groups.* New York: Wiley.

Thomason, (1967 & 1968). Managerial work roles and relationships, Part I and II. *Journal of Management Studies, 3,* 270–284, and *4,* 17–30.

Thompson, J.D. (1967). *Organizations in action.* New York: McGraw-Hill.

Thompson, S.C., & Kelley, H.H. (1981). Judgements of responsibility for activities in close relationships. *Journal of Personality and Social Psychology, 41,* 469–477.

Thornton, G.C., & Zorich, S. (1980). Training to improve observer accuracy. *Journal of Applied Psychology, 65,* 351–354.

Thurley, K.E., & Wirdenius, H. (1973). *Supervision: A reappraisal.* London: Heinemann.

Tosi, H. (1982). Toward a paradigm shift in the study of leadership. In J.G. Hunt, U. Sekaran, & C.A. Schriesheim (Eds.), *Leadership: Beyond establishment views.* Carbondale, IL: Southern Illinois University Press.

Toulmin, S. (1958). *The uses of argument.* Cambridge, U.K.: Cambridge University Press.

Toulmin, S., Rieke, R., & Janik, A. (1979). *An introduction to reasoning.* New York: Macmillan.

Trice, H.M., Belasco, J., & Alutto, J.A. (1969). The role of ceremonials in organizational behavior. *Industrial and Labor Relations Review, 23,* 40–51.

Trist, E.L., Higgin, G.W., Murray, H., & Pollock, A.B. (1963). *Organizational choice.* London: Tavistock.

Trower, P., Bryant, B., & Argyle, M. (1978). *Social skills and mental health.* London: Methuen, and University of Pittsburgh Press.

Tsui, A.S. (1982). The measurement of managerial effectiveness: Progress and problems (Working Paper). Fuqua School of Business, Duke University.

Tyler, L.E. (1981). *Annual Review of Psychology, 32,* 1–20.

Ungson, G., & Braunstein, D. (1982). *Decision making: An interdisciplinary inquiry.* Boston: Kent.

United States Department of Energy. (1980, April, September). *Statement of position* (DOE/NE-0007), Washington, D.C. and *Cross statement of position, (Suppl. 1).*

Urwick, L.F., & Brech, E.F.L. (1957). *The making of scientific management* (Vol. 1), *Thirteen Pioneers.* London: Pitman.

Valecha, G.K. (1972). *Construct validation of internal-external locus of control as measured by an abbreviated 11-item IE scale.* Unpublished doctoral dissertation, The Ohio State University.

Valentin, (1980). *Fordelingen af pavirkningsmuligheder.* Lavindkomstkommissionens sekretariat, Kobenhavn.

Van de Ven, A., & Delbecq, A. (1974). A task contingent model of work-unit structure. *Administrative Science Quarterly, 19,* 183–197.

Van de Ven, A., Delbecq, A., & Koenig, R. (1976). Determinants of coordination modes within organizations. *American Sociological Review, 41,* 322–338.

Van de Ven, A.H., & Ferry, D.L. (1980). *Measuring and assessing organizations.* New York: Wiley.

Van Maanen, J. (1976). Breaking-in: Socialization to work. In R. Dubin (Ed.), *Handbook of work, organization, and society.* Chicago: Rand McNally.

Van Maanen, J. (1980). Career games: Organizational rules of play. In C.B. Derr (Ed.), *Work, family and career.* New York: Praeger.

Van Maanen, J., & Schein, E. (1979). Toward a theory of organizational socialization. In L. Cummings & B. Staw (Eds.), *Research in organizational behavior* (Vol. 1), Greenwich, CT: JAI Press.

Van Sell, M., Brief, A.P., & Schuler, R.S. (1981). Role conflict and role ambiguity: Integration of the literature and directions for future research. *Human Relations, 34,* 43–71.

Von Bertalanffy, L. (1956). General system theory. *General Systems, 1,* 1–10.

Vroom, V. (1964). *Work and motivation.* New York: Wiley.

Vroom, V., & Yetton, P.W. (1973). *Leadership and decision-making.* Pittsburgh: University of Pittsburgh Press.

Wall, T.D., & Lischeron, J.A. (1977). *Worker participation: A critique of the literature and some fresh evidence.* London: McGraw-Hill.

Walton, R.E. (1969). *Interpersonal peacemaking.* Reading, MA: Addison-Wesley.

Walton, R.E. (1980). Establishing and maintaining high commitment work systems. In J.R. Kimberly, & R.H. Miles (Eds.), *The Organizational Life Cycle.* San Francisco: Jossey-Bass.

Walton, R.E., & McKersie, R.B. (1965). *A behavioral theory of labor negotiations: An analysis of a social interaction system.* New York: McGraw-Hill.

Walton, R.E., & Schlesinger, L.A. (1979). Do supervisors thrive in participative work systems? *Organizational Dynamics, 8*(3), 25–38.

Wanous, J. (1977). Organizational entry: Newcomers moving from outside to inside. *Psychological Bulletin, 84,* 601–618.

Watson, T. (1963). *A business and its beliefs: The ideas that helped build IBM.* New York: McGraw-Hill.

Watzlawick, P. (1978). *The language of change. Elements of therapeutic communication.* New York: Basic Books.

Watzlawick, P., Beavin, J.H., & Jackson, D.D. (1967). *Pragmatics of human communication: A study of interactional patterns, pathologies, and paradoxes.* New York: Norton.

Watzlawick, P., Weakland, J., & Fisch, R. (1974). *Change: Principles of problem formation and problem resolution.* New York: Norton.

Webber, R.A. (1975). *Management: Basic elements of managing organizations.* Homewood, IL: Irwin.

Weick, K. (1968). Systematic observational methods. In G. Lindzey & E. Aronson (Eds.), *Handbook of social psychology* (Vol. 4, 2nd ed.) Reading, MA: Addison-Wesley.

Weick, K. (1969). *The social psychology of organizing.* Reading, MA: Addison-Wesley.

Weick, K. (1974). Review of "The Nature of Managerial Work." *Administrative Science Quarterly, 19*(1), 111–118.

Weick, K. (1977a). Enactment processes in organizations. In B.M. Staw & G.R. Salancik (Eds.), *New directions in organizational behavior.* Chicago: St. Clair Press.

Weick, K. (1977b). Re-punctuating the problem. In P.S. Goodman & J.M. Pennings (Eds.), *New perspectives on organizational effectiveness.* San Francisco: Jossey-Bass.

Weick, K. (1978). The spines of leaders. In M. McCall & M. Lombardo (Eds.), *Leadership: Where else can we go?* Durham, NC: Duke University Press.

Weick, K. (1976). Educational organizations as loosely coupled systems. *Administrative Science Quarterly, 21* (1), 1–19.

Weiner, B., Frieze, I., Kukla, A., Reed, L., Rest, S., & Rosenbaum, R.M. (1971). *Perceiving the causes of success and failure.* Morristown, NJ: General Learning Press.

Weiss, D.J., Dawis, R.V., England, G.W., & Lofquist, L.H. (1967). *Manual for the Minnesota Satisfaction Questionnaire.* Minneapolis: University of Minnesota Industrial Relations Center.

Weissenberg, P., & Kupat, H. (1976). Another look at LPC score; What does it really mean? *Proceedings,* 13th Annual Meeting, Eastern Academy of Management, Washington, D.C.

Westerlund, G. (1952). *Behavior in a work situation with functional supervision and with group leaders*. Stockholm: Nordisk Rotogravyr.

Wexley, K.N., Singh, J.P., & Yukl, G.A. (1973). Subordinate personality as a moderator on the effects of participation in three types of appraisal interviews. *Journal of Applied Psychology, 58* (1), 54–59.

Whetten, D.A. (1978). Coping with incompatible expectations: An integrated view of role and conflict. *Administrative Science Quarterly, 23,* 254–271.

Whitehead, A.N., & Russell, B. (1910). *Principal mathematical.* Cambridge, U.K.: Cambridge University Press.

Whyte, W.F. (1941). *Street corner society.* Chicago: University of Chicago Press.

Wilkins, A. (1978). *Organizational stories as an expression of management philosophy: Implications for social control in organizations.* Unpublished doctoral dissertation, Stanford University.

Wilkins, A. (in press). Organizational control. In L. Pondy, P. Frost, G. Morgan, & T. Dandridge (Eds.), *Organizational symbolism, Greenwood, CT: JAI Press.*

Williams, R. (1976). *Keywords: A vocabulary of culture and society.* London: Fontana.

Williamson, O.E. (1975). *Markets and hierarchies: Analysis and antitrust implications.* New York: Free Press.

Wilson, J.Q. (1980). *The politics of regulation.* New York: Basic Books.

Winkler, J.T. (1974). The ghost at the bargaining table: Directors and industrial relations. *British Journal of Industrial Relations, 12,* 191–212.

Winogard, I.J. (1981). Radioactive waste disposal in thick unsaturated zones. *Science, 212,* 1457–1464.

Wirdenius, H. (1958). *Supervisors at work.* Stockholm: The Swedish Council for Personnel Administration.

Wish, M., Deutsch, M., & Kaplan, S.J. (1976). Perceived dimensions of interpersonal relations. *Sociometry, 40,* 234–246.

Witte, E. (1972). Field research on complex decision-making processes: The phase theorem. *International Studies of Management and Organization, 2,* 156–182.

Wofford, J.C. (1981). *An integrative theory of leadership.* Unpublished working paper, University of Texas at Arlington.

Woodward, J. (1965). *Industrial organization: Theory and practice.* London: Oxford University Press.

Wright, W. (1975). *Sixguns and society: A structural study of the Western.* Berkeley and Los Angeles: University of California Press.

Wynne, B. & Hunsaker, P. (1975). A human information processing approach to the study of leadership. In J.G. Hunt & L.L. Larson (Eds.), *Leadership frontiers.* Kent, OH: Comparative Administration Research Institute, Kent State Univ.

Yukl, G. (1981). *Leadership in organizations.* Englewood Cliffs, NJ: Prentice-Hall.

Yukl, G., & Nemeroff, W. (1979). Identification and measurement of specific categories of leadership behavior: A progress report. In J.G. Hunt & L.L. Larson (Eds.), *Crosscurrents in leadership.* Carbondale, IL: Southern Illinois University Press.

Zaleznik, A. (1977). Managers and leaders: Are they different? *Harvard Business Review, 55*(3), 67–78.

Zand, D.E. (1974). Collateral organization: A new change strategy. *Journal of Applied Behavioral Science, 10,* 63–89.

Zander, A. (1982). *Making groups effective.* San Francisco: Jossey-Bass.

Zelevy, M. (1981). Descriptive decision making and its applications. *Applications of Management Science, 1,* 327–388.

Abstracts and Works in Progress

001   Abelson, Michael A. Characteristics of chief executive officers of United States firms and effective organizational adaptation to change: An empirical investigation of causality. College of Business Administration, Texas A & M University, U.S.A.

002   Adler, Seymour. Subordinate imitation of supervisor leadership behavior: The role of supervisor power and subordinate self-esteem. Management Science Department, Stevens Institute of Technology, U.S.A.

003   Agersnap, Flemming, and Dreisler, Poul. Delegation as condition for democratization? Institute of Organisation and Industrial Sociology, Copenhagen School of Economics and Social Science, Denmark.

004   Ahn, Kenneth, and Taylor, Thomas G. Small is possible: The effectiveness of New England local government managers in rural administration. Department of Political Science, University of Maine at Orono, U.S.A.

005   Aldemir, M. Ceyhan. Managerial style and organizational structure. School of Business Administration, Aegean University, Turkey.

006   Aldrich, Howard. Environmental and contextual influences on managerial behavior. Cornell University, NYSSILR, Ithaca, NY, U.S.A.

007   Algera, J. A., and Koopman, P. L. User-oriented automation. Department of Work and Organizational Psychology, Free University of Amsterdam, The Netherlands.

008   Allen, Thomas J., and Katz, Ralph. Project effectiveness and the distribution of influence among project and functional managers within a matrix organization. Massachusetts Institute of Technology, Sloan School of Management, Cambridge, U.S.A.

009   Argyle, Michael. The social skills needed in the leader-follower relationship. Department of Social Psychology, University of Bradford, England.

010   Arvey, Richard D., Davis, Greg A., and McGowen, Sherry. An investigation of discipline and the effects of discipline in an organizational setting. Department of Psychology, University of Houston, Tx, U.S.A.

011   Ayman, Roya, and Chemers, Martin M. The relationship of managerial behavior to effectiveness and satisfaction in Mexico. Uni-

455

versidad Regio Monitana, Mexico, and Department of Psychology, University of Utah, U.S.A.

012   Baril, Galen L. Psychology Department, University of Scranton, PA, U.S.A.

013   Bass, Bernard M. Cross-national aspects of leadership. State University of N.Y. at Binghamton, School of Management, U.S.A.

014   Boss, R. Wayne. Toward increasing accountability and reducing regression following team building sessions. University of Colorado, College of Business Administration, U.S.A.

015   Boyce, James E., and Otalora, German. Untitled abstract. School of Business and Engineering Administration, Michigan Technological University, U.S.A., and Monterrey Institute of Technology, Mexico.

016   Braunstein, Daniel N. An examination of managerial roles as a function of centralized information-processing technology. School of Economics and Management, Oakland University, U.S.A.

017   Bresnick, David. Managerial behavior in a multipurpose human service agency and management improvement. Center for Management Development and Organizational Research, Baruch College, City University of N.Y., U.S.A.

018   Buchan, Bruce P. The unique role of business leaders on bank boards of directors. School of Business, Queen's University, Kingston, Canada.

019   Butterfield, D. Anthony. Sex, performance, and attribution theory: The "high-high" leader rides again. School of Business Administration, University of Massachusetts, Amherst, U.S.A.

020   Calista, Donald J. Marist College, Master of Public Administration Program, U.S.A.

021   Campbell, David. Untitled abstract. Center for Creative Leadership, 5000 Laurinda Drive, Greensboro, NC 27402, U.S.A.

022   Carroll, Stephen J., and Gillen, Dennis J. Differences in predictors of managerial effectiveness in mechanistic and organic organization structures. College of Business and Management, University of Maryland at College Park, U.S.A.

023   Chatterjee, Amitava. Systems approach to leadership effectiveness. Indian Institute of Technology, Kharagpur, India.

024   Chatterjee, S. R. Leadership approaches of West Australian managers: Issues of significance to others. School of Management, Western Australian Institute of Technology.

025   Chemers, Martin M. Managerial style in cross-cultural perspective: An analysis of culture and technology. Department of Psychology, University of Utah, U.S.A.

026   Chitayat, Gideon. A comparative study of leadership styles of senior executives in business and non-business organizations. School of

Business Administration, Hebrew University of Jerusalem, Israel.

027 Coelho, George V. Untitled abstract. Department of Health and Human Services, Public Health Service, Alcohol, Drug Abuse and Mental Health Administration, 5600 Fishers Lane, Rockville, MD 20857, U.S.A.

028 Connolly, Terry. Leaders and leading: A shift in the locus of inquiry. School of Industrial and Systems Engineering, Georgia Institute of Technology, U.S.A.

029 Conover, Gary G. Untitled abstract. 21 Meadow Heights, Hampden Highlands, Maine 04445, U.S.A.

030 Dansereau, Fred Jr. School of Management, State University of New York at Buffalo, U.S.A.

031 Dess, Gregory G. A step toward empirically validating the environment-strategy link: Implications for strategic decision making. College of Business Administration, University of South Carolina, U.S.A.

032 Dessler, Gary. The leadership theory jungle. School of Business and Organizational Sciences, Florida International University, U.S.A.

033 Dessler, Gary, and Shapiro, Gloria. A test of Dessler's dual-power theory of leadership. School of Business and Organizational Sciences, Florida International University, U.S.A.

034 Dickinson, Terry L. Host national and expatriate policies for selecting American managers. Department of Psychology, Colorado State University, U.S.A.

035 Dolan, Shimon L., and Tziner, A. Predicting and evaluating military leadership of female officers: Findings emerging from assessment centers. School of Industrial Relations, University of Montreal, Canada.

036 Dowling, John. School of Business, Queen's University, Kingston, Canada.

037 Dragon, Andrea C. Leadership and productivity in public service organizations. Rutgers University, New Brunswick, NJ, U.S.A.

038 Drenth, P. J. D., and Koopman, P. L. Department of Work and Organizational Psychology, Free University of Amsterdam, The Netherlands.

039 Eckerman, William C. The role of the company-level leadership in preventing drug abuse in the army. Research Triangle Institute, P.O. Box 12194, Research Triangle Park, NC 27709, U.S.A.

040 Erez, Miriam. A participative approach to goal-setting: A cross-cultural perspective. Faculty of Industrial Engineering and Management, Technion University, Haifa, Israel.

041 Evans, Martin G. Faculty of Management Studies, University of Toronto, Canada.

042 Evans, Mary Kathryn. Leadership as advocacy. Temple University, School of Business Administration, Philadelphia, PA, U.S.A.

043   Faltot, James C. What price results? An examination of managerial
       orientation toward process versus outcome variables. College of Busi-
       ness and Economics, Department of Business Administration, Uni-
       versity of Delaware, U.S.A.

044   Field, R. H. George. Theories of leadership: A jungle is not a jumble.
       Department of Business Administration, Simon Fraser University,
       Canada.

045   Fisher, Fred E. Resource exchange networks as an emergent manage-
       ment strategy: Metaphorical inventions in response to differentiated
       human needs in collectivist-oriented societies. Pennsylvania State Uni-
       versity, U.S.A.

046   Frohman, Alan L. 12 Todd Rd., Lexington, MA 02173, U.S.A.

047   Futamura, Toshiko. The effectiveness of organizationism in Japanese
       management. Tokyo Metropolitan University, Faculty of Economics,
       Japan.

048   Gaerthner, Gregory H., and Ramnarayan, S. Organizational effec-
       tiveness: An alternative perspective. Case Western Reserve University,
       U.S.A.

049   Galicia, Fernando Arias. Conflict approaches and leader effective-
       ness. Faculty of Commerce and Administration, City University,
       Mexico City, Mexico.

050   Gawthrop, Louis C. Public management and systems design: Toward
       an ethics of creative freedom. School of Public and Environmen-
       tal Affairs, Indiana University, Bloomington, U.S.A.

051   Gioia, Dennis A. The leader's use of automatic versus controlled
       information processes in the judgment of employee performance.
       College of Business Administration, Pennsylvania State University,
       U.S.A.

052   Gioia, Dennis A., and Manz, Charles C. Script processing and model-
       ing in leadership activity. College of Business Administration, Penn-
       sylvania State University and Department of Management, Auburn
       University, U.S.A.

053   Gillespie, Harry. Untitled abstract. 7960 Via Capri, La Jolla, CA
       92037, U.S.A.

054   Globerson, Arye. Integrating MD and OD. School of Industrial Rela-
       tions, University of Montreal, Canada.

055   Graeff, Claude L. College of Business, Illinois State University at
       Normal-Bloomington, U.S.A.

056   Greene, Charles N., and Podsakoff, Philip M. Influence in organiza-
       tions. Graduate School of Business, Indiana University and College
       of Administrative Science, Ohio State University, U.S.A.

057   Greenhalgh, Leonard, and Neslin, Scott A. Tuck School of Business,
       Dartmouth College, U.S.A.

058 Griffin, Ricky W. A social information processing approach to the study of leadership. College of Business Administration, Texas A & M University, U.S.A.

059 Grunwald, Wolfgang. Conflict-competition-cooperation: A theoretical-empirical concept analysis. Free University of Berlin, West Germany.

060 Harpaz, Itzhak, and Vardi, Moshe. Leadership styles and effectiveness of Israeli fire fighting commanders. University of Haifa, Israel.

061 Harrell, Thomas W., and Harrell, Margaret S. Fast Track MBA's. Graduate School of Business, Stanford University, Stanford, CA, U.S.A.

062 Hatcher, Myron E. Decision support systems characteristics and its relationship to management. Department of Health Services Administration, George Washington University, Washington, D.C., U.S.A.

063 Haynsworth, H. C., and McDonald, J. M. Data manipulation and managerial communications: Boon or boondogle. School of Business Administration, Winthrop College and Industrial Management Department, Clemson University, U.S.A.

064 Healy-Sesno, Alice, and Newman, Warren B. Utilizing an evaluation process model as a means to change managerial/leadership behavior. Attendance, Pupil and Administrative Services, Los Angeles County Education Center, 9300 East Imperial Highway, Downey, CA 90242, U.S.A.

065 Heller, Trudy. The leadership crisis: A developmental/maturational view. School of Business Administration, Temple University, Philadelphia, PA, U.S.A.

066 Hendrick, Hal W. Cognitive complexity, conceptual systems, and managerial behavior and effectiveness — structural cognitive style theory of leadership. University of Southern California, Institute of Safety and Systems Management, Los Angeles, U.S.A.

067 Hendrix, William H., and Ovalle, Nestor K. Effect of managerial behavior and situational variables on organizational effectiveness. Air Force Institute of Technology, Wright-Patterson Air Force Base, Ohio 45433, U.S.A.

068 Holliday, Sam C. The trait theory revised. School of Business Administration, Department of Management, Old Dominion University, U.S.A.

069 Horney, Heinz-Ludwig. The personal program for managers. 4630 Bochum 1, Am alten Stadtpark 55, West Germany.

070 Howell, Jon P. Leadership moderators: Neutralizers, substitutes, supplements, or mediators. College of Business Administration and Economics, New Mexico State University, U.S.A.

071 Jacobs, George W. Strategic behavior: Key to leader effectiveness.

Route 3, Lexington Court, Murfreesboro, TN. 37130, U.S.A.

072   Jenner, Stephen. The ideology of business management: An Asia-Pacific perspective. College of Business Administration, University of Hawaii at Manoa, U.S.A.

073   Jones, Allan P. The use and interpretation of leader punishment/reward behaviors. Department of Psychology, University of Houston, TX, U.S.A.

074   Kassover, Jodi. Managing boom towns: The new challenge for energy related industries. 3055 Austin Bluff's Parkway, Colorado Springs, CO 80907, U.S.A.

075   Katz, Ralph. A temporal investigation of the influence of managerial behaviors on project team effectiveness. Massachusetts Institute of Technology, Sloan School of Management, Cambridge, U.S.A.

076   Katz, Ralph, and Tushman, Michael. The influence of project managers on the turnover and promotional patterns of their project members: A longitudinal investigation in an R & D setting. Sloan School of Management, Massachusetts Institute of Technology, Cambridge, and School of Business, Columbia University, New York, U.S.A.

077   Keilson, Marilyn V. Cultural variables affecting managerial effectiveness. 5454 Wisconsin Ave. #725, Chevy Chase, MD 20085, U.S.A.

078   Kelley, C. Aaron. The effects of longevity and organizational level of subordinates' abilities to accurately perceive their superiors' values. School of Business, University of Louisville, KY, U.S.A.

079   Kelley, C. Aaron, and Young, John E. Planning managerial work: An assessment of organizational logic. School of Business, University of Louisville, KY, U.S.A.

080   Kelly, Joe. Observation study of executive behavior. Faculty of Commerce and Administration, Concordia University, Canada.

081   Kimmel, Melvin J. Senior leadership research and theory: The state of the art. Manpower and Personnel Research Laboratory, Department of the Army, Alexandria, VA 22333, U.S.A.

082   Komaki, Judi. Managers in action: A study in contrast. Engineering Experiment Station, Georgia Institute of Technology, U.S.A.

083   Krau, Edgar. Industrial unrest as a consequence of violating the established pattern of managerial attitude. University of Haifa, Israel.

084   Kremer, John. Pre-emptive game behaviour and the emergence of leadership. Department of Psychology, The Queen's University of Belfast, Northern Ireland, U.K.

085   Krieger, Joseph L. Studies of managerial work, managerial leadership behavior and effectiveness: 1955 versus present. Public Administration Department, Howard University, U.S.A.

086   Kriger, Mark P., and Barnes, Louis B. Executive decision processes in complex organizations. Graduate School of Business Administration, Harvard University, Cambridge, MA, U.S.A.

087   Kuipers, Herman. Leadership behavior in small groups. University of Technology, The Netherlands.

088   Kustin, Richard. A philosophy of Japanese leadership. Nova University, U.S.A.

089   La Van, Helen, and Welsch, Harold P. Role-related moderators between task structure and consideration. Department of Management, De Paul University, U.S.A.

090   Larson, James R. The supervisory performance feedback process: A preliminary model. Graduate School of Business, Columbia University, NY, U.S.A.

091   Lear, Daniel G. Personal characteristics of the effective manager. Nordli, Wilson Associates, Worcester, MA 01608, U.S.A.

092   Levin, Benjamin. The experience of managing: Managers' accounts of their work. Peel Board of Education, H. J. A. Brown Education Centre, 73 King Street West, Mississauga, Ontario L5B 1H5, Canada.

093   Lifson, K. A., Lifson, Herrman, Blackmarr, and Harvis, One Turtle Creek Village, Suite 606, Dallas, TX 75219, U.S.A.

094   MacCrimmon, Kenneth R. Risk and leadership. J. L. Kellogg Graduate School of Management, Northwestern University, Evanston, IL, U.S.A.

095   Macy, Barry A., and Mirvis, Philip H. Assessing rates and costs of individually-variable work behaviors in organizational effectiveness terms. College of Business Administration, Texas Tech University and School of Business, Boston University, U.S.A.

096   Macy, Barry A., and Mirvis, Philip H. Evaluating program costs and benefits. College of Business Administration, Texas Tech University and School of Business, Boston University, U.S.A.

097   Macy, Barry A., and Peterson, Mark F. Promoting participatory managerial behavior through a quality of work life intervention. College of Business Administration, Texas Tech University, and College of Business Administration, Cleveland State University, OH, U.S.A.

098   Maillet, Leandre. Royal Military College, Saint-Jean, Quebec, Canada.

099   Mangelsdorff, A. David. Dental management indicators: Development of a system. Academy of Health Sciences, Department of the Army, Fort Sam Houston, TX 78234, U.S.A.

100   Mangelsdorff, A. David. Organizational development intervention in health care settings. Academy of Health Sciences, Department of the Army, Fort Sam Houston, TX 78234, U.S.A.

101   Mangham, I. L. Centre for the Study of Organizational Change and Development, University of Bath, England.

102   Manz, Charles C. Toward a theory of self-leadership. Department of Management, Auburn University, U.S.A.

103   Manz, Charles C., and Sims, Henry P., Jr. Searching for the unlead-

er: Organizational member views on leading self-managed groups. Department of Management, Auburn University and College of Business Administration, Pennsylvania State University, U.S.A.

104   Margerison, Charles J. Chief executives' perceptions of leadership development. Cranfield School of Management, England.

105   Mark, Sandra F. Leadership in higher education: Consequences of career commitments. Genesee Community College, Batavia, NY 14020, U.S.A.

106   Martin, Harry J. Normative, informational, and organizational dependence as a basis for understanding effective leadership. College of Business Administraton, Cleveland State University, OH, U.S.A.

107   Mawhinney, Thomas C. Functional analyses of leadership: The need for integrating lab and field methods and results. School of Business, Indiana University, Bloomington, U.S.A.

108   McCann, Joseph E. Design guidelines for social problem solving interventions. Department of Management, University of Florida, U.S.A.

109   McElroy, James C., and Downey, H. Kirk. School of Business Administration, Iowa State University and College of Business Administration, Oklahoma State University, U.S.A.

110   McGuire, Jean B. Leadership as a strategy. Department of Management, School of Business Administration, University of Massachusetts, Amherst, U.S.A.

111   McKnight, Melvin R. Leadership behavior: A free-will based approach. School of Business, Montana State University, U.S.A.

112   McPhail, Thomas L. The NWIO and management strategies. School of Journalism, Carleton University, Canada.

113   Michael, Stephen R. A unified model of control. School of Business Administration, University of Massachusetts, Amherst, U.S.A.

114   Miller, V. V., and Crespy, Charles T. Managerial decisions that affect the financial performance of international corporations. University of New Mexico, U.S.A.

115   Mirvis, Philip H. Crisis leadership. School of Management, Boston University, MA, U.S.A.

116   Mitchell, Fred H. Leadership and social service programs in the 1980's: An international perspective. University of California, Davis, School of Medicine, Department of Family Practice, U.S.A.

117   Moskal, William F. An assessment of the effectiveness of management team-building interventions in a health care setting. Human Resource Development, Henry Ford Hospital, 2799 West Grand Boulevard, Detroit, MI 48202, U.S.A.

118   Murray, V. V., and Jick, Todd. Problems of leadership in periods of severe financial constraint in public sector organizations. Faculty

of Administrative Studies, York University, Ontario, Canada.

119 Neel, Robert G. A demonstration of two false positives in leadership behavior and personality. Department of Psychology, Indiana-Purdue University at Indianapolis, U.S.A.

120 Neel, R. G., Tzeng, O., Tekarslan, E., and Baysal, C. Relationship between personality characteristics and leadership styles of different supervisory levels. Indiana-Purdue University at Indianapolis, U.S.A., and Istanbul University, Turkey (third and fourth authors).

121 Niebuhr, Robert E., Manz, Charles C., and Davis, Kerry. An experimental approach to the assessment of attributional leadership theory. Department of Management, Auburn University, U.S.A.

122 Niehoff, M. S. Conceptual overview of changing managerial/leadership behaviors related to the changing sexual composition of the workforce. M. S. Niehoff, Ph.D. and Associates, 7702 Diagonal Road, Kent, OH 44240, U.S.A.

123 Noty, Charles. College of Business Administration, Roosevelt University, Chicago, IL, U.S.A.

124 Obi, H. U. Managerial behaviour and effectiveness: The Nigerian perspective. Department of Psychology, University of Nigeria, Nsukka, Nigeria.

125 Oppenheimer, Robert J. Testing three-way interactions among leader behaviors, task structure and personal characteristics of subordinates as indicated by the path-goal theory of leadership. Department of Management, Concordia University, Canada.

126 Pavett, Cynthia M., and Lau, Alan W. The effectiveness of managerial work. School of Business Administration, University of San Diego, CA, U.S.A.

127 Pavett, Cynthia M., and Lau, Alan W. The nature of managerial work: A comparison of MBA students and managers. School of Business Administration, University of San Diego, CA, U.S.A.

128 Pearce, Jone L. A model of subordinate loyalty to supervisors: Implications for organizational effectiveness. Graduate School of Management, University of California, Irvine, U.S.A.

129 Pekerti, Anugerah. Three-tier transorganizational model for management development. School of Business, University of Southern California, Los Angeles, U.S.A.

130 Pendergrass, Michael L. Studying and preventing "groupthink" in the military. Psychology Department, Wayne State University, U.S.A.

131 Pennings, Johannes M., and van Wijk, Gilles. Boundary spanning units and their organizational climate: A methodological exploration. Columbia University, Graduate School of Business, NY, U.S.A.

132 Perczel, Joseph. An approach towards a formal theory of managerial leadership. P.O. Box 15457, San Diego, CA 92115, U.S.A.

133   Poppleton, S. E. What makes for effective managerial leadership. Psychology Department, The Polytechnic of Wolverhampton, England.

134   Quaglieri, Philip L. The antecedents and consequences of accepting job performance feedback. College of Business, Northern Illinois University, U.S.A.

135   Ramsey, R. D. Why do they leave? Employee retention in the military as a function of managerial behavior. College of Business, Southeastern Louisiana State University, Hammond, U.S.A.

136   Ramsey, R. D. College of Business, Southeastern Louisiana University, Hammond, U.S.A.

137   Roberts, Karlene H. Conceptual and empirical issues in cross-nation research relevant to management. School of Business Administration, University of California, Berkeley, U.S.A.

138   Roberts, Karlene H. Cross-national organizational research relevant to management: One key problem limiting its usefulness. School of Business Administration, University of California, Berkeley, U.S.A.

139   Rohde, Kermit J. Leadership ability: An illusion. Department of Psychology, Oregon State University, U.S.A.

140   Rosenberg, Jerry M. Language and leadership. Graduate School of Management, Rutgers University, Newark, NJ, U.S.A.

141   Roskin, Rick. Untitled abstract. Faculty of Business Administration, Memorial University of Newfoundland, Canada.

142   Rowe, Alan J. Leadership styles: A derivative of decision styles. Department of Management and Policy Sciences, School of Business, University of Southern California, Los Angeles, U.S.A.

143   Rusmore, Jay T. Department of Psychology, San Jose State University, CA, U.S.A.

144   Rusmore, Jay T. Cluster analyses of executive positions. Department of Psychology, San Jose State University, CA, U.S.A.

145   Rusmore, Jay T. Organizational level: A moderator of validity for intelligence tests. Department of Psychology, San Jose State University, CA, U.S.A.

146   Sadek, Konrad E. Communication and information: Their influence on managerial effectiveness. International Information Systems, World Vision International, 919 West Huntington Drive, Monrovia, CA 91016, U.S.A.

147   Savoie, Andre. Psychology Department, University of Montreal, Canada.

148   Saxberg, Borje O. Effectiveness in managerial careers of engineers and scientists. Department of Management and Organization, University of Washington, Seattle, U.S.A.

149   Schappe, Robert H. Room 10-262, General Motors Building, Detroit, MI 48202, U.S.A.

ganizational Sciences, Florida International University, U.S.A.

165   Sheridan, John R. Contextual model of leadership influence. Neeley School of Business, Texas Christian University, U.S.A.

166   Shiflett, Samuel. Leadership style: Two broad dimensions or five situation-specific behavioral tendencies? Advanced Research Resources Organization, 4330 East-West Highway, Washington, D.C. 20014, U.S.A.

167   Shiflett, Samuel. Toward the identification and development of charismatic or personal leadership. Advanced Research Resources Organization, 4330 East-West Highway, Washington, D.C. 20014, U.S.A.

168   Shrivastava, Paul. Strategic leadership: A process view. Graduate School of Business Administration, New York University, U.S.A.

169   Singh, Ramadhar. Reward allocation by Indian managers: An information integration analysis. Indian Institute of Management, Ahmedabad, India.

170   Sooklah, Lessey. Design for generating hypothesis on the acquisition and use of managerial power. Faculty of the Business Administration, Memorial University of Newfoundland, Canada.

171   South, Lois L. Nurses' perceptions of nursing leadership behaviors. 161 Crescent Hills Road, Pittsburgh PA 15235, U.S.A.

172   Speroff, B. J. Leadership styles: Evolutionary concepts and formulations. 8145 Van Buren Avenue, Munster, IN 46321, U.S.A.

173   Start, K. B. Stress prone behaviour and personality. University of Melbourne, Victoria, Australia.

174   Straessle, D. Leadership training and effectiveness. Institut Fuer Betriebswirtschaft, Management Zentrum St. Gallen, West Germany.

175   Stybel, Laurence J. Helping managers deal with the trauma of dismissal: Implications for intervention theory and practice. Division of Management, Babson College, U.S.A.

176   Suojanen, Waino. Untitled abstract. College of Business Administration, Georgia State University, U.S.A.

177   Sweney, Arthur B., and Sweney, V. Ann. Subordinate performance predicted by role variables of superordinate/subordinate dyads in moderated samples. College of Business Administration, Wichita State University, KS, U.S.A.

178   Swezey, Robert W., and Mietus, John. Development of a complex management assessment and training simulation system. Behavioral Sciences Research Center, Science Applications, Inc., 1710 Goodridge Drive, P.O. Box 1303, McLean, VA 22102 and U.S. Army Research Institute for the Behavioral and Social Sciences, U.S.A.

179   Taylor, W. P. The role of leadership in strategic adaptation. Division of Business Administration, Bishop's University, Canada.

180   Terris, William, and Jones, John W. Psychological predictors of

managerial integrity. De Paul University, and London House Management Consultants, Inc., 1550 Northwest Highway, Park Ridge, IL 60068, U.S.A.

181 Tichy, Noel M. Technical, political and cultural dynamics of leadership. Graduate School of Business, University of Michigan, U.S.A.

182 Tivendell, John. Department of Psychology, Universite de Moncton, N.B., Canada.

183 Tjosvold, Dean, Andrews, I. Robert, and Jones, Hales. Business Administration Department, Simon Fraser University, Canada.

184 Toren, Nina. The management of scientists: With special reference to Soviet and Western scientists in Israel. School of Business Administration, Hebrew University of Jerusalem, Israel.

185 Tracy, Lane. Leadership: A living systems perspective. Ohio University, College of Business Administration, U.S.A.

186 Trentini, Giancarlo. Power, authority and freedom. Psychology Department University of Venice, Italy.

187 Tucker, Sharon. Beyond contingency theories: A proposal. Graduate School of Business Administration, Washington University in St. Louis, MO, U.S.A.

188 Wedley, William C., and Field, R. H. George. The managerial decision model: Selecting appropriate styles, methods, and members. Department of Business Administration, Simon Fraser University, Canada.

189 Withane, D. S. Organizational effectiveness: A contingency view. Nelson A. Rockefeller College of Public Affairs and Policy, State University of N.Y. at Albany, U.S.A.

190 Wlodarczyk, W. Cezary. Effects of the level of organizational structures uniformization on managerial behaviour: An example of the Polish health institutions. Institute of Occupational Medicine, Lodz, Poland.

191 Wofford, Jerry. Test of the leader-environment-follower interaction theory of leadership: A laboratory experiment. College of Business Administration, University of Texas at Arlington U.S.A.

192 Wong, Paul T. P. Locus of control and leadership effectiveness: A synthesis of Western and Eastern cultures. Department of Psychology, Trent University, Canada.

193 Wright, Peter. Untitled abstract. Southeastern Louisiana State University, U.S.A.

194 Young, Dennis R. Incentives in non-profit organizations. W. Averell Harriman College for Urban and Policy Sciences, State University of N.Y. at Stony Brook, U.S.A.

195 Yukl, Gary, and Clemence, James. Development and validation of a new leader behavior taxonomy. School of Business, State Univer-

sity of New York at Albany, U.S.A.

196 Zalesny, Mary D. Untitled abstract. Department of Psychology, Michigan State University, U.S.A.

197 Zammuto, Raymond F., and Cameron, Kim S. Environmental decline and managerial effectiveness. Organizational Studies Program, National Center for Higher Education Management Systems, P.O. Drawer P, Boulder, CO 80302, U.S.A.

Author Index

Subject Index

About the Contributors

Beverly Alban Metcalfe is Research Fellow, MRC/SSRC Social & Applied Psychology Unit, Dept. of Psychology, The University, Sheffield, UK.

Michael Argyle is Reader in Social Psychology, and Fellow of Wolfson College, Oxford University, U.K.

Bernard M. Bass is Professor of Organizational Behavior, State University of New York at Binghamton, U.S.A.

Brenda E. F. Beck is Professor of Anthropology, University of British Columbia, Vancouver, Canada.

Orlando Behling is Professor of Management, Bowling Green State University, U.S.A.

John Burgoyne is Research Director, Center for Study of Management Learning, School of Management & Organization Science, Univ. of Lancaster, U.K.

Peter A. Clark is Reader in Organization Behaviour and Director, SSRC/Work Organization Research Centre, University of Aston in Birmingham, U.K.

Patrick E. Connor is Professor of Organization Theory and Behavior, Willamette University, U.S.A.

Thomas G. Cummings is Associate Professor of Management & Organization, University of Southern California, U.S.A.

H. Peter Dachler is Professor of Psychology, Saint Gass Graduate School of Economics, Business and Public Administration, Switzerland.

Yves L. Doz is Associate Professor of Business Policy, Institute European d'Administration des Affaires, France.

Pieter J. D. Drenth is Professor of Psychology, The Free University, The Netherlands.

Peter Forsblad is Lecturer, Stockholm School of Economics and Business Administration, Sweden.

Janet Fulk is Assistant Professor of Communications Management, University of Southern California, U.S.A.

William L. Gardner is a doctoral candidate at Florida State University, U.S.A., and Research Associate for the Principal Competency Study.

Ilene F. Gast is Research Assistant, Army Research Institute for the Behavioral and Social Sciences, U.S.A.

Frank A. Heller is Senior Staff, Tavistock Institute of Human Relations, London, U.K.

Vivien Hodgson is Research Fellow, Center for Study of Management Learning, School of Management & Organization Science, University of Lancaster, U.K.

Dian-Marie Hosking is Lecturer in Organizational Sociology/Psychology, the University of Aston Management Centre, U.K.

Anne S.Huff is Associate Professor of Business Administration, University of Illinois, Urbana-Champaign, U.S.A.

James G. (Jerry) Hunt is Professor of Business Administration and Area Coordinator of Management, Texas Tech University, U.S.A.

Alfred Kieser is Professor of Business Administration and Organization Behavior, University of Mannheim, Federal Republic of Germany.

Bert King is Group Leader, Organizational Effectiveness Research Programs, Office of Naval Research, U.S.A.

Paul L. Koopman is Senior Researcher, Psychology Dept., The Free University, the Netherlands.

Edward E. Lawler III is Professor of Mgt. & Director, Center for Effective Organizations at the University of Southern California, U.S.A.

Diane Lee Lockwood is Assistant Professor of Management, Seattle University, U.S.A.

Fred Luthans is George Holmes Professor of Management, University of Nebraska, U.S.A.

Joanne Martin is Assistant Professor of Business Administration, Stanford University, U.S.A.

Mark J. Martinko is Associate Professor of Management, The Florida State University, U.S.A.

Larry F. Moore is Associate Professor of Organizational Administration, University of British Columbia, Canada.

Ian E. Morley is Chairman of the Department of Psychology, University of Warwick, U.K.

Frederic A. Morris is Research Scientist, Battelle Human Affairs Research Centers, Seattle, U.S.A.

Nigel Nicholson is Senior Research Fellow, Department of Psychology, University of Sheffield, U.K.

Richard N. Osborn is Senior Scientist, Battelle Human Affairs Research Centers, Seattle, U.S.A.

C. K. Prahalad is Associate Professor of Policy and Control, The University of Michigan, U.S.A.

Robert E. Quinn is Executive Director of the Institute for Government and Policy Studies, State University of New York at Albany, U.S.A.

Charles F. Rauch, Jr. is Assistant Professor of Management, University of Maine at Orono, U.S.A.

Chester A. Schriesheim is Associate Professor of Management, University of Florida, U.S.A.

Caren Siehl is a graduate student in Business Administration, Stanford University, U.S.A.

John W. Slocum, Jr. is Distinguished Professor in Organizational Behavior and Administration, Southern Methodist University, U.S.A.

Rosemary Stewart is Fellow in Organizational Behaviour, Oxford Centre for Management Studies, U.K.

Peter M. Storm is Associate Professor of Management, State University of Groningen, The Netherlands.

Philip M. Strong is Project of Officer, Biology Dept., Open University, Milton Keynes, U.K.

Anne S. Tsui is Assistant Professor of Organizational Behavior and Human Resource Management, Duke University, U.S.A.

Peter Weissenberg is Professor and Associate Dean, Faculty of Business Studies, Rutgers University, U.S.A.